History *of the* Deccan

J. D. B. Gribble was a member of the Indian Civil Services in India in the nineteenth century. However, he passed away before this monumental work could be completed and its conclusion had to be supervised by his daughter Mary Pendlebury.

History *of the* Deccan

J.D.B. Gribble

RUPA

Published by
Rupa Publications India Pvt. Ltd 2002
7/16, Ansari Road, Daryaganj
New Delhi 110002

Sales centres:
Bengaluru Chennai
Hyderabad Jaipur Kathmandu
Kolkata Mumbai Prayagraj

Edition copyright © Rupa Publications India Pvt. Ltd 2002

First published Vol. I (1896), Vol. II (1924)

All rights reserved.
No part of this publication may be reproduced, transmitted, or stored in a retrieval system, in any form or by any means, electronic, mechanical, photocopying,
recording or otherwise, without the prior permission of the publisher.

P-ISBN: 978-81-716-7945-4
E-ISBN: 978-81-291-4692-2

Ninth impression 2025

13 12 11 10 9

Printed in India

This book is sold subject to the condition that it shall not, by way of trade or otherwise, be lent, resold, hired out, or otherwise circulated, without the publisher's prior consent, in any form of binding or cover other than that in which it is published.

Dedicated
To
H.H. The Nizam

of
Hyderabad

VOLUME –I

CONTENTS

Volume-I

PREFACE

CHAPTER I
Introductory — 1

CHAPTER II
The Origin of the Bahmanee Kings of Gulbarga — 14

CHAPTER III
The Rise of the Hindoo Kingdom of Vijayanagar, and the End of the First Gulbarga Sultan — 23

CHAPTER IV
The Gulbarga Sultans – Muhammed Shah — 34

CHAPTER V
The Gulbarga Sultans from 1374-1397 A.D. — 47

CHAPTER VI
Sultans Ghazi-ud-din and Shams-ud-din — 56

CHAPTER VII
The City and the Kingdom of Vijayanagar — 60

CHAPTER VIII
  Sultans Feroze Shah and Ahmed Shah — 72

CHAPTER IX
  Sultan Aallah-ud-din II — 93

CHAPTER X
  Humayun the Cruel — 105

CHAPTER XI
  Sultans Nizam Shah and Muhammed Shah — 109

CHAPTER XII
  The End of the House of Bahmanee — 124

Part II
History of Bijapur and of the Deccan down to its Subjugation by Aurangzebe (A.D. 1500-1680)

CHAPTER XIII
  Yusuf Adil Shah of Bijapur — 131

CHAPTER XIV
  The Nizam Shahs of Ahmednagar — 142

CHAPTER XV
  Bijapur from 1509-1534. Ismael Adil Shah — 148

CHAPTER XVI
  Kingdoms of Berar and Golconda and Continuation of Bijapur — 159

CHAPTER XVII
  The Fall of Vijayanagar — 176

CHAPTER XVIII
Ahmednagar and Bijapur from the fall of Vijayanagar till the Death of Ali Adil Shah (1580)   189

CHAPTER XIX
The Story of Queen Chand and the Fall of Ahmednagar   201

CHAPTER XX
Restrospective Sketch of the Deccan   226

CHAPTER XXI
The Story of Malick Amber   235

CHAPTER XXII
The Beginning of the End   245

CHAPTER XXIII
End of Bijapur   262

CHAPTER XXIV
The Fall of Golconda — A.D. 1686   275

Part III
An Empire in Ruins

CHAPTER XXV
The King-Makers   288

CHAPTER XXVI
The End of King-Makers and the Birth of a New Kingdom   339

APPENDIX   357

Volume-II

PREFACE

CHAPTER I
   The Reign of Asaf-Jah, 1723-1748   1

CHAPTER II
   Asaf Jah's Successors   15

CHAPTER III
   The French in Hyderabad   27

CHAPTER IV
   Bussy in the Deccan and the Decline of French Influence   41

CHAPTER V
   The Rise of British Influence in Hyderabad   55

CHAPTER VI
   The British Resident and the First Mysore War   68

CHAPTER VII
   The Nizam and the Mahrattas   78

CHAPTER VIII
   Disbandment of Raymond's Contingent   94

CHAPTER IX
   The Mysore War   110

CHAPTER X
   The Mahratta Kingdom   127

CHAPTER XI
   The Hyderabad Contingent and the Pindari War   141

CHAPTER XII
    The Hyderabad Contingent and William Palmer and Co.   159

CHAPTER XIII
    Ministry of Maharajah Chandoo Lal (continued) Period – 1825-1845   171

CHAPTER XIV
    Period – 1845-50   184

CHAPTER XV
    Period – 1851-52   206

CHAPTER XVI
    The Berar Trust   215

CHAPTER XVII
    Death of Siraj-ul-Mulk Period 1853-58   235

CHAPTER XVIII
    Reforms Instituted by Sir Salar Jung Period 1853-83   245

APPENDIX   270

NOTE

Readers may kindly note that the following pages, with photographs on one side, have been reproduced at the end of Volume I.

65-66; 89-90; 135-136;
145-146; 159-160; 217-218;
227-228; 235-236; 259-260;
265-266; 271-272; 275-276;
313-314

PREFACE

The Deccan may be roughly described as that portion of Southern India which is bounded by the Vindhya Mountains and the River Godavery to the North, and by the Tungabadhra and Kistna Rivers to the South; the Gháts or mountain ranges which skirt the seacoast on either side being the Eastern and Western limits. It embraces an area about equal in extent to that of Great Britain and Ireland, and is a high-lying plateau with an elevation of from 1000' to 2000' above the sea. Previous to the Mahomedan invasion there exists no authentic record of the history of the Deccan beyond inscriptions and architectural remains. It is known that it contained rich and flourishing Kingdoms, but we know little of the conditions of the country, beyond what can be gathered from a name, a grant, a date or a coin. The Mahomedans did not venture South of the Vindhyas until the end of the 13th century. Their armies, commanded by generals of the Delhi Sultans, met with but little effectual resistance. But though they marched through the Deccan to the Southernmost limits of the Indian Peninsula, their invasions were for the purpose of plunder and not of occupation. They bent but they did not break; and as soon as the foreign army retired, the native Hindoo States at once sprang back to independence. Although there was a Mahomedan Governor at Deogiri (Dowlatabad), there was but a slender connecting link between him and Delhi. Towards the end of the first half of the 14th century this link was broken by the tyranny and oppression of Sultan Mahomed Toghlak; the Mahomedan generals and governors in the Deccan revolted; distance and

PREFACE.

internal dissensions prevented all interference on the part of the Delhi Sultans, and the result was that an independent Mahomedan Kingdom was established in the Deccan which lasted for more than 300 years. Of this Kingdom, subsequently divided into five, there exists no connected or continuous history. To Ferishta we owe almost all that we know of this period, and the information he gives us is to be found scattered, and in a greatly condensed form, in the various histories of India. A historian, however voluminous his work may be, when treating of a country as large as India is, with its huge population and its numerous races and peoples, has neither time nor space to give more than a broad outline. The interest centers round certain prominent figures, but outside this circle everything is confused. There is a luxuriant Eastern jungle of change names and events which must be recorded, but which like meteors, simply flash across the eye, and then disappear leaving no trace behind. Occasionally these broad outlines have been filled in. Historians such as *Pod*, *Wilkes* and *Grant Duff*, have cleared pieces of this huge jungle, and have enclosed each with a ring fence. This has been done for Rajputana, for Mysore and for the Mahrattas, but has not yet been attempted for the Deccan.

I was first struck with the necessity of a work of this kind by a conversation with the son of a Hyderabad Nobleman who had just finished his studies in the Nizam's College. I asked him who was the first of the Bahmanee Sultans of Gulburga, and he said that he did not know there had been any. He was equally ignorant of the fate of the last King of Golconda, although the remains of the old royal fortress are within an hour's drive of the city where he lived! In our Indian schools and colleges we teach the broad outlines of Indian history, but we pay very little attention to the details of the history of the different provinces. Now it seems to me that it is as essential for a Deccan boy to know something of the early history of the part of country in which he lives, as it is for him to know about Akbar, Aurungzebe, Clive or Warren Hastings. In the same way a Poonah boy should be thoroughly grounded in the history of the Mahrattas, and a Bangalore boy in that of Mysore. In the schools of Europe

PREFACE.

a boy goes through a detailed course of the history of his own country and is only given a general outline of the history of other nations. In India, the reverse seems to be the case. A general system is laid down for the whole of India, which does not embrace local and provincial history. The present volume therefore is an attempt to make Deccan readers more familiar with the history of their own country. Bearing this object in view, I have endeavoured to collect the fragments to be found in the various histories, and to piece them together, so as to form a connected history of the Deccan from the commencement of the 14th century up to the establishment of the present dynasty. This period of nearly 400 years is full of the most interesting and romantic episodes. Sir Henry Elliot's and Professor Dowson's most admirable history is a storehouse of raw material of which as yet but little use has been made, and the Bombay Gazetteers of the different Deccan Districts are replete with researches, archeological, historical and local, which comparitively unknown beyond an official circle, furnish admirable materials for a detailed history of the Deccan. These materials, old and new, I have made use of without scruple. I can claim nothing of originality; — in a history the absence of this quality is perhaps desirable — and what I have attempted is merely a collation of historical events relating to the Deccan from the time of the Mahomedan invasion.

It only remains for me to acknowledge the sources from which my information has been drawn. To Ferishta, as translated by Scott, a book which is now becoming scarce, my first thanks are due. The different historians collected by Elliot and Dowson, throw from time to time considerable light upon Deccan affairs, and I have transcribed from them *verbatim* whenever occasion required. My thanks are also due to the Bombay Government for permission to make use of the material provided in their most excellent Gazetteers of Kanara, Bijapur and Ahmednagar, a permission of which I have gladly availed myself. Colonel Meadows Taylor's historical romance of "A Noble queen" has enabled me to go at some length into a most interesting episode of Bijapur history, and the "Historical and Descriptive Sketch of the Nizam's

PREFACE.

Dominions" by Messrs. Wilmott and Seyd Hoossein Belgrami, has enabled me to give a description of those places which I have not been able to visit in person. To Mr. Herrman Linde my most cordial thanks are due for the beautiful original sketches with which he has so kindly provided me, and the excellent photographs of the Deccan cities have been furnished by the well-known photographer Mr. Lala Deen Dayal of Secunderabad and Sudore, whilst those of the Vijayanagar ruins are from Mr. Nicholas of Madras. Some of the portraits have been reproduced from a collection of old paintings found in the royal city of Bieder, and the genealogy of H.H. the Nizam (who has graciously accepted the dedication of the work) was kindly furnished to me from the palace by Nawab Sarvar Tung the Peshi Secretary to His Highness.

J. D. B. GRIBBLE.

CHAPTER I.

INTRODUCTORY

Up to the end of the thirteenth century the Mahomedans had not invaded the Deccan. It was to them an unknown country peopled by pagan idolaters, as they called them. Scarcely anything is known of the inner condition of the vast country in which are included the Deccan and Carnatic of modern times. There seems to be some doubt regarding the origin of the name itself, and it is supposed by some to be derived from the *Dandaka* or forest to which Rama went into voluntary banishment, but the most probable derivation is that Deccan is a corruption of *Dakkhin* the Prakrit form of the Sanscrit Dakshin, the left or south. The country was occupied by many ancient Hindoo kingdoms, the history and origin of which are lost. The two northernmost of these kingdoms had their capitals at Deogiri and Warangal. The former extended to the western coast, and far away south to Mysore, and the latter included Orissa and probably all the Telugu-speaking districts of Hyderabad and Madras. That these kingdoms were very great and powerful there can be no doubt, but there remain now nothing but ruins, which, however, are sufficient to show how advanced they were in civilisation. Deogiri, the modern Dowlatabad, was not only a large city but an important fortress, supposed to be impregnable. The wonderful caves of Ellora and Ajunta show how advanced was the art of architecture; and in Warangal the remains of immense irrigation tanks and channels show that the rulers of the country devoted great attention to the improvement of agriculture. In both these cities there were enormous accumulations of wealth, consisting of gold, precious stones, and elephants, all of which were found within their own boundaries. The people appear to have been brave, happy, and prosperous, and from west to east there were scattered about numerous holy shrines which brought together thousands of pilgrims. It was this wealth that attracted the cupidity of the Mahomedans.

In the year 1294 Ala-ud-Din was the governor of the Bengal provinces. He was the nephew and son-in-law of the Sultan of Delhi—Jelal-ud-Din—and was an ambitious, cruel man. He had heard stories of the wealth which was stored up in the cities of the idolatrous Hindoos, and, taking religion as his excuse, he determined to plunder them. In reality, what he wanted the riches for was to use them as a means of gaining his father-in-law's throne. Without mentioning his project to the emperor, Ala-ud-Din marched southwards with a large army, and was absent for more than a year. During this time no one knew what had become of him, but there were vague rumours that he was fighting with the Hindoos in Deogiri. This, indeed, was the case, and for a great part of this time he was besieging the fortress of Deogiri, afterwards Dowlatabad. This fortress is situated on an isolated hill, 640 feet in height. The hill is cone-shaped, and in addition to the steepness of the rock it was very strongly fortified with walls, bastions, and moats. There were in reality three distinct forts, one within another, and at the foot was the city which was the centre of a considerable trade. At the time of Ala-ud-Din's invasion, Ram Deo was king of Deogiri. Zia-ud-Din

INTRODUCTORY.

Barni, the Mahomedan historian, says: "The people of that country had never heard of the Mussulmans; the Mahratta land had never been punished by their armies; no Mussulman king or prince had penetrated so far. Deogiri was exceedingly rich in gold and silver, jewels and pearls, and other valuables." Ram Deo sent an army to meet the Mahomedan invader, but it was totally defeated, and Ala-ud-Din then invested the fortress of Deogiri. The fort was not taken, and the Rajah saved it only by agreeing to give up an immense amount of treasure, consisting of gold, jewels and elephants, with which Ala-ud-Din returned to Karra, his seat of government. So great was this treasure that it is said nothing had ever been seen like it before, and Ala-ud-Din used it to win over as many to his side as possible. When the Emperor Jelal-ud-Din heard that his son-in-law had returned after so successful a campaign, he sent to congratulate him and to ask why he did not come to Delhi to report the circumstances in person. Ala-ud-Din replied, that, having gone away without permission, he was afraid the Emperor would be angry with him, and therefore he had not ventured to come to Delhi, but if the Emperor would come and see him, it would satisfy the minds of his officers that no harm was intended to them, and he would then introduce them to the Emperor, and at the same time hand over to him the treasure which he had brought. The poor old Emperor, suspecting nothing, and anxious, perhaps, to receive the wonderful treasure of which he had heard so much, fell into the trap thus laid for him. He sent word that he would start at once, and, so as to show that he had no evil intentions, would come with only a slight retinue. Karra is situated on the Ganges, and was some five or six days' journey form Kilu-gadhi, where the Emperor was then encamped. Without listening to the advice of his counsellors, the Emperor set off on this journey in a boat, accompanied only by a few personal attendants and a body-guard of a thousand horse. The historian Barni thus relates the tragedy that followed: "Ala-ud-Din and his followers had determined on the course to be adopted before the Sultan arrived. He had crossed the river with the elephants and treasure, and had taken post with his forces between Manikpur and Karra, the Ganges being very high. When the royal ensign came in sight he was all prepared, the men were armed, and the elephants and horses were harnessed. Ala-ud-Din sent his brother Almas Beg in a small boat to the sultan, with directions to use every device to induce him to leave behind the thousand men he had brought with him, and to come with only a few personal attendants. The traitor Almas Beg hastened to the Sultan and perceived several boats full of horsemen around him. He told the Sultan that his brother had left the city, and God only knew where he would have gone to, if he (Almas Beg) had not been sent to him. If the Sultan did not make more haste to meet him, he would kill himself, and his treasure would be plundered. If his brother were to see these armed boats with the Sultan he would destroy himself. The Sultan accordingly directed that the horsemen and boats should remain by the side of the river, whilst he, with two boats and a few personal attendants and friends, passed over to the other side. When the two boats had started and the Angel of Destiny had come still nearer, the traitor Almas Beg desired the Sultan to direct his attendants to lay aside their arms, lest his brother should see them as he approached nearer, and be frightened. The Sultan, about to become a martyr, did not detect the drift of this insidious proposition, but directed his followers to disarm. As the boats reached mid-stream, the army of Ala-ud-Din was perceived, all under arms, the elephants and horses harnessed, and in several places troops of horsemen ready for action. When the nobles who accompanied the Sultan saw this, they knew that Almas Beg had by his plausibility brought his patron into a snare, and they gave themselves up as lost. Malik Khuram asked: "What is the meaning of all this?" and Almas Beg, seeing that his treachery was detected, said his brother was anxious that his army should pay homage to his master.

The Sultan was so blinded by his destiny, that although his own eyes saw the treachery, he would not return, but he said to Almas Beg: "I have come so far in a little boat to meet your brother, cannot he, and does not his heart induce him to advance to meet me with due respect?" The traitor replied: "My brother's intention is to await your majesty at the landing-place with the elephants and treasure and jewels, and there to present his officers." The Sultan, trusting implicitly in them, who were his nephews, sons-in-law, and foster-children, did not awake and detect the obvious intention. He took the Koran and read it, and proceeded fearless and confiding as a father to his sons. All the people who were in the boat with him saw death plainly before them, and began to repeat the chapter appropriate to men in sight of death. The Sultan reached the shore before afternoon prayer, and disembarked with a few followers. Ala-ud-Din advanced to receive him, he and all his officers showing due respect. When he reached the Sultan he fell at his feet, and the Sultan, treating him as a son, kissed his eyes and cheeks, stroked his beard, gave him two loving taps upon the cheek, and said: "I have brought thee up from infancy, why art thou afraid of me?" The Sultan took Ala-ud-Din's hand, and at that moment the stony-hearted traitor gave the fatal signal. Muhammad Salim of Samana, a bad fellow of a bad family, struck at the Sultan with a sword, but the blow fell short and cut his own hand. He again struck and wounded the Sultan, who ran towards the river, crying: "Ah! thou villain, Ala-ud-Din, what hast thou done?" Iktiyár-ud-Din Hud ran after the betrayed monarch, threw him down, and cut off his head and bore it dripping with blood to Ala-ud-Din. Some of those persons who accompanied the Sultan had landed, and others remained in the boats, but all were slain. Villainy and treachery and murderous feelings, covetousness and desire of riches, thus did their work." This happened on the 17th Ramazan 695. H. equal to A. D. 1296, and Ala-ud-Din at once ascended the throne and marched upon Delhi. The fatal treasure was largely used to make men forget the terrible tragedy that had been enacted on the banks of the Ganges. Every day five maunds of golden stars were discharged by a kind of engine amongst the people in front of the royal tent, and from far and near people flocked to his camp in order to share in the wealth that was being scattered about. Delhi was entered in the midst of a magnificent display, and there still remained enough of the gold to fill the treasury as it had never been filled before. Purses and bags filled with gold coins (*tankas*) were distributed, and men gave themselves up to dissipation and enjoyment. "Ala-ud-Din, in the pride of youth, prosperity, and boundless wealth, proud also of his army and his followers, his elephants, and his horses, plunged into dissipation and pleasure."

As was only natural, Ala-ud-Din was not likely to forget the place which had furnished him with the means of winning a throne. There must be more left in the country from which so much had already come. Deogiri had not been sacked and the Rajah had only bought off the invaders with a portion of his wealth. Besides, Warangal had not been touched, and, if rumours were true, this city was even wealthier than Deogiri. People said that in Telingana, of which Warangal was the capital, there were gold and diamond mines. It was a religious duty to take these treasures from the hands of infidels, and accordingly, in the year 1308 A. D. an army was sent to Deogiri, the Rajah of which had rebelled and had sent no tribute for several years. This time Deogiri was taken, and with it an immense amount of treasure. The Rajah with his family were sent as prisoners to Delhi, where they did homage to the Sultan, and were then pardoned.

Next year (1309) another expedition was sent to Warangal, the Rajah of which was called Rai Laddar Deo by the Mahomedan historians, but whose real name was Pratapa Rudra Deva. Malik Naib Kafur was appointed in command of this army, and his instructions were not to press the Rajah too hard, but to content himself with getting as much treasure as he could, with a promise of tribute in the future. The march lasted for more than three months and was through a wild and hitherto unknown country. Every day, we are told, it passed a new river until at length it reached the Nerbuddah, "which was such that you might say it was a remnant of the deluge." The Deogiri territories were respected as being those of a dependent, but when the fort of Sarbar was reached, which belonged to the Telingana country, it was taken by storm and the whole of the inhabitants were killed. "Every one threw himself, with his wife and children, upon the flames, and departed to hell," and those who escaped the fire were put to the sword. Soon after, the army arrived near Warangal, and an advance force was sent to occupy "the hill of An Makinda, for from that all the edifices and gardens of Warangal can be seen" (*Amir Khusru, Tarikh-i-'Alai*). This clearly refers to the hill of Hanumkunda, which is situated about four miles from the ruins of the ancient fort of Warangal. The city was surrounded by a double wall of fortifications, the outer one of mud and the inner one of stone. The circumference of the outer wall was seven miles and one-eighth. The whole of this wall was surrounded by the invaders with a wooden breastwork, to construct which all the trees of the sacred groves were cut down. "The trees were cut with axes and felled, notwithstanding their groans; and the Hindoos, who worship trees, could not at that time come to the rescue of their idols, so that every cursed tree which was in that capital of idolatry was cut down to the roots; and clever carpenters applied the sharp iron to shape the blocks, so that a wooden fortress was drawn round the army, of such stability that if fire had rained from heaven, their camp would have been unscathed." The siege was carried on with great fury in spite of an obstinate defence. Several sorties were repulsed, and in one the whole party was slain and "the heads of the Rawats rolled on the plain like crocodiles' eggs." At length the outer wall was taken and then the Rajah sued for peace. He was ordered to give up the whole of his treasure, and a general massacre was threatened if he should be found to have kept anything for himself. He also agreed to send tribute yearly. On the 16th Shawal (March 1310 A. D.) Malik Kafur left Warangal with his army, and with a thousand camels groaning under the weight of the treasure. He reached Delhi on the 11th Mohurram, and on the 24th the treasure was presented to the Sultan. Thus ended the first siege of Warangal, which had, however, to undergo several others before, thirteen years afterwards, it was finally sacked and destroyed.

The plunder thus obtained from the two excursions to the Deccan only excited the Sultan's desire for more, and the same general, Malik Kafur, was at once despatched to Deogiri with orders to organise another expedition to the regions further south. It is probable that Deogiri or Dowlatabad, as it will be called henceforth, was already governed by a lieutenant of the Delhi emperor, although the Rajah may have been left there with a certain amount of nominal power.

Not only was every assistance given towards the equipment of this new expedition, but the Rajah himself gave a Hindoo general to act as a guide to this unknown country. The King of Warangal also sent twenty elephants to Dowlatabad, with an intimation that he would be punctual in sending his tribute in future. Early in the following year (1311) Malik Kafur marched southwards. The territories of the Dowlatabad and Warangal kingdoms must have extended as far south as the boundaries of Mysore, for we do not read of the Mahomedan army having encountered any enemy until the "Bellal Deo of Dharwar Samoonder." This name evidently refers to one of the Vellala dynasty, which then ruled in Mysore, and the place is identified with a spot near Seringapatam, the word Samoonder being a Mahomedan corruption of Samudram, the word used in the Tamil, Telugu, and Canarese languages for a large tank or reservoir, the literal meaning being "sea." The Rajah was conquered and had to yield a large amount of treasure and elephants, which were despatched as a first instalment to Delhi. From Mysore the Mahomedan army marched to Madura where a quarrel had arisen between the two sons of the Hindoo king, who is called by the historian

Wassaf, Kales Dewar. This king is said to have been immensely rich, and the same author says that in his city of Mardi (Madura) there were "1200 crores of gold deposited, every crore being equal to a thousand lakhs, and every lakh to one hundred thousand dinars. Beside this, there was an accumulation of precious stones, such as pearls, rubies, turquoises, and emeralds, more than is the power of language to express." The whole of the country over which this king ruled, is called by the Mahomedan historians Ma'bar, and included not only that part which is now known as Malabar, but also the whole of the Madura country, Trichinopoly and Tanjore. The capital of this great kingdom was at Madura, and the dynasty is known as the Pandion race of kings.

When the King Kales Dewar died, about 1309, he left two sons, called by the Mahomedan historians Rai Sundar Pandiya and Rai Bir Pandiya. The latter name is clearly a corruption of Veera, an old Hindoo name. These two brothers quarrelled, and Veera Pandiya, the younger and illegitimate brother, drove the older one from the country, and it appears to have been on behalf of Sundar Pandiya that Malik Kafur invaded Madura. At the approach of the Mahomedan army, Veera Pandiya took refuge in the jungles, and was pursued from place to place. All the towns and temples on the line of march were sacked and destroyed, and on the 17th Zilkada the army arrived at Madura which shared the same fate. An immense amount of booty was obtained here, and Amir Khusru says that "when the Malik came to take a muster of the elephants, they extended over a length of three *parasangs*, * and amounted to five hundred and twelve, besides five thousand horses, Arabian and Syrian, and five hundred *máns* of jewels of every description—diamonds, pearls, emeralds, and rubies."

On the 4th Jumada Sani 711 H. (1311) Malik Kafur

---

* *Parasangs*, a Persian measure of distance = 3 miles.

arrived in Delhi with all this treasure and presented it to the Sultan Ala-ud-Din. But a curse seemed to attach to all the gold and jewels taken from the Hindoo idolaters, and in the same way as the Warangal treasure tempted Ala-ud-Din to murder his uncle Jelal-ud-Din, so now the same temptation brought upon him the same fate from the hands of Malik Kafur. In 1317 Ala-ud-Din died, his death having been hastened, it is said, by Malik Kafur, who at once seized the throne. He put out the eyes of two of Ala-ud-Din's sons, "by cutting them from their sockets with a razor, like slices of melon," and confined another (Mubarak Khan), intending him for the same fate. Before, however, he could do this, retribution overtook Malik Kafur himself. A conspiracy was formed amongst some of the nobles, who entered the palace at night and killed him when he was asleep. This being done, Mubarak Khan was placed upon the throne and assumed the title of Sultan Kutb-ud-Din (1317). In the following year another expedition was undertaken by the Sultan against Deogiri, which had revolted. The head of the revolt was Harpal Deo, but he was defeated without difficulty, taken prisoner, and then flayed alive, his skin being hung over the gates of the fort. A Mahomedan governor was then appointed, and from that time Deogiri, or, as it is now called, Dowlatabad, ceased to be the residence of a Hindoo king. In the following year the newly-appointed governor of Dowlatabad revolted, but was taken prisoner and sent to Delhi, where his ears and nose were cut off, and he was publicly disgraced. Khusru Khan, a favourite of the Sultan, appears to have replaced him, and to have made another invasion of Malabar; but the Hindoo gold seems to have laid upon him its curse also, for on his return to Delhi he abused the confidence placed in him by entering the palace with a band of assassins and murdering the Sultan. In this way died the last descendant of Ala-ud-Din, and the former murder of the poor old Sultan Jelal-ud-Din was avenged upon the murderer's descendents. Khusru Khan occupied the throne for a few months only, under the title of Sultan Nasir-ud-Din, when he in turn was slain by Ghazi Malik, a noble of Deobalpur, who then mounted the throne as the founder of a new dynasty, under the title of Sultan Ghiyas-ud-Din Tughlik Shah (1320).

One of the first acts of the new Sultan was to send an army under his eldest son to Warangal. Laddar Deo was still King of Warangal, and at first tried to purchase peace by delivering up his treasure. Ulugh Khan, the Sultan's son, refused any terms, and commenced laying siege to the fort. The Hindoos were reduced to extremity, and were on the eve of capitulating, when a revolt broke out in the camp in consequence of a false report of the Sultan's death. The Hindoos seized the opportunity, sallied forth, and plundered the baggage of the army, whereupon Ulugh Khan retired to Dowlatabad, and Warangal had another respite. The respite, however, was a brief one, for no sooner had the Sultan punished the instigators of the revolt, than he sent Ulugh Khan with another army to besiege the ill-fated city. This time resistance was of no avail, and after a short siege the fort was taken, the Rajah with all his family and treasures were captured and sent to Delhi, and the very name of Warangal was altered to that of Sultanpur. This occurred in 1323. But the curse attending the Hindoo gold was still at work, and again we find that the desire of possessing this fatal gold led to crime. This time it was parricide, and Ulugh Khan was led away to kill his own father. This is the way the murder was effected. The Sultan was returning from an expedition to Delhi, and Ulugh Khan built a pavilion in which to receive him. This pavilion was so contrived that by treading on a certain stone the roof would fall in. Whilst the Sultan was being entertained at dinner, Ulugh Khan and the conspirators went out, touched the secret spring, and the roof fell in and killed the Sultan and his companions. Ulugh Khan then mounted the throne under the title of Mahomed Tughlak Shah (1325).

We have now come to the time when we can find some authentic accounts of the Deccan country. The two great Hindoo kingdoms of Warangal and Deogiri have been destroyed, and in their place Mahomedan rule has been substituted. The representative of the Sultan of Delhi is an almost independent governor in the midst of on alien population. Except in the immediate vicinity of his capital, Dowlatabad, it is probable that he does not exercise more than a nominal sway. Though Mahomedan armies have marched far away to the south—it is said that Malik Kafur actually built a mosque at Rameswaram—they have left no permanent impression. All that they have done is to carry away plunder, and leave behind them ruins and heaps of corpses. There exists a bitter hatred against them on account of their cruelty and rapine, and already the Hindoos, driven away from Warangal and the Telingana, have founded a new kingdom at Vijayanagar, which is destined to be for two hundred and fifty years a bulwark against further invasion. In Delhi there is a constant struggle for the throne. Tempted by the enormous amount of treasure which has been carried away from the Hindoos, there are adventurers always eager to obtain a share. Already on the north-western frontiers has appeared the shadow of the Mogul conqueror, who before long will drive the Afghan Sultans away. Amid such scenes of disturbance it is not likely that the Sultans of Delhi can exercise a very effectual control over so distant a place as Dowlatabad. If this part of the country is to be preserved under Mahomedan rule, there must be a local leader to concentrate the scattered Hindoo provinces which have lost their ancient rulers. The time for the birth of a new kingdom has arrived, and when the hour has come the man is always ready. And so it was in this case.

CHAPTER II.

THE ORIGIN OF THE BAHMANEE KINGS OF GULBURGA.

IN the last chapter I have endeavoured to describe the state of affairs in the Deccan at the commencement of the reign of Mahomed Tughlak Shah. The character of this King was not one calculated to improve matters. During his long reign of twenty-seven years (from 1325 to 1352, A.D.) he brought his kingdom to the verge of ruin by his mad acts of tyranny and insane adventure. He was wise enough to see that if the new conquests in the Deccan were to be preserved to the Mahomedans, and the growing power of the young Hindoo kingdom at Vijayanagar kept in check, it would be necessary to have the central power nearer to the newly conquered province than Delhi. The distance from the capital, and the immense wealth hoarded up by the Hindoo princes offered too great a temptation to the loyalty of his lieutenants. The Governors at Dowlatabad were constantly being accused of disloyalty, and were frequently removed. In order to obviate this he conceived the mad idea of transferring his capital from Delhi to Dowlatabad. This was not done gradually, but, as it were at a moment's notice, the whole of the inhabitants of the great city, which for 180 years had been the capital of the Mahomedan Empire in India, were ordered to leave their homes and emigrate to Dowlatabad. The historian *Barni* thus describes the effect of this tyrannical order: "The city with its *sárais* and its suburbs and villages spread over four or five *Kos* (about 10 miles). All was destroyed. So complete was the ruin, that not a cat or dog was left among the buildings of the city, in its palaces or in its suburbs. Troops of the natives, with their families and dependents, wives and children, men-servants, and maid-servants were forced to remove. The people who for many years and for generations had been natives and inhabitants of the land were broken-hearted. Many from the toils of the long journey, perished on the road, and those who arrived at Deogiri could not endure the pain of exile. In despondency they pined to death. All around Deogiri, which is an infidel land, there sprung up graveyards of Mussulmans. The Sultan was bounteous in his liberality and favours to the emigrants, both on their journey and on their arrival: but they were tender and they could not endure the exile and the suffering. They laid down their heads in that heathen land, and of all the multitudes of emigrants few only survived to return to their home. Thus the city, the envy of the cities of the inhabited world, was reduced to ruin. One of these emigrants was a man who afterwards became very famous in the Deccan as the founder of a new kingdom. This man was called Hassan. He was born in the year 1290 (A. D.) and was in very humble circumstances. For the first thirty years of his life he was nothing more than a field labourer, and was employed by a Brahmin of Delhi named *Gangu*. This Brahmin gave him a piece of land near the city walls, together with a pair of oxen and two labourers. Hassan was a hard working honest man, and one day when he was at work with his plough, it struck in some hard body "and Hassan upon examination, found it was entangled in a chain round the neck of an earthen vessel, which proved to be full of antique gold coins. He immediately carried them to the Brahmin, who commended his honesty and informed the Prince of the discovered treasure" (Scott's Ferishta). This prince was the Sultan Ghaziuddin, who reigned from 1320 to 1325. The Sultan was so much pleased with Hassan's honesty, that he ordered him to be brought to his presence and bestowed upon him the command of one hundred horse. This sudden elevation from the position of a field labourer to that of a military officer of considerable rank would appear absurd now-a-days, but five hundred years ago it was no uncommon thing. The Brahmin Gangu, who employed Hassan, was one of the royal astrologers, and attracted by this promotion of his hitherto obscure servant he cast his horoscope. In this horoscope he found it foretold that Hassan would one day become a king. In repeating this prophecy to Hassan, the Brahmin made one request, *viz.*, that Hassan should adopt his name in future, and when he should some day become king that he would appoint him as his minister of finance. This Hassan promised, and from that time was known as Hassan Gangu*. It is said that his good fortune was also predicted by a Mahomedan saint named Shekh Nizam-ud-Din Oulea, whose memory is still venerated at Delhi, and whose tomb is resorted to annually by numerous pilgrims. These prophecies and his recent promotion, no doubt, fired Hassan's

---

* This name as translated from the Persian historians is generally spelt Kangoh, but it evidently refers to Gangu a not uncommon Hindoo name.

ambition, and he looked forward to some opportunity of adventure. The Deccan was then the El Dorado of the Mahomedan imagination, and no doubt Hassan hoped some day to employ his body of horsemen in slaying and plundering the infidel Hindoos. The opportunity was not long in coming. When Mahomed Tughlak Shah resolved to change his capital from Delhi to Dowlatabad, he appointed Kuttulugh Khan as Governor of the latter place, and allowed him to select his own officers. One of these was Hassan Gangu and he followed his new master to Dowlatabad, where he was assigned as jaghir the "town of Konechee with lands dependent on the district of Roy baugh" (Scott.) This town is situated in what is now H. H. the Nizam's Dominions. Here Hassan remained for some years increasing in influence and wealth. No doubt he made various raids for himself against his neighbours the heathen Hindoos, until at last he became a landholder and a military chief of considerable importance.

In the meantime matters throughout the kingdom of Mahomed Tughlak had grown from bad to worse. The unpopularity which the king had earned by the enforced emigration of the inhabitants from Delhi to Dowlatabad was increased by the arbitrary manner in which the jaghirdars were treated in the outlying provinces. All kinds of exactions were made, and whenever a landowner refused to pay he was treated as a rebel. Altogether Mahomed Tughlak seems to have behaved like a madman. *Barni* * enumerates six projects which led to the ruin of the country. The first was an attempt to extort from five to ten per cent more tribute from all the landowners in the Doab. These cesses, we are told, were collected so rigorously that the *raiyats* were impoverished and reduced to beggary. Those who were rich and had property became rebels; the lands were ruined and cultivation was entirely arrested. This, added to a failure of the rains, brought about a terrible famine, which

* Elliot and Dowson, Vol. III.

is spoken of as one of the worst that ever occurred in India. It continued, we are told, for some years, and thousands upon thousands of people perished of want. The second project was the change of the capital to which allusion has already been made. The third was even madder than the first two, and was nothing less than a conquest of the whole world. The King wished to become a second Alexander, and resolved upon raising an enormous army with which to carry out his designs. In order to provide the necessary funds to pay this countless host of soldiers, he introduced copper money, and gave orders that it should be used in buying and selling and should pass current, just as the gold and silver coins had passed. The promulgation of this order we are told by the same historian, turned the house of every Hindoo into a mint, and the Hindoos of the various provinces coined an enormous amount of copper coins. Of course, the natural result was a general depreciation of the currency, and so low did the value of the new coins fall, that they were not esteemed higher than "pebbles or potsherds." When trade was interrupted on every side, and when the copper *tankas* "had become more worthless than clods," the Sultan repealed his edict, and in great wrath he proclaimed that whoever possessed copper coins should bring them to the treasury and receive the old gold coins in exchange. "Thousands of men from various quarters, who possessed thousands of these copper coins, and caring nothing about them, had flung them into corners along with their copper pots, now brought them to the treasury and received in exchange gold *tankas* and silver *tankas, shashganis* and *du-garnis* which they carried to their homes. So many of these copper coins were brought to the treasury that heaps of them rose up in Tuglikábád (the new name of Dowlatabad) like mountains. Great sums went out of the treasury in exchange for the copper, and a great deficiency was caused. When the Sultan saw that his project had failed, and that great loss had been entailed upon the treasury through his copper coins, he more than ever turned against his subjects." The remaining three projects were military expeditions, all of which were attended by failure. The first two were against Khurasan and Persia, and the third against China. The latter was especially disastrous. A large army was shut in by the Hindoos in the defiles of what is now called the Black Mountain and was entirely cut to pieces. Out of the whole army only ten horsemen returned to Delhi to tell the news of their defeat.

The consequence of these rash enterprises was that everywhere the country broke into open revolt. In Multan, Bengal, and distant Ma'bar the Governors rebelled. It is difficult now to ascertain the exact boundaries of this province of Ma'bar. As has been said before, the whole of the southern portion of the Peninsula was called Malabar. * It is probable that the capital of the Mahomedan Governor was somewhere on the western coast, but if so, in a very short time all trace of this Mahomedan occupation vanished, for during the next two hundred years, until the time of Aurungzebe, the whole of this country was undoubtedly held by Hindoos. The Sultan marched with an army to put down this rebellion, but he did not get further than Warangal, when cholera broke out and he was compelled to return. When he reached Dowlatabad on his way home, he gave permission to those who wished to do so to return to Delhi. A large number availed themselves of this permission, but those who had become acclimatised resolved to remain. No sooner had the Sultan returned to Delhi than a revolt broke out at Warangal. A Hindoo named Kanya Naick raised an army of his co-religionists, and succeeded in driving out the Mahomedan Governor Malik Makbul, who fled to Delhi. The province of Warangal was then completely

* The west coast was known to the Arabs as Ma'bar long before this conquest, because it was the coast to which traders *crossed* over from Arabia (from *Abara* = he crossed).

lost to the Mahomedans and for some time the Hindoos established their rule. No attempt seems to have been made to recover this country, probably because the Sultan's attention was so fully occupied by other matters. In fact before long the only outlying provinces that remained faithful were Dowlatabad and Guzerat. But it was not long that the Sultan's folly caused him to lose these two provinces also. In 1344, a man named Aziz Khummar was appointed as Governor of Malwa and Guzerat with strict orders to collect as much tribute as possible. One of the first acts of this wretch was to collect eighty of the principal Amirs at his palace and cause them all to be beheaded. This brutal act, which was rewarded by the Sultan with a robe of honour and a complimentary letter, caused a general insurrection. This broke out first in Gujarat where the nobles rose and defeated the deputy Governor Mukbil. This occurred in 1345. The Sultan at once marched in person to suppress this revolt, which, after committing great cruelties, he succeeded in doing. Those nobles who were not captured fled with their families to the Deccan and many of them took refuge at Dowlatabad. The Sultan despatched an order that all these fugitives should be sent to him with an escort of fifteen hundred horse. On the way these prisoners rose against their guards, killed them and then returned to Dowlatabad where they proclaimed an open rebellion. The treasury was looted and distributed amongst the conspirators. They then declared the independence of the Deccan and elected as their first Sultan an Afghan chief named Ismael who assumed the title of Nusrud-din. Prominent amongst these conspirators was Hassan Kangoh, upon whom the title of Zaffir Khan was bestowed, together with several large districts in jaghir. So great was the general feeling of discontent against the Sultan of Delhi, that the rebels at Dowlatabad were assisted in their revolt by the Hindoos of Warangal, who thus made common cause with Mahomedans against their oppressor. Mahomed

Toghluk at once marched against the rebels and defeated them. He did not, however, succeed in capturing the ringleaders, and most of them escaped to their own districts, where the Sultan was unable to follow them, as his presence was again required to suppress a revolt at Delhi. He left behind him however a deputy named Imad-ul-Mulk, with orders to march to Gulburga, hunt up all the fugitives and bring the country into order. Gulburga was the part of the country in which Hassan Kangoh's jaghirs were situated, and this was the opportunity for which he had prepared himself. He collected his troops as quickly as possible, and went to meet Imad-ul-Mulk, who had remained at Bieder. The Sultan's General had about 30,000 men of all arms, and Hassan only about 15,000. The latter, therefore, avoided coming to a general action, but kept Imad-ul-Mulk in check, until reinforcements could arrive. At length he received 15,000 men from Warangal, and a body of 5,000 horse despatched by the confederate Sultan Ismael from Dowlatabad. With forces thus increased, Hassan did not hesitate to meet his opponent. A pitched battle ensued which was fought near Bieder. It commenced at daybreak and lasted till sunset. The result was that Imad-ul-Mulk was killed and his army utterly defeated with great slaughter. The fugitives made their escape to Malwa, but a large number appear subsequently to have taken service with the victorious general. Hassan, flushed with victory, now marched to Dowlatabad to join his forces with those of Sultan Ismael Nasr-ud-Din. Ismael came some distance to meet his general, and there was a scene of the utmost enthusiasm. Nasr-ud-Din saw that the whole of the army looked up to Hassan as its natural leader, and he therefore very wisely resolved to give place to his younger rival. He called an assembly of the nobles and told them that his great age rendered him incapable of conducting the government of so young a kingdom, surrounded by such powerful enemies. He therefore voluntarily resigned the throne, and advised them to elect Hassan Kangoh in his place. This proposal was received with the utmost enthusiasm and the former peasant was raised to the throne under the title of *Sultan Alla-ud-Din Hassan Kangoh Bahmanee.* (A. D. 1347). In the hour of his prosperity the new Sultan did not forget his old patron and, faithful to his former promise, he sent for Kangoh and committed to his care his treasury and finances. It is said that Kangoh was the first Brahmin who ever took service under a Mahomedan Prince, but, however this may be, he was most certainly not the last, for during the next two hundred years it became the universal custom throughout the Deccan for the different Mahomedan kings to appoint Brahmins to high posts of authority. This was a wise stroke of policy; for it had the effect of bringing the Government more in touch with the people, the vast majority of whom were Hindoos. In fact the Mahomedans throughout the Deccan were only employed in military posts, and the cultivation of the country was everywhere left in the hands of the Hindoos. Malik Seyf-ud-Din Ghoree was appointed Prime Minister, and the ex-Sultan resumed his name of Ismael, and was nominated *Amir-ul-Amra* or chief of the nobles.

Such was the commencement of the dynasty of the Bahmanee Sultans of Gulburga, for this was the capital of the new kingdom. In the succeeding chapters we shall see to what an extraordinary height of prosperity this kingdom quickly rose, under the wise and just rule of Sultan Alla-ud-Din the former servant of the Brahmin astrologer. Amongst the Mahomedans more than any other nation, there are to be found instances of a romantic and adventurous life, but even amongst Mahomedans there are but few examples of such a wonderful change of fortune, and still rarer are the instances where the success was unstained by cruelty. Sultan Alla-ud-Din was now 57 years of age, and he had still eleven years before him in which to finish the work he had thus gloriously commence'

CHAPTER III.

THE RISE OF THE HINDOO KINGDOM OF VIJAYANAGAR, AND THE END OF THE FIRST GULBURGA SULTAN.

WE have already seen that with the fall of Warangal in 1323 the Hindoo kingdom of Telingana came to an end. The city was plundered and destroyed and the King was carried off prisoner to Delhi. After some years he was permitted to return to find his capital in ruins and its inhabitants scattered.

He exercised a certain control over a few districts, but he never recovered his former power and position, and instead of being the head of a mighty kingdom, he became nothing more than a petty chieftain. There had been two brothers in the army of the King of Warangal, named *Bukha Raya* and *Hari-hara*. When the city fell, these two brothers made their escape with a small body of horse, and were according to one account accompanied in their flight by a Madhava Brahmin named Vidya Aranya, or the Forest of learning. This Brahmin had formed a strong attachment towards the two brothers, and had prophesied that they would some day become Kings *). During their flight they were joined by other remnants of the army of the King of Warangal until at last the following became quite a large one. This small army marched towards the south, and crossed the Kristna about the spot where it is joined by the Tungabadhra, near where the present town of Kurnool is situated. Following the course of the Tungabadhra the brothers marched on for more than 150 miles up the stream, until they reached a spot where they thought themselves safe from a Mahomedan invasion. Here they remained for some years, moving probably from one place to another until at last they selected a site for a town, which in honour of their Brahmin Counsellor they called Vidhyanagaram, or city of learning. The date of the building of this city is generally ascribed to the year 1336 A.D. The only records to be found of this new kingdom are in the grants which are to be found in the inscriptions on stone and copper in the temples. The earliest of these is several years subsequent to the year 1336. This, however, is only natural as it would only be after increasing in power that such grants would be made. The time was especially favourable for the growth of a new power. It will be remembered that the armies of the Delhi Sultans under Malik Kafur and others had between 1310 and 1324

* For another and more reliable account see Chap. VII.

swept away the Hindoo kingdoms of the Deccan. After this period, and especially during the reign of Mahomed Toghluk, there were so many disturbances in the Mahomedan kingdom that the Sultan had but little time to spare to look after the conquests in the South. The Mahomedan Governors of the provinces, amongst whom was Hassan Kangoh, were each too busy in schemes of personal aggrandizement to interfere with what was going on at a distance, so that whilst circumstances were bringing about the founding of a new Mahomedan Kingdom at Gulburga, Bukha Raya and Harihara were left undisturbed. So rapidly did their conquests extend, especially towards the East and South, that in a short time the name of their city was changed to Vijayanagaram, or the city of victory, and it is under that name, or that of Bisnugger that we find it mentioned in history. The city of Vijayanagar rapidly grew in size, and extended itself on both banks of the river Tungabadhra. The site is a favourable one, being protected by a ridge of hills, through which a narrow pass that can be easily defended protects the city. The rapid growth of this new kingdom is as striking as was that of the new kingdom of Golconda. For two hundred years they were rivals of each other. At first they were probably allies against the Delhi Sultans and so had time to extend their dominions without mutual interference. The Vijayanagar dynasty having been expelled from the Telingana or Warangal country, seems to have relinquished all thoughts of reconquering it, and devoted itself to recovering from the Mahomedans the outlying and detached provinces situated in the Ma'bar or Southern countries. The dissensions and civil wars, which lasted for the next twenty years in the North of India, enabled it to succeed in this endeavour, for by the end of that time we find that all trace of Mahomedan government in southern India had disappeared. It is probably soon after the establishment of this new Hindoo Kingdom that a geographical line was drawn between the Deccan and the Carnatic. The former represented that portion of central India which lies between the Godavery as a northern boundary and the Tungabadhra, and extended before long from one coast to the other. The latter comprised the rich valleys of the tributaries of the Pennair with their mountainous passes, and from thence extended to Conjeveram, Arcot, and subsequently Madura. There is throughout the history of the struggles between the Mahomedans and the Hindoos one remarkable feature. No sooner is a Hindoo kingdom established than it at once acquires enormous wealth in gold and jewels. These treasures, no doubt, attracted the cupidity of the Mahomedans, but a few years after a Hindoo Prince has been conquered and despoiled, we almost always find him in possession of fresh hoards of treasure which he again has to yield up. It is only when the Hindoo kingdom is annexed and the dynasty exterminated that we find the country ceases to produce gold and precious stones, and the Mahomedan conquerors have then to go against other Hindoo kingdoms in order to gain fresh treasure. Under Mahomedan rule it would seem that there was little or no natural production, and no development of the country's resources. Under Hindoo Princes, on the contrary, as long as they were left undisturbed, attention was paid to agricultural and irrigation works, and especially to mining industries. The consequence was that the Hindoo kingdoms became rich and prosperous, but as soon as they were conquered and annexed by the Mahomedans the indigenous industries were allowed to languish. No more striking instance of this is to be found than in the Deccan. It has already been told how often Deogiri and Warangal were attacked, and how on each occasion an enormous amount of treasure carried away. To this day the ruins of old irrigation works show how prosperous must have been the agricultural condition of the Telingana country. After the Mahomedan Governor of Warangal had been compelled to flee, as told in the last chapter, the Hindoos again ruled the country, and we shall again find them coming into collision with the Mahomedan Sultans of Gulburga, and being again in possession of treasures of gold and precious stones. When, however, eventually the Hindoo princes were finally overthrown, and their country subjugated to the Golconda Kings we hear but little more of the stores of treasure. It is, however, a fact that the whole of the Deccan, from Mysore up to the northern limits of the Nizam's dominions are covered with remains of old mining works. In Mysore it has been found that these old mines extend to a considerable depth, and traces of what, in mining language, is called "the old men" are found at three or even four hundred feet beneath the surface. In many of these mines the work had, no doubt, to be relinquished, because with the mechanical appliances of those days there was always a point beyond which the miners could not go, owing to the want of proper pumps, the cost of raising the ore by manual labour, &c. Other mines again were probably relinquished before this point had been reached, because the new conquerors paid no attention to the industry, and prized the spoil of the sword, higher than that of the spade and the pickaxe. They were, therefore, allowed to fall into ruin, and all tradition of the ancient industry passed away. Attention, however, is now being attracted to these old mines, and in some of the Mysore mines in which the work has been carried to a point beyond which the "old men" could not go, the yield of gold is so great, that they rank amongst the richest gold mines in the world. In course of time it is highly probable, that similar results will be obtained from the other old mines, hundreds of which are scattered all over the country. There is little doubt, that it was from these mines that the Hindoos obtained their vast wealth, and it is equally certain that the old miners must have left behind them a vast store of gold, which, with their appliances and primitive machinery, they were unable to touch. It would not be unsafe to prophecy, that a hundred years hence the Deccan will be one of the richest gold-producing countries in the world, and during the next century we may see the prosperity of six hundred years ago renewed to an even greater degree. The gold thus acquired, will be spent in restoring the old irrigation works, and the districts, which must at one time have borne a teeming population, but which now often carry less than one hundred meagrely-nourished persons to the square mile, will again be peopled by a prosperous and thriving peasantry. Having thus traced the origin of the Vijayanagar kingdom, we must now return to Gulburga and follow the events of the reign of the first of the Bahmani Sultans.

Sultan Alla-ud-Din was not slow to take advantage of the disturbances in Delhi to extend the boundaries of his new kingdom. He won over the Afghan, Mogul and Rajput Chiefs, stationed by the Emperor at Bieder and Candahar. This Candahar is not to be mistaken for the town in Afghanistan, but is a fort situated on the north-west of Dowlatabad. He also took Kailas from the Rajah of Warangal, with whom he then formed a defensive alliance. In a short time his dominions comprised almost the whole of the western and southern portions of what now forms the Nizam's Dominions. In 1352 (A.D.) Mahomed Toghluk died, and was succeeded by his nephew Firoz Shah. This Prince was a wise and humane ruler, and ranks amongst the best and greatest of the Delhi Emperors. He was wise enough to see that the only way to maintain the tottering empire was to consolidate it. Accordingly, he recognized the accomplished fact of the new kingdom of Gulburga, and devoted his attention to redressing the grievances of the provinces nearer his capital. Thus left undisturbed, Alla-ud-Din was at liberty to carry out his own designs. One of his first acts was to marry his son to the daughter of his Prime Minister, Malik Seyf-ud-Din Ghoree.

THE RISE OF THE HINDOO KINGDOM OF VIJAYANAGAR.

This ceremony was conducted with the utmost magnificence. We are told by Ferishta that "ten thousand robes of cloth of gold, velvet, and satin were distributed among the nobility and others. One thousand Arab and Persian horses, and two hundred sabres set with jewels were also divided. The populace were entertained with various amusements, and engines were erected in the streets of Gulburga, which cast forth showers of confectionery among the crowd. The rejoicings lasted a whole year, on the last day of which, the nobility and officers presented offerings of jewels, money and the rarest productions of all countries to the Sultan." This truly was a right royal wedding, and shows that the new King had already acquired a considerable quantity of wealth. It is probable, however, that festivities on so large a scale were organized from feelings of policy. In the same way as the Roman people was always attracted and conciliated by *Panes et circenses*, so, by a lavish expenditure of money, the founder of the new dynasty endeavoured to win over an alien people. In this he seems to have been eminently successful, and we read of no rebellions or revolts, amongst his Hindoo subjects. One conspiracy we do read of, but that was organized by the ex-Sultan Ismael, who had been made Amir-ul-Amra, or chief of the nobles. Although he had been wise enough to resign the throne in favour of Alla-ud-Din, it is probable, that he felt some jealousy towards the new King; in fact, it would be contrary to human nature if he did not. This jealousy was increased by the preference and precedence shown towards Seyf-ud-Din Ghoree, the Prime Minister. As chief of the nobles, he considered himself entitled to the first rank under the Sultan, and complained accordingly to his master. He received as an answer, that in every Government the pen ranked above the sword. With this reply, he pretended to be satisfied, but secretly he formed a conspiracy, the object of which was to assassinate the Sultan, and to place himself on the throne he had previously resigned. The plot, however, was revealed to the Sultan by some of the conspirators who repented. The Sultan at once called an assemblage of all his principal nobles and officers, and in their presence accused the Amir-ul-Amra of treachery. This accusation being denied on solemn oath, the Sultan called forth the informer and offered a pardon to all others who had joined the plot if they would reveal the truth. This they did, and his guilt being conclusively proved, the ex-Sultan was at once put to death. But though the Sultan showed that he could be severe, his conduct was a proof that he was neither cruel nor vindictive None of the traitor's property was confiscated, and his son Bahadur Khan was at once appointed to his father's post as Amir-ul-Omara, and the royal favour continued as before, to be extended to the family. Alla-ud-Din may have been brought up as a peasant, but he showed that he knew how to behave like a king.

"From this," to quote again from Ferishta, "and other instances of justice tempered with mercy, loyalty to the Sultan became fixed in every breast, and his power daily increased. The Rajah of Telingana,* who had become disobedient, but was treated with generous forbearance on account of his former assistance to the Sultan, was overcome by the sense of his virtues, submitted to his authority, and agreed to pay the tribute which he had heretofore remitted to the Sovereign of Delhi." An army sent into the Carnatic returned after several successful engagements, laden with booty, amongst which were two hundred elephants, and one thousand female singers. An invitation was sent from the representative of the old Rajah of Guzerat to invade that country, which was then left a prey to a number of turbulent and rebellious jagirdars, who were too distant from Delhi to be kept in control. Alla-ud-Din assembled a large army for this purpose, and sent off his

* The name generally used for Waragal.

eldest son Mohamed in command of the vanguard, he himself following with the main army. On the way, however, he was attacked by a severe illness, which compelled him to return to Gulburga. The Sultan seeing that his days were numbered, set about arranging the affairs of his kingdom. He divided his territories into four provinces at the head of each of which, he placed a governor. The capital and its dependencies, consisting of Dabul, a small port near Bombay, Bejoir and Mudkul were entrusted to Sey-fud-Din Ghoree; Choul, Kiber, Dowlatabad and Mheeropatan, to his nephew Mahomed; the Berars, Mahoor and Ramgur, to Kusder Khan Systain; and Bieder, Indore and the Telingana districts to Azim Humayun, son of Seyf-ud-Din Ghoree. It will thus be seen that Alla-ud-Din's dominions including not only a large portion of the present kingdom of Hyderabad, but also extended as far as the Western coast, though it is probable that his possessions there were detached and limited in extent. The Beejoir here mentioned is probably what was afterwards known as Beejapore, and of which we shall hear more hereafter. At this time the Mahrattas did not exist as a nation; and the country afterwards known as the Mahratta country was divided amongst a number of petty hill chieftains; some of whom submitted to the Sultan, whilst others remained independent in their inaccessible forts and fortresses.

For six months the Sultan continued to decline in health, and his end was fast approaching. During the whole of this time, in spite of his illness he gave public audience twice a day, and transacted business. He ordered all prisoners to be released except those accused of capital offences. These were sent to Gulburga, where they were examined by the Sultan himself. With the exception of seven, all these were set at liberty, and these seven the Sultan handed over to his son Muhammed to be dealt with as he thought proper after his father's death. "At length" says Ferishta "finding no benefit from medicine and feeling nature exhausted, he discharged his physicians, and waited patiently for the final cure of human ills. In this state, enquiring for his youngest son Mahmoud who had been reading with his tutor, what book he had that day perused, the Prince replied: "The Boseton of Saadi, and the following passage: 'I have heard that Jamshid of angelic memory had these verses engraved upon a fountain: Many like me have viewed the fountain, but they are gone, and their eyes closed for ever. I conquered the world by policy and valour, but could not overcome the grave.'" The Sultan sighed at this recital, and calling his sons Daood and Mahomed before him, said: "This is my last breath, and with it I conjure you, as you value the permanence of the kingdom to agree with each other. Muhammed is my successor; esteem submission and loyalty to him as your duty in this world, and your surety for happiness in the next." Having said this, he sent for the treasurer, and gave to each of his sons a sum of money to distribute to the poor. When they had obeyed him and returned, he exclaimed: 'Praise be to God!' and instantly resigned his life to the Creator. 'Constantly appears some one who boasts, I am Lord, shows himself to his fellows, and vaunts, I am Lord. When the affairs of mortals have become dependent on him, suddenly advances death, and exclaims: *I* am Lord!'" The death of Sultan Alla-ud-Din happened eleven years, two months, and seven days after his accession to royalty, and on the first of Rabee'-ul-Awal, 759, (A. D. 1359), in the sixty-seventh year of his age.

"It is related that Sultan Alla-ud-Din being asked, how, without great treasures or armies, he had acquired royalty in so short a space, he replied: "By affability to friends and enemies, and by showing liberality to all to the utmost of my power!"

There are unfortunately but very slight materials for a history of Sultan Alla-ud-Din, but those that exist are sufficient to show that he deserves a high place amongst the great men of the world's history. Born in the lowest ranks, he rose, by his own honesty of character, to be the founder of a great kingdom, and at no time was his career stained by cruelty or injustice. There are few characters in history that can compare with this, the first King of the Deccan, and there is probably no other nation in the world than the Mahomedan, which can furnish the example of a peasant raising himself to the throne of a monarch, who retains throughout his career, not only dignity of character, but honesty of purpose, and who relinquishes his life with such humble piety and simplicity. Mahomedans of the Deccan may well be proud of the first founder of their rule, and the history of the country shows that he was a rare exception to those who followed him.

CHAPTER IV.

THE GULBURGA SULTANS. — MUHAMMED SHAH.

SULTAN Alla-ud-Din was succeeded by his eldest son Muhammed (1st Rabee-ul-Awul 759 H—A.D. 1357). Everything in India depends upon personal influence, and no sooner did the news spread that Alla-ud-Din was dead, than the Hindoo Kings of Vijayanagar and Telingana, hoping to take advantage of a young king on a lately-established throne, not only refused to send tribute, but demanded the restoration of the districts taken from them by the late Sultan. Muhammed Shah was not at first in a position to punish this rebellion. His treasury was very low, owing to the enormous expenditure which he had incurred during the festivities which followed his accession, and to his having also sent his mother on a pilgrimage to Mecca accompanied by a large train of his nobles and chiefs. Accordingly, he prolonged negociations with the ambassadors sent to him, and sent others to the Courts of the Rajahs with instructions to gain as much time as possible. As soon, however, as he had completed his arrangements, and his mother had returned, he broke off all negociations and made a demand on the Rajahs of their arrears of tribute, together with a number of elephants laden with treasure. Upon this the two Rajahs at once declared war, and the Rajah of Telingana, assisted by an army from Vijayanagar, sent his son Nagdeo to recapture the fort of Kailas. The Hindoos, however, were met by a Mahomedan army under Bahadur Khan and were totally defeated. The Telingana Rajah was made to pay a large subsidy in gold and jewels, and for some years there was peace. This period, which seems to have lasted for thirteen years, the Sultan employed in strengthening his kingdom. He was fond of show and magnificence, and spent a considerable amount of money in beautifying his capital. It was probably during this period that the splendid mosque was built which still stands in the Gulburga fort, though all the other palaces have fallen into ruin. This mosque is said to be unique of its kind in India and is modelled after the great mosque of Cordova. * He also devoted a great deal of attention to his army, and established

---

* According to Mr. Fergusson's account ("Eastern Architecture." page 544) it measures 216 feet east and west, and 176 feet north and south, and consequently covers an area of 38,016 square feet. Its great peculiarity is that alone of all the great mosques in India the whole area is covered in. The roof is supported on square stone pillars which form a number of aisles all converging towards the pulpit platform, which is separated from the body of the masjid by a carved stone railing. Some portions of the building are sadly in need of repair. It would be a great pity if the building, which Mr. Fergusson styles "one of the finest of the old Pathan mosques in India," were allowed to lapse into the same decay and desolation as those which surround it.

his household forces on a system of great magnificence. In addition to a select corps of two hundred sons of noblemen, he formed a bodyguard of four thousand men commanded by an officer of high rank, styled the Meer Nobut, or Lord of the Watch. Fifty mounted horsemen and one thousand of the bodyguard were on duty every day at the palace. The Sultan himself gave public audience on every day of the week except Friday, and transacted business from the early morning until noon. The Nobut, or band of the Watch, was sounded five times during the day, a custom which is said to have been adopted by none of the other Mahomedan Princes of the Deccan except the Kings of Golconda. Gold coinage was also introduced, and we find that the system of hoarding gold was as prevalent five hundred years ago as it is now. The Hindoo bankers are said to have collected as much of the gold coinage as they could gather, and to have melted it down. Ferishta attributes this to the instigation of the Rajahs of Telingana and Vijayanagar who wished that their coins only should be current in the Deccan, but it is more probable that it was due to the inborn habit of hoarding which prevails amongst all Hindoos. The Sultan, however, put a most effectual stop to this custom by punishing such offences with death, and by confining the banking business to Mahomedans related to Delhi bankers.

Sultan Muhammed Shah was very jealous about his own dignity, and his two greatest wars arose from what he considered a personal slight. In 1371 some horse dealers arrived in Gulburga with some horses which were shown to the Sultan; they were a very poor lot, and the Sultan said that they were not fit to be given to a king, whereupon the dealers replied that the best of the horses had been forcibly taken from them by the Hindoo prince Nagdeo at Velunputtun. It is difficult to ascertain what port is meant by Velunputtun. Scott guesses it to be either Goa or Rajapoor, but Nagdeo was the son of the Rajah of Telingana, whose possessions most certainly did not extend to the Western coast. The name itself sounds more like a Telugu or Tamil name, and it therefore seems probable that it was some port on the Coromandel coast (perhaps Masulipatam). On the other hand, it seems difficult to understand why Arab horse dealers should have gone to the Eastern instead of the Western coast, and Ferishta expressly speaks of the Sultan halting on his march at a place called Kallean. This town was not the Kallean on the G. I. P. Railway below the Western Ghats but another Kallean situated in the Nizam's dominions considerably to the East of Gulburga. In order to revenge this insult, the Sultan marched into Telingana and took Velunputtun by storm, the young Rajah being taken prisoner. When the Rajah was brought before the Sultan, he was asked why he had dared to seize horses which were on their way to Gulburga. The Hindoo Prince is said to have given an insolent reply, which so enraged the Sultan that he ordered Nagdeo to be shot from an engine into a burning pile of wood, which barbarous sentence was duly carried out. On the return march, however, the Hindoos had their revenge. The country through which his journey lay was a very difficult one, and the enemy harrassed the Mahomedan army to such an extent that out of four thousand men only fifteen hundred reached Gulburga, after having lost all their tents, baggage and plunder, with the exception of the gold and jewels. The Sultan himself was wounded in the hand, and was forced to halt at Kailas. This fact is a proof that the expedition was to the Coromandel coast; for Kailas was a fort which had been taken from the Rajah of Warangal, in whose territory it was situated.

The Telingana Rajah in order to avenge the death of his son, now applied to Delhi for assistance, in return for which he promised to become a vassal of the Emperor. Feroze

Shah, however, was too much occupied with internal matters to comply with this appeal, and the Telingana king was left to his own resources.

In order to repair the disaster of this last expedition, the Sultan made large preparations and despatched two armies with which he intended to effect the complete conquest of Telingana. He left his Minister, Seyf-ud-Din Ghoree in charge of his capital, and himself marched with the army which had been sent to Warangal. A second army was sent to besiege Golconda, and the Rajah of Warangal was threatened with total ruin. The conquest, however, does not appear to have been an easy one, for the Sultan was detained for nearly two years in the Telingana country. At the end of this time the Rajah made overtures of peace, but the conditions imposed by the Sultan were very severe. They were the cession of the fort of Golconda, three hundred elephants, two hundred horses, and thirty-three lakhs of rupees. To these conditions the Rajah had to accede, and accordingly the main body of the Mahomedan army was sent back to Gulburga, the Sultan remaining with Bahadur Khan at Kailas in order to receive the treasure. When this had been handed over and the Rajah's ambassadors had been rewarded with presents, they asked the Sultan if he would sign a treaty of perpetual alliance with the Telingana Rajah, to be binding on the successors of both, in which case the Rajah would become his vassal, and present him with "a curiosity worthy to be laid at the feet of a great King only." This offer was no doubt agreeable to the Sultan, and a treaty was drawn up fixing Golconda as the boundary between the Sultan's and the Rajah's dominions, and the Sultan signed a paper conjuring his descendants not to molest the Telingana Rajahs as long as they kept faith. The ambassadors then produced the "curiosity," which consisted of a splendid throne covered with valuable jewels which had been prepared some time before as a present to the Emperor

Mahomed Toghluk Shah. With this present the Sultan was highly pleased, and the ambassadors were dismissed with every mark of honour. The treaty itself seems to have been faithfully kept, and for many generations we find no more mention of wars between the Gulburga and the Telingana Princes. It was in this way that Golconda came into the power of the Mahomedans, and from thenceforth it formed the capital of one of the Gulburga Governors, one of whom in course of time, when the power of the Bahmanee dynasty had declined, declared his independence and converted Golconda into the capital of a kingdom.

As regards the throne, Ferishta says that he had heard from an eyewitness that it was nine feet long and three feet broad. It was made of ebony covered with plates of pure gold, and set with precious stones of immense value. The jewels were so contrived as to be taken off and on. Every prince of the house of Bahmanee made a point of adding to it some rich stone; so that when in the reign of Sultan Mahmood it was taken to pieces to remove some of the jewels in order to be set in vases and cups, the jewellers valued it at one crore of pagodas or three and-a-half crores of rupees (about $3\frac{1}{2}$ millions sterling). This splendid throne was called Firozeh, owing, as Ferishta says, to its being partly enamelled of a sky-blue colour which in time was entirely concealed by the number of jewels.

This throne was carried to Gulburga, and set up in the Durbar-hall with great pomp and festivity, the old silver throne of Alla-ud-Din being relegated to the treasury. Public rejoicings were instituted, and there was high feasting and merriment. It was on occasion of one of these banquets that an incident occurred which led to another great war.

One evening, during the festivities with which the inauguration of the new throne was celebrated, three hundred singers, who had come all the way from Delhi, were introduced to the

Sultan. The Prince was flushed with wine, in which, at times he indulged to excess, and excited by the recollection of his recent victories he adopted the strange method of rewarding the singers by ordering the Minister to give them a draft on the treasury of the King of Vijayanagar. The Minister wrote the draft accordingly, but, remembering the saying that an appeal lay from Alexander drunk to Alexander sober, did not despatch it. On the following day, however, the Sultan asked him if the order had been sent to the Rajah, and, on being answered in the negative, he exclaimed "Think you that a word without meaning could escape my lips? I did not give the order in intoxication, but in serious design." Accordingly the royal seal was attached to the draft and it was sent by a messenger to Vijayanagar. Naturally the Rajah was greatly exasperated at this apparently uncalled for insult; caused the messenger to be paraded through his city on an ass and sent him back with every mark of contempt and derision. As this treatment of an ambassador was certain to be answered by a declaration of war, the Rajah resolved to take the first step and to carry the attack into the Sultan's territory. Accordingly, he at once marched with 30,000 horse, 100,000 foot and three hundred elephants, and making the fort of Adoni his base he ravaged that portion of the country situated between the Tungabadhra and the Kistna, which is now known as the Doab. Before Muhammed Shah could collect his army, the Rajah was able to surprise and capture the fort of Mudkul, in which was a garrison of 600 men. Of these, every one was put to the sword with the exception of one man, who was allowed to escape to carry the news to the Sultan who was still at Gulburga. When the news of this terrible disaster reached him, the Sultan was furious. He first ordered the unfortunate messenger to be put to death as being a coward to have survived the death of so many brave companions, and then swore a solemn oath that he would not sheath his sword until he had revenged this act by the slaughter of one hundred thousand infidels. He at once commenced his march, and in a few days reached the Kistna upon the opposite bank of which the Rajah was encamped. The river was then in high flood, and deeming it impossible to carry the whole of his army across in the face of the enemy, he sent the whole back, with the exception of a picked force of nine thousand horse and twenty elephants. With this small army he resolved to attack the Rajah, but as the enterprise seemed to be a desperate one, he appointed his son Mujahid Shah to succeed him with Malek Syef-ud-Din as regent. He then swore that he would neither eat nor sleep until he had crossed the river and put the enemy to flight. That same night the Sultan succeeded in crossing the river, which, as soon as he received the news, so alarmed the Rajah that he sent off all his elephants, baggage and treasure to the capital, meaning to fight the Sultan next morning. It was however the middle of the monsoon and heavy rain was falling. The roads were all impracticable and the elephants and baggage trains could not get on through the mud and slush, so that they were surprised by the Sultan just before dawn. There then followed an utter rout and indiscriminate slaughter. The Rajah himself managed to escape, but he left behind him the whole of his camp and treasure, and no less than seventy thousand Hindoos were put to the sword without regard to age or sex. The plunder was enormous, for without calculating what fell into the hands of the soldiery, the royal share alone is said to have amounted to two thousand elephants, three hundred pieces of cannon, seven hundred Arab horses, and a litter set with jewels. It seems difficult to understand how so large an army could have been so thoroughly defeated by so small a body of men, but apart from the confusion consequent on a night attack in blinding rain, it must be remembered that the Hindoos had little or none of the military discipline enforced by the Mahomedans. Under such circumstances their large numbers only served to add to the confusion, and those who could not escape were simply slaughtered like sheep. The Rajah now retired to the other banks of the Tungabadhra and, leaving his nephew in command of Adoni, encamped in the vast plain outside the fort at some distance, and assembled as large an army as possible. This army is said to have consisted of forty thousand horse and five hundred thousand foot, with a number of elephants, but it is probable that these numbers have been greatly exaggerated. The Sultan's army consisted of only fifteen thousand horse and fifty thousand foot, but there was also a train of artillery in which were employed a number of Europeans and Turks. With this army the Sultan crossed the Tungabadhra, this being the first occasion that a Mahomedan Prince had invaded the Vijayanagar dominions in person. The Rajah, Roy Kishen Roy, appointed a relative, named Hoji Mul, to be Commander-in-Chief of his army, and at once despatched him to meet the Sultan. Every endeavour was made by the Hindoos to excite the religious zeal of the soldiers, and Brahmins went about amongst them describing the butchery of cows, the desecration of temples, and the other enormities practised by the Mahomedan invaders. The two armies met somewhere near the Tungabadhra and a furious battle raged from early morning until about four in the afternoon. At first, fortune favoured the Hindoos, both wings of the advance army of the Mahomedans were broken and a defeat had almost ensued when the Sultan himself came up with a reserve of three thousand men. Thus strengthened, the Mahomedan centre advanced, and after a furious artillery fire a general charge was made. The confusion into which the Hindoos were thrown was increased by one of their elephants becoming unmanageable and breaking back through their ranks. Hoji Mul, the Hindoo general, was mortally wounded, and then the Hindoos broke and fled. A general massacre followed, in which not even pregnant women nor children at the breast were spared, and the vast Hindoo army was utterly broken up. After halting for a week on the field of battle the Sultan advanced to meet Kishen Roy, who thereupon fled to the jungles. The Sultan followed him without success for three months, until at last the Rajah was driven to take refuge in his capital, whereupon the Sultan sat down before Vijáyanagar with the whole of his army. This city, however, was too strong to be taken and after a month's siege the Sultan resolved to retire in order to draw the Hindoos out of their works. This *ruse* succeeded, and the Mahomedans recrossed the Tungabadhra followed on all sides by swarms of Hindoos. So completely had the Sultan disguised his intention that the greater part of his army believed that the retreat was a real one, and that the Sultan himself was either dying or dangerously ill. When, however, the army had reached a convenient plain, the Sultan ordered a halt, and assembling his principal officers directed them to hold their troops in readiness for another night attack. Kishen Roy's army was encamped at no great distance, and thinking a victory over the retreating Mahomedans certain, the Rajah and his officers passed the night in drinking and in the company of nautch girls. In the midst of their amusement, however, they were surprised by the Sultan, with such success that they were not even able to offer any opposition, but fled pell-mell. The Rajah managed to escape, but ten thousand of his soldiers were slaughtered and the massacre was extended to the innocent inhabitants of all the villages in the neighbourhood. Immense booty was gained from the plunder obtained from the camp, and the Hindoo power seemed to be entirely crushed. Kishen Roy now sent to treat for peace, and his ambassadors represented to the Sultan that the war might now well cease since he had only vowed to slaughter one hundred thousand Hindoos, and not to exterminate the whole race. The Sultan, however, replied that he would listen to no negociations until the musicians were satisfied, and the draft he had drawn upon the Vijayanagar treasury had been duly honoured. To this the ambassadors at once agreed, and the money was paid on the spot. The Sultan then exclaimed: "Praise be to God that what I ordered has been performed. I would not let a light word be recorded of me in the pages of time!"

Before returning to Gulburga the Sultan seems to have repented of the fearful slaughter he had wrought, and on the representation of the Hindoos, that, as in the future other wars might occur, it would be advisable to make a treaty to spare the innocent women and children, he swore an oath that in future he would not put to death a single enemy after victory, and would bind his successors to do the same. From that time, says Ferishta, it has been the general custom in the Deccan to spare the lives of prisoners in war, and not to shed the blood of an enemy's unarmed subjects.

No sooner had the Sultan returned to Gulburga than he was again called away to Dowlatabad, where a rebellion had broken out. The Governor hearing of the supposed retreat of the Sultan from Vijayanagar, had asserted his independence, and aided by a Mahratta chief named Geodeo, and one of the Rajahs of the Berars, had succeeded in diverting to his own use the revenues of Meerut and Berar. This is the first occasion on which we read of the term Mahratta as referring to a separate and distinct race. Ferishta speaks frequently of the Mahrattas as dwelling in the province of "Mheerut" or "Mharat" but it is probable that the Hindoo derivation of Maharashta, which is generally supposed to refer to the strip of country between Guzerat on the north, and Poonah on the south, is more correct. This region is bounded by the Konkan on the west and the Deccan on the east, and consists of a narrow hilly tract full of inaccessible valleys and thickly wooded hills, the inhabitants of which were from the nature of their country but little known. As soon as the Sultan heard of this rebellion he ordered his army to march to Dowlatabad, but he himself, followed by a small train of only three hundred horsemen, went on in advance, resolved if possible to put down the rebellion with this small force. Such was the terror of his name that his presence was sufficient to scatter the rebels' army without a blow being struck. The rebel chiefs fled to Dowlatabad, but finding themselves unable to hold the fort, escaped to Guzerat, which at this time seems to have been a kind of sanctuary for every one who was in difficulties. Before going they left their families in the protection of Sheikh Ein-ud-Din, a Mahomedan saint, who lived in Dowlatabad. As soon as the Sultan had taken possession of the fort he sent for the Sheikh, who alone of all other Mahomedan *fakeers* had paid no allegiance to him because of his habit of drinking wine. The Sheikh, however, was not to be intimidated, and sent back as answer the following story: "A scholar, a Syed, and a prostitute were once taken prisoners by the infidels, who promised to give them quarter if they would prostrate themselves before their idols. The scholar to save his life consented and so did the Syed. But the prostitute said: 'I have been all my life committing crimes, and am neither a scholar nor a Syed to atone for this sin by my other virtues. She refused to prostrate herself and was therefore put to death.'" This answer enraged the Sultan, who ordered the Sheikh to leave the city at once. This the holy man did, went to the tomb of Boorahan-ud-Din upon which he seated himself exclaiming "Where is the man who will drive me hence?" The Sultan, admiring this courage then sent him the following verse: "I am submissive to thee, be thou submissive to me." The Sheikh then sent a letter to the Sultan, whom he addressed as Muhammed Ghazi (victorious) and promised to pay him allegiance if, like his father, he would abstain from drinking wine, at all events in public, and would order his judges to enforce the laws against robbers. This delicate compliment appeased the Sultan, who ordered the title *Ghazi* to be added to his other titles, and then received the courageous Sheikh into his favour. True to his promise, on his return to Gulburga, the Sultan ordered all the distilleries to be destroyed, and so strictly enforced the laws against the Deccan banditti, who were even then famed for their lawlessness, that before long eight thousand heads of robbers were sent to the city, and placed on poles outside the gates as a warning to others.

Sultan Muhammed Shah's days of war were now over. The Hindoo Rajahs were reduced to obedience, and his country was quiet and at peace. The last few months of his life were spent in travelling about his kingdom, and in 1374 (19 Zilkad 776) he died full of honours, after a glorious reign of seventeen years.

Muhamed Shah seems to have been a passionate and impulsive Prince, easily offended and given to wrath, and ready to avenge the slightest offence to his dignity. He must, however, have had considerable military talent, and was personally as brave as a lion. His greatest expeditions were undertaken with a comparative handful of men, and by clever stratagems and surprises he was able to defeat an enemy immensely superior in force. The treasure he accumulated at Gulburga is said to have been enormous. "Three thousand elephants and half as much as treasure as any other Prince," was one of the results of his campaigns, but on the other hand another result was that nearly "five hundred thousand unbelievers fell by the swords of his warriors in defence of the faith of Islam, by which the districts of Carnatic were so laid waste that they did not recover their natural population for several decades."—(Ferishta).

CHAPTER V.

THE GULBURGA SULTANS FROM 1374—1397, A. D.

1374
to
1377

URING the twenty-four years which followed on the death of Muhammed Shah there were five sultans who reigned at Gulburga, four of whom were assassinated, the aggregate duration of whose reigns being only $4\frac{1}{2}$ years. The first of these Princes was Mujahid Shah, the only son left by the late Sultan. He is said to have been a tall, handsome man of great bodily strength, and of considerable intelligence and education. He chose as his favourite companions Persians and Turks, and thus sowed the first seeds of the jealousy which, for the last five hundred years, has existed between the Deccannee and foreign Mahomedans. It is mainly due to these jealousies that throughout the rest of the Deccan history we come across the constantly recurring intrigues, plots and assassinations, and which, a hundred and fifty years later, led to the dismemberment of the Gulburga kingdom, and eventually, three hundred years later, to the absorption of all the Mahomedan States of the Deccan into Aurungzebe's unwieldy empire. Sultan Mujahid was brave but revengeful, and during his father's lifetime committed an act which was destined to bring about his own premature death. When he was fourteen years old, he managed to break open his father's treasury and abstracted some bags of gold, which he divided amongst his playfellows. The treasurer, Mubarik, discovering this, reported the theft to the Sultan, who administered personal chastisement to the young culprit in so severe a manner as to draw blood. The Prince disguised his resentment towards the informer, and pretended an affection for him, until a month later he challenged him to a bout of wrestling, during which he threw him with such violence to the ground that the unfortunate treasurer broke his neck and died on the spot. No sooner had Mujahid ascended the throne than war again broke out between Gulburga and the neighbouring State of Vijayanagar. The cause seems to have been the possession of that debatable territory, the Doab. Mujahid called upon the Rajah to evacuate the whole of the districts between the Tungabadhra and the Kistna, and the Rajah replied by calling upon the Sultan to restore the forts of Raichore and Mudkul which had been conquered by his father, and to restore the elephants which had been given as part of the war indemnity. Mujahid at once marched with a large army and crossed the two rivers, leaving the veteran Seyf-ud-Din Ghoree as regent in his absence. On this occasion the Sultan is said to have killed an enormous tiger on foot by shooting it with an arrow through the heart, an act which struck such terror into the Hindoo Prince that he at once took to the jungles. Mujahid then advanced to Vijayanagar, but finding the city too strong went in pursuit of the Rajah. This pursuit is said to have lasted as far as Rameswaram in the extreme south, where the Sultan is reported to have repaired the mosque built fifty years before by the

Delhi general. There can be no doubt that at this time the rule of the Vijayanagar Prince extended over the whole of Southern India, and that his supremacy was recognized by the Rajahs of Madura and Tanjore. A little bit later we shall come across an instance of this, and it seems clear that at this time the Vijayanagar house was looked upon by all the Princes of Southern India as the head of the Hindoo nation, and as forming the last bulwark against the Mahomedan stream of invasion.

The Rajah seems to have hoped that by leading the Sultan through the jungle, the Mahomedans, who were accustomed to good living, would fall sick, and that he would then be able to harass them on their retreat. The only record of this campaign is to be found in Ferishta, and he says that the Rajah himself was attacked by jungle fever and, therefore, fell back upon his capital. Ferishta merely alludes to the Sultan having destroyed several towns; but as he makes no mention of any plunder, upon which the Mahomedan historians always lay great weight, it is probable that the Sultan was not strong enough to attack any of the great strongholds of the South. He pursued the Rajah back to Vijayanagar, and being joined by fresh forces attempted to besiege the city. It would seem that the Hindoos were dispirited, and the Sultan might have been successful in his attempt if he had not allowed himself to give way to a spirit of fanaticism. Outside the city there was a sacred temple, the shrine of numerous pilgrims. This temple Sultan Mujahid, fired by a zeal, either for religion or for plunder, attacked and destroyed*. Religious feelings,

* The story goes that a number of Brahmins took refuge in the shrine of Hanuman (the favourite monkey-God). They were all put to the sword and Mujahid Shah himself struck the image of the God in the face with his battle-axe, mutilating the features; a dying Brahmin then raised himself with a last effort and exclaimed: "For this act you will never see your kingdom again, and will not return to your capital alive!" A prophecy which proved to be only too true.

outraged in this manner, brought about what a sense of patriotism had not been able to effect. The Hindoos rose to a man, and so threatening was their attitude that the Sultan had to retreat. He was not, however, able to go very far before he was compelled to give the enemy battle. A furious conflict ensued, in which, although it is claimed for the Mahomedans that they killed forty thousand men, still their losses were so considerable that they had to retire. This was effected in good order, the Sultan holding the passes until his army had got through. There seems to be little doubt that on this occasion the Mahomedans suffered a defeat, which, had it not been for the Sultan's personal bravery, would have become a serious disaster. It is stated that it was mainly owing to the disobedience of Daoud Shah, the Sultan's uncle, that the battle was lost. This Prince had neglected to occupy an important post, which, being taken up by the Hindoos, the Mahomedans were compelled to retire. After the battle, the Sultan gave his uncle a sharp reprimand, so severe, indeed, that it rankled in the Prince's bosom, and led eventually to the catastrophe which ended Mujahid's reign. After his retreat from Vijayanagar, the Sultan laid siege to Adoni, but not only was his army greatly reduced in numbers, but it was hampered with an enormous number of prisoners, said to have amounted to between sixty and seventy thousand persons, mostly women. Malek Seyf-ud-din Ghoree who had been left at Gulburga in charge of the Kingdom, now advanced with reinforcements to his master's assistance. This veteran general soon saw that the capture of Adoni was likely to prove a serious matter. It is described as having had fifteen forts, all communicating with one another, and to have been of immense strength. The Vizier advised the Sultan to first of all reduce the forts on the north side of the river, and, in consequence of this advice, the Sultan resolved to raise the siege and retreat to his capital, which, however, he was not destined to reach.

After crossing the Tungabadhra, the Sultan, taking advantage of the peace which his Vizier had succeeded in forming with the Vijayanagar Rajah, left his army with a small bodyguard to enjoy the pleasures of the chase. His uncle, Daoud Khan, who was still sore over the public reprimand that had been administered, resolved to take this opportunity to carry out a conspiracy which he had hatched with the son of Mubarik Khan, the betel-bearer, who was burning to avenge the death of his father caused by the wrestling match, narrated in the beginning of the chapter. Before long, an occasion happened. One day the Sultan was amusing himself with fishing, but, being seized with a sudden pain in the eyes, retired to sleep in his tent alone. That night Daoud Khan and his fellow conspirators entered the tent with their daggers drawn. The Sultan's only attendant was an Abyssinian slave, who was rubbing his feet. He at once raised an alarm, but it was too late. Daoud Khan plunged his dagger into the Sultan's stomach, and Musaoud Khan, the son of the betel-bearer, then cut down the slave and gave the finishing stroke to the Sultan. As Mujahid left no children, his uncle, Daoud Shah, became the heir to the throne, and after having made the army swear allegiance to him, he marched upon Gulburga and ascended the throne amidst great pomp and magnificence. This deed of blood soon brought about its own revenge. Sultan Mujahid, who had just been murdered, was the grandson of the aged Vizier Sayf-ud-din Ghoree, whose daughter had been married to Sultan Muhammed. The old man asked to be allowed to resign his office, and he was permitted to retire. The rest of the Royal family appear to have acquiesced in the change of affairs, with one exception, the sister of the murdered Sultan, Rûh Parwar Ageh. This princess was looked upon by the rest of the ladies as the head of the harem, and she did not find it difficult to induce a young man, a favourite of the late Sultan, to avenge his patron's murder. The assassin's name is not mentioned, but the deed was committed in the mosque whilst the Sultan was prostrated in prayer. With one blow of the sabre he was killed, the murderer falling immediately afterwards by the sword of Khan Mahomed. In this way died Daoud Shah, the fourth Sultan of Gulburga after a short reign of one month and five days (A.D. 1378). There were four heirs to the throne after Daoud Shah's death, his son Mahomed Sunjer, nine years of age, together with two younger sons, Firoze and Ahmed, who afterwards succeeded to the throne, and the last surviving son of the first Sultan, Mahmood Shah, brother of Daoud Shah. Both these princes were in the harem, in the power of that strong-minded Princess Rûh Parwar Ageh. Khan Mahomed wished to place the former on the throne, but the Princess shut the gates and swore that the son of an assassin should never be Sultan with her consent. In order to prevent all further intrigue, she caused the poor little boy to be blinded and at once caused Mahmood Shah to be proclaimed. In this way the sins of the father were visited upon his innocent offspring.

Sultan Mahmood is said to have been a wise and humane prince. His first act was to punish the murderers of his nephew Mujahid. Khan Mahomed was imprisoned in the fort of Saugur, where he shortly afterwards died, and Musaoud Khan, the son of the betel-bearer, was impaled alive. It cannot be said that their punishments were not deserved, and, this act of retributive justice over, the new Sultan's reign, was devoted to peace, and the cultivation of literature and science. Seyf-ud-Din Ghoree was again appointed Vizier, though he was then nearly ninety years old. During a reign of more than nineteen years, the country was troubled by no wars, and it was only towards the end of this period that one rebellion occurred which, however, was promptly suppressed. So wide did the name of this Sultan spread, that poets and learned men from all parts of the Mahomedan

1378.
1396.

world flocked to the Court of Gulburga to share in his bounty. In return, they bestowed upon him the title of the Mahomedan Aristotle. The great Persian poet Hafiz even started to come to Gulburga, and got so far on his journey as to put to sea in the Persian Gulf. A heavy storm, however, came on, and the ship had to put back. Hafiz had had enough of sea voyages, and seems to have thought that the game of court favour was not worth the candle of seasickness and possible shipwreck, so he had himself reconducted to land, and, instead of his own person, sent the Sultan an ode. Put into rough English, the ode would run as follows:—

> For the wealth of the world I will not exchange
> The wind of my garden which softly blows;
> My friends may rebuke me, but I will not range:
> I will stop here at home with the bulbul and rose;
>
> Enticing, no doubt, is your beautiful crown,
> With costliest gems in a fair golden bed;
> But through perils and risks that ominous frown,
> I might win it, perhaps, but then have no head.
>
> When I thought of your pearls, it seemed then to me
> To risk a short voyage would not be too bold;
> But now I am sure, one wave of the sea
> Can *not* be repaid by treasures of gold.
>
> What care I for pearls or for gems rich and rare
> When friendship and love at home both are mine?
> All the gilding of art can never compare
> With the pleasure derived from generous wine!
>
> Let Hafiz retire from the cares of the world,
> Contented with only few pieces of gold;
> In the lap of repose here let him lie curled,
> Far removed from the sea and its dangers untold!

When this ode was read to the Sultan, he was so pleased that he observed that as Hafiz had actually started with the intention of coming to Gulburga, he was entitled to some recognition, even although he was not able to complete his journey. Accordingly, he had a thousand pieces of gold brought from the treasury, with which he ordered one of his courtiers to purchase specimens of Indian art and send them to the poet. This was accordingly done, and Hafiz received a splendid payment for his little ode. Sultan Mahmood was a very temperate man, both in his habit of living and of dress. Though fond in his youth of rich and costly attire, after his accession to the throne he wore nothing but plain white. He was in the habit of saying that kings were only trustees of the divine riches, and that to expend more than was actually necessary was to commit a breach of trust. This is a maxim which it were well all kings would bear in mind, but it is one unfortunately that is more honoured in the breach than in the observance. Great care and attention appears to have been bestowed during this reign on education, and schools were established at all the principal towns, and, amongst others, Gulburga, Bieder, Candahar, Elichpore, Doulatabad, Choule and Dabul. On occasion of a famine, the Sultan employed ten thousand bullocks in bringing grain from Malwa and Guzerat, which was then retailed to the poor at a low price. Shortly before the Sultan's death occurred the sole rebellion of his reign, to which we have already alluded. It was organized by Bahaud-din, the Governor of Dowlatabad, together with his two sons, but was quickly suppressed and the leaders of the revolt were killed. In A.D., 1396 (21st Rajab 799) the Sultan died of a putrid fever, and the day after the patriarch Seyf-ud-din Ghoree, who had accompanied the first Sultan from Dowlatabad to Gulburga, and who had ruled the country as Prime Minister for more than half a century, also passed away at the age of one hundred and seven years. Sultan Mahmood reigned nineteen years nine months and twenty-four days.

GENEALOGICAL TABLE OF THE BAHMANEE-SULTANS.

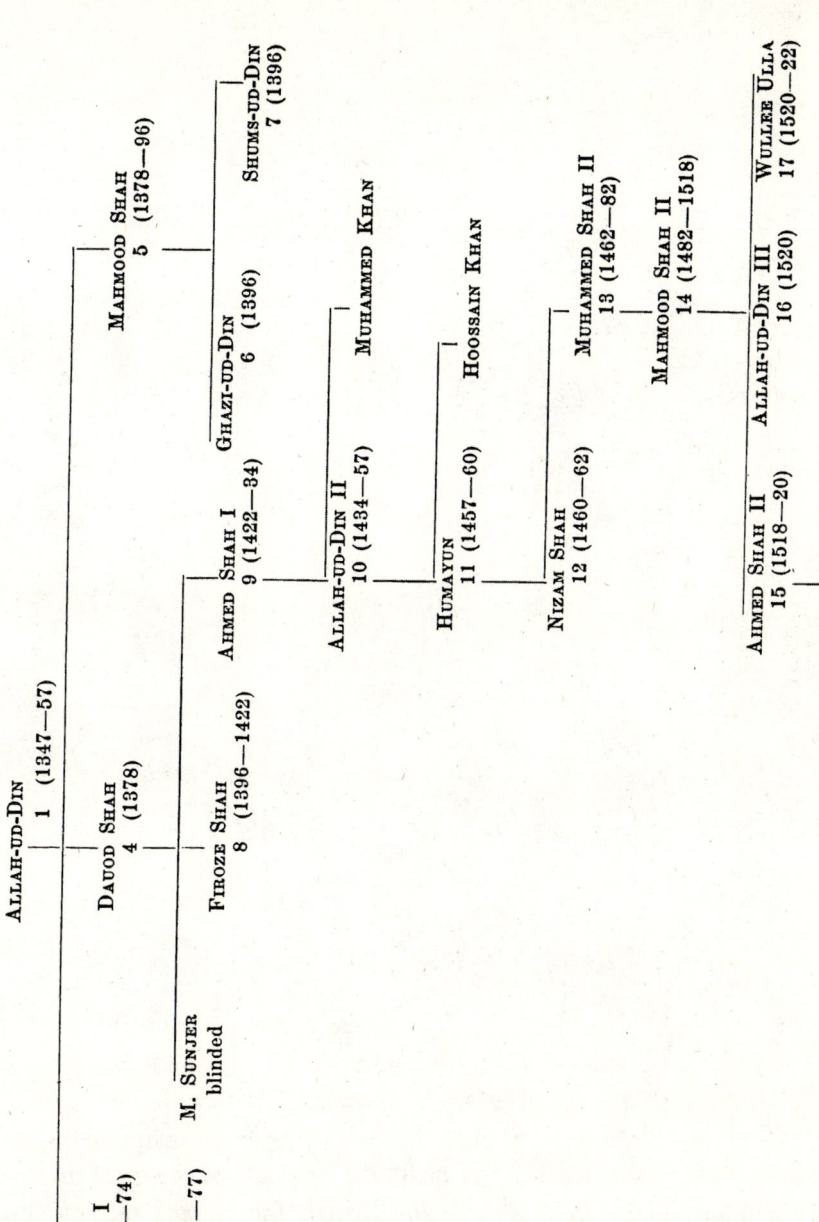

CHAPTER VI.

SULTANS GHAZI-UD-DIN AND SHUMS-UD-DIN.

A.D. 1396

THESE two Sultans commenced and ended their reigns in the short period of six months. They were both sons of Mahmood Shah. The eldest was Ghazi-ud-Din, who ascended the throne at the age of seventeen. He seems to have been an amiable young Prince, but he was unfortunate in at once exciting the jealousy of a powerful Turkish slave of the late Sultan, named Lallcheen. This person desired the post of Meer Nobut, or Lord of the Watch, for his son Hussan Khan, and when he expostulated with the Sultan for bestowing it upon another, he was told that it was not right that the sons of slaves should be promoted above the heads of the old nobility. Stung by this retort, Lallcheen resolved upon revenge, and he carried out his plan in the following manner:—The young Sultan was desirous of obtaining Lallcheen's daughter, and, accordingly, the slave invited his master to a feast. When the Sultan was half intoxicated with wine, Lallcheen drew him on one side as if to take him to the female apartments. When he had taken him into another room, he fell upon him, threw him down, and gouged out his eyes with a dagger. He then called in each of the attendants, one by one, and put them to death singly to the number of twenty-one persons so that no one remained alive powerful enough to obstruct his designs. The Sultan was then sent to the fort of Saugur, and his younger brother, Shums-ud-Din, was placed upon the throne. The reign of the unfortunate Ghazi-ud-Din lasted only one month and twenty days (17 Ramzan 799) (1396 A.D.).

Sultan Shums-ud-Din was only fifteen years old when he ascended the throne. Intimidated by the fate of his brother, he left all the power in the hands of Lallcheen. The latter, the more to strengthen his position, commenced an intrigue with the Sultan's mother, and in this way was able to do what he liked with the young Prince. As was to be expected, this absolute power soon excited the jealousy of the other members of the Royal Family. Sultan Daood Khan (the murderer of Sultan Mujahid Shah) had left three sons. The eldest of these, Mahomed Sunjer had, it will be remembered, been blinded, but there were two younger brothers, Feroze Khan and Ahmed Khan, who married two daughters of the late Sultan Mahmood Shah. They were therefore brothers-in-law and cousins of the unfortunate Ghazi-ud-Din, who had enjoyed so brief a period of power. Their wives incited these princes to avenge their brother which they resolved to do. Lallcheen, getting wind of this conspiracy sent orders to have the Princes killed, but they managed to escape in time and took refuge in the fort of Saugur which was commanded by one Suddoo, a slave of the royal family, who received them with kindness and respect. Here they found the poor young blinded Sultan Ghazi-ud-Din, and the three resolved to strike a blow to recover the throne. They gathered together an army, and marched upon Gulburga, but were defeated with considerable loss and had to fly again to Saugur. Flushed with this success, the insolence of Lallcheen overstepped all bounds. The Sultan Shums-ud-Din was treated as a mere puppet, and his mother no longer made any disguise of her intrigue with Lallcheen. This conduct so disgusted the chief noblemen that they entered into correspondence with the two Princes, who now resolved to attempt by stratagem what they had not been able to accomplish by force. Accordingly, they sent letters to Lallcheen and the Queen-mother praying for forgiveness and asking to be allowed to return to Gulburga. Lallcheen, delighted at the chance of getting the Princes into his power, at once consented, and they accordingly returned. For the first few days they remained quiet on their guard, and then carried out their plot by a surprise. Feroze Khan appeared in the Durbar with twelve followers, leaving three hundred adherents outside. The porters at the gate attempted to stop him, but they were at once cut down, and the Prince followed by his twelve friends rushed into the hall, leaving the gates guarded by the three hundred. The Sultan fled to an under-ground chamber, and Lallcheen's sons, who attempted to defend themselves, were cut down. Lallcheen was then taken and bound, and Feroze ascended the throne which bore his own name. Vengeance upon Lallcheen was reserved for the hand of his unfortunate victim Ghazi-ud-Din, who was sent for from Saugur. Lallcheen was placed, bound, before the blind prince, who called for a sword and killed him with one stroke. Ghazi-ud-Din, incapacitated by his blindness for Government, then asked to be allowed to go to Mecca. This request was granted, and we are told that the ex-Sultan lived for many years in that city provided with a liberal allowance from his cousin Feroze Shah. Shums-ud-Din, the boy king of fifteen, was then blinded and sent in captivity to Bieder, and so the country was once more restored to peace. Shums-ud-Din reigned only five months and seven days.

CHAPTER VII.

THE CITY AND KINGDOM OF VIJAYANAGAR.

It is necessary at this part of the history of the Deccan to glance at the manner in which Vijayanagar had risen to be so formidable a rival of the Mahomedan power. There can be little doubt that previous to the 14th Century, Vijayanagar was a place of such insignificance that it was entirely unknown. It may have been the residence of a petty Chieftain, and it is possible that the founders of the new city, Bukha Raya and Hari Hara, may have belonged to his family, and have returned thither after the fall of Warangal in 1323. The foundation of Vijayanagar is

THE CITY AND KINGDOM OF VIJAYANAGAR. 61

generally ascribed to the year 1336 A.D., and its completion to the year 1343, or a few years previous to the foundation of the Gulburga kingdom (1348), and there seems to be no doubt that the rapid growth of the young Hindoo Kingdom was in a great measure due to Sri Maha Vidyáranya, the eleventh successor of Sankarachariar; (according to Dr. Burnell, than whom there can be no safer guide), the same as Sáyana, the famous commentator on the Vedas. This sage's monastery was situated at Shringeri, in the Kadoor Taluq of West Mysore. Tradition says that after the fall of Warangal, the two brothers came to the sage and asked for help. The Hindoo High Priest was not slow to recognize the critical position. The fall of Deogiri and Warangal had left Southern India entirely unprotected from the invasions of the Mahomedans, and it was therefore absolutely necessary that a new bulwark of protection should be raised against this dangerous foe. It is said that the deity appeared to the sage in a vision, and revealed to him the existence of a hidden treasure, which he, recognizing their fitness for the new task, bestowed upon the two brothers, and with this money they founded the new city, which, in honour of their patron, they called Vidhyanagar. It is a strange thing that throughout the whole of Indian history we frequently find the foundation of a new city or dynasty connected with the finding of a hidden treasure. No doubt the custom of hoarding money goes back to the most ancient times, but it is also exceedingly possible that these hidden treasures were in reality mines, either of gold or precious stones, the existence of which was kept a profound secret. Within a few years after the founding of the new kingdom, its authority extended to the Western Coast. The great Mahomedan traveller, Ibn Batuta, who visited the Kánara Coast in 1342, says that at Honavar (the modern Honor) he found a Mahomedan Prince named Jamal-ud-Din, who was subject to an infidel King named Hariab (evidently

Hari Hara, or, as he is styled, Hariyappa) of Vijayanagar. It is probable that, owing to the influence of the sage Vidyáranya, all the Hindoo Kings of Southern India recognized the mission of the Vijayanagar Kings to protect them against the Mahomedans, and paid tribute in treasure and men for this purpose. On more than one occasion we find the Madura Kings recognizing the King of Vijayanagar as their overlord, and appealing to him for assistance. The resources thus placed at the disposal of the new kingdom were therefore enormous, and in a very short time its power and influence overshadowed that of all the other Hindoo kingdoms of South India. For more than two hundred years Vijayanagar performed its duty as Warden of the Hindoo marches, and during the constant wars that took place with the Mahomedan Princes she was as often victorious as she was conquered. Even when defeated, the Hindoos were able to at once replace the beaten armies by fresh levies, so that the Mahomedans were never able to get a firm footing in the Hindoo country until the final downfall of the kingdom. It was only seldom, indeed, that they were able to advance beyond the Tungabadhra, and the Raichore Doab or country between the Tungabadhra and the Kistna appears to have been the scene of most of the battles.

Vijayanagar lies on the right or south bank of the River Tungabadhra, which here rushes through some rocky hills and forms a wide bend. About ten miles further south there is a range of hills about 3,000 feet above the sea which form, as it were, a natural barrier. These hills shut in an extensive plain and the city itself was built in the north corner of this plain. The site of the city is full of rocky hills, some of which must be nearly 1,000 feet high, but most of which are only a few hundred feet. These hills are formed of huge boulders of stones piled upon each other in such a way as to form an almost insurmountable barrier. In order to fortify the city all that was required was to connect these hills by lls, which has been done in almost every instance. In this way the city was defended by a series of walls, the outermost one of which is said to have enclosed a space eight miles across (*Nicolo Conti*, early in the 15th Century, says that the city was sixty miles round). These walls seem all to have terminated in a rocky range of hills which intervened between the city and the river, thus rendering any approach from the river side impossible. Floating down the river now in boats from Humpi, the South-Westmost part of the city, there is nothing to show that on the other side of the rocks there are the ruins of what must have been a vast city. The stone piles of the old bridge communicating with the northern shore are still standing, but the approach to this bridge on the Vijayanagar side was by a natural tunnel through the hill, which could easily be defended by a small body of men against a large army. The only way in which the city could be approached was, therefore, from the south and southeast. At this latter point, advantage was taken of the lie of the country to build a large tank. The bund of this tank forms a natural rampart about a mile long. The water is about twenty feet in depth at the bund, and spreads over an area of at least three to four square miles. This large sheet of water would, therefore, form an insuperable obstacle to the attack of an army, and there remains, therefore, only the south-west from which the city could be attacked. Near the Calingula, or weir, at the western end of the tank bund, a massive wall runs off which probably formed the outer defence of the inhabited portion of the city. The moat of this wall was easily filled from the Calingula, and at different points the wall was defended by forts and redoubts, until at last it joined the rocky range of hills before alluded to. Immediately within this wall there were rice fields and gardens fed with water from the tank, and then came the different portions of the city each defended by its wall and rocky hills.

In the centre of the city, or innermost ring, was the King's palace, the mint and the palace of the Commander-in-Chief. The King's palace is said to have been on a hill, and formed the highest portion of the city. If so, all traces of it have now disappeared. At the foot of the hill there is still to be seen the ruins of what must have been a harem, or zenana, with a range of elephant stables and a concert hall. On the hill behind there are some old ruins. Possibly the palace was built here, but, if so, it is now impossible to identify it.

The first King was Hari Hara, and the date of his reign is ascribed to 1336—1350. He was followed by his brother, Bukka or Bukka Raya, who reigned till 1379, when he was succeeded by Hari Hara II., who reigned till 1401. This Prince, together with his son, Deva Raya (1401—1451), greatly extended the power of the kingdom, and added to the splendour of the city. A difference will be noticed in the names of these Kings and those with whom we find the Gulburga Sultans in conflict. The King of Vijayanagar, who so frequently fought with Muhammed Shah and Mujahid Shah of Gulburga (1357—1377) is called by Ferishta Krishen Roy or Raya. According to the dates, this King must, in reality, have been Bukka Raya, and it is impossible to explain how Ferishta gets the name of Krishen Roy. Muhammed Shah, as already related, no doubt committed a terrible slaughter amongst the Hindoos, but under Mujahid the Hindoo King certainly inflicted one severe defeat, which would have turned into a disaster, if the Sultan had not been able to hold the passes of the hills, which protect Vijayanagar on the south East, whilst the main army passed through. It was during the reign of Deva Raya that we have the first authentic account by a traveller of the city of Vijayanagar. Abd-er-Razzak, the Persian Ambassador, visited the city at the end of April, 1443, and found it "an exceedingly large and populous city, the seat of a King of great power, whose kingdom stretched from Ceylon to Gulburga and from Bengal to Malabar." (This latter must be an exaggeration, for it is certain that the Vijayanagar dominions never extended north of the Kistna River.)

"Most of the land was tilled and fertile, and there were about 300 seaports equal to Kalikat. There were 1,000 elephants, and over a million men. There was no actual "Rai" in India, except the King of Vijayanagar. The city had seven fortified walls, one within the other. The first or outmost circle enclosed a space of eight miles (two *parasangs*) across. Between the first, second, and third circles of wall were fields and gardens, and from the third to the seventh or inmost circle, the space was crowded with markets and shops. The seventh centre was on a hill, and in it was the palace of the King and four markets with a lofty arcade, and a magnificent gallery at the head of each. The markets were broad and long. There were always sweet and fresh flowers, and the different crafts had separate quarters. Many streams flowed along polished and level stone channels. On the right of the palace, which was the loftiest building in the city, was a pillared hall in which the Minister did justice. On the left was the mint, with hollow chambers full of masses of molten gold. Opposite the mint was the police office with 12,000 soldiers. Behind the mint was a market 300 yards long by twenty broad, where the dancing girls lived, very beautiful, rich and accomplished. The King was exceedingly young, of a spare body, rather tall and of an olive complexion. During Abd-er-Razzak's stay at Vijayanagar, the brother of the King killed many of the leading nobles, and all but succeeded in assassinating the King. The King sat on a throne of gold, inlaid with jewels, and the walls of the throne room were lined with plates of gold. During part of the time Abd-er-Razzak was there, a Christian was Minister; there was a wonderful festival at "Dassara" time, or *Mahan-*

avami, the September full moon. The great plain near the city was filled with enchanting pavilions covered with most delicate and tasteful pictures of animals, and there was one pillared mansion, nine stories high, for the King. For three days, with a most gorgeous display, dancing girls danced and sang, fireworks blazed, and showmen and jugglers performed wonderful feats. Abd-er-Razzak left Vijayanagar on the 5th of November, 1443, and reached Mangalore on the 23rd of the same month. It was impossible within reasonable space to give an idea of how well the country was peopled. All the people, high and low, even the workers in market places, wore jewels and gilt ornaments in their ears, round their necks, arms, and wrists, and fingers. From Mangalore he went to the port of Honavar or Honor, and there arranged for a vessel to take him back to Persia. He started on the 28th of January, and reached Ormuz on the 22nd* of April, after a voyage of sixty-five days."

Of the seven walls of which Abd-er-Razzak speaks, it is probable that the two outer ones were merely rows of forts. The village of Hospett, seven miles from the ruins, is still called the eighth gate of the ancient city; but a wall at this part enclosing a space eight miles across would have been a work too gigantic even for those days of forced labour. Nor is it likely that all traces of so large a work should have disappeared, and at present there is no sign of any wall until the Calingula of the tank is reached. The space enclosed by this latter wall might possibly be eight square miles or more, but cannot be more than about three miles across. Within these walls there are remains of many other walls, but, as said above, they do not form separate enceintes, but are for the most part connecting-links between different rocky hills. Abd-er-Razzak probably entered the city by means of seven different gates, and the distance between the outer and the

* Bombay Gazetteer—Kanara. Vol. XV. Part II.

inner gates was very possibly eight miles. This view is confirmed by the account of the Italian traveller, Vartherna, who visited Vijayanagar in 1503. He says that the city "stood on the side of a mountain with three circles of walls, the outermost circle seven miles round." This would exactly correspond with the wall leading from the tank-bund, and the other two inner circles can also be traced. Vartherna says that the King was the richest he had ever heard of. "His Brahmans said that he had £4,000 a day. He was always at war. He had 40,000 horsemen, whose horses were worth £100 to £226 each, for horses were scarce; 400 elephants; and some dromedaries. He was a great friend of the Christians, and the Portuguese did him much honour. He wore a cap of gold brocade, and when he went to war, a quilted dress of cotton with an over-garment full of golden piastres, and hung with jewels. The ornaments on his horse were worth more than an Italian city. He rode out with three or four kings, many lords, and five or six thousand horses." In 1514 another traveller, Duarte Barbosa, a Portuguese, says:—"Vijayanagar was on a level ground surrounded by a very good wall on one side, a river on a second side, and a mountain on a third. It was very large and very populous. There were many large and handsome palaces, and wide streets and squares. The King, a Gentile (= Gentoo) called Raheni, that is, Rayalu, always lived in the city. He lived very luxuriously and seldom left the palace. He was nearly white, well-made, and had smooth black hair. The attendance on the King was by women, who all lived in the palaces. They sang and played and amused the King in a thousand ways. They went to bathe daily, and the King went to see them bathe, and sent to his chamber the one that pleased him most, and the first son he had from any of them inherited the Kingdom. Many litters and many horsemen stood at the door of the palace. The King kept 900 elephants, each worth

1,500 to 2,000 ducats and 20,000 horses worth 300 to 600 ducats, and some of the choicest worth 1,000 ducats. The King had more than 100,000 men, horse and foot, and 5,000 women in his pay. The women went with the army, but did not fight, but their lovers fought for them very vigorously. When the King, which occasionally happened, went in person to war, he camped at some distance from the city, and ordered all people to join him within a certain number of days. At the end of the days he gave orders to burn the whole city, except his palaces, and some of the nobles' palaces, that all might go to the war and die with him.

"Among his knights many had come from different parts to take service, and did not cease to live in their own creeds. In times of peace the city was filled with an innumerable crowd of all nations. There were very rich local Gentiles, many Moorish merchants and traders, and an infinite number of others from all parts. They dwelt freely and safely in what creed they chose, whether Moor, Christian, or Gentile. The governors observed strict justice, and there was an infinite trade. Great quantities of precious stones poured into Vijayanagar, jewels from Pegu, diamonds from the Deccan, and also from a Vijayanagar mine, and pearls from Ormuz and from Cael in South India." *

One passage in this extract is especially important, as it supplies a reason why the only ruins of this large city are temples and a few public buildings. If the homes of the common people were liable to be burnt whenever the King went to war, they must, of course, have been built of the most unsubstantial materials. When Vijayanagar finally fell after the battle of Tellicotta (1565) the Mahomedans probably found the city in such a half-ruined state. The King had strained every nerve to meet the allied Mahomedan kings, and had possibly burnt the greater part of the city. All that the

* (*Ibid*).

Mahomedans found, therefore, were temples and public buildings, which they ruthlessly destroyed. In many of the temples it is still clearly visible how the pavement was torn up in order to search for hidden treasure. Of the public buildings, the most interesting ruins are: The elephant stables, very substantially built, and in a very good state of preservation and a grand stand where the King used to sit and watch the sports in the arena below. This stand is covered on all sides with excellent carvings in bas-relief of animals, sports, &c. On the north side the walls are hidden by *débris;* but a portion has been excavated, exposing some very delicate carving in an excellent state of preservation. Near the arena are the remains of an aqueduct, each section of which is built out of solid stone. The channel is a foot and a half wide by a foot deep. In communication with this aqueduct are the remains of a covered bath, evidently of Mahomedan architecture. This possibly is the bath which the King used to visit, as there are screened and latticed apartments like private boxes from which he could watch the bathers. Abd-er-Razzak speaks of the water flowing through the streets, and of the different handicrafts being located together. A very interesting example of this lies not far from the bath. There are the remains of a street, by the side of which is a stone channel, and on either side of the channel are a large number of square slabs of black stone with a round excavation like a plate in the middle, by the side of which are two, three, and sometimes five smaller excavations. These slabs were used for eating. The middle excavation was meant for rice, and the neighbouring ones for condiments. Here, probably, were the public eating houses. A traveller who wanted to dine came and sat down at a slab, and was served with his food, and he probably paid according to the kind of slab he selected. A five-condiment dinner cost more than one with only two. After eating he washed his hands in the channel, and then went away. These eating-slabs are probably in exactly the same position now as they were when they were last used, for they are of no value to the thief and are too heavy to be moved. Placed as they are, they form an interesting relic of Hindoo life of five hundred years ago.

The principal ruins are those of temples, of which there is an enormous number. They are scattered about everywhere, on the tops of hills and on the level ground. The most important of these are that of Hazara Ramaswamy, in the inner circle near the King's palace, with some beautifully carved pillars in black granite; the large temple at Humpi, which is in good repair and is even now largely frequented, and the temple of Vittelaswamy near the river. The latter has some beautifully carved pillars of a very rare and elegant pattern, and in front of the temple is what is probably a unique piece of carving in the shape of a large stone car, modelled on the pattern of an ordinary wooden car. This car unfortunately shows a number of cracks, and was in danger of falling to pieces; but the present Collector of Bellary Mr. R. Sewell, since retired, who takes not only an archæological, but also a keen personal interest in the ruins of this old city, has had the heavy superstructure of brickwork, with which the car was loaded, removed, and, relieved from this superincumbent weight, it is to be hoped that the car will stand for many more years to come, though it might be advisable to have it protected from the ravages caused by the weather.

At present the only two portions of the city which are inhabited are Kamalapoor, at the southwest end of the tank, which is called after its name, and Humpi, in the southwest corner of the city near the river. Kamalapur is a small village, the houses of which have a substantial appearance, being built from the stones of one of the walls. Here there is a small bungalow constructed out of an old temple.

A winding road leads from here through the ruins of the old city, past old temples and through crumbling gateways until Humpi is reached. Here there are the remains of a broad street fringed by what were shops and possibly noblemen's houses; some of these are pretentious, having columns in front, and a few of them are still inhabited. At the north end of this street is the temple, one of the towers or Goparams of which, was rebuilt by a former Collector of Bellary, Mr. Robertson, whose name is held in high reverence in consequence. None of the temples in or near the old city are of later date than the 14th Century, with the exception of one or two very small buildings, which Mr. Sewell is of opinion may be of an older period. This shows that, previous to the 14th Century, the place was one of insignificance, and that the whole of the vast mass of temples, which must at one time have existed, are due to the liberality of the Kings of the new dynasty. At present the very name of Vijayanagar seems in danger of being forgotten. The ruins are generally called the ruins of Humpi, and many who are familiar with that name are unaware that they form the only remains of what was once the largest and richest Hindoo city of Southern India. On the north bank of the river there was once a large suburb which was also defended by walls; a portion of this suburb now forms the small village of Anagoondy, where lives, in sadly reduced circumstances, the sole representative of the Vijayanagar Kings. But, poor though he is, he is still looked upon by all the inhabitants of the district with great respect, and whenever there is a family festival in his house, the Baiders turn out in large numbers to do him honour, and prostrate themselves before him when he appears in public. He is, however, but the shadow of a once great name.

CHAPTER VIII.

SULTANS FEROZE SHAH AND AHMED SHAH.

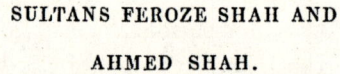

SULTAN Feroze Shah reigned for twenty-five years, and under his rule the kingdom of Gulburga may 1397 be said to have to reached its highest 1422 point of prosperity. He made twenty-four glorious campaigns; conquered the greater part of Telingana, and compelled the King of Vijayanagar to give him one of his daughters in marriage. It is said of him that he was strict in his religious observances, with the exception of drinking wine and listening to music, but he consoled himself for committing these two offences against Islam by saying that "music lifted his mind to contemplate the divinity, and that wine did not make him passionate, and, therefore, he hoped that hereafter he would not be questioned about them, but find mercy from a forgiving Creator."

Feroze Shah paid very great attention to the development of trade, and every year despatched vessels from the ports of Goa and Choule. These ships not only brought back merchandize of different countries, but, the captains were also charged to invite persons celebrated for their talents to visit the Sultan's Court. Another kind of visitors in whom the Sultan delighted were women, and in his harem were females of all nations: Arabians, Circassians, Georgians, Turks, Russians, Europeans, Chinese, Afghans, Rajputs, Bengalis, Guzeratees, Telinganees, and others. We are told that he could speak with each in her own language, but this is doubtless an exaggeration.

In the second year of the Sultan's reign, war broke out with the King of Vijayanagar whom Ferishta names Dewul Roy. According to the Hindoo inscriptions, the King of Vijayanagar in 1398 was Hari Hara II. The words "Deva" are more honorific titles than actual names. Almost all Hindoo Kings termed themselves Deva, and Roy or Raya is simply another form of Rajah. The names therefore of the Hindoo Kings as given by Mahomedan historians are not to be relied upon. The real names as now ascertained are derived from inscriptions which are far more to be depended upon, although not always absolutely so. The Vijayanagar King invaded the Doab with a large army in order to possess himself of Mudkul. At the same time the Rajah of the Telingana, (Nursinga) country, invaded the Berars, and the Sultan had to detach a large portion of his troops to defend this portion of his dominions. When the Sultan reached the river Kistna, he found the Vijayanagar forces camped on the other side, and the river being in flood, he was unable to cross. A Kazi in the Sultan's army, named Siraj, offered to cross the river and secure a passage. This he did by a most daring adventure. The Kazi with seven of his friends disguised themselves as religious mendicants, and crossing the river went to that part of the Rajah's Camp, which was frequented by dancing girls. The Kazi pretended to fall in love with the chief of these, and when night came on, and he found that the girl was going to an entertainment at the tent of the Rajah's son, he persuaded her to take him with her as one of the musicians, he being well-skilled in performing on the mandel, or Hindoo lute. This the girl consented to, and in the midst of the entertainment, whilst performing a dagger dance, the Kazi and one of his friends rushed in on the Rajah's son, and plunged their daggers into his body. In the confusion that ensued, the lights were extinguished and a number of Hindoos killed; a report was spread that the Sultan had crossed the river, and the whole camp was in a state of alarm. In the meantime the Sultan did actually cross with about four thousand picked men, and effected a landing without opposition. Surprised in this manner the whole army took to flight, and the King fled to Vijayanagar, where he shut himself up, an immense number of Hindoos being slain. A peace very shortly ensued, and the Rajah paid as a ransom for the Brahmins who had been captured eleven lakhs of pagodas, or *Hoons* or *Huns*; and upon this the Sultan returned to Gulburga. In the following year, he marched to punish Nursinga, who was driven out of Berar without much difficulty, and compelled to shut himself up in Kurleh, one of his own forts. Here after a siege of two months, he surrendered and went in person to the Sultan's camp at Ellichpore to make his submission. He was pardoned and reinstated, and is said to have been submissive thereafter. In 1401 Feroze Shah sent ambassadors to Timur the great conqueror, and proffered his allegiance. This was graciously accepted, and in return the Sultan was named sovereign of Malwa and Guzerat in addition to the Deccan. Considering, however, that both Malwa and Guzerat were already in the possession of two Mahomedan

Princes, this was something like dividing the lion's skin before the animal had been killed, and the sole result was to raise up two new enemies in the Kings, who feared that their dominions would be attacked. These princes at once formed a secret alliance with the King of Vijayanagar, who, being

assured of their assistance, discontinued paying any tribute. At first Feroze Shah did not feel himself in a position to resent this disobedience, but before long the smouldering quarrel broke into an open flame, and the ostensible cause was, as so often happens—a woman. In the fort of Mudkul there was a Hindoo farmer who had a beautiful daughter, who, contrary to the usual custom among Hindoos, had reached maturity without being married. A Brahmin returning from Benares saw this village beauty, and was so much struck with her that he remained a year and a half in her father's house, and instructed her in music and dancing. When her education was completed the Brahmin went to Vijayanagar, and reported to the King the existence of this peerless maiden. The King at once sent him back to Mudkul with orders to bring the maiden and her parents to Vijayanagar as he proposed to make the young lady his wife. This, no doubt, was a great honour, but still it was one that had its drawbacks. Nicolo Conti, to whom allusion has already been made, writing between 1420 and 1440, says that the King of Vijayanagar had 12,000, wives of whom 4,000 went on foot and served in his kitchen, 4,000 went on horseback, and 4,000 were carried in litters. Of the litter ladies 2,000 were chosen as wives on condition that they would burn when the King died. Now it is possible that the educated beauty of Mudkul knew of this custom, and did not relish having some day to perform the rite of Suttee. At all events the young lady declined the offer, and refused to accept the jewels which had been sent her. The reason she assigned was her love for her parents, because when once she should be made the wife of the King, she would be separated from them, and never see them again. Accordingly, the Brahmin was sent back with all his presents a disappointed man. After he had gone, the girl told her parents that she had long had an inward persuasion that she should become the wife of a great prince of Islam, and that, therefore, they must not be angry with her for refusing the Hindoo King. When the Brahmin reported the failure of his mission, the King's love became more inflamed than ever, and he resolved to carry off the fair Pertal—for this was her name—by force, even though in order to do so he had to invade the Sultan's country, for Mudkul was in the possession of Feroze Shah. Accordingly, he assembled an army, crossed the Tungabadhra, and marched upon Mudkul. Unfortunately, however, he stopped before he reached the fort, and the consequence was that the inhabitants, hearing of the approach of this large army, became alarmed and left the town. Amongst these were Pertal and her parents. The Vijayanagar troops had accordingly to retire without their expected prize, but on their way back they burnt and destroyed several villages and towns. When Feroze Shah heard of this unprovoked and insolent invasion, he assembled an army, and crossing the two rivers laid siege to Vijayanagar. Deva Raya was the Hindoo King, and he seems to have successfully defended his city. The Mahomedans were repulsed, and the Sultan himself wounded. In fact so hard pressed were the Sultan's forces that they had to withdraw into the plain, and entrench themselves in order to keep off the Hindoos. Deva Raya does not seem to have been able to force them from this position, and accordingly sent for assistance from his allies of Malwa and Guzerat. In the meantime, another army of the Sultan, commanded by his brother Ahmed, laid the Vijayanagar country waste, and rejoined Feroze in his camp with a large amount of booty and sixty thousand prisoners. The Sultan then left his brother Ahmed in the entrenched camp, and went with the rest of the army to besiege Adoni. In the meantime, the Rajah's application for assistance from Malwa and Guzerat had proved unsuccessful. His allies either could not or would not give him help, and he, therefore, found himself obliged to sue for peace. At first the Sultan refused, but at last agreed, under the condition, however, that in addition to an enormous indemnity he would give him his daughter in marriage. The indemnity consisted of ten laks of pagodas, five maunds of pearls (the maund of S. India is equal to 28 pounds), fifty choice elephants, and two thousand men and women slaves, in addition to the fort of Beekapore as a marriage portion. The first of these conditions was probably the most irksome one, but the Hindoo King was obliged to comply. The Sultan's brother went into the city of Vijayanagar, and brought out the bride, whereupon the marriage was celebrated with great pomp and magnificence. After the marriage had been celebrated, Feroze Shah paid Deva Raya a visit with his bride. The incident is thus related by Ferishta:

"A day having been fixed, he with the bride proceeded to Vijayanagar, leaving the camp in charge of Khan Khanan (his brother Ahmed). On the way he was met by Deva Raya with great pomp. From the gate of the city to the palace, being a distance of nearly six miles, the road was spread with cloth of gold, velvet, satin, and other rich stuffs. The two princes rode on horseback together, between ranks of beautiful boys and girls, who waved plates of gold and silver flowers over their heads as they advanced, and then threw them to be gathered by the populace. After this, the inhabitants of the city made offerings, both men and women, according to their rank. After passing through a square directly in the centre of the city, the relations of Deva Raya who had lined the streets in crowds, made their obeisance and offerings, and joined the cavalcade on foot, marching before the princes. Upon their arrival at the palace gate, the Sultan and the Raya dismounted from their horses, and ascended a splendid palanquin, set with valuable jewels, in which they were carried together to the apartments prepared for the reception of the bride and bridegroom, when Deva Raya took his leave and went to his palace. The Sultan after having been treated with royal magnificence for three days took his leave of the Raya, who pressed upon him richer presents than before given, and attended him four miles on his way back and then returned to the city. Sultan Feroze Shah was enraged at his not going with him to his camp, and said to Meer Fazl Oollah that he would one day have revenge for such an affront. This declaration being told to Deva Raya, he made some insolent remarks, so that, notwithstanding the connection of family, their hatred was not calmed. Sultan Feroze Shah proceeded to the capital of his dominions, and despatched persons to bring the beautiful Pertal and her family to court; which being done, her beauty was found to surpass all that had been reported of it. The Sultan observing that he was too old to espouse her himself gave her to his son, Hussan Khan, in marriage, and gratified her parents with rich gifts and grants of land in their country.

Pertal was committed to the care of the Sultan's aunt until the nuptial preparations were ready, when the knot was tied amid great rejoicings and princely magnificence."

The story of the beautiful Pertal and the war of which she was the innocent cause contain all the elements of a historical romance. Would that there were a Meadows Taylor still alive to give it to us, together with a graphic description of the country and the people amongst whom she lived!

Sultan Feroze Shah laid out a new city not far from Gulburga, which he named after himself Firozeabad. It was situated on the banks of the Bheemrah, or Bhima, one of the affluents of the Kistna. The site of this town was about 15 miles from the present railway station of *Wadi*, the junction of the G. T. P. and Nizam's State Railways, and is said to have been laid out with great regularity. Gulburga, however, continued to be the seat of Government, and the new town was more a pleasure resort than a residence. About 1412 a celebrated saint, named Mahummud Geesoo-Diraz, came from Delhi to Gulburga, but though the Sultan at first showed him considerable favour, he appears to have afterwards neglected him. The Sultan's brother, Ahmed, who held the post of Khan Khanan made it, however, his duty to show this saint considerable respect, and was constant in his attendance upon him. The result was that Ahmed stood high in the saint's favour, and when in 1415 the Sultan asked the latter to bestow his blessing upon his son Hassan, whom he had selected as his successor, and who is said to have been a weak and dissipated prince, the saint declined, giving, as his reason, that Providence had decreed that the crown should be bestowed on his brother, Ahmed. Upon this the Sultan ordered the saint to leave the city, which he did, and retired to a place outside, where his tomb now stands. This tomb is still highly venerated by the Mahomedans of the Deccan, and is visited every year by thousands of pilgrims. The walls are decorated with texts from the Koran in gilt letters, and none but true believers are admitted inside. Near it are some buildings consisting of a *serai*, a mosque, and a college, said to have been built by Aurungzebe in the seventeenth century.

In 1417 Feroze Shah made an unprovoked attack upon the fort of Bilkonda, belonging to the King of Vijayanagar, who was still Deva Raya. After a siege of two years, a pestilence broke out in the Sultan's army, and he had to retire. The Hindoos then advanced with a large force, and the Sultan, disregarding the advice of his chief officers, gave them battle, with the result that he suffered a serious defeat. His Commander in Chief, Meer Fuzl Oollah, was killed, and he himself had to fly in the greatest confusion. A general slaughter of the Mahomedans followed, and the Hindoos are said to have erected a platform of their heads. The Sultan was followed into his own country which was everywhere laid waste, mosques and holy places were broken down, and people were slaughtered indiscriminately. The Sultan appealed for help to Guzerat, but in vain, and it was only after some time and immense exertions that his brother, Ahmed, succeeded in driving the Hindoos back into their own dominions.

This reverse seems to have prayed so much upon the Sultan's mind that he fell ill. During his illness he left the affairs of his Government to two of his slaves, named Hoshiar Ein-ul-Mulk and Nizam Bedar-ul-Mulk. These two persons, alarmed at the growing popularity of Ahmed, advised the King to have him blinded. The Sultan, remembering the Saint's prophecy, resolved to do this, but his brother received timely notice and prepared with his son for flight. First of all, however, he went with his son to ask for the blessing of the holy Seyd. "The Seyd took the turban from his own son's head, and dividing it into two parts, tied one round the head of the father and son, and extending his hands over them, hailed them both with future royalty" (Ferishta.) After this Ahmed left the city, followed by four hundred trusty adherents. As soon as Hoshiar and Bedar heard that their intended victim had escaped, they set out in pursuit with four thousand horses. Ahmed had only a few followers, but is said to have gained the victory by means of a clever stratagem carried out by his chief supporter, one Khulif Hussan. A company of grain merchants with about two thousand oxen happened to pass, and Hussan purchased them all, and mounted a man with a red and white flag on each ox. Some cavalry were posted in front of this strange force with orders to appear at a distance when the engagement should commence. Next morning the attack was commenced, and whilst it was going on, Hussan's force was seen marching behind some trees. At the same time Ahmed made a vigorous charge, and the Sultan's army, thinking he was supported by a large force of cavalry, broke and fled. Ahmed gained a considerable amount of booty, and at once marched upon Gulburga, where he was soon joined by a large number of disaffected persons, who were encouraged by his success. The Sultan, in spite of his illness, had himself carried out in a palanquin and attacked his brother. His forces, however, were again defeated, and he had to take refuge in the citadel. Hoshiar and Bedar commenced defending the fort, but the Sultan, weakened by age and disease, resolved to abdicate. He first of all called his son, Hussan-Khan, and told him that as all the nobility had sided with Ahmed it would be better to submit. He then summoned his brother, and formally made over to him his kingdom, and his son. Ahmed Shah, then ascended the throne and ordered coins to be struck and the Khutba to be read in his name. A few days afterwards Feroze Shah died, and Ferishta adds that "it is said in some books that he was put to death through policy, by his brother; but no good foundation appears for the report." Ferishta is probably correct in this latter surmise, for by his subsequent behaviour to the late

Sultan's son, it is clear that Ahmed Shah was more generous than was the custom of the kings of that time towards their unsuccessful rivals. Feroze Shah's reign lasted twenty-five years, seven months, and fifteen days.

Sultan Ahmed Shah Wullee Bahmanee appears to have followed his brother's example of encouraging learning. As might be expected, he showed great gratitude to the holy Syed Geesoo Diraz; not only did he build for him a splendid college, but he also endowed him richly with villages and jaghirs. Ahmed Shah's accession was signalized by more than ordinary generosity. Rejecting the advice of his Minister to put the late Sultan's son to death, he gave him Ferozeabad as a residence with an ample revenue, and here the Prince continued in future to reside, without giving any trouble, for, being indolent and dissipated by nature, he preferred the pleasures of hunting and the enjoyments of the harem to the dangers and cares of sovereignty. As long as his uncle lived, he was unmolested, but in the next reign he was blinded and confined to his palace. The two Ministers of the late Sultan were also taken into favour, and Hoshiar Ein-ul-Mulk was appointed Ameer-ul-Umra, or chief of the Nobles, whilst Bedar-ul-Mulk was posted to the Government of Dowlatabad. Hussan the Merchant, owing to whose clever stratagem Ahmed had gained the throne, was appointed Minister (Vakeel-ul-Sultanat: Envoy of the Kingdom) with the title Malick-ul-Tijar, (Prince of Merchants) a rank which in Ferishta's time was still bestowed in the Deccan, and was held in high esteem.

One of Ahmed Shah's first acts was to declare war against Vijayanagar in revenge for the invasions during the late reign. Deva Raya was assisted by the King of Warangal, but the latter before long deserted his ally. The two armies met on the banks of the Tungabadhra, and after some delay the Sultan crossed the river, and attacked the Rajah early in the morning. A strange incident occurred in this surprise. The Rajah was sleeping in a garden near a sugar-cane plantation when the Mahomedans made their attack. He fled almost naked into the plantation, and there he was found hiding by some soldiers, who wanted to cut some of the canes. Thinking him to be an ordinary person, they made him carry a bundle of canes, and follow them. The Rajah, glad to escape recognition, said nothing, but followed his captors. When they reached the Rajah's camp, the Sultan's army was engaged in plundering, and so the soldiers, hoping to get more valuable plunder than sugar-cane, left their captive to his own devices, and joined their comrades. Deva Raya was not slow to make his escape, and soon after, coming up with some of his nobles, was brought into safety. The Rajah then retired to Vijayanagar, and Ahmed Shah devastated the country. He is said to have neglected the old compact made between the Sultan of Gulburga and the King of Vijayanagar, and to have slaughtered twenty thousand Hindoos, and to have destroyed a number of temples. So exasperated were the Brahmins that they formed a plot to assassinate the Sultan, and very nearly succeeded in their attempt. They surprised him whilst he was out hunting and separated from his companions, and pursued him so hotly that he was only just able to take refuge within a mud enclosure. Here he was joined by a few friends, but the Hindoos had succeeded in making a breach in the mud wall, and were on the point of entering, when they were attacked in the rear, and put to flight after a desperate struggle in which five hundred Mahomedans and one thousand Hindoos were killed. Abd-ul-Kadir, the officer who had luckily come to his master's rescue, was at once raised to the rank of two thousand, and the Government of Berar was bestowed upon him with the titles of Khan Jehan and the "Life bestowing Brother."

In the meantime, the city of Vijayanagar had been blockaded, and the inhabitants reduced to considerable distress, so that

Deva Raya felt himself compelled to sue for peace; this was granted on condition that he would send all arrears of tribute laden on his best elephants, and conducted by his son with drums, trumpets, and all the State pageantry to the Sultan's camp. This was done and the embassy was met outside the Sultan's camp and conducted into his presence. The Sultan, after embracing the Rajah's son, made him sit at the foot of the throne, and then invested him with a robe of honour, a jewelled sword, twenty horses, and elephants, and other gifts. After this the Sultan drew off his army, and returned to Gulburga.

In 1424 the Sultan marched against the Warangal King, who had withheld his tribute. Arrived at Golconda the Sultan halted, and sent on Khan Azim with a portion of the main army against Warangal, about 90 miles distant. This expedition was entirely successful. Not only were the Hindoos defeated with great loss, but Warangal itself was taken, and the Rajah killed. The Sultan then moved his camp to the captured city "and took possession of the buried treasures of ages which had till now been preserved from plunder, and accumulated yearly by the economy of the Rajahs" (Ferishta). These treasures, however, were only the accumulations of less than one hundred years, for after the former sack of Wàrangal in 1323 the city was for some time the seat of a Mahomedan Governor appointed from Delhi. Khan Azim, after being duly rewarded, was despatched to reduce other forts belonging to the Telingana country. This duty he accomplished in about four months' time, and Ahmed Shah returned to Gulburga.

From this time Warangal and a large portion of the Telingana country appears to have been incorporated with the Mahomedan kingdom of the Deccan. There were frequent risings of the Hindoos, subsequently, but we do not find that Warangal was ever afterwards a royal city. At the present day very few remains of its former grandeur are to be seen. The outer wall is built entirely of

The ruins of Warangal.

mud. It is very high, and encloses an area of about $2\frac{1}{2}$ square miles. The inner wall is of stone, and encloses an area of about one square mile or a little less. Almost the only ruins are four beautifully carved porches in the centre of the inner enclosure. They are placed at the four cardinal points, and probably formed the entrances to the palace. Close by is a large hall, possibly used as a treasure house. It is massively built in the shape of an ark. There is also a small temple with some fine carvings, and this is nearly all that remains of this ancient city. The walls themselves show signs of having been frequently rebuilt because old carvings and bas-reliefs are built in detached pieces into some of the upper portions, thus showing that after the fort had been destroyed, the old *débris* was used to reconstruct the walls. There is a great deal of resemblance in some of the stone carvings with those of the temple at Hanamkonda about $3\frac{1}{2}$ miles distant. This temple, which is now fast falling into almost total ruin, is one of the most perfect specimens of Chalukyan architecture in Southern India. Massive pillars of black granite, polished like marble, are carved into all manner of shapes with masterly skill. The shrines are protected by screens of the most delicate stone tracery, and the whole temple, or what remains of it, is a perfect gem of its kind. The following description is taken from the "Historical and Descriptive Sketch of H.H. the Nizam's Dominions" (Syed Hoossain Belgrami and C. Willmott 1884):—" Hanamkonda contains some very interesting remains, and, according to local accounts, was the capital of the surrounding country before Warangal was founded. The 'thousand-pillared temple' was constructed by the last Hindoo dynasty, and an inscription on a pillar at the gateway mentions that Rudra Deva was the reigning sovereign in Saka 1084, or A.D. 1162. The temple was built in the Chalukyan style, but was never finished. It consists of three detached cells of very considerable dimensions, with a portico supported by between 240 and 300 pillars arranged in a varied and complicated pattern. Opposite the portico, but at some distance from it, is a star-shaped structure, containing a hall and four entrances, without any recess for idols, and supported on about 200 pillars. This forms a sort of mandapam, and was connected with the main temple by a massive pillared pavilion covering a huge bull of polished black basalt. The pavilion has fallen down, but the bull is tolerably intact, and is a splendid specimen of a monolith. * The arrangement of the pillars and the variety of spacing are in pleasing subordination to the general plan. The pillars of the mandapam are plain, while those of the temple are richly carved, but without being overdone, and it is only in pairs that they are of the same design. Some of the other details are of great beauty, especially the doorways to the recesses, the pierced slabs used for windows, and the very elegant open work by which the bracket shafts are attached to the pillars. The arrangement of three temples joined together is capable of giving a greater variety of effect, and of light and shade than the plainer forms, and the appearance of the whole is further improved by the terrace about 3 feet high and from ten to fifteen feet wide on which the temple stands. There is a short inscription in Sanskrit on one of the pillars, and another in old Telugu on one of the walls. A black polished stone pillar about five feet high covered with inscriptions in old Telugu stands near the gate to the east of the temple, and a very fine well is close by. A similar pillar full of inscriptions stands in front of the temple to Padmakshi, the titular goddess of the Kakatya dynasty."

The country round Warangal is at present very thinly populated, the scale being about 80 to the square mile. It

---

* Since this was written, however, this beautiful bull has been greatly injured by the fall of massive stones. It is cracked in many places and unless steps are shortly taken will probably be totally destroyed.

must, however, at one time have been not only thickly populated but also highly cultivated. It is covered with the remains of old irrigation works which are everywhere to be found in the old Hindoo kingdoms, but which under Mahomedan rule were allowed to fall into ruin. About 25 miles from Warangal is one of the largest artificial lakes in India which is thus described in the same work:—"*Pakhal*—a lake situated close to a village of the same name in latitude 17° 57′ 30″ N. and 79° 59′ 30″ E. longitude. The lake or tank is some twelve miles square. It is enclosed on all sides, except the west, by ranges of low and densely-wooded hills. The western side is closed by a strongly constructed 'bund.' Tradition alleges the bund to have been constructed 1,600 years ago by Raja Khaldya, and a stone pillar, which stands on the bund, contains an illegible inscription, which is said to commemorate the name of the person who built it. The bund is about a mile in length. The average depth of the water in the lake is between thirty and forty feet. It is described as 'clear with a slightly bitterish taste, and considered by the inhabitants to be extremely unwholesome. It abounds with fish, some of a very large description and excellent flavour. It also contains otters and alligators.' The hills which surround the lake abound in game of every description, including a few wild elephants said to be the progeny of a pair of tame ones that escaped after the battle of Assaye. The Pakhal Lake has been made by throwing a bund across a river which has cut its way over a western outcrop of the Vindhyas, between two low headlands. Mr. King, of the Geological Survey of India, writing of the lake a few years since, said:—'It is a splendid sheet of water lying back in two arms on either side of a good big hill east-south-east of the bund, while from these are long bays reaching up behind low ridges of outcropping Vindhyas. On every side there is far-stretching jungle. Even below the bund for miles there is the thickest and densest jungle, only broken here and there by a few patches of rice cultivation. There is not the population even in the country below the tank to make use of its waters. In the old Telinga times, when Warangal was one of the great centres of the Telugu people, there must have been something more stirring in the way of human life than there is now in this desolate region of widespread jungle.' For six or seven months in the year the neighbourhood of the lake is very unhealthy; owing to this circumstance very little cultivation is carried on in the neighbourhood. There are, however, several small channels which convey water from the lake to some distance for irrigational purposes. In the centre of the bund are the ruins of a small pavilion styled the Chabutra of Sitab Khan. The best time to visit the lake for sport is during the first three or four months of the year. The nature of the country may be imagined from a native saying to the effect that a red squirrel can reach Badrachellum on the Godavari from the neighbourhood of Pakhal by leaping from tree to tree."

This vast jungle (which is now reserved by H. H. the Nizam for sporting purposes) has all grown up since the destruction of the Hindoo kingdom. What is now a marshy unwholesome forest was probably at one time a large expanse of rice fields.

But to return to Sultan Ahmed Shah. In the following year, 1425, Ahmed Shah made an expedition into the country of the Ghonds or what is now known as the Central Provinces. Here he is said to come into possession of a diamond mine, and to have destroyed several temples, erecting mosques in their places. After this he marched to Ellichpore, where he remained for nearly a year, and then returned to Gulburga. From this we see that the dominions of the Bahmanee house had at this time extended far up into the Central Provinces to the East, and to what are now called the Berars in the North. At this portion the kingdom was bounded by Malwa on the north, and Guzerat on the north-west. The hill country on the Western Ghauts, was probably still held by Mahratta tribes in a state of independence, but towards the south the limits of the kingdom must have extended nearly to Goa, whilst on the east they have reached to Masulipatam and the Coromandel Coast. It is also quite clear that the Delhi Sultans exercised no authority or control over any portion of this extensive kingdom. Mubarak Shah was then Sultan of Delhi, and his time was fully occupied in subduing rebellious Rajahs and petty Mahomedan princes. A number of these small States, such as Guzerat and Malwa, had arisen between the Deccan and the North of India, and further towards the east there were several independent Hindoo Chiefs who occupied that part of India now known as the Central Provinces. It was the vicinity of Malwa that gave rise to Ahmed Shah's next war. Hoshung Shah was then Sultan of Malwa, and was as independent in his own territory as Ahmed Shah was in the Deccan. Hoshung Shah began to be alarmed at the manner in which Ahmed Shah was increasing in power, and, perhaps, bore in mind the grant which had already been made by Timur of Malwa to the Sultan of the Deccan. Accordingly, he made overtures to the neighbouring Hindoo Rajah of Kurleh, named Nursinga to unite with him to check his dangerous rival. Nursinga had already come into contract with the previous Sultan of Gulburga, Feroze Shah, had been beaten, and agreed to pay tribute. Faithful to this compact, Nursinga refused the proferred alliance, and in consequence Hoshung Shah invaded his dominions. Twice he was repulsed, but on the third occasion he managed to take the Hindoo Rajah by surprise. Nursinga then applied to Ahmed Shah for assistance on the ground that this invasion had been made solely on account of his loyalty to the treaty which had been made with Feroze. Accordingly, Ahmed Shah marched to the relief of Nursinga, but before he was actually able to meet Hoshung

Shah, his religious advisers managed to persuade him that it was an unholy and wicked thing for a Mahomedan Prince to ally himself with an unbeliever in order to make war upon another true believer. Ahmed Shah yielded to the persuasions of his religious friends and wrote to Hushung Shah, asking him to retire, without coming to a fratricidal war. Ahmed Shah did in fact retire, but Hoshung Shah thinking that this was due to weakness, pursued him with a considerable force, and commenced to harass his rear. This affront was more than Ahmed Shah could stand, so, flinging his conscientious scruples to the winds, he told his Mollahs and Kazis that he had done enough for religion by retiring, and he must now protect his own honour by fighting. Accordingly, he ordered a halt and drew up his army in order of battle. He left the main army in command of his son, Alla-ud-Din, and his General, and himself took command of a select force, which he placed in ambush with the view of taking the enemy in the rear. Hoshung Shah, expecting to find an enemy in full retreat, was surprised to suddenly come across an army in full order of battle. His own army had been carelessly arranged, not expecting to meet with any opposition. Nevertheless he charged with much gallantry, but in the midst of his attack, Ahmed Shah emerged from his ambush, and taking the confused and serried masses in the rear put them entirely to flight. Hoshung Shah and his whole army fled in the utmost confusion, followed by Ahmed Shah, who took all his baggage, two hundred elephants, and the harem, besides putting some two thousand men to the sword. Nursinga, as soon as he heard of this defeat, made a sally from his fort, and intercepting the fugitive killed a large number, and thus made the victory complete. The Hindoo Rajah then visited the Sultan in his camp, and persuaded him to pay him a visit at Kurleh. After being splendidly entertained the Sultan returned towards Gulburga, the Hindoo Rajah accompanying him a considerable distance, and then being dismissed with marks of great honour. It was on this return march that Ahmed Shah halted at the ancient town of Bieder. Struck by its healthy situation and by the abundance of water, the Sultan resolved to build a new city here, and to make it his capital. This was accordingly done, and the new city, which was finished in 1431, was called Ahmedabad Bieder. The old Hindoo city is said to be the scene of the adventures of King Nal and his wife Damayanti, and was in times of antiquity the metropolis of a great Hindoo kingdom. A description of the modern Bieder will be given later on. Although the new city was not completed till 1431, the Sultan appears to have transferred his seat of Government to Bieder very soon after the building was commenced, because, already in 1429, we find him celebrating there the marriage of his son with the daughter of the Sultan of Khandeish—a marriage which seems to have originated from political motives, so as to form a bond of union between the Sultan of Khandeish and the bridegroom, Alla-ud-Din, the successor of Ahmed Shah. About this time the Sultan divided the Government of his dominions amongst his four sons. Alla-ud-Din, as the next heir, was kept at Bieder, with the youngest son Mahummad as his colleague; Muhamed Khan received Berar with Ramgeer, Mahow, and Koollum, and Daoud Khan was sent to Telingana; Malick-ul-Tijar was appointed Governor of Dowlatabad. In 1429 Sultan Ahmed sent an expedition into the Konkan under the leadership of Malick-ul-Tijar, which was at first very successful, several elephants and camels laden with jewels being sent to Court. The end of the expedition, however, was a terrible disaster. The Deccan General took the island of Mahim, which belonged to the Sultan of Guzerat, who thereupon sent an army to revenge this insult. Ahmed sent his son, Alla-ud-Din, with reinforcement, but in the engagement which ensued, the Deccan army suffered a total defeat, losing the whole of their baggage, tents, and elephants. Ahmed Shah now came down to the Konkan to lead the war in person, and the Sultan of Guzerat did the same. The two armies lay for some time opposite each other and a decisive battle seemed imminent, but the religious men interfered, and a peace was concluded, under which both parties were left in possession of their territories. The chief result of this war was that Hoshung Shah, the Sultan of Malwa, took advantage of the Deccan Sultan being employed elsewhere to invade the territory of Nursinga, the brave Hindoo Rajah of Kurleh. This Prince, left unassisted by his Mahomedan ally, was defeated and killed, and his country passed into the possession of the Malwa Sultan (1433). Ahmed Shah at first marched to revenge his death, but before a battle could be fought, peace was concluded between the two Sultans. Kurleh was left in possession of Malwa and the whole province of Berar was made over to Ahmed Shah. Soon after this, Ahmed Shah marched to Telingana to put down a rebellion, and this was his last public act, for he was taken ill and died, in 1434, after a reign of twelve years and two months.

CHAPTER IX.

SULTAN ALLAH-UD-DIN II.

1434 to 1457.

It will be remembered that Sultan Ahmed Shah appointed Muhammed Khan, his youngest son, to be the colleague of Alla-ud-Din, his eldest son and successor. Alla-ud-Din appears to have regarded his father's wishes, so far as to treat his younger brother with great and almost royal respect. He bestowed upon him costly presents, and despatched him to conduct the war against the King of Vijayanagar, who had again neglected to send his promised tribute. There is, however, an old saying, that there is no more room for two Kings in one country than there is for two swords in one scabbard. Muhammed's position was an anomalous one, and it is not, therefore, surprising that there should have been persons ready to inflame his imagination, and to suggest to him that, as partner to a King, he ought to have an equal share in the royal honours and privileges. Muhammed lent a willing ear to these representations, and being flushed with his success over the Hindoos, whose country he laid waste, and who were compelled to sue for peace by payment of a large sum, he resolved to raise the standard of rebellion. Alla-ud-Din had sent with Muhammed two of his principal noblemen, Khajeh Jehan, the Vizier, and Imad-ul Mulk Ghoree the son of the old Seyd-ud-Din, who had for more than fifty years been the Minister of the first Bahmanee Sultans. The latter was an old man who had retired from office, and was only induced to accompany the young Prince by the strong persuasions of the Sultan. The idea of rebellion having entered into Muhammed's mind, he endeavoured to induce these two noblemen to join him, but they, loyal to their rightful Sultan, not only refused, but pointed out to the young Prince the criminality of his intentions. This so incensed Muhammed that he caused both of them to be put to death, and then, not content with rebellion, committed the additional treason of calling upon the King of Vijayanagar to assist him with an army. Aided in this manner by the hereditary foes of his country, he succeeded in capturing the forts of Mudkul, Raichore, Sholapore, Beejapore, and Nuldroog.

Alla-ud-Din was greatly incensed at this rebellion, and especially at the murder of Imad-ul-Mulk, and he at once advanced with a large army to bring matters with his brother to an issue. A furious battle ensued, but after an obstinate struggle the rebel army was totally defeated, the principal leaders were killed, and Muhammed, followed by a few attendants only, had to take to the hills for shelter. The Sultan then returned to his capital, and not long afterwards, Muhammed submitted himself to his elder brother, was pardoned, and was sent as Governor to Telingana, which post had become vacant by the death of Daoud Shah. Here he lived undisturbed, and is said to have spent his life in a round of pleasures. This incident is interesting as accounting in some way for the unnatural custom which we find so prevalent throughout Mahomedan history, of kings blinding and confining their brothers and near relatives, who might be supposed to have pretensions to the throne. The splendour of an Oriental throne possessed fatal attractions to those whom the accident of birth had placed near to it, but whom circumstances had removed to a distance. The nearer the Prince was placed, the greater the danger to be expected, and experience seemed to show that the only way of preserving a kingdom from civil war was to remove all possible pretenders. The incident, however, forms a notable exception to the tragedies which were usually the result of such rebellions, and of which we shall find a terrible example in the next reign. Alla-ud-Din, in this instance, treated his brother with extraordinary and unusual generosity, and he does not, as is so often the case, appear to have received ingratitude in return.

In 1436 Alla-ud-Din despatched an expedition to the Konkan under Dilawar Khan. This General was successful, and returned after subduing the Rajahs of Amede and Sungeer with a considerable amount of booty. He also brought with him the daughter of the Rajah of Sungeer, a maiden of great accomplishments, whom the Sultan took into his zenana under the name of Peri-chera, or the "*Angel-faced.*" This lady soon became the Sultan's favourite wife, and for her sake he neglected his first wife, who, it will be remembered, was a Princess of Kandeish—a neglect which was to bear serious consequences. Dilawar Khan was on his return made Vizier, but he soon afterwards lost his master's favour and retired, his place being taken by a eunuch named Dustoor-ul-Mulk. This person soon excited universal disgust by his insolence, and amongst other enemies, he was foolish enough to cause the anger of the Sultan's son, Humayun, who already showed signs of that violent temper which was afterwards to earn for him the title of the "Cruel." This Prince, disgusted at the refusal of Dustoor to comply with some request, caused the Minister to be assassinated by one of his own retainers. Upon this a Deccanee nobleman, named Meamun Oollah, was appointed Minister, and matters resumed their former train.

In the following year (1437) war broke out with the

Sultan of Kandeish, to whom Malleeka Jehan, the neglected wife of Alla-ud-Din, had appealed for vengeance. This Prince claimed to be a lineal descendant of the Caliph Omar, and accordingly felt it as a personal insult that his daughter should have been set aside for an infidel Princess. He at once invaded Berar with a large army, assisted by a force sent by the Rajah of Ghondwarah. The Governor, Khan Jehan, was compelled to shut himself up in the fortress of Pernalleh, and the *Khutba* was read in the name of Nusseer Khan, the Sultan of Kandeish.

Alla-ud-Din, on receipt of this intelligence, at once ordered Malick-ul-Tijar to conduct an expedition to recover Berar. This General, it will be remembered, suffered a disaster in the late reign after taking the island of Mahim. He now represented to the Sultan that this defeat was mainly caused by the jealousy of the Deccanee and Abyssinian nobles, and he, therefore asked that on this occasion his army should be officered mainly by foreigners. Under this term were included the Turks, Persians, and Arabs settled in the Deccan. The Abyssinians and the Deccanees seem always to have been classed together and to have made common cause, and between them and the so-called foreigners there was always the greatest hatred. This request was granted, but in the sequel only added flames to the existing jealousy which has continued between the Deccanees and the foreigners down to the present day.

Malick-ul-Tijar's expedition met with eminent success. Not only was the Sultan of Kandeish defeated, but his kingdom was invaded, his capital, Burhanpoor, was taken, and his palace razed to the ground. Berar was recovered, and the General returned to Bieder laden with considerable plunder. He was received by Alla-ud-Din with every mark of distinction, was rewarded with presents; the Sultan's daughter was bestowed upon one of his principal officers, Shah Koolli Sultan, and finally it was ordered that in future the Moghuls should take the place in the army of the Deccanees and Abyssinians. It now becomes necessary to glance at affairs at Vijayanagar. Deva Raya was still King of this great country, and he appears to have come to the conclusion that if he was to make a successful stand against the Mahomedan Sultans he must reform his army. Although, during the last hundred years the Hindoos had been sometimes successful, the final issue of every conflict had been in favour of the Mahomedans. It is, indeed, surprising that after so many successful wars, the boundaries of the two States should have remained unaltered. In spite of their victories, the Mahomedans were never able to gain a footing in Hindoo territory, and after a lapse of nearly one hundred years the country between the rivers Kistna and Tungabadhra still remained a debatable land, in which the forts were continually passing from the possession of one King to that of the others. It was probably owing to their numbers that the Hindoos were thus able to make so successful a stand, but this in Deva Raya's opinion was not sufficient, and he wished to be able to carry the war into the enemy's country. Accordingly, he summoned a council of his principal officers and Brahmins, and asked why it was that with such infinitely greater resources in men and treasure than the Mahomedans, his armies should so constantly be defeated. "Some said that the Almighty has decreed a superiority of the Mussulmans over the Hindoos for thirty thousand years, or more yet to come, which was plainly foretold by their Scriptures; that, therefore, the Hindoos were generally subdued by them. Others said that the superiority of the Mussulmans arose from two causes; one, all their horses being strong, and able to bear more fatigue than the weak, lean animals of the Carnatic; the other, owing to a great body of excellent archers; being always kept up by the Bahmanee Sultans, of whom the Rajah had but few in his army." (Ferishta.) Deva Raya was sensible enough to see the justice of the latter opinion, and accordingly resolved to employ a large body of Mahomedan mercenaries. In order to attract such persons, he had a mosque built in the city of Vijayanagar, and allowed them the free use of their religion. Another remarkable step for a Hindoo Prince to take was, that he ordered a Koran to be placed on a desk in front of his throne, so that when Mahomedans appeared before him, they might go through the ceremony of obeisance without sinning against their own religion. By these means he succeeded before long in getting a Mahomedan force of two thousand men. These were employed in instructing and drilling the native levies, so that he managed to raise an army of sixty thousand Hindoos well-skilled in archery, besides eighty thousand horse, and two hundred thousand foot, armed in the usual manner with pikes and lances. We are not told that he had any artillery, although there can be no doubt that this arm was at this time regularly used by the Mahomedans.

It took some years for Deva Raya to get this large army ready, but at length when all his preparations were made, he commenced the war in 1443, by crossing the Tungabadhra and laying siege to Raichore, whilst the rest of his forces were employed in devastating the Doab.

In order to meet this invasion Alla-ud-Din summoned all his forces from Telingana, Dowlatabad, and Berar. He was not, however, able to collect more than fifty thousand horse, sixty thousand foot, and a large train of artillery. Compared with the Hindoo army this was but a small force, but it had the advantage of consisting for the most part of veterans, who had served through many campaigns. The Sultan himself marched against Deva Raya, who was encamped in front of Mudkul, and despatched Malik-ul-Tijar to raise the siege of Raichore. In this the latter was successful, and defeated the son of Deva Raya, who was wounded in the action and compelled to retire. In the meantime the Sultan was busy with the main Hindoo army. During the space of two months three general actions were fought. In the first of these the Hindoos were successful, but they were defeated in the two last. In the third, the eldest son of Deva Raya was killed, which created a panic, and caused the Hindoos to take refuge within the walls of Mudkul. In the heat of the pursuit two of Alla-ud-Din's chief officers pushed on too far, and were taken prisoners. Upon this Alla-ud-Din sent a message to Deva Raya that he regarded the lives of his two officers as each equal to one hundred thousand Hindoos, and that if they were injured, he would exact a full payment in return. Deva Raya was not unaware of how a former Sultan, Mahmood Shah, had made and carried out a similar promise, and so he thought it advisable to come to terms. A treaty was accordingly drawn up, in which the Hindoo King promised to respect the Sultan's territories in future, to restore the prisoners, and to pay his tribute regularly. Peace was then made; the Sultan bestowed presents upon the Rajah, and then returned to his own capital. During the remainder of the Sultan's reign, this peace was strictly observed by Deva Raya. *

On his return from this campaign the Sultan gave himself up to idleness, and the pleasures of the harem; he only appeared

We have other evidence of this war than that of Ferishta, for at the time it broke out, Abdar Razzak was staying at the Vijayanagar Court. He ascribes the initiative as having been taken by the Gulburga Sultan, who took advantage of the reported assassination of the Hindoo King to demand a heavy contribution. This traveller speaks of this departure of the Hindoo general or *Danaick* with a large army, and his return with a number of captives. He does not speak of any reverses or of the death of the King's son. It seems probable that the success of this campaign was principally on the side of the Hindoos. Ferishta admits that they were successful at first, and the fact of so advantageous a treaty being so easily granted would seem to show that the Hindoos had further successes. Ferishta's description of the reorganization of the Hindoo army is probably intended to excuse or account for the Mahomedan reverses.

in public once in four or five months, and spent the whole o his time "in drinking ruby coloured wines, pressing the lip of silver-bodied damsels, or listening to the melody of sweet voiced musicians."

Whilst the Sultan had thus withdrawn himself from business his Minister, Meamun Oolla had formed a plan for reducing the fortresses along the sea-coast, and despatched Malik-ul-Tijar with a force of seven thousand Deccanee and three thousand Arab horse, besides about seven thousand of his own troops. Malik-ul-Tijar made Jagneh, a port on the Malabar Coast, his headquarters, and from here sent forth expeditions against the various Rajahs, most of whom he managed to reduce to obedience. Amongst these was a Rajah named Sirkeh, of whom he wished to make a convert to Islam. This religion the Rajah promised to embrace, but said that first of all Malik should conquer his rival, the Rajah of Sungeer, because otherwise when the Mahomedans should leave the country, Sungeer would cover him with ridicule for having become a renegade to his religion. The road to Sungeer was said to lead to thick forests, and as Malik was unacquainted with it, the wily Sirkeh promised to lead him there in person. Accordingly, trusting in these promises

1453. Malik-ul-Tijar set out on his perilous expedition, but at the very outset was deserted by most of the Deccanee and Abyssinian troops, who refused to enter the woods Nothing daunted, Malik continued his march, followed by some seven thousand of his own troops. For two days the road was a fairly good one, but on the third Sirkeh led them through so horrible a jungle that, as Ferishta quaintly says "a male tiger through dread of the terrors of it, would have become a female; fuller of windings than the curly locks o the fair, and narrower than the path of love." Malik himsel was ill of dysentery, and could not look after his army When night came Sirkeh managed to make his escape, and left the Mahomedans, exhausted by their day's exertions, to camp as best they could in this desert region. In the meantime, Sirkeh sent word to the Rajah of Sungeer that he had decoyed the enemy into the trap, and that the rest of the work was left for him. "At midnight," says Ferishta, "the Rajah with a great force, with which was also the treacherous Sirkeh, rushed from dens, passes, and caverns, on the Mussulmans unsuspicious of surprise, and buried in the sleep of weariness and fatigue. Nearly seven thousand of the faithful were put to death like sheep with knives and daggers; for the wind being high, the clashing of the trees, which separated them from one another, prevented them from hearing the groans of their fellow-sufferers. Malik-ul-Tijar fell with five hundred noble Syeds of Medina, Kerballa, and Nujeef; as also some few Deccanee and Abyssinian nobles with about two thousand soldiers of those countries. When the Rajah thought his bloody revenge had been glutted sufficiently, he retired with his people from the forest."

The few survivors of this disaster, amounting to about three thousand in number, managed to retire by the way they had come, and rejoined the Deccanees and Abyssinians, who had refused to accompany Malick-ul-Tijar. A quarrel at once broke out between the Moguls (the foreigners) and the Deccanees, the former reproaching the latter that the disaster had been caused by their defection. The Moguls expressed their determination of taking refuge in the fort of Jagneh and of reporting the whole circumstances to the Court.

The Deccanees when they heard this resolved to be first with their complaints, and at once sent a distorted report to the Sultan, representing that Malick-ul-Tijar had undertaken the rash expedition in spite of the advice of his Generals; and that the Mogul survivors without waiting for the appointment of a new General had retired to the fort of Jagneh, where they had raised the standard of rebellion, intending to join the Konkan Rajahs. This false report was sent to two Deccanee noblemen—Sheer-ul-Mulk and Nizam-ul-Mulk Ghour—who, taking an opportunity when the Sultan had been drinking, told him the story embellished by their own exaggerations. The Sultan, carried away by passion, at once ordered the two nobles to march against the rebels and put them to the sword. The two noblemen were not slow to execute this commission, and marched with a large army to besiege the remnant of the Mogul force which had shut itself up in the fort of Jagneh. After a siege of two months, during which the Deccanees had not been able to gain any advantage, a false message was sent to the fort that a pardon had arrived from the Sultan, and the Deccanee Chiefs swore a solemn oath that the Moguls might come out unmolested. Deceived by these assurances the whole garrison, numbering some 2,500, with women and children, came and camped outside the fort. On the third day the Deccanee Generals invited three hundred of the chief Mogul officers to an entertainment, during which they were massacred to a man. At the same time a body of four thousand Deccanees fell upon the Mogul camp and put every male, even to the children at the breast, to the sword, and dishonoured the women. What made this outrage more infamous in the eyes of the Mahomedan world was that amongst the Moguls were a large number of Seyds or descendants of the Prophet. In this way the whole of the ill-fated garrison were destroyed, with the exception of about three hundred Moguls under Kassim Beg, who had encamped at some little distance. This small body, on hearing the alarm, at once made a march, with the object, if possible, of reaching the capital. In this they were successful, for, although a force of one thousand horse was sent in pursuit, they received timely aid from a friendly Jaghirdar, named Hassan Khan. The pursuing force was beaten off and its leader killed, and then after a long and weary march this small remnant of the Mogul army reached Bieder. When the Sultan heard the truth of the matter his rage passed all bounds. The officer who had suppressed the reports sent by the Moguls was at once beheaded. The two Deccanee nobles were recalled and disgraced, and others who had taken part in the plot were put to death. As a retribution of Providence, Ferishta says that Nizam-ul-Mulk and Sheer-ul-Mulk were seized with leprosy the same year, and their sons walked the markets for shameful purposes among the outcasts of the City. Kassim Beg, who had successfully brought home his small force, was promoted the Governorship of Dowlatabad, and all who had helped him were duly honoured. In 1453 a dangerous eruption broke out on the Sultan's foot which eventually four years afterwards proved fatal. In the meantime he was confined to his palace, and rumours went abroad that he was dead. These rumours induced his grandson (by his daughter) Secunder Khan, who was Governor of Bilcondah, to break into rebellion, and to call in the Sultan of Malwa to help him. Sultan Mahomed, who was then King of Malwa, at once complied and invaded the Deccan with a large army, where he was joined by Secunder Khan. Sultan Alla-ud-Din, in spite of his illness, at once marched to meet Mahomed Shah, and at the same time despatched Khajeh Gawan, a name we shall frequently hear of hereafter, to put down a rebellion which had also broken out in the Telingana country. As soon as Mahomed found that Sultan Alla-ud-Din was still alive, he retired and left Secunder Khan to himself, who then made his escape into Telingana, where he was soon reduced to submission by Khajeh Gawan. The Sultan, with great generosity, forgave Secunder Khan, and even restored him to his Government. In the following year Sultan Alla-ud-Din died from mortification after a reign of nearly twenty-four years.

Sultan Alla-ud-Din was a man of wit and learning, and is said to have been possessed of considerable eloquence. He

Character. sometimes preached in the mosque on Fridays and holydays, and read out the *Khutba* in his own name, styling himself "the just, merciful, patient, and liberal to the servants of God." On the last occasion when he so appeared, there was a horse-dealer present whose account had been left unpaid by the officers of the Court. This man was a zealous Mahomedan, and like many others had been greatly moved by the slaughter of the Moguls by the Deccanees. On hearing the Sultan read the *Khutba*, he rose and said:—"Thou art neither the just, the merciful, the patient, nor the liberal King, but the cruel and the false, who hast massacred the Prophet's descendants; yet darest to assume such vaunting titles in the pulpit of the true believers." The Sultan, we are told, was struck with remorse, and commanded the merchant to be paid on the spot; saying that those would not escape the wrath of God who had thus injured his reputation. He then retired to his palace, which he never left again till he was brought out to be buried.

CHAPTER X.

HUMAYUN THE CRUEL.

1457 to 1460.

Humayun's reputation for cruelty was so well-known and feared that no sooner was the late Sultan dead, than two of the chief amras—Syef Khan and Mulloo Khan—contrived a plot to seat his younger brother, Hassan Khan, on the throne. Whilst, however, they were so engaged, Humayun hearing the news of his father's death came to the palace and surprised them. Being aided by the palace servants, who had not been informed of the plot, he was soon able to overpower the conspirators. The poor young Prince was dragged from the throne he had only occupied a few minutes, blinded, and the conspirators were then summarily dealt with. A still more terrible fate was, however, reserved for the unfortunate young Hassan, as will be told further on.

Humayun was wise in his choice of a Chief Minister, since he selected Khajeh Gawan, who had already done such good service. Malick Shah, said to be a descendent of Chengiz Khan, was appointed Governor of Telingana, now one of the most important provinces, but Secunder Khan, one of the Sultan's companions, when Heir Apparent was left, unprovided for. Secunder Khan was the son of a daughter of Ahmed Shah, who had married Jellal Khan, and had for many years been the Governor of the Bilkondah District; he considered himself as entitled to a province, being, equally with Humayun, a grandson of Ahmed Shah. Disgusted at being superseded, Secunder Khan broke into rbeellion and induced his father to join him. Humayun had at once to march against this new rebel, and in consideration of his former friendship offered pardon, and the province of Dowlatabad. Secunder Khan, however, claimed equal rights as a grandson, and demanded the Telingana. This shows that although Warangal had fallen, there were still a number of unsubdued Hindoo princes on the East Coast. Telingana was therefore a favourite province, because there was booty to be gained. The Sultan's overtures being refused, a battle followed, in which Secunder Khan, who seems to have been a man of great personal courage, was defeated and slain. He actually charged the Sultan, but Humayun's elephant lifted the rebel from his horse, threw him on the ground, and trampled him to death. This ended the battle. As is usual when the leader is killed, the army took flight. Jellal Khan still held out a little longer, but finally submitted, purchasing a few more years of life by resigning all the hoarded wealth of forty years' high employment. But although in this instance, the rebellion was easily quelled, its example was followed elsewhere. Taking advantage of the Sultan's absence, a conspiracy was formed to release the young prince Hassan Khan and to set him on the throne. Yusuf Turk, a slave of the late Sultan, lent himself to this plot, and effected the release of the blinded young prince, together with his friend and tutor, the Saint Hubeeb Oolla. This he managed by a stratagem, and having obtained possession of the harem, where the political prisoners were confined, he set at liberty, not only the above two, but also two other sons of the late King, besides about seven thousand other captives. These are the figures given by Ferishta, but it seems incredible that so large a number could have been confined together. The captives, once released, armed themselves with sticks and stones, and managed to beat off the Kotwal, who, on hearing of the outbreak, hurried up to suppress it. During the night, the escaped prisoners dispersed to different places. Some of them, and amongst those Jellal Khan, an old man of eighty, and Yiah Khan, a son of the late Sultan, fell into the hands of the Kotwal, and were at once killed. Hassan Khan and Hubeeb Oolla shaved their beards and managed to get out of the city disguised as beggars. Once outside Hassan Khan made himself known, and was soon joined by a large number of the disaffected, amongst them Yusuf Turk. The rebels then possessed themselves of the town of Pur and the adjacent country. It was to suppress this revolt that Humayun returned burning with rage. He first of all punished the garrison, consisting of two thousand men, all of whom he put to death by the most cruel tortures that could be devised. The Kotwal was confined in an iron cage, and every day some member of his body was cut off, which he was made to eat, until at last he was released by death. The first force despatched against the rebels was defeated, which only increased the Sultan's rage. Thereupon, he reinforced his army, but kept the wives and children of the officers in confinement, swearing that he would kill them all, if the army was defeated, or made common cause with Hassan Khan. This threat had the desired effect, and the rebels were defeated and compelled to fly. Hassan Khan and his friends then fled towards Vijayanagar, hoping to find a refuge with the Hindoos, but passing Bijapur, then only a mud fort, on the way they were invited inside by the Governor, Seraj Khan, with a promise of protection. This promise, however, was treacherously broken.

The fugitives were all seized at night, and sent with their followers in chains to the Sultan at Bieder. The vengeance wreaked by the Sultan was terrible. He ordered stakes to be driven into the ground in the large square opposite the palace; elephants, and wild beasts were then brought in, and large cauldrons of boiling oil were placed in different parts. Upon this the Sultan seated himself in the balcony so as to preside over the execution. The first victim was his unfortunate brother, Hassan Khan, who was thrown before a tiger, who soon tore the wretched Prince to pieces. Yusuf Turk and his seven friends were then beheaded, and their wives and daughters publicly violated. Hubeeb Oolla had fortunately already been killed in Bijapur. The whole of the Prince's followers, even down to the cooks and scullions, numbering in all some seven thousand men, women, and children, were then put to death by the most fearful tortures —by sword, axe, boiling oil and water, and every means that cruelty could think of.

In order to avoid the possibility of another revolt, almost all of the other members of the royal family were put to death, and the Sultan spent the rest of his reign in practising the most abominable cruelties on the innocent as well as the guilty. "He would frequently stop nuptial processions in the street, and seizing the bride, would, after deflowering her, send her back to the husband's house. He put his women to death for trivial faults and when any of his nobility were obliged to attend him, so great was their dread, that they took leave of their families as if preparing for death."

It was impossible that such a state of things could long continue, and in 1460, after a short reign of three years and six months, this monster of cruelty died, "some say by natural disease, but others that he was assassinated by his own attendants."

CHAPTER XI.

SULTANS NIZAM SHAH AND MUHAMMED SHAH.

1460 to 1462.

Nizam Shah was only a boy when he ascended the throne, and the Regency was conducted by his mother, a woman of great ability, who consulted in all things the Vizier Khajeh Gawan and Khajeh Jehan, two men of great experience and integrity. It did not take long to restore peace and confidence, but the neighbouring States, thinking to profit by the youth of the new Sultan, resolved to attack his kingdom, which they hoped to find in a state of confusion. The first combination was made by the Rajahs of Orissa, Oriya, and the Zemindars of Telingana, who invaded the country by Rajahmundry, and plundered it as far as Kailas. This army advanced within ten miles of Bieder, but was there met by the young Sultan, with a force of forty thousand men. In a preliminary skirmish the Hindoos suffered so much loss that the whole army retreated, followed by the Mahomedans, who inflected great loss. The allied Rajahs were compelled to take refuge in a small fort, and there sue for peace, which, after payment of a large sum, was granted. The General commanding the victorious army was Khajeh Jehan.

The next invasion was from the side of Malwa, aided by the Rajahs of Oriya and Telingana. This also was met by Sultan Nizam Shah in person. A battle ensued, in which the two wings of Nizam Shah's army were completely victorious; the centre, however, where the Sultan himself was, was broken and compelled to retire to Bieder, so that the victory remained with the Sultan of Malwa, who then advanced to the capital, where he succeeded in taking the city, but had to lay siege to the citadel. Matters were now in a critical state, and many thought that the fall of the house of Bahmanee was inevitable, when suddenly help appeared in the shape of the Sultan of Guzerat with twenty thousand horse. He was joined by Khajeh Gawan with the remnants of Nizam Shah's army, and the two then advanced to raise the siege of Bieder, the citadel of which had been gallantly defended by the Queen mother and the young Sultan. The Malwa army was then compelled to relinquish the siege, and to retire towards Gondwara, followed by the allies. In the Hindoo country, the Malwa Sultan was purposely misled by a guide into a desert where he lost a large portion of his army, and had finally to retire to his country with great loss. In the following year he again invaded the Deccan, but was met near Dowlatabad by the combined forces of Guzerat and the Deccan, and compelled to retire. This invasion over, it was resolved to celebrate the young Sultan's marriage. This was done amid great pomp and rejoicing, which, however, was suddenly turned into mourning, for, on the night of the comsummation, the young King, who had begun life with so much promise, suddenly died.

Muhammed Shah was only nine years old, when he succeeded his brother, and the affairs of Government continued to be conducted by the two Ministers, and the Queen mother as in the last reign.

<small>1462 to 1482.</small>

Khajeh Jehan, however, was no longer the faithful servant he had hitherto proved himself. He seems to have entertained personal hopes of ambition, and appointed his own friends and creatures to the chief posts at Court. Khajeh Gawan was sent to the frontier, and had but little voice in the administration. The Queen mother, becoming alarmed at the growing power of the Minister, resolved to remove him, and this was done by assassinating him in open durbar in the presence of the Sultan. Khajeh Gawan was now the principal Minister of the State, and under his able guidance, matters went on prosperously.

When he was fourteen years old the Sultan was married to a Princess of his own family, and thereupon the Queen mother handed over to him the reins of Government and retired into privacy. Sultan Muhammed is said to have been a man of great learning and taste, Khajeh Gawan having paid great attention to his education. On the whole, he seems to have been actuated by noble impulses, but he was quick in temper and hasty, and it was owing to this defect in his character that he was destined to be the cause of the ruin of his house. It is necessary at this stage to go back somewhat in order to trace the history of a young man, who was now twenty-four years of age. This man was Yusuf Adil Khan Sewai, who was attached to the household of Khajeh Gawan (as I shall still continue to call him, though he had now received the additional titles of Malick-ul-Tijar and Khajeh Jehan). The story of Yusuf Adil Khan's birth and adventures is a most romantic one. He was born in 1443, and his father was no less a person than *Murad*, the Sultan of Turkey. Murad died in 1450, and was succeeded by his eldest son

<small>1467.</small>

Mahomed. Yusuf was then only seven years of age, but in conformity with the barbarous custom that has so long prevailed in Mahomedan courts, it was resolved to put the young Prince to death, in order to prevent the possibility arising of his being a claimant to the throne. The executioners were sent to the harem and told the Sultana that they had come with orders to bow-string the boy and show his body to the Sultan. The mother, distracted with grief, begged for a day's delay, which, on being granted, she employed in devising a plan to save her son. She sent for a slave-dealer and purchased from him a young Circassian boy who bore a strong resemblance to the Prince. She then gave her son to the merchant with a large sum of money and begged him to take the boy away and place him in safety. This the merchant promised to do, and started on his journey with the young Prince on the same night. Next morning the executioners came again. One was admitted, who strangled the unfortunate Circassian, and then carried out the body which was buried without further examination. In the meantime the merchant, whose name was Khajeh Imad-ud-Din, had carried off the real Prince to Persia, first of all to Ardebeel, where he was placed under the venerable Sheikh Suffee (founder of the Suffee royal family), and then to the town of Saweh, where the boy was educated with the merchant's own children. Whilst here the Sultana from time to time sent messages to her son and received reports of his progress. She also sent his old nurse together with a large sum of money for the Prince's support. Yusuf remained at Saweh till he was sixteen years old, and from this residence derived his name of "Sewai." He then resolved to go and try his fortune in Hindustan and having embarked at Jeroon, in the Persian Gulf, arrived safely at Dabul a port on the Malabar Coast to the south of Goa in 1458. From Dabul he went to Ahmedabad Bieder, where he was taken into the service of Khajeh Imad-ud-Din, who introduced him into the royal household as one of his Turkish slaves. Yusuf soon gained favour at Court, and was placed under the master of the house, who, dying soon after, he was appointed his successor in office. Yusuf then attached himself to the fortunes of Nizam-ul-Mulk Turk, who was the nobleman who had killed Khajeh Jehan in open Durbar, by command of the Sultan Muhammed, soon after he came to the throne. Nizam-ul-Mulk formed a great attachment to the young Prince in disguise, and called him his brother. This attachment was returned and, as will be seen further on, Yusuf, who was now honoured with the title of Adil Khan, was Nizam-ul-Mulk's faithful friend and follower until his death. It was this adventurous young Prince Yusuf who was destined before long to be the founder of another dynasty, which was to supplant the house of Bahmanee, and rule with splendour in the Deccan for nearly two hundred years, until at last conquered by the all-powerful Aurungzebe. This new dynasty was the Adil Shahi house of Bijapur.

No sooner had Sultan Muhammed Shah arrived at maturity, than he resolved upon conquest. In 1467 he sent Nizam-ul-Mulk to Berar as Governor, with instructions to take the fort of Kurleh, which had come into the possession of the Sultan of Malwa. Nizam-ul-Mulk was accompanied by his young friend and companion, Yusuf Adil Khan, who was in constant attendance on his person. Siege was laid to Kurleh, and, after defeating several armies sent to relieve it, Nizam-ul-Mulk managed by a bold assault to take the fort itself. The victorious soldiery seem to have indulged in abuse of the conquered Hindoos, which so enraged two Rajputs, that they resolved to murder the Mahomedan General. Asking to be admitted unarmed to salute so brave a man, they were allowed into his presence, when snatching a sword from a bystander, one of them plunged it into his body. Nizam-ul-Mulk fell mortally wounded, and the two Rajputs were cut to pieces.

Yusuf Adil Khan and another Turkish officer, named Direa Khan, then took command of the army, and after leaving a strong garrison in the fort returned to Bieder, carrying with them the body of the General, and a large amount of plunder. The Sultan was so pleased at the bravery of these two young officers, that he promoted them to the rank of one thousand with the fortress of Kurleh and its dependencies in jaghir. After this war, which was really in retaliation for the unprovoked invasion by the Sultan of Malwa during the previous reign, peace was made between the two Sultans, and a treaty drawn, based upon the former one, executed in the time of Sultan Ahmed. Under this treaty, Berar was confirmed to the Deccan, and Kurleh, as before, given to Malwa. Both princes bound themselves to respect each other's countries in future, and to live in peace and harmony together. The provision of the treaty were at once carried out, Kurleh was restored to Malwa, and we are told that no disagreements ever after happened between the two royal families.

Yusuf Adil Khan now attached himself to the person of Khajeh Gawan who held him in so high an estimation that he styled him his adopted son. In 1469, Khajeh Gawan was despatched with a large army to put down the pirates of the Western Coast. From time immemorial the pirates of the Western Coast of India had been the terror of the peaceful traders from the Persian Gulf. Pliny speaks of them "as having committed depredations on the Roman trade to East India." At the time in question the Rajahs of Songeer and Khaluch are said to have maintained a fleet of three hundred vessels. Khajeh Gawan's expedition lasted for three seasons, and was eminently successful. He captured most of the pirates strongholds, and also the capital of the Rajah of Songeer, when he took ample vengeance for the treacherous slaughter of Malick-ul-Tijar, on a former occasion. He also captured the important port of Goa, which, at that time, belonged to Vijayanagar.

After this, he returned laden with treasure to Bieder, where he was received by the Sultan with great honour and public rejoicings. The Sultan himself and the Queen mother honoured the successful General with a visit, and spent a whole week in his house, on which occasion the Queen mother called him brother. As soon as the Sultan left, the following incident occurred, as told by Ferishta. Khajeh Gawan retired to his chamber, disrobed himself, and began to weep with a loud voice. After this, he came out in the garb of a dervish, and calling together all the learned men, divines, and Seyds, distributed amongst them the whole of his jewels, money, and property, reserving only his elephants, horses, and library. He then thanked God that he had escaped from the temptations of his evil passions, and was freed from danger. On being asked for the reason of this strange conduct, he replied that when the Sultan had honoured him with a visit, and the Queen mother had called him brother, his evil passions began to prevail over his reason; and the struggle of vice and virtue was so great in his mind, that he became distressed, even in the presence of his Majesty, who kindly enquired the cause of his concern, on which he was obliged to feign illness in excuse, when the Sultan advised him to take repose, and then returned to his palace. He had, therefore, he continued, parted with his wealth, the cause of his temptations, that his library he intended for the use of students, and his elephants and horses he regarded as the Sultan's lent to him for a season only. From this time forward this great and good man always wore plain dress, lived simply, and on Fridays went about the city disguised, distributing money amongst the poor, and telling them that it was sent by the Sultan.

In 1471 the Rajah of Oristela, in which kingdom were included Rajahmundry and the present Godavery, Ganjam, and Vizagapatam Districts, applied to the Sultan for assistance against a slave who had usurped the throne. The Sultan was only too glad to have an opportunity of interfering in the affairs of this part of India, and at once despatched an army under Malick Hassan to the assistance of the Rajah, whose name is given as Himber. The rebel was defeated without difficulty, and Himber was reinstated. The Rajah thereupon proclaimed himself to be a vassal of the Sultan, and Malick Hassan returned to headquarters, with a large amount of plunder. In recognition of his success, he was appointed Governor of Telingana. Yusuf Adil Khan, who had now been actually adopted by Khajeh Gawan, was appointed to Dowlatabad. He took with him his old comrade Deria Khan, and in a short time recovered several forts, which had become alienated since the Malwa invasion. One of these was the fort of Weragur, which was the ancestral residence of a Mahratta Rajah, named Jey Singh. He appears to have been formerly tributary to the Bahmance Sultans, but assumed independence after the Malwa invasion. After sustaining a siege of six months, Jey Singh offered to give up his fort and treasure, if allowed to depart with his family unmolested. This was granted, and Yusuf Adil Khan was fortunate enough to acquire an immense booty and a new country without any bloodshed. A similar success was gained over the Chief of Ranjee, and Yusuf then returned to Bieder, laden with spoil which he laid before the Sultan. Muhammed Shah was highly pleased, and bestowed further honours upon Yusuf, at the same time remarking that whoever had Khajeh Gawan as a father could not fail to render important services. Yusuf was then by command of the Sultan entertained for a week by his adopted father, at the end of which the Sultan himself honoured the Khajeh with a visit, during which the Minister bestowed upon his master a vast number of valuable gifts, amongst which were " fifty dishes of gold with covers set with jewels, each large enough to hold a roasted lamb; one hundred slaves of Circassia, Georgia, and Abyssinia, most of whom were accomplished singers and musicians; one hundred horses of Arabia, Syria, and Turkey, and one hundred pieces of superb China, not to be seen except in the palaces of great princes." After this, we are told "the favour of Khajeh Gawan and Adil Khan became so great that they were courted and envied by all the nobility; and the Deccanees, like wounded vipers tormenting themselves, bound up the waist band of enmity against them." In 1472 the King of Vijayanagar made an attempt to recover possession of Goa, and sent the Rajahs of Belgaum and Bankipur with a large army for that purpose. Muhammed Shah with Khajeh Gawan at once marched to its relief, and sat down before Belgaum, which is described as having been a fort of great strength, encircled by a deep moat over which there was but one passage covered by redoubts. The Rajah, who is called by Ferishta, Pirkna, at first made overtures of peace to the Sultan, which, however, were refused, and the siege was prosecuted with vigour. The Rajah had placed the greatest confidence in his moat, but this the Sultan had filled in, and then breached the walls in three places by mines, which, we are told, had never been previously used for siege purposes. An assault was then made, in which, though he lost two thousand men, the Sultan was ultimately successful. Only the citadel remained, in which the Rajah shut himself up. Seeing, however, that defeat was inevitable, he went in disguise to the Sultan's camp, and being there admitted to an audience, he tendered his submission. This was accepted, and the Sultan then took possession of Belgaum, which, with its dependencies, he gave to Khajeh Gawan in jaghir. It was during this expedition that the Queen mother, who had accompanied the Sultan died. Her body was sent with great pomp to Bieder to be buried. A great deal of the prosperity of this reign was due to the able counsels of this lady, and there can be no doubt, that had she still been by the Sultan's side, he would not have committed a few years afterwards the great injustice which was to lead to the ruin of the Bahmanee Kingdom.

On his return to Bieder, the Sultan halted for some time at Bijapur, the climate and position of which pleased him greatly. Here he intended to stop for the wet weather, but was prevented, by the scarcity which prevailed over the whole of this part of the Deccan. This famine lasted for two years. No grain is said to have been sown during the whole of that time throughout the Bahmanee dominions, and thousands upon thousands of people died of hunger. Exaggerated reports of this famine and of the manner in which the Sultan's armies had been reduced, spread to the Telingana and Orissa country, and the Rajahs of Oriya and Orissa resolved to make a last attempt to shake off the Mahomedan yoke. Accordingly, they advanced with a large army, and compelled the Mahomedan Governor of Rajahmundry to shut himself up in the fort, and laid the rest of Telingana between the Godavery and Kistna waste. Muhammed Shah at once marched in person to oppose this invasion, and the Hindoos retired. The Oriya Rajah shut himself up in the fort of Kundapally, and the Orissa Rajah retreated across the Godavery into his own dominions. Here he was followed by the Sultan, who plundered all his towns, and drove the Rajah into the extreme limits of his kingdom. The Sultan had at first resolved to send for Khajeh Gawan and establish him in this province, but the Rajah hearing of his intentions began to sue for forgiveness. This was granted on payment of a large indemnity, of which twenty-five celebrated elephants formed a not unimportant portion, since the Rajah is said to have valued them next to his life. The Sultan then laid siege to Kundapally, which he also took, and with his own hands destroyed a temple and killed some Brahmin devotees. This act was looked upon by everybody as one of sacrilege, and popular opinion traced the misfortunes that subsequently occurred to the divine anger at so wanton an outrage.

Muhammed Shah remained nearly three years at Rajahmundry, and during this time settled the whole of the Telingana country. He appointed Nizam-ul-Mulk as Governor of Rajahmundry and Kundapally, with his son as deputy, and Azim Khan to Warangal and its dependencies, and then set out on an expedition to subdue Narsinga, a Governor of a portion of the Vijayanagar Kingdom. There seems to be some doubt as to the site of Narsinga's capital, but it is generally supposed to have been somewhere near the present Kurnool. Kurnool is situated just below the junction of the rivers Kistna and Tungabadhra, and according to Cunningham ("Ancient Geography of India") stands on the site of the Choliya (Chu-li-ye) mentioned by the Chinese pilgrim, Hwen Tsang, in the seventh century. This spot is also held by the same authority to be the old town of Zora—the Sora spoken of by Ptolemy—and he considers a branch of the ancient family of Sora founded the city of Shorapore, about one hundred miles to the west-north-west of Kurnool; the Rajah of which, he says, "still holds his patrimonial appanage, surrounded by his faithful tribe (Bedars), claiming a descent of more than thirty centuries." The last Rajah of Shorapore died in 1858, after a vain attempt at mutiny, and the tragic story of his end is told by Meadows Taylor in the "Story of My life." There are still some direct descendants alive, but the Raj is now incorporated with the Nizam's Dominions, and the surviving members subsist upon small pensions. This Narsimha or Narsinga was a man of considerable importance. Ferishta says that he held the whole of the country between the Carnatic and Telingana, extending on the sea coast to Masulipatam. There seems to be some doubt, whether he was an independent Prince or a Governor of a Vijayanagar province. The latter seems to be probable, for a few years hence we shall find him ruling at Vijayanagar, as the first of a new dynasty which had replaced that of Hari Hara.

Though Muhammed Shah was successful in his invasion of Nursinga's country, we do not read of any engagement between the Sultan and the Hindoo General, from which it seems probable that Nursinga was absent, possibly in Vijayanagar, following out his own schemes of ambition. The Mahomedan army met with but little opposition, and is said to have taken Masulipatam, and then to have marched against the sacred town of Conjeveram. This is the first time that a Mahomedan force had reached this centre of Hindooism, and fabulous accounts are given of the riches and splendour of the temple, the walls and roofs of which are described as having been plated with gold and ornamented with precious stones. Conjeveram was taken by assault, after the Sultan had killed a gigantic Hindoo in personal encounter. An immense plunder fell into the hands of the conquering army. Gold and jewels were in such profusion that the Mahomedans left everything of less value behind. Muhammed Shah stayed here for one week, and then marched back to his own country. In this expedition the Sultan had been accompanied by Khajeh Gawan, to whose counsel and assistance much of his success was due. The Khajeh's power and influence, however, was so great, that it had the effect of causing the long smouldering jealousy of the Deccanee nobles to break into open flame. Nizam-ul-Mulk, Nireef-ul-Mulk, and others formed a plot to ruin him, and the way it was carried out was as follows: Khajeh Gawan's right hand was Yusuf Adil Khan, and as long as these two were together, they were able to carry out all their plans of reform. These plans appear to have been conceived solely with the view of promoting the Sultan's interest, and of abolishing many of the abuses that had crept into the Government of the provinces. One reform was especially distasteful, as it consisted in a check upon the numbers of men maintained by the military Governors. Every Governor was required to keep up a definite number of men, for each of whom an allowance was fixed; thus a noble of five hundred received a lakh and a quarter of pagodas, and one of one thousand, two and a half lakhs; if the revenue of the jaghirs fell short of this amount, the deficiency was made up from the royal treasury; but on the other hand, strict rules regarding "men in buckram" were passed, and for every man found deficient, the full pay and allowance were deducted.

Touched in their pockets, the nobles all joined in hating Khajeh Gawan, and an opportunity occurring of Yusuf Adil Khan being sent against Masulipatam, they resolved to carry out their scheme. They managed to intoxicate an Abyssinian slave who had charge of the Khajeh's seals, and showing him a paper, said that it was necessary to get the Minister's seal in addition to certain others. The slave without looking into the paper affixed his master's seal, and then took the paper away. This paper was blank, and above the seal a letter was subsequently written purporting to be addressed by Khajeh Gawan to the Rajah of Orissa. In this letter the Khajeh was made to say: "I am weary of the drunkenness and cruelty of Muhammed Shah. Deccan may be conquered with little trouble, as at Rajahmundry and at that frontier there is no General of any note. You may invade that quarter without opposition, and as most of the nobles and the troops are devoted to me, I will join you with a powerful army. When we have in conjunction reduced the Sultan, we will divide his territories equally between us." This letter was given to the Sultan by Nireef-ul-Mulk and Mastah Hubshee when Nizam-ul-Mulk was present. The Sultan at once fell into the trap, his rage being artfully increased by Nizam-ul-Mulk, and at once sent for the supposed traitor. Some of the Khajeh's friends hearing what had happened, strongly advised him not to obey the order, but to take flight, promising to help him with ten thousand horse. Khajeh Gawan, however, refused all their offers, and simply remarked: "This beard has grown white in the auspicious service of the father, and it will be honourable should it be dyed with my blood by the fortunes of the son; there is no evading the decrees of fate, and to draw the neck from its sentence, is impossible." He then at once went to the Sultan's presence, and Ferishta thus relates what followed: "Muhammed Shah sternly exclaimed: "When anyone is disloyal to his sovereign, and his crime is proved, what should be his punishment?" The Khajeh replied: "The abandoned wretch who practises treachery against his lord, should meet with nothing but the sword." The Sultan then showed him the letter, upon seeing which he, after repeating the verse of the Koran ('O God, this is a great forgery!') said: "The seal is mine, but not the letter, of which I have no knowledge." He concluded by repeating the following verses: "By the God whose command the just have obeyed with their blood, false as the story of Yusuf (Joseph) and the wolf, is what my enemies have forged of me." As the Sultan was intoxicated with wine, and had resigned his soul to anger, and the decline of the house of Bahmanee was near, he attended not to the examination of facts, but rising from the assembly, ordered Johir, an Abyssinian, to put the Minister to death upon the spot. Khajeh Gawan addressed the Sultan and said: "The death of an old man like me is of little moment to myself, but to you it will prove the ruin of an Empire, and of your own glory." The Sultan attended not to his words, but abruptly retired into his harem. The slave then drawing his sabre, advanced towards the Khajeh, who kneeling down, and facing the Kibleh, said: "There is no God but God, and Mahomed is the prophet of God." When the sabre reached his neck, he cried: "Praise be to God for the blessing of martyrdom," and resigned his soul to the divine mercy. At the time of his death, Khajeh Gawan was seventy-eight years old."

This cruel murder of an old and faithful servant sent a

thrill of indignation throughout the whole of the Sultan's Dominions. Two of the principal nobles, Imad-ul-Mulk and Khodawund Khan, the Governors of the two provinces of Berar, at once removed with their troops to a distance, and refused to come to the Sultan's presence, until Yusuf Adil Khan should be sent for. This was done, and Adil Khan at once came, overwhelmed with grief at the death of his benefactor and adopted father. Overtures were now made to the disgusted noblemen, but although all their demands were granted, they refused to join the Sultan's camp, and pitched their own at a distance, paying their respects each day from afar off surrounded by their own guards. Before long Imad-ul-Mulk and Khodawund Khan retired, without taking leave, to their Government in Berar, and Yusuf Adil Khan having been confirmed in the jaghirs of Belgaum and Bijapur, marched with his army against Sivarajah, the King of Vijayanagar, who had broken into revolt. The Sultan, thus deserted by his principal Generals, was obliged to submit, and retired to Firozeabad, "seemingly spending his hours in pleasure, but inwardly a prey to grief and sorrow, which wasted his strength daily." From Firozeabad the Sultan returned to his capital, Bieder, and continuing to indulge in wine and debauchery, he at last succumbed to their effects. After a more than usual indulgence, he fell into fits, during which he frequently cried out that Khajeh Gawan was tearing him into pieces, till at length he died on the 1st Suffer, 887 H., after a reign of twenty years, and in the twenty-ninth year of his age. The date of his death, says Ferishta, is comprised in the following verses:—

"The King of Kings, Sultan Muhammed, when suddenly he plunged into the ocean of death, as Deccan became waste by his departure, 'the ruin of Deccan' was the date of his death."

CHAPTER XII.

THE END OF THE HOUSE OF BAHMANEE.

BIEDER.

With the death of Sultan Muhammed, the history of the house of Bahmanee as a separate and independent dynasty may be said to cease. It is true that his son Mahmood Shah was placed on the throne, as a boy of eight years of age; reigned for thirty-seven years, and was succeeded by three other Sultans; but these princes were nothing more than puppets, and their dominions were confined to the capital of Bieder, and its immediate vicinity. Taking advantage of the youth of the young Sultan, the powerful nobles of the different provinces asserted each his own independence. The first few years of the new reign were signalized by a series of struggles and intrigues. The capital itself was for many days the scene of a bloody struggle between the Deccanees and the Abyssinians on the one hand, and the Turks and Moguls on the other. Yusuf Adil Shah was the first to take advantage of this confusion. Supported by his old comrade and faithful follower, Deria Khan, he retired to Bijapur and there had the *Kutba* read in his own name. Malick Ahmed, the Governor of Dowlatabad, soon followed his example, and founded the capital of Ahmednagar, and the dynasty of the Nizam Shahee Sultans. In Berar Imad-ul-Mulk proclaimed his independence, and read the *Kutba* in his capital Burhanpore, and finally Kootb-ul-Mulk, the Governor of Golconda, who for some years had been practically independent, in 1510 proclaimed himself Sultan of Golconda and the Telingana country, and was the first of a dynasty called after his own name. In Bieder itself the Sultan was a mere tool in the hands of his Minister, a man named Cassim Bereed, who had been a Turkish slave, but who by intrigues had gradually risen to power. In 1490 an attempt was made by the Sultan to shake off the yoke of this too powerful Minister, in which attempt he was helped by one Delawar Khan. At first, Cassim Bereed was defeated, and had to fly towards Golconda. In a second encounter, however, Dilawar Khan was killed, and the royal army being defeated, Cassim Bereed returned to Bieder in triumph. A seeming reconciliation ensued between the Minister and the Sultan, and the former "seated securely on the *musnud* of administration left nothing but a nominal royalty to Mahmood Shah. The historians of the Bereed dynasty reckon the establishment of it from this period."

At the close of the fifteenth century, we find, therefore, five Mahomedan kingdoms in the Deccan, which had divided amongst themselves the territories of the Bahmanee Sultans.

By far the most important of these was the Bijapur kingdom of Yusuf Adil Shah. It extended from Sholapore and Gulburga in the north, down to Goa in the south. On the East its neighbour was the kingdom of Vijayanagar, and its boundary the River Kistna. The forts of Raichore and Mukdul were Mahomedan, but the country between the two rivers Kistna and Tungabadhra was still a debatable land. We have, therefore, arrived at the close of the first period of the Mahomedan occupation of the Deccan, and we shall be better able to trace the further sequence of events by following the fortunes of the Bijapur kings, noting from time to time the occurrences in the neighbouring States. But, before taking leave of the Bahmanee Sultans—for in future, their names will only occur incidentally—this would seem to be the place for a description of their capital, Ahmedabad Bieder. We quote again from the historical and descriptive account of Hyderabad :—

The city of Bieder in the days of its prosperity must have been of vast extent. A modern writer, referring to the rapidity of its erection, says:—"Soon, as if by magic, rose, some miles to the north of Gulburga, one of the most splendid cities of India or of the world. The great mosque of Ahmedabad Bieder was for centuries unequalled for simple grandeur and solemnity, and the more delicate beauties of the Ivory Mosque, inlaid with gems and mother-o'-pearl, was long one of the favourite themes with which travellers delighted to illustrate the wealth and prodigality of the realms of the Far East." Unfortunately, few authentic details as to the extent of the city have come down to us, Athanasius Nitikin, a Russian Armenian, who in 1470 visited Bieder as a merchant, "gives in his diary an interesting description of the country and its capital. There were villages at every *coss*. The land was laid out in fields, and the ground well tilled The roads were well guarded, and travelling secure. Bieder is described as a noble city with great salubrity of climate, and the king,

Mahmood Shah,* as a little man 20 years old, with an army of 300,000 men well equipped. Artillery is not mentioned, but there were many elephants, to the trunks of which scythes were attached in action, and they were clad in bright steel armour." When Aurangzebe invested the place in 1656 Bieder was described as 4,500 yards in circumference, having three deep ditches 25 yards wide, and 15 yards deep, cut in the stone.

Monsieur Thevenot, who visited Bieder in 1667, says:— "It is a great town; it is encompassed with Brick-Walls which have battlements, and at certain distances Towers; they are mounted with great Cannon, some whereof have the mouth three Foot wide. There is commonly in this place a Garrison of Three thousand Men, half Horse and half Foot, with Seven hundred Gunners; the Garrison is kept in good order, because of the importance of the place against Deccan, and that they are always afraid of a surprise. The Governor lodges in a Castle without the Town; it is a rich Government, and he who commanded in it when I was there was Brother-in-law to King Changeant (Shah Jehan). Auran-Zeb's Father; but having since desired the Government of Brampour (which is worth more,) he had it, because in the last War, that Governor had made an Army of the King of Viziapour raise the siege from before Bieder. Some time after, I met the new Governor upon the road to Bieder, who was a Persian of a good aspect, and pretty well striken in years; he was carried, before whom marched several Men on foot, carrying blew Banners charged with flames of Gold, and after them came seven Elephants. The Governor's Palanquin was followed with several others full of Women, and covered with red

* This statement is entirely opposed to Ferishta's chronology. According to the latter, Mahmood Shah did not ascend the throne until 1482, and was then only eight years of age. This is no doubt a mistake for Muhammed Shah, who, in 1470, had already been reigning for eight years, and was then 17 years of age.

Searge, and there were two little Children in one that was open. The Bamboons of all these Palanquins, were covered with Plates of Silver chamfered; after them came many Chariots full of Women; two of which were drawn by white Oxen, almost six Foot high; and last of all, come the Wagons with the Baggage, and several Camels guarded by Troopers."

The majority of the palaces and musjids, public buildings, gardens, baths, &c., with which the Bahmanee kings adorned their capital are now in ruins, but there is sufficient remaining to give an admirable idea of the vast extent and magnificence of the city. Perhaps the most remarkable of all the buildings was the College or Madrissah, built by Mahmud Gawan, the Minister of Mahmood Shah.

After the capture of Bieder by Aurangzebe, this splendid range of buildings was appropriated to the double purpose of a powder magazine, and barrack for a body of cavalry, when, by accident, the powder exploding destroyed the greater part of the edifice, causing dreadful havoc around. The explosion happened in the year 1695. Sufficient of the work remains, however, even at the present day, to afford some notion of its magnificence and beauty. The outline of the square, and some of the apartments, are yet entire, and one of the minarets is still standing. It is more than one hundred feet in height, ornamented with tablets, on which sentences of the Koran, in white letters, three feet in length, standing forth on a ground of green and gold, still exhibit to the spectator a good sample of what this superb edifice was. The College is one of the very many beautiful remains of the grandeur of the Bahmanee and Bereed dynasties, which flourished at Bieder; and they render a visit to that city an object of lively interest to all travellers.

Sir Richard Temple, who visited Bieder in 1861, says: "The bastions of the fortress had a rich colouring subdued by age, being built of the red laterite of which the hills are there formed. The style of the mosque was grand and severe, quite different from the polished and graceful manner of the Mogul architects in later times. The chief object of beauty in the place was the College. The exterior of the building had once been covered with exquisitely coloured glazing in floral devices, of which there was still much remaining to delight the spectator. This building is perhaps the finest of its kind surviving in India."

Bieder contains eight gateways four of which, however, are closed. The Fateh gate bears a Persian inscription to the effect that it was constructed by the Subedar of Bieder in 1082 Hijri (A. D. 1671). The Shah Ganj gate was constructed in the year previous. The Thalghat gate was built in the same year as the Fateh. The Sharzah or Lion gate, which is decorated with effigies of lions cut in the stone buttresses of the gateway, was erected in 1094 Hijri (A. D. 1682).

The fortifications of the place, which are very strong, are still well preserved, the battlemented walls of the city and the citadel having a most striking appearance, as they are approached. On the bastions, of which there are a large number many pieces of ordnance, made chiefly of bluish-coloured metal and highly polished, are found; some of them have the maker's name engraved upon them, together with the charge of powder to be used. The ruined buildings in the fort have all been constructed of trap. The Rang Mahal, so called from having its fronts adorned with coloured tiles, contains some apartments which are said to have formed portions of an old Hindoo temple. The citadel also contains the ruins of a mint, a Turkish bath, an arsenal and several powder magazines. There is also a well 150 feet deep. Another building of note in the citadel is the musjid close to one of the old palaces, which is probably the one alluded to, as having been long unequalled for grandeur and solemnity. It has evidently been a building of considerable beauty, but it is now much damaged, the roof has fallen in some places, and the building has suffered considerably by decay and neglect.

Between five and six miles north-east of the city are the tombs of the Bahmanee kings who died at Bieder. Close to the western gate is the tomb of Amir Bareed Shah, which is probably the best. It is of an imposing height, and has a richly ornamented interior. The tombs of the Bahmanee kings, of which there are ten altogether, are all built on large oblong platforms, and consist of huge square buildings surmounted by domes similar to those at Golconda. The largest of them is that of Ahmed Shah, who removed the capital from Gulburga to Bieder in 1432, and build this mausoleum, upon which is inscribed in Persian the following couplet:—

> "Should my heart ache, my remedy is this,
> A cup of wine and then I sup of bliss."

The tomb of the Minister Mahmood Gawan (Khajeh Gawan) contains a Persian inscription signifying "the unjust execution," and that "without fault he became a martyr."

Bieder is celebrated for the manufacture of a kind of metal-ware which is styled Bidri-work. The metal is composed of an alloy of copper, lead, tin, and zinc. It is worked into articles of most elegant designs, and inlaid with silver and occasionally gold. The articles manufactured consist chiefly of vases, hookahs, basins, &c. There is unfortunately not much demand now for these elegant manufactures, and proportionately but a small quantity is turned out. Many specimens of it have been sent to England, and a large number of articles were made in 1875 for presentation to the Prince of Wales.

PART II.

HISTORY OF BIJAPUR AND OF THE DECCAN DOWN TO ITS SUBJUGATION BY AURUNGZEBE (A. D. 1500—1680).

CHAPTER XIII.

YUSUF ADIL SHAH OF BIJAPUR.

THE period of two hundred years which this portion of the history of the Deccan comprises was one of great restlessness, and is full of important events. We have shown in the last chapter, that out of the ruins of the Bahmanee empire, there arose five Mahomedan kingdoms. Almost the whole of this period was taken up by internecine wars amongst these Mahomedan Kings. During the first portion of the sixteenth century the Hindoo Kingdom of Vijayanagar profited by the weakness of the various Mahomedan States, and rapidly rose in power. The original Hari Hara dynasty had come to an end towards the close of the fifteenth century. It was probably at its zenith about the time of Abdur Razzak's visit in 1444. Allusion has already been made to this traveller and to his glowing accounts of the splendour of the Vijayanagar Court. Under the successors of Deva Raya, the King who entertained Abdur Razzak, and who successfully fought against Sultan Alla-ud-Din of Gulburgah, the Hindoo power began to decline. Under Malikarjuna (1451—1465) and Virupaksha (1465—1479) several reverses were sustained, and the Russian traveller Athanasius Nikitin, who was in the Deccan in 1474, says that the King of Bieder attacked and took Vijayanagar, killing some 20,000 Hindoos. The Sultan of Bieder at this time was Mahomed Shah the King, who, by the murder of Khajeh Gawan, brought about the ruin of the kingdom. Ferishta's account of this Prince is a very full one, but, strange to say, he makes no mention of any capture of Vijayanagar. We read of two wars waged by Mahomed Shah against outlying provinces of Vijayanagar such as Belgaum (1472) and Kurnool and Conjeveram later on (1474—75), but nothing is said of a siege of the capital. It is, therefore, probable that Nikitin's account is a mistake, and the defeat alluded to was of the Vijayanagar army only. The last King of the Hari Hara dynasty was Virupaksha, and he was succeeded or supplanted about 1480 by Narasimha or Narsinga, the founder of a new dynasty. This Narasimha is the same man against whom Sultan Mahomed Shah sent an army. He was the Governor of Kurnool, and of all the East Coast. This expedition has been described in Chapter XI. Narasimha is said by some to have been a slave of the last King Virupaksha, and by others to have been a Telugu Chieftain, and it is possible that he was a descendant of the old Choliyan family, which was ruling in the Kurnool portion of the Deccan in the seventh century. At all events about 1780 Narasimha was the *de facto* sovereign of Vijayanagar, and in a very short time he had established his rule over the whole of Southern India, for the Portuguese called the country south of the Kistna as far as Cape Comorin the Narsinga country. How long Narasimha reigned seems to be doubtful. By some authorities it is stated that he was succeeded by his son of the same name in 1487, but Dr. Burnell is of opinion that Virupaksha reigned until 1490. It is, however, certain that a Narasimha reigned until 1509, when he was succeeded by Krishna Deva Raya, the greatest and most powerful of all the Vijayanagar Kings. About Krishna-Deva Raya there can be no doubt. Not only does he live in tradition, but his name is found in numerous inscriptions, and authentic (Hindoo) histories exist regarding his reign. But, strange to say, the Mahomedan authorities, to whom we owe so much, are absolutely silent regarding this King. His name is not even mentioned by them, and his reign is passed over in silence. The various Ministers are frequently spoken of, and the Mahomedan writers say that the Ministers possessed the actual authority and kept the real Rajas in subjection. This is especially noticeable towards the end of the Hindoo period just before its downfall. Mr. Sewell, however, in his "Antiquities of Southern India" (Vol. 2) points out that, however this may have been, in the inscriptions the names of the ruling sovereigns are always mentioned. It is certain that from 1509 until 1530 Krishna Deva Raya ruled over the whole of the south of India, from coast to coast. He does not seem to have meddled much with the Mahomedan Kingdoms, unless first attacked, but his own Kingdom was thoroughly consolidated. Krishna Deva Raya's conquest extended as far north as Cuttack, and we shall see later on how he defeated the Bijapur Sultan and retook Raichore with an enormous army. Some writers think that it was through jealousy that the Mahomedan writers omit all mention of this victorious Hindoo King.

At the same time as the Hindoo Kingdom of Vijayanagar was threatening the Mahomedan supremacy in the south, the foundations of another Hindoo power were being laid in the West. During this period of two hundred years, the Mahrattas grew from scattered freebooters into a great nation, and early in the sixteenth century the first of the European nations settled at Goa. The division therefore of the great Bahmanee Kingdom into five smaller ones was singularly unfortunate, and, weakened by their own jealousies and quarrels, and by the constant struggles with their Hindoo and European neighbours, it was not a difficult task for Aurangzebe to eventually conquer them, one by one. After this slight glance at the state of affairs, we will now revert to Bijapur the first, the greatest, and the last but one of the new Mahomedan Kingdoms to survive.

It has been narrated how after the murder of Khajeh Gawan, Yusuf Adil Shah, in 1489, declared his independance. The romantic early history of this King has also been narrated, and his subsequent reign of twenty-one years fully justified the promises of his youth. Bijapur, the capital of the new Kingdom, stands on the site of an old Hindoo town, called Bichkhanhalli, and five other villages. There are still to be found some inscriptions from the eleventh and twelfth centuries, and some Hindoo columns of victory, from which the name of the city is derived—Vijaya-pur, or City of Victory. Yusuf Adil Shah at once set himself to work to complete the defences of his new capital, which for many years had been the seat of a Governor of the Bahmanee King. He built the citadel, or Ark-killah, which was subsequently improved and beautified by his successors, until it became "a perfect treasury of artistic buildings" (Silcock in *Bombay Gazetteer*), and commenced the city walls, which were not completed until fifteen years later. As was to be expected, the new King was not allowed to maintain his independence without having to fight for it. He was at once attacked by Kassim Bereed, the all powerful Minister of the Bieder Sultan. Narasimha, the Regent or Ruler of Vijayanagar, joined Bereed in this enterprize, but the combination was beaten off without much difficulty, and for two or three years Adil Shah was left in peace. In 1792, Adil Shah felt himself strong enough to attack Vijayanagar, and taking advantage of certain dissentions, endeavoured to surprise Raichore. Ferishta calls the Ruler of Vijayanagar *Heem* Rajah, and speaks of him as the Regent or guardian of the young Rajah. The word Heem is clearly a corruption of the word *Nara-shim*, and the fact of a "young Roy" or Rajah being spoken of, would seem to show that nominally the old dynasty had not yet been set aside, and that Narasimha conducted the Government in the name and under the authority of the titular King. Narasimha advanced to relieve Raichore, and crossed the Tungabudhra, accompanied by the young Rajah. An engagement followed, in which the Sultan's attack was at first repulsed, but on the Hindoos scattering in search of plunder, the Sultan charged them with his reserve, with such desparation that they broke and fled in all directions. The plunder that was left behind was enormous, no less than two hundred elephants, one thousand horse, and sixty lakhs of *oons* (equal to one million eight hundred thousand pounds). Ferishta says that in this engagement, the young Rajah was wounded, and died on the road to his capital, after which "Heem Rajah" seized the Government of the country. Although there seems to be no doubt that Narasimha, the former ruler or Governor of Kurnool, was the *de facto* Ruler of Vijayanagar from about 1480, it will be probably safest to fix the date of the extinction of the Hari Hara or first Vijayanagar, dynasty, as 1492. Whether the "Heem Rajah" who then succeeded was the original Narasimha, or his son of the same name, cannot now be decided, and does not seem to be very material.*

* The inscriptions collected by Mr. Robert Sewell ("Lists of Antiquities of Madras," Vol. II.) show conclusively that Narasimha I. had two sons, the elder of the same name, and the younger named Krishna

The plunder obtained by Adil Shah in this war was of immense use to him, in establishing his new Kingdom. A large portion was spent in strengthening and beautifying his capital, and by liberal presents he attached several able officers to his fortunes. Nor did he forget the old master, from whom he had rebelled, but sent Mahmood Bahmanee at Bieder two splendid robes embroidered with precious stones, two horses shod with gold, and saddles and bridles set with jewels. Indeed, for some time to come, the Adil Shahi Kings, although independent, continued to acknowledge the Bahmanee Sultans, and afforded them assistance whenever called upon. Shortly afterwards, Sultan Mahmood Bahmanee paid Adil Shah a visit at Bijapur, where he was royally entertained. When the Sultan was about to leave a number of costly presents were sent to him, but with the exception of one elephant he refused them all, on the ground that he would not be able to keep them, as Kassim Bereed would be certain to seize them, and that, therefore, Adil Shah had better keep them in trust, until, "like a faithful servant, he could deliver him from the usurpation of his Minister."

In 1495 Dustoor Deenar, the Governor of Gulburga, revolted

Deva. The author of the *Bombay Gazetteer*, Vol. XV., Part. II., distinctly states that in 1487, Narasimha I. was succeeded by his son Narasimha II. who reigned until 1508. Dr. Burnell, however (Dravidian Paleography), carries on Virupaksha, the last of the Hari Hara dynasty until 1490. Now, Dr. Burnell is a singularly careful and reliable authority, and it, therefore, seems that the explanation as given in the text is a correct one, and that from 1480 until the date of the battle between Adil Shah and "Heem Rajah" the Narasimhas were Regents on behalf of Virupaksha, and on his death, the son Vira Narasimha II. mounted the throne and founded a new dynasty. We find exactly the same confusion in the succession of the Mohamedan Sultans of Bieder. After the death of Mahomed Shah, the dynasty continued until late in the first half of the sixteenth century, but the Bereeds were the real Rulers and actually date their dynasty, from 1489, and are called by the Mahomedan historians, the Bereed Shahs of Bieder.

from the Bahmanee rule and assumed the royal title. Sultan Mahmood, or rather Kassim Bereed, the real Ruler, called upon Adil Shah for assistance, which was at once given, and the combined forces defeated and took the rebel prisoner. Kassim Bereed wished to put Dustoor Deenar to death, but from motives of policy Adil Shah interceded, and not only obtained his pardon, but contrived to get his Government of Gulburga restored. Two years afterwards a marriage was arranged between Adil Shah's daughter (an infant in the cradle) and Mahmood Shah's son, Ahmed, and a secret arrangement was made under which Adil Shah was to take possession of Gulburga and of Dustoor Deenar's provinces. In this way, the powerful Minister, Kassim Bereed, would be cut off from his estates. Bereed, alarmed at this, at once retired from Bieder and collected an army, but was defeated by Adil Shah near the town of Kinjooty (1497), and Mahmood Shah was taken back in triumph to his capital (Bieder). In the following year the different Deccan sovereigns came to a definite arrangement, under which they divided the Deccan between themselves. Adil Shah received the provinces of Dustoor Deenar, including Gulburga; Imad-ul-Mulk, the Sultan of Berar, received Mahore, Ramgeer, and the surrounding country; and Ahmed Nizam Shah, of Ahmednagar, got as his share Dowlatabad, Antore, Kalneh, and all the country up to the borders of Guzerat. Kassim Bereed was allowed to come back to his post at Bieder, but all the territory that was left to him was a small strip of land round the capital, with, however, the country then in the possession of Kutb-ul-Mulk. This, however, was not much of a gift, because in order to obtain it he would first of all have to dispossess Kutb-ul-Mulk, who resided in Golconda. This was a feat which Kassim Bereed never effected, for a few years later (1510) Kutb declared his independence, and became the founder of the Kutb Shahi dynasty of Golconda. The unfortunate Bahmanee Sultan, therefore, was the principal loser by this war, in which Adil Shah had rendered him assistance. This help was dearly bought, and his great vassal Kings enriched themselves at their over lord's expense, leaving him the barren honour of ruling in a capital to which scarcely any territory was attached with a Minister who was virtually his master.

Dustoor Deenar made one more attempt to regain his provinces, and; assisted by three thousand horse sent to him by Ameer Bereed, the son of Kassim Bereed (who had now succeeded to his father's post), met Adil Shah on the banks of the Bhimrah. A fierce engagement ensued, which was won chiefly by the valour of the Sultan's brother, Guzzunfir Beg, by whose charge the enemy was put to rout and Dustoor Deenar killed. Ferishta thus describes the end of the battle:—"Ghuzzunfir Beg, who had received a severe wound, kneeling down with the rest of the Amras, performed the ceremonies of congratulation, and waved money and jewels over the Sultan's head in offering for the victory. Adil Shah kissing his eyes and forehead, clasped his noble brother in embrace, and superintended the dressing of his wounds, but all was vain; and the hero, according to the declarations of holy writ *(when their death comes they shall not delay an instant nor abide)*, after three days and nights, having drunk the Sherbet of martyrdom, speeded to the world eternal."*

This victory was the flood of Adil Shah's fortunes, and left him firmly established in his kingdom, which now extended from Gulburga and Sholapore to Goa, being bounded on the east by the Kistna, and on the west by the mountains of the Konkan.

---

* Ferishta calls Guzzunfir Beg the Sultan's brother, but it is difficult to understand how this could be, because Adil Shah, it will be remembered, was sent away from Constantinople to escape being killed as an infant, and only arrived in India, alone, after a series of adventures. Perhaps, however, he was the Sultan's *adopted* brother, as we are told by Ferishta that Adil Shah was *adopted* by Khajeh Gawan.

In 1502, Adil Shah resolved upon a very important step, which was to change the religion of the State from the Sunnee to the Sheah creed. During his stay in Persia, Adil Shah had imbibed the Sheah doctrine, and was a disciple of the House of Suffeewee, which had now succeeded to the Government. This change of religion at first excited great animosity amongst his brother Sultans in the Deccan, who at once declared against him what is known as the "holy war of the four brothers." In introducing this change Adil Shah behaved with singular moderation. Converts or Perverts are generally very bigotted, but Adil Shah publicly let his subjects know that, whatever he might believe, he was not going to interfere with their beliefs. "My faith for myself and your faith for yourselves," was his tolerant maxim, and the result was that, although a few of his officers withdrew from his service, the majority remained loyal. At first the combination of the other Mahomeden Sultans seemed likely to crush Adil Shah, who throughout seems to have preferred maintaining a well-disciplined but numerically small standing army to the large and disorganized hordes that were then the fashion. Adil Shah's army was rarely more than 25,000 in strength, and he therefore, had to fight a cautious game. He never gave his enemies the chance of meeting him in a pitched battle, but carrying the war into their own territories, constantly avoided an engagement, hovering round the allied army and cutting off its supplies. Retreating before them as they advanced, he led the allied kings, not into his own territory, but into that of Imad-ul-mulk, the Sultan of Berar, who was favourably inclined towards him. Negociations were then commenced, and the allies were told that the war had been made against Adil Shah, not so much on religious grounds, as because Ameer Bereed wished to possess himself of Bijapur, in which case he would become too dangerous a rival. By way of concession, Adil Shah sent orders to restore the Sunnee rites, and then all cause of quarrel being removed, the allies broke up their confederation and retired each to his own dominions. Ameer Bereed was thus left alone, and Adil Shah promptly seized the opportunity to surprise his camp, in which he was so successful, that Ameer Bereed just managed to escape with the Sultan of Bieder and a few followers. The whole war only lasted three months, and Adil Shah returned in triumph to Bijapur and quietly continued the practice of the new faith without further opposition.

Although the rest of Adil Shah's reign was quiet as far as his own countrymen was concerned, he was brought into contact with another power which was but the pioneer of the present rulers of India. In 1498 on the 26th August, Vasco de Gama sighted Mount Dely, in South Kanara, and effected a landing on the island of Anjidiv. Subsequently, they landed on the mainland, near the mouth of the Kalinadi. Adil Shah—or Sabayo—as he is called by the Portuguese writers, sent an expedition against the foreign invaders, which, however, was destroyed. The leader of this expedition, a Mahomedan Jew, was taken captive and brought by Vasco de Gama to Europe, where he was converted and received the name of Gasper de Gama. In 1503 Vasco de Gama returned, and effected a treaty with the Honavar Chief, then a subject of Vijayanagar. From this time each year saw a fresh arrival of the Portuguese ships. Ferishta says that in 1509 they surprised and took Goa, but were afterwards driven out by an army sent by Adil Shah. The Portuguese writers are silent regarding this, though they speak of a victory gained over sixty sail despatched against them in 1506 by Adil Shah and commanded by a Portuguese renegade named Abdullah.

In the midst of this continued fighting on the Western Coast, Yusuf Adil Shah died at Bijapur of a dropsical complaint (1510), and was succeeded by his son, Ismael Adil Shah, a boy of about 14 years of age.

Yusuf Adil Shah ranks high in the Deccan, not only as a soldier but also as a statesman. Like Hassan Gangu, the founder of the Bahmanee dynasty, he was just, humane and tolerant, but enjoyed the additional advantage to be gained from being highly educated. He wrote elegantly, and was not only a good judge of verses, but himself a poet and *improvisatore*, singing his own verses to his own music. We read of none of the acts of bigotry and cruelty which disgrace the memories of so many of the Deccan Kings. Even his change of faith, so calculated to excite fanatacism and bloodshed, was carried out with such tolerance and moderation, as to excite no opposition among his subjects. He was a patron of art and literature, and especially that of Persia, and numbers of learned and scientific men found their way to his Court. He spent his money liberally on buildings and public works, an example which was followed by his successors, so that his dynasty, with the exception of that of the Kutb Shahs of Golconda, has left nobler memorials of the building art than any other in the Deccan. Lastly, his private character was eminently temperate and virtuous. He was the husband of one wife, a Hindoo, the daughter of a Mahratta chieftain, by whom he had one son and three daughters. The lady is said to have been not only of great beauty, but of singular ability, and we shall have a proof of her strength of mind when we come to the history of the next reign. The title bestowed upon her after having embraced Islam was Booboojee Khanum. The three daughters were subsequently married to the three Sultans of Berar, Ahmednugger, and Bieder (Bahmanee), so that family ties joined the Mahomedan kingdoms closely together. Adil Shah was seventy-five years of age when he died, and Ferishta says of him that he was "handsome in person, eloquent of speech, and eminent for his learning, liberality, and valour."

Character.

CHAPTER XIV.

THE NIZAM SHAHS OF AHMEDNAGAR.

The father of the first Nizam Shah was a Brahmin, who was taken prisoner in one of the wars of Ahmed Shah Bahmanee, made a Mussulman, and educated as a royal slave under the name of Malick Hoossein. He was a lad of considerable ability, and being educated together with the Sultan's eldest son, Mahomed, acquired a considerable knowledge of Persian and Arabic. When Mahomed ascended the throne (1462) Malick Hoossein was promoted to the rank of one thousand, and placed in charge of the royal falconry, from which he derived the name of Beherce (*Beher* meaning a falcon). He was subsequently made Governor of the Telingana provinces, and after Khajeh Gawan's death, succeeded him in office with the title of Malick Naib. Under Sultan Mahomed he was the Prime Minister, and received the additional title of Nizam-ul-Mulk. Whilst the father was thus employed in the capital, he sent his son, Malick Ahmed, to the Konkan, where he carried on a very successful war against the hill Chieftains, reducing a number of forts, gaining a considerable amount of treasure (especially at Seer), and eventually reducing the whole country as far as the coast. In 1486, Nizam-ul-Mulk rebelled, and after having seized the city of Ahmedabad Bieder, was eventually assassinated, as related in the account of the reign of Mahomed Shah. The son, who was on the way to join his father, at once retired to Khiber, where he assumed the titles of the deceased, and was generally known as Ahmed Nizam-ul-Mulk Beheree, to which, although he did not as yet assume it, the people added the title of Shah. Khiber was situated in the hills not far from the town of Junar, which, for some time, was the seat of Government of the new Sultan. Ahmed Nizam Shah, as we shall call him, although he actually claimed the title a few years subsequently, was an able and gallant soldier, and some of his sudden raids resemble those of that prince of robbers, the Mahratta Sivajee. Kassim Bereed was now the moving power at Bieder, and he sent an army under Nadir-ul-Human to reduce this new rebel. After some fighting, this army was completely defeated, and its General slain, whereupon a larger force under eighteen of the principal noblemen was sent to reduce Ahmed to subjection. Ahmed Shah, however, by a clever stratagem, managed to elude this army, and getting into its rear with a picked force of three thousand cavalry, made a sudden attack upon the capital (Bieder). Here he was admitted by the guards, and for a day remained in possession of the city. He appears to have behaved with considerable moderation, releasing only the members of his father's family, but at the same carrying off the wives and families of the noblemen who had been sent against him; whom as hostages he treated with all honour.

Stung by this daring escapade, the Bieder Sultan removed the General in command of his army, and appointed in his place Jehangir Khan, the Governor of Telingana, who had a considerable reputation for bravery and ability. Ahmed Shah, vastly outnumbered, now retired into the hills of the Konkan, whither he was followed by Jehangir Khan, who for a space of a month-blockaded him. On the rains setting in, Jehangir Khan, thinking himself safe, relaxed a good deal of his discipline, with the result that one night Ahmed Shah surprised his camp and finding the army in a state of intoxication, put the whole, including the General, to the sword. On the site where this victory was won, Ahmed Shah laid out a garden and built a magnificent palace, which he called Bagh Nizam. This was in 1489, and from this date, acting under the advice of Adil Shah, of Bijapur, whose policy it was to weaken the power of Bieder as much as possible, he commenced reading the *Khutba* in his own name, and assumed the White Umbrella as a sign of royalty. This assertion of independence, however, offended some of his nobles, whereupon the Sultan replied that he had assumed the umbrella, not as a sign of royalty, but in order to shelter himself from the sun. The nobles then withdrew their objection on condition that he would allow his subjects to do the same. "As he could not well refuse," says Ferishta, "permission was given; and from that time to this, in his country the King and the beggar carry it over their heads; but to distinguish the Sultan from his subjects, the royal umbrella has a piece of red upon it, while the others are all white. This custom spread throughout all Deccan, contrary to that in the Moghul Empire, where no one but the sovereign dare use an umbrella." *

In 1493 Ahmed Shah resolved upon the reduction of Dowlatabad, which for some time had been in possession of

---

* Scott translating Ferishta in 1794 adds a note to this effect: "This is the case at present, except in the English dominions."

two brothers, to one of whom, Malick Wojah, his sister, was married. On a child being born, the other brother Malick Ashruff, afraid that he would be removed, assassinated both brother and nephew, in consequence of which the wife sought the protection of her brother Ahmed Shah. The Sultan thereupon advanced to besiege Dowlatabad, but on his way gave assistance to Cassim Bereed at Bieder, who was then besieged by Adil Shah. The policy of the Deccan Kings was to maintain the balance of power, and so we continually find them taking first one side and then the other, so as to prevent any of their rivals from becoming too powerful. After raising the siege of Bieder, Ahmed Shah advanced upon Dowlatabad, but found it too strong to be taken by assault. Accordingly he resolved to build himself a city nearer the fort, and by continuing a constant state of siege, and by devastating the country around, to compel the garrison to capitulate. This led to the building of a city about half way between Juna and Dowlatabad, situated on the banks of the River Seer. This city is said to have been completed in two years' time, when, according to Ferishta, it "rivalled in splendour Bagdad and Cairo." Calling it after his own name, the new City was called Ahmednagar. From this time the siege of Dowlatabad continued for more than seven years, interrupted occasionally by other small undertakings, and the fort was not finally taken until 1449 or 1500, when, upon the death of Malick Ashruff, the keys were surrendered to Ahmed Shah. From this time Dowlatabad continued in the possession of the Ahmednagar Kings. The remainder of Ahmed Shah's reign was a comparatively peaceful one, and he employed it in improving the condition of the country. In 1508 he died, leaving a son seven years of age, to whom he made his nobles take an oath of allegiance.

    Ahmed Shah has left a reputation not only for singular ability, but also for great virtue and self-control. It is related

Character. of him that when he rode through the city "he never looked to the right or the left, lest his eyes might fall upon another man's wife." Upon one occasion when a young man, he had captured the fort of Kaweel, and among the captives was a young lady of extraordinary beauty with whom he fell desperately in love. Upon being told, however, that she had a husband who was also a prisoner, he not only restored her to him unmolested, but dismissed them both with valuable presents. Towards his officers he was generous and forgiving. Instead of dismissing a man after failure, he stimulated him to further efforts, giving him another chance to retrieve his character, and in this way enjoyed the strong attachment of all his nobles. Ferishta says that the custom of duelling was introduced by this Sultan, who, when young men came before him with mutual complaints, ordered them to fight the quarrel out in his presence, deciding in favour of the one who first wounded his adversary. In consequence of this encouragement, a crowd of young men attended the hall of audience each day, hoping to win fame and distinction in the Sultan's presence, until at last matters came to such a pass that every day two or three combatants were killed. At length the Sultan, disgusted at so much slaughter, ordered that all such combats should take place, not in his presence, but on a plain outside the city. Regulations for such duels were laid down, bystanders and relations were not allowed to interfere, and all blood feuds in consequence of the death of one of the combatants was strictly prohibited. This custom of duelling found great favour in the Deccan, and spread throughout the country where all noblemen were especially skilled in the use of the sword. Ferishta speaks of having been an eyewitness to such a duel in which six grey-bearded men were killed in the streets of Bijapur. He speaks of the custom as an "abominable" one, and trusts that under "the auspices of wise and just princes, it may be altogether done away with, so that this country resembling paradise may be purified from such abomination."

It is now time to revert to Bijapur, where about the same time the first King, Yusuf Adil Shah had died, also leaving a minor son, whose fortunes we will for the present follow.

THE GRAND STAND VIJAYANAGAR RUINS.

CHAPTER XV.

BIJAPUR FROM 1509—1534.   ISMAEL ADIL SHAH.

THE exact age of Ismael Adil Shah, when his father died is not given, but he appears to have been about 13 or 14 years old. The late King on his death-bed had appointed one of his most trusted nobles as Ismael's Guardian and Regent, and had made the other Amras swear to obey him. For some time Kamil Khan—for this was the Regent's name—governed well and wisely. He lived on terms of friendship with the other Mahomedan Kings, and appears to have gained considerable popularity amongst the nobles as well as the people. The Portuguese were confirmed in the possession of Goa, and a treaty was drawn up with them, which was faithfully observed on both sides. As times went on, however, and the period approached when the young King would attain his majority. Kamil Khan, attracted by the sweets of power, began to entertain the ambition of usurping the throne. With this object in view, he from time to time distributed amongst his own relations and adherents the estates of those noblemen who died, or who were convicted of crimes. With the examples of Narasimha, in Vijayanagar, and Cassim Bereed, in Bieder, before him, he resolved upon founding a new dynasty. Accordingly, he formed an alliance with Ameer Bereed, and after having confined the young Sultan and his mother, Boobajee Khanum, in the citadel, he marched with an army against Sholapore, which he reduced after a siege of three months, and then returned to Bijapur to finish his work of usurpation. He first of all banished all persons who were adherents of the late King, and then raised a large force with which he held the command of the city. All preparations being made, Kamil Khan, consulted the astrologers as to which would be the best day to depose the young King. The astrologers gave as their opinion that for the next few days the combinations of the stars were against Kamil Khan, and that, therefore, it would be advisable to wait. Accordingly, the first of the next month was fixed for the revolution, and in the meantime Kamil Khan shut himself up in the citadel so as to escape the danger threatened by the adverse conjunction of the planets. The Queen-mother, however, had been informed of what was contemplated, and resolved to seize the opportunity of this temporary seclusion to strike the first blow. Accordingly, she applied to Yusuf Turk, the foster-father of her son, and asked him to help her. Yusuf replied that he was an old man, and that his life was at her service. The Queen thereupon told a female attendant to go and make enquiries regarding Kamil Khan's health, and just as she was leaving for the purpose, added, as an after-thought, that she should take Yusuf Turk with her, as he was anxious to obtain permission to go to Mecca. The woman accordingly went, and after having delivered the Queen's message and present, introduced Yusuf to Kamil Khan. The Regent at once gave Yusuf the required permission, and as he held out to him the betel leaf as a sign that he might go, Yusuf pulled out a dagger which he had concealed under his cloth and plunged it into Kamil Khan's body. Yusuf and the female attendant were at once cut down, but it was too late, and the would-be usurper had met his deserved fate. As soon as the news of this murder was spread abroad, an immense commotion arose. The Queen closed the gates of the royal palace, and though Sufder Khan, the son of the late Regent, at once attacked the palace with the object of getting possession of the young Sultan, he found it obstinately defended. The citadel and the royal palace were situated in the same enclosure, and Sufder Khan, keeping the citadel gates shut against the city, endeavoured to take the palace by storm, so that there was a bloody struggle taking place inside the citadel walls, whilst outside the citizens were assembled in a state of excitement. The Queen had only a few adherents, but the guards made common cause with her, and defended the palace most obstinately. Whilst the fight was going on, a party of Deccanee matchlock men managed to climb the wall and afford relief to the Queen and her party. The Queen and the Sultan's foster-aunt, Dilshad Aga, the latter with a veil over her head, animated and encouraged the defenders by their presence and promises. Sufder Khan now brought up cannon, with which he managed to break down the gate, but as he was on the point of entering, the gallant Dilshad fired a volley of arrows and gun shot into his party. One of these arrows wounded Sufder Khan in the eye, and in order to recover himself he took refuge under a wall. It so happened, however, that the young King was seated on the wall just above the place, and, seeing his enemy beneath him, he succeeded in rolling over a large stone, which, hitting Sufder Khan on the head, killed him on the spot. As soon as their leader had fallen, his troops took to their heels. The city was then cleared of the rebels, and the mutiny was at an end, thanks to the bravery of the Queen and Dilshad Aga, and to the ready wittedness of the young Sultan. When everything was quiet, the young Sultan went to the mosque to return thanks for his escape, and then conducted the funeral procession of his foster-father Yusuf to the tomb of a saint outside the city, by whose side he was buried, and eventually a dome was raised over the graves of both. During the rest of his reign, the Sultan went once a month to visit the tomb of the faithful Yusuf (1511-12).

Ismael Shah was now about seventeen years of age, and no opposition was made to him on the score of age. Ameer Bereed, on hearing of the failure of the plot, at once raised the siege of Gulburga, which he had attacked, and retired to Bieder. The Vijayanagar King who had made an attack upon Raichore pressed the siege and succeeded in taking the fort, which during previous hundred years must have changed masters fifteen or twenty times. Ferishta still calls the Vijayanagar King Heem Raja, but this is clearly a mistake, as Heem Raja, or rather Narasimha, had been succeeded in 1508 by his brother Krishna Deva Raja. This capture of Raichore was one of Krishna Deva's first exploits, and only a prelude to a long career of victory.

Ameer Bereed, repulsed from Gulburga, called upon the Kings of Ahmednagar, Berar, and Golconda to come to his assistance, and after some delay succeeded in collecting a large army, with which he advanced to besiege Bijapur. Ismael Shah met this army a short distance from his capital, and though only at the head of twelve thousand horse, he attacked with such vigour that he put the whole force to flight, and took the Sultan of Bieder, together with his son Ahmed prisoners. The whole of the camp and baggage fell into the hands of the conquerors, and Ismael returned to his capital in triumph The two royal prisoners were treated with the greatest courtesy. Splendid presents were made to them, and Sultan Mahomed asked for Ismael's sister as the wife of his son (Ahmed). The espousals having been celebrated, the two Sultans went together to Gulburga for the marriage ceremony, which was carried out with much magnificence. As a guard of honour, Ismael sent a troop of five thousand horse to conduct the newly-married pair, and Sultan Mahomed to Bieder, and Ameer Bereed was so alarmed at the approach of this force that he made haste to evacuate the city. For a short time Sultan Ahmed was therefore freed from the tyranny of his Minister, but as soon as the Bijapur troops had taken their departure, Ameer Bereed returned, and the Sultan reverted to his former state of subjection. A few years of peace followed, one of the most important events of which was the reception by Ismael Shah of an embassy from the Persian monarch, despatched on purpose to thank him for an act of courtesy shown to an ambassador, who a few years before had been detained at Bieder. This embassy arrived in 1519, and was met by Ismael Shah twelve miles outside the capital. The King of Persia in his letter addressed the Sultan as a Sovereign Prince, and Ismael was so pleased with this recognition that he ordered in future on Fridays and holidays prayers should be recited in all the mosques for the royal family of Persia.

In the following year (1520), Ismael attempted to carry out his long-intended project of recovering the forts of Raichore and Mudkul. For this purpose he assembled an army of more than fifty thousand horse and foot, and encamped on the banks of the Kistna. The river, however, was in flood, and the enemy was in command of all the ferries. Instead of waiting for a favourable opportunity, Ismael one evening when fired by wine gave orders to force a passage by means of rafts. Heedless of the remonstrances of his officers, Ismael plunged his own elephant into the river and succeeded in crossing with about two thousand men. Here he was attacked by the whole of the Hindoo army, and though the Sultan and his army fought with the utmost bravery, the whole were either cut to pieces or drowned, with the exception of the Sultan and seven soldiers. After this repulse Ismael had to give up all further thought of vengeance for the present, and retired to Bijapur after having sworn an oath never to indulge in wine until this defeat should be revenged.

In 1523 an alliance was made between Boorahan Nizam Shah and Ismael, and the sister of the latter was given to the former in marriage. This marriage instead of cementing the alliance between the two Kings, unfortunately led to another war, for Ismael had promised to give the fort of Sholapore as dowry with his sister. This promise he neglected to keep, and so Nizam Shah, calling in the assistance of the Berar Sultan and of Ameer Bereed, who was always ready to join any one of the Deccan Kings against another, advanced with an army to take it by force. This time, Ismael Shah was more successful, and after having put the allied camp into disorder by a night surprise, he attacked early on the following morning, and defeated the enemy with great slaughter, taking all his elephants and baggage. This concluded the war, and the Sultan returned in triumph to Bijapur.

In 1528, Nizam Shah and Ameer Bereed attempted another invasion of Bijapur, but were again defeated with great loss, and Ismael then formed an alliance with the Berar Sultan, to whom he gave his remaining sister in marriage.

In the following year, we find that Ismael Shah sent a large supply of money, together with six thousand horse, to assist Nizam Shah against an invasion of the Sultan of Guzerat. The invasion was repelled, but Ameer Bereed, who had also joined Nizam Shah, endeavouring to corrupt Ismael's troops before their return, Sultan Ismael resolved to put an end to this restless old intriguer's plots. Binding over Nizam Shah to neutrality, he accordingly assembled an army of ten thousand cavalry, and laid siege to Bieder. Ameer Bereed at once fled with the object of bringing assistance from Golconda. After some delay a reinforcement of four thousand Telinganas arrived, and attacked Ismael's force at the same time as the garrison made a sally. Both attacks were, however, beaten off with great loss, and the city was still more closely invested. Imad Shah, the Sultan of Berar now attempted to conciliate Ismael, and visiting him in his camp, asked him to forgive Ameer Bereed. The Sultan, however, replied that Bereed had done him and his family more injuries than could be enumerated—which was quite true—and refused to make any terms. Upon this Imad Shah retired to Oodgir, where he was joined by Bereed. Ismael Shah hearing that his enemy had joined Imad Shah resolved upon surprising him, and despatched Assud Khan, who throughout all these wars had taken a most distinguished part, with a body of two thousand picked horse. Assud Khan reached Bereed's camp at the conclusion of a big banquet. All the guards and sentinels were asleep amidst their broken wine pots, and Bereed himself was so hopelessly intoxicated, that he was carried in a state of insensibility, tied to his bed, and did not recover consciousness, until he was a long way on the road to Bieder. Bereed at first thought that he had been carried away by evil spirits, but on being told of the real state of things, was overcome with shame.

On the morning after the arrival of the surprise party in Ismael Shah's camp, Ameer Bereed, now a man of a very advanced age, was placed before Ismael Shah with his hands tied behind his back. After he had stood in this way for two hours in the sun, the Sultan ordered him to be put to death, and an executioner advanced for this purpose. Bereed then begged that his life might be spared, and offered if this were done to persuade his sons to hand over the fort and citadel of Bieder. The sons, on being called upon, replied that their father's life was of but little more worth, since in the ordinary course of nature he must die soon. Ismael, thinking that this was merely a ruse in order to gain time, ordered Bereed to be put to death, but consented to have him placed in such a position that the sons could see the extremity to which he was reduced. This had the desired effect, and the sons now offered to give up the fort on condition only that they and their women should be allowed to depart with the clothes on their persons without search. In this manner, they managed to carry off a considerable portion of the royal robes and jewels, and with them retired unmolested to Oodgir.

Ismael Shah, who had been joined by Imad Shah of Berar, now entered the city with great pomp, and seated himself on the royal *musnud* of the Bahmanees. Of the real representative of this ancient house, we hear nothing, he had probably been taken away with the Bereeds. An immense amount of treasure and jewels were found in the fort, of which Ismael Shah would not take any portion, but distributed it amongst his followers and the Berar Sultan. It is narrated that he told the poet Molana Seyd Kumi that he might take as much from the treasury as he could lift with both hands. The poet replied that as he had grown old and weak in the Shah's service he should be allowed two attempts. This was granted, and the poet then said that he should like to wait until he had quite recovered his strength. The Sultan then quoted a verse to the effect: "There is danger in delay, and it hurts the petitioner," thereupon the poet made shift to carry as much as he could. Nor was he entirely unsuccessful, for we are told that at each attempt he carried away bags containing 25,000 gold *oons*, equal to about £ 10,000.

At Imad Shah's intercession, Ismael now pardoned Ameer Bereed, and gave him the Government of Kalean and Oodgir, but made him swear fealty to him and also to accompany him with three thousand horse on an expedition to recover Raichur. This expedition proved successful, and Raichur was re-taken after a siege of three months, it having been for seventeen years in the possession of the Hindoos. It will be remembered that, on a previous occasion, when he had been defeated, Ismael Shah had sworn to refrain from wine until he should have revenged the defeat. This having been accomplished, he held a grand banquet, at which Imad Shah, Ameer Bereed, and his Commander-in-Chief, Assud Khan, were present. Fifteen hundred captives were taken, and Ameer Bereed was again granted the Government of Ahmedabad and Bieder, on condition, however, that he would surrender Kalean and Candahar. After this, Imad Shah and Ameer Bereed were allowed to return to their respective countries.

Once at liberty, the wily old intriguer Bereed forgot to fulfil the promise he had made of surrendering the two forts, and entered into an alliance with Boorahan Shah of Ahmednagar (1531). The result was another campaign in which Boorahan Shah was defeated. An alliance was then formed between the two Sultans, one of two conditions of which was that Ismael Shah was to be at liberty to conquer what he could of the Kutb Shadi dominions, and Boorahan Shah was to add (if he could) Berar to his kingdom. In consequence of this agreement, Ismael Shah, who was now joined by Ameer Bereed, laid siege to Koilconda, one of the Kutb Shahi's forts (1533). Before, however this fort could be taken, Ismael Shah fell ill and died on the way to Gulburga (1534). Assud Khan at once raised the siege, and returned with the body of the deceased king and his two sons to Bijapur, where, after burying his master near his father, Yusuf Adil Shah, he installed the eldest of the young princes on the throne.

Ismael Adil Shah was prudent, patient, and generous. He was more inclined to forgive than to punish, and his clemency was sometimes taken advantage of. He had artistic tastes, and was skilled in poetry and music. He was also very fond of painting and of making arrows and saddle cloths. He was quick at repartee, and had a large stock of quotations, which he made in an apt and appropriate manner. In manners, he was more polished than the Deccannees, and had been early trained in the Turkish and Persian habits and customs. Although he did not make much head against the Hindoos, he was acknowledged as the principal of the Mahomedan kings of the Deccan, and though jealous of his power and often combining to oppose him, they seem to have admitted his superiority. His reign lasted for twenty-five years.

Character.

GENEALOGY OF THE BEREED DYNASTY.

[*Usurpers of the Bahmani Kingdom*].

(BIEDER).

1. KASIM BEREED. . .   1492—1504
2. AMIR BEREED (son) . . . . 1504—1549
3. ALI BEREED SHAH (son) . . . .   1549—1562
4. IBRAHIM BEREED (son) . . . .   1562—1569
5. KASIM BEREED (brother) . . . .   1569—1572
6. MIRZA ALI BEREED (son) . . . .   1572—1609
7. ALI BEREED   1609

After No. 7. BIEDER was incorporated with Bijapur.

(NOTE. KASIM BEREED was originally a Georgian Slave but rose to be minister of MAHMUD BAHMANI, during whose reign the other Deccan Kingdoms revolted. KASIM kept the king MAHMUD II a prisoner and virtually ruled till his death in 1504. His son AMIR continued to reign under three other puppet kings until 1527 when the last king KATAM ULLAH fled to Ahmednagar when AMIR assumed royalty. ISMAIL ADIL SHAH conquered BIEDER and restored it to AMIR BEREED as his vassal. AMIR died in 1549 having lost almost all his territory and his son assumed the title of Shah).

CHAPTER XVI.

THE KINGDOMS OF BERAR AND GOLCONDA AND CONTINUATION OF BIJAPUR.

It is necessary now to glance backwards in order to trace the foundations of the two kingdoms of Berar and Golconda which have already been frequently mentioned in the previous chapter.

Berar was the smallest and least important of the Mahomedan kingdoms of the Deccan, and its independence was the most short-lived. Like his rival king in Ahmednagar, the founder of the Imad Shahi dynasty of Berar was a Hindoo by descent. He is said to have been a Canarese Brahmin taken in war by the Bahmanee Governor of Berar. He adopted Islam, and rapidly rose to high office, receiving the title of Imád-ul-Mulk. He asserted his independence about the same time as Yusuf Adil Shah (1484), and in the partition of 1498 he was recognised by the other kings, and received as his share Mahar and Ramgarh, or the territory between the Godavery and the Pain Gunga rivers. The first Imad Shah died early in the 16th century, and was succeeded by his son, Alla-ud-din, who was on the throne throughout the whole of the reign of Ismael Adil Shah, as related in the last chapter. This prince was constantly at war with Ahmednagar, and generally got the worst of it. He lost his outlying districts of Mahar and Pathri, and had to call in the Sultan of Guzerat, whom he afterwards found it very difficult to get rid of. His dominions comprised the province of Berar as nearly as possible as it exists at the present day, lying between the Rivers Taptee on the north and Godavery on the south. The present southern boundary of the province is the river Pain Gunga. The capital was at Ellichpore, and with the exception of this city there were few other towns of importance. The people were quiet and devoted to agriculture, and as the province lies out of the line of march of the great kingdoms, it had enjoyed a long period of peace. It formed a sort of irregular square comprising an area of about 20,000 square miles. Sultan Alla-ud-din was succeeded by his son, Daria Imad Shah (1550), and he in turn was succeeded (1568) by his infant son, Burhan Imad Shah. The infant king was confined by his Minister, Tufal Khan, who usurped the Government. He was, however, attacked by the Kings of Bijapur and Ahmednagar, defeated, and after some time spent in flight, was put to death together with the young prince whom he had dethroned (1572). From this time Berar was annexed to Ahmednagar, to which kingdom it belonged, until it in turn was conquered by an army from Delhi in 1607. This brief summary of the history of Berar must suffice for the present, and further notice of any events of importance will be made as they have reference to the general thread of the story.

A kingdom that was destined to play a much more important and lasting part in Indian history was that of Golconda, which, under a different dynasty and another name exists unto the present day. During the time of the Bahmanee Sultans, Golconda was the capital of the Governor of the Telingana provinces, and his rule extended to the eastern coast with ports at Musalipatam and Coconada. The Hindoo Kings of Warangal had disappeared, but a number of petty chiefs survived. These Chiefs were continually breaking out into rebellion, and gave the Mahomedan Governor a good deal of trouble. The Telingana province was therefore one of considerable importance, and the Governor was an officer of high dignity.

The founder of this new kingdom was Barra Malick Kull Kutb-ul-Mulk, a Persian by descent, who entered the service of Sultan Mahmoud Bahmanee towards the close of the 15th century. When in 1490 an attempt was made to assassinate Sultan Mahmoud, Barra, Malick was one of those who saved the King, and eventually quelled the rebellion. For this he was created Ghazi Malick Kutb-ul-Mulk, and sent as Governor to Telingana. When in 1489 the other Deccan Sultan threw off all semblance of submission to the Bahmanee house, Kuli Kutb-ul-Mulk still remained loyal, and it was not until 1510 that he finally declared his independence.

His first thought was to strengthen the fortifications of his capital Golconda, and to improve its buildings. The fort as it now exists shows signs of great strength, and 170 years later it baffled the whole of Aurungzebe's army, and was only won by treachery. In the middle of the fort is a hill, from the top of which the country is visible for miles around. The King's palace and most of the houses in the interior of the fort are now in ruins, but the walls are still intact, and seen from the outside, the whole has a very gloomy appearance, as the high walls frown down on the waters of the lake which washes the northern portion of the fort.

The first campaign of the new Sultan was an unprovoked one, against Krishna Deva Raya, of Vijayanagar. After a great battle near Pangal, in which the Hindoos were worsted, the Sultan succeeded in capturing the two forts of Kovilconda and Ganpoora, and then returned with a considerable amount of plunder. In the following year, the Rajah of Khammamett broke into rebellion, and on being defeated managed to make his escape and organized a confederation of all the Hindoo Rajahs. A number of actions ensued, in which the Mahomedans were successful, and at last a treaty was signed, in which the River Godavery was made the northern boundary. No sooner had peace been restored in the north, than war broke out again in the south. Sultan Ismael, of Bijapur, instigated by the King of Vijayanagar, laid siege to Kovilconda. Kutb Shah advanced to its relief, and during an engagement that followed, received a sword cut in the face which disfigured him for life, part of the nose and cheek being cut off. It was whilst this siege was in progress that Sultan Ismael Shah was taken ill and died, and Assud Khan, (his minister and general in chief) deeming that a settlement of the succession was of more importance than the capture of the fort, raised the siege, and retired to Gulburga, after making peace with Kutb Shah. This Sultan continued to reign for eleven years longer, and during almost the whole of that time he was occupied in quelling the rebellions of the Hindoo Chiefs. Under Krishna Deva R ya, the Vijayanagar kingdom was gradually spreading in extent, and Kutb Shah found himself being cut off from communication with the seashore. He does not seem to have held much land south of the Kistna, and the Vijayanagar influence rapidly extended along the coast, until it predominated as far north as the Godavery. In 1543 Kuli Kutb Shah was assassinated whilst saying his prayers in the mosque at Golconda, in consequence of a plot organized by his son, Jamshid Kuli who succeeded him. This first Golconda Sultan had ruled in the Telingana Province for sixty years, during sixteen of which he had been a Governor, and forty-four an independent prince. He was ninety years of age when he died.

As we have now brought the string of events down to the death of Ismael Adil Shah, it will be as well to revert to the Bijapur Province, round which for the next forty years the principal interest centres.

We have already told how Assud Khan considered it advisable to raise the siege of Kovilconda, and return with the dead body of the late Sultan and the two young princes to Gulburga. The names of those two princes were Mulloo and Ibrahim. The former was the eldest, and had been designated as his successor by the dying Sultan. He was, however, a passionate, licentious young man, and there was a general feeling against making him Sultan, but Assud Khan thought himself to be bound in duty to carry out his master's last commands. Assud Khan was now the most prominent man in the kingdom. On frequent occasions he had during the reign of Ismael Adil Shah given instances of his military talents and devoted bravery. He now, and during the rest of his life, showed himself to be a statesman, not only of ability, but also of integrity. During the march to Gulburga, he kept both the young princes in a kind of honourable confinement, and prevented them from having access to one another, or to the rest of the army, for he was afraid that intrigues would be set on foot. Arrived at Gulburga, a consultation was held with the ladies of the harem and the Chief nobility, and it was decided to follow the wishes of the late Sultan and place the eldest son, Mulloo, on the throne. This was done, but it soon became apparent that the apprehensions of Assud Khan were amply justified. The young King showed himself to be thoroughly vicious, and gave himself up to reckless debauchery. Disgusted at his conduct, Assud Khan retired with his family to his Jaghir of Belgaum, and left Sultan Mulloo to his own devices. Before six months were passed, the young tyrant had made himself thoroughly hated, and had alienated from him all the adherents of his house. The crisis was brought by his sending to Yusuf Turk, a nobleman of high rank, to demand his son for the satisfaction of his unnatural lust. On this demand being treated with contempt, the King sent a body of followers with orders to bring the father's head. These men were beaten off, and Yusuf Turk retired with his family to his estates in a state of righteous indignation. The Sultan's grandmother, Booboojee Khanum, who, in the former reign had shown herself to be so capable of action, now made up her mind that the young Sultan must be deposed. Accordingly, she wrote to Yusuf Turk to give his assistance, which, after consulting Assud Khan, and obtaining his co-operation, he promised to do. On an appointed day, Yusuf Khan suddenly entered the capital with a large force. He met with little or no opposition, and Mulloo was at once seized, together with his youngest brother. They were both blinded, and the second brother, Ibrahim, was then proclaimed amidst universal rejoicing. This short reign, so full of infamy and disgrace, lasted only six months.

The new Sultan's first act was to change the State religion from the *Sheeah* to the *Sunnee* creed, and his next was to dismiss all the foreigners such as Turks, Persians, Moguls, &c., in his service, with the exception of 400 men, whom he retained

Sultan Ibrahim Abdil Shah (1535).

as a special guard. In their place he enlisted Deccanees and Abyssinians. The latter race never seem to have been reckoned as foreigners, and throughout Deccan history we always find them making common cause with the Deccanees. Under the latter name it must not be supposed that the Hindoos of the Deccan were included. The appellation is used exclusively with reference to the descendants of the first Mahomedan or Afghan families that had accompanied Sultan Alla-ud-Din to the Deccan. This summary dismissal was by no means a wise step, for the men thus sent away formed some of the best fighting material of the Bijapur army. Rama Rajah of Vijayanagar at once enrolled them in his service, and not only gave them great indulgences, but allowed them to build a mosque in his city. He also had a copy of the *Koran* placed before his throne, so that when his Mahomedan servants came to pay their respects, they could do so without a breach of the rules of their own religion. In this way he succeeded in collecting a well-disciplined force of three thousand Mahomedans, which proved of considerable use to him.

Soon after Ibrahim Shah's accession, a revolution broke out in Vijayanagar which led to the Sultan's interference in the affairs of that kingdom. Rama Rajah the son of Krishna Deva Raya, had succeeded to the throne in 1530, and being a descendant of the usurping dynasty, strengthened his position by marrying a daughter of the old Hari Hara family. Ferishta speaks of the throne being then held by an infant of the original dynasty, and goes on to say that on Rama Rajah endeavouring to put this family entirely aside, a revolution broke out amongst the nobility, whereupon Rama Rajah put an infant descended from the female line on the throne, and, leaving him in charge of his own uncle, Hojè Permal Row, went on an expedition against some refractory Rajahs in the Malabar and Madura countries. During his absence a rebellion took place in the capital. Hojè Permal Row was induced to liberate the young Rajah and place him on the throne. Several other Rajahs then joined the revolution, and for a time Rama Rajah was deprived of power. Before long, Hoje Permal Row had the young King strangled and usurped the throne himself. Finding, however, that he was too weak to hold his own against Rama Rajah, who still kept the field, he invited Ibrahim Shah to come to his assistance, offering him a subsidy of three lakhs of *oons*, (£ 40,000) for each day his army should march. This was an offer which Ibrahim Shah was by no means loth to accept. He marched with a considerable army to Vijayanagar, was there received by Permal Row and entertained for seven days. This alliance with a Mahomedan sovereign, however, excited such dissatisfaction amongst the Hindoo Rajahs that a strong protest was made, and Permal Row, trusting to their promises that if he would dismiss the Sultan they would recognize him as Rajah, paid his new ally fifty lakhs of *oons* (£ 1,700,000) and allowed him to return. No sooner, however, had Ibrahim Shah crossed the Kistna than Rama Rajah and his confederates returned and laid siege to the capital. Permal Row shut himself up in the citadel, and becoming "mad from despair, blinded all the royal elephants and horses, also cutting off their tails that they might be of no use to the enemy. All the diamonds, rubies, emeralds, other precious stones and pearls, which had been collected in the course of many ages, he crushed to powder between heavy mill stones and scattered them on the ground. He then fixed a sword-blade into a pillar of his apartment, and ran his breast upon it with such force, that it pierced through, and came out of his back; thus putting an end to his existence just as the gates of the palace were opened to his enemies" (*Ferishta*). Rama Rajah then became undisputed King of Vijaganagar, and we hear of no other revolts or rival claimants until the final downfall of the kingdom nineteen years later.

Ibrahim Shah took advantage of the confusion in Vijayanagar to send an army under Assud Khan to surprise the important fortress of Adoni. This, however, he was not able to do, as Rama Rajah despatched his brother Venkatadri (or, as Ferishta calls him, Negtaderee) with a force far exceeding his in number. Assud Khan then commenced a retreat, but being harassed closely by the Hindoos, was able to surprise their camp one night, and take the General's family captive. Thereupon negociations were opened, to be followed shortly by a peace, and Assud Khan returned to Bijapur.

Assud Khan was now the principal man in Bijapur, and as always occurs, his power and influence excited considerable envy and jealousy. For some time the Sultan refused to allow his mind to be poisoned with stories against his Minister. After a time, however, they prevailed, and Ibrahim Shah sent for Assud Khan, intending on his arrival to put him to death. The plot, however, had been overheard, and Assud Khan, forewarned, retired to Belgaum, where he was too strong for even the Sultan to attack him. Various intrigues were then set on foot in order to gain possession of the too-powerful Minister, and one Yusuf was granted a jaghir near Belgaum for the express purpose of enabling him to carry out a surprise. This, indeed, he attempted, but was beaten off with disgrace.

A disagreement of this kind was an opportunity which the ever-watchful and jealous neighbouring States were not likely to let pass. Accordingly, giving out that Assud Khan was prepared to join them, Nizam Shah and Ameer Bereed invaded the Bijapur territories, and after investing the Sholapur districts, marched upon Belgaum. Assud Khan was now placed in a very awkward position. The invading princes appear to have used his name without authority, but if he refused to act with them, they were in a position to compel him or to annex his jaghirs. Accordingly, he temporized, and although he joined the enemy's camp, he wrote to Imad Shah of Berar begging him to come to the assistance of Bijapur. This Imad Shah at once did, when Assud Khan joined him, and represented to him the whole of the circumstances that had brought about this crisis. Imad Shah then took Assud Khan before Ibrahim, who, on being convinced of his loyalty, at once received him with favour. This at once changed the aspect of affairs, and the invaders had to retreat. Ibrahim followed them well into their own territories, and Ameer Bereed, dying on the road, Nizam Shah had to sue for peace. This was granted on condition of restoring the five districts of Sholapore, and promising not to again invade the Bijapur dominions (1542). This peace, however, did not last long, for in the following year Nizam Shah made an alliance with Ali Bereed, who had succeeded his father Ameer, Kutb Shah of Golconda, and Rama Rajah of Vijayanagar. These princes all entered Bijapur territory by three different routes—Nizam Shah by Sholapore, Kutb Shah by Gulburga, and Rama Rajah by the usual bone of contention, Raichore. Ibrahim Shah, at a loss how to meet these three invasions, sent for Assud Khan, whose advice was that Nizam Shah being at the bottom of the confederacy he should be pacified first. Rama Rajah could be bought off by concessions and promises, and then Kutb Shah could be dealt with alone. As Ibrahim was unable to meet the combination in the field, this appears to have been the best advice possible. Nizam Shah professed himself satisfied by the restoration of the Sholapore district, and Rama Rajah was bought off by some small concessions. Assud Khan then marched against Jumsheed Kutb Shah, recovered from him Gulburga and its districts, and then followed him up to the walls of Golconda, within which he compelled him to take shelter after defeating his army and wounding the King in an engagement. Assud Khan then returned to Bijapur, where he was received with great distinction. In a short time, however, the war broke out afresh, Nizam Shah being again the agressor. This time the attempt was upon Gulburga, but the invading force was met by Ibrahim Shah on the banks of the Bhimrah, and defeated with great loss. Ibrahim Shah fought personally in this battle with great gallantry, but the credit for the victory was due, and was given, to Assud Khan. This victory appears to have turned Ibrahim's head, and he behaved with such arrogance to the ambassadors of Nizam Shah, that they retired in disgust, and the war broke out afresh. This time, fortune was against Ibrahim, and his armies were twice defeated in the space of six months. Ibrahim attributing these defeats to the disaffection of his Hindoo officials, caused a number of them to be put to death, and others to be tortured in the public square. This cruelty excited general disgust. Assud Khan retired to Belgaum, and a conspiracy was formed to depose Ibrahim and place his brother, Abdulla, on the throne. The conspiracy was discovered, and Abdulla went to Goa, where he was sheltered by the Portuguese, and there commenced a correspondence with Nizam Shah and Kutb Shah. An attempt was made to gain Assud Khan over to this conspiracy, but though he was again in disfavour with the suspicious Sultan, this loyal old veteran refused the proposal with indignation. But Assud Khan's name was one to conjure with, so high was the general feeling of affection and confidence. He himself was sick, but the Portuguese, after having proclaimed Abdulla, marched with him towards Bijapur, and giving out that Assud Khan was on their side, induced a number of the disaffected nobles to join their army. Nizam Shah hearing of Assud Khan's illness at once marched upon Belgaum hoping in case of his death to secure this important fortress. On his arrival Assud Khan was somewhat better, and Nizam Shah then attempted to win the garrison by bribery. For this purpose he sent a Brahmin as his emissary, who had nearly succeeded, when the plot was discovered by Assud Khan, who at once put the Brahmin and seventy of the soldiers he had corrupted to death. This act showed clearly that Assud Khan was still loyal, and on hearing of it, the Bijapur nobles at once forsook Abdulla. The Goanese, disappointed of a junction with Nizam Shah, had now to retire, and Nizam Shah deserted by his allies, had also to return to his country. In the mean time, Assud Khan was really dying. The man who had so often saved the State when alive had rendered it a final service on his death-bed, for if, as had been originally intended, Nizam Shah had effected a junction with the Portuguese, Bijapur must have fallen, and Abdulla been placed upon the throne. The whole incident is especially worthy of record, because it is the first occasion in which we find a European nation taking an active share in the intrigues of a Native State, a policy which has had such successful results in subsequent years. When Assud Khan felt that his end was approaching, he sent a message to his master, Ibrahim, whom he had served so well, but who had so often requited his services with ingratitude. The Sultan at once set off for Belgaum, but arrived too late. All that he could do was to comfort the mourning family with *khilats* and assurances of royal favour, but this comfort must have been of a nature not altogether gratifying, for we are told that the Sultan took the opportunity of annexing all his deceased servant's treasures and estates for his own use.

Assud Khan had for nearly forty years been one of the most prominent characters in the Deccan. He was universally respected not only for his military talents, but also for his judgment and wisdom. He lived with a magnificence that was almost royal, and his household servants alone numbered more than two hundred and fifty persons. In his stables were sixty elephants of the largest, and one hundred and fifty of a smaller size, besides four hundred Arab and Persian horses, in addition to a number of country-breds. In his kitchen there was consumed each day one hundred maunds (8,000lbs.) of rice, fifty sheep, and one hundred fowls and other provisions in proportion. The treasures and jewels which he left are said to have been of immense value, and in this respect he formed a striking contrast to that other great nobleman, Khajeh Gawan, who, under the Bahmanee Sultans, may well be compared with him.

No sooner was this war terminated than another broke out. In accordance with Assud Khan's last wish, Sultan Ibrahim made an alliance with, and gave his daughter in marriage to, Ali Bereed, of Ahmedabad Bieder. This at once excited the jealousy of Nizam Shah, who thereupon made an alliance with Rama Rajah of Vijayanagar, who recommended him to attack Kallean, a fortress belonging to Bereed. Ibrahim marched to assist his son-in-law, but suffered a severe defeat, and the fort was taken by Nizam Shah. Ibrahim, compelled to retire, made a diversion into the enemy's country towards the west. He devastated a considerable amount of country, and succeeded in surprising Porundeh, a fort which subsequently became very famous as Sivajee's favourite stronghold. Here he left a garrison, which surrendered without a struggle as soon as Nizam Shah advanced to retake this important post. Next year (1551) the war recommenced. As usual, the Vijayanagar army commenced operations by besieging Raichore and Mudkul. The Hindoo Prince then marched to join Nizam Shah, and the two armies took Sholapore without much trouble.

In 1553 Boorahan Nizam Shah died, and his successor, Hoosein Nizam Shah, made peace with Bijapur, which, however, did not last long. Hoosein Shah having degraded his father's Commander-in-Chief, Khajeh Jehan, the latter escaped to Bijapur, together with a younger brother of the Sultan. It did not require much persuasion on the part of these refugees to induce Ibrahim Shah to support the claims of this pretender, especially as the fort of Sholapore was held out to him as a bait. He at once proclaimed Shah Ali (for this was his name) Sultan of Ahmednagar, and marched with an army to take possession of Sholapore. Here he was met by Hoosein Nizam Shah, and an engagement ensued, in which Ibrahim Shah was worsted. The defeat appears to have occurred through a mistake. His General, Seyf Eyn-ul-Mulk, had in reality broken the enemy's centre, but was left unsupported. Ibrahim Shah being told that he had gone over to the enemy, made a precipitate retreat, leaving his General in the lurch. The latter managed to cut his way through the enemy's ranks, and followed his master, who, however, received him at Bijapur with such disfavour that the General retired to his own estates. Ibrahim sent an army after him but it was defeated, and another and stronger force met with the same fate. Eyn-ul-Mulk now asserted his independence, and so dangerous did matters look, that Ibrahim Shah had to march against him in person with the whole force that he could raise. The Sultan, however, fared no better than his generals, and was severely defeated with the loss of his baggage and royal paraphernalia. Ibrahim himself escaped and fled in haste to Bijapur, which was at once invested by the rebel. In this last extremity, Ibrahim applied to Rama Rajah of Vijayanagar for assistance. The Hindoo King at once complied, and sent his brother Venkatadri with a large army. The Hindoo General, by a clever night attack, succeeded in surprising Eyn-ul-Mulk's camp, and put the whole of the army to the sword, the rebel himself just managing to escape with two hundred followers. Eyn-ul-Mulk fled to Ahmednagar, where, however, he was assassinated by order of the Sultan (1551).

Ibrahim Shah, thus saved by the Hindoos, gave himself up to debauchery, and very soon fell ill. He called in a number of doctors, but as they were not able to cure him, he put them to death, beheading some and having others trodden to death by elephants.

As might be expected, this treatment was not calculated to encourage the rest, who left his court in a body. The Sultan, left without medical aid, was equally unable to cure himself, and died in 1557 after a reign of twenty-four years.

Ibrahim Adil Shah was a passionate and headstrong man. As long as Assud Khan was his chief adviser, his reign was a prosperous one, but after he had quarrelled with him, and especially after Assud Khan's death, he degenerated into a licentious tyrant. Although constantly at war, he seems to have had little or no military talents, and all his successes were due to his Generals. When left to himself, he seems generally to have been defeated. The frequent manner in which both he and his rival Sultans appealed to Rama Rajah for assistance shows how rapidly the Hindoo kingdom had been growing in importance. Whilst the Mahomedan States, like Kilkenny cats, were destroying each other, the Hindoos were rapidly becoming the arbiters of the Deccan. During Ibrahim Shah's reign several important changes were made, which were destined to prove of importance in Deccan history. These were the employment of Brahmins and Hindoos in the Revenue and Accounts Departments, the use of the Vernacular in the preparation of accounts, and the enlistment of *Bergees* or Mahratta soldiers in the army. In Ahmednagar, the Nizam Shahs adopted the same policy, and the Sultan even appointed a Brahmin Minister with the title of *Peshwa*, the origin of the title which was subsequently to become so famous. The *Bergees* were enlisted from among the Mahratta villagers, almost all of which were situated in either Bijapur or Ahmednagar territories. They were mercenaries, and replaced the old Silladarees, who provided their own horses, and ranked more as gentlemen soldiers than as ordinary rank and file. These Mahratta troops, which in

Bijapur numbered as many as 30,000, introduced an entirely new system of warfare, which was subsequently brought to perfection by the great Sivajee. This system consisted in eluding the enemy as much as possible, and in harrassing him in every way, whilst on the line of march; cutting off supplies; night surprises and a general harrying of the country in front of the enemy. This led to a desultory predatory kind of warfare, in which the country and the cultivators suffered more than the armies. The change of the State religion, to which allusion has been made, did not have any political results. As a matter of fact, the Bijapur Sultans seem to have belonged alternately to the Sheeah and the Sunnee sects. Ibrahim Shah's son and successor at once reverted to the Sheeah, and his successors belonged sometimes to the one, and sometimes to the other sect. The only effect of this was to bring about a spirit of tolerance, not only towards each other, but also towards the Hindoos.

GENEALOGY OF THE IMAD SHAHI DYNASTY.

(Berar — Capital Ellichpore and Burhanpore).

---

1. **FATHULLAH IMAD SHAH BAHMANI**
(a Hindoo boy captured by the Bahmani
King in a war with Vijayanagar and
turned Mahomedan. Revolted.
1483—1504.

2. **ALLA UD DIN IMAD SHAH**
1504—1528

3. **DARIYA IMAD SHAH**
1528—1560

4. BURHAN IMAD SHAH 1560—1568	BIBI DOULAT married HUSSAIN King of Ahmednagar.

(N.B. In BURHAN'S reign TUFAL KHAN seized the throne but was killed by MURTAZA NIZAM SHAH of Ahmednagar and Kingdom annexed.

CHAPTER XVII.

THE FALL OF VIJAYANAGAR.

In the year 1560, the Vijayanagar Kingdom was at the height of its splendour. Rama Rajah had subdued all his rebellious chiefs, and ruled without dispute from the Kistna to Cape Comorin. He had gradually extended his sway up to the mouths of the Godavery, was in alliance with the Hindoo Rajahs, who still maintained their independence north of that river, and was married to the daughter of the King of Orissa. In Madura, the ruler of the whole of the south was a Deputy of Vijayanagar. In Taylor's "Oriental Manuscripts" there is an interesting account of the manner in which Visvanatha Naick, a General of the Hindoo King, reduced his own father who had assumed independence in Madura to obedience. The date of this transaction is fixed at A.D. 1432, or about one hundred years after the founding of Vijayanagar. Even at this time the Vijayanagar Rajah's rule is said to have extended over "fifty-six kingdoms, and he entertained in his service forty thousand cavalry, four thousand elephants, and ten thousand camels," and foot soldiers innumerable. The kingdom was bounded on the east and west by the sea, though the ports on the Western Coast were limited to those between Goa to the north and Calicut to the south. The only portion of the Southern Peninsula which did not acknowledge the sovereignty of Vijayanagar appears to have been that portion of the Western Coast in which the kingdoms of Cochin and Travancore are now situated. The whole of this enormous territory was sub-divided amongst minor Rajahs and petty Chiefs, all of whom paid tribute, and rendered feudal service to their over-lord. From time to time they occasionally asserted their independence or turned refractory, but they were generally reduced without much difficulty. The country was watered by several magnificent rivers, the Kistna, the Pennair, the Poniar, and the Cauvery. The mountains in Mysore and Travancore formed vast forests, which were full of wild elephants; the valleys were rich and fertile, and there runs throughout the whole extent from north to south a belt of gold-bearing quartz which must have been extensively worked. From a country so rich in natural resources the Kings derived an enormous revenue. We have already given extracts from the accounts of some of the travellers who visited Vijayanagar in the early part of the 15th century, all of whom speak in enthusiastic terms of the splendour and riches of the capital. An immense amount of the gold and silver was melted into solid masses, and buried in cellars under the King's palace. But though fond of accumulating gold and jewels, the Hindoo Kings were always liberal in their expenditure on agricultural and irrigation works. The rivers were all dammed at different parts, and irrigation channels dug to the rice fields, and where no rivers existed, the whole face of the country was covered with a network of irrigation tanks and reservoirs, some of enormous size, covering many square miles in extent. At the beginning of this century, when Sir Thomas (then Captain) Munro was appointed to settle the Districts which had just been ceded after the Mysore War, he thus describes the country which is situated around the capital, Vijayanagar (the present districts of Bellary, Anantapoor, Cuddapah, and Kurnool):—"To attempt the construction of new tanks is perhaps a more hopeless experiment than the repair of those which have been filled up, *for there is scarcely any place where a tank can be made to advantage that has not already been applied to this purpose by the inhabitants*" (*Cuddapah Manual*, page 10). In the sub-division of the Cuddapah District, where the author was for some years the Principal Revenue Officer, there were in an area of 3,574 square miles no less than 4,194 tanks of various sizes. All these public works were built and maintained by an ingenious revenue system, under which none of the cost of maintenance was borne by the Government, and only in the case of the larger works, the cost of construction. Under this system called *Dasbandham* a portion of the land irrigated was allotted rent-free on condition of the grantee keeping the tank in repair, and in many cases of constructing it. The remainder of the land paid the usual rent to Government, and in this manner the Government whilst improving the country, added to its own revenues with but little additional expenditure.

Politically speaking, the importance of Vijayanagar had increased in the same way as its prosperity had done. During the time of the Bahmanee Kings, although there were numerous wars, the boundary of the Tungabadhra or the Kistna was rarely over-stepped by either side. The fighting was almost entirely confined to the country lying between these two rivers, known as the Doab. With the ruin of the Bahmanee dynasty and the constant quarrels of the Mahomedan Kings, who established themselves in its place, the importance of Vijayanagar rapidly increased. The Doab became virtually Vijayanagar territory, and though the forts of Raichore and Mudkul were frequently retaken by the Bijapur Kings, they were not held for long. In course of time Rama Rajah assumed the aggressive, and we find him being called in, first on one side, and then on the other, and occasionally being subsidized by both. The reason why the Hindoo Kings had been able for so long to more than hold their own against the Mahomedans, in spite of the greater bravery and discipline of the latter, seems to have been their enormous recuperative power. Having so vast a population under their rule, they were, after each defeat, able to bring new hordes into the field, so that by mere force of numbers they were able to compel the Mahomedans to retire. The time, however, had now come for the final blow which was to crush Vijayanagar for ever, and we will now narrate the incidents that led up to it.

When Ibrahim Adil Shah died in 1557, Hussein Nizam Shah was ruling in Ahmednagar. He at once took advantage of the confusion attendant upon a new accession to invade the Bijapur territory, which he did in conjunction with Kutb Shah, who, however, soon deserted him, and he had to retire within his own dominions. Ali Adil Shah, who had succeeded his father Ibrahim, at once resolved to revenge the unprovoked attack, and at the same time endeavoured to regain Sholapore and Kallean. For this purpose he formed an alliance with Rama Rajah and Kutb Shah, whilst Hussein Shah made overtures to Imad Shah of Berar, and strengthened the alliance by giving the latter his daughter in marriage. A proof of the value which was attached to the friendship of Rama Rajah is to be found in the unusual step which Ali Adil Shah took in order to gain his alliance. A son of Rama Rajah happening at this time to die, the Sultan, accompanied by only one hundred followers, went all the way to Vijayanagar to pay the Rajah a visit of condolence. He was hospitably received, and Ferishta says that the wife of Rama Rajah adopted Ali Adil Shah as her son, in order to cement the friendship between the two Kings.

But this visit instead of strengthening the friendship was, in reality, the cause of its dissolution. Rama Rajah, who was now an old man of over ninety years of age, displayed a considerable amount of arrogance, and made Adil Shah feel that he was a suppliant. The author, from whom we have so often quoted, says that, when leaving the city, Rama Rajah did not accompany the Sultan, and that this affront rankled in his mind, though he did not consider it prudent to show any signs of dissatisfaction at the time. It will be remembered that a similar want of respect excited the anger of Feroze Shah Bahmanee, when he paid a visit to Deva Rajah, one hundred and fifty years previously. The local tradition adds another reason why Adil Shah bore a grudge against Rama Rajah. It is said that they were riding together through the city, and the Sultan seeing a number of pigs, observed to the Rajah that he could not understand how Hindoos could eat the flesh of such uncleanly animals. The Rajah is said to have replied: "You Mahomedans eat fowls, do you not?" Of course the answer was in the affirmative. "Well," said the Rajah, "fowls pick their food from out of the dung of the swine, so that they must be even more uncleanly than the pigs which you despise." This the Sultan treasured up as an insult to his religion, and resolved to avenge it when the opportunity should come.

In 1558, the war which had been delayed by negociations broke out, since Nizam Shah indignantly refused to restore Sholapore. Rama Rajah, true to his promise, assisted Adil Shah with a large army, and Kutb Shah, who had at first promised to join Nizam Shah, speedily forsook him for the other side. This combination was too strong for Nizam Shah to withstand. The whole of his territory was laid waste and ravaged, and he himself was shut up in his capital, Ahmednagar. Here the Hindoo allies committed all kinds of excesses, mosques were desecrated, and Syeds and holy men slaughtered, whilst their wives and daughters were deflowered. All this excited the indignation of the Mahomedan princes, but what probably inflamed them still more was the pride and arrogance of Rama Rajah himself. He would not allow them to be seated in his presence, and made them to walk in his train, until he gave them permission to mount. At the close of the war, he compelled both Kutb Shah and Adil Shah to give up certain districts as the price of his assistance. In this way Kutb Shah gave up Kovilkondah, Bankul, and Kunbore, whilst Adil Shah had to resign Outingpur and Bakrukobe.

This termination of the war filled Adil Shah with disgust. He had gained nothing for himself, for Sholapore had not been taken, and Ahmednagar had managed to hold out, but, on the other hand, he had been made to resign two districts, and had been disgraced and dishonoured in the eyes of his co-religionists.

He is said to have been a man of considerable intelligence, and, if so, his eyes cannot but have been opened to the inevitable consequences of the growing power of Vijayanagar in the face of the suicidal quarrels of the Mahomedan Kings. Accordingly, he conceived the idea of a league of the Mahomedan Kings with which to crush the rival, who was now overshadowing them all. The first prince to whom the idea was revealed was Ibrahim Kutb Shah, of Golconda. He at

once signified his consent, and offered his services as a
mediator to obtain not only the alliance of Nizam Shah, of
Ahmednagar, but also the restoration to Adil Shah of the fort
of Sholapore. In order to effect this design, he despatched
Mustafa Khan, one of the most intelligent of his nobles, to
Bijapur. Adil Shah, proving himself to be thoroughly in
earnest, the ambassador, went on to Ahmednagar, and after a
negociation lasting for some days, an arrangement was made.
Hussein Nizam Shah agreed to give to Ali Adil Shah, Chund
Bibi, his daughter, as wife, and with her the fort of Sholapore
as a dowry. In return, Adil Shah was to give his daughter
to Nizam Shah's eldest son, Sultan Murtiza. This double-
marriage was carried out with great pomp, and the mutual
treaties having been solemnly ratified, the two princesses started
on the same day from their respective homes, in order to join
their husbands. In Chund Bibi Adil Shah gained a prize
infinitely more valuable than the fort of Sholapore. The
history of the world has preserved the memory of many
Queens, who have also been heroines, and Chund Bibi deserves
to take a place in the foremost of their ranks. Tradition in
the Deccan still honours her, and more recently the story of
her life has been told in enthusiastic terms by Colonel Meadows
Taylor. The holy league being thus formed, was also joined
by Bereed Shah of Bieder. The Sultan of Berar does not
seem to have been invited, and took no part in it. In the
year 1564 the four princes met in the plains of Bijapur and
then marched to Tellicotta, on the Bijapur bank of the Kistna.
Though the preparations for this undertaking must have
lasted some time. Rama Rajah seems to have at first treated
it with contempt. But when convinced of the fact of the
alliance, he despatched his younger brother, Timma Rajah,
with a large army, said to have consisted of one hundred
thousand foot, twenty thousand horse, and five hundred
elephant, to guard the passages of the Kistna. His second

brother, Venkatadri, he sent with another large army as reserve, and himself followed with the whole of the rest of his forces The allied armies by a series of clever feints managed to draw the Hindoos away from the only practicable ford, after which, returning by a forced march they succeeded in crossing the river without opposition, and then drew up their forces in order of battle. Hussein Nizam Shah, as was due to his age, took the lead, and commanded the centre; Ali Adil Shah commanded the right, and Kutb Shah with Bereed Shah the left wing. The artillery was fastened together by chains, and drawn up in front of the line, flanked on each side by the war elephants. Ferishta, who doubtless heard an account of the battle from eye-witnesses, gives a very graphic account of it, which we cannot do better than reproduce:—"Rama Rajah entrusted his left to his brother Eeltum (Timma?) Rajah, and his right to his other brother, Venkatadri, against Ali Adil Shah, while he himself commanded in the centre. Two thousand war elephants and one thousand pieces of cannon were placed at different intervals of his line. About twelve o'clock in the day, Rama Rajah mounted a litter in spite of the remonstrances of his officers, who wished him to be on horseback, as much safer; but he said there was no occasion for taking precautions against children who would certainly fly at the first charge. Both armies being in motion, soon came to battle, and the infidels begun the attack by vast flights of rockets and rapid discharges of artillery which did not discourage the allies. A general action took place, and many were slain on both sides. Rama Rajah, finding a different behaviour in the enemy from what he had expected, descended from his litter, and seating himself upon a rich throne set with jewels, under a canopy of crimson velvet, embroidered with gold and adorned with fringes of pearls, ordered his treasurer to place heaps of money all round him, that he might confer rewards on such of his followers, as

13

deserved his attention. There were also rich ornaments of gold and jewels for the same purpose. The infidels, inspired by the generosity of their prince, charged the right and left of the allies with such vigour, that they were thrown into disorder; and Ali Adil Shah and Kutb Shah began to despair of victory, and prepare for retreat. Hussein Nizam Shah remained firm in the centre, and pushed so vigorously, that of Rama Rajah, that it began to be confused; upon which the Rajah again mounted his litter, which was soon after let fall by the bearers upon the approach of a furious elephant belonging to Nizam Shah, and before he had time to recover himself and mount a horse, a body of the allies took him prisoner, and conducted him to Chela Roomi, who commanded the artillery. He carried him to Nizam Shah, who ordered instantly his head to be struck off and placed upon the point of a long spear, so that his death might be proclaimed to the enemy. The Hindoos, according to custom, when they saw their chief destroyed, fled in the utmost confusion and disorder from the field of battle, and were pursued by the allies with such successful slaughter that the river which ran near the field of battle was dyed red with their blood. It is computed by the best authorities that one hundred thousand infidels were slain in the fight, or during the pursuit. The plunder was so great that every private man in the allied army became rich in gold, jewels, effects, tents, arms, horses, and slaves, as the Sultans left every person in possession of what he had acquired, only taking a few elephants for their own use. *Firmans*, with accounts of this very important victory, were despatched to their several dominions, and the Sultans after the battle marched onwards into the country of Rama Rajah as far as Anagoondy, and the advanced troops penetrated to Vijayanagar, which they plundered, razed the chief buildings, and committed all kinds of excess." (*Scott's Translation*.) The Portuguese historian Faria-y-Suza (Kerr

VI., 422) writes:—"The trade of India in 1566 was reduced to a very low ebb by the desolating war between Vijayanagar and the Mahomedan Kings of the Deccan. The Vijayanagar King, who was then ninety-six years of age, was at first successful, but in the end was defeated and slain. The Mahomedans spent five months in plundering Vijayanagar, although the natives had previously carried away 1,550 elephant loads of money and jewels with above a hundred millions of gold, besides the royal chair, which was of inestimable value. In his share of the plunder Adil Shah, got a diamond, as large as an ordinary egg and another of extraordinary size, though smaller, together with other jewels of inestimable value." The temples which still remain almost all show traces of this search for plunder, and every hole and corner seems to have been ransacked. Two years afterwards, the city was visited by the Venetian traveller, Caêsar Fredericke. He speaks of the houses as still standing, but in parts of the city there were nothing but tigers and wild animals. Timma Rajah, brother of Rama Rajah, had then come back, and was endeavouring to re-people the city. In this, however, he never succeeded, and he also had to retire further south.

The battle of Tellicotta was a crushing blow to the Hindoo rule of South India. The representatives of the old reigning family withdrew first to Penna Konda, and then to Chandragiri in the North Arcot District, which remained the capital for more than two hundred years. But the country attached to this portion of the Hindoo family was very small in extent. After the defeat of Rama Rajah, all the vassal Rajahs asserted their own independence. Mysore, Madura, and Tanjore formed themselves into independent States, and the country round Vijayanagar was parcelled amongst petty chieftains and zemindars. If anything, the fall of Vijayanagar was a loss rather than a gain to the Mahomedan States. For some time to come the mutual jealousy which existed amongst the Sultans prevented them from allowing the one or the other to extend his dominions. It is true that subsequently both Golconda and Bijapur did annex considerable tracts of the Vijayanagar territory, but they did not benefit to anything like the extent we should have imagined after such an utter collapse. Again, the near presence of a powerful Hindoo Kingdom compelled the Sultans to be always in a state of preparedness for war. This check removed, they seem to have reduced their armies, and to have spent their strength in perpetual struggles between each other, thus making it easier for them, subsequently, to fall victims to the Emperor of Delhi. Rama Rajah, the last of the Vijayanagar Kings, seems to have been a man of very considerable ability and force of character. A passage from the writer above mentioned, Cæsar Fredericke throws some light upon the disputed question, as to whether he was a usurper or a descendant of the Second or Nursimha dynasty, He says that Rama Rajah and his two brothers, Timma and Venkatadri, had been captains of Krishna Deva Rajah (1509—30), and that on his death they assumed the power, and kept his son, an infant, named Sadashiva Rajah, in prison, showing him to the people once a year. This explains the reason of the rebellion of Hojè Perumal Rajah alluded to before (1535). He took advantage of Rama Rajah's absence to kill the young King, and to seat himself on the throne. The manner of his death has been narrated. When this occurred, Rama Rajah, who had married Krishna Deva's daughter (see Sewell's Tables, "Antiquities of South India," Vol. II., 248), would be the next representative of the family. There seems to be little doubt that if the battle of Tellicotta had ended differently, Rama Rajah would have crushed the Mahomedan States. The struggle to them was one for very existence. Rama Rajah's arrogance in his later years shows to what an extent he had asserted his supremacy over the Mahomedan Kings, and his final disaster seems to have been partly due to the contempt in which he held them. It is clear that he must have been a man of extraordinary energy and bodily power to have taken a leading part in the battle, at so advanced an age. As already stated, a descendant of the last Vijayanagar dynasty still lives at Anagoondy, close by the ruins of the old city.

GENEALOGY OF THE VIJAYANAGAR KINGS.

First dynasty

BUKKA
|
SANGAMMA

1. HARIHARA I   2. BUKKA
A-D. 1336—50   1350—79

         3. HARIHARA II
         1379—1401

         4. DEVA RAJAH I
         1401—1412

         5. VIJAYA BHUPATI
         1418

         6. DEVA RAJAH II
         —1447

         7. VIRU'PAKSHA

Second dynasty.

     1. NARASIMHA
        1487(?)—1509

     2. KRISHNA DEVA RAJAH   *Third dynasty*
        1509—1530

daughter TIRUMA LAMBA =   RAMA RAJAH
                                       1530—1564
                                       Killed at | Tellikotta

(*Taken from Sewell's tables*).

CHAPTER XVIII.

AHMEDNAGAR AND BIJAPUR FROM THE FALL OF VIJAYANAGAR TILL THE DEATH OF ALI ADIL SHAH (1580).

It was not long after the fall of Vijayanagar that dissensions again broke out between the Mahomedan Kings of the Deccan. Shortly after his return to Ahmednagar Hussein Nizam Shah died, and was succeeded by his son, Murtaza (1565—1588), who is known by the name of the Madman. For the first few years of his reign, Murtaza was a minor, and the regency was conducted by his mother, Khunza Sultana. Ibrahim Adil Shah, taking advantage of Murtaza's infancy, led an army against Venkatadri, Rama Rajah's brother, in the hope of annexing more of the Vijayanagar territory. Venkatadri appealed to Ahmednagar for help, and, true to the old Deccan policy of preventing any one of the roial Kings from becoming too powerful, the Queen Regent sent an army to assist Venkatadri, and the Bijapur troops were compelled to retire. Peace was then concluded, and a stipulation made that neither of the Mahomedan Kings should conquer any of the Hindoo territory without mutual consent. The two Mahomedan armies then coalesced and marched against Berar, where Tufal Khan, the Prime Minister, had usurped the authority. The combined armies, after having ravaged the country, marched back to Ahmednagar, where Ali Adil Shah, the Bijapur King, attempted to surprise the young Sultan Murtaza. Khunza Sultana, however, was warned in time, and managed to escape at night with her son and the Bijapur King returned to his capital *re infectá*. For the next three years continual fighting took place between Ahmednagar and Bijapur with varying success, until at last, in 1569, Kishwar Khan, the Bijapur General, invaded the Ahmednagar territory with a large army. The Queen Regent, with the young Sultan, marched to oppose this invasion, but whilst in camp, Murtaza, having gained over some of his nobles, suddenly asserted his own independence, took his mother prisoner, and having sent her away, placed himself at the head of the army. He then laid siege to the fort of Dharur, which he carried by assault, the Bijapur General being killed by an arrow in the heart. In this war Murtaza was assisted by Kutb Shah of Golconda, and the two Sultans then prepared to attack Bijapur. Dissensions however, soon arose between them, and on Murtaza attempting to seize the person of Kutb Shah, the latter made his escape, but had to leave his camp behind, which was plundered by the Nizam Shahis. Murtaza then concluded peace with Ali Adil Shah, and returned to Ahmednagar. In the following year an attack was made by the Ahmednagar troops upon the Portuguese fort of Revdanda, which, however, proved a failure, the General, according to Ferishta, having been bought off by large presents, especially of Spanish wine. After this repulse Murtaza appointed Chengiz Khan to be his Minister and he succeeded in effecting several reforms. Chengiz Khan seems to have been a man of considerable ability, and he soon saw that the jealous policy pursued by the Deccan Kings was likely to bring about their own ruin. Accordingly, he formed a treaty with Ali Adil Shah of Bijapur, under the terms of which the latter was to be allowed to conquer as much of the Vijayanagar country as he could, whilst Ahmednagar was to be at liberty to annex Berar (1572). Sultan Kutb Shah of Golconda was not a party to this treaty, but he, on his part, was employed in extending his dominions towards the Eastern Coast, and in subduing the Hindoo Rajahs towards the mouth of the Godavery. Ali Adil Shah being thus free, at once attacked the strong fort of Adoni, which up to that time had been considered impregnable. Adoni was defended by eleven strong walls, and the citadel is situated on the top of a hill. It had long been used by the Hindoo kings as a place of safe refuge. As it seemed impossible to carry the fort by storm, it was closely invested, and at length yielded to hunger. Flushed with this success, Ali Adil Shah penetrated further into the Carnatic, and took several forts, and amongst them Darwer, which was held to be one of the strongest forts in the Carnatic. Binkapore also fell to his arms, together with Gandikota, on the right bank of the Pennair river, in the present district of Cuddapah. This fort is also one of considerable importance, and later on when it belonged to Golconda, it was still more strongly fortified by the celebrated Mir Jumla. It is situated on the top of a hill just at the entrance of the gorge, through which the Pennair rushes. This gorge is very narrow, and the sides of the hills are almost perpendicular. The name itself signifies the fort of the gorge (Gandi-gorge; Kota-fort), and it was for many years held to be of considerable importance. It was here, a hundred years later, that the European traveller, Tavernier, had an interview with Mir Jumla.

Whilst the Bijapur King was thus successfully extending his conquest into the Carnatic, Murtaza Shah had turned his arms against Berar, where Tufal Khan was still at the head of the Government, and kept the person of the young King, Imad Shah, in confinement. He was soon driven from Ellichpur, and for some months wandered about together with the young Sultan, from place to place. He applied to Khandeish for assistance and shelter, but the King refused both, for fear of the vengeance of Murtaza Nizam Shah. At last Tufal Khan applied to the Emperor Akbar for help, and a letter was written to Murtaza Shah ordering him to desist. It is, however, a far cry from Berar to Delhi, and Murtaza took no notice of the command, the authority of which he did not recognize. Soon afterwards Tufal Khan and the young Sultan fell into Murtaza's hands, and whilst in confinement both died, it is said, by poison. But though Murtaza had thus met with a temporary success, his neglect of the Imperial command brought him into contact with another power which was destined ere long to overshadow, not only Ahmednagar, but the whole of the Deccan. Akbar, stung at the slight offered to his letter, as soon as he heard of the death of Tufal Khan and of the last of the Imad Shah Sultans, resolved to take an active part in Deccan affairs, and for that purpose began to march towards Berar with an army of observation (1576). The ostensible reason assigned was hunting, but the real reason was to gain a footing to the south of the Vindhyas. Murtaza Shah had, moreover, allowed himself to become jealous of the power of Chengiz Khan, his Minister. It was whispered to him that Chengiz Khan contemplated assuming royal honours in Berar, and, when later on, the Minister suggested to the Sultan that he should be left there with an army to defend the recent conquest from attacks, either on the part of Khandeish or Delhi, the Sultan deemed this to be a confirmation of the accusation. He accordingly ordered the Minister's physician to give him a dose of poison in his medicine. Chengiz Khan when told of the order, at once submitted. He protested his innocence of any rebellious intentions, and swallowed the fatal draught, after leaving a message to the King that his body should be sent to Kerbela.*

After his death, the King found out his mistake, but it was too late, and Murtaza retired in disgust to his capital, where, for some time, he shut himself up in his palace. During this time his favourite, named Sahib Khan, with a

---

* Ferishta (Scott's Translation) gives the latter in full. It ran as follows:—"The faithful servant, Meeruk, the sun of whose age has passed through sixty mansions, and was hastening to the seventieth, having laid the head of submission on the threshold of your Majesty, represents that the draught mixed with the water of life, he has knowingly drunk, and with eager desire. Having placed the treasures of duty and loyalty to the Sultan by whose bounty I was cherished in the casket of my bosom, I shut my eyes from the observance of strangers. As lasting as the grave may well be to me, so be the life of your Majesty. I hope this much from the Sultan, that, esteeming me, both in life and death, among the number of loyal servants, he will act according to the maxims I send by my own hand; that he will send my body to Kerbela; that he will esteem certain Amrahs named in the petition, as worthy of distinction, and entertain my foreign servants among his own guards." The murder of Chengiz Khan is another example of the inveterate feud between the Deccanees and the foreigners. As soon as a foreign Mahomedan by his ability and honesty raised himself above the heads of the Deccanee nobles, he was the object of their relentless hatred. The most faithful services were not able to overcome the suspicion which they were able to instill in the minds of the Sultan, and we constantly find the King himself ordering the death of his most devoted servants, to discover when, too late, that they had been unjustly accused.

band of depraved associates, committed all kinds of excesses in the city, not scrupling to seize the daughters and even the sons of noblemen for the vilest purposes. One nobleman of ancient family was even killed, whilst protecting the honour of his daughter, and another was ordered to change his name, because it happened to be the same as that of the insolent favourite. The Sultan himself seems to have been half-insane. On one occasion he left his palace alone, and made his way towards the tomb of the Saint Imam Reza. He was, however, recognized by a country-man, and persuaded to return. The indignation in the city at the insolent behaviour of the favourite, Sahib Khan, was so great, that he found it necessary to escape, but the Sultan followed and overtook him, and induced him to return. Salabat Khan, destined to be one of the best of the Ahmednagar Ministers, was the representative of the nobleman as against Sahib Khan, but for the time he had to retire from Court. The Sultan, in order to please his favourite, now made an unprovoked attack upon Bieder, where Ali Bereed was ruling. The malcontents in Ahmednagar took advantage of this absence to proclaim the Sultan's brother, Boorahan Shah, and Murtaza had to return in haste to his capital to suppress the rebellion. In this extremity, the Sultan had to send again for Salabat Khan, who insisted upon the favourite being dismissed. This was done, and a body of troops were sent with him as an escort, but instead of defending him, they murdered him on the way. Salabat Khan succeeded in quelling the revolt without difficulty, and Boorahan Shah fled to Bijapur, where he was kindly received by Ali Adil Shah. Salabat Khan now became Minister of Ahmednagar, and ruled the country well for several years. Ferishta says:—"The country of Mheerut was never so well governed as by him, since the reign of Sultan Mahmoud Bahmanee."

For the time the threatened interference of Akbar was

averted. Either he thought the time had not yet come, or that his army was not strong enough. At all events he did not cross the Vindhya mountains, and shortly afterwards marched back to Delhi.

It is now time to revert to the affairs of Bijapur. We left Ali Adil Shah in the midst of his conquests in the Carnatic. It must always be remembered that the Mahomedan conquests, not only in the Deccan, but also throughout India, were the conquests by a foreign army of the forts and strongholds. The country itself was left untouched, and the fort once taken, it was either razed like Vijayanagar, or a garrison being left there, the army marched on. The Hindoo ryots were left to till their fields as before, and the only difference to them was, that they paid their land-tax to a Mahomedan, instead of a Hindoo landlord. The artizans and merchants still plied their crafts as formerly, it was only the members of the royal families who retreated before the conquerors. A large number of the landed proprietors were also allowed to remain, with authority to collect the land revenue on condition, however, that they paid a fixed rent to the Government. Over each small district was placed a Mahomedan Governor, who was supported by a small body of troops, with which he kept order. It was the presence of these outposts, with the army at headquarters ready to back them up, that kept the country in order. There was no occupation of the country by the Mahomedans, and no settlement of the conquerors in the rural parts. The Hindoo population remained a nation as separate and as apart as it had been when they were ruled by their own countrymen. Their customs and their religious rites remained the same. When the wave of war swept over their villages, then temples and shrines were desecrated, but in those places which had not been visited by the foreign army, the old structures still remained, and during times of peace, they were not molested. Some of these Hindoo

Zemindars proved faithful servants, and brought with them their own retainers to serve in the Mahomedan armies. In this way the constitution of the Mahomedan armies of the Deccan underwent a gradual change. Whether it was owing to constant feud between the foreign and the Deccanee Mahomedans, or whether foreigners found greater attractions in the armies of the great Delhi Emperors, cannot now be said, but it seems certain that there was no longer the same quantity of volunteer adventurers from foreign parts, from whom to recruit the Deccan armies. It therefore became the custom to recruit the ranks largely from among the Hindoo warlike tribes—the Beydars, Mahrattas and Rajputs. The chief commands were still bestowed upon Mahomedans, and there were also special regiments composed exclusively of Mahomedans amongst whom were also Arabs and Abyssinians. The armies, however, were very largely made up of Hindoos, and not only did this cause a change in their system of warfare, but it led eventually to a weakening of the army itself. The Mahratttas, or Bergees, as they are termed by the Mahomedan historians, especially distinguished themselves as irregular cavalry, and were greatly employed in the hilly country which ends in the Western Ghauts. Mahomedans at no period seem to have had any partiality for hills and jungles. When they received a jaghir, (or estate) they preferred that it should be in the plains, if possible, not far from the capital. Even then, they seldom resided in their country seats, except occasionally for hunting or purposes of sport. They preferred the vicinity of the Courts with all their intrigues and their luxury. They therefore left the wilder portions of the Deccan in the hands of these Hindoo chieftains, stipulating only that each Zemindar should bring a certain number of retainers into the field. In this way there gradually grew up a hardy race of mountaineers, always the best stuff for soldiers, who, brought up in their own faith and traditions, were yet taught the art of war by their conquerors, and only awaited a time of danger and of weakness to raise the standard of revolt, and assert their own independence. This was, in fact, the origin of the Mahratta nation, and the Sultans of Bijapur and Ahmednagar may be said to have educated and brought into existence the nation which, before long, was to take, not only their places, but very nearly to acquire the sovereignty of India.

It was about this time (1578) that the first signs of the coming danger showed themselves. A number of the Bergee chiefs broke into excesses, and an army was sent into their hilly country by Ali Adil Shah. The disciplined forces of Bijapur could make no head against these hill robbers, and after skirmishing for nearly a year, they had to retire with considerable loss. Mustafa Khan, the Sultan's Minister, perceiving the impossibility of using regular troops in so inaccessible a country, then devised the perfidious scheme of enticing the chiefs to Bijapur, and of there slaughtering them. To this plan Adil Shah agreed, and an instrument having been found in the person of a Brahmin, named Vasoojee Punt, he was despatched to entice them by promises A few refused to fall into the snare, and amongst them the principal chief, Handeattum (Hanumanta?) Naick, who retired with his followers to Bilkonda. The rest came to Bijapur, and there they were all assassinated. No details of this foul act of treachery are given by the Mahomedan historians, and it is merely alluded to in passing. There can, however, be little doubt that this act of cruelty must have long lived in the memory of the Mahrattas, and was possibly a principal factor in exciting a race-hatred which was to serve eventually to bind them together as a nation. Up to this time there seems to have been a certain amount of cordiality between the Mahomedans and the Hindoos, but soon after this period, we find this spirit to be entirely changed, and it may not therefore be unreasonable to assign this treacherous act as one of the causes of this estrangement.

In 1580, Ali Adil Shah died, assassinated by one of his servants in a brawl, and was succeeded by his nephew, Ibrahim, then in his ninth year. Ali was a munificent patron of architecture, and many of his buildings at Bijapur still remain. The Jumma mosque, the large masonry pond near the Shahapur Gate, and the water-courses which carried water through all the streets of the city are attributed by Ferishta to this King. During his reign, the first ambassadors were sent from Delhi to Bijapur, and many learned men visited his court from Persia, Arabia, and Turkey.

GENEALOGY OF THE NIZAM SHAHI DYNASTY.

(AHMEDNAGAR).

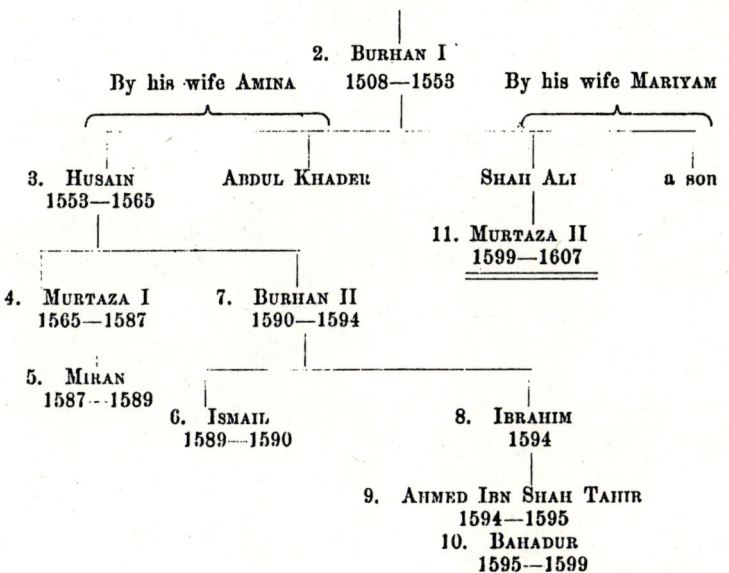

(N.B. After BAHADUR Ahmednagar was annexed to Delhi, but Malik Amber maintained his independence at first as deputy of MURTAZA II and afterwards as sole ruler at Dowlatabad and Aurangabad until his death in 1626 when his son was conquered and the whole of the kingdom annexed to Delhi).

GENEALOGY OF THE ADIL SHAHI DYNASTY. (BIJAPUR).

1. ABU'L MUZAFFAR YUSUF ADIL
   1489—1511

2. ISMAEL ADIL SHAH — daughter MARRIED — MARIYAM married
   1511—1534   AHMED SHAH BAHMANI   BURHAN SHAH of
                                           AHMEDNAGAR

3. MALU ADIL SHAH
   1534—1535
            4. IBRAHIM ADIL   a daughter
               1535—1557   MARRIED ALA-UD-DIN
                                 IMAD SHAH of BERAR

       5. ALI ADIL   TAHMASP
          1557—1579

          6. IBRAHIM ADIL   ISMAIL
             1579—1626

             7. MUHAMMED ADIL
                1626—1656

             8. ALI ADIL
                1656—1659

             9. SIKANDER
                1659 - 1686.

MAIN STREET.   HYDERABAD.

CHAPTER XIX.

THE STORY OF QUEEN CHAND AND THE FALL OF AHMEDNAGAR.

In 1580, the year after the death of Ali Adil Shah, there died also Ibrahim Kutb Shah of Golconda. He was the fourth in succession from his father, the first King, Sultan Kuli. It has been narrated how Sultan Kuli was assassinated whilst in the mosque in 1543, and was succeeded by his son, Jamshid Kuli. This King reigned for seven years only, until 1550,

During this time he was frequently engaged in the various quarrels between Bijapur, Bieder, and Ahmednagar, either on one side or the other. He was a man of considerable political sagacity, and always contrived to be on the winning side, so that out of each quarrel he managed to draw some advantage for himself. For almost the whole period of Jamshid's reign, his brother, Ibrahim, was living at Vijayanagar, protected by the Hindoo King Rama Rajah. When Jamshid died, his son, Sultan Kuli, was proclaimed King, but reigned only for six months. His Minister, Saif Khan, made himself very unpopular; the nobles revolted, called in Ibrahim and placed him on the throne. At first in gratitude to Rama Rajah for the protection which he had received, the relations between Vijayanagar and Goleonda were of a very friendly character. Soon after his accession Ibrahim Shah was invited by Nizam Shah to join in an alliance against Bijapur, and was only dissuaded from so doing by a letter from Rama Rajah. The following is the text of the letter:—

"Be it known to your Majesty that it is now many years since the two courts of Bijapur and Ahmednagar have been in a constant state of warfare, and that the balance of power between them was so equal, that, although every year each of these sovereigns had been in the habit of making a campaign on the others frontiers, yet no advantage accrued to either. It now appears that your Majesty (whose ancestors never interfered in those disputes) has marched an army to turn the scale in favour of Hussein Nizam Shah, without having any cause of enmity against Ibrahim Adil Shah of Bijapur, who has accordingly sought our alliance. As a friendship has long subsisted between our court and your Majesty, we have thought fit to lay these arguments before you to induce your Majesty to relinquish the offensive alliance which your Majesty has formed, and by returning peaceably to your capital, show a friendly disposition towards both parties, who will afterwards conclude a peace and put an end to this protracted war." (*Historical Sketch*, Vol. II., p. 476.)

Ibrahim Kutb Shah yielded to this request, and not only withdrew his army, but in the following year sent a body of troops to assist Rama Rajah in the revolt of his uncle, to which we have already alluded. For the next few years we find Kutb Shah engaged with his own affairs, but in the meantime Rama Rajah's power had gone on steadily increasing. The letter quoted above shows what the Hindoo Rajah's policy was, and we have seen how he played off Bijapur against Ahmednagar, first siding with the one, and then with the other, until he had made himself the arbiter of the affairs of the Deccan. And now we find another instance of how in politics there can be no sentiment and no feelings of gratitude. Rama Rajah's arrogance increased with his power, until, as we have seen, he would not allow the Mahomedan Sultans to sit in his presence, or to mount their horses until he gave the order. Then it was that Ali Adil Shah, the adopted son of the Hindoo Rajah's mother, proposed the alliance of Mahomedans against the infidel, and Ibrahim Kutb Shah, who owed his very existence to Rama Rajah, concluded the negociations. The result of this alliance was the battle of Tellicotta, and the downfall of the Hindoo Kingdom. Golconda does not seem to have benefited much in an extension of its boundaries towards the south. Kutb Shah had his hands full with the Hindoo Rajahs on the Eastern Coast, all of whom had been allied with Vijayanagar. Whilst he was subduing these, Ali Adil Shah spread his conquest into the Carnatic, and the Golconda boundary towards the South still remained the Kistna. It is probable that Kutb Shah began to realise how rich this country was in gold and precious stones, and throughout the rest of the Golconda history, we find the Sultans more engaged with their own affairs and abstaining— comparatively speaking—from interfering in the constant disputes between Bijapur and Ahmednagar. We have spoken of the wealth of the Golconda country in jewels and gold. The mines of Golconda are a proverb, but it is as well to state at once that there never was a diamond mine at Golconda, or anywhere within eighty miles of the fort. The celebrated diamond mines were all situated in the country that now forms the British districts of Kurnul, Cuddapah, and Nellore, and the diamonds were brought to, and stored in, the royal fort of Golconda, but as the merchants mostly resorted there, they gave the name of Golconda diamonds to stones that were really found elsewhere.

From the battle of Tellicotta up to the end of his reign, Ibrahim Kutb Shah was engaged in very few of the Deccan wars. The policy of the Golconda Kings seems always to have been to mix themselves as little as possible in Deccan affairs. The consequence was that he was able to devote himself to the improvement of his country. The fort at Golconda was entirely rebuilt and strengthened, many fine palaces were erected there, and several large irrigation tanks, among them being the beautiful sheet of water now known as the Hussein Saugur Tank, situated between Hyderabad and Secunderabad; the dam at Budwal, &c., &c. Ferishta says that during his prosperous reign "Telingana, like Egypt, became the mart of the whole world. Merchants from Turkistan, Arabia, and Persia resorted to it; and they met with such encouragement that they found in it inducements to return frequently. The greatest luxuries from foreign parts daily abounded at this King's hospitable board." Ibrahim Kutb Shah died in the thirty-first year of his reign, and out of thirty children, six sons and thirteen daughters survived him.

We must now return to Bijapur. When Ali Adil Shah died (1579), the most popular personage in Bijapur was his wife, Chand Bibi, who, it will be remembered, was the sister of the Ahmednagar Sultan. She was a woman of great intelligence and activity. She accompanied her husband in his campaigns and rode by his side to battle. During times of peace a large portion of the public affairs were entrusted to her, and she gave audiences and transacted business in open durbar. She was beloved by all, not only for her daring, but also for her justice and firmness. When her husband died, Chand Bibi assumed the direction of affairs, associating with herself Kamil Khan Deccanee. Every day, except Wednesdays and Fridays, public halls of justice were held, at which the young Sultan, who was only nine years old, appeared seated on the throne. For some time matters went on well, but then the co-regent appears to have been guilty of some insult to the Queen. She called in Kishawar Khan, and on his appearance Kamil Khan fled, but was overtaken four miles from the city and killed, his head being cut off and carried back. Kishawar Khan was now made co-regent, but he very soon began to indulge in ambitious designs. He excited the hostility of the nobles, who advised the Queen to send for Mustafa Khan, the Governor of Binkapur. Kishawar Khan hearing of this, despatched an order to a Jaghirdar living near Binkapur to assassinate Mustafa Khan—and had this order sealed with the royal seal. The order was carried out, and Mustafa Khan was bow-strung whilst at prayers. Matters now came to an open outbreak between the Queen and Kishawar Khan, and for a time the latter was successful. Acting in the young King's name, he procured an order confining Chand Bibi in the fort of Satara on the accusation that she had invited her brother to invade Bijapur from Ahmednagar. Kishawar Khan had now possession of the King's person, and for some time exercised despotic power. As soon as the troops heard of the Queen's imprisonment, they at once marched upon Bijapur, determined to depose the tyrant. In this movement they were supported by the people whose love for Queen Chand was unbounded. Indeed, when Kishawar Khan rode through the city in company with the young King, he was greeted by the populace with hoots and hisses, and even the women threw dirt and ashes at him, reviling him as the oppressor of the Queen, and the murderer of a holy Seyd (Mustafa Khan). Kishawar Khan, seeing that the whole people and the army were against him, escaped from the city, and leaving the young King in one of the royal gardens, fled first to Ahmednagar, but being refused shelter there, went on to Golconda, where he was soon afterwards assassinated by a relative of Mustafa Khan. At this point I cannot do better than quote the words of one far better qualified to write the history of the Deccan and who, in his historical romance of "A Noble Queen," has done full justice to the memory of Chand Bibi.* I give the extract verbatim:—

"Delivered from Kishawar Khan, the young King at once sent for his aunt, and her office of Regent was resumed. The new Minister, Ekhlas Khan, was an Abyssinian, and, like all his tribe, violent and uncontrollable, and the factious dissensions which ensued between Deccanees and Abyssinians, which led to bloody contests in the streets, encouraged the invasion of the kingdom by the Kings of Berar, Bieder, and Golconda, and the close investment of the city followed at a time when there were not two thousand troops for its defence. Ekhlas Khan, though turbulent as a Minister, was, however, a brave and faithful soldier, and the city was well defended. The Queen, accompanied by her nephew the King, went from post to post at night, though the weather was the severest of the rainy season, cheering, encouraging, and directing all. Two divisions of cavalry without the walls did good service in cutting off supplies and forage from the enemy, and harassing their flanks, but at last twenty yards of the city wall fell down after a night of heavy rain, and an assault was imminent, but, owing to dissensions in the enemy's camp,

* The late Colonel Meadow Taylor.

did not take place. Meanwhile the Queen, taking advantage of the respite, not only guarded the breach in person, but collected the masons of the city, and setting the example herself, and freely distributing rewards, had the breach completed in time to prevent any chance of attack by storm. She had never left the spot by day or night, and all entreaties for her to spare herself from the inclement weather and take rest were unavailing.

"The sore straits to which the kingdom had been reduced by the violence and obstinacy of the Abyssinian party now struck them so forcibly, that their leaders went in a body to the Queen and laid down their authority, beseeching her to do what she pleased with them so long as she and the King were safe. The Queen received this evidently earnest submission in a generous spirit. A new Minister, who possessed the confidence of all, was appointed, and in less than a month an army of twenty thousand of the old troops had collected at the capital. The Queen's devotion and spirited personal valour had inspired confidence in all, which now amounted to positive enthusiasm. The city had been invested for more than a year, its weak garrison was often mutinous and despairing, a large breach had occurred in the works, and anarchy prevailed throughout the whole kingdom. Yet this noble woman had redeemed all by her personal example, and the siege was raised, the several allies retiring to their own dominions. And now the Queen hoped for peace.

"Alas! it was not to be yet. Dilawar Khan, one of the military commanders, attacked the Minister, and blinded him, usurping the executive power. Many other atrocities were committed, and again the Queen's authority was reduced to the mere control of the palace and education of the King. But, in spite of many cruelties, Dilawar Khan was an able administrator; the resources of the kingdom were again developed, its Government began to be respected, and no more attacks were made upon its possessions. The events I have detailed were crowded into the space of four years, and as the King was approaching the age at which his majority could be declared, the Queen hoped, that with it the rest and peace she so intensely longed for would come to her. But there was still more to be done.

"Not at Bijapur, but in her native city Ahmednagar. The King Murtuza asked for the hand of Khodeija Sultana, the sister of his ward the King, for his son the Prince Hussein, and considering that all trouble at Bijapur was at an end, the Queen Chand accompanied the bride-elect, the Royal party being escorted by the choicest of the Ahmednagar cavalry. She had hoped to find peace in her old home; but she found that home more convulsed with faction, and more distracted within and without, than when she had left it. Her brother, Murtuza, always violent, had become in reality mad, and had attempted the life of his son Meeran, who, in revenge, attacked his father in the palace at Ahmednagar, and caused him to be suffocated in a hot bath. An account of this revolution is given minutely by the historian Ferishta, who was in command of the palace guards, and which is very dramatic in its details, but too long for extract. He does not, however, mention the Queen Chand, who must have been in the fort at the time of the tragedy. The new King did not long survive this act of parricide, and, after a few months, was seized by his Minister and publicly beheaded amidst the execrations of the people. After his death a frightful tumult arose; the fort was carried by the mob, and hundreds of persons of distinction, chiefly foreigners, perished. A period of anarchy then ensued, when Ismail, a son of Boorhan, who was brother of Murtuza Nizam Shah, and, therefore, nephew of Queen Chand, was declared King; and Jumal Khan, head of the Deccanee party, constituted himself Regent and Minister. This revolution was opposed by Bijapur and Berar;

and the troops of the latter were defeated by Jumal Khan; but peace was concluded with Bijapur, and Queen Chand, wearied by constant strife and atrocities which she had no power to control, was allowed to join the Bijapur army then in the field, and returned with it, though with no authority, to the capital, there, as she trusted, to end her days in peace. She was received by the people with their former enthusiasm, and by the young King with no diminution of his old affection; but she took no part in public affairs, which, under the young King, were very prosperous. At Ahmednagar other revolutions followed with which this tale has no concern. Ismail, who had succeeded, was, after some time, attacked by his father, Boorhan, who had obtained the aid and sympathy of Akbar, Emperor of Delhi, and was deposed, and Boorhan himself reigned till his death in 1594 in comparative peace. He was succeeded by his son Ibrahim, a weak, violent prince, and the fortunes of the kingdom will be understood from the course of the present story to its close. At Bijapur Queen Chand lived in peace, and only assumed local authority at the request of her nephew, whenever his temporary absence was necessary on tours of his dominions or in the field.

"Such were the real antecedents of our 'Noble Queen.' I trust they may not be considered out of place in a work professedly of fiction, but tend to make more intelligible that which would be otherwise, perhaps, strange and confused. Few in England know that the contemporary of our Queen Elizabeth in the Deccan kingdoms was a woman of equal ability, of equal political talent, of equal, though in a different sense, education and accomplishments, who ruled over a realm as large, a population as large, and as intelligent, and as rich as England; a woman who, surrounded by jealous enemies, preserved by her own personal valour and endurance her kingdom from destruction and partition; who through all temptations and exercise of absolute power, was at once simple, generous, frank, and merciful as she was chaste, virtuous, religious, and charitable—one who, among all the women of India, stands out as a jewel without flaw and beyond price."

In the extract given above reference is made to the tragedy which occurred at Ahmednagar, of which a more detailed account seems to be called for here. We have already alluded to the favourite of Murtaza Shah, Saheb Khan. After this minion's death, he was succeeded by another, a dancer, named Futteh Shah. This person took advantage of his influence over his royal master to obtain large grants of lands and gifts of jewels. At length, he asked for two necklaces which had formed a part of the plunder of Rama Rajah, and which were composed of the most valuable rubies, emeralds, and pearls. The Sultan ordered them to be given to him; but Salabat Khan, the Minister, unwilling that such treasures should be alienated, substituted two strings of mock jewels in their place. Futteh Shah soon discovered this imposition, and complained to the King, who, thereupon ordered all the jewels to be laid out for his inspection. Salabat Khan, however, concealed the most precious, and the King on discovering this, became so angry that he threw all the rest into the fire. His Minister endeavoured to save them, but the pearls were all destroyed. It now became apparent that the Sultan was a mad man, and, indeed, from this time forward he threw off all control. First of all he refused to allow his son Meeran's marriage with the Bijapur Princess, or to send her back again unless Ibrahim Adil Shah would first hand over the fortress of Sholapore, which, it will be remembered, had been given as the dowry of Chand Bibi. This led to a declaration of war from Bijapur. Salabat Khan, recognizing the impossibility of serving a madman, now resigned office, and was sent in honourable confinement to the fort of Rajapur. The new Minister, Kassim Beg, at once concluded peace with Bijapur, and then proceeded to celebrate the long deferred marriage. The Sultan's madness now took another form, and he conceived an unnatural jealousy of his son, Meeran Hussein, who had just been married. He made the young prince sleep in a room near his own, and then, when he was asleep, set fire to it. The young prince awoke in time, and calling for help was rescued by the favourite Futteh Shah, and made his escape to Dowlatabad. On ascertaining that the victim had escaped, the Sultan was highly enraged, and ordered his Ministers to send orders to have him killed, and when they refused, deposed them from office. The new Minister, Mirza Khan, wrote to Bijapur, and represented how everything was in confusion, owing to the Sultan's insanity, and asked for a despatch of a force to the borders. This request was complied with, and then, under the pretence of meeting this hostile force, Mirza Khan left the city with the available troops. He did not, however, march far, and the historian Ferishta, who was then employed in the Ahmednagar Court, was sent to enquire the reason of the delay. Ferishta soon suspected the treachery, and managing to escape from the Minister's camp, returned to the capital and reported matters to the Sultan. The latter, now thoroughly alarmed, sent for Salabat Khan from his place of confinement. It was, however, too late. Mirza Khan, instead of attacking the Bijapur forces, advanced by forced marches to Dowlatabad, and at once returned with the young prince, Meeran Hussein. Ferishta was appointed to guard the palace, but he says that being deserted by all, he could not do so. The young prince then entered with forty followers, putting all to death who came in his way. Ferishta's life was spared, as he had been a schoolfellow of the prince. But the same mercy was not shown to the Sultan, though bound to him by a closer and holier tie. Ferishta thus relates the last scene:—"Having reached the presence of his father, the prince behaved to him, both in word and action, with every possible insult and abuse.

Nizam Shah was silent, and only looked at him with contempt, till the prince putting his naked sabre across his breast, said: 'I will put you to death.' Nizam Shah, then breathing a deep sigh, exclaimed:—'Oh, thou accursed of God, it would be better for thee to let thy father be for his few remaining days thy guest, and to treat him with respect.' The prince relenting for a moment at this expression, stopped his hand, and withdrew from his father's apartment. Not having patience, however, to wait for his death, though he was then in a mortal illness, he commanded him to be put into a warm bathing-room, and, shutting fast the doors and windows to exclude all air, lighted a great fire under the bath, so that the Sultan was speedily suffocated by the steam and heat. The parricide was perpetrated in the year 996 (1587). The deceased Sultan was buried with great pomp in the garden Roseh; but his bones were afterwards taken up and carried to Kerbella, where they were deposited near those of his father and grandfather.

The reign of the new Sultan lasted only two months and three days. Not only did he at once give way to cruelty and debauchery, but the whole country was horrified at the crime by which he had gained the throne. Ferishta appears to have made his escape, together with Queen Chand, and went to Bijapur, where they were gladly received. In the meantime at Ahmednagar there was a revolt against Meeran Shah. The Minister, Mirza Khan, seized his person, and, as mentioned above, cut off his head in public, and sent for the two surviving sons of Boorahan Shah, the brother of the late Sultan Murtaza, one of whom Sultan Ismael, a boy of twelve years of age, was proclaimed. A counter revolt was made by a Deccanee named Jamal Khan and there ensued a terrible riot and massacre. The Deccanees got the best of it, and they at once commenced to slaughter all the foreigners they could find. The Minister, Mirza Khan, managed to escape, but was caught, brought back, and cut to pieces. Some of his friends were rammed into cannons and blown into the air. Altogether in the space of seven days, nearly a thousand foreigners were murdered. At length, matters quieted down, and Jamal Khan then recognized Ismael as Sultan, and appointed himself as Minister. The usurpation, however, did not last long, Boorahan Shah, the father of Ismael, was then with the Emperor Akbar, who offered to give him an army to retake the throne of his ancestors. Boorahan declined the army as likely to excite the people's jealousy, but went alone in order to see what he could do by his own personal influence. He was at once joined by a large number of nobles, and though at first repulsed, he soon afterwards defeated and killed Jamal Khan. He then entered Ahmednagar, deposed his son Ismael, who was sent into confinement, and ascended the throne in his place (1519).

But we must now revert to Bijapur and the fortunes of Queen Chand.

When Queen Chand returned to Bijapur, after having escaped the massacre at Ahmednagar, she found the position of affairs to be somewhat altered. Sultan Ibrahim was now old enough to take over the conduct of public business himself, and though he still maintained cordial and even affectionate relations with his aunt, the latter very wisely withdrew from any public interference in affairs of State, although in private she gave her advice whenever called upon to do so. Ibrahim was a young man of considerable ability and promise. He had advanced with an army to assist in placing his brother-in-law, Meeran Hussein, on the throne of Ahmednagar, but when he heard of the latter's act of parricide, as related above, he declined all further alliance with him, and leaving him, as he said, to the vengeance of the Almighty, retired to Bijapur (1587). When after a short time, Meeran Hussein himself was assassinated, Ibrahim, taking advantage of the dissensions at Ahmednagar again advanced with an army. Very little seems to have been done in this campaign, probably owing to the jealousy between the two leading Bijapur Generals, Delawar Khan, the Minister, and Bulleel Khan, who had been recalled from the Malabar district, where he had been engaged with some refractory Rajahs, to assist the main army. Bulleel Khan was favoured by the Sultan, whose object it was to weaken the power of Dilawar Khan. The Minister, on the other hand, endeavoured to cast odium on his rival by representing that if he had shown more energy in the campaign in Malabar, he would have been able to bring more tribute, and a larger contingent to assist in the invasion of Ahmednagar. Bulleel Khan retorted that this was due to the suddenness of his recall, and, throwing himself on the Sultan's mercy, was rewarded by a rich *Khilat*. Dilawar Khan for a moment stifled his resentment, and when the audience was broken up, carried off Bulleel Khan to his own tents in order to celebrate their reconciliation by a splendid feast. Bulleel Khan was thus thrown off his guard, and returned with the army to Bijapur. Arrived there, however, Dilawar Khan threw away the mask of friendship, and suddenly seized his rival without the King's knowledge, and caused him to be blinded. This outrage greatly incensed the Sultan, and though for the time he was unable to resent it, he resolved to get rid of his insolent Minister at the earliest opportunity. This opportunity soon came. In 1589, as already related, Boorahan Nizam Shah, who had taken refuge with the Emperor Akbar, advanced to recover the throne of Ahmednagar, from his son, Ismael, who, as related above, had been proclaimed by Jamal Khan. Jamal Khan advanced to meet the Bijapur troops, and contrary to Ibrahim's orders, Dilawar Khan gave him battle. At first he was successful, but when his followers dispersed to plunder the camp, some of the enemy rallied, and attacking Dilawar Khan who was left with only a few followers, compelled him to take flight. In the meantime, the Sultan with the main body of the army had retired, and Dilawar Khan was only able to join him after much difficulty. The Sultan now determined to shake himself free of Dilawar Khan, and for this purpose arranged with Amir-ul-Oomara, Eyn-ul-Mulk, to come over to his camp. This he did one night by stealth, whilst Dilawar Khan (who though more than eighty years of age was not past the pleasures of love) was engaged in amorous dalliance with a "beautiful virgin of Deccan, whom he had long sought after and just obtained." Next morning when too late, Dilawar Khan found that his royal captive had escaped, and at once proceeded to bring him back. He found the Sultan with Eyn-ul-Mulk's forces drawn up behind, and he at once told him that "marching by night was improper," and that he should therefore return The Sultan incensed at his insolence exclaimed: "Who will deliver me from this traitor?" Whereupon one Asout Khan spurred up to the Regent, and struck him with his sabre. The horse reared and threw Dilawar Khan, who, in the confusion that followed managed to escape, leaving his son, Khan, behind, who was taken and put to death. Ibrahim Shah was now for the first time really independent, and news arriving that Boorahan Shah had defeated Jamal Khan, and taken possession of Ahmednagar, he sent him letters of congratulation, and retired to Bijapur.

In the meantime Dilawar Khan had taken refuge with Boorahan Nizam Shah, who, forgetful of the assistance given by the Sultan of Bijapur, employed him to reduce the fort of Sholapur, which for so long had been the subject of contention between the two kingdoms. This led to another war, and the Ahmednagar troops took the initiative, and headed by the traitor Dilawar Khan, marched upon Bijapur. Ibrahim Adil Shah pretended to take no notice of this invasion, and allowed the enemy to advance as far as the river Bhimah, pretending in the meantime to give himself up to pleasure. In this way Dilawar Khan was misled into thinking that Ibrahim was too weak to oppose him, and when messengers came from his late master offering to take him back into his service, he at once consented, hoping in this way to be restored to his former absolute power. Ibrahim received his former Minister in his capital, but soon disillusioned him by ordering him to be blinded. Dilawar Khan in vain represented that he had come to court solely on his Majesty's assurance of pardon and safety. The Sultan told him that he had only promised him life and property, and that depriving him of sight could effect neither. Accordingly, he was blinded and sent to the fortress of Satara, where he remained a prisoner until he died. Ferishta was an eyewitness of these proceedings, of which he gives a graphic account, the side he was on being that of the Sultan of Bijapur.

Ibrahim Shah having thus rid himself of his rebellious subject, at once marched against the invaders. Boorahan Shah was compelled to retreat, and dissensions breaking out in his camp, was only too glad to sue for peace. This was granted after some delay, on condition that he razed the fortress he had built on the banks of the Bhimah. To this the Sultan had to consent, and, after with his own hands pulling down the first stone, he marched back to Ahmednagar in disgust, "heartily repenting of his unprovoked invasion of the territories of Ibrahim Adil Shah."

Peace being restored at home, Ibrahim Shah turned again to the reduction of the Malabar Rajahs, whom Bulleel Khan had left only partially subdued. The duty was entrusted to Munjum Khan (1593), who succeeded so well that in a short time he had taken the fort of Mysore, which was then in possession of Vencatadri Naick, the brother's son of the late Rama Rajah of Vijayanagar, when he was recalled by news of a fresh rebellion.

It will be remembered that the late Sultan Ali Adil Shah, the husband of Queen Chand, had left no sons but two nephews, the eldest of whom, Ibrahim, succeeded him. The younger of these two, Ismael, was appointed to the Government of Belgaum, where, however, he was kept in a kind of honourable confinement. This restraint becoming irksome, the young prince, having associated several noblemen with him, suddenly seized the fort and proclaimed his independence (Ramzan 9th, 1593). A general revolt now occurred, and for a time it seemed as if Ibrahim would be crushed by his enemies. The old nobleman, Eyn-ul-Mulk, disgusted, probably that he was allowed so little share in the Government, secretly favoured Ismael, under whom he hoped to enjoy more power. Boorahan Nizam Shah, anxious to revenge his former humiliation, also marched an army to assist the pretender, and the noblemen generally espoused his cause. The Hindoo Rajahs also broke into revolt, and the Portuguese, anxious for some excuse to interfere, promised to send a reinforcement to Ismael. But the young Sultan Ibrahim managed to extricate himself from his awkward dilemma with considerable skill. He had an able and courageous adviser in his aunt, Queen Chand, and he resolved to strike the rebels singly before they could effect a junction. Hummeed Khan was despatched with a force to meet Eyn-ul-Mulk, who had now openly joined the young prince at Belgaum. Hummeed Khan pretended to favour the rebellion, and, thus misled, Eyn-ul-Mulk left the protection which the walls of Belgaum afforded, and advanced towards Hummeed Khan without waiting for Boorahan Shah, who was only a few marches distant. He probably thought it more advisable to bring the rebellion to a successful issue by the help of Hummeed Khan, than to be under obligations to the rival King of Ahmednagar. But he was deceived. Preparations were made to receive the supposed rebel Hummeed Khan in a splendid pavilion which was pitched for the purpose in a large plain some distance from Belgaum. As soon as Hummeed Khan had advanced near enough, he threw off all disguise, and suddenly charging the unsuspecting Eyn-ul-Mulk, threw him from his horse, and cut off his head. The young prince Ismael was also taken prisoner, and then the rebels fled in dismay. Hummeed Khan at once returned to Bijapur, where he was received with great honour, and the head of Eyn-ul-Mulk was blown from the great gun *Malik-i-Maidan* (the Lord of the Plain), Boorahan Nizam Shah hearing that the rebellion had been quelled, thereupon returned to Ahmednagar, where, wasted by illness and the dissensions in his country, he soon afterwards died (1594). Boorahan Shah was succeeded by his son Ibrahim, who signalized his accession to the throne by treating the Bijapur ambassadors with such rudeness that they returned to their own country. This affront led to another war, and Ibrahim Adil Shah at once marched with an army to avenge the insult. The two armies met on the frontiers, and a very hotly contested battle ensued, in which the Ahmednagar forces were at first successful, the left wing of the Bijapureans being broken and put to flight. The right wing, however, commanded by Hummeed Khan, stood their ground with such obstinacy that the tide of battle turned, and the young Ahmednagar King rashly advancing with only a small retinue was surprised by a troop of the Bijapur horse, and killed by an arrow, upon which the Admednagar army took to flight.

The death of Ibrahim Nizam Shah created the utmust confusion in Ahmednagar. Two factions arose, each proclaiming a rival king. One of these was Bahadur Shah, the infant son of Ibrahim, and the other was Ahmed Shah, a boy twelve years of age, who, it was pretended, was the grandson of Hussein Nizam Shah's brother. Mian Manju was then at the head of affairs, and was the protector of the young pretender Ahmed Shah. On it being proved that Ahmed had no claim to royal descent, a third faction put forward another infant as the rightful heir of Ibrahim, and Mian Manju, thereupon despairing of bringing about a restoration of order, sent a message to Prince Murad, Akbar's son, who was then in Guzerat, waiting for an opportunity to interfere in Deccan affairs, to come to his assistance. Murad was only too glad to accept the invitation, and marched with an army of thirty thousand men, with the ostensible object of placing Ahmed on the throne, but with the real intention of annexing Ahmednagar to the Delhi Empire. But before he could reach the capital, Mian Manju repented of his venture, and after consulting with the chief noblemen, it was resolved to ask Queen Chand to undertake the Regency and to defend the State from Murad and the Mogul army. Chand Bibi must have been at that time nearly fifty years of age, and was happy in Bijapur, where she was beloved by all. But she was a Princess of Ahmednager by birth, and she immediately responded to the call that was made upon her, though it involved the taking up of a post surrounded by danger. She at once set off for Ahmednagar, and when she had taken charge of the State, Mian Manju started for Golconda and Bijapur to endeavour to obtain help. In the meantime, the toils closed round the city of Ahmednagar, but it had a noble defender in Queen Chand. This courageous woman at once placed the city in a proper state of defence, and at the same time proclaimed the infant Bahadur as King. Murad invested the city and actively commenced to push the siege, but in spite of his large train of artillery, he was able to accomplish very little. The kings of Golconda and Bijapur had now become thoroughly alarmed, and despatched armies to raise the siege, and Murad hearing that these reinforcements were on the way, resolved to attempt a storm before their arrival. "In a few days fire mines were carried under the bastions on one face of the fort, all were charged with powder, and built with mortar and stones, excepting where the train was to be laid, and it was resolved to fire them on the following morning (20th February 1596). During the night Kwaja Mahomed Khan Shirazi, admiring the resolution of the besieged, and unwilling that they should be sacrificed, made his way to the walls, and informed them of their danger. At the instance of Chand Bibi, who herself set the example, the garrison immediately began to countermine. By daylight they had destroyed two of the mines, and were searching for the others, when the prince, without communication with Khan Khanam, ordered out the line, and resolved to storm without him. The besieged were in the act of removing the powder from the third and largest mine, when the prince ordered them to be sprung. Many of the counterminers were killed and several yards of the wall fell. When the breach was made, several of the leading officers of the garrison prepared for flight. But Chand Bibi, clad in armour, and with a veil thrown over her face, and with a drawn sword in her hand, dashed forward to defend the breach. The fugitives to a man returned and joined her, and as the storming party held back for the other mines, the besieged had time to throw rockets, powder, and other combustibles into the ditch, and to bring guns to bear upon the breach." * From the early morning until sundown, the heroic Queen remained in the breach, encouraging her soldiers and endeavouring to repair the damage. For some reason or other, the general assault was delayed until the afternoon, by which time the defenders were better prepared to resist it, but from about two o'clock until sunset force after force of Moguls was hurled against the breach to be each time repulsed, until the moat was filled with the bodies of the slain. Throughout the whole of this desperate attack, Queen Chand was foremost amongst the defenders.

* *Bombay Gazetteer* Vol. XVII., by James Campbell.

Her green-veil was seen everywhere, and her voice was heard, calling out in its shrill treble her late husband's battle cry. At length, as darkness set in, the Moguls, repulsed in each attack, had to retire discomfited, and by next morning the breach had been repaired and rendered impracticable. Prince Murad, finding that his assault had failed, and that the reinforcements were within a day's march, now resolved to raise the siege. He first sent ambassadors to the Queen, who were ordered to compliment her on her heroic defence, and to inform her that in future the Imperial Forces would style her a Sultana or Queen, instead of Begum as before, and at the same time to request a truce for burying the dead. This was granted, and after it had expired, a regular treaty was drawn up, under which Prince Murad agreed to retire on receiving the cession of the Sovereignty of Berar. At first Queen Chand refused these terms, but eventually she consented, and Prince Murad, whose army was weakened, not only by want of provisions, but also by internal dissensions, withdrew to take possession of his new acquisition, which gave to the Delhi Emperors their first firm footing in the Deccan. Soon afterwards Prince Murad died from the effects of hard drinking, and for three years Ahmednagar remained unmolested by the Moguls.

No sooner had the invaders retired, than dissensions broke out amongst the Ahmednagar people. Main Manju was in favour of young Ahmed being recognized Sultan, but the Queen would have no one but Bahadur, the infant son of the late Sultan. In order to settle this dispute, the Queen sent for her nephew, Ibrahim Adil Shah, of Bijapur, who soon arrived with a sufficient force to keep the peace between the two factions. A lengthened enquiry was then held, and on it being proved that Ahmed Shaw was not a lineal descendent of the Nizam Shah's family, an estate was settled upon him, and Bahadur was placed upon the throne. For a short time there was now peace in Ahmednagar and Queen Chand turned her attention to the restoration of the affairs of the kingdom. But she was not fated to complete the reforms she commenced, for in 1597, war again broke out with the Moguls in consequence of encroachments made by them. Prince Daniyal had succeeded his brother Murad as Governor of the Deccan, and his policy was to take advantage of every opportunity to reduce, and if possible to annex, Ahmednagar. But before the final struggle with the Moguls took place, Queen Chand had again to call in the assistance of her nephew, Ibrahim, of Bijapur, against her turbulent subjects in Ahmednagar. He at once complied, and sent Soheil Khan with a considerable force, and with orders to place himself entirely at the Queen's disposal. Mahomed Khan, the Queen's Minister, against whom chiefly this force was intended, refused to admit it into the citadel, and despatched a letter to the Mogul Commander-in-Chief in Berar, offering if he would come to his help to hold the country as a vassal of the Emperor of Delhi. This piece of treachery, however, became known to the garrison, who then seized Mahomed Khan, and handed him over to the Queen. In this way the Queen's authority was restored, but unfortunately the invitation to the Moguls was only too readily accepted. A Mogul force was sent to seize the town of Paithri, which had not been included in the Berar Concession, and thereupon Soheil Khan was ordered by his master to recapture it. In this expedition he was assisted by an army from Golconda, the Sultan of which had begun to be alarmed by the close neighbourhood of the Delhi army. The allied force consisted of no less than 60,000 cavalry, besides infantry, and the engagement that ensued was a decisive one for the fate of the Deccan. The battle was fought on the banks of the Godavery, not far from the town of Sonpat. The Delhi forces were commanded by the Khan Khanan, assisted by the redoubtable old warrior, Raja Ali Khan, of Khandeish.

by Raja Jaganath, and other Hindoo subsidiaries. Abu-l-Fazl* thus describes the battle:—

"The army of Nizam-ul-Mulk (Ahmednagar) was in the centre; the Adil Khan's (Bijapur) was on the right; and the army of Kutb-ul-Mulk on the left. On the 21th Bahaman (26th January, 1597), after the first watch of the day the River Godavery was passed, and the battle began by an attack on the right wing of the enemy. But they held their ground firmly in a strong position, and kept up a heavy fire. Great bravery was exhibited on both sides, and a long and desperate struggle was maintained. The enemy was numerous, and the superiority of his fire checked the Imperial ranks, and made them waver. Jaganath and several other Rajputs drew rein, and did not move, while the Adil Khan troops made an onslaught upon Raja Ali Khan of Khandeish. He made a stubborn resistance and fell fighting bravely, with thirty-five distinguished officers and five hundred devoted followers.

"Mirza Shah Rukh and Khan Khanan had been successful in their part of the field, so also had Saijid Kasim and other leaders. The enemy was under the impression that the Ruler of Khandeish was in the centre and thought that Mirza Shah Rukh and Khan Khanan were involved in his defeat. During the darkness of the night, the opposing forces remained separate from each other, each supposing that it had gained a victory. In the course of the night many of the scattered troops rejoined their standard. Under the impression that Raja Ali Khan had gone over to the enemy, the imperial troops plundered his baggage. Dwarka Das, of the advance and Said Jalal, of the left, retired to Nilawi. Ram Chandar, who fought bravely and had received twenty wounds with the forces under Raja Ali Khan, remained among the wounded during the night, and died a few days after.

* Elliot and Dowson., Vol. VI., page 95.

"When morning came the Imperial Forces 7000 in number, found themselves in face of 25,000 of the enemy. They had all night suffered from thirst, and they now carried the river Sugam. The enemy was only half-hearted, and being dismayed by this demonstration, took to flight and made but little resistance * * * Worn out by the protracted conflict, the imperial Forces were unable to pursue. At the beginning of the campaign the imperial Forces numbered only 15,000, while the enemy were 60,000 in number. Still they had gained victory and had captured forty elephants and much artillery."

This quotation has been given at some length as a good specimen of the manner in which Deccanee warfare was conducted. The troops were, no doubt, brave, but very undisciplined. Though outnumbering their opponents, they were unable to take advantage of their first successes, owing to their want of cohesion and discipline. The extract is also important, as showing the support which Akbar's wise rule received from the Rajputs, who formed the flower of his army. It was only Aurungzebe's subsequent bigotry and intolerance that alienated this hardy race of soldiers.

After this defeat, the allied army dispersed, and Nehang Khan and the Ahmednagar Minister and General retired to the capital, where he formed a plan to seize Queen Chand and the young King. The Queen, however, shut the gates of the citadel against him, and refused to allow him to enter. Whilst Ahmednagar was thus torn by civil war, the Imperial Troops were steadily advancing. They were now commanded by Prince Daniyal and the Khan Khanan (1599). Nehang Khan fled to Junar, and the Imperialists then invested Ahmednagar, and the unfortunate Queen had to sustain another siege. And now unfortunately the garrison was divided in itself. A portion wished to fight the matter out to the bitter end, but the Queen seeing the hopelessness of resistance was inclined to make terms by again confirming the treaty made with Prince Murad at the previous siege. Her idea was to give up the fort, and retire with the young King to Junar. Hamid Khan, one of the principal officers in the fort, and the head of the opposite faction, came to know of this, and at once ran into the streets exclaiming that the Queen wished to betray the people. The excitable and turbulent soldiers of Ahmednagar, forgetting all the noble devotion which Queen Chand had always shown, at once assembled in front of the palace. Headed by Hamid Khan they rushed inside, sword in hand, and not finding the Queen in the audience hall, they broke open the private apartment. There they were confronted by this courageous woman who was undismayed, though she saw that the end had come. Too excited to listen to her, the crowds rushed on, and Hamid Khan cut her down, and so died Chand Bibi, one of the noblest characters in the History of India.

Deprived of its courageous defender, the fort of Ahmednagar did not hold out much longer. In a few days the mines were sprung, and the garrison making but a feeble resistance, the fort was easily carried. A scene of indiscriminate slaughter then took place, the treasury was pillaged, and the young King Bahadur was taken and sent to the Emperor Akbar, who was then at Burhanpore. Bahadur was subsequently sent to the fortress of Gwalior, where he remained in honourable confinement until his death. From this time (1599), we hear nothing more of the independence of the Kingdom of Ahmednagar. The Moguls had now taken firm footing in the Deccan, and the beginning of the end had commenced.

CITADEL AND MOAT. BIJAPUR.

CHAPTER XX

RETROSPECTIVE SKETCH OF THE DECCAN.

Before leaving Ahmednagar, which now disappears from all independent share in the history of Deccan affairs, a slight sketch of the civil administration of the kingdom under the Nizam Shahi Kings will not be out of place, and I cannot do better than quote from Mr. Campbell:—

"The Ahmednagar dominions extended over the greater part of Berar, and the whole of what was afterwards included in the *Subha* of Aurungabad, Jalna, and some other districts in Nassik and Khandeish, and the district of Kalyan in the Konkan from Bankot to Bassein. Under the Ahmednagar Kings, though perhaps less regularly than afterwards under the Moguls, the country was divided into districts or *sirkars*. The district was distributed among sub-divisions, which were generally known by Persian names, *pargana*, *karyát*, *sammat*, *mahal*, *taluka*, and sometimes by the Hindu names of *prant* and *desh*. The hilly west, which was generally managed by Hindoo officers, continued to be arranged by valleys with their Hindoo names, *Khora*, *Mura*, and *Marval*. The collection of revenue was generally entrusted to farmers, the farms sometimes including one village. Where the revenue was not farmed, its collection was generally entrusted to Hindoo officers. Over the revenue farmers was a Government agent or *Amil*, who, besides collecting the revenue, managed the police and settled the civil suits. Civil suits relating to land were generally settled by juries or *panchayets*. Though the chief power in the country was Mahomedan, large numbers of Hindoos were employed in the service of the State. The garrison of hill forts seem generally to have been commanded by Hindoos, Marathas, Kolis, and Dhangars, a few places of special strength being reserved for Mahomedan commandants, or *killedars*. Besides the hill forts, some parts of the open country were left under loyal Maratha and Brahmin officers with the title of estate holder or *jaghirdar*, and of district head or *Deshmukh*. Estates were generally granted on military tenure, the value of the grant being in proportion to the number of troops which the grant-holder maintained. Family feuds or personal hate, and, in the case of those whose lands lay near the borders of two kingdoms, an intelligent regard for the chances of war often divided Maratha families, and led members of one family to take service under rival Musulman States. Hindoos of distinguished service were rewarded with the

Hindoo titles of *raja*, *naick*, and *rav* or *rao*. Numbers of Hindoos were employed in the Ahmednagar armies." (*Bombay Gazetteer*, vol. xvii.)

In the same year as Ahmednagar fell, an incident occurred which was destined to have a most important effect upon Indian history. During the Holi festival of that year (March-April), a Maratha, named Majoli Bhonsla, who commanded a small body of Silledar horse, took his son, Shahji, a boy of five, to pay his respects to his commanding officer, Lukhji Jadhavrao. Lukji's little daughter, Jiji, a child of three, was present, and whilst the elders were talking, the two children began to play together. Lukhji asked his daughter in joke: "How would you like that boy for your husband?" and on the girl saying "Yes," Majoli at once rose and called the guests to witness that Lukhji had offered his daughter in marriage to his son Shahji, which offer he, as Shahji's father, accepted. Taken thus at his word, Lukhji and his wife were exceedingly angry, but Maloji remained unshaken, and eventually (1604) the marriage really took place. The issue of this marriage was the great Sivaji, the founder of the Maratha nation. Mr. Campbell, whom I have quoted above says (*ibid*) that Lukhji's objections were overcome by purchasing from "a falling court like that of Ahmednagar," a command of 5,000 and the title of Rajah for Maloji, and that then, Lukhji having no longer any excuse "for not performing what he was urged to by his sovereign," consented to the marriage. The passage is quoted word for word from Grant Duff's "History of the Marathas" (vol I., p. 78), but it is clearly an error, for, as we have seen, there was no longer a sovereign at Ahmednagar in 1604, to give or to withhold promotion. What seems most probable is that Maloji, in the interval between 1599 and 1604, did good service for the Moguls, and received his promotion from them for assisting them in the settlement of their new conquest. The story of Sivaji has, however, been so exhaustively told by the great historian Grant Duff, that it is out of our province to go into it here, and the incident is only alluded to as marking an important epoch in the history of the Deccan. We shall, of course, frequently come across Sivaji, in the future course of our history, but except as far as he is brought into contact with Bijapur, it is not proposed to recapitulate what has already been so well told.

To return to Ibrahim Adil Shah at Bijapur. After the catastrophe at Ahmednagar, the Sultan took but little active share in the affairs of the Deccan. Alarmed at the growing power of the Moguls, he made overtures to the Emperor Akbar, and an alliance was agreed upon, one of the conditions of which was that he should give his daughter in marriage to the Emperor's son, Daniyal. An ambassador was sent by Akbar to bring the Princess, but he remained so long at Bijapur that another, Asad Beg, was sent to bring him and the Princess back, with orders to stay at Bijapur only one night. The Princess seems to have been very reluctant to enter upon this marriage, and when at length she was despatched with the ambassador, accompanied also by the historian Ferishta, together with rich presents, she managed one night to escape from her guardians in order to return to her father. In the morning, however, she was caught and was eventually safely handed over to her husband. At this time Bijapur must have been at the height of its splendour and magnificence. Asad Beg, coming from Delhi, where Akbar's court was at the summit of its grandeur, speaks most enthusiastically of the Southern city. His description is worthy of being quoted, as it is not likely to be tinged with any partiality.—*

"That palace, which they called Hajjah, was so arranged that each house in it had a double court. Where there are

---

* Elliot and Dowson, vol. vi., p. 163, *et seq.*

two courts they call it in those parts Hajjah. All round the gate of my residence were lofty buildings with houses and porticos; the situation was very airy and healthy. It lies in an open space in the city. Its northern portico is to the east of a *bazaar* of great extent, as much as thirty yards wide and two *kos* (four miles) long. Before each shop was a beautiful green tree, and the whole bazaar was extremely clean and pure. It was filled with rare goods, such as are not seen or heard of in any other town. There were shops of cloth sellers, jewellers, armourers, vintners, bakers, fishmongers and cooks. To give some idea of the whole bazaar I will describe a small section in detail. In the jewellers' shops were jewels of all sorts, wrought into a variety of articles, such as daggers, knives, mirrors, necklaces and alse into the form of birds, such as parrots, doves, and peacocks, &c., all studded with valuable jewels, and arranged upon shelves, rising one above the other. By the side of this shop will be a baker's with rare viands placed in the same manner upon tiers of shelves. Further on a linen draper's with all kinds of cloths shelved in like manner. Then a clothier's. Then a spirit-merchant's with various sort of China vessels, valuable crystal bottles, and costly cups, filled with choice and rare essences arranged on shelves, while in front of the shop were jars of double-distilled spirits. Beside that shop will be a fruiterer's filled with all kinds of fruit and sweetmeats, such as pistachio nuts and relishes, and sugarcandy and almonds. On another side may be a wine merchant's shop, and an establishment of singers and dancers, beautiful women adorned with various kinds of jewels, and fair faced choristers, all ready to perform whatever may be desired of them. In short, the whole bazaar was filled with wine and beauty, dancers, perfumes, jewels of all sorts, palaces, and viands. In one street were a thousand bands of people drinking, and dancers, lovers, and pleasure-seekers assembled; none quarrelled or disputed with another, and this state of things was perpetual. Perhaps no place in the wide world could present a more wonderful spectacle to the eye of the traveller."

At Bijapur Asad Beg for the first time came across tobacco. "Never having seen the like in India, I brought some with me, and prepared a handsome pipe of jewel work. The stem, the finest to be procured at Achin, was three cubits in length, beautifully dried and coloured, both ends being adorned with jewels and enamel. I happened to come across a very handsome mouth-piece of Yaman cornelian, oval shaped, which I set to the stem; the whole was very handsome. There was also a golden burner for lighting it as a proper accompaniment. Adil Khan had given me a betel bag of very superior workmanship this I filled with fine tobacco, such that if one leaf be lit, the whole will continue burning. I arranged all elegantly on a silver tray. I had a silver tube made to keep the stem in, and that too was covered with purple velvet." Then follows a very amusing description of the Emperor's reception of this novel present. Akbar ordered Asad Beg to prepare and give him a pipeful, but no sooner had he begun to smoke, than the physician approached and forbad him to do so. Then followed a discussion between the druggist, the physician and at last the priest. The general verdict of these learned men was against the use of tobacco as being an unknown thing, and, therefore, unfitting for his Majesty to try. Asad Beg said: "The Europeans are not so foolish as not to know all about it; there are wise men among them who seldom err or commit mistakes. How can you, before you have tried a thing, and found out all its qualities, pass a judgment on it that can be depended on by the physicians, kings, great men and nobles? Things must be judged of by their good or bad qualities, and the decision must be according to the facts of the case." The physician replied: "We do not want to follow the Europeans, and adopt a custom which is not sanctioned by our own wise men without a trial." I said: "It is a strange thing, for every custom in the world has been new at one time or the other; from the days of Adam until now, they have gradually been invented. When a new thing is introduced among peoples and becomes well-known in the world, everyone adopts it; wise men and physicians should determine according to the good or bad qualities of a thing; the good qualities may not appear at once. Thus the China root, not known anciently, has been newly discovered, and is useful in many diseases." This answer so pleased Akbar that he gave Asad Beg his blessing, and said: "Did you hear how wisely Asad spoke? Truly, we must not reject a thing that has been adopted by the wise men of other nations merely because we cannot find it in our books; or how shall we progress?" The result was that the noblemen of Delhi took kindly to the new practice of smoking, but his Majesty, we are told, 'did not adopt it.'

After Asad Beg's vivid description of the charms of Bijapur one can understand why it was that the first ambassador from Delhi was so reluctant to come away, and why Asad had been ordered not to stop longer than one night. It is said that his predecessor, Jamal-ud-Din, was paid by the Sultans of Bijapur and Golconda at the rate of £105,000 to £140,000 a year, and this probably accounts for the reason why he spent three years in the Deccan, and why Asad's orders were so peremptory. The message which he tells us he was directed to give to Jamal-ud-Din was very significant: "If thou dost not return to Court with Asad, thou shalt see what will happen to thee and thy children." This had the desired effect, and the two ambassadors returned together. Asad Beg had been so successful in his mission that he was sent to the Deccan a second time, on which occasion Akbar is reported to have said: "You went before, in great discomfort to fetch Mir Jamal-ud-Din and the daughter of Adil Khan and the presents, because it was necessary. But this time you must go in state to the four provinces of the Deccan, and remain in each place so long as may be necessary, to collect whatever they may have of fine elephants and rare jewels throughout their dominions, to bring back with you. Their money you may keep. I want nothing but their choice and rare elephants and jewels. You must secure things of this kind for the Government, the rest I give to you. You must not relax your effort as long as there is one fine elephant or rare jewel out of your grasp in the Deccan." How Asad fared in this embassy we are not told, for soon afterwards the great Emperor died, but the instructions give a very clear idea of the tributary state to which the Sultans of the Deccan had by this time been reduced. Mr. Stanley Lane Poole estimates that at the accession of Aurungzebe the tribute from the Deccan amounted to about ten crores of rupees (say £ 10,000,000 (Aurungzebe, p. 128). This sum divided between Golconda and Bijapur, which were the only two independent kingdoms left, would amount to a considerable impost, but it is probable that is was very irregularly paid, especially towards the latter end of the seventeenth Century.

Ibrahim Adil Shah lived until 1626, and during his time Bijapur was at the height of its glory. Ibrahim was a great patron of architecture, and some of the finest buildings in Bijapur arose during his reign. His tomb, the Ibrahim Roza, is a splendid group of buildings, which, according to Mr. Fergusson, is more elaborately adorned than any in India. It was commenced soon after Ibrahim's accession to the throne and took thirty-six years to complete, and according to an inscription, the cost was 1,50,900 *huns*, or about £ 52,815; this, however, represents only the cash expenditure, since the workmen, as pointed out in the *Gazetteer* (vol. xxiii. p. 611), were probably paid in grain. Ibrahim is said to have been a man of learning and taste, and though the first years of his reign were stormy, the latter were spent in almost profound peace. When he died he left a full treasury, a flourishing country, and an army whose strength is stated at 80,000 horse and upwards of 200,000 foot. His memory is cherished as one of the best of the Bijapur kings (*ibid*). The noble example of Queen Chand, who was the guardian of the King's youth, no doubt left a deep impression upon him, and he himself has left a poem in which he praises her virtues, which is full of love and gratitude to her memory. We reproduce it here as translated by Mr. H. F. Silcock, C.S.:—

> In the gardens of the blest, where the happy *houris* dwell,
> In the palaces of men, where earth's fairest ones are seen.
> There is none who can compare in beauty or in grace
> With the noble Chand Sultana, Bijapur's beloved Queen.
> Though in battle's dreadful turmoil her courage never failed.
> In the softer arts of peace she was gentle and serene,
> To the feeble tender-hearted, to the needy ever kind,
> Was the noble Chand Sultana, Bijapur's beloved Queen.
> As the *champak* flower in fragrance is the sweetest flower that blows.
> As the cypress trees in form all other trees excel,
> So in disposition tender, in beauty without peer,
> Was that gracious Queen whose praise no human tongue can tell.
> In memory of that mother who with watchful tender care
> Ever guarded her poor orphan in a weary troubled land,
> I, Ibrahim the Second, these feeble lines indite
> To the honour of that Princess, the noble Lady Chand.

CHAPTER XXI.

THE STORY OF MALICK AMBER.

At the time of the fall of Ahmednagar, one Malick Amber was the Governor of Dowlatabad. Malick, or Sidi Amber, as he is often called, had been originally an Abyssinian slave. He was a man of considerable talents, especially in administrative matters. During the time of Queen Chand he was her faithful deputy, and when the Queen was murdered, and the capital fell, he remained faithful to the old dynasty, and proclaimed Murtaza II, grandson of the second Nizam Shah, to be the King. The new King fixed his capital at Kirki, a city which had been founded by Malick Amber, and which is now known as Aurangabad. Malick Amber was the Regent and virtual ruler of what portion of the kingdom was left. It is probable that at first this little kingdom consisted of but one or two districts with which the Moguls in Ahmednagar did not think it worth their while to interfere, as they had sufficient to do in settling the western portion of the kingdom. In 1607, Malick Amber placed the King Murtaza into confinement, where he remained for the next nineteen years; and then declared his independence, ruling the country that was left in his own name. His rule appears to have been a wise and able one, and especially so as regards revenue matters. He made a thorough survey and settlement of the country under his charge, which remained in force until the middle of this century, and his name is still highly-spoken of as the founder of the country's prosperity. The country itself is very rich and fertile, and consists for the most part of the valley of the Upper Godavery. Circumstances favoured Malick Amber, for soon after his accession to power dissensions broke out amongst the Moguls. Soon after Jehangir's accession, his son, Sultan Khusroo, revolted. This took away the attention of the Emperor for some time from the affairs of the Deccan, and by the time he had quelled the revolt, Amber had managed to make himself so strong that he was never really conquered. Gradually he extended his possessions until they reached within eight miles of the fort of Ahmednagar to the west; and to Bieder on the east, whilst in the south they bordered on the Bijapur country. Malick Amber was the Emperor Jehangir's especial object of detestation. He frequently mentions him in his memoirs, but scarcely ever without some adjective of abuse, such as "black-faced," "wretch," or "cursed fellow." Numerous expeditions were sent against him, but though he was sometimes defeated, he was never conquered, and he was as often successful as not. In 1609, Jehangir recalled the Khan Khanan on account of the mismanagement of affairs in the Deccan. Jehangir in his diary thus summarises the state of affairs at that time:—"From the time of the conquest of Ahmednagar by my late brother Daniyal to the present time, the place had been under the command of Khwaja Beg Mirza Safawi, a relation of Shah Tahmasp, of Persia; but since their late successes, the Deccances had invested the town. Every effort was made to defend the place, and Khan Khanan and the other *Amirs* who were with Prince Parwez at Burhanpur marched forth to relieve it. Through the jealousies and dissensions of the leaders, and from want of supplies, the army was conducted

by inproper roads, through mountains and difficult passes, and in a short time it was disorganized, and so much in want of food that it was compelled to retreat. The hopes of the garrison were fixed on this force, and its retreat filled them with fear. They desired to evacuate the place. Khwaja Beg Mirza did his best to console and encourage them; but in vain, so he capitulated on terms and retired with his men to Burhanpur. When the despatches arrived, and I found that the Khwaja had fought bravely and done his best, I promoted him to a *mansab* of 5,000 and gave him a suitable Jagir." *
A letter written to Jehangir at this time by Khan Jehan, the Second-in-Command, shows the state of affairs:—"All the disasters have happened through the bad management of the Khan Khanan. Either confirm him in his command or recall him to court, and appoint me to perform the service. If 30,000 horse are sent as a reinforcement, I will undertake in the course of two years to recover the Imperial territory from the enemy, to take Kandahar, and other fortresses on the frontier, and to make Bijapur a part of the Imperial dominions. If I do not complish this in the period named, I will never show my face at court again." This suggestion was adopted, and the Khan Khanan was recalled, Khan Jehan being appointed in his place. It does not appear that Khan Jehan was able to fulfill all his promises; he did so, no doubt, in part, but as for reducing the whole of the Ahmednagar country, let alone Bijapur, we find the latter left untouched, and in the former Amber was as strong as ever. In 1612, Jehangir speaks of the defeat of another Imperial expedition in a battle fought near Dowlatabad. Jehangir thus notices it: "Amber the black-faced, who had placed himself in command of the enemy, continually brought up re-inforcements till he had assembled a large force, and he constantly annoyed

---

* Elliot and Dowson, Vol. VI., p. 323.

Abdullah with rockets and various kinds of fiery missiles, till he reduced him to a sad condition. So, as the Imperial force had received no reinforcement, and the enemy was in great force, it was deemed expedient to retreat, and prepare for a new campaign." This was done, and soon afterwards proposals of peace were made by the Deccanees, which appear to have been accepted. Two years afterwards an attempt was made to assassinate Malick Amber, which, however, failed, and the Emperor in recording it adds:—"A very little more would have made an end of this cursed fellow." In the same year (tenth of the reign = 1616), we find a victory recorded over the army of the "wretched" Amber:—"Some good officers and a body of *Bargis* (Mahrattas), a very hardy race of people, who are great movers of opposition and strife, being offended with Amber desired to become subjects of my throne. * * * Having thus brought them in to the interests of the throne, Shah Sarvar Khan marched with them from Balapur against Amber. On their way they were opposed by an army of the Deccanees: but they soon defeated it, and drove the men in panic to the camp of Amber. In his vanity and pride, he resolved to hazard a battle with my victorious army. To his own forces he united the armies of Adil Khan and Kutb-ul-Mulk, and with a train of artillery, he marched to meet the royal army, until he came within five or six *koss* of it" (*ibid*, p. 344). A hotly contested engagement ensued, which resulted in the total defeat of the Deccanees, and the flight of the 'black-faced' Amber, who left his capital Kirki to be occupied by the Imperialists. After this defeat, Malick Amber sued for peace, which was granted, and the Imperial troops withdrew, but they had no sooner withdrawn than another outbreak occurred. Jehangir had gone to Cashmere, and Malick Amber thinking this a favourable opportunity, made an inroad into the Berars, and shut the Imperial garrison up in Burhanpur. The rebels remained for six months in this part of the country, and annexed several districts of Berar and Khandeish. Matters were in so critical a state, that Prince Shah Jehan was sent to reconquer the Deccan. At first (1621) he was successful. Kirki was invested and taken, and so destroyed "that the town which had taken twenty years to build will hardly recover its splendour for another twenty years." Amber now again had to submit, and was compelled to cede fourteen *koss* (28 miles) of Imperial territory and pay an indemnity of fifty lakhs of rupees. In 1622, Shah Jehan broke into rebellion, and Amber seems to have given him very considerable assistance. For the next three years this rebellion continued, and operations were at first conducted in the Deccan. Amber profited by the confusion to annex fresh territory, and pushed on his boundaries to within a short distance of Ahmednagar. In 1623, Shah Jehan was beaten and compelled to raise the siege of Burhanpur, upon which he left the Deccan, and the Imperialists were able to pay attention to Malick Amber. The following quotation from Mutamad Khan (Elliot and Dowson, Vol. VI., pp. 414-15) shows how important a person Malick Amber had become:—"Malick Amber proceeded to the frontiers of Kutb-ul-Mulk, to receive the annual payment of his army, which was now two years in arrears. After receiving it, and making himself secure on that side by a treaty and oath, he proceeded towards Bieder. There he found the forces of Adil Khan, who were in charge of that country, unprepared, so he attacked them unawares and plundered the city. From thence he marched against Bijapur. Adil Khan had sent his best troops and officers along with Mulla Mahomed Lari to Burhanpur (to assist the Imperial Forces), and not deeming himself strong enough to resist the assailant, he shut himself up in the fortress of Bijapur, and doing all he could to secure the place, he sent a messenger to recall Mahomed Lari and his forces." Sarbuland Rai was the Imperial Governor at Burhanpur, and he at once allowed Mahomed Lari to return, sending with him a large portion of his army. Amber now raised the siege of Bijapur, and retreated to his own country, but was followed by the combined Adil Khani and his Imperial troops. Amber, hardly pressed, was at length compelled to give battle about ten miles from Ahmednagar. Mahomed Lari, who commanded the Bijapur troops, was killed, and his fall throwing his followers into confusion, Malick Amber obtained a complete victory. "Malick Amber, successful beyond his hopes, sent his prisoners to the fortress of Dowlatabad, and marched to lay siege to Ahmednagar. But although he brought up his guns and pressed the siege, he met with no success. He, therefore, left a part of his army to complete the investment, whilst he marched against Bijapur. Adil Khan again took refuge in the fortress, and Malick Amber occupied all his territories as far as the frontiers of the Imperial dominions in the Balaghat (Berar). He collected an excellent army and laid siege to Sholapur, which had long been a subject of contention between Nizam-ul-Mulk and Adil Khan. He sent a force against Burhanpur, and having brought up guns from Dowlatabad, he took Sholapur by storm" *(ibid)*. Orders were now sent to the Imperial Forces to stay all further proceedings until the arrival of reinforcements, and until his death, Malick Amber seems to have been supreme in the Deccan. This occurred in 1626, and the same historian whom we have quoted above, thus records it:—"Intelligence now arrived of the death of Amber, the Abyssinian, in the eightieth year of his age, on the 31st Ardebthist. This Amber was a slave, but an able man. In warfare, in command, in sound judgment, and in administration, he had no rival or equal. He well understood that predatory warfare, which in the language of the Deccan is called *bargi-giri*. He kept down the turbulent spirit of that country, and maintained his exalted position to the end of his life, and closed his career in honour. History records no other instance of an Abyssinian slave arriving at such eminence."

During the whole of this time (1607-26) the King Murtaza II. had been kept in confinement, chiefly in the fort of Dowlatabad, where he spent his time in drink and sensual excess. Malick Amber left two sons—Futteh Khan and Chenghiz Khan—of whom the former, the elder, succeeded to his father's authority. The King, however, managed to make his escape, in which he was aided by a favourite slave, named Hamid Khan. Futteh Khan was then seized and sent in confinement to the fort of Khiber. Here, however, he did not remain long, but making his escape, he raised the standard of rebellion. Hamid Khan appears to have been an able man, and succeeded in raising an army and again capturing Futteh Khan, who was now confined in the fort of Dowlatabad. Shah Jehan was then on the Delhi throne, having succeeded on 6th February, 1628. Soon after his accession, one of his principal Generals, Khan Jehan, who for some time had been Governor of the Deccan, revolted, and took refuge with Murtaza Shah in Kirki and Dowlatabad. This led to considerable fighting with the Imperial troops, who were sent to capture the rebel, and Khan Jehan at length had to escape to the Punjab. This was in 1630, and in the same year a terrible famine ravaged the Deccan and Guzerat. We are told by Abdul Hamid Lahori (*ibid.* Vol. VII., p. 24), "that the inhabitants of these two countries were reduced to the direst extremity. Life was offered for a loaf, but none would buy; rank was to be sold for a cake, but none cared for it; the ever bounteous hand was now stretched out to beg for food, and the feet which had always trodden the way of contentment, walked about only in search of sustenance. For a long time dog's flesh was sold for goat's flesh, and the pounded bones of the dead were mixed with flour and sold. When this was discovered, the sellers were brought to justice. Destitution at length arrived at such a pitch that men began to devour each other, and the flesh of a son was prefered to his love. The numbers of the dying caused obstructions in the roads, and every man whose dire sufferings did not terminate in death, and who retained the power to move, wandered off to the towns and villages of other countries. Those lands which had been famous for their fertility and plenty now retained no trace of production."

During this time Futteh Khan had been in confinement, but through an intrigue by means of his sister, who was in the King's zenana, he not only was released, but was appointed Commander-in-Chief. Futteh Khan, however, felt that this change was only a temporary one. The King Murtaza was now very old, and was given up to all kinds of debauchery. He was surrounded by evil advisers, and so to save himself, Futteh Khan placed his master in the same prison from which he had just been liberated. He then at once entered into correspondence with the Imperial Court, and offered to hold the country as a vassal of Delhi. "In answer he was told that if he wished to prove his sincerity he should rid the world of such a worthless and wicked being (Murtaza II.) On receiving this direction, Futteh Khan secretly made away with Nizam Shah, but gave out that he had died a natural death" (*ibid*, Vol. VII., p. 27). Futteh Khan, however, soon repented of what he had done, and placed Hussein, the son of Murtaza, a boy ten years of age, on the throne, and when the ambassadors from Delhi arrived, he refused to hand over the fort. Shah Jehan thereupon sent an army under Mahabut Khan to reduce Dowlatabad. Futteh Khan's change of mind appears to have been caused by the attitude of the Bijapur forces, whom Adil Shah had sent against Dowlatabad, but who now made an arrangement to assist Futteh Khan in its defence, against the Imperialists. Shahjee, who was rapidly becoming a person of importance, appears in this matter on the side of Bijapur, and did good service in harassing the march of the Imperial army. But in spite of all opposition, the post was at last invested, and the siege commenced. The defence was a very obstinate one, and when at last the lower fort was taken, Futteh Khan retired with the young King to the upper fort which was held to be impregnable. Abdul Hamid (*ibid*, Vol. vi., p. 41) thus describes it:—"The old name of the fortress of Dowlatabad was Deo-gir, or Dhárágar. It stands upon a rock which towers to the sky. In circumference it measures 5,000 legal *gaz*, and the rock all round is scarped so carefully, from the base of the fort to the level of the water, that a snake or an ant would ascend it with difficulty. Around it there is a moat forty legal yards (*zara*) in width and thirty depth, cut into the solid rock. In the heart of the rock there is a dark and tortuous passage like the ascent of a minaret, and a light is required there in broad daylight. The steps are cut in the rock itself, and the bottom is closed by an iron gate. It is by this road and way that the fortress is entered. By the passage a large iron brazier had been constructed, which, when necessary, could be placed in the middle of it, and a fire being kindled in the brazier, its heat would effectually prevent all progress. The ordinary means of besieging a fort by mines, &c., are of no avail against it." But in spite of the strength of the fort, Futteh Khan saw that further resistance was useless, and that sooner or later he would have to yield. In order, therefore, to get as good terms as possible, he offered to submit. The offer was accepted, the keys handed over, and the *Khutba* was read in the name of the Emperor. The young King Hussein was sent to Gwalior to join the young prince who had been sent to the same place from Ahmednagar, thirty-four years before. Futteh Khan was loaded with honours, and was offered a high command in the Imperial army, which he was about to undertake, when he developed symptoms of insanity from an old wound in the head. He was, therefore, allowed to retire to Lahore, where he lived for many years in receipt of a pension of two lakhs of rupees. His younger brother, Chengiz Khan, had already entered the Emperor's service, where he was appointed an Amir of two thousand, with the title of Munsoor Khan. This was the end of the Nizam Shahs, and from this time, the whole of their territory sunk into a province of the Empire.

The story of Malick Amber is very slightly mentioned by Indian historians, and he is frequently spoken of as being a Governor of the Delhi Emperor. There can, however, be no doubt that for nineteen years he not only ruled in his own name, but that he very nearly reconquered the whole of the Ahmednagar Kingdom. He must have carried his conquests as far as the sea, for he is spoken of as doing damage to the Imperial shipping. He was evidently held in great respect in the Deccan, and both Golconda and Bijapur paid him tribute. As long as he lived, the Moguls could retain no firm hold, and he went near to forming a large independent kingdom which, had he lived a few years longer, might possibly have been able to withstand the Imperial arms. But it was not to be, and when he died, the last capable defender of the Deccan passed away, so that the end now became merely a question of time. With the fall of Dowlatabad the beginning of the end had commenced.

CHAPTER XXII.

THE BEGINNING OF THE END.

THE fall of Dowlatabad was followed by the reduction of several other strongholds. Shahjee was negotiating for the surrender of Jalna, but was anticipated by the Moguls, who induced the Governor of the fort to hand over possession to them. Shahjee then managed to get hold of a relative of the Nizam Shah, and keeping him in confinement in one of the hill forts, proclaimed him as successor to the Ahmednager Kingdom. This led to an expedition by the Imperial army, commanded by Prince Shah Shujah, and the Khan Khanan, against the hill fort of Purenda, but though the siege was pushed with a considerable amount of vigour the besiegers were not able to effect a breach, and on the rains setting in, they had to retire. In 1635, we find that an ambassador was sent from Delhi to both Golconda and Bijapur with *firmans* specifying the amount of tribute they should pay, and for the *khutba* being read in the Emperor's name. Nominally, however, the Kings were still independent, but an officer, similar to our Residents of modern times, was appointed to reside at the court of each, who kept the Emperor informed of what was going on. We read that these officers were met by the Sultans to whom they were accredited with every mark of respect; both Adil Shah and Kutb Shah going five *koss* from their capitals to meet them. It is also significant that from this time we find that the Delhi historians omit the title of Shah, and merely style the Kings, Adil Khan and Kutb-ul-Mulk. But though Bijapur made a show of submission, the King privately kept up negotiations with, and sent assistance to, the Mahratta Shahjee. This led to a punitive expedition against him by an Imperial Force, and there was a good deal of desultory fighting. The country was ravaged and laid waste, and finally Adil Shah had to sue for peace, which he obtained by payment of twenty lakhs in jewels, elephants, &c., and by promising to restrain Shahjee from molesting the Imperial territory. If Shahjee agreed to surrender the Ahmednager strongholds, such as Junar, &c., he was to be at liberty to enter the Sultan's service, but if he did not, the Sultan was to assist the Imperial army in crushing his rebellion. During the whole of this transaction, the Emperor himself was present in the Deccan with the main body of his army, but on peace being settled, he agreed to return to Delhi, and thus relieve the country from the enormous strain which the presence of the huge Imperial camp laid upon it. In his place the Emperor left his son, Prince Aurungzebe, as Viceroy and Governor of the Deccan. Abdul Hamid (*ibid*, p. 88) states that the Imperial province in the Deccan contained sixty-four forts, fifty-three of which are situated on hills, the remaining eleven being on the plains. It is divided into four *subas*— (1) Dowlatabad with Ahmednager and other districts, which they call the *suba* of the Deccan. The capital of this province, which belonged to Nizam-ul-Mulk, was formerly Admednager, and afterwards Dowlatabad; (2) Telingana, this is situated in the Balaghat (the capital was Nander with the fort of Kandahar); (3) Khandeish, the capital of which was Burhanpur, and the fort Asir; and (4) Berar (the capital of which was Ellichpur, and the fortress Gawil). The revenue of the four provinces is stated to have amounted to five crores of rupees (equal five millions sterling).

Shahjee did not submit without a struggle, but the combined forces of the Emperor and Adil Shah were too much for him, and he was at length compelled to surrender Junar, and at the same time to give up the young Nizam whom he had proclaimed. The young prince was then taken by Aurungzebe to Delhi, and eventually sent to join his two other relatives in Gwalior. Shahjee now entered the service of Adil Shah, who employed him in the campaign he was carrying on in the Carnatic. Here Shahjee continued for almost the rest of his life, leaving his younger son Sivajee under the care of his mother at Poona. In the Carnatic, Shahjee proved himself a most useful servant. He reduced Mysore, Arcot, and the whole of the Tanjore country down to the River Cauvery, the latter portion being bestowed upon him by the Sultan as a personal jaghir. For more than seven years Shahjee did not see his son Sivajee, who during this time grew up to manhood, and developed qualities which enabled him to infinitely surpass his father in daring, intrigue, and in statesmanship. Mahmud Shah was now on the throne of Bijapur. He had succeeded his father in 1626, and reigned until 1656. During this long period of thirty years, the Sultan, though not very successful against the Imperial army, extended his dominions far into the south and east. He did not himself go into the field, but remained for the greater part of his time in the capital, where he raised many handsome buildings. Amongst those is the celebrated Gol Gumbaz, or, as it is often called, the Bol Gumbaz (*Gol* means round, and *Bol* speaking). This is in some respects one of the most remarkable buildings in the world. The dome is bigger than that of the Pantheon at Rome, and covers an area of 18,225 feet (one-eighth more than that of the Pantheon.) The tomb—for in it the body of

Mahmud was buried—took ten years to build. The dome itself is built in pendatives* of a very peculiar form, and in Mr. Fergusson's opinion, they are the happiest thought in dome-building that has yet come to light. The *Bombay Gazetteer* (Vol XXIII.) thus describes the way it is built:—"In ordinary Saracenic domes, the lines of the square are carried up to the dome, and the octagon, at the springing of the dome, has the same diameter as the square; at Bijapur this space is contracted by inscribing in it two squares resting on alternate piers of an imaginary octagon. These by their intersection form an inner octagon whose angles are opposite the centre of the sides of the larger octagon. By these means an enormous mass of masonry is hung as a bracket inside the square. The inward drag of this mass is counteracted by the circular gallery, but at the same time it balances the tendency of the dome to spread at the base, and thrust the walls outward. This beautifnl building serves for a landmark, and is seen from a distance of twenty-five miles. It is, however, necessary to stand at some distance from it in order to take in the exact proportions. When too close, the dome seems to sink into the body of the building. Its great outward defect is want of height, though in this it is said to be superior to either the Pantheon or St. Sophia."

Prince Aurungzebe's tenure of the vice-royalty lasted for about seven years. When he was appointed, he was a youth of seventeen, and his rule was only a nominal one. Indeed at this time the young Prince seems to have been more devoted to religion than to the pomps and vanities of the world. It was whilst he was residing at Kirki, which, after him is called Aurangabad, that Aurungzebe conceived the extraordinary idea of retiring from the world as an ascetic, and, indeed, did for about one year actually live in a cell in

* A pendative is an architectural device by which a square is gradually contracted into a circle.

the rocky hills, that abound in the neighbourhood. The sacred caves of Ellora and Ajunta are situated not far from Aurangabad, and about the whole neighbourhood there exists a sort of *aura* of asceticism and sanctity, and it is possible the young prince's imagination was fired by this tradition, though it related to a religion different to his own. During the first Viceroyalty of Aurungzebe in the Deccan, matters seem to have been comparatively quiet, and they remained so for the ten years during which Aurungzebe was employed in the military operation in Balkh. In 1654, however, Aurungzebe was again appointed Viceroy of the Deccan, and the causes which led to this appointment call for detailed notice. We have seen how from time to time during the commencement of the Seventeenth Century the Golconda armies had taken a share in the various wars of the Deccan, and how Malick Amber levied tribute from the country. Subsequently peace was restored, and the Sultan became a tributary of the Empire. Abdulla Kutb Shah was then reigning at Golconda, or rather at Bhagnagar, the old name of Hyderabad. This town is situated on the south or right bank of the River Musi, one of the tributaries of the Kistna. Though surrounded by a wall, the city could never have been used for purposes of defence. It was founded originally by Mahomed Kutb Shah at the end of the sixteenth Century, and named by him after his favourite wife or mistress, Bhagmati. The city has no architectural pretensions with the exception of the Char Minar or four minarets, situated in the heart of the city at the meeting of the four main thoroughfares, and the Jumma or Mecca Musjid, of which a description will be given later on. In the seventeenth Century Hyderabad was a centre of mercantile enterprise, and merchants and dealers flocked there from all parts of the world, one of the special attractions being the market for diamonds which was held in the fort of Golconda, five miles distant. Amongst these adventurers was the son of an oil merchant of Ispahan, who came to Golconda about the year 1630. He was a man of extraordinary talents, and in a short time rose to a position of a great wealth and influence. The name by which he is known in history is Mir Jumla, and he forms one of the principal characters in the history of India during the seventeenth Century. The travellers Tavernier and Thevenot who visited Golconda in 1648 and 1667 have left behind graphic accounts, not only of Golconda and Hyderabad, but also of Mir Jumla, who at the first date mentioned was the principal personage in the State. The former says:—"Mir Jumla was a person of great wit and no less understanding in military than in State affairs. I had occasion to speak to him several times, and I have no less admired his justice than his despatch to all people that had to do with him; while he gave out several despatches at one time, as if he had but one business on hand. * * * On the 15th, in the morning, we were admitted to wait upon him again, and were immediately admitted into his tent, where he sat with his two secretaries by him. The Nawab was sitting according to the custom of the country, barefoot like one of our tailors, with a great number of papers sticking between his toes, and others between the fingers of his left hand, which papers he drew sometimes from between his fingers and sometimes from between his toes, and ordered what answers should be given to every one." It was during Mir Jumla's period of power in Golconda that the valuable diamond mines were acquired and developed. These mines, as already stated above, were situated at a considerable distance from Golconda, but under Mir Jumla's orders they were most carefully and systematically worked. It is not clear whether the Minister did not work some of them on his own account; possibly he farmed them from the King. Thevenot speaks of his having twenty maund's weight of diamonds which he had obtained either from the mines or from conquests in the Carnatic. Mir Jumla also owned a large jaghir adjoining the Carnatic, about 300 miles long by 60 miles wide, yielding a revenue of forty lakhs of rupees, and rich in diamond mines. His power and wealth were so great that he was able to entertain a force at his own expense of 5,000 horse. As was only natural, this enormous power and wealth of a foreigner excited the jealousy of the Deccanees, and endeavours were made to poison the King's mind against him. His son, Mahomed Amin, was also a young man of dissipated habits and incurred the King's displeasure. Mir Jumla saw that his disgrace and fall were inevitable, and he therefore resolved to throw himself into the arms of the Imperialists. Prince Aurungzebe had just arrived in the Deccan, and accordingly Mir Jumla wrote to him and invited him to invade Golconda. Bernier gives a copy of the letter,* which runs as follows:—"You need but take four or five thousand horse of the best of your army, and to march with expedition to Golconda, spreading a rumour by the way that it is an ambassador from Shah Jehan who goes in haste to speak about confidential matters to the king at Bhagnagar. The Dabir, who is the first to be addressed, to make anything known to the King, is allied to me, and is my creature and altogether mine. Take care of nothing but to march with expedition, and I will so order it that without making it known you shall come to the gates of Bhagnagar, and when the King shall come out to receive the letters according to custom, you may easily seize on him and afterwards or all his family, and do with him what shall seem good to you; in regard that his house of Bhagnagar, where he commonly resides, is unwalled and unfortified." Bernier goes on to say that on receipt of this letter, Aurungzebe at once marched as proposed, and Mir Jumla kept his word, everything falling out as predicted. "The King, being advised of the arrival of this pretended ambassador, came forth into a garden

* "History of the late Revolution of the Empire of Mogul," Vol. I., pp. 38-39.

according to custom, received him with honour and having unfortunately put himself into the hands of the enemy, ten or twelve slaves were ready to fall upon and seize him, as had been projected, but that a certain Omrah touched with tenderness, could not forbear to cry out, though he was of the party, and a creature of the Amir: 'Doth not your Majesty see that this is Aurungzebe? Away, or you are taken!' Whereat the King being affrighted, slips away, and gets hastily on horseback, riding with all his might to the fortress of Golconda." It is possible that this account may be true, for Aurungzebe was quite equal to such a piece of treachery. No doubt it is the story which Bernier heard, and in his position of surgeon to the Emperor he would have exceptionally good sources at his command. But it must always be remembered that in every country, and especially in India, stories which are current at court are generally tinged with exaggeration. In this case not only is there internal evidence that the story is not correct, but there is also the history of Ináyat Khan, which gives a very different version but one which contains the element upon which the more sensational one could easily be built. Apart from the impossibility of Prince Aurungzebe being able to start on a raid of this kind without it being known, we know that he was essentially a cautious man, and one who laid his plans after much deliberation. An expedition of this kind would, no doubt, have had attractions for a man like Sivajee, but not for Aurungzebe, and further, if he had succeeded so far as to have got the King actually in his power, he would not have allowed him to escape. Now, Ináyat Khan says Mir Jumla came himself to Aurungzebe because he had fallen into the displeasure of his master, the King. He was received with high honour, and a *khilat*, and *mansab* of 5,000 was bestowed upon him. It is very possible that on the occasion of this visit Mir Jumla laid before the Prince the plan of an invasion; but as yet there was no excuse. As soon, however, as Sultan Abdullah heard that Mir Jumla had gone to Aurungzebe, he placed his son, Mahomed Amin, in confinement, and attached all his Minister's property. This furnished the excuse for interference, and we are told that the Prince at once despatched "a quiet letter to Kutb-ul-Mulk regarding the release of the prisoners, and the restoration of Mahomed Amin's goods and chattels." At the same time he reported the matter to Delhi, and asked for permission to march with an army to insist upon the order being carried out. This permission being granted, the Prince despatched his eldest son, Mahomed Sultan, with an advance force with orders to encamp near Hyderabad, and insist upon the letter of his father being obeyed. Abdulla Shah at first delayed, but when the army arrived within a short distance of Hyderabad, he complied so far as to send out Mahomed Amin, but not his and Mir Jumla's property. The Sultan is said to have taken refuge in the fort of Golconda, and to have sent out a messenger with a box of jewels, but at the same time to have made a sortie which attacked the camp of the young Prince whilst the jewels were being presented. The attack was beaten off, but as the messenger was supposed to have been an accomplice, he was put to death. If Bernier's story were true, Mir Jumla must have still been with the Sultan, but it seems clear that previous to the despatch of this advance force he had joined Aurungzebe. There can be no doubt that the Sultan's flight was a very rapid one, and that after he had escaped, the city of Hyderabad was partially plundered; but there seems to be no ground for the accusation of treachery on the part of Aurungzebe. When Aurungzebe heard that the Sultan had only partially obeyed his orders, he at once joined his son with the main body of the army, and proceeded to invest the fort. Some fighting ensued, in which the Imperialists were not always successful, but the siege was being pressed actively when orders came from Delhi to the Prince to allow terms, and not to press the matter to the end. This probably was due to the jealousy which Prince Dara Shukoh entertained of Aurungzebe, and as the former was the emperor's favourite son, he was able to influence his father's actions. From Tavernier's account it would appear that Aurungzebe was by no means so successful in his siege as the historian Ináyat Khan tries to make out. This history is overladen with fulsome flattery of Aurungzebe, who is never mentioned without some qualifying adjective such as the "ever victorious," "the fortunate Prince," or the "ever triumphant." Tavernier visited Golconda for the third time soon after the conclusion of the war, and his account, obtained, no doubt, from eyewitnesses, cannot be open to the suspicion of partiality which that of a courtier is. Tavernier speaks of one distinct repulse, in which the Imperialists had to flee for several leagues after leaving their General on the battle-field. Under Ináyat Khan's plastic pen, this defeat becomes a victory, and as the passage is a good example of his style of writing which makes every enemy a "wretch" and every Imperialist a "hero," it is worth reproducing:—

"After two or three days had elapsed in this manner, a vast force of the Kutb-ul-Mulk's made their appearance on the northern side of the fort, and were about to pour down upon the entrenchment of Mirza Khan, who was engaged in the defence of that quarter; when the latter, becoming aware of their hostile intention, made an application for reinforcements. The renowned and successful Prince immediately despatched some nobles with his own artillery to his support, and their reinforcements having arrived at full speed, took part at once in the affray Under the magic influences of his Majesty's never-failing good fortune, the enemy took to flight, whereupon the ever-triumphant troops began putting the miscreants to the sword, and allowed hardly any of them to escape death or captivity. After chasing the vain wretches as far as the fort, they brought the prisoners along with one elephant that had fallen into their hands into his Royal Highness's presence. *On this date a trusty person was deputed to go and fetch Mir Jumla.*" This last sentence proves two things: one, that at this stage of affairs Aurungzebe considered it advisable to have a third party through whom negociations could be carried on; and secondly, that Mir Jumla was not with the King of Golconda, which he would have been had Bernier's story been true. Pending Mir Jumla's arrival there was continued fighting and also negociations. The King's mother * was admitted to an audience, not only with the Prince's son Mahomed, but also with Aurungzebe himself. The terms offered to the King's mother were an indemnity of one crore of rupees in cash, jewellery, and elephants, which the "chaste matron," as she is termed, agreed to pay. The narrative of Ináyat Khan goes on to say: "At this time the news of Mir Jumla's arrival in the vicinity of Golconda was made known; so the Prince forwarded to him the *firman* and *khilat* that had come for him from court." Mir Jumla then joined the Prince's camp, and soon afterwards peace was definitely settled, Abdullah Shah's daughter being given in marriage to Aurungzebe's son Mahomed. Ten lakhs of rupees in money and jewels were given as her dowry, and then Aurungzebe evacuated his camp, and retired to his seat of Government. So far Ináyat Khan; but when Tavernier's account is examined, it becomes clear that the native historian in a courtier-like manner has glossed over the whole proceedings. The traveller says: "Some days after the enemy had laid siege to the fortress, a gunner, perceiving Aurungzebe upon his elephant visiting the outworks whilst the

---

* Tavernier tells us that this lady was a Brahmin. She was of great intelligence, and owing to her influence the Brahmins were largely employed by the King.

King was on the bastion, said to the latter that if his Majesty wished he could destroy the Prince with a shot of the cannon, and at the same moment he put himself in position to fire. But the King seized him by the arm, and told him to do nothing of the sort, and that the lives of Princes should be respected. The gunner, who was skilful, obeyed the King, and instead of firing at Aurungzebe, he killed the General of his army, who was farther in advance, with a cannon shot. This stopped the attack, which he was about to deliver, the whole camp being alarmed by his death. Abdul Naber Beg, General of the army of the King of Golconda, who was close by with a flying camp of 4,000 horse, having heard that the enemy were somewhat disordered by the loss of their General, at once took advantage of so favourable an opportunity, and going at them full tilt, succeeded in overcoming them; and having put them to flight, he followed them vigorously for four or five leagues till nightfall. A few days before the death of this General, the King of Golconda, who had been surprised, seeing himself pressed, and supplies being short in the fortress, was on the point of giving up the keys; but as we have before related, Mirza Mahomed, his son-in-law, tore them from his hands, and threatened to slay him if he persisted any longer in such a resolution; and this was the reason why the King, who previously had but little liking for him, thenceforward conceived a great affection for him, of which he gave daily proofs. *Aurungzebe having then been obliged to raise the siege*, halted some days to rally his troops and receive reinforcements, with which he set himself to besiege Golconda. The fortress was as vigorously attacked as it was vigorously defended". *
Tavernier then goes on to describe the manner in which Mir Jumla brought about a peace; how the marriage was celebrated, and how Mir Jumla then returned with Aurangzebe

* Edition of V. Ball, LL.D., 2 Vols. (Macmillan, 1889).

THE BEGINNING OF THE END.

to his seat of Government at Burhanpur. There can be no doubt that Aurungzebe was checked in his operations against Golconda by orders from Delhi, and this check was most likely due to the jealousy of his elder brother. It would, however, be necessary to assign a reason which could pass current. This reason might have been that Aurungzebe had taken an unfair advantage of the Sultan. Hence the story which Bernier heard and has recorded. The letter of Mir Jumla may possibly be genuine, but it is impossible that the scheme could have been carried out as suggested in it, and it was not until Mir Jumla had left the Sultan that the invasion was actually carried out. From this time forward Mir Jumla threw in his lot with Aurungzebe. He first of all went to Delhi, where he presented the Emperor with a splendid diamond, believed to be the Koh-i-noor which is now amongst the British crown jewels.* Mir Jumla continued to be Aurungzebe's confidential adviser, and no doubt much of the latter's success was due to this clever schemer's advice. This aid was afterwards rewarded by Aurungzebe when he gained the throne by the viceroyalty of Bengal.

For a time therefore Golconda was spared, and Aurungzebe's chief attention was devoted to Bijapur and to the turbulent Sivajee, who was now beginning to give the Moguls a great deal of trouble. It is not within the scope of this work to follow Sivajee's fortunes; this has already been done by a far abler pen, and it must suffice here to say that the whole of the Mogul forces in the Deccan were insufficient to curb his growing power; and he continued in open rebellion, not only against them, but also against his own Sovereign of Bijapur.

As soon as Aurungzebe returned to his province, he commenced an expedition against Bijapur, one of the excuses for which was that the Sultan had not kept Sivajee in restraint,

* Bernier, and also Ball's Tavernier, Appendix I., Vol. II.

and was therefore responsible for his depredations. The Sultan of Bijapur was Ali Adil Shah II. (1656-1672), who was then a boy of nineteen. Tavernier and Thevenot, who both visited Bijapur about this time, say that he had been adopted by the late Sultan's wife before her husband's death. There is no confirmation of this in the Mahomedan histories, but it seems probable that this formed one of the reasons of Aurungzebe's invasion; another was that on ascending the throne the new Sultan had not paid homage or sent tribute to the Emperor. Mr. Campbell, in the *Bombay Gazetteer* (Vol. XXIII., p. 429) speaks of the young King as being the son of the late Sultan Mahomed, and calls the invasion an utterly unwarrantable one. He does not, however, give his authority for this statement, and a certain amount of credit is due to the two European travellers who could have had no reason for misrepresenting matters. Tavernier is very explicit. * "Some years before the death of the King, the Queen, as she had no children, adopted a young boy, upon whom she had bestowed all her affection, and whom she brought up, as I have already said, with the greatest care in the doctrines of the sect of Ali (*Sheah*). On the death of the King she caused this adopted son to be declared King, and Sivajee, as he then possessed an army, continued the war, and for some time caused trouble to the regency of this Queen. But at last he made the first proposals for peace, and the treaty was concluded, on the condition that he should retain all the country he had taken as a vassal of the King, who should receive half the revenues —and the young King, having been established on the throne by this peace, the Queen his mother undertook the pilgrimage to Mecca, and I was at Ispahan when she passed on her return." Thevenot says the same. † "The King (who reigns in Bijapur at present) was an orphan, whom the late King and Queen

* Ball's Edition. Vol. I., p. 183.
† Lovell's Translation, 1686.

adopted for their son, and after the death of the King, the Queen had so much interest as to settle him upon the throne; but he being as yet very young, the Queen was declared Regent of the kingdom. Nevertheless, there has been a great deal of weakness during her Government, and Rajah Sivajee hath made the best on't for his own elevation" (part III., p. 92). Now, adoption is not recognized in Mahomedan law, and it would therefore seem that Aurungzebe was justified in putting forward a claim that the kingdom had lapsed to the Empire. Certainly similar claims have been put forward by the British Government during the last hundred years, as regards not only Mahomedans but also Hindoos, under whose law adoption is a recognized custom. Aurungzebe accordingly marched an army into Bijapur, and refusing all overtures made by the young King, who offered almost everything short of surrender, laid siege to the capital. The defence was an obstinate one, and the city was on the point of surrender, when news arrived of the illness of Shah Jehan. If Aurungzebe was to make a bid for the throne, it was necessary for him to at once proceed to Delhi, and accordingly he made a hasty peace, received from the young King his professions of homage and a large payment of tribute, and then marched his army back to the north. Prince Dara Shukoh, the eldest son of Shah Jehan, seems to have made a very correct forecast of Aurungzebe's intentions. Mahomed Saleh Kambu * says that the Prince told his father that Aurungzebe would first of all help Murad Baksh, who was then Governor of Khandeish, to rebel, and then, making use of the money he had received from Golconda and Bijapur, would march with a large army to Delhi in order to assume the Government. This, indeed, is what actually occurred. The above-mentioned author says: "Although the Emperor showed no haste in adopting those views, he was quite willing to send the letters (of recall).

* Elliot and Dowson, vol. vii,., p. 129,

He could not resist the influence Prince Dara had obtained over him. So letters of the unpleasant import above described were sent off by the hands of some Imperial messengers. The messengers reached Prince Aurungzebe as he was engaged in directing the operation against Bijapur, and he had the place closely invested (1656-57). The arrival of the letters disturbed the minds of the soldiers, and greatly incensed the Prince, so much confusion arose." Accordingly, Aurungzebe started on the expedition which was to gain for him a throne. On his way he passed through Dowlatabad, where he left Mir Jumla in confinement. This, however, was merely a blind, for there can be no doubt that he was helped by the crafty Persian, both in advice and money. With the story of this expedition, and with the unhappy fate of Dara Shukoh and Murad Buksh, we have nothing to do in this history. It is, however, strange that we again find—as they had done 350 years before—the treasures of the Deccan being used by the victorious Governor for the purpose of rebellion against his own father, and for parricide. The curse that rests upon the Deccan gold had not yet been removed, and it is easy to understand how it has become a matter of belief amongst natives of India, that hidden treasures are guarded by demons. They are the demons of avarice and ambition.

In the meantime the Deccan for a period of twenty years had a breathing time. The end was not yet to be.

GENEALOGY OF THE KUTB SHAHI DYNASTY. (GOLCONDA).

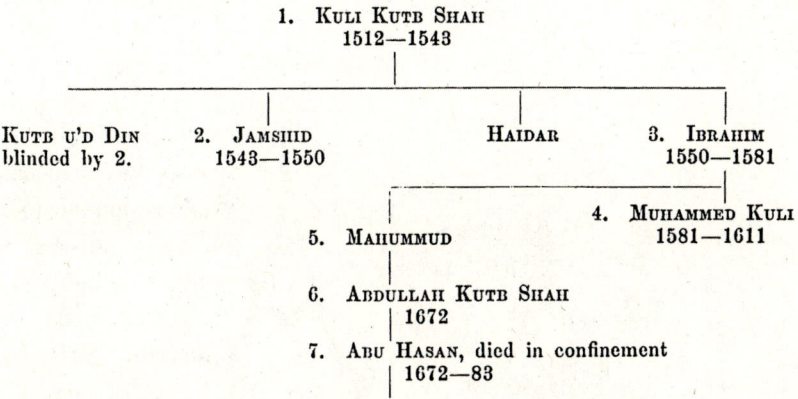

1. KULI KUTB SHAH
   1512—1543

KUTB U'D DIN   2. JAMSHID   HAIDAR   3. IBRAHIM
blinded by 2.   1543—1550   1550—1581

                                  4. MUHAMMED KULI
           5. MAHUMMUD   1581—1611

           6. ABDULLAH KUTB SHAH
               1672

           7. ABU HASAN, died in confinement
               1672—83

CHAPTER XXIII.

THE END OF BIJAPUR.

AURUNGZEBE'S absence from the Deccan, was Sivajee's opportunity, and he at once commenced a series of raids, not only into Imperial territory, but also against Bijapur. The Sultan determined to make an effort to crush him, and for this purpose collected a large army, which he entrusted to Afzul Khan, one of his most trusted and experienced Generals. Afzul Khan, though a brave and talented soldier, was by no means a match for the wily Mahratta. In 1659 Afzul Khan set out on his expedition with an army of 5,000 horse and 7,000 picked foot, besides a large supply of rockets and light artillery. Sivajee gradually retreated until he had enticed the

THE END OF BIJAPUR. 263

Mahomedan General into the defiles of the Mahabaleshwar hills, and then when the latter had arrived in front of the hill fort of Pratabgarh, he proposed a conference in which to discuss the terms of peace. A small plateau below the fort was elected as the place of meeting, and it was arranged that the two Commanders should meet there unattended by any followers. Afzul Khan, unsuspicious of any treachery, was the first to arrive at the place of meeting. Soon afterwards, Sivajee was seen descending the hill, stopping frequently as he approached as if in fear. Arrived at the plateau, Afzul Khan came forward to meet him, and then as Sivajee advanced as if to embrace him, he suddenly plunged the sharp tiger-claw dagger he held in his right hand into Afzul Khan's back, and at the same time followed up the stroke with a blow of the dagger he held in his left. Afzul Khan attempted to draw his sword, but it was too late, and he fell covered with wounds at the Mahratta's feet. Whilst this tragedy was taking place, the Mahratta troops had been gradually closing round the Mahomedans, and just as the latter were struck dumb with the foul act of treachery that was being committed before their eyes, a sudden onset was made. The Mahomedans, horror-struck and taken unaware, at once took to flight and were almost entirely cut to pieces, only a small remnant escaping to tell the tale. Flushed with this success, Sivajee broke into the open country and plundered up to the walls of Bijapur itself. The King, however, was soon able to raise another army which he entrusted to Fazl Khan, the son of Afzul Khan, and himself accompanied his troops to the field. Sivajee at once retreated, and when he had regained his hilly country was able to prolong the war indefinitely. Whenever it came to a battle, the Royal Troops were successful; but the Mahrattas then retreated to their inaccessible hills, and, eluding the Mahomedan forces, broke out in a fresh place. Although Fazl Khan distinguished himself by bravery and skill, he was not able to bring the war to a definite conclusion, and it dragged on until 1662, when a peace was concluded, under which Sivajee's conquests were confirmed to him on condition of his recognizing the Sultan as his Suzerain. "By this treaty Sivajee became Ruler of the whole of the Konkan Coast from Kalyan to Goa, and above the Sahyadris from the Bhima to the Varna, a strip of land about 130 miles long by 100 broad." * This peace lasted for six years, and though during this time Bijapur still continued to show signs of its former splendour, it was gradually crumbling away. It still continued to be a centre of commercial enterprise, and the European travellers who visited it about this time speak of the wealth of its merchants, and especially of the jewellers. Tavernier, who visited the city about 1648, does not appear to have been struck by its architectural beauties, and mentions only the goldsmiths and jewellers. Thevenot's account is so similar to that of Tavernier's, and is otherwise so vague about the surrounding country, that one cannot help suspecting that he merely wrote down what he heard from Tavernier, whom he certainly met in Surat after the latter's visit. Baldœus, the Dutch traveller in 1660, says that the Bijapur kingdom was 250 leagues long and 150 broad, and that its army consisted of 150,000 horse, besides a large number on foot. The same traveller also says that the Kingdom abounded in saltpetre works. In 1666, a Mogul force advanced against Bijapur under the command of Jey Singh, and though the Sultan offered to pay all arrears of tribute, he refused to accept any terms. But Bijapur was not yet quite dead, and rousing himself in despair the Sultan succeeded in raising a large force, to which it would seem that Sivajee also contributed. With these combined armies, the Sultan was able to defeat the Moguls, and the plague breaking out, they had to retire to Aurangabad, pursued by the Bijapur

* Campbell, *Bombay Gazetteer*, Vol. XXIII.

forces. But the effort was not a national one, and in the reaction that followed Bijapur was so weak that the Sultan had to make first concessions to Sivaji, and stooped indeed so far as to agree to pay him a yearly tribute of three lakhs of rupees on condition that he would abstain from levying *chouth* * throughout his dominions. Soon after this, the Sultan Ali Adil Shah died (1672) and was succeeded by his son, Secunder Adil Shah, a boy five years of age. For the next four years the kingdom was torn by rival factions. Khawas Khan was the Regent, and a rivalry between the two other Ministers, Abdul Karim and Muzafur Khan, was formed by the Brahmin agents of Sivajee. The quarrels between these two were so fierce that the Regent finding himself helpless, made overtures to the Emperor, offering to give the Sultan's elder sister to one of his sons in marriage. The offer was accepted, and an army was despatched under Khan Jehan to annex the kingdom and bring back the princess. Before, however, the army could reach Bijapur the Regent's treachery was discovered and the people rising in indignation, assassinated him and electing Abdul Karim as their Regent, flocked together to oppose the Moguls. Abdul Karim at once made every disposition for defence, and so patriotically was he backed up, that he was enabled to defeat the Mogul General and send him in retreat across the border. Bijapur not as yet being ready for conquest, Aurungzebe now attempted diplomatic measures, and an Agent or Resident was sent to Bijapur nominally as a mark of friendship, but in reality to intrigue and gain over the nobles. During these times of disorder Sivajee had not been idle.

* *Chouth* was the one-fourth of the revenue which the Mahrattas always levied in the districts which were at their mercy. It was a kind of blackmail, and by paying, the district obtained immunity from their raids. A hundred years later, this *chouth* was levied throughout the greater part of India, from the Cauvery to the Ganges.

He had declared himself a Rajah in 1674, and was now busy in securing the country of Tanjore and Gingee which had been granted as a Jaghir to his father Shahjee. It is not unusual to find it stated in histories that the kingdom of Tanjore was conquered by the Mahrattas. This, however, is scarcely correct. Tanjore and the hitherto impregnable fort of Gingee were in reality conquered by a Bijapur army despatched by Mahmud Adil Shah, 1637. Shahjee, who about this time had submitted to the Sultan of Bijapur, after a career of rebellion, which has already been described, was appointed to the chief command of this expedition. He was eminently successful, and carried the Bijapur armies through the Carnatic as far as Tanjore. Subsequently Tanjore and Gingee were granted to Shahjee as a Jaghir by the Bijapur Sultan in reward for his services. Tanjore was therefore a portion of the Bijapur kingdom, and Shahjee merely held it as a fief of the Sultan. Indeed, when during his father's absence Sivajee broke into revolt, the Sultan recalled his father, and holding him responsible for his son's actions, confined him in a dungeon, the door of which was partially built up (1648). Eventually, however, he was released and sent back to Tanjore to quell a rebellion. Sivajee's claim to this Jaghir was therefore a very shadowy one, but the weakness of the Bijapur State enabled him to make the best use of it. He marched into the Carnatic and succeeded in ousting the Bijapur troops from Vellore, Gingee, and Tanjore, and placed his brother Vencojee in charge of the country as his own deputy. This was only done after some considerable time, as Vencojee considered himself entitled to the whole Jaghir, but as it is not within the scope of this history to follow the fortunes of the Mahrattas, the matter need not be now discussed, and is only referred to in order to show that the Mahratta dynasty in Tanjore was not the result of a Mahratta conquest of the country, but of a Mahratta rebellion against the Suzerain power, which was only rendered possible by the Sultan's weakness. As a matter of fact, Vencojee became the founder of the Tanjore dynasty, which has only recently become extinct by the death of the last female descendant, the Princess of Tanjore.

In the meantime matters in Bijapur were thrown into a still greater state of confusion by a repulse which the Bijāpur troops met in an attack upon Golconda. The Golconda Sultan had made an alliance with Sivajee, the object of which was to divide the Bijapur kingdom between them. In anticipation of this attack the Bijapur Regent, together with the Mogul General Dilawar Khan, undertook an expedition against Golconda, but were compelled to retreat by Madhanna Punt, the Golconda Minister. On their return to Bijapur an *emeute* broke out in the army, which was largely in arrears, and it was only quelled by Masud Khan, the wealthy Abyssinian Governor of Adoni, agreeing to pay the arrears, if he was appointed Minister. This arrangement was accordingly made, and Masud Khan by paying off a portion of the forces and disbanding the remainder succeeded in restoring quiet. The Emperor Aurungzebe, however, was by no means pleased, when he heard of this arrangement and informed Dilawar Khan, his General, that he should have taken advantage of the opportunity to interfere himself; he was now instructed to demand payment of arrears of tribute and also the fulfilment of the arrangement regarding the Princess. Masud Khan refused to carry out this latter request, and at once regained his popularity, a portion of which had been lost by the disbandment of the troops. Thereupon Dilawar Khan advanced with an army to lay siege to Bijapur, and the Princess, though personally strongly against the match, voluntarily went over to the Mogul Camp, in order, if possible, to save the City from the horrors of a prolonged siege. The sacrifice, however, was of no avail. She was courteously received and sent on with an escort to Aurungzebe, but the Mogul army still continued to press the siege with vigour (1679). In despair the Regent applied for help to Sivajee, and offered the Raichore Doab if he would come to his assistance. This offer Sivajee accepted, and taking possession of his new territory, ravaged the country to the rear of the Mogul army right up to the gates of Aurangabad; Dilawar Khan, however, continued to press the siege of Bijapur and the Regent implored Sivajee to return as soon as possible. This the Mahratta did, and so galled the rear of the Mogul army, that at length, being unable to make any impression on the gallant defenders of the city, Dilawar Khan was compelled to retire. Bijapur was thus again saved, but at a heavy cost. The cession of the Doab was exceedingly unpopular, for it reduced Bijapur from a large kingdom to a mere isolated province, shut in on both sides by Mahratta territory. So great was the general disgust at the heavy price paid by the Regent Masud Khan, that he was compelled to resign and to return to Adoni. In the meantime Sivajee had died, and the new ministers at Bijapur, Shirza Khan and Seyd Mackhtum, endeavoured to regain popularity by recovering from his son and successor Sambhajee, a portion of the territory granted to his father. The attempt failed, and was especially injudicious because it alienated Sambhajee, who never forgave it, and thus Bijapur lost the only ally whose help might have enabled it to hold out against the Emperor.

The end was now near. For three years Bijapur enjoyed a brief time of peace, but it was only the lull before the storm. Aurungzebe had never relinquished his intention of subjugating the Deccan. He was led to form this resolve, not only on account of his personal ambition, but, as he openly said, from religious motives. The "vile dog" Sivajee had for years defied his authorities, and that still "viler dog" Sambhajee treated it with an even greater want of respect. The Mahrattas were "accursed heathen" who must at all hazard be swept away. But Aurungzebe regarded the Sultans of Golconda and Bijapur with feelings of detestation, almost equal to those he entertained towards the Mahrattas. Though they were not actually infidels, they were heretics, for not only did they belong to the unorthodox sect of Shias, but they also allowed infidels to thrive in their dominions. In Golconda the principal Minister was a Hindoo, and in both States a tolerance was shown toward Christians, such as was not to be found elsewhere in the Mahomedan world. Colonel Meadows Taylor has given in "A Noble Queen" a most interesting account of the protection afforded by the Bijapur Rulers to the Christian community at Mudkal, and there were many other similar Settlements throughout the kingdom. The following note from the *Bombay Gazetteer* (Vol. XXIII., p. 435) may be reproduced here:—

"According to Colonel Meadows Taylor the Adil Shahi kings were tolerant in regard to different sects of Mahomedans and the same tolerance seems to have been shown to Christian missions from Goa. It is evident from the churches that still remain in the Deccan, that the movements of the Jesuit friars and their communication with the people were not restricted, and that in some instances large communities were made their converts, which still remain firm in their faith. One mission church is at Aurangabad; another, the members of which are distillers and weavers, at Chitapur on the Bhima, about twenty miles southeast of Gulburga; a third at Raichur which consists of potters; a fourth at Mudkal, the largest, containing upward of 300 members, who are shepherds and weavers; a fifth at a place between Raichur and Mudkal, who are farmers. In all these places there are small churches furnished with translations in excellent Canarese of the Breviary and of Homilies and lectures, which in the absence of the priest, are read by lay-deacons or monks duly accredited. They have also schools attached to them. These churches, under the late Concordat are now permanently subject to the jurisdiction of the Archbishop of Goa, all of them possess *firmans* or grants of endowments by Ibrahim, Ali, and Mahmud Adil Shah; some of lands, others of grain, cloths and percentage upon the local custom and excise revenues, which are still enjoyed under the local grant. The early Portuguese missionaries introduced into the Deccan, where they still flourish, the Cintra orange, and the black and white fleshy grapes of Portugal."

A similar tolerance to heretics was also shown by the Golconda Sultan, and Tavernier tells a most interesting story of how the Sultan formed a strong attachment to a certain Father Ephraim, and when afterwards the same Father was imprisoned by the Jesuits of St. Thome, and sent to the Inquisition at Goa, the Sultan ordered Mir Jumla, who was then in the Carnatic, to kill and burn the whole Jesuit settlement, if within two months the Father was not released. The threat had the desired effect, and the authorities in Goa had to go in procession to Father Ephraim's prison, open the doors and bring him out in triumph (Ball's Edition of Tavernier, Vol. 1., Chapter XV.) This dallying with heresy was an abomination in the eyes of the bigotted Emperor, and he resolved to go in person and sweep the Deccan of the infidels and heretics that abounded there.* In 1683 Aurungzebe's preparations were made, and he started on that great expedition which lasted for twenty-four years, and from

* To this day it is remarkable what a number of Hindoo superstitions and habits have crept into the Mahomedan families of the Deccan. There can be no doubt that during the three hundred years of independence there was a far closer intimacy between the two races than existed anywhere else in India. There seems to have been not only a mutual toleration but a strong affection between the Hindoo subjects on the one hand and the Mahomedan rulers on the other which was weakened only towards the decline of the Bijapur kingdom, by unnecessary cruelty towards the rising power of the Mahrattas as related *supra* in the text.

which he never returned. So vast was the army that accompanied the Emperor, that the advance was necessarily slow. Mr. Stanley Lane Poole ("Aurungzebe") has given a description of the enormous moving city which accompanied the army, and it need not therefore be reproduced here. But though the mills of the gods grind slowly they grind very fine, and the gradual advance was like an avalanche that destroyed everything in its way. In 1685 the campaign against Bijapur was commenced by the fall of Sholapur. At first the Bijapur troops, aroused from their quarrels by the presence of the common enemy, had some few successes, and defeated the Mogul outposts on the banks of the Bhima; but gradually the net was gathered closer round the devoted city. The Bijapur army is said to have been in a very high state of efficiency, well officered and full of brave and efficient soldiers. But they had gradually to fall back, and Bijapur was closely invested by Prince A'zam. The defence, however, was nobly conducted, and the Mogul army suffered greatly from want of provisions, for the neighbourhood of Bijapur is a desert and the season had been a bad one. For some time the Imperial army could make no impression upon Bijapur, until at last the Emperor who had remained at Sholapur, came in person to conduct the siege. But still the defence was vigorously conducted. Although a practicable breach had been effected no storm was attempted. But hunger did its work more effectually, and at last on the 15th October, 1686, the garrison, reduced to the last extremities, capitulated. The Emperor entered the city in state, moving through crowds of weeping inhabitants and proceeded to the great Durbar hall, where he received the submission of the nobles. The unfortunate Sultan Sikander was brought before him laden with silver chains, and was ordered to be kept in confinement in his own capital. He received an allowance of one lakh of rupees per annum for his maintenance, but did not long survive to draw it, for a few years afterwards he died, not without suspicion of having been poisoned by the Emperor's orders. This was the end of Bijapur as an independent kingdom, and from henceforth it became an Imperial province.

The English Geographer Ogilby, writing in 1689, gives the following account of Bijapur compiled from old travellers:

"Bijapur had many jewellers who traded in diamonds and pearls of great value. The diamonds were brought from Golconda and were sold to Surat or Cambay merchants, who re-sold them in Goa and elsewhere. The arms used by the people, both by horse and foot, were broad swords, pikes, lances with a square iron at the end about a span long, bows and arrows, shields and darts. Their defensive arms were coats of mail and coats lined with cotton. When they marched afield they carried calico tents, under which they slept. They used oxen to carry their baggage. Their common mode of fighting was on foot, though when they marched, some walked, others rode on horses, and some on elephants, of which the King kept a large number. The King was very powerful, and able in a short time to bring eighty thousand to two hundred thousand armed men into the field, both horse and foot. The King had diverse great guns in his magazine, and about two hundred cannons, demi-cannons and culverines. The King was called 'Adelcan' or 'Adel Shah,' meaning the Lord of Justice, or the King of Keys—that is, the keeper of the keys that locked the treasure of the Bisngar (Vijayanagar) King. The land had no written laws, the King's will was the law. At the capital civil justice was administered by the high sheriff or *Kotwal*, and criminal cases were administered by the King. The criminals were executed in the King's presence with great cruelty, throwing them often before elephants and other wild beasts to be eaten, and sometimes cutting off their arms, legs, and other members.

A debtor who failed to pay his debt within the period named by the judge was whipped and his wife and children were sold by the creditor as slaves. Persons taking oaths were placed in a round circle made on the ground and repeated some words, with one hand on ashes and the other laid on their breast (*Bombay Gazetteer* Vol, XXIII., p. 434.)

It is clear from Bernier's résumé of the history of the Deccan that most erroneous impressions existed in Delhi regarding the history and the condition of the Deccan. Bernier of course tells us what he heard, and there seems to be little doubt that these false stories were purposely propagated in order to make Aurungzebe's invasion of Mahomedan states popular. Bernier's story regarding the origin of the Deccan Kingdom is utterly opposed to the real facts. He says: "Two centuries have scarcely elapsed since the great peninsula of India, stretching from the Gulf of Cambay on the West, and extending southerly to the Cape of Comorin and to the Gulf of Bengal near Juggernath on the east, was with the exception perhaps of a few mountainous tracts under the domination of one arbitrary despot. The indiscretion of Rajah, or King, Ram Ras the last Prince under whom it was united, caused the dismemberment of this vast monarchy, and this is the reason why it is now divided among many sovereigns professing different religions. *Ram Ras* had three Georgian slaves in his service whom he distinguished by every mark of favour and at length nominated to the Government of three considerable districts. One was appointed governor of nearly the whole of the territory in the Deccan which is now in the possession of the Mogul; Daulatabad was the capital of that Government which extended from Bieder, Paranda and Surat as far as the Nerbudda. The territory now forming the Kingdom of Visiapour was the portion of the second favourite, and the third obtained the country comprehended in the present Kingdom of Golconda. These three slaves became exceedingly rich and powerful and as they professed the Mahomedan faith and declared themselves of the Chyas (Shea) sect, which is that of the Persians they received the countenance and support of a great number of Mogols in the service of Ram Ras. They could not even if so disposed, have embraced the religion of the Gentiles, because the gentiles of India admit no stranger to the participation of their mysteries. A rebellion in which the three Georgian slaves united, terminated in the murder of Ram Ras, after which they returned to their respective Government, and usurped the title of *Chah* or King." *—A more incorrect or garbled account of Deccan history than this cannot be imagined. Bernier, however, was a most accurate and conscientious observer, and his record of contemporary events is more reliable than those of the Mahomedan historians. He was moreover for many years at the Imperial Court and had access to the highest and best informed of the nobility. It is therefore clear that he can only have recorded the version which he heard and as it is impossible, (from the fact of the histories being still extant) that the true history of the Deccan could not have been known, there seems to be good ground for the belief that this garbled version was purposely published in order to give a colour to Aurungzebe's invasion and conquest, for which, once interrupted, he was at that time only wanting another opportunity.

* Berniers Travel's.—Constables Oriental Miscellany.—Constable & Co 1891. Vol. I.

CHAPTER XXIV.

THE FALL OF GOLCONDA.—A. D. 1686.

T the same time as Aurungzebe sent an army from Sholapur to attack Bijapur he also sent an army under Prince Muhammed Muazzam and Khan Jehan against Hyderabad. Abu'l Hassan was the reigning Sultan, having succeeded his uncle Abdulla in 1672. His two principal Ministers were Hindoos, named Madanna and Akanna, and this fact of employing infidels formed one of the protests which Aurungzebe put forward for his destruction.

Abu'l Hassan appears to have contemplated relieving Bijapur, but his forces were met by the Imperial army between the two kingdoms, and though greatly superior in numbers, the Hyderabad General was beaten with considerable loss. The Imperial troops, however, were not strong enough to follow up this advantage, and remained encamped on the field of battle for some months. This delay excited the Emperor's anger, and he despatched a strong letter of censure to the Prince and to Khan Jehan, who thereupon sent a message to Muhammed Ibrahim, the Hyderabad General, that they would conclude a peace if certain districts which had been seized from the province of Ahmednagar were restored. Ibrahim taking this offer as a sign of weakness, refused peremptorily, and thus left the Imperial forces no other resource than to recommence hostilities. There seems to have been good reasons for the Emperor's displeasure at the Prince's inaction, for in the battle that followed the Imperialists won an easy victory, and the Sultan's troops fled in confusion to Hyderabad, whither they were followed by the Mogul army. There is some reason to suspect that Ibrahim, the Hyderabad General, had been bought over. At all events, his master, the Sultan, was so enraged at his discomfiture that he sent an order for his arrest, and Ibrahim, afraid of the result, then actually went over the Prince's camp and made his submission. On hearing of this defection, Abu'l Hassan at once left the city of Hyderabad and took refuge with his servants and family in the fort of Golconda, situated about four miles distant. This step appears to have been taken against the advice of his Hindoo Ministers, who would rather that he should have retreated to Warangal, in the Telingana country, where he could easily have collected a fresh army with which to raise the siege of the capital. The flight was so hurried that it was only next day that the nobles of the city heard that their Sultan had gone. As might be expected, a panic ensued, and knowing that the Imperial army was close at hand, they followed him pellmell, leaving their palaces and their effects behind. A scene then occurred which was somewhat similar to that which took place in Paris after the Franco-Prussian war, in the days of the Commune. The city was for some hours in the hands of the rabble, which rose and looted every thing that it could lay hands upon. The palaces of the two Hindoo Ministers were first of all pillaged, then followed the palace of the Sultan and those of the nobility. More than four millions sterling are said to have been carried off in this manner, and everything was in a state of anarchy. "The women of the soldiers and of the inhabitants of the city were subjected to dishonour, and great disorder and destruction prevailed. Many thousand gentlemen, being unable to take horse, and carry off their property, in the greatest distress took the hands of their children and wives, many of whom could not even seize a veil or sheet to cover them, and fled to the fortress." *

As soon as the Prince heard of what was going on he marched upon the city, but before he could arrive, it had been for some time in the hands of the rioters. They do not seem to have made any opposition. "Nobles, merchants, and poorer men, vied with each other as to who by strength of arms and by expenditure of money, should get their families and property into the fortress. Before break of day, the Imperial forces attacked the city, and a frightful scene of plunder and destruction followed, for in every part and road and market there were lakhs and lakhs of money, stuffs, carpets, horses and elephants belonging to Abu'l Hassan and his nobles. Words cannot express how many women and children of Musulmans and Hindoos were made prisoners, or how many women of high and low degree were dishonoured, carpets of great value, which were too heavy to carry, were cut to pieces with swords and daggers, and every bit was struggled for."

The Prince appointed officers to prevent the plunder, but a considerable time elapsed before order could be restored, and there seems little doubt that when the rioters were

*Khafi Khan—Elliot and Dowson, Vol. VII.

subdued the Imperial troops themselves plundered on their own account. Letters were now received from Abu'l Hassan offering submission, and after some negociation the Prince promised to withdraw on payment of one million two hundred thousand sterling in addition to the usual tribute; the Hindoo Ministers were to be dismissed and the districts which had been taken from Ahmednagar province were to be restored. No sooner were these conditions accepted than the Mahomedans of Golconda rose against the Hindoo Ministers, attacked them whilst coming from the Durbar to their own houses, and killed them, sending their heads to the Imperial camp. As soon as news of these occurrences reached the Emperor he sent a letter openly approving of what had been done, but privately he censured both the Prince and the General Khan Jehan, not only for sparing the Sultan, but also for not having taken prompter steps to quell the riot. But as already related, Aurungzebe required for the present all his available forces for the siege of Bijapur. Accordingly Golconda had a brief respite, and the Prince and Khan Jehan, with the main body of the army were recalled, and only a small force of observation was left with orders to watch events from a safe distance. Saadat Khan was sent to Hyderabad as Vakeel or Ambassador, with instructions to keep Abu'l Hassan quiet with negociations regarding the indemnity and tribute, until the Emperor should be at liberty to come in person. Saadat Khan did his work well, and kept on procrastinating until he received information that Bijapur had fallen and the Emperor had arrived at Gulburga on his march to Hyderabad. Abu'l Hassan now became thoroughly alarmed, and although he still said that he was unable to send the requisite cash, he offered to send the jewels of his family, and did, in fact, send to Saadat Khan a large number of trays of jewels, on the understanding that they should be sealed up and subsequently valued. Aurungzebe, however, continued his march, and in a few days had arrived not far from Hyderabad. Abu'l Hassan now gave up all hopes of escape by mere payment, and sent to Saadat Khan to return the jewels, but was told that they had already been sent to the Emperor. The Sultan then despatched a humble letter to Aurungzebe, but received in reply a stern letter, of which the following is the purport:*—

"The evil deeds of this wicked man pass beyond the bounds of writing, but by mentioning one out of a hundred, and a little out of much some conception of them may be formed. First, placing the reins of authority and Government in the hands of vile tyrannical infidels; oppressing and afflicting the Seyds, Shaikhs, and other holy men; openly giving himself up to excessive debauchery and depravity; indulging in drunkenness and wickedness day and night; making no distinction between infidelity and Islam, tyranny and justice, depravity and devotion; waging obstinate war in defence of infidels; want of obedience to the Divine commands and prohibitions, especially to that command which forbids assistance to an enemy's country, the disregarding of which had cost a censure upon the Holy Book in the sight both of God and man. Letters full of friendly advice and warning upon these points had been repeatedly written and had been sent by the hands of discreet men. No attention had been paid to them; moreover, it had lately become known that a lakh of pagodas had been sent to the wicked Sambha. That in this insolence and intoxication and worthlessness, no regard had been paid to the infamy of his deeds, and no hope shown of deliverance in this world or the next."

When Abu'l Hassan received this letter, he prepared for the worst. In his sudden flight from the city to Golconda, the Sultan seems to have displayed a great amount of weakness and pusillanimity which stands out in strong contrast to

* Khafi Khan—Elliot and Dowson. Vol. VII.

his final defence. It is, however, with the abrupt manner in which he left his capital that fault can be found, but not with the fact, for Hyderabad city, although surrounded by a wall, on the river front, is an utterly indefensible place, whereas it took the Imperial Army more than eight months before it could gain Golconda, and then only by treachery. The defence was a heroic one, and was well worthy of the brave struggles that we have already narrated as having taken place at Ahmednagar, Dowlatabad, and Bijapur before they had to yield to the Mogul arms. We shall be excused for going more into detail as regards this memorable siege, for not only is it the record of the end of the last Deccanee kingdom, but we are fortunate in having a full account written by Khafi Khan,* who was present throughout and who does ample justice to the principal hero, whose friend he afterwards became. We have the more excuse for these details, because in the ordinary histories the episode is dismissed with a few words only.

When Abu'l Hassan saw that there was no hope of mercy or of consideration from Aurungzebe, he set his shoulder manfully to the wheel. A large body of horse, numbering about 15,000 was stationed to the rear of the Mogul army, and help was called for from Sambhajee, which was duly sent. This force gave great assistance in cutting off supplies, harassing convoys, &c. We are not told what was the strength of the garrison, but we are told that the Sultan had ample stores of provisions, and ammunition, and a very powerful battery of artillery. The men seem to have been imbued with a spirit of patriotism and hatred of the Moguls, but as regards the principal officers, the Sultan was, with two notable exceptions, deserted by almost all his nobility, who, seeing that the end was near, went over to the Emperor's camp. Ibrahim, the former Commander-in-Chief, had been given high

* Elliot and Dowson, Vol. VII.

rank in the Imperial army and was now one of the foremost amongst the besiegers. These two exceptions were Abdur-Razzak Lari and Abdullah Khan Pani. The former performed miracles of heroism, and as the sequel will show, ranks most deservedly amongst the bravest and most faithful of Indian soldiers. The latter unfortunately was a traitor at heart, and it would have been better for his master the Sultan if, like Ibrahim, he had openly gone over to the besieging army. The siege commenced on the 24*th Rabi-ul-awal*, (September 1687) and from this date for more than eight months not a day passed without a hot encounter. Before long the Sultan's troops outside the fort, swelled by Sambhajee's reinforcements, amounted to between forty and fifty thousand horse, and though not strong enough to engage the Imperial army, afforded the garrison considerable relief. The Emperor's son, Prince Shah Alum, was nominally in command of the army, but he soon incurred his father's displeasure from the favour with which he regarded the Sultan's overtures for peace. The same thing had already occurred at Bijapur, and the Prince's policy as heir-apparent seems to have been to gain over these Deccan Sultans, and to make peace or war dependent upon his own approval. Aurungzebe, however, was not the man to be thwarted by his own son, and as soon as he became aware of his intentions, he had him arrested and sent away in confinement. Day by day and week by week the trenches were pushed forward. Almost daily the garrison made sallies, some of which were successful, but the defenders were never able to break the line, and the toils gradually closed in on the fortress. So hot was the fire on both sides that the smoke is said to have removed the distinction between day and night. Large mounds were erected so as to command the interior of the fort, and one is still pointed out as that on which Aurungzebe's tent was pitched. In about a month's time the trenches were carried up to the edge of the moat, and attempts were then made to fill it up by throwing in cotton bags filled with earth. Fifty thousand bags were ordered to be sent from the cotton-producing tracts of Berar, and the Emperor himself sewed the seams of the first bag thrown in. At last matters were brought so far that an escalade could be attempted. This had become necessary, for not only was there great scarcity in the Imperial camp, but pestilence had also broken out. Accordingly, after three months a surprise was attempted one dark night. Ladders were fixed and a few men succeeded in gaining the ramparts. But at this moment the garrison was alarmed by the barking of a dog, and the defenders succeeded in throwing down the ladders and in beating off the storming party. The dog which had thus given the fort another respite was given a golden collar and a plated chain, and was kept tied near the Sultan himself. Heavy rain now came on, in the midst of which another sally was made, which caused the Imperialists heavy loss, both in killed and prisoners. The latter were treated with generosity and kindness. One of them, an officer of distinction, Sarbhara Khan, was taken by the Sultan over his granaries and magazines, and then sent back to the Emperor with overtures for peace. The Sultan offered to present a crore of rupees (one million sterling) and a further crore for every time that Aurungzebe had besieged the fort; he also offered a free present of 600,000 maunds of grain; but Aurungzebe was inflexible. In spite of the straits to which his army was reduced, he replied: "If Abu-l Hassan does not repudiate my authority, he must come to me with clasped hands or he must be brought bound before me. I will then reflect what consideration I can show to him." By the month of Shaban three mines were ready to be exploded, but Abdur Razzak by countermining, succeeded in withdrawing the powder and match from one, and in drowning the other two with water. Only one mine was partially exploded, and the result was more damage to the besiegers than to the besieged. The garrison then made a sortie, and succeeded, after desperate fighting, in gaining the trenches, which were only recovered after much slaughter. Another assault delivered under the eyes of the Emperor himself, was also repulsed, and again the garrison occupied the trenches, spiked a number of the guns, and pulled out of the moat the logs of wood, and many thousands of the bags which had been used to fill it up, using them to repair the breaches in the walls. Aurungzebe now almost despaired of success, and, force failing, tried what he could do by bribery. Abdur Razzak refused all overtures, although he was offered a high post and a *munsab* of 6,000 horse. He even went so far as to exhibit the Emperor's letter to the men in his bastion, and tore it to pieces in their presence, sending back as a message that he would fight to the death. Abdullah Khan, however, was of a different nature, and yielded to the Emperor's offers. After a siege of eight months and ten days, he one night caused a wicket to be opened and admitted Prince Muhammad Azam. The gates were then thrown open, the army entered, and the shout of victory was raised. "Abdur Razzak heard this, and springing on a horse without any saddle, with a sword in one hand and a shield in the other, and accompanied by ten or twelve followers, rushed to the open gate through which the Imperial forces were pouring in. Although his followers were dispersed, he alone, like a drop of water falling into a sea or an atom of dust struggling in the rays of the sun, threw himself upon the advancing force, and fought with inconceivable fury and desperation, shouting that he would fight to the death for Abu'l Hassan. Every step he advanced, thousands of swords were aimed at him, and he received so many wounds from swords and spears, that he was covered with wounds from the crown of his head to the nails of his feet. He received twelve wounds upon his face alone, and the skin of his forehead hung down over his eyes and nose. One eye was severely wounded and the cuts upon his body seemed as numerous as the stars. His horse also was covered with wounds and reeled under his weight, so he gave the reins to the beast, and by great exertions kept his seat. The horse carried him to a garden, called Naquina, near the citadel, to the foot of an old cocoa-nut tree, where by the help of the tree he threw himself off. On the morning of the second day a party of men belonging to Husaini Beg passed, and recognizing him by his horse and other signs, they took compassion upon him, and carried him upon a bedstead to a house. When his own men heard of this, they came and dressed his wounds."

In the meantime Abul Hassan had met his fate in a kingly manner. When the noise and the groans convinced him that all was over, he first went into his harem to comfort his women, to ask their pardon and to take their leave. He then went into the reception hall, and placing himself upon the throne (*musnud*) he waited for his unbidden guests. As the day broke and the time came for taking his food, he ordered it to be served to him where he was. At last Ruhu-llah Khan, the Commander of the Emperor's forces, was announced and entered with his suite. The Sultan greeted them all with courtesy, conversed with them at his ease, and never for a moment forgot his dignity. He then called for his horse, and wearing on his neck a splendid row of pearls, he went with his captor to the Imperial camp. He was first taken to Prince Muhammad Azam, to whom he presented the pearls. The Prince accepted them, and placing his hand upon the Sultan's back, endeavoured to console him. The Prince then took the Sultan to the Emperor, to whom he introduced him. Aurungzebe received him courteously, and after a few days sent him to be confined in the fort of Dowlatabad, where he was kept as a state prisoner until the time of his death, some years later. A suitable allowance was given to him, and he was allowed the society of his wives.

This was the end of the last of the Deccan Sultans, and whatever may have been the faults of Abu-l Hassan's life, it must be acknowledged that he met his misfortunes in a manner worthy of a king.

It now only remains to narrate the fortunes of his brave general Abdur Razzak. We cannot better do than quote from Khafi Khan, the generous enemy who has already paid tribute to his prowess:—"Abdur Razzak, senseless, but with a spark of life remaining, was carried to the house of Ruhu-llah Khan. As soon as the eyes of Saf-Shikan Khan fell upon him, he cried out: 'This is that vile Lari! Cut off his head, and hang it over the gate!' Ruhu-llah replied that to cut off the head of a dying man without orders, when there was no hope of his surviving was far from being humane. A little bird made the matter known to Aurungzebe, who had heard of Abdur Razzak's daring and courage and loyalty, and he graciously ordered that two surgeons, one a European, the other a Hindoo, should be sent to attend the wounded man, who were to make daily reports of his condition. The Emperor also sent for Ruhu-llah Khan and told him that if Abu-l Hassan had possessed only one more servant devoted like Abdur Razzak, it would have taken much longer time to subdue the fortress. The surgeons reported that they had counted nearly seventy wounds, besides the many wounds upon wounds which could not be counted. Although one eye was not injured it was probable that he would lose the sight of both. They were directed carefully to attend to his cure. At the end of sixteen days, the doctors reported that he had opened one eye and spoken a few faltering words, expressing a hope of recovery. Aurungzebe sent a message to him forgiving him his offences, and desiring him to send his eldest son, Abdu-l Kadir, with his other sons, that they might receive suitable *munsabs* and honours. When this gracious message reached that devoted and peerless hero, he gasped out a few words of reverence and gratitude, but he said that there was little hope of recovery. If, however, it pleased the Almighty to spare him and give him a second life, it was not likely that he would be fit for service; but should he be ever capable of service, he felt that no one who had eaten the salt of Abu-l Hassan, and had thriven on his bounty, could enter the service of King Aurungzebe. On hearing these words a cloud was seen to pass over the face of his Majesty, but he kindly said: "When he is quite well let me know."

Eventually Abdur Razzak recovered, and again refused to come to the Emperor's presence, asking to be allowed to make the pilgrimage to Mecca. Aurungzebe now became angry, and orders were sent to arrest him but Firoz Jung managed to convey him away to his own house, and there kept him in concealment. After a year Abdur Razzak thought better of the Emperor's offer, he could no longer do any good to his fallen master, and so he entered the Imperial service with a *mansub* of 4,000 and 3,000 horse.

The plunder taken at Golconda amounted to eight lakhs and fifty-one thousand *huns* (golden coins or pagodas) and two crores and fifty-three thousand rupees, altogether six crores eighty lakhs and ten thousand rupees (*circa*, seven millions sterling), besides jewels, inlaid articles and vessels of gold and silver; the copper coin (*dams*) amounted to 1,15,16,00,000, equal to about $2\frac{1}{2}$ millions sterling.

We have now arrived at the close of the Mahomedan kingdoms of the Deccan. For the next thirty years this portion of India remained a province of Delhi. The Great Delhi Emperor had succeeded in absorbing the Mahomedan States, which had to a certain extent kept the Mahrattas in check, and he was now left face to face with the despised infidels. But in spite of all its magnificence and apparent power, Imperialism was rotten to the core. Aurungzebe continued to reign for about fifteen years, but during the whole of that time, in spite of all attempts, he was unable to exterminate the Mahrattas. Their power continued to increase, and was a rock upon which the flood of Imperialism was destined te be broken. But this belongs to another period of Deccan history, and at present there only remains to tell how after thirty years another Mahomedan kingdom arose and took the place of that of Golconda.

PART III.

AN EMPIRE IN RUINS.

CHAPTER XXV.

THE KING-MAKERS.

In this section the scene lies principally in Delhi and the North of India, but as the events led to the establishment of a new Kingdom in the Deccan and the persons are intimately connected with Deccan affairs it has been deemed advisable to relate the incidents at some length, especially as the period referred to is very summarily treated in the usual histories.

After the fall of Golconda, Aurungzebe was free to turn his attention to the Mahrattas. Mr. Stanley Lane Pool seems to think that the conquest of the Deccan kingdoms was chiefly intended as the first step towards the destruction of this nation of robbers and freebooters, since with their fall the large subsidies paid by them to the Mahrattas would cease. Accordingly a governor was placed in charge of Hyderabad and Golconda, and the Emperor marched westwards in order to finally crush that 'hell-dog' Sambajee. At first the Emperor's arms were everywhere successful. The whole of the territories belonging to Bijapur and Golconda were taken possession of by his generals down as far south as Tanjore. So great was the respect shown to the Emperor's authority that it was the custom of his generals to send one of his slippers placed on a splendid howdah, carried by an elephant in gorgeous trappings and conducted by a force of cavalry and infantry. When the slipper arrived at the capital of a native Prince he was expected to meet the slipper outside his capital and conduct it, followed by his nobles and troops with their ensigns lowered, to the Durbar hall in the Palace. There the slipper was placed upon the throne and the Prince himself had to pay it obeisance. This having been done, the general in charge was presented with costly presents, the tribute money was sent to him in sealed bags, and the slipper marched on in state to the next kingdom, where a similar pageant was gone through. On the occasion of a ceremonial procession of this kind soon after the accession of a new king (Runga-Kistna-Naicker, circa 1698) * the slipper, accompanied by twelve thousand cavalry, from thirty to forty thousand infantry, and two Nawabs, arrived outside Trichinopoly and a message was despatched by means of peons with silver sticks and silver breast-plates, that the Imperial mandate had come. "As the king was young he enquired of the *sirdars* about him what this meant. They replied: 'It is the *Padshah's* firman, *i.e.*, a slipper placed in a howdah attended with various banners and troops, which is sent to the rulers of kingdoms, and these kings go forth to meet it; treat it with respect; take it with those that accompany it to their capital; give presents to these, and paying to them tribute money, send them away. As this is the established rule, and the mandate is now sent to this capital we also treat it in the same respectful manner.' On hearing this the young king became angry, but dissembling his intentions gave presents to the peons and sent out his own ambassadors, who were instructed to plead sickness on his behalf, but to contrive so that the embassy was brought into the town. This the emis-

* Taylor's *Manuscripts*, Vol. II. p. 205.

saries appear to have done with success, and by first fixing one place and then another as the spot where the king would meet them, induced the Nawabs to come inside the fort gate. There being still no king the Nawabs said with anger: 'Is your king not come? have you such obstinate pride?' But the others said: 'Our king from the effect of sickness is not able to enter a palankeen, come with us to the gates of the palace.' They accordingly came with the mandate to the gates of Sri-Runga-Kistnappa-Muthu-Virapa-Naicker's palace. As the king still did not appear, they came still closer to the palace entry; when, thinking that a want of respect was implied by waiting there, they took the mandate from the howdah, placed it in a palankeen, and, not without anger, carried it into the hall of the throne. Meanwhile the king had invested himself with all the paraphernalia of his dignity, and in the midst of a great number of his friends was seated on his throne, when the Padshah's Nawabs, and principal men, having taken the *Farmana* in their hands, had brought it into the hall of the throne. Seeing that the king did not pay the smallest token of respect either to the *Farmana* or themselves, they were excessively angry, and pushing aside such persons as stood in their way in the hall of audience, they came near and offered to give the *Farmana* into the hands of the king. The king, being very angry, bid them place it on the floor. But paying no attention to his command and not putting the slipper down, they again offered to give it into his hands. Thereupon the king called for people with whips: and adding. 'Will the Padshah's people put the *Farmana* down or not? let us see,' further summoned people with rattan canes. As the king was calling aloud, they became terribly afraid and put the *Farmana* down on the floor. The king, seeing this, placed one of his feet within the slipper and addressing the people said: 'How comes it that your Padshah has lost even common sense? When sending foot furniture for such kind of persons as ourselves, why does he not send two slippers instead of one? Therefore do you speedily go back, and bring here another slipper!' While he thus spoke they answered with all the vivacity of anger. On which the king became excessively incensed and had them all beaten and driven away. In consequence, on going outside the fort they assembled all their troops and began to make war. The king on hearing this intelligence, sent outside the fort five thousand cavalry and a great force of infantry which fell upon the Padshah's troops and cut them up piecemeal. As they could not make a successful stand, they ran away, and reported these occurrences to the Padshah. He, thinking on the matter, considered that if he were for the future to send such a message, the disgrace done to it now, by the daring of one, would be imitated by others: he was therefore induced by this high bearing of Raja-Runga-Kistna-Muttu-Virapa-Naicker, thenceforwards to cease the sending of the *Farmana* to the different rulers of countries."

The foregoing account is from a Hindoo source, and there is nothing in any of the Mahomedan histories which in any way confirms it. It is probably exaggerated, especially as regards the numbers of the Mahomedan army who were put to flight. It shows, however, that previous to the incident, which occurred before the end of the seventeenth century, the custom of sending the slipper had been for some years in force, since the Trichinopoly Sirdars were acquainted with it, and that the Emperor's over-rule was recognized; for as the first impulse of the Sirdars was to show respect to the slipper, it is clear that for some time previously the Emperor's rule extended and was recognized as far south as Trichinopoly. In the account of the transactions of the latter years of Aurungzebe's reign, translated by Scott from the narrative of a Bondela officer, we are told that in 1693 Zulficcar Khan, the Emperor's great general, of whom we shall hear more later on, marched sixty coss from Gingee into the territories of Trichinopoly and Tanjore and collected considerable contributions from the Zemindars. The slipper embassy was probably subsequent to this expedition and it was only five or six years later, when Aurungzebe's whole attention was taken up with the Mahrattas, that so flagrant an insult could have been committed. Without therefore relying on the exact accuracy of the incident as here given, it proves that soon after the fall of Golconda the Emperor's armies over-ran the whole of the territories of that State and of Bijapur and exercised a certain amount of control over the hitherto independent Pandia kingdom of Trichinopoly.

But we must now return to the affairs of the Deccan proper. The Emperor with the main body of his army marched from Hyderabad through Gulburga to Bijapur. A number of the Deccanee nobles and generals came in and submitted and were rewarded with munsabs and military charges. Amongst others was Sheikh Nizam Hyderabadee, who was honoured with the title of Khan Humman and despatched on an expedition against Sumbajee, that "vile dog" who for so long had defied the great Emperor with impunity. Sumbajee had at this period almost entirely withdrawn himself from the field. His armies were despatched in various directions on marauding expeditions, and he himself remained shut up in the fort of Sungumeshwar, where he imagined himself safe amongst his native hills. Khan Humman, however, was able to take him by surprise, and making a rapid march from Kolapur arrived at the gates of the fort and succeeded in entering before they could be closed. Sumbajee himself was intoxicated, and though most of his followers succeeded in making their escape, twenty-four of his principal chiefs defended him with bravery. They were, however, all taken prisoners; and Sumbajee together with his prime minister Kuloosha were brought before the Emperor.

It is said that Aurungzebe intended to spare him, so as to induce him to restore the forts which were still in his possession, and with this object in view offered him his life if he would become a Mussulman. "Tell the Emperor," said Sumbajee, "that if he will give me his daughter I will become a Mahomedan," and concluded his reply by an invective on the prophet.* Exasperated by this insult the Emperor ordered him to be executed, which was done in a most barbarous manner. A red hot iron was drawn across his eyes, his tongue was cut out, his skin flayed from his body, and his head cut off. (August 1689.) The news of this barbarous murder of the son of the great Sivajee only served to exasperate the Mahratta nation still more against the Moguls, and the war was therefore carried on on both sides with even more bitterness than before.

Aurungzebe's Prime Minister at this time was Assud Khan, and his son Yeatikad Khan was despatched with a large force to invade the Concan. He was fortunate enough to obtain possession of Yessoo Bhai, Sumbajee's widow, and her son Sivajee, who had been declared as his father's successor, with his uncle Rajah Ram as regent. These two prisoners were taken to the Emperor's camp, where they were kindly received, and the boy, being only six years of age, was adopted by Aurungzebe's daughter. He seems to have been taken notice of by the Emperor, who called him Sahoo or Shao, and by this name he was always afterwards known. Yeatikad Khan was highly honoured for this capture, and the title of Zulficcar Khan was bestowed upon him, under which name he henceforward played a conspicuous part.

Rajah Ram, with a large force, then set off for the strong fort of Gingee, which is situated in the present district of South Arcot, about 50 miles inland from Pondicherry. The remains of the fort show that it must at one time have been

* Grant Duff, Vol. I. p. 306.

of considerable strength. It is built on a small circular range of rocky hills which are isolated in the plain. A wall connects the whole of this range, and strong forts are built at the mouth of each entrance or valley. The ground thus enclosed contains several square miles, and is capable of growing grain required for the garrison. There are also large reservoirs which are fed not only by springs but by water-courses from the hill sides, so that the place was capable of maintaining a lengthened siege without any relief from outside. This fort formed the stronghold of the Mahrattas in the south of India, and the outpost of their possessions in Tanjore. The siege of this important place lasted for very nearly ten years from 1689 until 1698, but there seems to be no doubt that operations were purposely delayed owing to intrigues amongst the generals. The Bondela officer, from whose journal Scott has compiled his history of this portion of Aurungzebe's reign, says that the total ruin of the Mahratta power might have been effected with ease many years before but the Amras delayed on purpose, and secretly assisted each other to draw out the war to a never-ending length for their own advantage, also dreading that when the Emperor should have finally reduced the Deccan, he would carry his arms to Candahar and Balkh, which expeditions were disagreeable to the nobility, who did not wish to encounter the hardships of the north.* During the greater part of the siege of Gingee. Zulficcar Khan was in chief command, though for a portion of the time he was superseded by Prince Kaum Buksh, Aurungzebe's favourite son. Soon after the Prince's arrival rumours began to circulate that the Emperor was ill and was not likely to recover. In the event of the throne becoming vacant it was necessary for the success of any aspirant that he should be at headquarters in order to assert his claim. Accordingly the Prince began

* It is alleged that documents exist which show that Aurungzebe's secret intention was ultimately to found a great Empire in Central Asia.

to make secret overtures to the Mahrattas and on this coming to the ears of Zulficcar Khan he promptly had the Prince arrested and confined in his own tent. This was an act of masterfulness that Kaum Buksh never forgave, and he never let an opportunity pass of showing the dislike he felt for the general, a dislike which seems to have been cordially and implacably returned. Nevertheless the siege of Gingee had to be raised, for the imperial army was so reduced by sickness and want of provisions that it had to withdraw into quarters. Zulficcar Khan and the Prince were summoned to the Emperor's camp, and although Aurungzebe openly accepted his son's explanation and blamed the general, as a matter of fact he kept the Prince for some time in honourable confinement and employed his lieutenant on active service. Zulficcar Khan was a brave and ambitous general. When he really meant fighting he invariably beat the Mahrattas, but it is said that he secretly intended to establish himself in the Carnatic with the object, when the opportunity came, of making himself independent. If this is true, it was unfortunate for him that he relinquished the idea, for though after Aurungzebe's death Zulficcar Khan enjoyed for a few years the power and the wealth of a king-maker at Delhi, his career ended at last with murder and spoliation, whereas another, following out his original ambition, actually achieved independence and became the founder of a royal line that still rules in the Deccan.

The date of this incident was 1696, and from this time Aurungzebe seems to have adopted a fresh policy in his campaign against the Mahrattas. A new force was despatched into the Carnatic to besiege Gingee, and the Deccan army was divided into two portions. The one, a flying column, was sent under Zulficcar Khan to beat up the Mahrattas wherever they could be found, whilst with the main body the Emperor himself sat down to besiege the hill forts one after the other, Chin Koolich Khan, a name destined to become famous in the Deccan, was left as Governor of Bijapur.

In pursuance of this plan the Emperor successively besieged and captured Sattara, Panalla, Vishalgurh, Singurh, Purunda, Rajgurh, Poona, and Waikankara; whilst in the open field Zulficcar Khan constantly defeated the Mahratta armies when he could meet them face to face. But in spite of this marvellous perserverance of an old man bordering on ninety, Aurungzebe was never able to make any lasting impression on the "mountain rats." Young Sahoo was still kept in the Emperor's camp. Rajah Ram, his uncle, who at first acted as Regent, was dead, and the real leader of the Mahratta nation was Tara Bhai, Sumbajee's widow and stepmother to Sahoo. Tara Bhai was a second Queen Chand, and deserves a lasting place in the ranks of noble queens and heroines. She became the life and soul of the Mahrattas, and sent out army after army with instructions to avoid all conflict in the open field, but to harass the imperial armies in the rear, to cut off their supplies, and to carry raids far beyond the confines of the Deccan. Aurungzebe' spersistency and doggedness in his attempts to break up the Mahratta confederacy had the very opposite effect to what he intended, and it is said that the Mahrattas themselves offered up prayers for the preservation of the Emperor's life and therefore for the prolongation of his policy. So successful were the Mahrattas in their raids that on several occasions the huge imperial camp was reduced almost to starvation, and was so hemmed in on all sides that no one dared to leave its limits. The Deccan itself was reduced to the state of a desert. All the Emperor's supplies and money had to be drawn from the north. His governors at Hyderabad and Bijapur could only with difficulty make small collections, and even there they had to dispute with the Mahratta tax collectors, who boldly levied their *chouth*, or one quarter of the revenue, throughout the imperial provinces. But nothing could bend the will of the stern old Emperor. Hunger and reverses did not subdue it, and though on at least two occasions his camp was well nigh carried away by floods, he still pursued his life of self-abnegation, resolved to conquer or to die. Zulficcar Khan was again despatched to carry on the siege of Gingee, and received a hint that it would be well for him to show more energy. This time he was not trammelled by the presence of a royal Prince, and Gingee at last yielded to his arms (1698), and, the strength of the Mahrattas in the South Carnatic being broken, the general was left free to return to the principal seat of the war in the Deccan. Here the same system of operations was carried on. Aurungzebe laid siege to one fort after another, and Zulficcar Khan hurried from province to province in pursuit of the elusive Mahrattas. In one campaign alone he is said to have marched 2,000 coss, or about 4,000 miles, a distance which is surely somewhat exaggerated. It is scarcely within the province of this work to follow in detail all Aurungzebe's movements. It is true that the scene of them lay in the Deccan, but they have been so exhaustively discussed by Grant Duff that it would be useless to go over the same ground. Each year was a repetition of the previous one. Nothing decisive was ever gained by the Emperor. The forts he took one year were frequently retaken in the following one, when he had moved on to begin again the same wearisome story. During the whole of this time the Mahrattas gradually increased in strength and daring. Their bands harried the country from Mysore up to Guzerat, and a strong central system of Government was organized at Poona. Fifty years before, Aurungzebe had found Sivajee at the head of a comparatively small body of robbers. When he died Sivajee's grandson ruled over a well organized Government and a nation imbued with the spirit of plunder.

The time had at last come for the great Emperor to leave this life of unrest and struggles. Nearly ninety years of age, he had ruled for almost fifty. All those who had crossed his path, whether father, brothers, sons or nephews, had come to a violent end, in battle, or else by the more secret means of the dagger or the poison bowl. For the last twenty years of his life he had lived in a camp and endured hardships far greater than some of his luxurious followers. Right or wrong he had unswervingly carried out the line of policy he had laid down for himself, and now, as he felt his end approaching, he saw his plans thwarted, his enemies flourishing, his sons at discord with one another, and the whole fabric of Empire crumbling away as it were to pieces. Towards the end of 1706 he marched into Ahmednagar, the capital of the old Nizam Shahi kings, and on the day he marched in, he himself exclaimed that his last campaign was finished. Remembering his own fight for the throne, he sent his three sons away to their different governments, separated as far as possible from one another. The eldest, subsequently known as Bahadur Shah, was in Cabul; Azim Shah was sent to Malwa, and Kaum Buksh, his youngest and favourite, to Bijapur. To the eldest son the Emperor seems to have sent no message, and to have made no sign, and he probably thought that he was too far removed to have a chance of succeeding. But shortly before he died he wrote a letter to Azim Shah and another to Kaum Buksh, both of which are so pathetic that they must be given *in extenso*.*

To Shah Azim Shah.

"Health to thee! My heart is near thee! Old age has arrived: weakness subdues me, and strength has forsaken all my members. I came a stranger into this world, and a stranger I depart. I know nothing of myself, what I am, and for what I am destined. The instant which passed in power has left only sorrow behind

* Eradat Khan, translated by Scott (also Elliot and Dowson). These letters are not to my knowledge reproduced in any of the histories. Mr. Stanley Lane Poole gives an extract from one in his monograph. *Aurangzib.*

it. I have not been the guardian and protector of the empire. My valuable time has been passed vainly. I had a patron in my own dwelling (conscience) but his glorious light was unseen by my dimmed sight. Life is not lasting; there is no vestige of departed breath, and all hopes from futurity are lost. The fever has left me, but nothing remains of me but skin and bone. My son Kaum Buksh, though gone towards Bijapur, is still near; thou my son art yet nearer. The worthy of esteem Shah Alum (Bahadur Shah) is far distant and my grandson (Azim Ushan) by the orders of God is arrived near Hindoostan. The camp followers, helpless and alarmed, are like myself full of affliction, restless as quicksilver. Separated from their lord, they know not if they have a master or not.

I brought nothing into this world, and except the infirmities of man carry nothing out. I have a dread for my salvation and with what torments I may be punished. Though I have a strong reliance on the mercies and bounties of God, yet regarding my actions fear will not quit me; but when I am gone, reflection will not remain. Come then what may I have launched my vessel to the waves. Though Providence will protect the camp, yet regarding appearances, the endeavours of my sons are indispensably incumbent. Give my last prayers to my grandson (Bedar Bukht son of Azim Shah) whom I cannot see but the desire affects me. The Begum (his favourite daughter) appears afflicted but God is the only judge of hearts. The foolish thoughts of women produce nothing but disappointment. Farewell! farewell! farewell!"

To the Prince Kaum Buksh.

"My Son, nearest to my heart. Though in the height of my power, and by God's permission, I gave you advice and took with you the greatest pains, yet, as it was not the divine will, you did not attend with the ears of compliance. Now I depart a stranger, and lament my own insignifiance, what does it profit me? I carry with me the fruits of my sins and imperfections. Surprising Providence! I came here alone, and alone I depart. The leader of the caravan has deserted me. The fever which troubled me for twelve days has left me. Wherever I look I see nothing but the Divinity. My fears for the camp and followers are great, but alas! I know not myself. My back is bent with weakness and my feet have lost the power of motion. The breath which rose is gone, and left not even hope behind it. I have committed numerous crimes and know not with what punishment I may be seized. Though the Protector of mankind will guard the camp yet care is incumbent also on the faithful, and my sons. When I was alive no care was taken and now the consequence may be guessed. The guardianship of a people is the trust by God committed to my sons. Azim Shah is near. Be cautious that none of the faithful are slain or their miseries will fall upon my head. I resign you, your mother and son to God, as I myself am going. The agonies of death come upon me fast. Bahadur Shah is still where he was, and his son has arrived near Hindustan. Bedar Bukht is in Guzerat. Hyut al Nissa (his daughter the Begum), who has beheld no afflictions of time till now, is full of sorrows. Regard the Begum as without concern. Odeypooree*, your mother, was a partner in my illness and wishes to accompany me in death; but every thing has its appointed time.

The domestics and courtiers, however deceitful, yet must not be ill treated. It is necessary to gain your views by gentleness and art. Extend your feet no lower than your skirt. The complaints of the unpaid troops are as before.

* It is questioned whether this is not a mistake for Jodhporee, as a princess of Jodhpore was sent to Aurungzebe's zenana. The house of Odeypore claims to have never contributed a Princess to the Mahomedan Emperors.

Dara Shakoh, though of much judgment and good understanding, settled large pensions on his people, but paid them ill, and they were ever discontented. I am going. Whatever good or evil I have done, it was for you. Take it not amiss, nor remember what offences I have done to yourself, that account may not be demanded of me hereafter. No one has seen the departure of his own soul: but I see that mine is departing."

Reading between the lines of these letters there seems little doubt that Aurungzebe's sympathies were in favour of Kaum Buksh. Both this Prince and Azim Shah, though they had purposely been sent off to their respective governments of Bijapur and Malwa, were cognizant that their father's death was imminent, and remained therefore as near as possible. Bahadur Shah was supposed to be too far away to be dangerous, but as the sequel showed, he also had laid his plans with the greatest care and caution. Azim Shah's general was the redoubted Zulficcar Khan, between whom and Kaum Buksh there was an undying hatred dating back from the incident which occurred at the siege of Gingee, already alluded to.

Eradat Khan, who had for a long time been in attendance on the Emperor, gives a touching sketch of his last interview with his old master, which must have taken place only shortly before the latter's death. Eradat Khan had been appointed to an important command at Aurungabad, and "on the evening before my departure, the Emperor, opening the window of his sleeping apartment, called me to him and said: 'Absence now takes place between us and our meeting again is uncertain. Forgive then whatever willingly or unwillingly I may have done against thee, and pronounce the words, *I forgive!* three times with sincerity of heart. As thou hast served me long, I also forgive thee whatever knowingly or otherwise, thou mayest have done against me.' Upon hearing these words my sobs became like a knot in my throat, so that I had not power to speak. At last after his majesty had repeatedly pressed me I made shift to pronounce the words, *I forgive!* three times, interrupted by heavy sobs. He shed many tears, repeated the words, and after blessing me, ordered me to retire."* There is something very pathetic in the picture of this old man dying alone in the midst of a large camp, haunted by the memories of past crimes, and by the forms of those nearest to him in blood who had crossed his path and had been done to death, and with a vague dread of a retribution to come. "I have committed numerous crimes and know not with what punishment I may be seized." Such is his own confession, and the feeling must have been rendered acute by the consciousness that his "valuable time had been passed vainly." His long life had in fact been a failure, and the work which during the last twenty years of his life he had set himself to do with stubbornness of purpose and inflexibility of will, was not only undone but he was leaving his empire in a far worse position than it had been when he took it by force from his father's grasp. "Every plan that he formed came to little good; every enterprize failed," is the verdict of the Mahomedan historian who praises him for his "devotion, austerity and justice; and for his incomparable courage, long-suffering and judgment." But in spite of the admiration which is due to the many great qualities in Aurungzebe's character it seems difficult if not impossible to join with those who regard him as a martyr, as a man who "had pitted his conscience against the world, and the world triumphed over it," or as one who "lived, and died in leading a forlorn hope, and if ever the cross of heroic devotion to a lost cause belonged to mortal man it was his."† The real truth is that the cause he was devoted to was his own advancement, and in order to achieve that he did not

---

* Scott's Translation.
† Stanley Lane Poole, *Aurangzib*, p. 205.

scruple to wade through blood towards the throne he longed for. Fratricide had for him no terrors, and the obligation of filial respect or paternal love no weight. To us he seems more like a narrow-minded bigot with such a load of guilt on his conscience that he mistrusted all mankind. No doubt his conscience reproached him for the crimes of his youth, but can it be said that this deterred him from the commission of others in his old age? The relentlessness with which, for no reason, he brought about the ruin of the Deccan kings, and the barbarous manner in which he treated the Mahratta Sumbajee, show that the old Adam was still alive in him, and that what he had done in 1656 he would not have hesitated to do forty years later had the same obstacles been in his path.

Aurungzebe's death occurred on the 21st of February, 1707, and three days afterwards Azim Shah, who was then 54 years of age, arrived at Ahmednagar, took possession of the Imperial camp, and a week later formally ascended the throne. The remains of the deceased Emperor were despatched to Aurungabad, where they were buried in a tomb which he had prepared during his life-time. Azim Shah at once commenced a leisurely march for Agra, having been joined by several of the important chiefs, such as Chin Koolich Khan, with his father Feroze Jung, and Mahomed Ameen Khan, who for this purpose deserted the service of Kaum Buksh. This latter Prince evidently felt himself too weak to make an attempt for the throne. He was only forty years of age and could bide his time. Accordingly he retired to his seat of Government at Bijapur, and leaving his two elder brothers to fight it out, occupied himself with collecting an army in the Deccan with which he resolved to encounter the conqueror. The route chosen by Azim Shah was, though shorter as the crow flies, a very hilly and difficult one, and the consequence was that before he reached Agra a number of his men were lost by disease and by want. Bedar Bukht, Azim Shah's son, who was in Guzerat, was ordered to march in order to join his father's army near Agra. This order was at once obeyed and the Prince set off with only three thousand men, without waiting to raise a larger army, although at the time there was a considerable amount of money in the treasury. The fact is that Bedar Bukht had been greatly attached to his grandfather, Aurungzebe, and had therefore excited his father's jealousy, and he was afraid that, if he met him with anything like a considerable force, Azim Shah might suspect him of entertaining designs against the throne. Eradat Khan, who was in this Prince's confidence, tells us much of the strained relations between father and son, and there seems to be very little doubt that the Prince did really harbour the thought of supplanting his father.

In the meantime Bahadur Shah, although far off in Cabul, and already an old man of 64, had not been idle. When despatched to this distant government, he had accepted what was really a banishment without a word of complaint. To his own sons, who were with him, and to his friends he said that he had given up all idea of ever succeeding to the throne. When news of Aurungzebe's sickness reached him, he said that in the event of his father's death he would not dispute the throne with Azim Shah, but would retire into Persia and claim hospitality from the Shah. So persistent was he in these statements that not only were they believed by his own family but they also served to dispel all suspicions at headquarters, and he was looked upon accordingly as a negligeable quantity, too far removed by age and by distance from any chance of rivalry. Bahadur Shah's Dewan or principal minister was one Monuaim Khan, who was thoroughly faithful and attached to his master. This officer had for some time been employed in organizing and reforming the Prince's army and household. He had therefore a claim to his confidence, and accordingly he one day questioned him regarding his future plans. Subsequently he related what took place to Eradat Khan, who has given us his statement in his own words:

"When I perceived that my attachment, sincerity, and abilities had properly impressed Shah Alam's mind, and that he was convinced that I was a prudent, faithful, and secret servant, being alone with him one day, conversing on the affairs of the Empire, I took the liberty of thus addressing him: 'It is reported that your Highness intends flying to Persia, with so much confidence that even the Princes your sons assure me by sacred oaths of its truth.' He replied: 'In this rumour their lies concealed a great design, to forward which I have spread it abroad and taken pains to make it believed. First, because my father, on a mere suspicion of my disloyalty, kept me nine years in close confinement, and should he even now think I cherished the smallest ambition, he would immediately strive to accomplish my ruin. Secondly, my brother Mahomed Azim Shah, who is my powerful enemy, and valiant even to the extreme of rashness, would exert all his force against me. From this report my father is easy and my brother lulled into self-security; but by the *Almighty God, who gave me life* (laying his hand on the Koran by him) and on this holy book, I swear, though not one friend should join me, I will meet Azim Shah in single combat, wherever he may be! This secret which I have so long maintained, and even kept from my own children, is now entrusted to your care. Be cautious that no instance of your conduct may betray it.'"*

The confidence thus shown was not misplaced. Monuaim Khan at once went to Lahore, which formed the key of the road to Delhi, and there quickly made the necessary preparations, so that everything should be ready when the time came to strike the decisive blow. Bodies of troops were

* Eradat Khan, *Memoirs of the Mogul Empire.* Scott, Vol. II.

collected and stationed in garrisons, so that they could be picked up completely equipped *en route*. A regular stage of communication was opened out towards the Deccan on one side and through the Khyber pass to Cabul on the other, so that any news could be transmitted with the utmost despatch. Tavernier tells us that messages of importance were generally conveyed by foot-runners instead of by horsemen, and that runners were able to beat horsemen over a long distance. "The reason is," says this entertaining traveller (Ball's edition, vol. i. 291) "that at every two leagues there are small huts, where two or three men employed for running, live and immediately when the carrier of a letter has arrived at one of these huts he throws it to the others at the entrance, and one of them takes it up and at once sets off to run. It is considered unlucky to give a letter into the hand of a messenger; it is therefore thrown at his feet and he must lift it up. It is still to be remarked that throughout India, the greater part of the roads are like avenues of trees, and those which have not trees planted, have at every 500 paces small pieces of stone which the inhabitants of the nearest villages are bound to whiten from time to time, so that the letter carriers can distinguish the roads on dark and rainy nights." The distance which the messengers would have to travel between Ahmednagar, where Aurungzebe died, and Cabul, could not have been less than 2,000 miles, and the road by which troops could march from Cabul to Agra is not less than 1,200 miles, but yet so great was the despatch used by Bahadur Shah that although the old Emperor only died on the 28th Zilkad, in little more than $2\frac{1}{2}$ months from that time the Prince had forestalled his brother; had taken possession of Agra, and was able to deliver a decisive battle on the 80th day after Aurungzebe's decease. Immediately Bahadur Shah received the news of his father's death he started off post haste for Lahore, where he found a body of troops ready and

a strong force of artillery prepared and kept in readiness by the faithful Monuaim Khan. Without a day's delay the Prince hurried on, picking up fresh levies on his way, and in this manner was able to reach Agra several days before his brother, who had leisurely marched up from the Deccan never dreaming of finding a rival to dispute his throne. Eradat Khan, who was with Azim Shah's army, attached to the person of his son Bedar Bukht, says that "such vanity took possession of the mind of Azim Shah that he was convinced his brother, though supported by the myriads of Toor and Sullum, durst not meet him in the field. Hence those who brought intelligence of his approach he would abuse as fools and cowards, so that no one cared to speak the truth. Even his chief officers feared to disclose intelligence, so that he was ignorant of the successful progress of his rival."*
From this dream of security, however, there was a rude awakening; for, when he arrived at Muttra, about 20 miles from Agra, he was met by a message from Bahadur Shah offering to divide the kingdom with him. So magnanimous was the elder brother that he even left to the younger the choice of the division. The offer was, however, haughtily refused, and on the following day. (18 Rubbee ul Awal A. H. 1119=23rd May 1707) the two armies met for the decisive struggle. Prince Bedar Bukht commanded the advance guard, Zulficcar Khan the left wing, and Azim Shah the main body of the army. Bahadur Shah had with him a considerable army, and, assisted by his four sons, advanced to the attack in a compact form. Azim Shah's order seems to have been very loose, and he foolishly left the main body of his army and advanced to the support of his son Bedar Bukht, who was engaged with the vanguard. Zulficcar Khan on the left wing was also attacked, and, though he was able to hold his own, his

* Scott's Translation.

force was greatly weakened by the defection of his Rajpoot allies, who fled at the fall of their chiefs, Ram Singh and Dulput Row, who were killed by the same cannon ball. The day was actually decided by the defeat of the vanguard of Azim Shah's army, and the main body does not seem to have been engaged. Azim Shah and Bedar Bukht both fell fighting bravely, and when this occurred the rest of the army took to flight. Zulficcar Khan, seeing that the day was lost, escaped to Gwalior and took refuge with his father Assud Khan. In this manner, after a comparatively easy victory, Bahadur ascended the throne.

Zulficcar Khan's conduct in the battle is open to some doubt, and there were certainly many who suspected him of having wilfully refrained from assisting Azim Shah. The result seems to justify these suspicions, because although Monuaim Khan was with justice made Vizier, Zulficcar Khan was created Ameer-ul-Amra, with the post of chief paymaster and the government of the Deccan. His father, Assud Khan, received the honorary post of Vakeel Muttaluk, which though of considerable dignity, carried with it no real power.

"Shah Alam Bahadur Shah was generous and merciful, of a great soul tempered with affability and discerning of merit. He had seen the strict exercise of power during the reigns of his grandfather and father and been used to authority himself for the last fifty years. Time received a new lustre from his accession, and all ranks of people obtained favours, equal, if not superior, to their merits, so that the public forgot the excellences and great qualities of Aurungzebe, which became absorbed in the bounties of his successor." (Eradat Khan). His court was a very splendid one and his throne was surrounded by seventeen princes of the blood, for he permitted even the sons of those princes who had fallen in battle against him to appear fully armed in his presence.

The only danger remaining to the Emperor was in the

Deccan. There, Kaum Buksh had the Khutba read in his name, in Bijapur and Hyderabad coins had been struck, and he had assumed all the signs of royalty. This Prince was a man of considerable intelligence but of a very violent and hasty temper. Although the favourite son of Aurungzebe, it is said by Eradat Khan that he seldom remained for more than a month in his father's society without getting into some trouble or disgrace. He was rash and impulsive, very overbearing in manner, and at the same time possessed of an inordinate self-conceit. Aurungzebe probably with a view of helping him, had attached some of the most powerful of the nobles to his service. One of the principal of these was Ghazee-ud-Din Feroze Jung, a Turanian Mogul whose power and influence in the Deccan was very great. As already mentioned, the son of this nobleman was Chin Koolich Khan, the future founder of a new dynasty. Forgetful of the assistance which these two powerful chieftains could have rendered to him, Kaum Buksh not only made no attempts to conciliate, but estranged and disgusted them by his arbitrary and domineering conduct. Feroze Jung, who had for some time been blind, withdrew from the Deccan entirely, and having accepted a small Government in Guzerat relinquished for good all prominent share in public affairs. Koolich Khan remained in the Deccan but kept aloof together with his retainers from all connection with the headstrong young Prince who was evidently bent upon consummating his own destruction. This example was followed by several other noblemen, until at last the Prince was left unsupported except by his own personal retainers. Kaum Buksh made Hyderabad his headquarters, and nothing daunted at the defection of his followers refused all overtures of the Emperor and declared that he would fight out the struggle for the throne until the bitter end.

In the meantime Bahadur Shah, after having made the

arrangements necessary for the settlement of his new Empire, collected an immense army, with which he started to subdue his rebellious brother. It is said that the expedition contained a hundred thousand more men than did any army of Aurungzebe's, but this seems to be scarcely likely. Before entering the Deccan with this strong force Bahadur Shah made another and last attempt at conciliation, and wrote to Kaum Buksh a letter in which he said: "Our ever honoured father resigned to you Bijapur; but we give you in addition, Hyderabad. These two extensive countries, long famous for great kings, producing a revenue more than half of Hindustan, we leave to you, without interference or reluctance, and shall esteem you dearer than our own children. Think not then of contention nor consent to shed the blood of the faithful nor disturb the repose of our Government. If you give the ear of acceptance to this advice, we will further confer upon you the Nizamat of Deccan if agreeable to you; and after visiting the sacred tomb of our father we will return to Hindustan." * Kaum Buksh paid no attention to this overture, which was made with all sincerity, but continued to make his preparations. But as the Emperor drew nearer the defections of his noblemen continued to increase. Many were gained over by messages from the Vizier Monuaim Khan promising them pardon and reward; and others, seeing the hopelessness of the cause, left him to return to their homes. When Bahadur Shah had arrived within 25 miles of Hyderabad, Kaum Buksh's army consisted of only 10,000 of the worst Deccan horse and a small force of artillery. With this insignificant army the infatuated Prince even yet expected to gain a victory, and giving up the protection of the city walls marched forth to meet the Imperial army. Bahadur

* The word Hindustan is always understood to refer to the upper Ganges valley, and is not used as we use it to apply to the whole Peninsula.

Shah, still willing to spare his brother, forbade his troops to attack, but the Prince, mistaking this forbearance for fear, himself led the charge. Zulficcar Khan, his old enemy, then obtained permission to advance with a small force, and if possible to capture the Prince alive. As soon as the Prince's followers saw that an attack was really intended they fled in all directions, leaving their leader almost alone. "Notwithstanding this, he continued as long as he had strength to use his bow and arrows from his elephant, till at length he sank down on his seat through loss of blood from several wounds. He was then taken prisoner by Daoud Khan, and carried to the Prince Jehan Shah, who with his brothers (sons of the Emperor) had stood at some distance during this extraordinary skirmish."* He was carried to the Imperial tents and there treated by his brother with every kindness, but it was all of no avail and he died the same evening from the effects of his wounds. Kaum Buksh in the violence of his ambition threw away the chance of an empire even greater than that of his brother. The Deccan, united under one Prince, who was also a member of the Imperial family, and acknowledged by and allied to the Emperor himself, would before long have developed into a strong and homogeneous kingdom extending from sea to sea, and from the Vindhyas to Cape Comorin. Such a kingdom was the only possible means of subduing the Mahrattas, and by it the disjointed Hindoo kingdoms of the south would have been conquered without difficulty. It is probable that the course of history would have been far different if, when some forty years later the English began to take an active interest in the political affairs of South India, they had come into contact with a strongly established Mahomeden king of the Deccan.

Bahadur Shah resolved to return at once to his capital, and was perhaps deterred from remaining any longer in the Deccan

* Eradat Khan. Scott's Translation.

by the memory of his father's fate, who, thinking after the capture of Sumbajee that only two or three matters remained to be settled, stopped on and then got entangled in so many operations that he was never able to leave the country. Before leaving, however, the Emperor took one important step with the object of conciliating the Mahrattas. This was the release of Sahoo, Sumbajee's son who had for the last twenty years been following the Emperor's camp.* This step was taken in consequence of the advice of Zulficcar Khan, who as before stated had been appointed Viceroy of the Deccan. Sahoo's mother, brother, and family were, however, kept as hostages of his good conduct. This being done, the Emperor leaving Sahoo to establish himself, marched back to Agra, where for the present we will leave him in order to follow the affairs of the Deccan.

During Sahoo's long confinement, his uncle Rajah Ram and afterwards his father's second wife Tara Bhai had conducted the Mahratta affairs. Tara Bhai governed in the name of her son, who, however, was an idiot, and the real power remained in her hands. This power she did not feel disposed to at once relinquish, and, pretending that Sahoo was nothing but an impostor, called upon her ministers to help her in opposing him and to swear fidelity to her son. Daoud Khan, who had been left by Zulficcar Khan as Deputy Governor of the Deccan, had been instructed to give Sahoo every assistance in his power. Accordingly the latter was soon able to raise an army of 15,000 well equipped men, with which he marched from the Godavery towards Poona. Here he found the people by no means unanimous in their support of Tara Bhai, and many came forward and recognized him as the legitimate

* It is not quite certain whether this step had not already been resolved upon or even taken by Azim Shah before he marched to encounter Bahadur at Agra. Looking at the dates, however, I am inclined to think the text is correct.

descendant of the great Sivajee. Having obtained possession of Satara, Sahoo caused himself to be formally seated on the throne. Tara Bhai and Sahoo both sent representatives to the Imperial Court, asking for the Emperor's countenance and support. Sahoo was backed up by Zulficcar Kkan, but Tara Bhai, on the other hand, found an advocate in Monuaim Khan, the Vizier, and the result was that though letters were made out in the latter's name as regent for her son Sivajee, they were not delivered but kept in abeyance until the dispute between the two rivals should be fought out.

The result of this struggle belongs more to the history of the Mahrattas, and as this has been already exhaustively treated, it is not our intention to go over the same ground here. Suffice it to say that Sahoo remained at Satara whilst the rival court was held at Kolapur. The former received the moral and active support of the Mahomedan governor of the Deccan, and the latter was followed by many of the principal Mahratta chiefs. The practical result of this rivalry was the growth of the Brahmin influence in Poona, which finally resulted in the representatives of royalty being reduced to the position of puppets, whilst the Brahmin Peishwas, arrogating to themselves all the actual power and influence, ruled the Mahratta people and directed the course of its armies.

Before passing on to the next period it will be as well to take a glance at the state of the Deccan after twenty years of warfare. The whole extent of country lying between Hyderabad, Bijapur, and Ahmednagar seems to have been reduced to the condition of a desert, not only by the ravages of contending armies but also by the progress of the vast imperial camp, numbering over a million of soldiers and followers, which like a swarm of locusts ate up the country as it moved slowly from place to place. The Mahomedan governors found the greatest difficulty in collecting the revenue, and were compelled to treat the jaghirdars and zemindars with the utmost severity, and they in their turn exacted from the cultivator whatever they could. Villages were depopulated and fields left uncultivated, and whenever the Mahomedan army had removed to some distance there appeared in its track a marauding body of Mahratta horse, which if not satisfied by the blackmail of *chouth*, harried what little the Mahomedans had left. A more deplorable state of things cannot be imagined. Aurungzebe was compelled to draw not only his treasure but even his supplies from the north, and these caravans were constantly being plundered by the Mahratta cavalry. More than fifty years before, Mir Jumla, the able Minister who forsook the Golconda king for Shah Jehan's service, had, it is said, endeavoured to persuade the latter Emperor to leave the north of India and fix his capital in the Deccan which was the site where gold and diamonds could be found, and where a more splendid kingdom could be maintained than in the north. It was on this occasion that Mir Jumla gave to the Emperor the Kohinoor as a specimen of the wonderful diamonds which the country produced. Had Mir Jumla been able to visit the Deccan in the beginning of the 18th century he would have marvelled at the change that had taken place. On all sides were villages ruined, fields neglected, and irrigation works destroyed. The people from harmless peasants had turned into organized gangs of robbers, who endeavoured to recover their own losses by despoiling others. Tavernier, Thevenot, and the other European travellers of the 17th century speak of Hyderabad as the emporium of Indian trade, and of Bijapur as one of the richest and most populous cities in the world. At the time we are writing of, all trade had ceased, for no caravan was safe, and a merchant travelling with goods or money would not have gone twenty miles without being robbed and probably murdered.

Bahadur Shah's reign was only a short one, for he died in

1711 while on an expedition against the Sikhs. At the time of his death his four sons were with him in his camp, and again there occurred the fratricidal struggle for the throne which had taken place at the close of the two former reigns. The actual scene was in the Punjaub, but as the results materially affected the Deccan, we propose to describe it with some detail, especially as the circumstances are passed over by the usual histories with a few words, although they afford a graphic sketch of how the passion for empire destroyed all natural ties and feelings in the members of the royal family, and of how the empire was tottering on the verge of ruin by being split up into contending parties and factions.

Bahadur Shah died near Lahore in his seventieth year. (18th Feb. 1711.) His four sons were Jehander Shah the eldest, Jehan Shah, Raffiu-sh-Shah and Azimu-sh-Shah. All four resolved to try for the throne, and the youngest, Azimu-sh-Shah, had apparently the best chance of succeeding. Each of the Princes had his own camp and following, but Azimu-sh-Shah was in possession of his father's camp and treasure, and had therefore the proverbial nine points of the law in his favour. He at once caused himself to be proclaimed, upon which the other three brothers combined and agreed to sink their own rivalry in order to crush the pretensions of the youngest. The young Prince commenced badly by offending the powerful Zulficcar Khan. This general, who had for so long been accustomed to a prominent place in the affairs of the Empire, and who with some justice regarded himself as a maker of Emperors, sent a message to Azimu-sh-Shah asking how he could be of service him. The answer to this overture was couched in so supercilious a tone that Zulficcar Khan withdrew in disgust and embraced the cause of the eldest brother Jehander Shah. *

* Eradat Khan thus relates the incident which is of interest, as throwing some light upon the rules of oriental etiquette, any breach of

Instead of at once attacking his brothers, Azimu-sh-Shah made another mistake in entrenching himself in his camp. He may perhaps have thought that if he waited his time, and kept hold of the treasure, his brothers would gradually be deserted by their followers, so that they would eventually have to submit. The reverse, however, actually happened. Zulficcar Khan threw himself into the cause of the three Princes, and with his usual energy drew all the artillery from the city of Lahore, beneath the walls of which they were encamped. The truth of the proverb, *l'audace, l'audace et toujours l'audace*, especially as regards oriental warfare, was illustrated on this occasion. Azimu-sh-Shah's hesitancy was attributed to fear, and instead of his brothers being deserted by their followers, fresh levies were attracted, and many even deserted from Azimu-sh-Shah, who unwisely at such a time showed no disposition to spend any of his treasure. By shutting himself up in entrenchments Azimu-sh-Shah gave Zulficcar Khan an opportunity which this veteran soldier was not likely to let slip. Though his inferior numbers prevented him from meeting Azimu-sh-Shah in the field he was much stronger in artillery, and accordingly commenced an active cannonade from which the Prince's army, shut up in the entrenchments, suffered

which is calculated to cause bitter offence: "The Ameer-ul-Amra now desired me to send my grandson to Azimu-sh-Shah to ask him how he could serve him on the present occasion. I sent him but he returned with a reply, laconic and slight, as if from a nobleman of high rank to the commander of a hundred. 'As the Imperial servants can know no place of support but this court, and most have already repaired to it, the Ameer-ul-Amra may also pay his duty, with assurance of a gracious reception in the Presence.' When the Ameer-ul-Amra read this, he shed tears, and said to me with some emotion: 'You see the manners of the Prince and his advisers! Whatever is the will of God must taken place. Alas! the errors of a favourite, unacquainted with government often endanger the very existence of his master. When fortune frowns on any one, he is sure to do that which he should not.' After saying this he left and went to Prince Moiz-ud-Din (Jehander Shah)."

severely. After allowing himself to be fired at for five days, a proceeding which served to dispirit his army still more, the misguided Prince issued forth to attack the combined Princes. At the first meeting with Jehan Shah his followers fled. Azimu-sh-Shah and his son Mahomed Kurreem were left almost alone, and the Prince, disdaining to fly, was shot as he was fighting from the back of his elephant.* His son managed to mount a horse and escape, but he was captured a few days afterwards and cruelly put do death. There remained therefore the three Princes, Jehander, Jehan, and Raffiu-sh-Shah. According to their compact the treasure was to be divided equally between them; and Jehan Shah, who appears to have been a loyal and generous prince, at once placed a guard over the treasure, prevented his followers from pillaging the camp, and sent the whole of the ready cash to Zulficcar Khan for division. This was what this wily old intriguer wanted. He had determined to support Jehander Shah, who was a foolish and dissipated man, as being the one over whom he was likely to exercise the greatest influence. With this object in view he delayed a division of the treasure, since he knew that the troops of Jehan and Raffiu-sh-Shah were clamouring for pay and were therefore likely to create trouble. He played with each Prince in turn, visiting first one and then the other, promising with fair words, but always putting off a settlement. Jehan Shah was advised by his friends to seize the traitor at his next visit and put him to death, but this he refused to do, and when he came contented himself with reproaching him for his duplicity, adding: "Even now, perhaps, thy family is dreading that I may put thee to death, which, however politic, I scorn to do

* This is Eradat Khan's story, and, as he was an eyewitness of the battle, it is probably true. Khafi Khan, on the other hand, says that Azimu-sh-Shah 'disappeared', and was supposed either to have been drowned or assassinated.

by fraud. Rise, then, and go in peace to thine own house." We are told that "the Ameer-ul-Amra departed with a speed and precipitation which declared his guilt." This magnanimity was however thrown away, and Zulficcar Khan openly put aside all disguise and announced his intention of ruining Jehan Shah. Raffiu-sh-Shah in the meantime remained quiet. He had on former occasions greatly befriended Zulficcar Khan, and thought him bound to him by ties of gratitude. He therefore counted on his support, and leaving his two elder brothers to settle their own quarrel, reserved himself to fight the conqueror. Jehan Shah, seeing that nothing was to be gained by delay, resolved to attack Zulficcar Khan, but the night before he could carry out his intention a fire broke out in his camp which destroyed the whole of his ammunition. Some fresh supplies were obtained, but they were utterly insufficient, and many of his followers began to desert. Jehan now determined to stake all on a sudden attack. He made a furious onslaught on Jehander's camp, and nearly surprised his brother in his tent. Zulficcar Khan, however, was ready with his whole force drawn up. Jehan Shah was surrounded, his followers fled, and he was struck by a musket ball. His son, Ferkhander Akhter, who fought by his side, descended from the elephant and defended his father with his sword, until he also fell covered with wounds. During this skirmish Raffiu-sh-Shah had drawn off his forces, and remained a passive spectator. When it was over he advanced with the intention of engaging Jehander Shah, firmly believing that Zulficcar Khan would come over to his side. He was, however, advised to wait until the following day, when if he attempted a surprise there was a better chance of success. This he did, and early in the morning an attack was made on Jehander's camp. But owing to the treachery or rashness of the attacking force a premature cannon shot gave the alarm, and they found a strong force drawn up and commanded by their supposed ally Zulficcar Khan. The unhappy prince thus disappointed and betrayed resolved to sell his life as dearly as possible. As usual he was forsaken by his soldiers, but descending from his elephant he "drew the sabre of glory from the scabbard of honour and fought singly on foot against thousands of assailants." He, too, soon fell covered with wounds, and Jehander Shah left without a rival, was proclaimed Emperor and sounded the march of victory.

Dreadful as were these fratricidal quarrels it is impossible to deny to the sons and grandsons of Aurungzebe the one virtue of courage. The word "fear" seems to have been unknown to them, and they were always ready to expose their persons without scruple. They fought with the courage of despair, and though they were void of the ordinary natural feelings of family affection, ambitious, false, and revengeful, they were undoubtedly brave. This was apparently their one virtue.

Zulficcar Khan had been the moving spirit in this intrigue, and he was the principal person to profit by it. Jehander Shah was a man of weak mind and of low and dissipated tastes. He cared nothing for the duties of government, and left the whole power in the hands of his minister. During his short reign of nine months the Emperor set all public opinion at defiance. He went about publicly with a common courtesan as his companion, and not content with holding drunken orgies in the palace, he went with her to the bazaar and frequented the lowest houses. On one occasion he went with his mistress and a herb-woman named Zohera to the house of a common prostitute where they remained drinking until late in the night. "After rewarding the woman with a large sum and the grant of a village, they returned in a drunken plight to the palace, and

"linked to a thousand crimes."

all three fell asleep on the road. On their arrival Lall Koor (the mistress) was taken out by her women, but the Emperor remained sleeping in the chariot, and the driver, who had shared in the jollity of his royal master, without examining the conveyance, drove it to the stables. The officers of the palace after waiting till near morning for his arrival, on finding that the mistress had entered her apartments without the Emperor were alarmed for his safety, and sent to her to enquire concerning his situation. She desired them to immediately examine the coach, where they found the wretched prince fast asleep in the arms of Zohera, at a distance of nearly two miles from the palace. After this he still more exposed his vices to the public; often he passed through the streets, seizing the wives and daughters of the lower tradesmen. Once a week, according to the vulgar superstition, he bathed with Lall Koor concealed only by a single cloth in the fountain of the Lamp of Delhi (a celebrated saint) in hopes that this ceremony would promote pregnancy." * On another occasion the same woman Zohera met Chin Kulich Khan who was living in Delhi in strict retirement, in the streets. Finding that the Khan's palankeen did not get out of the way soon enough, Zohera's attendants began to insult him, and she herself called out to him from the top of her elephant, "Are you the son of a blind man?" This wanton insult led to an affray in which Zohera got roughly treated by the Khan's followers. Zohera complained to her mistress and she in turn to the Emperor, who ordered Zulficcar Khan to punish the nobleman. This however he did not dare to do, and Chin Kulich Khan, disgusted at the profligacy of the Court, kept himself in even stricter retirement awaiting the opportunity which was not far off. Zulficcar Khan was at this time not only Minister but also Viceroy of the Deccan and made use of his position to enrich himself and his near

* Eradat Khan, *Memoirs of the Mogul Empire*, Scott's Translation.

relatives. On all sides there was nothing but injustice and oppression. "He studied to ruin the most ancient families, inventing pretences to put them to death, that he might plunder their possessions. Unhappy was the person he suspected to be rich, as wealth and vexatious accusations always accompanied each other. He took enormous emoluments and revenues for himself, while he disposed of money to others with a hand so sparing that even his own creatures felt severe poverty with empty titles, for he never allowed *jaghirs* to any. The minds of high and low, rich and poor, near or distant, friends or strangers were turned against him, and wished his destruction. Hindoos and Mussulmans agreed in praying to Heaven for the fall of his power, night and day. Often does the midnight sigh of the widow ruin the riches a hundred years." *

In the meantime in the Deccan everything was playing into the hands of the Mahrattas. Having nothing to fear from a debauched Emperor they extended their conquest on every side. Where they could not actually annex territory they levied their black-mail of one quarter of the revenue, and the Mahomedan deputies, too weak to oppose their exactions, were content to purchase immunity by allowing them to collect their *chouth*. The actual administration of the Mahratta Empire was conducted by the Peishwa at Poona, and gradually the Rajah at Sattara became a mere puppet in his hands. The great feature of the Mahratta armies was their cavalry, for which they were in a considerable measure indebted to Aurungzebe. This Prince had during the last twenty years of his life devoted much attention to the improvement of the breed of horses in the Deccan. He imported a vast number of Arab sires from the north and distributed them amongst the villages. When he died, and the Imperial army left the Deccan, these horses fell into the hands of the

* *Ibid.*

Mahrattas, who were not slow to use them for military purposes until the Deccanee mare or stallion became famous throughout India.*

Whilst everything at Delhi was in confusion, an avenger was rapidly preparing an army in the distant province of Bengal. Azimu-sh-Shah, the first of the four sons of the late Emperor who fell in the struggle at Lahore, had left a son named Ferokshere who was Governor of Eastern Bengal. His principal supporters were two brothers, descendants of the well-known Seyds of Barha, a race celebrated for its bravery. These two men, Seyd Abdullah and Hussein Ali, had already distinguished themselves in the engagement between Azim Shah and Bahadur Shah after the death of Aurungzebe. On this occasion they had fought on Azim Shah's side, and when Bahadur Shah proved victorious they withdrew to Bengal. Here they attached themselves to the service of the young prince Ferokshere, and received, the one the Government of Allahabad, and the other that of Behar. When Ferokshere commenced his march on Delhi he was at once joined by Seyd Hussein Ali with a large force from Behar. It was hoped at Delhi that the other brother at Allahabad would remain loyal, and flattering letters full of promises were sent to him, but in vain. Seyd Abdullah, disgusted at the profligacy

---

* There can be no doubt that the Deccan plains, with their vast stretches of waste land, are eminently suited for horse-breeding purpose. Of late years considerable attention has been bestowed on the revival of horse-breeding in the Nizam's Dominions, and annually from 1.200 to 1,500 young colts by thoroughbred Arabs out of country mares are brought to the great horse fair at Mallagaom in the Bieder district. In course of time the new Deccanee breed bids fair to rival if not surpass the historical Deccan cavalry of the last century. It is only, just in reference to this, to mention the name of Mr. Ali Abdoolla, the well-known sportsman, who for about ten years has been at the head of the Hyderabad Government Stud. The headquarters and principal breeding farm are at Singareddy, about 30 miles from Hyderabad.

of the Court and the despotism of Zulficcar Khan, only waited for the Prince's approach to hand over to him the fort and to join him with the whole of his force. This accession raised the number of Ferokshere's army to about 70,000 horse and foot, and without waiting for further additions he commenced the march from Allahabad on Delhi. Thirty miles to the east of Agra the Prince met the force which had been sent to oppose him. This was commanded by Aiz-ud-Din, a son of the Emperor, and consisted only of six thousand veteran troops, a fine park of artillery, and a large rabble of Jâts and Rajputs. A slight skirmish followed, which though unattended by any important result was sufficient to terrify the Imperial general, who, taking with him the heir-apparent, fled to Agra. Of the army he left behind a large number went over to Ferokshere and the remainder dispersed. Ferokshere remained encamped upon the field of battle, and instead of marching upon Agra in pursuit, awaited there the return of the Imperial army. The Emperor finding that Ferokshere did not advance, and attributing his delay to fear, left Delhi, and marched to Agra. Here he was joined by the rest of his army which now numbered "seventy thousand horse, and foot without number." The two armies were separated by the river Jumna, and for the space of a week their time was occupied in marching and countermarching on either bank, endeavouring to gain a ford. This the two Seyds first succeeded in doing, and although the Emperor with an advance guard came up to them before the whole army had succeeded in crossing, he did not venture to attack them. Next day a general engagement took place, and the following is the description by Eradat Khan who was an eyewitness, and who was engaged on the Emperor's side. "After a cannonade of some time I saw two bodies from the enemy's line charge ours, one with a red and the other with a green standard. The former was the corps of Rajah Judboolla Ram and the latter of Seyd Hussein Ali Khan. Observing that our right flank was much exposed, I remarked it to Zulficcar Khan, who immediately ordered Abdul Summad Khan to move with the mistress's troops to that quarter. The first body of the troops charged, and the second pushing through the line of our artillery, which was deserted as it approached, attacked the centre in which was Jehander Shah. Our troops fell back upon the camp and great confusion took place." This charge practically decided the fate of the Emperor. Although Seyd Hussein Ali had fallen desperately wounded, the Imperial troops never attempted to rally. They did not even wait to be attacked, but broke their line and scattered in every direction, leaving the women, the jewel office, and the treasury to shift for themselves. Zulficcar Khan with a few veterans still held out, hoping that the presence of the Emperor might have the effect of rallying the troops. This probably would have been the case even at this late hour, for the enemy, finding that Seyd Hussein Ali had been carried off wounded, had halted in hesitation. A bold charge might then have saved the day, but Jehander Shah was not made of the same stuff as the rest of his family, and had not the courage to risk his person to save his throne. He had already mounted a fast elephant and was on his way to Delhi. Zulficcar Khan held out till dark, and then, seeing that further resistance was hopeless, followed his master and reached Delhi shortly after him.

The Governor at Delhi was Assud-ud-Dowlah, father of Zulficcar Khan, and to him the Emperor appealed for protection. Jehander Shah's personal vices, however, had long since forfeited the loyalty and affection which were his due. His army was defeated and scattered, and his nobles were therefore no longer in fear of his power. Assud-ud-Dowlah at once placed him in confinement, and, anxious only to save himself and, if possible, his son, sent word to Ferokshere that he held the ex-Emperor at his disposal. In the meantime Ferokshere had caused himself to be publicly proclaimed, and was joined by many of the chief generals of his defeated rival. Amongst these was Chin Kulich Khan, who, as we have already seen, had just cause for resentment against Jehander Shah; and who, there can be no doubt, had entered into a private arrangement with the Seyds to hold aloof. He was welcomed by Ferokshere, and was rewarded with a *munsab* of 7,000 horse and the appointment of Subadar of the Deccan with the title of Asaf Jah, NIZAM-UL-MULK, by which name he will be designated in future. Naturally the principal rewards fell to the share of the two Seyds, to whom Ferokshere's victory was entirely due. The elder brother Seyd Abdullah was appointed Vizier, with the title of Kutb-ul-Mulk, and a *munsab* of 7,000, whilst the younger, Hussein Ali, was created Ameer-ul-Amra, with a similar *munsab*.

Ferokshere received the message of Assud-ud-Dowlah with an appearance of satisfaction, and returned a gracious reply, telling him that his services would be rewarded by a confirmation in his office of Vizier and Governor of Delhi, and ordering him to keep Jehander Shah in close confinement. This message raised the spirits of Assud-ud-Dowlah and of his son Zulficcar Khan, and instead of attempting to seek safety by flight they remained in Delhi, kept everything quiet, and awaited the arrival of Ferrokshere.

When the new Emperor had arrived within a few marches of Delhi he sent word to Assud-ud-Dowlah to join him in his camp, and bring with him Zulficcar Khan. This order was at once obeyed with a feeling of mingled hope and fear. The father, who was advanced in years, was graciously received, and presented with jewels and robes, and the Emperor then told him to return home and leave behind him his son Zulficcar Khan, as the Emperor wished to transact some business with him. The father, says Khafi Khan, saw that his son was doomed, and with a swelling heart and tearful eyes he repaired to his tent. Eradat Khan gives a more detailed account of the tragedy that followed. Zulficcar Khan was first of all kept waiting in one of the apartments of the Imperial tent. A dinner was then brought to him, but it being against the court etiquette for a subject to eat in the Emperor's tent, he was asked to adjourn to a square of screens. Arrived here the door was at once shut upon him, and after he had been kept for some time in suspense, Abdullah Khan, the superintendent of the household, of whom we shall hear more hereafter under the name of Mir Jumla, came to him with a question he was desired to answer. He was asked to explain why at the siege of Gingee he had put the Emperor's uncle Kaum Buksh into confinement. The reply was: "I confined the prince by order of Aurungzebe, his sovereign and mine. Had he commanded me to imprison my own father, I should have at once complied." He was then asked why in the battle between Azim Shah and Bahadar Shah he had deserted the former and sought safety in flight. The reply was: "While Azim Shah was alive I kept the field, but when he was dead I dared not oppose a prince of the blood without a rival of equal dignity at the head of our army." The next question was: "What were the circumstances of your conduct to the martyred prince, His Majesty's father, Azimu-sh-Shah?" Zulficcar Khan replied: "He behaved inattentively to me, and I then attached myself to his brother; but in this did no more than other nobles, who each embraced the cause of the prince he loved best, and from whom he received the greatest favours." Then followed the last question, which, however, was unanswerable, "Why was his majesty's brother inhumanly murdered in cold blood, many days after the battle, when other princes were allowed to live?" The fallen general now saw that no submission or entreaty would spare his life, and so he angrily exclaimed, "If I am to die, kill me instantly, nor vex me longer with vain interrogation." Thereupon Lachin Beg, a person who earned an unenviable notoriety in reference to executions, and other followers rushed in and strangled Zulficcar Khan with a bowstring, afterwards plunging their daggers into his body. The body was drawn outside the camp with ropes, and allowed to lie as an example of fallen greatness. His estates, and those of his father, were confiscated, but his father was allowed to go into retirement, where soon afterwards he died, not without suspicion of poison.

At the same time an order was sent to despatch the ex-Emperor Jehander Shah, and as Ferokshere made his triumphal entry into Delhi, the head of his uncle was carried round the city on a spear whilst the body was placed on an elephant, from which also was hung the corpse of Zulficcar Khan, head downwards. Some days were then occupied with other executions, and for some time there was in Delhi a reign of terror. Lachin Beg, who was a prominent performer in these murders, received the nickname of *Pasma Kash* (thong-puller). Khafi Khan says: "As men were subjected to this punishment of the bow-string without ascertainment or proof of offence, such a terror of it seized the hearts of the nobles of the reign of Aurungzebe and Bahadur Shah that when anyone left his home to attend upon the Emperor, he took farewell of his sons and family ... Hakim Salim had been one of the personal attendant upon Azimu-sh-Shah, and it was said that the Prince was killed at his suggestion. Mir Jumla invited the Hakim to his house, and treated him sumptuously at night, but before morning men were sent to his door and they strangled him." This Mir Jumla was a great favourite of the new Emperor, Ferokshere, and he appears to have been the Emperor's confidential agent in contradistinction to the two Seyds, to whom the affairs of the State were entrusted. As might be expected, before long this dual power led to considerable friction, and the constant endeavour of the Seyds was to remove Mir Jumla from his post near the Emperor's ear. Kulich Khan, or rather Asaf Jah, Nizam-ul-Mulk, with the caution which characterized all his actions, withdrew from this scene of bloodshed and intrigue, and, making Aurungabad his headquarters, did his best to bring the Deccan into order and repose.

The Emperor Ferokshere was a man of low mind and manners, but was at the same time extravagant in his profusion and display, and so succeeded in gaining a certain popularity amongst the vulgar. He was imbued with a strong jealousy of the two Seyds, which however he dared not openly show because of their power and of the obligations he was under to them for their assistance in raising him to the throne. This jealousy was secretly fostered by Mir Jumla, who, having quickly squandered the accumulated wealth of Zulficcar Khan, was meditating the downfall of the Seyds. Seyd Abdullah, to whom were entrusted the duties of Vizier, was much addicted to the pleasures of the zenana, and left most of his business to his dewan, named Ruttun Chund, who took advantage of the trust confided in him to levy exactions from all who were brought into contact with him. The more active and talented of the two brothers was Seyd Hussein Ali, who was Amir-ul-Amra, or Commander-in-Chief. With the object of separating Hussein Ali from his brother, Mir Jumla persuaded the Emperor to despatch him against Ajeet Singh, Rajah of Marwar, who had been in a state of rebellion since the death of Aurungzebe. Ajeet Singh submitted very quickly, and, agreeing to give a daughter to the Emperor in marriage, received more lenient terms than he was entitled to, for Hussein Ali was anxious to return to Delhi, where the hostility between his brother the Vizier and Mir Jumla had broken into open flame. The cause of this rupture was the monopoly of the patronage and power in the hands of the Vizier and his brother. Mir Jumla, in order to share in the perquisites attached to the patronage, insisted that all orders and petitions should receive his counter-signature as confidential minister of the Emperor. As Vizier Seyd Abdullah claimed to be the official representative, and Ruttun Chund, his deputy, openly defied the pretensions of the palace favourite. The latter, however, had the ear of the Emperor, and it had been resolved to effect the Vizier's arrest when suddenly his brother appeared on the scene. It is said that the Emperor's mother, who had guaranteed the arrangement between the Emperor and the two Seyds, when the revolt against the late Emperor was resolved upon, betrayed to them the conspiracy that was being hatched and caused Hussein Ali to be warned that he should return quickly if he wished to save the influence of his brother. This unexpected return disconcerted the conspirators, and a fresh combination was brought about. It was proposed to elevate Hussein Ali to the Viceroyalty of the Deccan and to remove Asaf Jah to Malwa. Hussein Ali did not object to this as long as he was allowed to govern by a deputy whilst he remained at Delhi, where his influence at the head of the army was sufficient to counteract Mir Jumla's intrigues. This, however, was exactly what the Emperor wished to avoid, and matters were nearly coming to an outbreak when the Emperor's mother interfered. She visited the two Seyds and persuaded them to come to the Emperor's presence, agreeing, as a guarantee of good faith, that during the audience their troops should garrison the palace. Accordingly the two brothers went, and having made a nominal submission a compromise was effected, under which Mir Jumla was sent to the governorship of Behar and Hussein Ali agreed to go to his post in the Deccan. Such, however, was the power of the haughty soldier that before leaving the Emperor's presence he openly said that if Mir Jumla were recalled, or if anything should be attempted against his brother Seyd Abdullah, he would within twenty days return to Delhi at the head of his army. These matters having been satisfactorily arranged, the Emperor celebrated his marriage with Ajeet Singh's daughter with considerable pomp.*

Mir Jumla actually went to Behar, but the intrigues in his favour still continued at Delhi, and a message was sent by the Emperor to Daoud Khan, the former Deputy of Zulficcar Khan in the Deccan, to oppose Hussein Ali on his march. Daoud Khan was a brave man and from his long connection with this part of the country had considerable influence with the Mahrattas. He therefore accepted the dangerous mission, and calling in Neemajee Scindia, marched from Aurungabad to meet the new Viceroy. It is worthy of remark that during this struggle Asaf Jah had quietly accepted his removal. His time had not yet come, and without attempting to oppose Hussein Ali, he withdrew to Moradabad and left his successor to fight out his quarrel with Daoud Khan. The latter was easily beaten, and being killed during the engagement, his followers at once dispersed. Daoud Khan's body was dragged round Burhanpore at the tail of an elephant, and a despatch was sent to the Emperor apprising him of the death of a rebel. Ferokshere is said to have remarked that Daoud Khan had been unjustly killed, whereupon the Vizier boldly replied that had the same fate happened to his brother Hussein Ali, His Majesty would possibly have been of a different opinion.

*At this time the Emperor had just recovered from a severe illness during which he had been treated by an English physician, Mr. Hamilton. When the grateful Emperor wished to reward Mr. Hamilton, the latter refused to accept any fees, and the only recompense he asked for was a charter for the East India Company allowing them free trade at Calcutta. This was at once granted, and the fees of office were remitted.

For some months there existed a state of armed neutrality between the Emperor and his two powerful nobles. Mir Jumla was no longer at headquarters to take any active part in intrigues, and the two Seyds were on their guard against any overt act. But the Emperor chafed daily at his state of dependence and resolved as soon as he could to remove the two men who overshadowed his throne. It is said (Khafi Khan) that the Emperor's own mother, who, as already stated had been a party to the agreement between the Seyds and her son, before he struck a blow for the throne, and who had stood security for her son's good faith, kept them informed of any plots against their well-being. This may be true but the real reason of the Emperor's state of feebleness lay in the disorganization of the Empire. He had no friends to whom he could turn for help. It was evident that a great Empire was crumbling to pieces, and that every one was scrambling to secure something for himself. The skies were falling and there was a chance of catching larks. An example of the general feeling of unrest and of the weakness of the Government is to be found in certain riots which occurred in Ahmedabad in the third year of Ferokshere's reign. The origin of the riots was the same as that which brought about the riots in Bombay and elsewhere during the last eighteen months, namely, the cow question. It is remarkable that this is the first instance, on record of the Hindoos having taken up arms in this matter since the commencement of the Mahomedan rule. The striking difference between the riots of 1713 and those of 1893 lies in the manner in which the rioters were treated. Religious disturbances are always likely to occur between rival creeds in a country like India, but the ease or difficulty with which they are suppressed is the test of the strength or weakness of the Government. The riot originated in a Hindoo on the night of the *Holi* feast attempting to burn the *Holi* on a vacant piece of ground in front of his house common to himself and a Mahomedan neighbour. The neighbour prevented him, and the Hindoo appealed to the Mahomedan Governor, who decided that he had a right to do as he liked in his own house, and accordingly the *Holi* was burnt. Next day the neighbour brought a cow to the same piece of ground and slaughtered it there, putting forward as an excuse that he also had a right to do as he liked on his own ground. The Hindoos at once rose *en masse* and attacked the Mahomedans, who had to take refuge in their houses. Flushed with their success the Hindoos seized the son of a cow-butcher, a lad of 14 or 15, dragged the boy off, and slaughtered him. This act of revenge drew all the Mahomedans from their quarters, and to their assistance came a number of Afghans in the Governor's employ, who were always ready for a fight. The Mahomedans commenced to fire the Hindoos' quarters, but met with a check at the house of a rich Hindoo jeweller, which they found barricaded and defended by a number of match-lock men. A regular pitched battle ensued, and numbers were killed on both sides. For three or four days all business and work was suspended, and the citizens were occupied in fighting with each other. At last both parties appealed to Delhi, and petitions were sent to the Emperor. But similar riots were going on at Delhi, and nothing seems to have been done. Matters gradually settled down in Ahmedabad, but no steps appear to have been taken to punish the rioters.

Another example of the brutality and lawlessness of the time is to be found in the treatment of the Sikhs in the same year (1714). This strange sect had always been an object of peculiar abhorrence to the Mahomedans. Goaded by persecution they frequently retaliated in kind. They erected a strong fortification at Gurdaspur in the Panjab, about ten or twelve days journey from Delhi, and an expedition was sent to reduce it. The Sikhs, a strong and warlike race, as we have since discovered, fought with the utmost bravery. On several occasions they almost succeeded in overpowering the Imperial forces, but at last they had to yield to superior numbers and suffered a crushing defeat, after which they shut themselves up in the fort. A long siege followed, in which, owing to the determined bravery of the defenders, no advantage could be gained, and it was only when their supplies were cut off that they could be reduced to sue for terms. The only condition they asked for was that their lives should be spared. This would seem to have been promised, for the Mahomedan historian (Khafi Khan) who relates the incident says: "Diler Jung *at first* refused to grant quarter, but *at length* he advised them to beg pardon of their crimes and offences from the Emperor. Their chief *Guru* with his son of seven or eight years old, his *diwan*, and three or four thousand persons, became prisoners and received the pre-destined recompense for their deeds." There followed a massacre which is probably unsurpassed in history for the brutality of its details. Khafi Khan goes on to say: "Three or four thousand of them were put to the sword, and the extensive plain was filled with blood as if it had been a dish. Their heads were stuffed with hay and stuck upon spears. Those who escaped the sword were sent in collars and chains to the Emperor." Two thousand stuffed heads and one thousand prisoners were sent to Delhi, and among them the Guru and his son. They were all paraded before the Emperor, who ordered them to be killed in batches of several hundreds each day, reserving the Guru and his son for the last. When all had been slain the Guru was made to cut off his own son's head, and was then himself slaughtered as a finale.

In the meantime matters were becoming very critical in the Deccan. After the defeat of Daoud Khan by Seyd Hussein Ali, the Emperor secretly instigated the Mahrattas to oppose his Viceroy in the hope of crushing his power through them. One Khunde Row had established a chain of posts along the commercial road from Surat to Burhanpur and black-mailed or robbed all the caravans that passed. Trade was almost paralysed, and two expeditions sent by Hussein Ali against this freebooter were surprised and defeated. Rajah Sahoo at Sattara, secretly encouraged by the Emperor, was also putting forward pretensions to the levy of *chouth* throughout the Mogul possessions in the Deccan. At Delhi affairs seemed to be coming to a crisis. Mir Jumla suddenly returned to Court without leave, and though apparently received with disfavour, he remained in Delhi and was supposed to be intriguing against the Seyds. Seyd Abdullah kept his brother in the Deccan fully informed of how things were going on, and urged him to come in person and by his presence put matters right. Hussein Ali saw that there was no time to be lost, and fearing to leave an unsettled country behind him determined to come to terms with the Mahrattas. A treaty was accordingly drawn up between him and Rajah Sahoo, in which the claim of the latter to *chouth* was recognized. The Rajah on his side made himself responsible for the peace and security of the districts over which he levied this species of blackmail. He became, as it were, the head of the Deccan Police, and in case of robbery was bound to make good the value of the property stolen. He actually styled himself not the independent rival, but the servant and vassal of the Delhi Emperor. The annual amount of the chouth thus levied from the Provinces of Aurangabad, Berar, Bieder, Bijapur, Hyderabad, and Kandesh, was valued at no less than 18 crores of rupees, equal in those days to nearly £ 20,000,000.* In order to aid in the collection of the revenue and to keep the peace, the Mahratta Rajah engaged to keep up a force of 15,000 men, to be placed at the disposal of the

* Grand Duff, *History of the Mahrattas*, Vol. I. p. 383.

Mogul Governors. No doubt a treaty of this kind was humiliating in the highest degree, but it left Seyd Hussein Ali free to go to Delhi and settle matters for himself, and the Seyd's personal interests were to him a matter of greater importance than those of the Empire. Besides, not only did it leave him with free hands, but it also gave him two important allies in the shape of his recent enemy, Khunde Row, and Ballajee Wishwanath, who joined him with a considerable force. As might be expected, the Emperor Ferokshere refused to ratify a treaty which so completely thwarted his intentions, but this was a matter of small importance to the Seyd who now felt himself strong enough to openly set the Emperor at defiance. Accordingly (1718) he commenced his march towards Delhi, resolved if he could not bend the Emperor to his will to depose him and put a more pliant instrument in his place.

In Delhi everything was ripe for a revolution. Ferokshere had disgusted every one by his vacillation, his tyranny, and his unworthy favourites. The last was a Kashmiri of low birth, named Mahomed Murad, who had been rapidly promoted to the highest rank. Several of the old nobility, and amongst others Nizam-ul-Mulk were recalled from their posts, and though received with apparent favour were not granted other appointments. The Emperor openly spoke of removing Seyd Abdullah from the post of Vizier and of appointing Mahomed Murad—who was now called Itakad Khan—in his place. Accordingly the old nobility formed a secret combination, and rather than submit to the authority of a low upstart, agreed to support the two Seyds.

When Ferokshere heard of Hussein Ali's march from the Deccan he became alarmed, and a peace was made between him and Seyd Abdullah. The Emperor visited the latter in his house and protested with oaths that he would do him no harm. It was, however, felt on both sides that this reconciliation was a hollow one, and Abdullah's private letters to his

brother urged him to hasten his march as much as possible.
Early in 1719 (end of Rabi-ul-Awal A.H. 1131) Hussein Ali arrived near Delhi, and, as if in defiance, caused his drums to be beaten within earshot of the Emperor's palace. Ferokshere at this crisis showed his usual hesitation. At one time he would be transported with rage and vow to be revenged on the two brothers, while at another he would pretend that he was anxious for a reconciliation. The few friends who remained by him saw that the end was coming, and began to desert him. One of the last to do so was the Rajput prince Jey Singh. He left when the Emperor granted the demand of Seyd Abdullah that he and his brother should be placed in supreme power over all affairs of state and that various posts in the palace and in the Government should be filled by their adherents. Two days after Jey Singh's departure the two brothers entered the citadel, the Emperor's guards were removed and their own men were placed in charge. "Of all the great men near the Emperor, none were left near him, or near the gates of the fortress except Imtiyaz Khan, registrar of the Privy Council, whose absence or presence made no difference, Zafar Khan, who for his complaisance and time serving was called 'the pea in every soup', and some helpless attendants and eunuchs." (Khafi Khan). At the first audience of the two Seyds with their royal master only a few words passed, but at a second on the following day the brothers openly upbraided him for his intrigues and treachery and denounced the ingratitude with which they had been treated in return for placing him on the throne.

Whilst this discussion was going on in the palace the city was in a state of excitement. For the first time the Mahomedan capital of the Empire was in the hands of infidels, for a large force of Mahrattas was used to garrison it. This unusual sight seems to have excited the rage of some Mahomedan horsemen, fifteen or twenty of whom attacked a band of Mahrattas and put them to flight. A panic followed in which most of the Mahrattas attempted to leave the city, but the people rose and a massacre ensued in which some fifteen hundred Mahrattas, including Santa, a chief of note, were killed. When this riot was at its height the drums were beaten and a declaration was made that Ferokshere had abdicated and was succeeded by Rafi-ud-Darajat, grandson of Bahadur Shah. This diverted the attention of the rioters, who now attempted to enter the palace and rescue the Emperor, for though Ferokshere had disgusted the nobility he was still popular with the masses. Here, however, they were met by the Seyds' garrison and repulsed. Inside the palace everything was in confusion. Ferokshere had taken refuge in his zenana, but he was soon dragged out from amongst the shrieking women, taken to a small chamber in the top of the fort, and there blinded. "In this corner of sorrow and grief they left him with nothing but a ewer, a vessel for the necessities of nature, and a glass to drink out of." * (18 February 1719)

* Khafi Khan.

TABLE OF THE DESCENDANTS OF AURUNGZEBE.

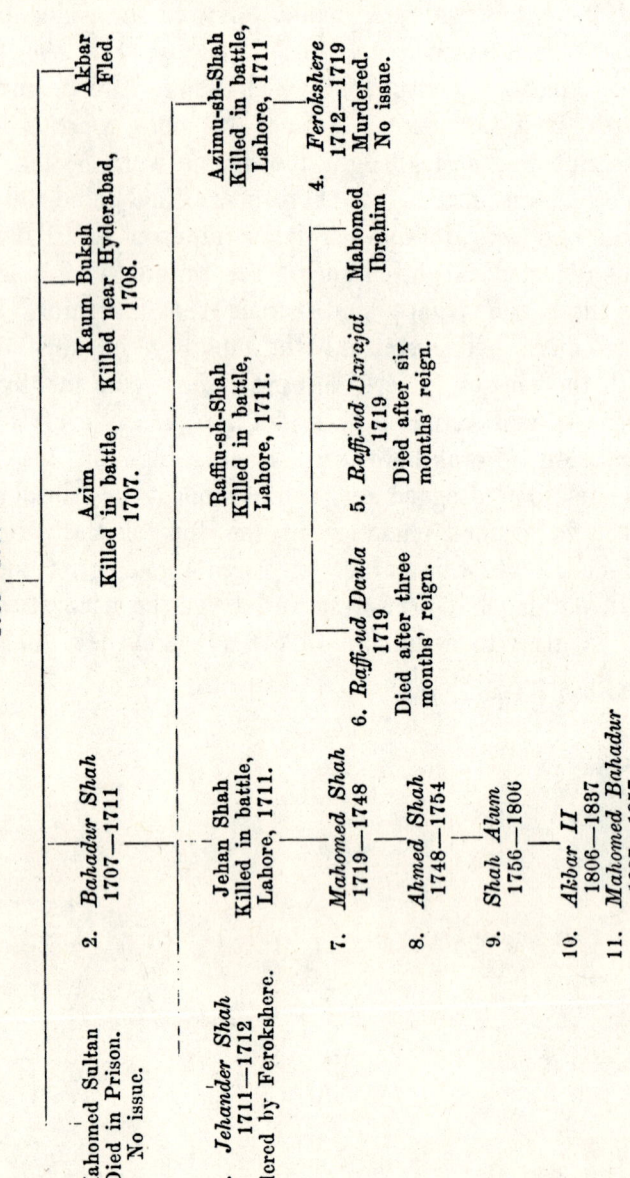

1. Aurungzebe 1658—1707

2. *Bahadur Shah* 1707—1711

— Azim, Killed in battle, 1707.
— Kaum Buksh, Killed near Hyderabad, 1708.
— Akbar, Fled.

Mahomed Sultan. Died in Prison. No issue.

3. *Jehander Shah* 1711—1712. Murdered by Ferokshore.

Jehan Shah Killed in battle, Lahore, 1711.
— Raffiu-sh-Shah Killed in battle, Lahore, 1711.
— Azimu-sh-Shah Killed in battle, Lahore, 1711.

6. *Raffi-ud Daula* 1719. Died after three months' reign.
5. *Raffi-ud Darajat* 1719. Died after six months' reign.
4. *Ferokshere* 1712—1719. Murdered. No issue.

Mahomed Ibrahim

7. *Mahomed Shah* 1719—1748
8. *Ahmed Shah* 1748—1754
9. *Shah Alum* 1756—1806
10. *Akbar II* 1806—1837
11. *Mahomed Bahadur* 1837—1857

CHAPTER XXVI.

THE END OF THE KING-MAKERS AND THE BIRTH OF A NEW KINGDOM.

THE new Emperor Darajat was a young man of less than twenty years. He was placed with such haste on the throne that there was not even time to change his clothes, all that could be done being to throw round his neck a string of pearls. He appears to have been weak both in body and mind, and was a mere puppet in the hands of the Seyds, who not only garrisoned the fort and palace with their own soldiers but placed their friends and dependants in every post of importance. With the object of getting rid of Nizam-ul-Mulk he was sent to Malwa, and again he went without a murmur. There followed him, however, a number of men who, discontented with their treatment by the Seyds, looked to Nizam-ul-Mulk as their patron. These men he attached to his service by payment and by kindness, and they formed the nucleus of a force which was destined to win him a kingdom.

In the meantime in Delhi the Seyds did exactly as they liked. They scrambled for the royal treasures, and the elder brother took a number of Ferokshere's ladies and transferred them to his own zenana. It is said that the two brothers quarrelled over the division of the plunder, and that for some time jealousy and hatred took the place of the union that had hitherto existed between them. As for the unhappy

Ferokshere, he lingered for two months in his miserable prison. The operation performed on his eyes had not been thoroughly done, and he gradually recovered their use, so that he was able to attempt an escape by letting himself out of a window. He was, however, discovered and dragged back. He then attempted to bribe his jailor to let him escape, and on this failing he broke into a passion and abused the two Seyds for their ingratitude towards him. This was reported and the order went forth that Ferokshere was to be killed. The executioners entered his cell with the bow-string. "When the thong was thrown upon his neck, he seized it with both hands, and struggled violently with hands and feet, but the executioners beat his hands with sticks and made him leave go his hold. There is a common report that daggers and knives were used in that desperate struggle, but from what the author has heard no such weapon was used." (Khafi Khan). The unfortunate Emperor was then 38 years of age, and from the time of his victory over Jehander Shah he had reigned six years, nine months, and twenty-four days. His tragic end was due in a great measure to his own fault and to the manner in which he worked against the Seyds whilst openly acknowledging them as his chief ministers. He had forfeited the confidence of all the nobles, but he was still regarded by the people with affection, and when his body was carried to the tomb of Humáyún, it was followed by a crowd of men and women, "chiefly the vagabonds and mendicants of the city, who had partaken of his bounty. They cried and groaned, tore their clothes, threw dust upon their heads, and scattered their abuse. The *bakshis* of Hussein Ali and Seyd Abdullah were ordered to attend the funeral, and they did so with several of the principal men of the city. Stones were cast at them. No one would take the bread or the copper coins which were offered in charity. On the third day some vagabonds and beggars met, cooked food, and distributed it among the poor and remained assembled all night." (*Ibid.*) In the meantime the new Emperor was dying of consumption, and by the time he had reigned six months, he begged that he might be allowed to die in peace and that the throne might be bestowed upon his elder brother Raffiu-ud-Daula. This was done, and three days afterwards Daraját died. The new puppet Emperor was, like the last, weak in body and in intellect. He received the title of Shah Jehan the Second, but beyond the fact that coins were struck and the Khutba read in his name, he had nothing to do with the Government. He was surrounded by creatures of the elder Seyd and was not even allowed to leave the palace in order to go to mosque or hunting, or to speak to a courtier, except in the presence of one of the Seyds. His very clothes and food were chosen for him, and a guardian was appointed who looked after him as a nurse does after a child. In the meantime a revolution had broken out at Agra. One of Aurungzebe's grandsons named Neku Siyar, the son of Mahomed Akbar, had been confined in the fort, and him some of the soldiers of the garrison proclaimed Emperor and at the same time garrisoned the fort. Seyd Hussein Ali marched against the rebels with a considerable army, and after a short siege the fort capitulated. Neku Siyar was taken prisoner and sent back to confinement, and the vast treasures which for three or four hundred years had been accumulated at Agra fell into the hands of Hussein Ali. The jewels of Nur Jehan and Mumtaz Mahal alone were valued at between two and three crores. Most of this plunder the younger Seyd kept for himself. The elder got nothing until after about four months he received twenty-one lakhs of rupees. This settlement between the brothers was brought about by the intervention of Ruttun Chund, but the ill-feeling rankled in the minds of both. But before this reconciliation could take place the young Emperor Shah Jehan II. died after a short reign of three months and some days (Sept. 1719). The cause of his death was dysentery and mental disorder. This unexpected death of their puppet completely disconcerted the plans of the Seyds. They did not know what to do. It was necessary to place a scion of the royal house on the throne, but it was also necessary that he should be of such a character that he would not interfere with their plans. At last they selected Prince Mahomed Roshan Akhtar a youth eighteen years of age, great-grandson of Aurungzebe and son of Jehan Shah, who had been living in retirement at Fathpúr, with his mother, a woman of much intelligence and tact. The death of the late Emperor was kept a secret for a week and not announced until the new one had been proclaimed, on Zilkada A. H. 1131 (end of Sept. 1719) under the title of Mahomed Shah Bádsháh.

The new Emperor was a man of some character, and he was fortunate in having an able counsellor in the person of his mother. This lady would do nothing to excite the jealousy of the two Seyds, and, acting under her advice, the young Emperor at first allowed his two powerful ministers to do as they liked. The Emperor's person, as before, was surrounded by creatures of the two ministers, and there gradually arose a general feeling of discontent throughout the country at their absolute power. This discontent was increased by the behaviour of Ruttun Chund, who, acting in the name of the elder Seyd, disgusted every one by his rapacity and injustice. Added to this there no longer existed the same bond of union between the two brothers, and their enemies began to gather courage and to watch for an opportunity of causing their downfall. Throughout all this web of intrigue the one personage who held aloof and won the respect of all was Nizam-ul-Mulk, who in his Government at Malwa was quietly strengthening his position by gathering round him a body of adherents devoted to his person, who, when the time should come, would be ready to fight for him to the death.

Seyd Hussein Ali was not slow to perceive the increasing popularity of his great rival, and resolved to bring matters to an issue. Accordingly he formulated against him a number of charges, and called upon him for an explanation. This Nizam-ul-Mulk furnished, and in so satisfactory a manner that Hussein Ali had no other recourse than to boldly throw off the mask. He informed him that as he wanted the province of Malwa for himself, in order the better to regulate the affairs of the Deccan, Nizam-ul-Mulk might select any one of the governments of Agra, Allahabad, Multan, or Burhanpur. This demand brought matters to a crisis. The young Emperor and his mother secretly looked to the Nizam as their liberator from the Seyds, and letters from Delhi warned him that there was no time to be lost, and that what he had to do he must do quickly. Accordingly Nizam-ul-Mulk resolved to openly break with the Seyds, and leaving Ujain, he first of all made three marches as if towards Agra, and then turned sharply round and marched southwards towards the Deccan. Town after town rapidly submitted, and at Burhanpur he captured the family of Hussein Ali's brother. These he refrained from molesting, and in a true spirit of chivalry despatched them unharmed with a strong escort to the capital. When the Seyds heard of the revolt of Nizam-ul-Mulk they at once determined to do all in their power to crush him. Orders were despatched to all the Governors of districts and forts to oppose him in every way, and Hussein Ali began to collect a large force in order to march against him in person. In the meantime Alam Ali Khan endeavoured to surprise Nizam-ul-Mulk between two forces. Whilst he marched on Burhanpur from Aurungabad with a strong force, a large army, principally composed of Mahrattas, advanced against it from the West. This army was commanded by Dilawar Ali Khan, a general of some repute. The Nizam, however, was not the man to allow himself to be caught in a trap like this.

He first of all marched against Dilawar Ali Khan and defeated him with considerable slaughter. The general and some five thousand men, chiefly Rajpoots, were left on the field, and the conqueror then turned back to meet Alam Ali Khan, detaching a small force to guard Burhanpur. Before engaging his opponent the Nizam sent him a conciliatory message, but this was rejected with scorn and a general engagement ensued. This was fought on the banks of the Purnah about twenty-five miles to the west of Burhanpur. Khafi Khan thus describes the battle: "On the 6th Sharwál, 1132 A. H. (1st August 1720 A. D.) the battle was fought. Alam Ali Khan received a severe wound, but for all that he kept the field. The elephant which carried him, unable to bear any longer the arrows and swords-cut that he received, turned tail. Alam Ali Khan, dripping with blood from his wounds, turned his face towards the army of Nizam-ul-Mulk, and cried out that his elephant had turned his back but he had not. All his arrows were exhausted, but such of the enemy's arrows as had struck his face or his body, or his *howda*, he quickly pulled out and returned. He received so many wounds in succession that he sank under them and sacrificed his life for his uncles (the Seyds). He was only twenty-two years of age, but he was distinguished by all the determination and the bravery of the Barha Seyds." (Elliot and Dawson, Vol. VII.) The leader being killed, his army scattered, and the whole of the camp fell into the hands of the Nizam, who was at once joined by several other chiefs of influence. It is worthy of remark how important a part bows and arrows play in all these engagements. There were muskets in use and artillery, but the bow seems to have been the favourite weapon of the leaders.

The news of this catastrophe warned the Seyds that no further time must be lost, and it was accordingly resolved that Seyd Abdullah should return to Delhi and keep things quiet there, whilst Hussein Ali, accompanied by the Emperor, should march at once against Nizam-ul-Mulk. This was done and Hussein Ali set off with an army of about 50,000 men and the imperial camp. But scarcely had the two brothers been separated by a few days march when the conspiracy which had for some time been hatching broke out. This conspiracy had received the sanction of the Emperor's mother, although the Emperor himself was left in ignorance. Besides the Queen-mother only three men appear to have been in the plot, Mahomed Amin Khan, Saadat Khan, and an artillery officer named Haidar Khan. It was the last who was selected as the actual assassin. "On the 6th Zilhijja, in the second year of the reign, the royal army was encamped at Tora, thirty-five *koss* from Fattipur. Mahomed Amin Khan, having accompanied the Emperor to his tent, made a show of being unwell, and retired to the tent of Haidar Kuli Khan. When the Emperor entered his private apartment, Hussein Ali also retired. As he reached the gate of the royal inclosure, Mir Haidar Khan, who had a speaking acquaintance with him, approached. Washing his hands of life he placed a written statement in the hands of Hussein Ali and complained of Mahomed Amin as his victim read it." (*Ibid.*) While he was thus engaged Haidar Khan drew his dagger and plunged it into his side. The Ameer-ul-Amra struck the assassin a violent blow with his foot, at the same time crying out, "Put the Emperor to death!" The shock of his motion overset the palankeen, and he fell dead to the ground. A hundred swords were drawn in an instant, and the daring assassin was cut in pieces, but a band of Moguls who had been placed ready by Mahomed Amin Khan, now approaching, dispersed the attendants, and cutting off the head of the Ameer-ul-Amra carried it to the Emperor. (Scott's Translation). As soon as the news of this tragedy spread there was an uproar in the camp. One of the deceased's nephews, Izzat Khan, rushed sword in hand to the Emperor's tent, resolved to avenge his uncle, but was cut down in the attempt. The Emperor was quickly mounted on an elephant and brought out by Mahomed Amin, and an attack was made on Hussein Ali's camp. Those of his dependants who resisted were cut to pieces, and the rest escaped, leaving the encampment to be first plundered and then set on fire. Such was the end of the great Seyd, the maker of four Emperors and for about eight years the virtual ruler of India. His career and his fate were not dissimilar to those of Zulficcar Khan, whose story has been related, and the history of both, like that of others who have attempted the same rôle in other countries, shows the inevitable fate of overweening ambition.

The news of the assassination of Seyd Hussein Ali spread with marvellous rapidity throughout India, and there was generally a feeling of relief. Nizam-ul-Mulk was one of the first to tender his services to the Emperor, but none the less he was not slow to seize the opportunity to strengthen his position in the Deccan and to render it secure. Seyd Abdullah in Delhi received the news with consternation and grief, and at once prepared to revenge his brother's death. His first act was to place another Prince on the throne in opposition to the Emperor, but this was a post of danger that none cared to accept. The two sons of Jehander Shah flatly refused to accept the throne, Neku Siyar, who had already once tasted for a few weeks the sweets and dangers of royalty, also declined the honour, and it was only after much persuasion that Sultan Ibrahim, youngest son of Raffiu-sh-Shah, at length allowed himself to be proclaimed. The singular device was resorted to of making him Emperor for a temporary purpose (*àriyát*=by way of loan). The next step was to gather together an army, and in this the Seyd showed unusual energy. He opened his treasure-house and distributed more than a crore of rupees amongst various noblemen and chiefs.

Horsemen were enlisted at the rate of eighty rupees each man, and lavish promises were made of promotion and prize-money. In this manner a considerable force was rapidly collected, but as was to be expected it consisted for the most part of raw recruits. Many of Hussein Ali's old soldiers, who at first had taken service under the Emperor, deserted when they heard that the brother of their old master had taken the field. These and a body of the brave Seyds of Barha formed the backbone of Seyd Abdullah's army. But little reliance could be placed on the rest. In spite of the large sums spent in recruiting, most of the horses were ridden bare-backed, and the foot-soldiers were badly equipped. About 70 miles from Delhi Seyd Abdullah was joined by a fresh force of Barha Seyds, who brought with them ten or twelve thousand horses. By degrees the army swelled to the number of from 90,000 to 100,000 horsemen. In the meantime the Emperor had advanced to meet his rebellious Vizier, with an army far inferior to his in numbers, but well equipped and disciplined. The two armies met near Husainpur, and on the 17th Muharram they were both drawn up in battle order. Before commencing the fight the Emperor ordered the head of Ruttun Chund, the Hindoo Dewan of the Seyds, to be struck off and thrown at the feet of his elephant. This man was execrated by everybody, and this act therefore was regarded as one of good omen. The royal army seems to have been the stronger in artillery, and a furious cannonade was opened which caused some of Seyd Abdullah's recruits to take to their heels. The Barha Seyds performed miracles of gallantry, and frequently charged the Imperial batteries with such impetuosity that at one time it seemed as if they would turn the tide of battle in their favour. But they were numerically too weak, and were at last beaten back, and in their turn lost their guns. Night fell and the Imperial army still continued the cannonade, causing numbers to run away. On the following morning out of the 100,000 horsemen only seventeen or eighteen thousand remained in Seyd Abdullah's camp. When daylight broke, the Emperor, who had remained on his elephant for the greater part of the night, ordered a general advance. The Barha Seyds still fought with great gallantry and made several desperate charges. Seyd Abdullah placed himself at their head, and at one time the royal forces began to waver. But a fresh body of troops was brought up, the Seyds were surrounded, and at length beaten. Seyd Abdullah was taken prisoner, having been wounded in several places. A few others of the Seyds were also taken, but the greater number fell under the swords of the Imperialists, and the power of this clan was for ever broken. The unfortunate young Ibrahim, who had for a few days been on the throne, was found hiding in the jungle, but as he had had but little choice in what he had done, he received the royal pardon. Seyd Abdullah himself was kept in confinement, and was carried with the army, which now marched upon Delhi. Before it could arrive there the Seyd's relatives and family made their escape, taking with them as much of their property as they could collect. On the 22nd Muharram the Emperor entered Delhi in state, and there followed a distribution of rewards to those who had supported him. Letters were also despatched to Nizam-ul-Mulk asking him to come to Delhi and take up the duties of Minister. This was a post which the Nizam was by no means anxious to occupy. His experience of the intrigues at the Imperial Court had disgusted him with the life; his great rivals were now removed; and he had resolved to make himself independent in the Deccan. For the time, however, he deemed it advisable to consent, and so, after regulating his affairs in the Deccan, he marched leisurely towards Delhi, where he arrived in the middle of 1721. Nizam-ul-Mulk was now the most prominent personage in the Empire. He enjoyed a reputation for great shrewdness and caution, but at the same time for boldness in seizing and utilizing his opportunities. A man of this stamp was not likely to be long without enemies, and no sooner had he arrived in Delhi and taken up the duties of his post than intrigues were organized against him. On every side he found himself opposed and thwarted, and there were not wanting unworthy favourites to warn the Emperor that he was only substituting another king-maker in the place of those who had been removed. Nizam-ul-Mulk was too wise and shrewd to throw away the substance of power which he had already won in the Deccan for the shadow which depended on the fickle favour of a royal master, and accordingly he made up his mind to leave at the earliest opportunity, and never to return in the capacity of a subject. On the pretence of wishing to recruit his health by hunting he left Delhi for a few days, and then, taking the opportunity of an uprising of the Mahrattas in Malva, advanced to Ahmedabad. Here he was met by news both from Delhi and Hyderabad. From the capital he heard that his son Ghazi-ud-Din, whom he had left as his Deputy, had been removed by the intrigues of his enemies, that the faction of his opponents was in power, and that the city was in a state of wholesale corruption. From the Deccan on the other hand he learnt that Mubariz Khan, the lieutenant whom he had left at Hyderabad, had revolted and had given out that he had been appointed Subadar of the Deccan. This decided him. He resolved to renounce for ever Delhi ambition and intrigue and to devote the rest of his life to independence. He therefore turned his back upon Hindustan and marched rapidly towards Aurungabad. Arrived there he sent several conciliatory messages to Mubariz Khan, reminding him of former obligations; but finding them disregarded, he marched to meet him. The two armies met near Shakar Kerar in Berar, and though Mubariz

Khan fought very bravely he was totally defeated, himself and his two sons being killed. The Nizam then advanced to Hyderabad, which from this time he made his headquarters. From this time (1723) the independence of the Hyderabad State may be dated, and the Emperor was obliged to recognize the accomplished fact. He did this with as good a grace as possible, and sent to his powerful vassal a present of elephants and jewels, with the title of *Asaf Jah* and directions "to settle the country, repress the turbulent, punish the rebels, and cherish the people." This the Nizam did, and Khafi Khan thus concludes his interesting history of this period: "In a short time the country was brought under the control of the Mussulman authorities—it was scoured from the abominations of infidelity and tyranny. Under former Subadars, the roads had been infested with the ruffianism of highway robbers and the rapacity of the Mahrattas and rebellious *zemindars*, so that traffic and travelling were stopped, but now the highways were safe and secure. The Mahrattas had exacted the *chouth* with all sorts of tyranny from the jaghirdars, and in addition to it ten per cent under the name of *surdeshmukh*. By this means odious *kumaish-dars* were removed and changed every week and month; orders beyond all endurance of the ryots were issued, and annoyances and insults were heaped upon the collectors of the jaghirdars. Nizam-ul-mulk so arranged that instead of the *chouth* of the *Suba* of Hyderabad a sum of money should be paid from his treasury, and that the *surdeshmukh* which was levied from the ryots at the rate of ten per cent should be abandoned. He thus got rid of the presence of the *kumaish-dars* (collectors) of the *chouth* and the officials of the *surdeshmukh* and *rahdari* passport system), from which latter impost great annoyance had fallen upon travellers and traders."

From this time forward the Nizam was practically independent. He had brought with him to the Deccan a band of devoted adherents, and upon them he bestowed large gifts of land. Some of these were Mahomedans, but some also were Hindoos. The former were utilized for military service, and in return for their valuable jaghirs they were bound to furnish large bodies of soldiers—foot, horse, and artillery. So greatly did the Nizam depend upon the noblemen for support and loyal service that he divided his newly acquired kingdom roughly into thirds. One third was reserved for his own privy purse, and was termed the *Sarf-i-Khas;* one third was allotted for the expenses of the Government, and was called the *Dewan's* territory, and the remaining third was distributed as jaghirs or feudal estates. Of these the military fiefs were the most important, and are still known as the *Pagah* estates. So extensive were the powers granted to the holders of these fiefs that they formed a kind of *imperium in imperio* and in their own jaghirs possessed sovereign rights. They had the power of life and death, and were excluded from all State taxation. This division of power and wealth was probably necessary in order to safeguard the new ruler of the country from rivalry and rebellion, but it contained in it the seeds of future difficulties and complication. The Hindoo noblemen were chiefly employed in administrative work. This was a wise measure, for a large proportion of the population of the country say 90 out of 100, consisted then as it does now of Hindoos. In this policy Asaf Jah showed great sagacity and knowledge of Deccan traditions. From the time of the first Gulburga Sultan, Allah-ud-Din, it had been the custom for the Mahomedan princes to employ Hindoos to manage the land revenue and finance. This work they had done with eminent success until the twenty years campaign of Aurungzebe revolutionized the condition of the Deccan. The first Nizam had a new element to deal with, that of the Mahrattas, and he therefore showed great wisdom in reverting to the old policy of entrusting Hindoos with the task of dealing with their Hindoo rivals in the matter of land revenue and finance, and of relying upon his Mahomedan followers to furnish his military contingent. But the old Deccan nobility disappeared or fell into obscurity. Under this term we refer more especially to the Mahomedan families of the Deccan. The Hindoo Rajas and landholders remained. They gave their allegiance to the new master, and were confirmed in their old privileges and possessions. But the Deccannee or Mahomedan nobles were all more or less pledged to former Viceroys, and followed with them their changes of fortune, their estates being bestowed upon the adherents of the new regime. Thus the *proteges* of the first Nizam gladly accepted the title of *Asaf Jahis* or followers of Asaf Jah, and to the present day this designation is highly prized as a proof of honourable descent.

Asaf Jah, by prudence, caution, self-restraint and by boldness, thus succeeded in raising himself to a position of the highest importance in India. One of his great rivals was killed, and the other was kept in confinement in which he shortly died, some say of a natural death, but Khafi Khan says: "God forbid that his (the Emperor's) counsel should have been given for poison, but God only knows!"

Indian history is for the most part a record of daring adventurers, who gain power and sometimes the throne by a series of crimes and utilize it for purposes of extortion, tyranny, and oppression. In the lives of Zulficcar Khan and of the two Seyds we have a striking example of such careers and of the inevitable catastrophe. Asaf Jah presents a remarkable contrast to the general rule. His rise to power is stained by no crime, domestic or public, and his story is simply that of a man who bided his time, who seized his opportunity, and who was loyal to those who treated him loyally.

The time has now come to close the first portion of this history. The days of the Empire were fast drawing to a close.

THE BIRTH OF A NEW KINGDOM.

Beyond the Khyber Pass began to loom the shadow of the Persian conqueror, and in Maharashtra a nation had been formed that was to make a bid for the Empire. It did so and failed, and in the meanwhile in the West and the East and North-East the small clouds of British power, at the time scarcely bigger than a man's hand, gradually increased in size, until a few years later the English were called in first as the aids and then as the arbiters of the Mahomedan Emperors. With the death of Aurungzebe the decay of the Mogul Empire commenced and at the death of Mahomed Shah the Empire had practically ceased to exist. If Asaf Jah had had successors worthy of him, the Delhi Emperors would have been followed by as glorious a dynasty in the Deccan.

GENEALOGY OF ASAF JAH, THE FIRST NIZAM.

1. Mohomed bin Abi Bukr.
2. Aboo Mohomed Mukkee.
3. Aboolkasim Makee.
4. Abdul Rehman Makee.
5. Abdulla Basri.
6. Mohomed Kasim Khushkee.
7. Nasruddin Basri.
8. Kasim Ali Roomi.
9. Mohomed Saeed Kushkee.
10. Abdulla Soofi.
11. Abdul Razzak Bagdadi.
12. Abdulla Bagdadi.
13. Mohomed Baha ooddin Bagdadi.
14. Shiekh Mohomed Bagdadi.
15. Shiekhulsheyookh Shahab ooddin Sohurverdi.
16. Abi Mohomed Hafiz.
17. Zenooddin Qutbul-aktak.
18. Shiekh Alâ ooddin.
19. Shiekh Tajooddin.
20. Shiekh Fateh oollah.
21. Shiekh Najib oollah.
22. Fatehulshiekhussani.
23. Shiekh Javid Ulmolukub Sirmusp.
24. Fatehoolla Shiekhussani.
25. Shiekh Javid Shah Sani.
26. Huzrut Mohomed Durvesh.
27. Shiekh Mohomed Moomin.
28. Mohomed Alumulshiekhul Saddikiul Alvi.
29. Khawaja Azizau Aluna.
30. Khawaja Mir Ismail.
31. Mir Abid Khan Ulmokhatib Ba Kooleej Khan Walid-i-Kamruddin Khan.
32. Foroze Jung.
33. Chin Koolich Khan *Asaf Jah* 1st Nizam.

Kindly furnished by the private Secretary to H.H. the Nizam.

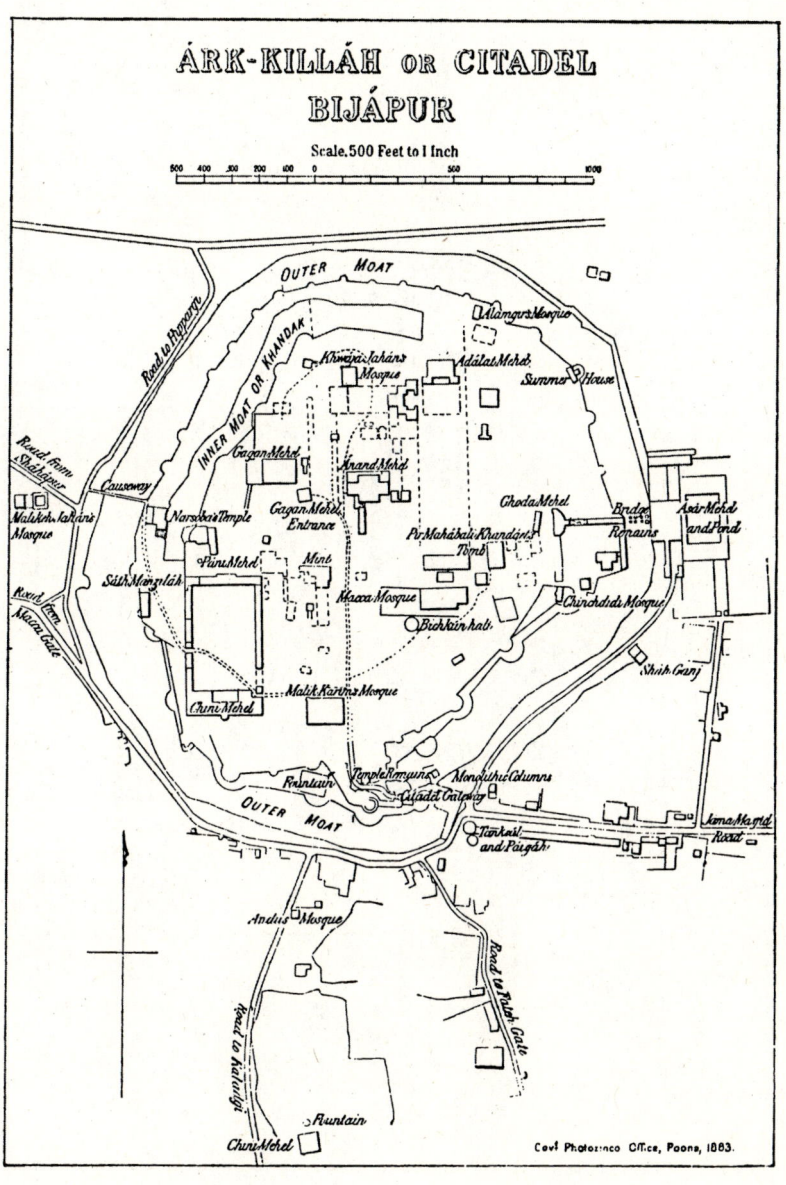

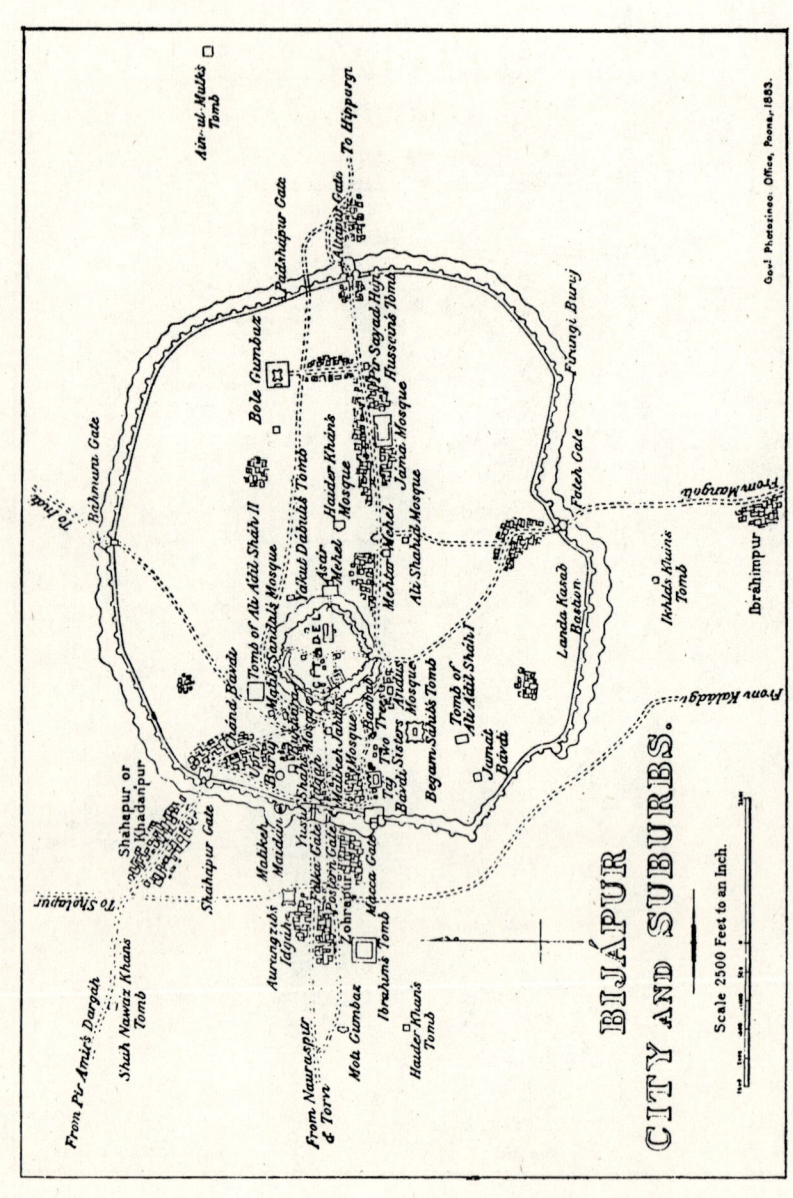

APPENDIX.

Owing to the kind permission of the Government of Bombay I have been permitted to reproduce the description of Bijapur and the plans of the city as they appear in Vol. XXIII of the Bombay Gazetteer. The description of Hyderabad I propose to reserve for the second portion of this history which will consist for the greater part of the history of modern Hyderabad under the present dynasty founded in the first quarter of the last century.

Bija pur,[1] during the sixteenth and the greater part of the seventeenth centuries (1490-1686) the capital of the Adil Sháh dynasty and the mistress of the Deccan, is in north latitude 16° 50' and east longitude 75° 48', about 1950[2] feet above the sea, on the north slope of the ridge which forms the water-shed of the Kistna and Bhima rivers. It is a station on the Hudgi-Gadag or East Deccan railway sixty miles south of Sholápur. Its surroundings have nothing striking or picturesque. On all sides for long distances stretch waving treeless downs, the uplands covered with a shallow stony soil, bare except during the south-west rains (June-October), and separated by dips or hollows of comparatively rich soil. To the north the country is peculiarly desolate, nothing but ridge after ridge, scarcely a village as far as the eye can see. To the very walls the country is the

[1] Contributed by Mr. H. F. Silcock, C. S.
[2] The levels taken in different parts of the city are 1932 feet at the Ásar Mehel, 1940 at the Boli Gumbaz, 1960 at the plinth of the Two Sisters, 1972 at the mámlatdár's office in the Macca Gate, and over 2000 feet near the Idgáh. Mr. E. K. Reinold, C. E.

same, except that outside of the city the monotony of the rolling plain is relieved by tombs and other buildings. From the north the first glimpse of Bijápur is about fifteen miles distant, where the dome of the Boli Gumbaz rises above the intervening uplands, and, as the city is neared, fills the eye from every point, looming large against the southern horizon. At five miles the whole city breaks suddenly into view, and far on every side the country is covered with buildings of varied shapes and in different stages of decay. The numbers of tombs, mosques, palaces and towers which lie scattered in every direction, give the scene a strangely impressive grandeur. To the right, the white domes of Pir Amin's tomb gleam in the sunlight, a brilliant contrast to the dark gray ruins in the foreground. In front lie the city's massive walls and bastions, with here and there a stately building towering over the fortifications, while, on the left, the colossal proportions of the Boli or Gol Gumbaz' dwarf its surroundings. Still further to the left, the plain, the old battlefield, is dotted with tombs, among which is conspicuous the massive dark gray mausoleum of Ain-ul-Mulk. Close round the city the land is surprisingly barren. The ground in front is bare of trees and all vegetation, and is broken into large irregular hollows, the quarries from which the city was hewn. On the west miles of ruins of the old town of Shahápur (1510-1636) prevent cultivation. Close to the walls on the south are traces of tillage, but none of it shows from a distance. The only object is the great city stretching far and near in a waste whose desolate glimpses of noble buildings, some fairly preserved others in ruins, make the more striking.

South of Bijápur the country changes. On the southern side of the ridge which overlooks the city there is considerable cultivation. The same treeless ridges remain, but between the ridges are fairly rich hollows, and, within eight miles of the walls, is the valley of the Don now as of old the granary of Bijápur. The slope of a barren ridge, surrounded on three sides by a treeless cropless plain, seems a strange site for a capital. The desert to the north where no invading army could find food or fodder was no doubt a valuable defence to Bijápur on the side most open to attack. But the crest of the ridge to the south, commanding the approaches on both sides, seems at first a better site for a fortress. The reason for the choice of the present site seems to have been that the crest of the ridge is waterless while within the walls of Bijápur the supply of water is abundant. The under rock teems with splendid springs of which, to judge by the remains of wells and gardens, full advantage was taken. Later on the local supply was increased by artificial means, and the Torvi conduit and the Begam Lake made the city almost independent of its local resources.[1]

Bijápur within the walls covers about 1600 acres or two and a half square miles. The suburbs even now spread over a large area, and in the city's prime stretched for miles. The walls, which are still in fair order, are about six and a quarter miles round and form an irregular ellipse of which the major axis from the Macca Gate in the west to the Allápur Gate in the east is about two and three-quarters and the minor axis from the Bahmani Gate in the north to the Fateh Gate in the south is about one and three-quarters miles.

The city walls are surrounded by a deep moat forty to fifty feet broad. They are massive and strong, and, not counting ten at the gates, are strengthened with ninety-six bastions of various designs and different degrees of strength. In height the walls vary from thirty to fifty feet, and have an average thickness of twenty feet which in places they greatly exceed. The general plan of construction is much the same in the different sections, though the design and

[1] The Torvi water works are described at page 403.

finish vary.[1] They seem to consist of two massive stone walls twenty to thirty feet high and twenty to thirty feet apart, with the space between filled with earth, well rammed, and covered with a masonry platform. This platform which runs all round the walls, was protected on the inside by a battlemented curtainwall about ten feet high running from bastion to bastion and loopholed for both artillery and small arms. On this platform there was ample room for the movements of the garrison, who, from their superior station, could with ease command the ground outside. The construction of the walls was undertaken by Ali Adil Sháh I. (1557-1580),

[1] Major Moor (Little's Detachment, 310, 311) describes the walls in May 1792 as, A thick stone building about twenty feet high with a ditch and rampart. Capacious towers of large hewn stone were at every hundred yards much neglected and many fallen in the ditch. The curtain was of great height perhaps forty feet from the berme of the ditch entirely built of huge stones strongly cemented and frequently ornamented with sculptured representations of lions and tigers. The towers were very numerous and of vast size built of the same materials and some with top ornaments like a cornice and otherwise in the same style with the curtain. Captain Sydenham (Asiatic Researches, XIII, 435) describes the walls in 1811 as a rampart flanked by 109 towers of different dimensions, a ditch and covert way surrounding it, and a citadel in the interior. These works were very strong and were still in fair repair, their outer and inner faces being of hewn stone laid in mortar. The parapets which were nine feet high and three feet thick were composed entirely of stone and mortar. The towers were in general semicircular with a radius of about thirty-six feet. The curtains, which appeared to rise from the bottom of the ditch, varied from thirty to forty feet in height, and were about twenty-four feet thick. The ditch was in many places filled and was so covered with vegetation that not a trace of it appeared. In other parts it seemed to have been formed through rock, forty to fifty feet broad and about eighteen feet deep. A faced counterscarp showed in many places and the remains of a line of masonry running parallel about seventy yards in front pointed out the boundary of the covert way. In 1792 Major Moor found this covert way almost perfect. He says it was one hundred and fifty and in places two hundred yards broad. (Little's Detachment, 311). At present hardly a sign of the covert way remains. The Honourable Mountstuart Elphinstone (Colebrooke's Life, II. 70) describes the walls in 1819: The ditch and the rampart enclose a circle of six miles circumference. The rampart is of earth supported by strong walls and large stones. It is twenty-four feet thick at top, and has Indian battlements in tolerable order and large towers at moderate distances. We mounted a very lofty tower separate from the wall. From this height we saw the plan of the town, now scattered with ruins and in some places full of trees. The most conspicuous object next to the great dome is the citadel. On the whole I find Bijápur much above my expectations and far beyond anything I have ever seen in the Deccan. There is something solemn in this scene and one thinks with a melancholy interest on its former possessors. The proofs of their power remain while their weaknesses and crimes are forgotten and our admiration of their grandeur is heightened by our compassion for their fall.

on his return from the decisive victory of Tálikoti (1565) in which the power of the great Hindoo kingdom of Vijayanagar (1335-1587) perished. They are said to have been completed in two years and a half, though as necessity arose strong bastions were added at intervals down to the overthrow of the Adil Sháh dynasty in 1686. It is locally reported that the nobles of the realm were each entrusted with a bastion and curtain wall; and that this explains the great variety in the design and detail of the different sections which adds much to the handsomeness and impressiveness of the whole. On each of the leading bastions a stone tablet commemorating its building was let into the wall. Some of these tablets remain, but many have fallen out and been carried away.

Of the ninety-six bastions, three, the Sherzi bastion on the west and the Lánda Kasáb and Firangi bastions on opposite sides of the Fateh Gate on the south, greatly exceed the others in size and strength.

The SHERZI BURUJ or Lion Tower takes its name from two heraldic lions carved in stone to the right of the entrance which leads to the tower platform.[1] The bastion is not very high, but is of great diameter and is very strong. In the centre are two raised circular platforms for cannon, on one of which lies, supported on beams of wood, the great bronze gun of Bijápur the Malik-i-Maidán or Monarch of the Plain till recently almost the largest piece of ordnance in existence, and a splendid specimen of the founder's skill. The bastion is furnished with bombproof powder-chambers and water-tanks, and apparently it was never exposed to fire as the masonry is untouched. Dread of the Malik-i-Maidán prevented attacks, which was well for the garrison, as from its unwieldy size and peculiar construction the gun could not have done much harm, and, as the bastion was so low, it might have been comparatively easily scaled. The inscription tablet states that this tower

[1] Bird in Journal Bombay Branch Royal Asiatic Society, I, 354.

was built about A.D. 1658 by Nawab Munzli Sháhin in the reign of Ali Adil Sháh II, (1656-1672). It was therefore almost the last addition to the defences. The inscription runs:

"During the reign of the victorious king Ali Adil Sha'h, who, through the favour of God gained a glorious victory, this bastion was in five months made firm as a rock by the successful efforts of Munzli Sha'h. An angel in delight gave the date of the building saying, The Sherzi bastion is without an equal."

The numerical value of the angel's words is 1069 that is A.D. 1658. Near the Fateh Gate on the south, and about 530 yards west-southwest of it, a bastion towers above its neighbours. This is locally known as the LÁNDA KASAB. On it is the largest gun in Bijapur, though as it is in a seldom visited part of the city, its existence has been overlooked and the Malik-i-Maidán is generally considered the largest. The bastion was built about A.D. 1609 by Hazrat Shah in the reign of Ibrahim II. (1580-1626). A second inscription tablet seems to show that it was not finished till 1662, as this tablet, let into the inside wall of the bastion, records the completion of the walls in that year. The Lánda Kasáb seems to have been the most formidable in construction and armament of all the bastions on the south side, as, in addition to the large iron gun referred to, two other pieces of artillery were mounted on it, one of which, something like a modern mortar, still lies on it. Against this bastion Aurangzeb in 1686 seems to have directed the whole fire of his artillery, and pitted it with shot-marks.[1] Little damage was done to the tower itself, but a breach was made in the curtain-wall close by, and, as the garrison could be relieved from that side only, the steps leading to the top of the bastion were open to the fire, and the place was no doubt untenable. Both guns seem to have been more than once struck, and the larger one lies dismounted, probably from a shot which struck it near the muzzle.

[1] Outside the walls, near the Lánda Kasáb bastion, is the tomb of Eklas Khan the dome of which was destroyed by shots during Aurangzeb's siege. The whole tomb bears marks of heavy fire. From the direction of the shot-marks it seems that it was seized as an advanced post by Aurangzeb's army, and recovered by the defenders.

APPENDIX. 363

The FIRANGI BURUJ or Portuguese Tower, about 1000 yards east of the Fateh Gate, is the most complete of all the bastions, and from its peculiar construction is extremely interesting. It is a hollow semicircular tower, in the middle of a strong battlemented curtain-wall, along every few yards of which are small raised platforms for cannon. The tower rises about thirty feet above the general platform of the walls, and about half-way up a passage-way or corridor was built running round the interior, access to which was gained by steep flights of stone stairs at each end of the tower. On this corridor masonry platforms for small cannon were constructed, while at each end are small ammunition chambers. The hollowness of this tower takes greatly from its value as a defence. It is called the Portuguese Tower because it was built by a Portuguese general who took service with Ali Adil Shah I. (1557-1580) in 1576. As far as inscriptions show his name was Yoghris Khán, and, on the tablet in the tower, he is called the Slave of Ali Adil Sháh. Nothing else is known of this man. The name Yoghris was probably taken on entering the Bijápur service. To judge from the works entrusted to him he must have stood high in the king's favour. Their inscriptions seem to show that the Fateh Gate was one of the bastions of the Macca Gate, and one or two other parts of the walls were built by him or under his supervision. The north face of the walls has several fine bastions. But the Sherzi, Lánda Kasáb, and Firangi are the best worth seeing, as each is remarkable to Sherzi bastion for its armament, the Lánda Kasáb for its historical importance, and the Firangi for its construction and architecture.

Five large gates led into the city. [1] Four of these are still

[1] Near the Boli Gumbaz was a sixth gate called Pádshápur. It was undefended and appears to have been used for much the same purpose as the postern gate near the Macca Gateway. Several small postern gates in different parts of the city opened into the moat. The Pádshápur Gate was built up for many years and has only lately been opened.

in use; the fifth has been closed and turned into Government offices. These gates were, the Macca in the west, the Sháhápur leading to the Sháhápur suburb in the north-west, the Bahmani leading to the Bahmani kingdom in the north, the Allápur close to the Allápur suburb in the east, and the Mangoli to the south. Close to the Macca Gate a small postern gate led west into the Zohrápur suburb. The Macca Gate has been closed for more than a century, but communication with that quarter of the city was kept through the Postern Gate. In later years another western entrance was made close to the Sherzi Tower, the wall being knocked down and a bridge thrown across the moat. This gate, which is known as the Futka or Broken Gate, is now the chief western entrance to the city. Another gate to correspond with the Futka Gate was opened close to the Allápur Gate in the east, and a broad road has been lately made to join the two and open this part of the city which ruins and brushwood made wholly inaccessible. The ancient gateways are models of building, and are immensely strong. The general plan in all is much the same; two massive circular towers with the doorway between, and above the door a platform guarded by a battlemented wall. In front of these towers a broad clear space is surrounded by lofty fortified walls joined with the towers and loopholed for musketry. These walls also end in small castellated towers with another gateway between, facing parallel to the city-walls, so that in addition to the fire from the gateway the approach was swept by the fire from the walls. The gates themselves, some of which remain, are of thick wooden beams about six inches square fastened together with iron clamps, strengthened with massive bars, and bristling with twelve-inch iron spikes. With the siege appliances of the days of the Bijápur monarchy, gateways such as these were impregnable, and no attempt seems to have been made to force them. Aurangzeb did not enter the city till it surrendered, and made no attempt to gain the gateways. The name Fateh or Victory, by which the Mangoli Gate is known, preserves the conquest of Bijápur by the Emperor Aurangzeb. Through this gateway he entered the captured city in state and to mark the circumstance ordered the name of the gate to be changed from Mangoli to Fateh or Victory. A handsome gun, cast-iron inlaid with brass in a scroll pattern, which is said to have been dropped by the Emperor's troops while filing through this gateway, has been lately raised and placed on the platform of the Two Sisters. The Macca Gateway, which is now closed and used as the offices of the mámlatdár and subordinate judge, is by far the strongest and most complex of the gates. Its appearance is so changed by the houses built inside of it that the general plan is difficult to master. Outside it is somewhat like the others, the walls ending in two round towers with a doorway between. Inside the construction is peculiar. The gateway looks like a large bastion furnished with several platforms for the working of heavy guns and with covered ways loopholed for musketry. On the city side too it was strongly fortified, for, though the guns could not be trained on this side, a passage ran along the front loopholed for musketry and communicating with the interior of the fortification. The whole plan is more that of a strong fort than a gateway, and great pains seem to have been taken to make it impregnable not only to enemies without but to treachery within. One of the guns, which lay dismounted on the southern tower, has been raised on a masonry platform. It is interesting for its inlaid muzzle and from having apparently burst at the breech and been repaired by welding round it a massive coil of iron. Two or three fine trees on the gun platforms add to the picturesqueness of this part of the fortification which is well worth a visit. The gate is said to have been closed and garrisoned by order of the Peshwa's government about 1762 to protect the city from robbers.

From whatever direction it is approached, Bijapur has an air of striking grandeur. Its perfect walls and bastions and the glimpses of noble buildings pleasantly shaded combine to give the impression that the city is peopled and prosperous. When the gate is passed the waste inside is a sudden surprise. From the west the approach through the modern village of Torvi is some preparation for the ruin within the walls. Long lines of fallen houses, with here and there a palace wall or a mosque mark the site of the old town of Sháhápur. Nearer the city on the south, is the beautiful tomb and mosque of Ibráhim II. (1580-1626) and in front above the almost unharmed walls Kháwas Khán's tomb now known as the Two Sisters and the Seven-Storeyed Palace rise in the middle distance, and further on is a glimpse of the dome of the Jáma Mosque and of the Boli Gumbaz of Sultán Máhmud (1626-1656). The greater part of the people of modern Bijápur are settled close to the western gate, and though their lowly huts are a marked contrast to the stately monuments of the past, the air of life and cheerfulness is a not unpleasing relief among the waste of ruins. When the peopled western quarter is passed the ruin and loneliness of the inside become more and more painful, though shady gardens round tombs and other ancient buildings relieve the monotony and mask the desolation. Towards the centre of the city a road well lined with trees leads to the Citatel or Ark-killáh with the royal palaces and other public buildings. On all sides are splendid specimens of the builder's art. The Sát Mazli, Anand Mehel, and Gagan Mehel within the citadel, and the Malika Jahán mosque, the Asar Mehel, and the unfinished tomb of Ali Adil Sháh II. immediately without, form a group rarely equalled for picturesqueness, each in itself a gem of art. Beyond the Citadel north towards the Bahmani or east towards the Allápur gates, is a dreary waste, with almost nothing save fallen palaces and roofless dwellings overgrown with custard-apples and other wild shrubs, while an occasional unharmed tomb or mosque makes the surrounding desolation the more complete. Even these ruins have glimpses of the Bijápur of the author of Tára. Amidst the ruins are enclosures that were once gardens in which broken fountains and dry water-courses suggest visions of elegance and comfort, and where low brushwood and tangled grass have choked fragrant flowers and rich fruit trees. Here and there a jasmin, run wild, trails over ruined walls and once trim terraces. Mournful as is the desolation the picturesque beauty of the buildings, the fine old trees and the mixing of hoary ruins and perfect buildings form an everchanging and impressive scene. Striking as they are, the imagination is perhaps less stirred by the grandeur of the public buildings than by the countless other ruins. Palaces, arches, tombs, and minarets, all carved from rich brown basalt, garlanded by creepers and broken and wrenched by *pipal* and banian roots, furnish fresh interest even after days spent in the ruins. In the height of prosperity Bijapur must have been a noble city. Still it may be questioned if its buildings were so effective in their prime as they now are deserted and in ruins.

The Árk-killáh[1] or Citadel, nearly in the centre of the city, is one of the most interesting parts of Bijápur, a perfect treasury of artistic buildings. It was chosen by Yusuf Adil Sháh (1489-1510) as the site for his fort, but was so changed and improved by his successors as to leave little of the old village of Bichkanhali.[2] The present citadel is nearly circular, a little less than a mile round measuring by the counterscarp of the ditch. Its defences are a strong curtain, with, on the south and east, several bastions of considerable strength, a

[1] The Ark of Ark-killáh is of doubtful origin. It is probably taken from the Sanskrit *ark* the sun.
[2] Captain Sykes (Bom. Lit. Trans. III. 61) says this village was called Kejganhalli.

faussebraye or rampart mound and ditch, the whole well built and massive.[1] The faussebraye is very wide, especially on the north and north-west, where a second wet ditch was cut at the foot of the rampart, which on these sides was very low, apparently to give the royal palaces whose fronts all look in that direction an unbroken view over the city and country round. The citadel was begun by Yusuf Adil Sháh shortly after his revolt in 1489. A mud fort then stood on the site.[2] The mud wall was taken down and a strong stone wall built in 1493,[3] many of the stones being apparently taken from Hindoo temples as this wall contains much carving like that found in temple stones. The citadel was not completely fortified till the reign of Ibráhim Adil Sháh I. (1534-1557). A stone tablet in one of the bastions near the gateway marks its completion in A.D. 1546 (A.H. 953) under the superintendence of Khán A'zam Ekhtiar Khán. The original design seems to have been to build a double wall round the fort with two moats, and to have the space between the walls a garden. This design seems never to have been carried out. On the south and south-west the double wall was built, and the space between turned into a garden with ponds and fountains, but this inner wall passed only a short way west. On the east only one wall was built, though its base was guarded by a curtain-wall running from bastion to bastion. On the north side the main wall of the citadel was very low, apparently not to block the view, but on this side the double moat sufficed for protection. Though the walls are strong and massive, and several formidable bastions were built at prominent points, it seems unlikely that such a fort could have ever stood for any time against an enemy

---

[1] Little's Detachment, 320. In 1819 the citadel which had a double rampart and a moat enclosing numerous and magnificent palaces was in a state of ruin and decay. The courts were overgrown with trees and choked with weeds and everything looked dismal and forlorn. Colebrooke's Elphinstone, II. 71.
[2] Briggs' Ferishta, II. 462.   [3] Briggs' Ferishta, III. 14.

armed with artillery who had forced the city fortifications. The site is unfavourable. It is almost the lowest part of the city and is commanded by the rising ground on the north-west, on which is built the cavalier called the Upri Buruj. No doubt the deep moat, even if not swarming with crocodiles as Tavernier reports,[1] made the place difficult of approach. Still this was but a slight obstacle, to a well-armed enemy in possession of the north-western height, as all the palaces would be open to his fire and the place be untenable. This unprotected state of the public buildings tends to show that in later years the Ark-killáh was never used as a citadel, but simply as a royal residence. It may have been owing to its defenceless position that Ali Adil Shah I. (1557-1580) resolved on fortifying the whole city instead of trusting to the central castle.

At present the main entrance to the citadel is on the south-east by two traversed gateways of considerable strength. Originally[2] five well fortified gates are mentioned but of three of these no trace remains. Apparently the gateways were added after the fortifications were complete. The original or south-east gate lay between the two lofty circular bastions in which the fort-walls ended, and the entrance seems to have led through an old Hindoo temple much of which was left standing and the column used in making the gateway and the guard-house attached.[3] Additions were built to the outside of

---

[1] Harris' Voyages, II. 360.   [2] Ogilby's Atlas (1680), V. 246.

[3] Some hold that there was no temple here and that the columns were gathered from different places to form a guard-room. Looking to the peculiar character of these columns, which differ greatly from the others in the Ark-killáh, and to the copious Kánarese inscriptions, also to the fact that the distance of the columns from each other is much the same as if they were parts of an old Hindoo temple but is not what it would have been had they been brought to form a guard-house it is difficult to believe that the columns are not the remains of an unmoved temple. Some on each side of the gateway correspond so exactly that it is hard to believe that they are not in their original places. Moreover all the architectural remains close by are Hindoo. The large slab spanning the entrance is raised on stones undoubtedly part of a temple, and close by are the remains of Hindoo victory pillars. If all these were brought from a distance it is strange that they should have been centred in so comparatively narrow a space.

these bastions in the form of flanking walls, and a second gate, with a guard-room above it, was made in front of the earlier gate and strengthened by a fortified wall which ran parallel with the entrance and at right angles to the bridge leading over the moat.[1] Every precaution seems to have been taken to make this gateway impregnable. In itself it is very strong, and ample quarters for a large garrison were provided, while the powerful end bastions commanded all approaches. This was the only entrance till, in the reign of Máhmud Adil Sháh (1626-1656), a causeway was thrown across the moat on the west, but it is so narrow as to be of use only to walkers. On entering by the main gateway, after passing through beautifully carved basaltic Hindoo columns, the height and massiveness of the side walls at once attract attention. No guns remain on any of the bastions, but the platforms are untouched. They are said to have formerly been armed with 100 guns, but considering their size and number this is scarcely probable.[2] After passing the old temple the road crosses the centre of the Ark-killáh and leaves on the left another so-called Hindoo temple or college which is evidently a mosque built of temple remains.[3] Beyond this it sends off one branch on the left to the Granary or Chini Mehel I. and the Sát Mazli which in later years was the favourite residence of the kings and is still a singularly beautiful palace. Another branch leads to the right in the direction of the Macca mosque and passes close to a low circular wall

---

[1] It is curious that in this fortification, which is evidently a subsequent addition, the guard-room over the bridge is built in very much the same style as the small chambers in the towers of the Idgáh near the Upri Buruj, which is said to have been constructed by Yusuf. The main gateway and bastions were no doubt built by him and he may have also built the outer line of defence subsequently, but with the exception of this guard-room, the rest of the towers and walls seem of a later age than the main gateway.

[2] Ogilby's Atlas, V. 247.

[3] Some hold that the four centre columns under what may be styled the dome as well as the entrance gateway are remains of a Hindoo temple in place. But the rest of the building has been undoubtedly formed from the stones of other temples brought for the purpose of building the mosque.

APPENDIX. 371

which is said to mark the centre of the old village of Bichkanhali. Following the straight road towards the north, after passing the Mint and one or two other ruined buildings, the Anand Mehel or Joy Palace is reached, one of the most beautiful palaces in Bijápur, surrounded by remains of terraced walks, fountains, and gardens. On the opposite side lies the Gagan Mehel famous for the large arch which spans its front, while the gateway which opens on the road, now being turned into a church, is no less remarkable for the exquisite stucco ornament of the interior. The main building of this palace which is now in ruins is one of the oldest in the city and for many years was the residence of the kings. Afterwards when the Sát Mazli and Chini Mehel I. were built the Gagan Mehel was turned into a reception-hall. Here in 1686 the Emperor Aurangzeb received the submission of the last of the Adil Sháh kings, the youthful Shikandar, amid the passionate tears of the nobles and the wailing cries of thousands, which rose to the throne of God as a witness against the causeless aggressor.[1] The only other public building which can be identified is the Adálat Mehel on the north-east, and of this only the bare walls are left. On the western side near the causeway the Hindoo temple of Narsoba stands picturesquely on the side of the inner moat. In this temple it is said king Ibráhim II. (1580-1626) used to worship, when for some years he forsook the faith of his fathers.

With the rays of the morning sun streaming through the oriel windows of the Sát Mazli and the waters of the inner moat lapping its base and reflecting its climber-clothed walls, few places in Bijápur, until recent changes, were more beautiful than this Ark-killáh. Few places also are fuller of memories than the Ark-killáh. Here in 1510 the young

Colonel Meadows Taylor in Architecture of Bijápur. 47.

Ismáil (1510-1534) was besieged by his traitor minister Kamál Khán; here between 1511 and 1585 the noble queen Chánd Sultána held her court, and from here was (1580) sent prisoner to Sátára; here Máhmud the Merry (1626-1656) spent happy hours with his favourite the beautiful Rhumba; and this same citadel, the scene of many a glorious pageant, witnessed also the overthrow of the dynasty of which it was the glory and the pride. Though its palaces are in ruins, its gardens choked with tangled grass and thorns, and its water-courses and fountains dry, an air of kingly dignity clings to the Árk-killáh, and rouses a feeling of reverent admiration for the noble dynasty.

Excluding the citadel, Bijápur within walls, during the days of the monarchy, seems to have been divided into thirty-three wards or *peths* most of which remain and are used for municipal purposes. Of ten the position is forgotten, and even since 1848 all trace of two has been lost. Of the twenty-three wards[1] into which the present city is divided, the five most important are Bara Khudan Bazár in the north-west, Máhmud Khán Bazár in the west, Ane-kendi Bazár in the east-centre, Jáma Mosque Peth in the east, and Sháh Peth in the north-east.

BARA KHUDA BAZÁR, a corruption of Bara Khudávand in the northwest close to the Shahapur Gate is one of the oldest parts of the city. In it is the large Chand well built by Ali Adil Sháh I. (1557-1580) in honour of his queen Chand Bibi. This ward is still fairly peopled. MÁHMUD KHÁN BAZÁR, in the west close to the Macca Gate, is the business

---

[1] The names of these wards passing west to east, are, 1 Bara Khudan Bazár; 2 Puráni Peth; 3 Langar Bazár; 4 Haidar Bazár; 5 Pali Bazár; 6 Fateh Jama Bazár; 7 Máhmud Khán Bazár; 8 Mubárak Khán Bazár; 9 Karanjin Bazár; 10 Rumi Khán Bazár; 11 Kamál Khán Bazár; 12 Murád Khán Bazár; 13 Ane-kendi Bazár; 14 Jáma Masjid Bazár; 15 Nághtán Bazár; 16 Jhakti Bazár; 17 Thána Budruk Bazár; 18 Shabutra Bazár; 19 Pádshápur Bazár; 20 Daulat Khán Bazár; 21 Sháh Peth; 22 Shikár Khána Bazár; and 23 Rangin Masjid Bazár. The site of the Murkho Khurd and Murkho Budruk wards is forgotten.

centre of the city, where the weekly market is held. It was named in honour of Sultán Máhmud (1626-1656) but all the present houses are modern. To the north of this ward may be seen the ruins of Afzul Khán's palace, the victim of Shiváji's treachery at Pratápgad in 1659 The Táj well, built by Ibrahim Adil Sháh II. (1580-1626) in honour of his queen Táj Sultána, is the most famous well in the city, and with the surrounding rest-houses, is an interesting piece of architecture, the large arch which spans the entrance to the well being particularly fine. The Ánekendi Bazár, in the east centre to the north of the Jáma Mosque road, is interesting from its fine large entrance gateway. It contains the mosque of Mustápha Khán in which is some handsome stone carving, and the remains of several old palaces notably the palace of Kháwas Khán, minister to Ali Adil Sháh II. (1656-1672). The ward is said to take its name from *áne* the Kánarese for elephant, as the royal elephant stables were in this quarter. The Jáma Mosque Peth has some fine old houses inhabited by the descendants of old Bijápur families. The great mosque is in this ward, and this is the headquarters of the Musalmán community. Sháh Peth, in the north-east near the great dome, is interesting from its being inhabited almost wholly by Gavandis or masons, who, though they no longer follow the craft, are said to be the descendants of the masons who built Bijápur. The place is frequently called the Gavendis' ward. No interest attaches to any of the other wards inside the walls most of which are almost deserted.

Were it not for its suburbs, which even now are pretty thickly peopled, the city would present a still more unfavourable comparison than it does with that Bijápur which less than three centuries ago counted its inhabitants by the hundred-thousand. Of eight suburbs only five are of importance. Of tho five three are close to the city walls, Sháhápur also called Khudanpur that is Khudávandpur and Fakirabad in the north-west, Zohrápur called after Ibráhim II.'s wife in the west, and Ibráhimpur called after Ibráhim II. in the south. The remaining two are at some distance Sháhápur or Pir Amin's Darga about two miles to the north-west and Torvi about four miles to the west. The other suburbs are Allápur built by Yusuf Adil Sháh (1489-1510) a mile and a half, and Ainápur with a large unfinished tomb of Sultán Máhmud's wife Jahán Begam about two and a half miles, to the east of the city. Exactly opposite the Boli Gumbaz and about 150 yards from the wall is the railway station approached by the Hipargi road which runs east and west through the city to the north of the Árk-killáh.

Sháhápur Darga or Pir Amin's Darga, from the tomb of a Musalmán saint of that name, lies about two miles north-west of the Khudanpur Bazár, also known as Sháhápur Peth, on the side and crest of a hill which overlooks the city walls on the east and some fine mango groves on the west. The houses are clustered round the saint's tomb which is an object of great veneration and is well cared for. The tomb is gaudy, and the grounds round it are pretty and well kept, and, as the domes are regularly whitewashed, their colour from a distance forms a pleasing contrast to the gray ruins which surround them. Between Pir Amin's tomb and the city is the rest-house of Nawáb Mustápha Khán, a large quadrangular building made during the reign of Sultán Máhmud (1626-1656) for the use of travellers and lately (1883) turned into a jail.

West from Pir Amin's tomb, still part of Bijápur, is the hamlet of Takki or Afzulpur, called after Shiváji's victim Afzul Khán (1659) whose summer palace was in this quarter. The village itself has nothing of mark. Some little distance off is the family burial-ground of Afzul Khán, to which a curious story belongs. On a broad platform stretching along one side of what was once a large masonry pond or well, but which is now silted and embowered in mango and tamarind

APPENDIX. 375

trees, are rows of tombs, all very closely alike. Examination shows from the device carved on their tops that these are all women's tombs and that they are ranged in eleven rows of seven tombs each. All are of the same size and shape and the same distance apart, except one on the north-west corner which is a little larger. The Bijápur story of these tombs is that when in 1659 Afzul Khán volunteered to lead the fatal expedition against Shivaji the astrologers warned him that he would never return. On the strength of this warning he set his house in order by drowning his seventy-seven wives in the palace pond, burying their bodies in the pond bank, and adorning their graves with rows of neat tombs. The story may be false; there are no means of testing its truth. Still it is strange to find so many tombs of precisely the same pattern and apparently of the same age, in what was originally a part of the private grounds of Afzul Khán's palace. The legend explains their presence fairly well, though the character of its hero is somewhat out of keeping with Meadows Taylor's chivalrous tender-hearted Afzul Khán. Near Afzulpur are the remains of some fine reservoirs made as feeders to the Torvi water-course which was the main source of the city's water-supply. The four western suburbs Sháhápur, Zohrápur, Pir Amin's Darga, and Takki are remains of the great city of Sháhápur finished in 1557 by Ali Adil Sháh I. (1557-1580),[1] which, in the days of Bijápur's greatness, from the Bahmani Gate in the north stretched as far as the present village of Torvi and appears to have covered a larger area than Bijápur itself. Both towns were known under the general name of Bijápur, but Sháhápur seems to have been the centre of business. The population is stated at one time to have amounted to nearly a million, and judging by the wide area the streets and houses covered this is not improbable. For three miles from the

[1] Briggs' Ferishta, III. 116. According to Scott (Deccan, II. 72-73) Sháhápur was begun in 1510 and was improved by Ibráhim Adil Sháh I. (1534-1557).

walls of Bijápur the country is covered with the ruins of Sháhápur, and the city apparently spread still further, as the walls with which Ibráhim II. (1580-1626) intended to enclose the two cities are almost a mile beyond the modern village of Torvi. The greater portion of Sháhápur was destroyed by Máhmud Sháh in 1635, when he wasted the country round Bijápur to prevent the advance of the Moghals. Later on when the city underwent several sieges, it was no longer safe to live outside of the fortifications, and Sháhápur was gradually deserted. The present suburbs of Khudanpur and Fakirabad in the north-west are still known by the name of Sháhápur, though the houses are all comparatively modern, and the gateway in that quarter preserves the memory of the time when Shahapur was a large and flourishing city not inferior to Bijápur.

To the west of Sháhápur lay the suburb of Nauraspur, which Ibráhim II. (1580-1626) wished to turn into a new capital, and about 1600 began to raise magnificent palaces and other buildings. Had his design been carried out, the new capital would have been much more picturesque than Bijápur. It is at the head of a considerable valley surrounded by lofty hills, which it was intended to fortify with a strong wall, part of which was built and is still standing. Even now Nauraspur is more striking than Bijápur whose uniform flatness is monotonous. Ibráhim failed to carry out his design. The astrologers warned him that the removal of the seat of government from Bijápur would ruin the state and he desisted. Still palaces and gardens were completed, and Nauraspur became the favourite hot-weather residence of the Bijápur court. The ruins attest the magnificence of the place. One of the buildings, the Sangit or Nauras Mehel, a splendid ruin, compares favourably with any Bijápur palace. The front arches are very fine, while the site of the palace is extremely picturesque with the Torvi hills in the back ground and in front a valley stretching for miles full of mango and other trees.

However rich Bijápur might be in springs, so large a population could not wisely be left wholly dependent on the local supply. According to Ferishta, Ali Adil Sháh I. (1557-1580) was the first king who paid attention to the water-supply.[1] He built the large well in Sháhápur now known as Chánd's well and made channels to lead the water through the city. Ferishta's mention of water channels suggests that the under-ground Torvi channels were the work of Ali Adil Sháh I. not as is locally believed of Sultán Máhmud (1626-1656). The channel which brings water from Torvi, three miles west of Bijápur, and distributes it through the city, is a vast work of no slight engineering skill. A site was chosen on a stream about a mile above Torvi, and a masonry dam was built across the valley. From the lake thus formed, a masonry channel sunk in the bed of the stream carried the water to within half a mile of Torvi, and from there an under-ground water-course was hollowed, which passed under Torvi and was continued about a mile to Afzulpur where it seems to have ended in a large reservoir. Another small masonry pond or well at the base of a hill about 400 yards west of Torvi supplemented this supply. Here the water of some very powerful springs was gathered in a reservoir and carried along an underground channel to Torvi, where it joined the larger channel. The reservoir at Afzulpur seems to have been also fed by another pond made in the hills, half a mile south of that village, whose water was carried on arches over the intervening houses. Traces of this high level conduit remain where it crossed the old road to Torvi, and though nothing about it is locally known, the site of the pond and the direction in which the remains of the conduit seem to lead, leave no doubt that it was intended to supplement the Torvi water-supply. The remains of the reservoir at

Briggs' Ferishta, III. 143.

Afzulpur show that it was a work of great size. The dam, which is now breached in two places, is nearly sixty feet high, a huge mass of masonry and earth, with curious chambers in the embankment. Below the main lake is another smaller reservoir to catch the overflow and supply the neighbouring parts of the city. From the main lake a canal, which at its start is about eight feet by six, carried the water under ground nearly three miles to the city. The cutting of this canal must have been a work of great difficulty, as in places it is sixty feet below the surface in solid rock. During part of its length it is lined with brick masonry, but in general the water flows along a rocky channel. Communication was kept with the surface by a number of vertical air shafts or *usvás* as they are locally called. These shafts which are about forty yards apart may be traced along the whole length of the canal as far as the Ibráhim Roza. There the line is lost. It is recovered in the middle of the city in a garden near the Two Sisters. Between this garden and the Ibráhim Roza the channel seems to have split in two, as a line of air shafts runs a good deal to the south towards the Jáma mosque. Some of these shafts are fitted with steps probably to aid in cleaning the channel which has now silted to such a depth that it is next to impossible to discover its true dimensions. Water still flows into the city by this channel. It supplies the Ásar Mehel reservoir and the outer moat of the Árk killáh, but this water can hardly come from Torvi unless there is another unknown underground connection, as the Afzulpur lake is dry. Probably the channel is filled from springs tapped on the way. Even in the part of the canal above Torvi, water seems still to flow from the spring at the head of the water-course, as it is not uncommon to find it bubbling through holes in the masonry and forming miniature fountains in the stream bed.

In later years (1580-1686), when the number of palaces

and the love of luxury and ease increased, it was felt that Torvi water-supply was not enough for the wants of the city. It was at too low a level, and could not bring water into many palaces or be used for fountains or gardens. For this a lake at a much higher level than the city was required. A site was chosen among the hills to the south of the city, and a large lake was formed by throwing a dam about a mile in length across the valley.[1] The lake thus formed covered an area of about 500 acres, and as it was much higher than Bijápur there was ample pressure to raise the water to the required height. The water was carried through a pipe 15" in diameter cased in a mass of masonry 8' by 6' and at a depth varying from 15' to 50' below the surface, for two and a half miles to the Sháh Ganj or main distributary tower, a little to the south-east of the Ark-killáh. Along its course from the lake large square towers were built about 800 feet apart to relieve the pressure of the water and prevent the pipes bursting. Owing to the height of this lake above the city and the consequent pressure, the water in the towers inside of the walls was raised 20' to 30' above the ground. Some of the towers are very fine pieces of workmanship and many of them are still standing and show how the supply of water was conveyed all over the city from the Boli Gumbaz to Sháhápur. The largest supply of water was in the Ark-killáh, where two fine distributary towers are still standing. Here, as appears from the remains of fountains in the Sát Mazli, the water could be laid on some 30' above ground. All were supplied with water on the ground-floor and all the palaces had small channels and reservoirs of running water. Countless fountains embowered in trees played in every quarter,

[1] Below the embankment of this lake are the remains of a second lake which from the traces of conduits was apparently also connected with the city. Nothing is now known in Bijápur regarding it. It is not improbable that is was the work of Ali Adil Sháh I. who, according to Ferishta, brought water into the city. The conduits run in the direction of the Jáma mosque, and as Ali began that building it is not unlikely that he also provided it with water.

and fragrant flowers filled the air with their perfume. Few places can have been more beautiful than this Ark-killah with its stately palaces and grounds, and the air full of the coolness and the flow of water.

To Sultán Máhmud (1626-1656) Bijápur owed most of its comfort and luxury. Other kings adorned the city with buildings, but Máhmud by making the Begam Lake which he named after his queen Jahán Begam, in 1653, made gardens and fountains possible all over the city. For this and for other reasons Máhmud's name is locally in such high repute that every work of importance, regarding which there is doubt, is attributed to him. Besides the Begam Lake, he is said to have made the Torvi water-course; and though from the works he did take in hand, it might be safe to attribute this water-course to him, still, considering his comparatively short reign of thirty years, during nearly two-thirds of which he was engaged in war with the Moghals, it is improbable that he could have made his own mausoleum and the palaces in the Ark-killáh, nearly completed the Jáma mosque, constructed the Begam Lake, and in addition have undertaken the vast labour of cutting the underground Torvi water-channel. It is more likely that, as stated by Ferishta, the city is indebted to Ali Adil Sháh I. (1557-1580) for the Torvi works. Still Sultán Máhmud did enough to raise above question his claim to be considered the greatest of the Bijápur kings, a monarch whose energy, perseverance, and genius would have dignified any time or country. During the 1876-77 famine the Begam Lake which was silted was taken in hand. A dam was built and the whole of the water-course and the twelve water-towers between it and the Asar Mehel have been thoroughly cleaned out. Its weak point is the smallness of the catchment area.

GENEALOGICAL TREE OF THE PRESENT NIZAM OF HYDERABAD

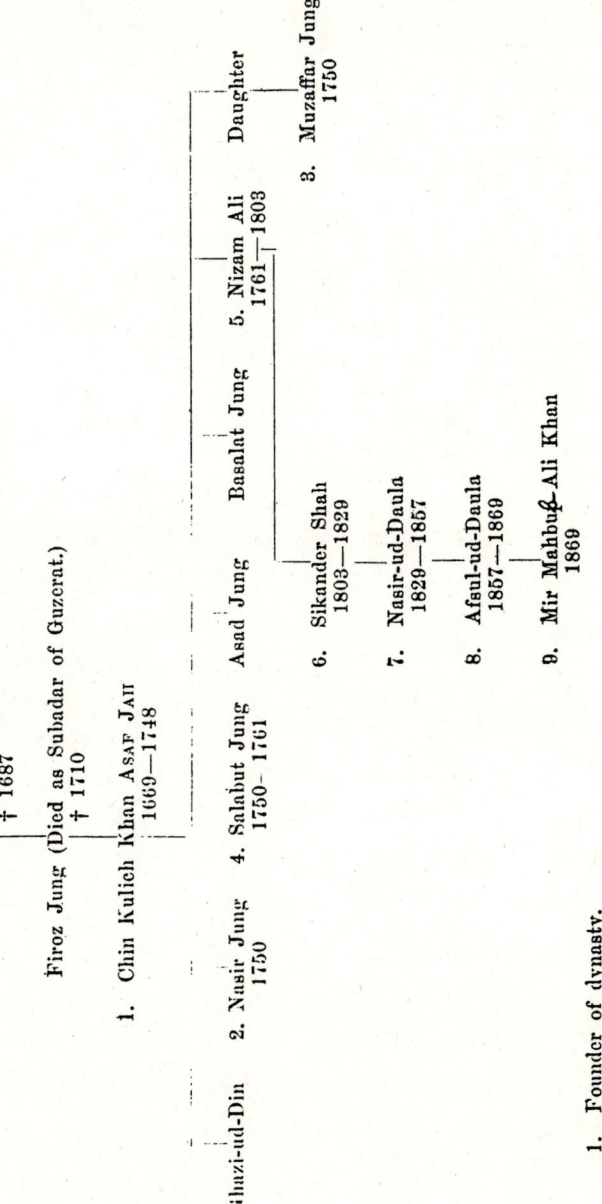

1. Founder of dynasty.
2. Killed before Gingee.
3. Placed on the throne by Dupleix, but killed in an affray at Cuddapah on his return from Pondicherry.
4. Deposed and eventually killed by his brother Nizam Ali.

NOTE.—Descent is claimed from Khalif Abu Bekr on the male, and from the Prophet, on the female side. Abid Kuli Khan had been Kazi of Bokhara, and came to Delhi about 1658.

Elephant Stables
(Pages 65-66)

Remains of Entian ci 5 Temple in Warangai. Fort
(Pages 89-90)

Modern Tomb at Secunderabad
(Pages 135-136)

GREAT MOSQUE, GULBURGA FORT
(PAGE 145-146)

TEMPLE, VIJAYANAGAR
(PAGE 159-160)

Jumma Musjid Hyderabad
(Page 217-218)

Elephant trough (43 Long x 10 circumference)
(Page 227-228)

LADIES BATH
(PAGE 235-236)

GOLCONDA FORT
(PAGE 265-266)

Scarped Rock Dowlatabad Fort
(Page 259-260)

ABUL HASAM, KUTOB SHAH
(PAGE 271-272)

THE LAST KING OF GOLCONDA IMPRSIONED BY AURUNGZEBE
(PAGE 275-276)

ASAF JAH (FROM AN OLD PICTURE)
(PAGE 313-314)

THE RESIDENCY, CHUDDERGHAUT

THE NAWAB FAKHR-OOL-MOOLK
(*SEE APPENDIX NO 2*).

Nawab Sir Faridoon Mulk, K.C.I.E., C.S.I., C.B.E.
(*See Appendix No 3*).

The Nawab Sir Salar Jung,
Grandson of The Eminent Statesman
and Prime Minister.
(*See Appendix No 4*)

COLONEL R. NEVILL.,
COMMANDING H.H. THE NIZAM'S TROOPS

A.J. DUNLOP, ESQ., C.I.E., C.S.I.,
MINISTER OF REVENUE
(SEE APPENDIX NO 5-6).

THE AUTHOR,
JAMES D. B. GRIBBLE, I.C.S.,
DIED 1906.

EDITOR AND COLLABORATOR,
MRS. PENDLEBURY,
WIDOW OF COLONEL W. PENDLEBURY,
AGENT N.G.S. RLY., 1886-1913.

MIR ALAM LAKE, HYDERABAD.

VOLUME –II
Edited and Finished by
Mrs. M. Pendlebury

PREFACE

THE author of this History of the Deccan, my father, J. B. D. Gribble, I.C.S., died before completing this work, which originally appeared in a series of articles in an Indian periodical, entitled "Tales of a Deccan Grandfather."

The task of editing and completing my father's work has fallen on me.

The second volume deals principally with an important alliance entered into between the Nizam and the British, in order to afford His Highness the necessary protection required to defend him from the turbulent foes that surrounded his dominions.

From this resulted the formation of the little army known as the Hyderabad Contingent that won fame and distinction in several campaigns. Then followed the Nizam's financial embarrassment incurred by the upkeep of the troops in question. Finally on account of the debt thus incurred several districts were ceded to the British under certain conditions as security for money advanced by them.

For ten years Mr. Gribble had keenly and closely studied this question and was considered an expert on the same. His death occurred just before he had finished dealing with these matters in the chapter entitled the Berar Trust which was to be one of the most important in the second volume. Unfortunately I have had to cast this

PREFACE

chapter from a few notes and the substance of certain articles which the author had written for the *Pioneer* and the *XIX Century Review*. It was through these very articles that public attention was first drawn to the question of the Berar Trust, and to the fact that the Nizam's claims had not been dealt with adequately. Later through Mr. Gribble's efforts a debate was held in Parliament. Subsequently a settlement was arrived at in 1902, which, however, did not cause universal satisfaction as it did not meet the claims in question.

My thanks are due to H.E.H. the Nizam, who has graciously accepted the dedication of this volume.

It has been a great pleasure to go over matters relating to Hyderabad, with the life of which I have been intimately connected for more than twenty years.

My one regret has been that the author did not live to complete his own work and that the points on which he was an expert should have been dealt with by another hand wielding a pen less able than his own.

MARY PENDLEBURY

CHAPTER I

THE REIGN OF ASAF JAH. 1723-1748

PREVIOUS chapter in the first volume dealt with the accession of Nizam-ul-Mulk Asaf Jah to the Dominion of the Deccan, and in the present chapter the fortunes of the Asaf Jah dynasty will be followed, which will constitute a history of Hyderabad rather than of the whole of the Deccan. At the period at which we have now arrived, the Mahrattas had acquired a considerable portion of what was originally known as the Deccan and which was ruled over by the Bhamanee Kings and the other Mahomedan dynasties, the history of which has been given in previous chapters. The history of the

Mahrattas, however, has already been written and therefore it is not proposed to go over the same ground in the present work, but to refer to them only in so far as they are brought into direct relationship with the Subahdar of the Deccan, or, as he was afterwards called, the Nizam of Hyderabad.

When Asaf Jah compelled the Delhi Emperor to recognize him as the Governor of the Deccan, his jurisdiction extended over a far larger extent of territory than is now covered by the Hyderabad State. With the exception of the comparatively narrow strip of country on the western coast, which belonged to the Mahrattas, his jurisdiction reached from the river Taptee, west of Aurangabad, Ahmednagar and Bijapur, over the Mysore country and the Carnatic right down as far as Trichinopoly and probably also to Madura. The incident of the slipper narrated in a previous chapter shows clearly that, although on one occasion the Raja of Trichinopoly refused to pay tribute to the Ambassadors of the Mogul Emperor, still it had for some time, at all events, been the custom to acknowledge the overlordship of the Delhi Emperor. In the Carnatic proper, there was a Nawab with his head-quarters at Arcot who acknowledged the supremacy of the Deccan Viceroy and was, indeed, appointed by him. On the East Coast the whole of the country from Chicacole right down to the south acknowledged the suzerainty of the Deccan Viceroy, and the semi-independent Rajas paid him their tribute as the representative of the Emperor at Delhi. For the purpose of receiving their tribute, the Nizam had a Governor stationed at the town of Rajahmundry It will thus be seen that the Viceroyalty of the Deccan extended over almost the whole of the peninsular south of the Taptee. To the north of this river and in the province of Malwa, of which he had been Viceroy previous to his coming to the Deccan, Asaf Jah held or laid claim to a number of jaghirs and fiefs, but here he already had come in contact with the Mahrattas who had commenced to spread over Guzerat, Malwa, and Nagpur, levying *chouth* wherever they could and acquiring for themselves territorial possessions. The Mahratta generals thus employed were the ancestors of the afterwards great houses of Scindia, Holkar, Nagpur and Baroda, who eventually made themselves independent of the Peshwa at Poona, although they professed to regard him as their overlord.

For the first few years after his accession, Asaf Jah was engaged in reducing his dominions to a state of order. It will be remembered from the previous volume that, when Syed Hoossein was Viceroy of the Deccan in 1714-15, he acknowledged the right of the Mahrattas to levy *chouth* in some of his western districts. For the next sixty or seventy years the Poona Mahrattas were constantly striving to enlarge the sphere over which they levied this oppressive tax and Asaf Jah was as constantly employed in endeavouring to repel their aggression without coming to open war.

The following extract from *Orme* shows how the Mahrattas built up their claim to this tax. The matter is of importance since a great deal of the history of the next fifty years turns upon it, and no apology is therefore necessary for introducing it here:

"The country of the Mahrattas lies between Bombay and Golconda; its limits are not known with any degree of certainty to Europeans, and we are equally ignorant of the origin of the people. It is now a century that they have made a figure as the most enterprising soldiers of Hindustan, and as the only nation of Indians which seems to make war an occupation by choice; for the Rajputs are soldiers by birth. Of late years they have often been at the gates of Delhi—sometimes in arms against the throne, at others in defence of it against the Afghans or Pathans. The strength of their armies consists in their numerous cavalry, which is more capable of resisting fatigue than any in India, large bodies of them having been known to march 50 miles in a day. They avoid general engagements and seem to have no idea in making war but that of doing as much mischief as possible to the enemy's country. This they effect by driving off the cattle, destroying the harvest, burning the villages and by exercising such cruelties as makes the people of the open country take flight on the first rumours of their approach. The rapidity of their motion leaves the prince with whom they wage war little chance of striking a decisive blow against them, or even of attacking with effect any of their detachments. Hence the expense of maintaining an army in the field, also of very little probability of even fighting such an enemy, and the greater detriment arising from the devastations they commit, generally induce the governments they attack to purchase their retreat with money. Great parsimony in their expenses and continued collections of treasure by the means now described have been the principal causes of raising them in less than a century, from a people of inconsiderable note, to a nation which at present strikes terror into all the countries between Delhi and Cape Comorin. They often let out bodies of men, and sometimes whole armies, but the hiring of them is a dangerous resource; for the offer of better terms seldom fails to make them change sides, and they seldom relinquish their practice of plundering, even in the countries which they are hired to defend. But, notwithstanding their warlike character, they are, in other respects, the most scrupulous observers of the religion of Brahma—never eating of anything that has life, nor even killing the insects which molest them; however, a buffalo sacrificed with many strange ceremonies, atones for the blood of their species which they shed in war."—(Orme's "Description of the Mahrattas," Volume I, Chapter 2.).

Asaf Jah had brought with him from Malwa a number of followers, Mahomedans and Hindus, who were attached to his person and fortunes. To the Mahomedan nobles he granted jaghirs or estates on military tenure and employed them as his generals. In this way he was enabled to raise, when necessary, an enormous army amounting on some occasions to as many as 300,000 men. They were, of course, very primitively armed, according to our modern notions, but as the enemies they met were similarly equipped, this did not so much matter. The time had not yet arrived when the superiority of small highly disciplined forces, thoroughly equipped, was recognized over these huge rabble-like hosts which devastated the country over which they passed and which were unwieldy from their very numbers. The Hindus whom Asaf Jah brought with him, he employed principally in administrative work in the departments of revenue and finance. To them he also granted jaghirs as a remuneration for their services, and all these jaghirs, whether granted for civil or military purposes, came to be considered as hereditary in the different families. The vast majority of the population of the Nizam's dominions consisted of course of Hindus; and scattered over the country was a large number of indigenous Rajahs and Chiefs who held, most of them, sunnads or grants from former kings, many of which had been confirmed subsequently by the Delhi Emperors. The Rajahs were all recognized and confirmed in their possessions on payment of tribute, being allowed to exercise a kind of semi-independent jurisdiction within the limits of their estates. The whole of the Hyderabad country was divided into three distinct portions, consisting. first, of these feudal jaghirs; secondly, of scattered portions of territory reserved for the Nizam's privy purse, now known as Sarf-i-khas lands; and, thirdly, of the so-called Dewani or Government lands, the revenues of which were devoted to the expenses of administration. A great many of these districts were farmed out to noblemen and others who paid large nazars or tribute for the privilege. These persons were supposed to retain a certain proportion (2 to 4 annas in the rupee) for administrative charges, and to remit the balance to the central treasury. There was, of course, considerable laxity in this respect, and it depended upon the personal character of the deputy whether the people were oppressed or not. No attempt was made to spend any money on roads or communications; almost all traffic was carried on quadrupeds, generally by the indigenous nomadic tribes. Even the old Hindu irrigation works were allowed to fall into neglect and disrepair, for very few of the local deputies ever dreamt of spending public money on such objects. They kept for themselves as much as they could out of the revenues, and when subterfuges would no longer answer, they sent the remainder to head-quarters. Still, however, the revenue which the Nizam derived from such an enormous extent of territory was very large and his court was the most splendid in India after that of Delhi.

It is difficult to ascertain with anything like correctness what the actual revenues of the Nizam's large province were, but Grant Duff, in his *History of the Mahrattas*, has compiled from the original Mahratta records a statement showing the revenues of the six Deccan Subahs or Divisions over which the Mahrattas claimed the right of levying *chouth* at 25 per cent. and *Surdeshmookee* at 10 per cent. The six Subahs which constituted the Hyderabad Dominion proper and the revenue they yielded are given below :

	Rs.
Aurangabad	12,376,042
Berar	11,523,508
Beejapur	78,508,560
Bedar	7,491,879
Hyderabad	64,867,483
Candeish	5,749,819
	180,517,291
Say	£18,000,000

It was upon these revenues that the Mahrattas demanded their *chouth* of 25 per cent., which was supposed to be a payment for the protection of the villages from raid and rapine. This protection was given by irregular horse, which, when the *chouth* was not punctually paid, raided the villages on their own account until it was produced. In other words, it was a species of blackmail. But the right to levy this *chouth* had been previously sanctioned by an imperial order at the time when Syed Hussein was Viceroy of the Deccan (1714-1719). The *Surdeshmookee* had also been sanctioned at the same time, but was not levied with the same regularity ; in fact, it was part of the Mahratta policy to allow these taxes to fall into arrears so as to give them a *casus belli* on some future occasion, when possibly they might have an opportunity of acquiring more than their just dues by virtue of the sword. For the first few years after Asaf Jah's accession, his time was fully employed in arranging these complicated affairs. In so doing, he was on several occasions brought into collision with the Mahrattas. This occurred in 1727 and subsequently in 1729, and in both campaigns the Nizam was only partially successful, but such was his astuteness that he contrived to draw as much profit out of a reverse as he did from a victory. He was also frequently assisted by the internal dissensions amongst the Mahrattas, for, although the Rajah at Satara was still the virtual King of the Mahrattas, his authority was gradually being overshadowed by that of the Peishwa, whilst the different prominent chiefs and generals were in their turn jealous of the Peishwa's growing influence. Grant Duff (*History of the Mahrattas*, Volume I, Chapter 13) has described the policy of the Nizam in a few well-chosen words which are here reproduced :

"On a general view, his plans were calculated to preserve his rank at court, and his power in the Deccan; to keep alive the old, and to create new dissensions amongst the Mahrattas: to preserve a connection with that nation in case it should ultimately be useful to direct their attacks from his own to the imperial territories; and, however inconsistent some of these designs may seem, in this system of political artifice through the remainder of a long life Nizam-ul-Mulk not only persevered but generally prospered."

In 1731 the dissensions between the Mahrattas reached a climax, and Trimbuk Rao Durbari came to open conflict with the Peishwa. The Nizam secretly supported the former, thus forsaking an alliance he had previously formed with the Peishwa. A battle was fought in Guzerat in which Trimbuk Rao was defeated and killed, and Baji Rao was left supreme with all but a nominal control of the Mahratta sovereignty. The Peishwa then returned to Poona, and, highly indignant with what he considered the treachery of the Nizam, was prepared to proceed against him with the whole of his available force—a crisis which Asaf Jah would have found it difficult to overcome. But this crafty politician found a means of escaping from this danger, and of saving himself and his dominions from the devastating inroads of the Mahrattas. He managed to persuade the Peishwa to turn his arms against the Emperor at Delhi, he himself promising to remain neutral. In consequence of this arrangement, the Mahratta armies overran the province of Malwa, crossed the river Chembul, and threatened the imperial capital itself. The fighting continued from 1734 until 1738, when, overtures having been made to him by the Emperor Mahomed Shah, the Nizam proceeded to Delhi and threw his support upon the imperial side. But even with this support the Emperor was only able to buy off the Peishwa at a heavy price. He had in fact to comply with the whole of Baji Rao's demands, which now exceeded all bounds. "At different stages during the discussions, he required the whole province of Malwa in *jaghir*; the Rohillas, who had established themselves, to be dispossessed; the forts of Mandoo, Dhar and Raiseen; the *jaghir* and *fouzdaree* of the whole tract south of the Chambul; fifty lakhs of rupees from the royal treasury, or an equivalent assignment on Bengal, Allahabad, Benares, Gya and Muttra in *jaghir*; and a hereditary right as Surdeshpandya of the Soobah of the Deccan." (*Grant Duff.*) For the moment the

Emperor managed to evade all these concession with the exception of the last, to which he acceded on Baji Rao's agreeing to pay him a nuzzer of six lakhs of rupees. This was a stroke levelled by the Delhi minister against the Nizam, and had the immediate effect of arousing the latter's jealousy and of deciding him to actively support the Emperor in order to overthrow the minister, Khan Dowran. Several skirmishes occurred in front of Delhi with varying success, but ending generally in favour of the Peishwa, who, having received the concessions which he had asked for of the Government of Malwa, at length returned to the Deccan, where for some time he was engaged in military operations with the Portuguese.

In the meantime, taking advantage of the Peishwa's absence, the Emperor prevailed at last upon the Nizam to repair to his court, and bestowed upon him the governments of Malwa and Guzerat in the name of his eldest son, Ghazi-ud-Din, but on the condition that he should drive the Mahrattas out of these provinces. Baji Rao at once returned with an army of 80,000 men, and crossing the Nerbudda met the Nizam near Bhopal in January, 1738. No pitched battle ensued, but by means of a series of skilful manœuvres he managed to hem the Nizam into such a position that he was practically helpless, and in the following month had to sign a convention in which he granted to the Peishwa the whole of Malwa and the complete sovereignty of the territory between the Nerbudda and the Chambul. But here again, we have an example of Asaf Jah's diplomacy and ability : the price by which the peace was bought was in reality paid by the Emperor and not by the Nizam. He gave away the province of Malwa, which had never been really in his possession, whilst his own dominions remained intact. In 1735, Nadir Shah invaded

Hindustan and after having sacked Delhi returned to
Persia on the 5th May. The Nizam Asaf Jah had been
with the Emperor throughout these proceedings but had
been powerless to help him. Indeed, Orme says that he
himself invited Nadir Shah to come to India, but he cites
no authority for this assertion and all the probabilities
are in the opposite direction ; for it was much more in
the interests of the Nizam that there should be a weak
ruler like Mahomed Shah on the throne than a man of
the stamp of the Persian conqueror ; but, after Nadir
Shah had retired and had taken with him the accumulated treasures of Delhi, Asaf Jah must have seen
that any further attempt to uphold the Emperor's authority was hopeless. Accordingly he resolved to devote the
rest of his life to the consolidation of his own kingdom in
the Deccan. He must now have been nearly 90 years of
age, but was still endowed with an immense amount
of energy and physical strength. Affairs in the Carnatic
urgently required his presence, for the French under
Dupleix had already begun to interfere, and Safdar Khan,
the Nawab of the Carnatic, had been assassinated by his
brother-in-law. Everything in the south was in confusion, and to add to this confusion the Mahrattas had
come down with a large army with the object of taking
Trichinopoly. In spite therefore of his advanced age,
Asaf Jah marched down to Arcot with a large army,
which Orme refers to as 80,000 horse and 200,000 foot.
His presence served to restore order and for the present
he appointed Anwar-ud-Din as Nawab (1744). It is
narrated that so great was the confusion in the Carnatic
and so many the rivals who put forward their claims to
the Nawabship, calling themselves Nawab in anticipation of success, that the old Nizam gave orders to his
attendants that eighteen Nawabs having been to see

him that day, the next person who presented himself under the style of Nawab should be beaten out of his camp with whips. (*Orme*, Volume VII, Chapter 1.) It was whilst engaged on this expedition that the Nizam first came into contact with the English merchants of Madras, who despatched an embassy to him whilst he was in camp near Trichinopoly. The chief of this embassy was Mr. Eyre and a very interesting diary of what occurred is preserved in the records of the Government of Madras. From this diary I quote an extract:

"*March 30th*.—About 8 this morning the Nawab's officer came to us with a guard of horse and foot and two elephants with drums and colours, and told us the Nabob was glad to hear of our arrival in camp, and had ordered him to conduct us to him. After the usual compliments, we presented him as by the list of presents. After his taking betel, we proceeded with him and were carried to the public Durbar, where the Nabob was sitting attended by his Omrahs, Nawabs, Rajahs, and other great men; and, making our obeisances in front at a considerable distance, we were shown a place on the carpets and to sit down there. About an hour after, when the Nabob rose from the Durbar, he sent for us into private apartments, whereupon his speaking our welcome we paid the Governor's respect to him; and he bade us sit down and then honoured us with a great deal per discourse on indifferent matters. Coffee was also served to us with the honour of the fans. This being the first audience nothing was said of the presents, and in something more than an hour he gave us betel and we withdrew and returned to our tents, where the Nabob and Imam Saheb each sent us a dinner. In the afternoon received a list from Imam Saheb of what goods he had assigned for the presents to the Nizam, which we got unpacked and sorted that night and sent early next morning to the Nabob.

"31st.—The goods being sent and opened in the Nabob's tents, went to wait on him at the Durbar, and, that business being over, the Nabob sent for us to a private tent where the goods lay opened and we were desired to sit. The Nabob observed them very nearly and took many of the parcels in hand and said they were very good, and of the painted looking-glass and some others that he would keep some himself and send also some of them to the Mogul (Emperor) and would tell him that he had them of the Government of Chennapatnam.* Coffee was served and after an hour's discourse we retired."—(Talboys Wheeler's "Madras in the Olden Time.")

Mr. Eyre remained in the Nizam's camp for seventeen days and then returned to Madras. This appears to have been the first introduction to the Nizam of the English merchants, and for many years afterwards there was an interchange of courtesies, if not with the Nizam himself, at all events with his deputy, the Nawab of Arcot, so much so that, when three years later hostilities broke out between the French and the English, the Nawab not only wrote to the former asking them why they had made war without his permission, but also sent a body of troops to assist the latter. The connection thus formed led to most important results. The English merchants in Madras regarded themselves as under the special protection of the Nizam and of his deputy the Nawab and, although the latter was at first inclined to side

* The old name for Madras.

with the French, when in 1746 La Bourdonnais attacked and took Madras, he ultimately sent an army under his eldest son, Mahfug Khan, to oppose them. An engagement took place at St. Thome, in which the French, under Paradis, marked a new departure in Indian warfare by signally defeating the whole of the Nawab's army with a few battalions of sepoys or native soldiers, trained, disciplined and officered by Europeans.

From this time, however, the connection between the rightful Nawab of the Carnatic, Anwar-ud-Deen, and the English became more intimate, especially when, as we shall see in the next chapter, the French openly espoused the cause of a rival Nawab.

In the meantime, the Nizam Asaf Jah returned to Hyderabad (1744), and for the next four years his life was passed in comparative quiet. Orme says that he was now over 100 years old, and his various enemies were content to wait until his death, when a general cataclysm seemed to be inevitable. This actually occurred in 1748, a few months after the death of the Emperor Mahomed Shah, and thus passed away one of the most notable of Empire-builders to be found in the annals of Indian history.

CHAPTER II

ASAF JAH'S SUCCESSORS

ASAF JAH left six sons and one daughter. The eldest of these sons was named Ghazi-ud-Din, and in the ordinary course would have succeeded his father. But for the present, at all events, Ghazi-ud-Din had no wish to come to Hyderabad. He was in high office in Delhi, and, a new Emperor having ascended the throne, he preferred remaining at court. The next son was Nasir Jung, and he at once placed himself on the *musnud*, seized the treasury and proclaimed himself Nizam. The other sons were Salabut Jung, Asad Jung, Basalut Jung and Nizam Ali, of whom the first, the fourth, and the fifth eventually became Nizams. The daughter had a son named Muzaffer Jung, who had been the old Nizam's favourite, and was generally supposed to have been designated as his heir.

For some time before his father's death Nasir Jung had been in disgrace. In 1841 he had broken into open revolt and had actually met his father in battle. At the last moment, however, he surrendered, and, after being kept in confinement for some time in the fort of Nander, was afterwards retained near the Nizam's person. Muzaffer Jung, the favourite grandson, had been appointed Governor of the upper or Balaghaut portion of the Carnatic, with his head-quarters at Bijapur, the ancient capital of the Adil Shahi kings. Muzaffer Jung resolved to oppose the succession of his uncle, Nasir Jung, and for this reason made a combination with Chanda Saheb, who was then a prisoner of the Mahrattas and kept in honourable confinement at Sattara. In order to explain who Chanda Saheb was it will be necessary to go back somewhat, but this retrospect is of the utmost importance, since it was owing to Chanda Saheb's connection with the French that European interference in the politics of the Deccan originated.

In 1732 Saadut Ullah, the Nawab of the Carnatic, died He had ruled since 1710 before the time that Asaf Jah made himself independent. Although nominally the Carnatic was a portion of the Deccan, Saadut Ullah had always exercised a certain amount of independence, and, when he died, having no sons, he appointed his eldest nephew Dost Ali, to succeed him in the Nawabship. This appointment, however, was never recognized by Asaf Jah and no *sunnad* confirming him was ever despatched. Dost Ali however remained in power and practically ruled the whole of the Southern Carnatic Dost Ali had a son named Safdar Ali and one of his daughters was married to his Dewan Chanda Saheb. At this time (1736) Trichinopoly was an independent Hindu kingdom, but, the Rajah having died, Dost Ali resolved to endeavour to attach it to his dominions. Accordingly he sent an army under his son Safdar Ali and Chanda Saheb to lay siege to the town. Chanda Saheb managed to persuade the Ranee to admit him into the fort with a body of troops and then treacherously seized the queen, put her in prison, where she died, and took possession of the kingdom in the name of Dost Ali.

Chanda Saheb then remained in Trichinopoly as Governor and Safdar Ali returned to his father.

Asaf Jah was by no means pleased with these events in the Carnatic since they dangerously increased the power and influence of Dost Ali, whose object was to create an independent kingdom in the south of India and to throw off all allegiance to the Nizam. At that time, however, he was busily occupied at Delhi, whither he had been summoned by the Emperor on the occasion of the invasion of the Persian conqueror Nadir Shah. He therefore encouraged the Mahrattas to attack Trichinopoly, which they were only too willing to do, and in conjunction with the Hindu Kings of Mysore and Tanjore they marched upon Arcot. On its way the Mahratta army was met by Dost Ali, who however was defeated and killed. After this victory the Mahrattas came to terms with Safdar Ali, whom they recognized as successor to his father, but compelled him to pay a tribute of ten lakhs of rupees and then ostensibly returned to Mysore. Chanda Saheb had expected the Mahrattas to lay siege to Trichinopoly and had made every preparation for defence and had also sent his wife and family to Pondicherry, the French settlement, where they were hospitably entertained as guests by the French Governor, M. Dupleix, of whom we shall hear a great deal later on. Chanda Saheb deceived by the retreat of the Mahrattas, and thinking himself to be safe, sold off his stores of grain and dismissed a large portion of his army. No sooner had he done this, however, than the Mahratta army returned and laid siege to Trichinopoly, which after a gallant defence had to yield on 26th March, 1741. It was at this siege that Hyder Ali, afterwards Sultan of Mysore, but then an officer in the Rajah's army, distinguished himself. Chanda

Saheb was taken prisoner and brought by the Mahrattas to Sattara, where he was kept in confinement until he could pay a heavy ransom. This he was unable to do, and remained accordingly a prisoner whilst his wife and family were still residing at Pondicherry. In the following year Safdar Ali, the Nawab of the Carnatic, was assassinated, and it was after this event that Asaf Jah proceeded to the Carnatic, as related, and left behind him Anwar-ud-Din as Nawab. Whilst the family of Chanda Saheb had been left at Pondicherry, Safdar Ali's family had been sent to Madras for safety. Anwar-ud-Din, although practically appointed as Nawab, was not confirmed in the appointment, but Asaf Jah sent for the young son of Safdar Ali from Madras and placed him under Anwar-ud-Din's guardianship with a view of his becoming the Nawab hereafter. In the following year, however, this unfortunate prince named Syed Mahomed was assassinated and then Anwar-ud-Din was confirmed as Nawab.

This, therefore, was the condition of affairs at the death of Asaf Jah. It will be seen that there were two rival claimants to the Nawabship of the Carnatic. Chanda Saheb who by marriage to Dost Ali's daughter represented the family which for many years ruled in the Carnatic, and Anwar-ud-Din, who having been appointed Nawab by the Nizam, was legally constituted ruler. Anwar-ud-Din was in actual possession and it is therefore clear that less was to be expected from a dispossessed pretender than from a man supported by the legally constituted authority. It was, however, hopeless to expect that the Nizam would allow his nominee to be displaced and accordingly it was necessary to find another Nizam who in return for being raised to the throne would support the appointment of Chanda

Saheb. The latter had a great reputation for bravery and military talents, and owing to his family being in Pondicherry he was in frequent communication with the French. The French Governor, M. Dupleix, was one of the ablest and most ambitious of Europeans who ever came to India. It was he who had first grasped the idea of assisting the native princes in their quarrels with each other and in return for that assistance to get power and influence for himself and his country. He was quick enough to see that an opportunity had offered itself and he was only too willing to take advantage of it. In the coming struggle between Nasir Jung and Muzaffer Jung he resolved to take the side of the latter, and if he could succeed in getting him to be made Nizam of the Deccan there could be no doubt that his reward would be a magnificent one. Accordingly he resolved to make use of Chanda Saheb, and, by promising the Mahrattas to be security for payment of the ransom, obtained his release. Chanda Saheb then joined Muzaffer Jung at Bijapur, and the two raised a small force with which they marched towards the Carnatic. Chanda Saheb promised to make Muzaffer Jung Nizam, and as a price for help obtained the promise of the Nawabship of the Carnatic. A small success at Chitteldroog attracted more followers to the flag of Chanda Saheb, and on the borders of the Carnatic they were joined by a force sent by Dupleix consisting of 400 Europeans and 2000 sepoys. On the 23rd July this army was met by Anwar-ud-Din at the fort of Amboor with the result that the latter was totally defeated and killed Muzaffer Jung now openly proclaimed himself as Nizam of the Deccan, and appointed Chanda Saheb to be Nawab of the Carnatic. As the victory of Amboor had been gained principally by the valour of the French force sent by Dupleix, the allies now proceeded together to Pondicherry in order to thank Dupleix in person. Dupleix gave them a magnificent reception, and after entertaining them for several days, urged upon them to at once march and obtain possession of Trichinopoly. This Muzaffer Jung promised to do, but unfortunately delayed on his way in order to get payment of a large sum of money from the Rajah of Tanjore.

The French had now openly espoused the cause of rebellion against the hitherto recognized authority of the Nizam in the Carnatic. It was probably this reason more than any other that induced the English to offer their services in support of the other side, that of law and order. Anwar-ud-Din was dead, but his second son, Mahomed Ali, escaped from the defeat at Amboor and took refuge in the fort of Trichinopoly Here he collected a small army and was shortly joined by 150 English troops sent by the Governor of Madras. Everything depended upon crushing this small force as soon as possible before the Nizam could have time to march from the Deccan and vindicate his outraged authority If instead of delaying at Tanjore Muzaffer Jung, as arranged with Dupleix, had at once marched to Trichinopoly, there is little doubt that he would have easily obtained possession of this important fort, and have thus rendered the task of the Nizam considerably more difficult. But an opportunity once lost seldom occurs again.

In the meantime the Nizam Nasir Jung had collected a large army, but delayed to march against Muzaffer Jung because he was afraid that in his absence his brother, Ghazi-ud-Din, would attempt some intrigue at the Emperor's court. In fact, he had resolved to go to Delhi himself when he received the news of the battle of Amboor. For the time being this meant the conquest of the Carnatic and it therefore became necessary to quell this rebellion at all hazards. Accordingly he collected a large army and sent orders to his tributary chief to join him on the line of march. He was also accompanied by three bodies of Mahratta horse who were employed as advance scouts. Altogether the army consisted of 300,000 fighting men, of whom one-half were cavalry; 800 guns and 1,300 elephants. This enormous force was the largest which had ever entered the Carnatic, and it struck awe into the hearts of all who had been inclined to waver in their allegiance. So unwieldy an army could only march by slow stages, and it was about the middle of March, 1750, before the different portions collected at the old fort of Gingee, which is situated about 40 miles to the west of Pondicherry. The French having taken the side of Muzaffer Jung, it was only natural that their rivals the English should support the other side, apart from the fact that Anwar-ud-Din's family, of whom Mahomed Ali was now the surviving representative, had received shelter at Madras. The first success, however, of Muzaffer Jung and Chanda Saheb had made them doubtful as to the real power of Nasir Jung, but, now that the latter had shown himself to be thoroughly in earnest, they resolved to send a body of 600 Europeans under Major Lawrence to join him at Gingee. This fort is a very old and celebrated one. It is built on a number of hills in the form of a circle, each hill is connected by strong walls. Under the great Emperor Auranzebe it had undergone a siege of about 12 years, and it was held to be the strongest fort in Southern India. Nasir Jung drew up his army under the walls of the fort, and there awaited the attack of Muzaffer Jung, who with

Chanda Saheb and the French force was at a short distance away. The French were under the command of M. Atenil who was the same officer who had so distinguished himself at Amboor.

On this occasion, however, he was suffering under very great disadvantages. A number of his officers were in a state of great dissatisfaction bordering upon mutiny, because they had obtained no share in the plunder which the others had brought from Tanjore. A cannonade was opened between the two armies, which, however, owing to the distance, did but little damage though it had the effect of still further discouraging the French who were convinced of Nasir Jung's superior strength. That evening thirteen of the French officers went in a body to their commanding officer and resigned their commissions, whilst at the same time others left the army and returned to Pondicherry. Muzaffer Jung and Chanda Saheb changed their plans, the former refused to retreat, so he remained alone, whilst Chanda Saheb, not daring to trust himself to the mercy of Nasir Jung, followed the French. One reason that induced Muzaffer Jung to remain was that for some days past he had received messages purporting to come from Nasir Jung in which he was promised forgiveness and protection. The overture he resolved to accept, and sent some of his officers to Nasir Jung's presence. Nasir Jung was of course delighted that the rebellion should be so easily put down and is said to have sworn on the Koran that he would neither make his nephew a prisoner nor deprive him of the governments he enjoyed during his grandfather's life.

Accordingly Muzaffer Jung left his camp and proceeded to make his submission, but no sooner had he arrived near his uncle's tent than he was seized, carried off to a neighbouring tent and placed in chains. His camp was then attacked and his followers dispersed and put to the sword, the Mahratta cavalry following the French force up to the very wall of Pondicherry.

In this sudden and unexpected manner the shortlived rebellion of Muzaffer Jung had apparently come to an end. He himself was in captivity, his army dispersed, and his friends and allies compelled to retreat. His very life was in danger, for he had everything to fear from Nasir Jung's anger. Muzaffer Jung's career, however, was not yet over, and even a more sudden and unexpected change was destined to take place in his fortune.

Although Nasir Jung had been so successful there was a good deal of discontent amongst some of his chiefs. Three of the principal of these were the Nawabs of Cuddapah, Kurnool and Savanur. From the commencement of this struggle between the son and the grandson of the Great Nizam-ul-Mulk, to whom they owed everything, these and other old officers of Asaf Jah had endeavoured to bring about a reconciliation. They were moreover greatly disappointed at Nasir Jung's breach of faith in seizing his nephew after promising his liberty, since, relying on this promise, they had been chiefly instrumental in persuading Muzaffer Jung to surrender. For the present, however, these chiefs took no open step, but when M. Dupleix, hearing of their discontent, commenced a correspondence with them, they did not hesitate to reply. M. Dupleix's conduct at this critical time showed what a remarkable man he was. All that was left of his army was a small body of Europeans. Almost the whole of his native allies and followers had been scattered or destroyed, and there was opposed to him the enormous army of the infuriated Nizam, which was now flushed with a victory in which it had scarcely lost a man, and was further supported by a strong body of English allies. But Dupleix by no means despaired, and, although for the present he was unable to use open force, he arranged his plans with so much skill that ultimately he proved successful. Dupleix's first act was to send ambassadors to Nasir Jung's camp, ostensibly to obtain lenient terms for Muzaffer Jung and Chanda Saheb, but in reality to gain time and also to enter into closer conspiracy with the dissatisfied Nawabs. After eight days these ambassadors returned, and the plot was now approaching completion. This plot was further aided by Nasir Jung's own conduct. He first of all fell out with Major Lawrence by making delays in the appointment of Mahomed Ali as Nawab of the Carnatic, so that, in disgust, Major Lawrence retired with his force to Fort St. David about 50 miles distant. At the same time, Nasir Jung, considering the campaign to be practically over, retired with the whole of the army to Arcot, where he himself remained whilst he sent back the greater part of his army and two of his generals to Hyderabad. This was an opportunity which Dupleix was not slow to seize. He resolved to attempt a daring enterprise, which if successful would establish the French name over the whole Carnatic. Nasir Jung was at Arcot enjoying himself with hunting and other amusements. Mahomed Ali and the English force was further south and were fully occupied by the army of Chanda Saheb, and so he resolved to attack the so-called impregnable fort of Gingee. A small force of 250 Europeans and 4,200 sepoys was sent out under the command of M. Bussy, who was afterwards to become so celebrated in Hyderabad itself. This small force did not attempt a regular siege, but simply carried the place by storm at night supported by only four guns. The defenders.

not expecting so bold an attack from so small a force, were taken by surprise and surrendered, so that next morning this handful of Frenchmen found to their surprise that they were in possession of an historical fort that years had held powerful armies at bay and had now yielded without inflicting a loss of more than two or three men.

The news of this daring feat aroused Nasir Jung from his indolence and lethargy. Summoning as many of his discharged forces as he could reassemble, he at once marched to Gingee, accompanied by 60,000 infantry, 40,000 horses, and 350 guns. He had resolved to crush the daring Frenchman who had struck his prestige so serious a blow. It was, however, in the middle of the rainy season, and his progress was delayed by flooded rivers, so that it took him almost two months to march 50 miles. During this time Dupleix had opened out negotiations for peace, and, being now in a more advantageous position owing to his success at Gingee, his demands were that Muzaffer Jung should be released, his estates restored to him, and Chanda Saheb should be appointed Nawab of the Carnatic. At first Nasir Jung would not hear of these conditions, but as, owing to the rains, disease had broken out, and supplies were running short, he resolved at last to grant the demands, the only condition being that Duplex and Chanda Saheb should acknowledge his sovereignty. But Dupleix was carrying on a double game. At the same time that he was negotiating with the Nizam he was also corresponding with the discontented Nawabs in his camp In fact, when Nasir Jung's officers arrived in Pondicherry with the news that the Nizam would sign the required treaty, at the same time as he delivered to the officers the treaty to be taken back for ratification, Dupleix sent secret instructions to his force in Gingee to march against Nasir Jung, leaving it to chance to decide which event should happen first, the return of the ratified treaty or the carrying out of the long-planned conspiracy.

As soon as they received Dupleix's letters, the French numbering 800 Europeans and 3,000 sepoys marched out of Gingee to where the Nizam was encamped 16 miles away. The advance guards of the Hyderabad army fell back and then the small French force came upon the whole of the army drawn up in line, in front of which was an elephant with a white flag. This being the signal agreed upon with the conspirators, the French halted The troops in front were those of the Nawabs of Cuddapah and Kurnool who remained stationary. On this being reported to the Nizam he came upon his elephant and riding up to the Nawab of Cuddapah called him a coward for not advancing against the enemy. The Nawab in reply rose in his howdah and shot the Nizam through the heart. His guards dispersed and then after cutting off Nasir Jung's head the Cuddapah Nawab went to Muzaffer Jung's tent and hailed him as Nizam of the Deccan (14th December, 1750). Nasir Jung's assassination was brought about by his unpopularity and his breach of faith towards Muzaffer Jung, but the plot to which he fell a victim was a very treacherous one and was the more unexpected by him since he had only the day before sent the treaty to Dupleix duly signed and ratified. As regards the army the change of masters appears to have been welcomed. It was known that Muzaffer Jung was the favourite grandson of the great Nizam-ul-Mulk and all hastened to pay him their respects.

CHAPTER III

THE FRENCH IN HYDERABAD

AFTER this sudden change from a prison, threatened hourly with death, to a throne and the undisputed command of an enormous army, Muzaffer Jung was transported with joy. He looked upon Dupleix as his deliverer and at once marched to Pondicherry to thank him in person. Here for several days there was an endless series of festivals. The new Nizam appeared everywhere with Dupleix in public and showed him every honour and respect. The whole of the treasure found in the camp of Nasir Jung was handed over to the French Governor who was asked by Muzaffer Jung to decide all cases of disputes between himself and his chiefs and a promise was given that in all matters Dupleix's advice would be asked for. A grand Durbar was held in Pondicherry in which Muzaffer Jung was installed as Subadar of the Deccan and Dupleix's chair was placed next to that of the Subadar so as to show that he was of equal rank. At this Durbar the Subadar declared Dupleix to be Nawab of all the country south of the river Krishna down to Cape Comorin including Mysore and the whole of the Carnatic, besides bestowing upon him a personal present of a Jaghir worth one lakh of rupees every year. He was also made a Mansabdar of 7,000 horse with the right to bear the ensign of the fish, and the Nizam further promised never to grant a favour without his previous approval, and to be guided in all things by his advice. But Dupleix was too wise to accept all these favours. He knew that if he did so he would only create enemies amongst his former friends, and so he presented Chanda Saheb to the Nizam and asked that he should be appointed the actual Nawab of the Carnatic. This was done, but the real power remained in the hands of Dupleix. Muzaffer Jung now expressed his intention of returning to Hyderabad and asked Dupleix to send with him one of his trusted officers and a force of Europeans to act as a body-guard. This Dupleix was very glad to do because by this means he would be able to maintain his influence with the Nizam, when far away in the Deccan. Accordingly M. Bussy was appointed with a force of 300 Europeans and 2,000 sepoys to form the Nizam's personal guard. This having been arranged, Muzaffer Jung accompanied by his French escort and followed by his army commenced his march back to Hyderabad. But Muzaffer Jung was not destined to see his capital again. After a march of only a few weeks,

THE FRENCH IN HYDERABAD

whilst passing through the Jagirs of the Nawab of Cuddapah, a disturbance occurred in that part of the army where the ladies travelled, which was attacked by some of the Cuddapah ryots. The Nawab supported his ryots and when Muzaffer Jung came up and reproached him for the disturbance an engagement took place Bussy's troops soon decided the quarrel, and the Nawab commenced to retreat. Muzaffer Jung instead of waiting for his cavalry followed on his elephant, the Nawab of Kurnool who had also taken part in the engagement, but fell dead, pierced through the brain by a spear thrown by the Kurnool Nawab, who was immediately afterwards cut to pieces It is probable that the whole of this incident was a pre-arranged conspiracy ; for the three Nawabs of Cuddapah, Kurnool and Savanoor, all of whom took part in it, and who had also been implicated in the assassination of Nasir Jung, were dissatisfied with the rewards they had received and were jealous of the influence of the French. Savanoor and Kurnool were both killed and Cuddapah escaped grievously wounded. Muzaffer Jung's reign had only lasted about six weeks and now everything was again in confusion. The presence of Bussy, however, with his small but disciplined force soon set matters right. Nizam-ul-Mulk's third son, Salabut Jung, was following his brother in a sort of honorary confinement. Bussy being in charge of the royal camp at once had him brought forward and publicly installed as Subadar The other chiefs presented their nuzzers and before the day was over order was restored and the march resumed (March, 1751.)

This change of Nizams made no difference to the position occupied by the French. If anything, their influence was made stronger than it was before, because the Nizam saw how valuable was this disciplined force and he felt that it was due to Bussy's prompt action that he had been placed on the *musnud* without any further disturbance. Besides he knew also that there was further trouble to be expected; for his elder brother Ghazi-ud-Din had published his intention of asserting his right to the Subahship of the Deccan. He felt therefore that it was necessary to have near him a force that could be trusted and an officer who by interest was attached to his person.

Salabut Jung's first act was to confirm all the concessions and privileges that had been granted by his brother to the French, and in addition he gave them the towns of Masulipatam and Chicacole. The march was then resumed. On the way Kurnool was stormed and taken; Hyderabad was reached on the 12th April and a triumphal entry was made into Aurungabad on the 29th June. It is necessary now that a glance at the state of affairs generally should be taken. At this period the most powerful man in the South of India was the French Governor, Dupleix. He was regarded by all as the maker of Subahdars and Nawabs. His fame reached as far as Delhi, and the Emperor himself sent him a *sanad* confirming all that had been granted by the Nizam. The English influence seemed to be at its last gasp. Chanda Saheb was generally acknowledged as Nawab throughout the Carnatic, and his rival Mahomed Ali was besieged in the fort of Trichinopoly, supported by a small army of only 7,000 or 8,000 men and a small body of some 300 Englishmen. It was believed that it was only a question of time before the chief power in the South of India would be that of France. As a matter of fact, however, this was not the case. The power of Dupleix had now reached its height, and from this time commenced to decline. The English determined to make every effort to support Mahomed Ali. A strong force was thrown into Trichinopoly and an army, to which was attached a young lieutenant named Robert Clive, who was a few years hence to become so famous, was sent to take the field. It is not intenfled to follow the history of events in the south; for the object of this work is to trace the connection of Hyderabad with the European powers, and it will therefore be sufficient to say that the siege of Trichinopoly by Chanda Saheb and the French continued for 18 months more (June, 1752) when the French general, Law, was at last compelled to surrender. Chanda Saheb was taken prisoner and handed over to the Mahrattas by whom he was put to death, and Mahomed Ali, the protégé of the English, was recognized as Nawab of the Carnatic.

But the losses which the French prestige suffered in the south were more than compensated for by the immense influence which Bussy succeeded in gaining by the side of the Nizam. Salabut Jung was a man who had been brought up more or less in confinement. He had not enjoyed a soldier's training and now that he was raised to a throne he devoted himself to pleasure. In order to do this in safety he put his whole trust in Bussy and his French force, and Bussy did everything to justify that trust. His force of 300 Europeans and 2,000 sepoys was kept in the strictest discipline. The men were lodged in the Aurungabad fort and no soldier was allowed to leave his barracks except at a fixed time. There were no quarrels or disturbances with the townsmen, and the French troops really acted as the police of the town, so that the richest and most valuable goods were freely displayed under their protection. The first against whom Bussy had to defend the Nizam Salabut Jung was Nizam-ul-Mulk's eldest son, Ghazi-ud-Din. In order to recover the kingdom of his father, Ghazi-ud-Dın made an alliance with the Mahrattas, and, whilst the latter under Balajee Baji Row advanced from Poona with 100,000 men, the former marched with 150,000 from Delhi. Bussy had managed to increase his force to 500 Europeans and 5,000 sepoys in a high state of discipline, and in addition there was the large but irregular army of Salabut Jung. Bussy resolved to deal with these two invading forces separately, before they could effect a junction. As the Mahrattas were the nearest he dealt with them first, and then, marching via Bidar, continued on towards Poona as if he were going to attack the Mahratta capital. By this move Balajee was compelled hastily to return, or else he would have been cut off from his base This he did with 40,000 of his best horse, and met the Nizam with his French contingent soon after he left Bidar. An engagement followed in which the Mahrattas for the first time met a disciplined force of Europeans and trained sepoys. The Mahratta horse charged with their usual dash and gallantry, but were met by Bussy's steady ranks armed with muskets and bayonets. These were immovable, and, unable to stand the withering fire of the artillery, the Mahrattas retreated broken and in disorder. Bussy continued his march, and again came across Balajee at Rajapur on the river Gur. Taking advantage of an eclipse of the moon when the Hindus were engaged in worship, Bussy made a night attack surprised their camp, and scattered them in all directions, gaining at the same time an immense amount of booty. (November 12th, 1751.) This victory not only greatly increased Bussy's reputation, but also marked an epoch in the methods of Deccan warfare. For the first time in regular battle had a small, but highly disciplined and well-equipped force, succeeded in annihilating an army ten times its strength ; and henceforward it will be seen that all the states of Southern and Central India endeavoured to organize contingents drilled and disciplined according to the European system. Bussy continued his victorious march till within 20 miles of Poona, and, after inflicting another defeat some five days later, peace was made with the Mahrattas and the Nizam, and Bussy was at liberty to return to Aurungabad in order to meet Ghazi-ud-Din. It was not until September, 1752, that the latter arrived in the neighbourhood of Aurungabad with an army of 150,000 men. Instead of hostilities, negotiations were commenced, and, whilst these were in progress Ghaz-ud-Din suddenly died. The story of his death is thus told by Colonel Malleson (*History of French in India*, p. 367) : " The right of Ghaz-ud-Din as the eldest son of his father gave him a moral influence which was not without its effect on the nobles of the Deccan, and which very much disturbed Salabut Jung himself. It is possible that, under the circumstances, and in the face of the Mahratta alliances which Ghaz-ud-Din had at length cemented by the offer of a considerable sacrifice of territory, he might have been inclined to listen to a compromise, when an event occurred which removed the necessity for further negotiation. Living at Aurungabad in the ancient palace of the Subahdar was one of the widows of Nizam-ul-Mulk ; she had borne him but one son, the next in order to Salabut Jung, Nizam Ali. All the hopes of this lady were concentrated in the ardent desire to see this son sitting on the viceregal seat of his father. Between that wish and its accompaniment, however, there were two obstacles. One of these, Salabut Jung, was out of her reach, the other Ghazi-ud-Din, was at Aurungabad. To thrust him out of the path she wished her son to follow, she had no scruple as to the means by which such a result might be obtained. She accordingly invited Ghazi-ud-Din to a feast and in a dish of which she had persuaded him to partake, telling him truly that it had been prepared by her hands, she poisoned him. Ghazi-ud-Din died that night."

His rival being removed, it was not difficult for Salabut Jung to make terms with the Mahrattas. Balajee Row had collected another army and had been joined by the Holkar and Bhomsla, Rajah of Nagpur. Balajee had had one experience of the quality of the Nizam's general, Bussy, and had probably little desire for another, as long as he could get something out of the negotiations. Accordingly, he agreed to retire himself and to make his allies evacuate the Nizam's dominions on the cession of some territory to the west of Berar between the rivers Taptee and Godavery and situated in the province of Khandesh. At Bussy's advice this was granted, since it was deemed wiser to cede this outlying portion than to risk a war. This occurred at the end of the year 1752.

At this time, as has been briefly noticed, Chanda Saheb had been captured and killed at Trichinopoly, and in his place Dupleix had been nominated by the Nizam as the Nawab of the Deccan. The appointment was, however, more or less a nominal one. The English army was still in the field, and their protegé, Mahomed Ali, was recognized as Nawab over a large portion of the Deccan. There was still occasional fighting with varying results, but on the whole the ascendancy appeared to be passing away from the French. Moreover, Dupleix's period of office was drawing to a close Peace had been proclaimed between France and England, and the French authorities, instead of being grateful to Dupleix for the enormous results which he had obtained, were getting

THE FRENCH IN HYDERABAD

alarmed at the growth of his sphere of influence, and were about to make a change of policy.

In Hyderabad, also, a change of feeling had taken place. Although the Nizam was still as warmly attached to Bussy as ever, his power and influence were regarded with jealousy by many of the noblemen at his court. Amongst these was the Dewan Syed Lashkar. This noble had been appointed a year previously at Bussy's recommendation, who believed that he was his friend and supporter; in reality, however, he was determined, if possible, to get rid of the French, and was on the side of the mother of Nizam Ali, whom he hoped some day to raise to the Deccan throne. But whilst Bussy was present his personal influence was sufficient to put an end to all intrigues and so the Dewan had to wait for a better opportunity. This opportunity was not slow in coming. Soon after the conclusion of the peace with the Mahrattas, Bussy fell ill, and leaving his second in command at Hyderabad, whither Bussy had come together with the Nizam from Aurungabad early in the year 1753, he himself went for a change of air to Masulipatam, about 150 miles distant, on the eastern coast. This was Syed Lashkar's opportunity.

One of the principal reasons why Bussy had been able to maintain the discipline of his troops at so high a standard was that he never allowed their pay to fall into arrears. His personal influence with the Nizam was so great that he was always able to draw regular supplies from the treasury, whilst the greater portion of the irregular army of the Nizam was often left for months in arrears. No sooner was Bussy's back turned than Syed Lashkar began to raise difficulties in the matter. Remittances only came very irregularly and at last, pretending friendship, he told the commandant Goupil that he was very sorry that there was no money in the treasury, and recommended that he should send bodies of troops into the districts in order to collect the revenue. In this way not only was the force scattered over the distant parts of the country, but the restraint of discipline was relaxed, and from time to time outrages were committed which were made use of to prejudice the Nizam against the French. But Syed Lashkar was not contented with this. He first of all induced the Nizam to move from Hyderabad to Aurungabad, leaving the main body of the French at the former city and taking only a small escort with a junior officer in command of the latter. At the same time the Dewan commenced a correspondence with Mr. Saunders, the Governor of Madras, in which he engaged to get Bussy and the French troops sent back to Pondicherry. Malleson gives an extract from one of the letters in which the Syed says : " Have no fear of the result ; for I have arranged the mode in which to rid myself of your enemies. The plan is in action and with the assistance of Providence the result will be what you wish. I expect to be with you at the end of the rains and to arrange then everything in a satisfactory manner."

In the meantime, the Dewan continued his policy with the French in Hyderabad and the districts. They were kept without money or supplies, and separated from each other they naturally fell into a state of despondency. Matters were rapidly coming to a crisis, and would probably have ended in a mutiny if suddenly Bussy had not appeared on the scene. When the condition of affairs in Hyderabad was reported to him, he saw at once how serious it was, and, although not yet entirely recovered, he resolved to return at once. He was also informed of Syed Lashkar's correspondence with the English ; for the letter, from which the above extract is taken, had fallen into the hands of French agents. This news was at the same time sent to Dupleix at Pondicherry, and he at once wrote to Bussy begging him, even at the risk of his health, at once to return to Hyderabad in order to set matters right. Bussy saw that there was no time to be lost and sent orders that the whole of his force should assemble at Hyderabad, and himself started off to meet them and arrived at Hyderabad in May. His presence soon effected a change and the Government of the city, overawed by the threatening aspect of the troops, paid up some of the arrears due and furnished supplies. Bussy, however, was not satisfied with this, and resolved to go at once with the whole of his force to Aurungabad and there demand an explanation from the Dewan in presence of the Nizam. Although it was the middle of the hot weather, the long march of nearly 300 miles was performed in two months, a rate of progress which in those days was considered almost incredible. Syed Lashkar now became thoroughly alarmed and sent out messages to Bussy that he would act in every way in accordance with his wishes and, if he liked, would resign the Dewanship. This, however, was a step which Bussy did not like to take, but he took care to let the Syed know what his wishes were and told him that if he should assist him in carrying them out he would not interfere as regards the Dewanship. Syed Lashkar accordingly met Bussy outside Aurungabad and conducted him and his force to the presence of the Nizam who received them most cordially. In the negotiations that followed Bussy insisted that unless a proper guarantee were given for the punctual payment of his force, it would be impossible for him to maintain it in a state of efficiency. He, therefore, asked that the East Coast Districts should be given to him as Jaghirs, from the revenue of which he undertook to pay the force himself. These districts, since known as the Northern Circars in the Madras Presidency, were for the greater part semi-independent Zemindarees extending over a sea-coast length of nearly 500 miles from Chicacole to Masulipatam. They were under the Nizam and were governed by his Deputy at Raj Mundry. Bussy now proposed to take the Governor's place, not as a tributary to the Nizam, but on account of the French Government, and in return to maintain the French contingent. This arrangement was an entirely new departure from any arrangement which as yet had been made between a native and European Power. Hitherto, the English and the French had been content with small coast-settlements to which were attached a few towns and villages, which were made use of for trading purposes. Now for the first time the French were made the practical rulers of a province the tribute from which amounted to 40 lakhs of rupees every year. The country itself was divided into numerous Jaghirs and Zemindarees, all of which were quasi-independent in the hands of Hindu Rajahs such as Vijayanagaram, Bobbilli, Jaipur, etc. These had hitherto regarded the Nizam as their overlord and paid him tribute. Under the new arrangement the overlordship and the tribute were transferred to the French, and Bussy's position at the Nizam's court was almost that of an independent ally. But the intrigues against the French power did not cease. Syed Lashkar endeavoured to persuade the Nizam that Bussy, having obtained all he could get from him, would now intrigue to place one of his brothers Basalut Jung or Nizam Ali on the throne, in order to obtain fresh grants as a reward. He accordingly advised the Nizam to place these two princes in confinement, thinking that Bussy would probably interfere on their behalf. This was done, but Bussy was far too clever to fall into the trap, although several of the noblemen tried to persuade him to do so. He said that the Nizam's family affairs were no concern of his; all that he had to do was to defend the prince against his enemies and leave him to settle his own private affairs. Thereupon, Syed Lashkar, disgusted at having again failed, sent in his resignation and was succeeded by Shah Nawaz Khan, a nobleman of high character and position, believed by Bussy to be attached to French interests (*Malleson.*)

Opportunity was taken at the same time to remove the French in India from office. All the adherents of the fallen Minister were replaced by others professing devotion to the French, but in reality being against them.

In the Deccan, therefore, for the time, everything in the middle of 1753 seemed to be in favour of the French. Bussy's influence was stronger than ever, and the Nizam regarded him as his principal protector against the intrigues of his brothers and his noblemen. In the Carnatic, however, the French influence received at this very time a most severe blow. The French directors, alarmed at the ever increasing circle of Dupleix's influence, had resolved to alter the French policy in Southern India, and with this object in view had sent out M. Godehen to replace Dupleix. This took place in August, 1753, and in October of the same year Dupleix left India disgraced and ruined in fortune. Although there was upwards of a crore of rupees due to him by his own Government and others in India, he received not a rupee, and died a few years afterwards in poverty. This was the unhappy fate of one of the most brilliant and daring Europeans who ever came to India. He had laid the foundations of a new empire for his country, and in return he received nothing but ingratitude. The seed he had sown, however, was not thrown away; for his rivals, the English, as we shall see, stepped in and reaped the harvest.

CHAPTER IV

BUSSY IN THE DECCAN AND THE DECLINE OF FRENCH INFLUENCE

WITH the fall of Dupleix and the change in the policy of the French in the Carnatic, there was a corresponding fall in their prestige. Chanda Saheb, whom the Nizam had recognised Nawab of the Carnatic, nominated by the Nizam to succeed him, was gone, and the new French Governor seemed to have no inclination to interfere in the politics of the various rival states. Mahomed Ali, the protégé of the English, was now universally acknowledged as the ruler of the Carnatic, and was therefore practically an independent rival of the Nizam, who by tradition was his overlord, but who in fact did not recognize him. But Mahomed Ali had to pay a price for his advancement. The Mysoreans had greatly helped towards his final victory, and Hyder Ali, who was then the leading chief of the Mysore army, utilized the position to increase his own power and influence, until, later on, he was able to depose the Hindu Rajah and make himself the independent ruler of Mysore. In this way two vassal states were detached from the rule of the Nizam, whose sphere of influence was confined entirely to the

Deccan, where, however, it was challenged by the yearly increasing power of the Mahrattas.

But whatever losses the French prestige may have suffered in the further south of India, ample compensation was obtained by the increase of their influence in Hyderabad and the Deccan. The possession of the extensive seaboard districts gave them, not only increased opportunities for trade, but also enormous prestige. But this prestige also brought with it the penalty of jealousy. The new French system of small but highly disciplined and equipped armies was entirely opposed to the traditions of the old nobility, whose enormous revenues were granted for the nominal upkeep of large forces, in the constitution and equipment of which quantity was more regarded than quality. Bows and arrows, spears and javelins were the principal weapons, and their victories were gained chiefly by numbers. If the new system of small but highly disciplined armies became general, not only would there be no occasion for their forces, but, even if they undertook to raise similar troops, smaller jaghirs would probably be required for their maintenance. In addition, a number of the nobles were jealous of Bussy's influence over the Nizam, and secretly wished to remove Salabut Jung and place his brother, Nizam Ali, on the *musnud*. The minister himself, although openly he pretended that Bussy was his friend and patron, was secretly working against him and Shah Nawaz Khan—for this was the minister's name—was in reality only waiting for Bussy to turn his back and absent himself in his newly granted province to put himself at the head of the conspirators. It was just at this time that Dupleix was recalled to France, and his successor, Godehen, agreed to recognize the English nominee as Nawab of the Carnatic. After a short visit to the coast, Bussy returned to Hyderabad in January, 1755, and found that his enemies had not been idle in trying to prejudice the Nizam's mind against the French as allies. At the Durbar which was held on his arrival, Bussy explained the terms of the new treaty arrived at between the French and the English. Malleson thus describes the interview :

"The Subadar (Nizam), instructed beforehand by his advisers, inveighed bitterly against the new policy that had been inaugurated at Pondicherry. ' Your Sovereign,' said he, ' promised to support me against my enemies to establish my authority and to make it respected. Of this you yourself have given me assurances on which I have always depended. Yet now I hear that it is the King of England who especially concerns himself with the affairs of India, even with those that affect me.' Bussy endeavoured to put the best possible gloss upon the proceedings of Godehen. The Subadar and the Minister heard him but without being convinced. They were indignant that the fate of the Carnatic should have been settled without reference to the Subadar, its liege lord. ' You have put me,' said Salabut Jung, ' in the balance against Mahomed Ali ; you have allowed to be placed at the head of one of my tributary provinces a man whom I have never employed and who has always rebelled against my authority. Nay, if I were to proceed to the Carnatic to drive him out of it, the English would support him ; and you, on account of this truce, would hold back. You, who are engaged to support me on all occasions, would aid me neither against the English nor against Mahomed Ali.' He then went on to say, ' You know that the state of my affairs necessarily demands the support of a European power ; on this condition I am able to govern. Either you must remain here or I must enlist the English in my interest. Are you disposed to render me the services which you have rendered hitherto? I must do you the justice to say that I am grateful for them, but it would appear now that you have neither the power nor the inclination.'"

This is a very important conversation to remember, for it shows in how critical a state were Salabut Jung's affairs. With rivals in his own family and disaffection amongst his nobles, he was surrounded on all sides by enemies. The Mahrattas were yearly increasing in influence, and were stealing every inch of territory that they could lay hands on. In Mysore, Hyder Ali was rising to power, and was casting jealous eyes upon the Nizam's districts of Bellary and Cuddapah. Further south Mahomed Ali was his avowed enemy, and ready to take any advantage offered. Salabut Jung was therefore in a position of great danger, and feared that if forsaken by the French he would be attacked by all his enemies at once. For the present, however, Bussy was able to show that he had no intention of forsaking the Nizam, but on the contrary was able to give him active and useful support. The Nizam, as Subadar of the Deccan, was supposed to exercise authority, not only over the Carnatic, but also over Mysore, which was nominally bound to pay him the tribute as the representative of the Emperor of Delhi. This tribute was seldom paid and only when the Nizam was strong enough to compel its payment. Salabut Jung now determined to make use of his French troops to levy this tribute, and the opportunity was a good one, since the greater part of the Mysore army was employed at Trichinopoly. The only difficulty was that the French were on terms of alliance with Mysore, so that Bussy had no right to take up arms against them. Bussy was therefore in an awkward position; for, if he refused to help the Nizam, the latter's suspicions regarding him would be confirmed. He, therefore, wrote to the Mysore Dalwai or Minister and advised him to pay and in the meantime set out with Salabut Jung at the head of his 500 Frenchmen. Bussy marched with such despatch that the Rajah was unable to get any reinforcements, and, as the Mahrattas took the opportunity of threatening an invasion of Mysore from the west, he was only too glad to comply with the Nizam's demand. He paid seventeen lakhs of rupees in cash and jewels, and gave bills for thirty-eight lakhs more, whereupon the Nizam with Bussy returned to Hyderabad. For the moment, Bussy's influence over Salabut Jung was greater than ever, but at the same time the opposition against him increased. It was not long before an opportunity occurred of which Bussy's enemies took advantage. In February, 1756, the Nizam, having made peace with the Mahrattas, resolved to subdue the Nawab of Savanur, who, it will be remembered, had been one of the three leading Nawabs who brought about the assassination of Nasir Jung and the death of Muzaffer Jung. Since the last event, the Nawab had been in open rebellion against the Nizam, who now resolved to reduce him to order. In this expedition the Nizam was helped by the Mahrattas, who were following out designs of their own and wished by helping the Nizam to prevent any attack on their recent conquest of Gooty. Morari Row was also playing a double game, and, recognizing the importance of the French contingent as a support to the Nizam's army, wished to attract Bussy to himself. The Nawab of Savanur, seeing that resistance was useless, at once came to terms. The Nizam left the negotiations to

Bussy, and there seems little doubt that he utilized his position to gain advantages for the French to the detriment of the Nizam. Savanur was in possession of a bond given to him by Dupleix for his services in the revolutions to which Nasir Jung had fallen a victim. Bussy, on behalf of his own nation, wished to have this bond cancelled, and in order to gain this end gave the Nawab favourable conditions, in which the Mahrattas also shared. This transaction could not remain long secret, and the minister, Shah Nawaz Jung, at once represented to the Nizam that his interests had been betrayed by his French general for his own private interests. Salabut Jung yielded to the advice of his minister and signed an order dismissing Bussy from his service. It seems difficult to defend Bussy in this matter, and there can be little doubt that in order to get back back the bond he sacrificed the Nizam's interests and gave better terms to the Savanur chief and the Mahrattas than he otherwise would have done, although it does not appear that in the transaction he was in any way actuated by personal motive.

The minister, Shah Nawaz Jung, at once took steps to crush Bussy entirely. He wrote to the Madras Governor asking him to send up an English force, and to the Peshwas he suggested that Bussy should be assassinated (*Malleson*, p. 485). Bussy was in a very critical position. His communication with Pondicherry was cut off by the Carnatic. He had only a small force with him, and he was far away in the Gooty country from his supports on the eastern coast. His only communication with the Circars on the coast was through Hyderabad, which, under the circumstances, must be considered hostile country, since he was a disgraced and dismissed man. Bussy was quite equal to the occasion ;

as soon as he received his order of dismissal he at once started back via Hyderabad for Masulipatam. Shah Nawaz sent off a body of troops to intercept him, but the Mahratta general, who wished to gain Bussy over to himself, sent an escort of Mahratta cavalry to protect him. This enabled Bussy to cross the Krishtna river, just before a flood came down, which detained the Nizam's troops and enabled him to reach Hyderabad some fifteen days before they did. The Mahratta overtures Bussy refused. He dismissed the escort that was sent to protect him, with presents and compliments but said that he still regarded the Nizam as his master and should proceed to Hyderabad to await his further orders.

Arrived at Hyderabad Bussy established himself and his force which consisted of 200 European cavalry and 5,000 sepoys, on the north side of the River Musi, in an old palace known as Char Mahal,* and sent off an urgent message to Masulipatam for reinforcements. The flooded condition of the rivers delayed for several days the approach of the Nizam's army. When at last the main body appeared, Bussy had to undergo a regular siege. His sepoys gradually deserted him, and he was left with his Europeans only.

Bussy's appeal for help had been promptly attended to, and M. Law was despatched from Masulipatam with 160 Europeans, 700 sepoys and 5 guns on the 16th July, 1756, and his force was strengthened on the way by further reinforcements. Until within 15 miles of Hyderabad the relieving force met with little or no opposition, but here, on arriving at some hilly and difficult country, they found a large portion of the

* This must not be confused with the Chow Mahal where the Nizam now resides. This palace is in the city and the quarters occupied by Bussy were separated from the city by the River Musi.

Nizam's army together with 6,000 Mahratta horse, drawn up to meet them. Law was on the eve of giving up the attempt, but Bussy sent him an urgent order "in the name of the King," to push on at all hazards. This was done, and after three days of hard fighting, in which, however, the Mahrattas, who were secretly desirous of gaining the services of Bussy for themselves, took but little part, he managed to reach Haiatnagar, about six miles from Hyderabad. Here he was joined by a small force, and then marched into Bussy's camp in the Char Mahal. The minister, Shah Nawaz Khan, now saw that Bussy was master of the situation, and at once sent proposals for an amicable arrangement. Bussy's sole conditions, beyond the punishment of two of the principal deserters, were that he should be reinstated in his honours and dignities, and should, as hitherto, be regarded as the officer next in authority to the Nizam. This was agreed to, and on the 20th August, after having been besieged for nearly six weeks by the whole of the Nizam's army, Bussy was received in public Durbar and reinstated by the Nizam in all his titles, dignities and honours.

This incident is not only a remarkable instance of Bussy's marvellous courage and personal influence, but also serves as a striking proof of the great value of a small but highly disciplined force when opposed by large numbers, badly disciplined and badly armed. It was a lesson which the Mahrattas learnt, and henceforward we shall find them organizing similar forces themselves, and, as they were unable to detach Bussy from his allegiance to the Nizam, they looked round for others to take his place.

Bussy remained for three months and a half at Hyderabad, and then, on the 16th November, marched to Masulipatam with about 100 Europeans and 400 sepoys, in order to re-establish his authority, which had been considerably weakened by the occurrences at Hyderabad. This he did without difficulty, and during a stay of about nine months succeeded in capturing all the English settlements on that coast, and in establishing friendly relations with all the large Zemindars and Rajahs. There was, however, one exception, viz., the young Maharajah of Vizianagaram. The late Rajah had been very friendly with the French, and when Bussy was supposed to be in extremities in Hyderabad, and on the verge of ruin, had actually sent him a large supply of money.

When Bussy came to the coast in 1757, the Rajah persuaded him to accompany him in an expedition against his hereditary enemy, the Rajah of Bobbili. whose fort was captured, and he with almost the whole of his family and retainers were massacred. A day or two afterwards the Rajah of Vizianagaram was himself assassinated, and his son succeeded him. Bussy was himself disgusted at all this barbarous slaughter, and made some disparaging remarks to the young Rajah regarding his father's cruelty, which caused very great offence. The Rajah said nothing at the time, but the incident rankled in his mind, and subsequently led to important results.*

In the meantime, Bussy's long absence on the East Coast had left his enemies in Hyderabad leisure to revive their intrigues. Shah Nawaz Khan persuaded the Nizam to appoint one brother Nizam Ali to the government of Berar, and the other brother Basalut Jung to Bellary. He also managed to obtain possession of the

* My authority for this statement, which is not alluded to by other historians, is a monograph drawn up by the late Maharajah Ananda Gajpati Raj and given to me by him in 1895.

strong fort of Dowlatabad, where was the treasure of Syed Lashkar, the late minister, who had just died. His object was to confine Salabut Jung in Dowlatabad and proclaim Nizam Ali minister, and then to expel Bussy and the French from the Deccan. To help him in the conspiracy he did not hesitate to invite the Mahrattas, who, always ready to take a share in any quarrel out of which there was a chance of getting substantial profit, sent an army under the Peshwa's son, Wiswas Row, which took up a position not far from Dowlatabad. Shah Nawaz Khan now called Nizam Ali to Aurungabad, and invested him with the administrative work of the kingdom, while the other brother Basalut Jung was appointed keeper of the Great Seal. The whole of the power was now in the hands of the two brothers, and the real Nizam, Salabut Jung, was a mere puppet. It is probable that his life would have been sacrificed if it had not been for his faithful escort of 200 French soldiers, whom Bussy had left behind as his body-guard. As soon as Bussy heard of the critical position of the Nizam he resolved to come to his aid. Aurungabad was over 500 miles from Rajamundry, but Bussy, with 500 European infantry, 200 cavalry, 500 sepoys and 10 field pieces, managed to cover this distance in 21 days, or an average of nearly 20 miles a day. When he arrived at Aurungabad, he found himself in the midst of four armies gathered together like birds of prey. There were Nizam Ali from Berar, the Nizam's army of which Nizam Ali had assumed the command, Basalut Jung, with an army from Adoni, and finally the Mahrattas under Balajee Row who, as Orme remarks, had come as usual to take advantage of the confusions of the Government! Bussy's first step was to secure the safety of the Nizam's person, and, in order to do so effectually, surrounded him with his Frenchmen. He then entered into negotiations with Nizam Ali and the minister Shah Nawaz Khan, employing for this purpose his most confidential Mahomedan Captain, Hyder Jung; whilst these negotiations were proceeding, Bussy by a clever surprise, succeeded in seizing the fort of Dowlatabad, having been admitted by the Killedar, or Governor, together with 300 Europeans. This fort, together with the treasure of the late minister, Syed Lashkar Khan, had, it will be remembered, on the latter's death, been seized by Shah Nawaz Khan. In order to prevent the latter from resenting this bold act, at the same time as the fort was seized, a party of Bussy's force surrounded Shah Nawaz Khan's tents and took him prisoner.

Nizam Ali now found all his plans disconcerted by Bussy's bold action, but pretended that it was a matter of indifference to him who was in possession of Dowlatabad, and gave out that he would leave for Hyderabad, of which he had been appointed governor. On the day of his departure Nizam Ali held a large Durbar, at which Hyder Jung, who was Bussy's most confidential man, was present. After the Durbar had been dismissed, Hyder Jung was detained for a private interview, and, as he was rising to take leave, was assassinated by two of Nizam Ali's officers. This deed at once led to a great uproar; Bussy immediately placed all his troops under arms, and drew them up in order of battle; at the same time he despatched a strong body of horse to escort the Nizam, Salabut Jung, from Roza, whither he had gone to visit his father's tomb, and another to bring in Shah Nawaz Khan. The latter was found surrounded by armed followers, and some fighting took place in which Shah Nawaz Khan and one of his sons were killed. Nizam Ali was now so alarmed that he quitted the camp, and followed by a small body of his best horse rode off in the direction of Burhanpor, a distance of 150 miles, which he is said to have accomplished in 26 hours.

On the following day Salabut Jung returned from Roza and found the conspiracy broken, owing to Bussy's promptitude, who had thus once again saved him from dethronement and probably from death. At first Salabut Jung wished to follow and punish Nizam Ali, but Bussy persuaded him that it would be safer to avoid a civil war and return to Hyderabad. This accordingly was done, and the Nizam accompanied by Bussy arrived at Hyderabad on the 15th July, 1758.

Here they were met by news which was destined to alter the whole condition of affairs, but to understand which it will be necessary to go back a little in the course of our history.

In the previous year, war had broken out between the French and the English, and the former determined to use every endeavour to regain their old influence in the Carnatic, and if possible to drive the English out of Southern India. Clive was then in Calcutta, and was busy in settling the affairs of Bengal after his victory at Plassey in the previous year, and it was not expected that he would be able to send any assistance to Madras. Accordingly large reinforcements were sent out to Pondicherry, together with a new Governor, Count Lally, who was ordered to concentrate the whole of his strength upon the capture of Madras. Lally arrived in Pondicherry early in May, 1758, and at once sent a letter to Bussy, warning him that he would soon be recalled. This letter reached Bussy on his march from Aurungabad to Hyderabad, and he took his precautions without telling the Nizam the real reasons. As soon as he had crossed the river Gaunga and had left the main body of the army on the other side, he called a halt, and, saying that he could not march any further until he had been joined by the detachment of 150 Europeans and 400 sepoys whom he had left at Dowlatabad, he sent express orders to this body of troops to join him at once. On their arrival the march was continued, and therefore when the army arrived at Hyderabad Bussy had the whole of his force with him ready for any emergency. Here he found a letter from Lally ordering him to march at once with the whole of his force, leaving only sufficient for the defence of the coast settlements, and to join Lally immediately by way of Masulipatam.

It will not be difficult to understand the dismay and the disappointment with which Nizam Salabut Jung received this news. He had come to regard Bussy with his French army as his only help and saviour. He was surrounded by enemies, conspiracies and intrigues, and he knew that his own brother Nizam Ali was only waiting for an opportunity to make another attempt for his throne. But Bussy's orders were peremptory, and he could only obey. Before Bussy left, Nizam held a large Durbar, at which he embraced Bussy with every show of affection and grief; he called him the Guardian Angel of his life and fortune, and foreboded the unhappy fate to which he would be exposed by his departure. (*Orme*, Book IX.) This foreboding was unfortunately destined to prove true, as we shall see hereafter, and though Bussy promised that he would return, when the Nizam said good-bye to him, he did so for ever. Bussy never again set foot in the Deccan, and left the country where for nearly seven years he had enjoyed a series of victories and successes for another scene where the fortunes of war had reserved for him nothing but defeat and disgrace. The whole of the French forces left with Bussy and Salabut Jung was left alone to face as best as he could the plots and intrigues by which he was surrounded. The French influence in the Deccan was thus broken, never to be revived except for a short period 30 years later. The door was now open for a new influence, that of the English, and we shall see how they availed themselves of the opportunity.

CHAPTER V

THE RISE OF BRITISH INFLUENCE IN HYDERABAD

THE coming struggle between the French and the English for supremacy in the Deccan was watched by all the Native States with the utmost interest. As soon as it was known on the East Coast that the greater part of the French troops were to be withdrawn from the Deccan and the Circars, there was a feeling of unrest. In particular, the Rajah of Vizianagaram, who had never forgiven the affront put by Bussy on his father's memory, as related in the last chapter, resolved to strike a blow. Raja Anandaraj—for this was his name—at once wrote to Calcutta and stated that the French were about to be withdrawn, and, if Clive would send down to Vizagapatam a body of troops, he would assist with his own forces and would guarantee that the French would be cleared out of the Circars. These letters reached Calcutta in August and were at once laid before the Council. In the opinion of the majority of the Council the despatch of such an expedition would be very hazardous. Matters were by no means settled in Bengal, and the attitude of the new Subadar Meer Jaffer was not such as to inspire much confidence. A really effective army could not safely be spared, and, if it could be, the majority was of opinion that it would be better to send it to Madras. Clive, however, was of different opinion and thought that an invasion of the Circars would compel the French to divert a large portion of their army from the siege of Madras, and would thus indirectly help the garrison. Accordingly Clive resolved to accept Anandaraj's proposal, and without delay despatched an expedition under Lieutenant-Colonel Forde. This force consisted of 500 Europeans, 200 sepoys, six field-pieces, six 24-pounders, a howitzer, and an 8-inch mortar. The expedition left Calcutta towards the end of the September and reached Vizagapatam on the 20th October. As soon as Anandaraj knew that it would start, he attacked the fort of Vizagapatam, which had formerly belonged to the English, but which was then in possession of the French, reduced it without difficulty, and then handed it back to the English, whilst he with his army encamped at Cossimkota, a small fort five miles inland. On the 1st November, Colonel Forde moved off from Vizagapatam and joined the Rajah and, after some days' delay spent in arranging the terms of alliance, the two armies moved on towards Rajamundry, distant about 130 miles. Forty miles from this town the combined armies came in sight of the

French under M. Conflans, who were strongly encamped near the village of Condoor. The two forces were of about equal numerical strength, though the French had the greater number of guns. Here a battle was fought in which the French were completely beaten and fled in disorder, not halting until they had crossed the Godavery, after which they proceeded more leisurely until they reached Masulipatam. Forde was not able to follow them at once, for a disagreement had arisen between him and the Rajah, which took some time to settle. It was the 6th of February before the combined armies reached Ellore, some 50 miles from Masulipatam, and it was not until 3rd March that Colonel Forde was able to invest Masulipatam. In the meantime, after his defeat at Condoor, M. Conflans, the French commander, had despatched a letter to the Nizam Salabut Jung begging him to come to his assistance. This Salabut Jung did, and together with his brother, Basalut Jung, marched with an army of 35,000 men to Bezwada, where he arrived about the same time as Colonel Forde commenced the siege of Masulipatam. With this force threatening him, Colonel Forde pushed on the siege as quickly as possible and with such success that on the 4th April, after nine days' hard fighting, the town had to capitulate. It is a remarkable fact that the prisoners taken in this brilliant feat of arms exceeded the number of the assailants.

Too much importance cannot be attached to these two events, the battle of Condoor and the taking of Masulipatam. The latter particularly was the crowning blow to French influence on the Coramandel Coast. Nor did it occur a day too soon. The French, alarmed at this unexpected invasion from Calcutta, had detached a body of troops from Madras, and no doubt this weakening of their main body was one of the causes which had led to Lally being compelled to abandon the siege of Madras, which he had done on the 17th February. This body of troops was ready to co-operate with the Nizam's army, and, had they been able to join hands, Colonel Forde would have been in a position of great danger. But after the fall of Masulipatam the British were masters of the position and Salabut Jung was ready to come to terms with them, for news had reached him that, taking advantage of his absence, his brother, Nizam Ali, was endeavouring to bring about a rising in Hyderabad. There can be no doubt that Nizam Ali was encouraged to take this step by letters he had received from Calcutta and from Colonel Forde; for both Clive and the latter officer hoped that, by creating a disturbance in his capital, Salabut Jung would be prevented from taking any active part on behalf of the French. This, in fact, turned out to be the case. Salabut Jung, anxious to return, was only too willing to treat with the English and the result was that a treaty was drawn up in which the French alliance was finally relinquished. This treaty is dated the 14th May, 1759, and under it the Nizam ceded to the English the whole of the Circar of Masulipatam, together with eight districts, as well as the Circar of Nizamapatam and two other districts as an inam, or free gift, together with the *sanads* which had been given to the French. The Nizam further undertook to drive the French out of the Deccan within 15 days and to compel them to retire to the south of the river Krishna and in future never to allow them to have a settlement in his country nor to retain them in his service or give them any assistance. The Rajah of Vizianagaram was to continue to pay tribute to the Nizam, but was not to be called upon for any arrears. Both parties to the treaty agreed that they would not assist the enemies of the other, nor give them protection of any kind. This therefore was the first occasion on which the Nizam of Hyderabad was brought into direct relations with the English, and it is worthy of remark that in return for his concession the Nizam himself received little or nothing. The English were now placed in the same position as that which the French had, and became the possessors of the line of coast extending 80 miles from north to south, and stretching some 20 miles inland, with a revenue of 40 lakhs of rupees, in return for which they were not even bound to assist the Nizam with any permanent army These terms show clearly how great the moral effect of the successes of Colonel Forde, and of the English in Madras, had been, and how urgent was the necessity of the Nizam to return to Hyderabad. With the loss of his French troops Salabut Jung was deprived of the only protection from his enemies. On his return to Hyderabad he found that his brother, Nizam Ali, was so strong that he could resist him no longer. He had to accept him as his Minister or Dewan and dismiss his brother, Basalut Jung, to his government at Adoni. All real power passed into the hands of Nizam Ali, who at last threw off all further disguise and in 1761 deposed Salabut Jung and threw him into prison, where he soon afterwards died.

During the interval between the treaty between Salabut Jung and Colonel Forde, and the assumption of the *musnud* by Nizam Ali just alluded to, the remaining brother, Basalut Jung, finding himself deprived of all power and influence at the Court of Hyderabad, had from his jaghir of Adoni entered into negotiations with the French with the object of creating for himself, assisted by them, an independent kingdom in the Carnatic. Basalut Jung's object was to add the districts of

Circar and Cuddapah to his own adjacent jaghirs of Adoni and Guntoor, since he saw that Salabut Jung, deprived of Bussy's help, would be unable to hold his own, and forseeing that Nizam Ali would inevitably, sooner or later, assume the Subadarship, he hoped in the meantime to make himself independent. Accordingly he marched into the Cuddapah country, and there he was joined by Bussy. This alarmed Nizam Ali, who feared that Bussy would return to Hyderabad and regain an ascendancy over Salabut Jung, which would effectually destroy his schemes. He accordingly became profuse in his offers to Basalut Jung of an increase of territory if he would return to his jaghir (*Wilks*, Vol. I, Chapter 3.)

Bassalut Jung was joined by Bussy in Cuddapah. He disclosed to him his plans, which were that he should be recognized as Nawab of the whole of the Carnatic or districts south of the Krishtna and Tungabudra rivers. These negotiations, however, fell through, and the difficulties in which the French Governor Lally now found himself by the march of the British upon Pondicherry compelled Bussy to join his chief. A detachment of sepoys under the command of French officers was, however, left with Basalut Jung, who for the present had to keep his ambitious projects in abeyance, projects indeed which the subsequent victory of the English rendered impossible of accomplishment. But Nizam Ali in order to carry out his own designs found it advisable to come to terms with Basalut Jung, who was accordingly left in possession of Guntoor, the south position of Cuddapah, and his own jaghirs of Adoni, which comprised a large portion of the present district of Bellary.

After Nizam Ali had succeeded in carrying out his designs Basalut Jung passes out of any further share in

Hyderabad affairs. He continued unmolested in his jaghirs, where he enjoyed a kind of semi-independence, assisted still by a French contingent, until his death, when the contingent was passed into the service of Nizam Ali, in spite of British protests that this was a breach of treaties—the Nizam's excuse being that he had stipulated not to employ French troops, but that there was no stipulation against his employing natives officered by Frenchmen. This contingent formed the nucleus of the celebrated contingent raised subsequently by Raymond, of which we shall hear hereafter.

In the meantime the struggle between the French and the English for supremacy had come to an end. Disaster followed disaster to the French arms. After the decisive battle of Wandiwash (21st January, 1760) the English gradually reduced the various forts in the Carnatic and pressed the French back to Pondicherry, which they besieged, and, after a siege of four months, captured on the 17th January, 1761. Lally, Bussy and the other French officers, together with some 2,500 men were all taken prisoners and sent to Europe and the French influence, which for some time had threatened to overshadow the whole of Southern India, was for ever broken. It is true that, when peace was proclaimed between England and France, 1763, Pondicherry was restored, but, though fifteen years later the French made another final attempt to regain power, their influence as a nation ceased for ever. Individuals, as we shall see later on, achieved for themselves power and influence, but France was no longer a power to be reckoned with, and the eyes of all South India were now directed towards the English, who in so marvellous a manner had taken the place of her rivals.

In 1765 Lord Clive returned to India, and on his way

stopped at Madras. Here he pointed out to the authorities the importance of securing the whole of the coastline of the Circars, and it was resolved to apply to the Emperor at Delhi for a *sunnad* for these districts. It will be remembered that under Forde's treaty with the Nizam only Masulipatam and some of the districts were given to the English as *inam*; for the remainder the Rajah of Vizayanagaram had to pay tribute to the Nizam who was still nominally the sovereign. Clive now desired to obtain a grant to the English of the whole of this portion of the country and accordingly, without any reference to the Nizam, applied to and obtained from the Emperor a *sunnad*, which freed the Circars from the Nizam and bestowed them upon the British (1766). At the same time General Calliaud was despatched with a large force to take possession of these provinces, which he did without any difficulty being raised by the various Rajahs and Zemindars.

It may be imagined that the news of this new step excited Nizam Ali's rage and indignation. Although the Nizams invariably acknowledged the Emperor as their sovereign, and obtained his signature to their *sunnads* of appointment, it was most unusual for a *sunnad* to be granted by the Emperor direct to a stranger for districts which were under their immediate jurisdiction and which had hitherto paid tribute to them as the representatives of the Emperor. When he received the news Nizam Ali was engaged with the Mahrattas on the western frontier, but he at once returned with his army to Hyderabad, and declared that he would avenge himself for the usurpation, as he deemed it, of so important a part of his territories by an invasion of the Carnatic. The Governor of Madras was not then prepared to embark upon another war, and accordingly General Calliaud was directed to go to Hyderabad and if possible to settle the matter amicably with the Nizam. This was done, and on the 17th November a treaty was signed between Calliaud and the Nizam. This important document commences thus: "A treaty of perpetual honour, favour, alliance and attachment between the great Nawab, high in station, famous as the Sun, Nawab Asaf Jah Nizam-ul-Mulk, &c., &c., and the Honourable East India Company." Under this treaty the two contracting parties solemnly engaged themselves to mutual assistance and to esteem the enemies of one the enemies of the other and contrariwise the friends of one the friends of the other. In return for the "gracious favours received from His Highness" consisting of the sunnads of the five circars as a free gift, the British undertook to maintain a body of troops to settle the affairs of His Highness's Government and only to withdraw the same in the event of the peace of the Carnatic being threatened, and that only after timely notice to His Highness. As a consideration for this free gift the Company undertook to pay for Rajamundry, Ellore and Mustafanagar five lakhs of rupees yearly, and for Chicacole and Mustafanagar, when obtained, two lakhs each, or a total of nine lakhs. Chicacole was to be taken possession of at once, but Mustafanagar, or Guntoor, was to remain in possession of the Nizam's brother, Basalut Jung, unless he or his agents should create any disturbances, in which case the Company was authorized to take possession at once. The nine lakhs referred to were to be used for the payment of the troops which the Company engaged to maintain, and the Company was to account to the Nizam for any balance if the expense should fall short of that sum, but must themselves bear any excess. These troops, however, were to be maintained only when required by the Nizam, and when not required the payment as fixed above was to be made annually in three instalments. The Nizam promised to give three months' notice when he required the troops, and, on his part, promised to assist the Company with his own troops, reserving to himself the same right of withdrawal on necessity occurring. These were the principal points of the treaty, which concluded with a declaration that in future all doubts and suspicions should cease between the respective, parties and in their room a perpetual, just and sincere confidence should be established.

No sooner was this treaty concluded than the Nizam called upon the British to furnish assistance in reducing the fort of Bangalore. This was done, but Hyder Ali, who was then the actual ruler of Mysore, took the opportunity of the Nizam's presence to persuade him to throw over the English alliance and to join him in an invasion of the Carnatic. It is difficult to understand why so soon after the signing of the treaty the Nizam should have consented to break it, for the English had carried out their conditions, and there was apparently no reason for the breach. However this may be, the English force was dismissed, and the Nizam joined forces with Hyder Ali and invaded the Carnatic in two columns. A battle was fought near Trinomaly in which Hyder was beaten and compelled to retire, after which the Nizam separated from his new ally and withdrew to the neighbourhood of Caveripatam, but 40 miles west of Madras. Here ambassadors from Madras were received and the Nizam declared himself willing to enter into a new alliance with the English and the Nawab of the Carnatic, Mahomed Ali, who now for the first time was recognized by the

Nizam. This treaty was signed by the Nizam upon the 26th February, 1768, or 22nd Shawal 1181 Hijri.

This new treaty confirmed the provisions of the former treaty but went considerably further and commences by reciting the grants given by the Emperor to the British, in consequence of which the Nizam confirmed the grant of the five Circars with the exception of Murtuzanagar which was to be held by Basalut Jung until his death, and agreed to write orders to the various Rajahs and Zemindars to recognize the English Company as their sovereign in future. The terms of payment were reduced to two lakhs (with one more as soon as the Circar of Condavir should be handed over) for the next six years, after which, if they had been left in undisturbed possession by the Nizam, the Company should pay five lakhs, or seven if Condavir was in their possession, such payment to cease if either the Nizam, or, at his instigation, the Mahrattas should attack the Circars. The stipulation about mutually furnishing assistance with troops is specially omitted in this treaty as likely to give rise to "misunderstandings," and it is simply provided that the enemies of either shall be regarded as the enemies of the other (the Nizam and the Nawab) and the friends of either as the friends of all. They all three agreed to give no assistance to any invaders, and the Company and the Nawab promised to send to the Nizam two battalions of sepoys and six guns whenever he should require them and circumstances would permit, to be maintained at the Nizam's cost as long as they should be in his service. The treaty goes on to provide for the recognition of Mahomed Ali as Nawab of the Carnatic, and releases him from all tribute in consideration of payment of five lakhs of rupees. It finally concludes by declaring "Hyder Naik" to be a rebel and a traitor, and bestows the territories held by him in the Carnatic Balaghat on the English, who, on coming into possession of them, agreed to get a *sunnad* for them from the Emperor and pay to the Nizam seven lakhs of rupees annually. This latter clause was something like the hunters dividing the lion's skin before he was shot, for a good many years were to elapse before the British were able to obtain the possession now bestowed upon them. On obtaining these districts the English also agreed to pay the *chouth* for them, which up to that time had been paid to the Mahrattas. *Chouth*, as explained in a former chapter, was a species of blackmail levied by the Mahrattas in all districts over which they could gain any influence. It consisted of 25 per cent. of the revenue, and if this was not paid the Mahrattas sent a force to harry and raid the district in question, so that it was only by regular payment of this tax that the villagers could count upon safety from ravage or plunder. In return, however, the Mahrattas agreed to protect such districts from any other robbers. This claim for *chouth* had been recogized early in the century when, as we have seen, Syed Hussein had been appointed Subadar of the Deccan, and from that time the claim had been asserted by the Mahrattas whenever they could do so. It was originally a kind of tax for nominal police protection. A further account of the origin of this claim will be found in Chapter VII. On the whole the terms of the treaty were much less favourable to the Nizam than those of General Calliaud. Not only did he recognize the validity of the Emperor's *sunnads* of which no mention was made in the former treaty, but the payments were greatly reduced and finally he was made to recognize Mahomed Ali as the independent ruler of the Carnatic. It is therefore only fair to assume that the advantages gained by the British in the short war with Hyder Ali had been very considerable, and that the Nizam bitterly repented ever having yielded to the temptation to break the former alliance. At all events the Nizam never again showed the slightest wish to sever his connection with the English, and from that time forward the two countries have remained in a state of perpetual friendship and alliance, the bonds of which, as we shall see, were in the course of time drawn still more closely together.

CHAPTER VI

THE BRITISH RESIDENT AND THE FIRST MYSORE WAR

THE circumstances that led to the appointment of the first British Resident to Hyderabad are interesting and important. It will be remembered that one of the circars, Murtuzanagar—or as it is now called Guntoor—was to be reserved for Basalut Jung during his lifetime. In 1779, Hyder Ali sent an army to reduce Cuddapah, which for some years had been tributary to Mysore.

This alarmed the Madras authorities, since they feared that Hyder would prove to be a dangerous neighbour. They were besides dissatisfied with the way in which Basalut Jung had behaved, for he had retained a body of French troops in his service, and, in spite of protest and representation made through the Nizam as far back as 1776, he had not dismissed them. Accordingly the Madras Government opened out negotiations with Basalut Jung direct without first communicating with the Nizam, and the result was that Basalut Jung executed a treaty (January, 1779) under which he agreed to dismiss the French from his service and to cede the district of Guntoor on condition of a fixed annual payment. The amount of this payment was not settled, but it was agreed that it should be the same as the Nawab then received. It was further agreed that, if the Nawab required protection, the Madras authorities would send him the troops, the cost of which would be deducted from the Jaghir rents. As soon as this had been arranged, a body of troops was sent in April, under Colonel Harper, to take possession of the district and to protect the person of Basalut Jung. The manner in which this march was conducted was extremely foolish. After reaching Guntoor, Basalut Jung asked that the troops should join him at Adoni, of which he was Governor, and accordingly they marched through the Cuddapah district, which then belonged to Hyder, without first asking for permission. Hyder's officers refused to allow them to pass, and Colonel Harper had to retire with the best grace he could. This thoughtless conduct, however, was quite sufficient to enrage Hyder, and there can be no doubt that it was one of the many causes that led to his next desperate struggle with the British power.

Hyder Ali, however, was not the only person who was offended with the arrangement about Guntoor. Soon after concluding the treaty with Basalut Jung, the Madras Government resolved to send an officer to the Nizam's court in order to sound him regarding his relations to other Indian powers and also to the French. The first Resident selected was a Mr. Holland, who arrived at

Hyderabad on the 6th April, 1779, or about the same time as Harper arrived at Guntoor. Mr. Holland was received with every mark of respect and courtesy, but, when he had to explain the transactions which had taken place between the Madras Government and the Nizam's brother, Basalut Jung, he found that his Highness was extremely indignant. He said, and quite truly, that the treaty with Basalut Jung, his subject, was most improper and uncalled for; that the sending of troops to Guntoor, a portion of his dominions, was, without his permission, a breach of the treaty of 1768; and, if the troops were not stopped, he would be compelled to oppose them. Probably the real reason why the Nizam was jealous of a body of English troops being attached to the person of his brother, was that he feared lest, aided by them, his brother should endeavour to assert his independence. As regards the French troops whom Basalut Jung had dismissed, they had been taken on by the Nizam, in order, as he explained, to prevent them from passing into the service of Hyder Ali or of the Mahrattas. There can be no doubt that the Nizam was justified in being indignant at the manner in which he had been treated and this indignation was still further increased when Mr. Holland presented to him a request from the Madras Government that the tribute of five lakhs of rupees, which was already two years in arrears, should be remitted altogether. This unjustifiable proposal threw the Nizam into a state of extreme agitation and he declared his conviction that the English no longer meant to observe the treaty, for which reason he must prepare for war. But it is the boast of the English Government that, though individuals may commit wrong and injustice, the Government itself will see that justice is done, and this is what happened in the present case. Mr. Holland had been authorized to communicate with the Supreme Council in Calcutta, and accordingly he sent copies of all the correspondence which had passed between the Madras Government and the Nizam.

The Supreme Council at once recognized the mistakes and injustice committed by the Government of Madras, and wrote a letter to the Nizam reassuring him of the pacific intentions of the Company; they ordered Mr. Holland to suspend further negotiations till he should receive fresh instructions from his own Presidency, and at the same time wrote to the Government of Madras, pointing out the mistakes that had been committed. (1st November, 1779.) The Nizam expressed himself as completely satisfied by the friendly assurances of the Supreme Council, but the Madras Government accepted the rebuke in a very different spirit. Sir Thomas Rumbold who was then the Governor of Madras (father of another Rumbold who had afterwards a good deal to do with Hyderabad), drew up a minute in which he denied the right of the Supreme Council to interfere and attacked that body in respect of its own policy in the conduct of the Mahratta war. This minute was forwarded to Bengal, together with a resolution of the Government couched in the same strain, and at the same time an order was sent recalling Mr. Holland. The Supreme Council now determined to assert its authority. The whole matter was reported to the directors in London, and in the meantime Sir George Eyre Coote was sent to Madras with orders to suspend Sir Thomas Rumbold, and, as the Madras Government had suspended Mr Holland, the Supreme Council appointed him as their representative at the Nizam's court. It only remains to mention that the decision of the Supreme Council was confirmed by the Board of Directors. Sir Thomas Rumbold and two members of Council were dismissed from their service, two other members were deprived of their seats, and the Commander of the Forces, Sir Hector Munro, was severely reprimanded. (*Mill*, II, 471.) From this time the authority of the Madras Government over the affairs of the Hyderabad ceased, and the Resident continued to be appointed by the Supreme Government in Calcutta, with whom he was placed in direct communication, a custom which continues to the present day.

For the present, therefore, the affair of the District of Guntoor was satisfactorily settled, but it was destined to lead to still further correspondence and negotiations. In 1782 Basalut Jung died, and, according to the treaty, the Guntoor District should have been handed over to the Company. This, however, was not done, and in return the Madras Government withheld the *Peshkash* due on the other four Circars. At this time the whole of Southern India was in a very disturbed state. Hyder Ali had also died in 1782, and was succeeded by his son, Tippoo, who at once embarked upon a career of conquest. He attacked and annexed districts on the western coast, and then put in a claim for Bijapur against the Nizam. As a consequence a junction was formed between the Hyderabad and Mahratta armies, and it was expected that the British would join their alliance in order to put a check to Tippoo's ambition. The English, however, had made a treaty of peace with Tippoo after he had taken Mangalore (1786), and Lord Cornwallis, who was then Governor-General, let it be known that he did not intend to commence fresh hostilities. A peace, therefore, was patched up between the different rival powers, and Lord Cornwallis resolved to take advantage of this to press the Company's claims to Guntoor. Accordingly, Captain Kennaway was despatched as Resident at Hyderabad to conduct the negotiations. Mr. Briggs in his work, *The Nizam*, makes the following remarks regarding the position : " The situation of the Nizam was such that he regarded himself as having more to hope and less to apprehend from a connection with the English than with either of the four Powers which bordered upon the dominions. Generally inferior to either the Mahrattas or Tippoo, he was ever in dread of being swallowed up by one of those formidable neighbours. An alliance with one of those Powers threatened hostility with the other." An alliance with the English, therefore, was more likely to bring safety as not being likely to cause these two, with so many conflicting interests, to combine against him. Captain Kennaway therefore arrived at Hyderabad at the time when the Nizam was inclined to listen to his proposals in regard to the cession of Guntoor, and, without discussing any other points which were reserved, he at once consented to hand over the District (1788). At the same time Meer Abdul Kassim, more generally known as Meer Allum, was sent to Calcutta with a letter to the Governor-General, couched in friendly language, in which, after urging the settlement of certain pecuniary claims, it was suggested that a new treaty of offence and defence should be formed between the Nizam and the British. The pecuniary claims were easily settled, with the result that a balance of nine lakhs of rupees, which were found to be due to the Nizam, were paid to him. Lord Cornwallis, however, was not equally disposed to enter into a treaty, and he replied that he had no power to do so without the permission of Parliament, but he wrote to the Nizam a letter which he said should have the force of a treaty (July, 1789), in which certain articles of the treaty of 1768 were modified or explained. This letter was afterwards confirmed by

Parliament and declared to have the same force as a treaty. The chief points in this letter are : (1) a definition of the force to be supplied to the Nizam. It was agreed that two battalions, each of 800 sepoys, commanded and officered by Europeans, with six guns, should be supplied to the Nizam at his cost, *whenever he should apply for their services*, thus modifying the words in the former treaty, "if the condition of the affairs of the Company should allow it," but it was stipulated that these troops should not be used against certain Powers then in alliance with the Company, namely, the Mahratta States, the Nawab of the Carnatic, and the Rajahs of Tanjore and Travancore. (2) It will be remembered that in the treaty of 1768 a stipulation was made about taking certain districts in the Carnatic Balaghaut from Mysore, for which tribute should be paid to the Nizam. Abdul Kassim had been instructed to point out that this stipulation had never been carried out, and to urge the advisability of its being put into effect. Lord Cornwallis, however, replied that circumstances had altered since 1768, and that we were then at peace with Mysore, but promised that, if in future the Company should come into possession of those districts, the terms of the treaty of 1768 should be strictly carried out. It is significant that, although the Company was then at peace with Tippoo, that king's name was not mentioned as one of those against whom troops supplied to the Nizam should not be used. The reason of this appears to have been that Lord Cornwallis thoroughly distrusted Tippoo's intentions, a suspicion which, as was shown by subsequent events, was amply justified. At the same time as these negotiations were being carried on at Calcutta the Nizam appears to have sounded Tippoo in respect to an alliance. This statement is on the authority of Colonel Wilks, who also states that negotiations were broken off because Tippoo added as a condition a matrimonial connection between the two families. Tippoo's father, Hyder Ali though of a respectable family, had begun life as a common soldier and his nickname of "Naik" shows the estimation in which he was held. It was not likely, therefore, that the Nizam with his long line of descent from the Prophet would agree to such a condition, and so the negotiations by whomsoever commenced were abruptly broken off, much to Tippoo's disgust. The probabilities in fact would seem to point to the overtures having been made, in the first place, by Tippoo and not by the Nizam. One Hafizjee had been the ambassador at Seringapatam on this occasion, and, as Tippoo attributed to him the subsequent failure of his overtures, he became the special object of the tyrant's hatred. The negotiations at Calcutta were successfully terminated in 1788, and in the following year (December 24th, 1789) Tippoo made an unprovoked attack upon the British ally, the Rajah of Travancore. This led to war being declared by the British, and the contingency provided for by the treaty of 1788 having occurred, the Nizam and the Mahrattas were both called upon to furnish contingents. This they did, and the Nizam promised to provide a body of cavalry of not less than 10,000, to be maintained at the cost of the Company. It was agreed that all country conquered from Tippoo should be equally divided between the three contracting parties, and, should eventually Tippoo attack or molest any one or other of the contracting parties, the others should join to punish him in such manner as might be afterwards settled. Both the Mahrattas and the Nizam fulfilled their part of the agreement and sent bodies of troops to act on the Mahratta and Hyderabad frontiers of Mysore. The Mahrattas were assisted by a body of British troops under Captain Little, and the Nizam by two battalions of Madras troops with six guns. The chief command of the army against Tippoo was taken over by Lord Cornwallis, the Governor-General, and the campaign did not come to a close until 1792, when Tippoo had to agree to the terms of peace dictated by the allies. In the final operations before Seringapatam the Nizam and the Mahrattas each sent a body of ten thousand horse to assist the main army. The Nizam's troops were accompanied by his son Sekunder Jah and by Meer Allum, both of whom took a prominent part in the final negotiations. There was also a detachment of the French contingent raised by Raymond numbering 150 men and commanded by Raymond himself. It is not necessary here to go into the details of the campaign, which are fully given in the works of Wilks and Grant Duff, but one incident may be mentioned as it forms a sequel to the marriage proposal just mentioned. During the march to Seringapatam the Nizam's contingent passed through his old possession of Cuddapah and on its way proceeded to recover the different forts. One of the principal of these was Gurramkonda, a hill fort of great strength about 30 miles from the present Mysore frontier. The lower fort was taken by a British force under Captain Reed, who then went on to join the main army, leaving Hafizjee with a sufficient force to continue the siege of the upper fort. This command, however, he did not long retain. As soon as Tippoo heard of the fall of this important fortress, he despatched an army of 12,000 men under his own son, Futteh Hyder, then about 18 years old, assisted by Ghazi Khan and Ali Reza. This army succeeded in surprising Hafizjee, who was then taken prisoner; the lower fort was evacuated by the Nizam's troops and the upper fort was relieved. The unfortunate Hafizjee had fallen into bad hands. Futteh Hyder was the young prince for whom Tippoo had desired a Hyderabad bride, and Ali Reza was fully aware of Hafizjee's share in the transaction and of Tippoo's hatred towards him. In order to please his master he practised upon his prisoner the most cruel insults. He was stripped naked, and, after being taunted and mocked, was at last put to death, whilst at the same time a French officer in the Nizam's service was assassinated. On hearing of this disaster the whole of the Nizam's army marched back and recovered the lower fort, though the upper fort held out till the close of the war. (*Cuddapah Manual*, p 102.) It is not our object to describe the details of this campaign. The Prince Sekunder Jah assisted by Meer Allum distinguished himself and was especially mentioned by Lord Cornwallis. Tippoo was defeated and was compelled to cede a large portion of his territory, and this was divided between the allies, each of whom received districts yielding about 40 lakhs. The British received the Salem Baramahl and Coimbatore districts to the south of Mysore, the Nizam obtained the Gurramkonda, Gooty and the Doab districts, which had been overrun by Hyder Ali, and the Mahrattas received extensive territory in Bijapur and Dharwar. The result, therefore, of the campaign was satisfactory and profitable to the Nizam, not only in prestige and the accession of valuable territory, which although it had belonged to him formerly, had been taken by Hyder, but also in the weakening of the power of this dangerous rival Tippoo. These incidents occurred during the years 1791 and 1792.

CHAPTER VII

THE NIZAM AND THE MAHRATTAS

DURING the course of our narative up to this point the Mahrattas have been frequently alluded to, and it now seems necessary to explain in more detail their relations with the State of Hyderabad. It will not be necessary to trace the rapid growth of this strange nation, which, in the course of a hundred years, grew to such enormous power that at one time it seemed as if the whole of the Indian Empire would be under its sway. The story of Sivajee, the "mountain rat" as he is often called by the Mahomedan historians, is a most romantic one, but can find no place here. His son, Sambajee, that "vile dog" as the Emperor Aurangzebe called him, met with a tragical end, being flayed to death by the Emperor's orders, but, although the last 20 years of Aurangzebe's life were devoted to the task of crushing the Mahrattas, he failed in his attempts, and at his death in 1707 they were stronger than ever. As a matter of fact it was this

20 years' campaign that was one of the principal causes of the rapid rise of the Mahrattas. After Aurangazebe had conquered the two last Mohamedan kingdoms of the Deccan, Bijapur and Golconda, he remained in the country moving from place to place with his vast army and leaving everywhere ruin and desolation behind him. The governors whom he left in charge of the conquered provinces had their hands more than full in preserving order in the districts surrounding the capitals. As soon as the grand army left one position in the country and moved to another, it was followed by the hordes of the light Mahratta horse, who, avoiding anything like a pitched battle, continually harassed the flanks and the rearguard, and, as soon as the army had moved to any distance, occupied the district it had left, and commenced levying tribute from the unfortunate villagers, or, if this were refused, harrying, devastating them with fire and sword. Whenever the villagers agreed to these exactions the Mahrattas installed a collecting officer, who often worked side by side with the Mogalai official. In this way gradually a custom grew up for the Mahrattas to levy their tribute, which they called *chout* and *surdeshmuckee*, sometimes one, sometimes the other, and sometimes both, over a great part of the Deccan, and over territory which belonged to the Imperial provinces. As a *quid pro quo* they professed to protect the villagers from aggression on the part of anyone else. In this way they created a kind of " sphere of influence " as it is now termed, and a claim of this kind once enforced was never afterwards relinquished. Even if it fell into abeyance owing to temporary disasters, as after the battle of Panipat, it was sure to be subsequently put forward with a claim of arrears when the Peshwa felt himself strong enough. In this way there was

always an open question between the Imperial governors and the Mahrattas, and, when subsequently the Nizam made himself independent, between them and the Nizam.

In the meantime, whilst Aurangzebe was occupied in the Deccan, the large tract of country between the Nerbudda and Delhi, occupied by the great province of Malwa, was left unprotected. Thither some of the predatory Mahratta chiefs went, followed by their depredating armies, creating each for himself a separate sphere of influence though still professing allegiance to their sovereign at Sattara, and afterwards to his deputy at Poona. This was the origin of Scindia, Holkar, Baroda and the Bhonslah Rajahs of Nagpur, or, as they are generally called in history, the Rajahs of Berar. But these Mahratta chiefs, although they were occupied in extending their respective spheres of influence north of the Narbudda, always retained a strong affection for, and interest in the villages from which their ancestors had come, and where their relatives resided. These villages they generally managed to acquire by grant or by purchase, and so, whilst exercising their chief power at a considerable distance, they managed to get, and to keep with the utmost jealousy, jaghirs and villages situated in the south some of which were actually in the Nizam's territory. In the provinces to the north of the Narbudda, their chiefs did not always exercise an actual sovereignty for the country was full of semi-independent chiefs and Rajahs, really vassals of Delhi. Some of the country the Mahrattas succeeded in annexing entirely, and this was then called *Suraj* or *Swaraj*, as for instance, Oojjaein, Gwalior, Indoor, Baroda and Nagpur, with their surrounding districts; whilst the semi-independent Rajahs were made to pay *chouth, surdeshmucki,*

THE NIZAM AND THE MAHRATTAS

and other exactions, to the extent sometimes of 65 per cent. of the revenue. In the wars that followed, the Mahrattas were at liberty to pursue their dreams of conquest, which were to convert India into a Hindu Raj. The 14 years of interregnum in the Deccan served to consolidate their power, and, when Asaf Jah made himself independent, the Mahrattas were the only enemies he had to dread. The descendants of Sivajee still maintained the royal title and style. Their residence was at Sattara, but in course of time they had become mere puppets in the hands of their ministers, the Peshwas, who ruled at Poona. Further away, other Mahratta noblemen had conquered for themselves independent kingdoms. Scindia, Holkar, and the Gaekwar at Baroda were among the most powerful of these, and they, together with the Mahratta Rajah of Nagpur, surrounded the Hyderabad State on the north, the west and the south-western frontiers. Scindia especially was the most ambitious and powerful amongst these princes, although he, together with the rest, nominally accepted the overrule of the Peishwas at Poona. Whilst Asaf Jah was Nizam of Hyderabad, he was continually at war with one or other of these princes, and in these wars he was not always successful in arms, although he was more than a match for them in diplomacy. During the disturbances that followed Asaf Jah's death, the Mahrattas increased their power and levied *chouth* over almost all the western portions of the Nizam's dominions. And, as regards the Princes of Malwa, Scindia succeeded in asserting his supremacy over all the districts north of the Tapti. We have seen how, soon after his arrival, Bussy was sent against the Mahrattas, and succeeded in defeating them with his small but well-disciplined army. We have also seen how they were waiting near Aurungabad to take advantage of the quarrel between the Nizam Salabut Jung and his brother Nizam Ali; but were prevented from interfering actively, although, in the negotiations that followed, the Nizam had to concede several of his outlying districts in Khandesh, thus giving the Mahrattas a continuous run of territory all along the western boundry of Hyderabad right up to the dominions of Scindia and Holkar. It has also been narrated how, soon after Bussy's withdrawal from Hyderabad, Nizam Ali, who was acting as Dewan, usurped his brother Salabut Jung's power and confined him in the State prison of Bider, where he soon afterwards died. This was in 1761. In the previous year, whilst Salabut Jung was still on the throne, and Nizam Ali was acting as his minister and commander-in-chief, the Nizam had suffered a severe defeat at the hands of the Mahrattas at Udgir about 150 miles from the western boundary at Ahmednagar, and had been compelled to cede the greater portion of the district of Bijapur, in the south-western portion of his dominions. This portion passed into the possession of the Mahrattas, who further exacted a claim of *chouth* over the neighbouring districts of Hungund, lying to the south of the river Krishtna, and between it and the Tungabhra. On the 7th January, 1761, occurred the third great battle at Panipat, in which for the time the power of the Mahrattas was almost entirely crushed by the Afghan Abdali, who came forward as the champion of the Emperor. Taking advantage of this disaster, Nizam Ali, who, as narrated above, had deposed Salabut Jung soon after the defeat of Udgir, thought that an opportunity had come for recovering from the Mahrattas some of the territory which had been taken away. Accordingly he marched with an army to the neighbourhood of Poona,

THE NIZAM AND THE MAHRATTAS 83

which, the main army being away in the north of India, was not able to offer any resistance. The city was sacked, and many of the houses which did not pay a ransom were pulled down. The remnants of the Mahratta army were on their return, and, hearing of the invasion, took advantage of Nizam Ali's absence and laid siege to Aurungabad, where, however, they were repulsed. They then marched to Hyderabad, where also they were defeated, and had to retire, although not without levying a considerable amount of blackmail. (1763.) Neither party seems to have gained any great advantage in these operations but there can be no doubt that the plunder of Poona greatly irritated the Mahrattas, who for that time were resolved to take ample revenge at the earliest opportunity. The Mahrattas continued in this unsettled state for some years, and, as the British were allies of both the Nizam and the Peshwa, they were often placed in a very awkward and dubious position. As the Mahrattas recovered from the defeat they suffered at Panipat, their power and influence again increased, whilst that of the Nizam appeared to be on the decline. But a new power was then growing in South India, that of Mysore, and for some time the attention of the Mahrattas was fully taken up with the ambitious schemes of Hyder Ali, who had designs equally upon them and the Nizam. We have seen how, in 1768, after first joining Hyder Ali, Nizam Ali concluded a treaty with the British, and how, from that time forward, the alliance between the two Powers was gradually and continually strengthened. The common enemy of both was Hyder Ali, and after him his son Tippoo Sultan.

At the time of Kennaway's (afterwards Sir John Kennaway) visit to Hyderabad as Resident, and of the negotiations with regard to an alliance previous to the

Mysore War, which has been mentioned in the last chapter, the only Powers in South India, from whom danger was to be expected, were Tippoo Sultan and the Mahrattas, and of these, owing to his violent and passionate character, Tippoo was the most to be feared, at all events from the English point of view. The Nizam's power had been greatly reduced from what it had been at the time of Asaf Jah's death. He had entirely lost the Carnatic. On the east coast, the northern circars, Guntoor and Masulipatam, had passed into the hands of the British. Hyder had conquered, and Tippoo was in possession of the districts of Bellary, Gurramkonda, Cuddapah (Kurpa), and asserted a claim to Kurnool, whilst the Mahrattas were asserting their claim to *chouth* and levying it, when they could, over the whole of the Mahratwari Provinces. In Berar a large portion had been actually annexed by the Bhonsla Rajah of Nagpur, and in the remainder there was a kind of double administration known as the *do-amil*, in which the Nagpur officials levied 60 per cent. of the revenue as *chouth* and *surdeshmookhee*, side by side with the Nizam's officers. who had to be content with the balance. So predominant was the influence of the Bhonsla Rajah in his province that he is generally spoken of in official documents as the Berar Rajah. Scindia and Holkar both held outlying districts in the Nizam's territory near the Ajunta Hills and Jalna, and the Peishwa held tracts of country stretching right up to the Godavery and the fort of Dowlatabad, whilst his horsemen harried all the neighbouring districts which did not protect themselves by paying *chouth*.

The Nizam dared not make an alliance with either Tippoo or the Mahrattas for fear of attracting the hostility of the other. He was himself too weak to with-

stand the arms of either, and was therefore compelled
to fall back upon the protection of the British. Hence it
was that he was only too ready to enter into negotiations
with Kennaway. But the British on the other hand,
though willing to combine against Tippoo, were by no
means anxious to excite the hostility of the Mahrattas,
who were at that time equally their allies as well as the
Nizam. Therefore it was that, in the treaty with Kennaway, the Mahrattas, equally with the Kings of Travancore
and Tanjore, were excluded as powers against whom
the British should not be liable to fight. As long as
Tippoo was the common enemy, this arrangement worked
very well, but after he had been conquered in 1792, and
the danger averted, at all events for a time, the difficulty
again arose. The Mahrattas again pressed their claims
against the Nizam for arrears of *chouth*, and Nizam Ali
appealed to the British for protection. But the British
urged with justice that they had no more right to side
with the Nizam against the Mahrattas than they would
be justified in taking the part of the Mahrattas against
the Nizam. It is true that they were bound to give the
Nizam support, but not against their own allies to whom
they were equally bound by treaty. It must be remembered that the condition of affairs at the end of the
seventeenth century was very different from what
it is now. The British power was not then strong enough
to oppose in South India the combined power of the
Mahrattas princes, especially as in such a case the latter
would probably be helped by Tippoo, who, though
beaten in the last war, was still formidable. Accordingly,
the Governor-General declined to interfere, and, as
neither the Mahrattas nor the Nizam would give way,
after some time spent in useless negotiations, war became
inevitable. At this time the Nizam had in his service a

body of well-disciplined troops, commanded by Monsieur Raymond and other French officers, and upon these, in addition to his own regular army, he had to rely in the coming struggle. It will be as well here to give a short sketch of Raymond, who was a remarkable man, and, though not so fortunate in his career as Bussy, is, next to him, the most important Frenchman who had any connection with Hyderabad, and one whose memory is still, after more than a hundred years, held in high esteem.

Michel Joachim Marie Raymond* came out to India at the age of 20 in 1775. His father was a merchant and sent him with a consignment of goods to Pondicherry, After having sold these at a profit, the young man resolved on a career of adventure and entered the service of Hyder Ali as a sub-lieutenant in a corps commanded by Chevalier de Lasse. With this corps he fought against the British in the campaign of Trinimoly, and afterwards, when Bussy came out to India for the second time, in March, 1783, he joined this distinguished veteran. But Bussy was not then the same man that he had been thirty years before. He was in poor health, had grown very stout and had no longer the energy of his younger days. When Bussy died at Pondicherry in 1785 (January), Raymond went to seek employment in the Deccan. He did not at once come to Hyderabad, but joined the French corps under Basalut Jung at Guntoor, which, as we have seen, became the subject of correspondence with the British Government. After five years, Basalut Jung was compelled to dismiss this corps, which was at once taken over by the Nizam. It would at first appear as if this act was a breach of the

* For these notes on Raymond's career I am indebted to Colonel Malleson's interesting little book, "Foreign Adventure in India."

former treaties, under which the Nizam had promised
not to entertain a corps of Frenchmen in his service.
This difficulty was got over by the Nizam contending
that the promise did not refer to native battalions officered
by Frenchmen or foreigners. To this construction of
the treaty the British Government were obliged to
consent, although with great reluctance, and with the
frequently expressed displeasure of the Madras Government. Raymond was placed at the head of this force,
which, with the large European element at his disposal,
he was able to bring to a considerable state of efficiency.
It was divided into regiments, and in the year 1795
consisted of 15,000 men formed into twenty battalions
and officered by 124 Europeans. These troops were
regularly paid from the revenues of certain districts
near Bider, which were assigned to Raymond's management for this purpose. The corps was made self-sustaining in every respect and possessed storehouses,
workshops, arsenals, gun foundries and powder mills.
The ruins of the old gun foundry still form a conspicuous
object on a piece of waste ground nearly opposite the
Fatteh Maidan in Chudderghaut. Malleson thus sums
up Raymond's character: "No adventurer in India
ever stood higher than he did. He was brave, magnificent, generous, affable and vigilant. To great abilities
he united the most consummate prudence. The one
dream of his life was to carry out by the means still
open to him the schemes of Dupleix, of Lally, and of
Suffrin. He deserves to be ranked with those illustrious
warriors in the hierarchy of patriotic Frenchmen."
It was, therefore, upon Raymond's force that the Nizam
principally depended in the approaching struggle with the
Mahrattas.

Whilst angry correspondence was passing between

Hyderabad and Poona, Mahodajee Scindia died on the 12th February, 1794. He was by far the most powerful and ambitious of the Mahratta princes, and, indeed, overawed the Peshwa himself. The intrigues and disturbances which followed his death were still further increased by the sudden death of the young Peshwa, and the Nizam considered that this was the opportunity to declare war. This declaration on the part of the Nizam rendered it still more impossible for the British to lend him the active support of their forces, and all that the Resident, Captain Kirkpatrick, could do was to allow the two battalions of British troops to preserve the internal peace of the dominions whilst the army was engaged in the campaign.

Accordingly early in 1795 both armies took the field. The Nizam's forces consisted of 70,000 irregular infantry, 25,000 regular troops under Raymond, including his own battalion of about 11,000, and a due proportion of artillery. To meet this army the Peshwa summoned all his vassal princes. Daulut Row Scindia sent a portion of De Boigne's army under his second-in-command, Perron, numbering 25,000; Raghojee Bhonsla of Nagpur, 15,000; Holkar, 10,000; and Parasaram Bhow, 7,000. Other contingents increased the total number to 130,000, and there were besides 10,000 Pindaries. The greatest strength of the Peishwa's army consisted of the brigades commanded and disciplined like Raymond's force, which had been sent by De Boigne, of whose career further notice will be found hereafter. These consisted of about 18,000 men commanded by European officers, together with a similar brigade of 4,500 brought by Holkar and commanded by Dudrence and Major Boyd. There was, therefore, the strange spectacle of French officers fighting on both sides, in some instances aided also by English private adventurers. The Residents at both the courts also accompanied the armies. Sir C. Malet was with the Peshwa and Captain Kirkpatrick with the Nizam. The latter was often placed in a very awkward position. Fraser (" Our Faithful Ally," p. 13) describes the difficulties in which he found himself : " The Nizam made several attempts to elicit from Captain Kirkpatrick his opinion in regard to the disposition he had made of his forces, the Resident always replying that his inexperience in tactics totally disqualified him for judging of such matters. As an illustration of the adroitness with which these questions were put and the prudence required in answering them, Captain Kirkpatrick was one day invited by his Highness to one of his tents on the pretence of viewing the river Manjerah from a remarkably favourable point. Here he found the minister, Azimul Omrah, who led on the discourse until, in the most natural manner, he commenced describing the several passes by which the army might descend from Balaghaut. So talking, he by and by asked the opinion of Captain Kirkpatrick as to which of these routes he thought the most eligible. Instead of directly replying to this question, the Resident, addressing himself to the Nizam, appealed to his candour whether he could with the smallest propriety, considering the friendship subsisting between the Company and the Peshwa, offer any opinion on so delicate a subject. The minister then demanded what was to prevent Captain Kirkpatrick, and observed that the privacy of his present audience had been purposely arranged to guard against the disclosure of his advice. Captain Kirkpatrick, still addressing himself to the Nizam personally, demanded in his turn what His Highness would expect from W. C. Malet were the Peishwa to consult with him respecting the best mode of attacking the army of Hyderabad. 'I know,' interrupted Azim-ul-Umrah, that the answer of Sir Charles Malet would be the same that you have so often given me; he would advise a speedy adjustment of all subsisting differences as absolutely necessary to the welfare of both sides. 'And this,' said Captain Kirkpatrick, 'is the only reply it is now possible for me to give to the question which has been put to me.'" With this the interview terminated. The two armies met midway between the forts of Parenda and Khurdla, near the river Manjera. According to Briggs, it was almost entirely a skirmish, ending in some night firing, a panic, and the flight of the Nizam's troops. Malleson, however, goes into much greater detail in his account of the life of Perron, and the following description is taken from that writer (*Foreign Adventurers*, p. 197) : " The battle began by an advance of the Mahomedans on the right wing and centre of the Mahrattas. The attack completely succeeded. The Mahratta right wing was driven on to its centre, at the same time as the centre itself was completely broken by the steady advance of Raymond's drilled troops. These divisions fled in confusion carrying Dudrence's and Boyd's men with them and endeavouring to seek a refuge behind the still unbroken left. Towards this left, covered and supported by a cavalry flushed with victory, Raymond now advanced. Perron allowed him to approach almost within musket shot and then suddenly opened a concentrated and continuous fire from the thirty-five guns, loaded with grape, which he had placed on the eminence. At the same time, Raghojee Bhonsla resisted the Mahomedan cavalry with a shower of rockets, the materials for firing which he had obtained on the ground during the general fight of the right wing. This simultaneous discharge sent the Moghal cavalry to the right-about. Raymond's infantry, however, not only stood firm, but succeeded for a time in making a successful opposition to all the efforts of Perron. It is difficult to say how the battle would have ended had Nizam Ali been endowed with the most ordinary qualities of a leader. But, like most Asiatic commanders, he trusted only to his horsemen; when these fled, he fled with them, sending order after order to Raymond to follow him. Meanwhile, the Mahratta horse, rallying, were hastening to support Perron. Raymond then most unwillingly was forced to follow his master. He did so, however, in the most perfect order, prepared to renew the fight on the next day." An accident, however, occurred during the night which converted the orderly retreat into a panic. Towards the middle of the night a small patrol of Mahrattas in search of water for their horses came upon a party of the Nizam's troops near a stream. Firing commenced, in which Raymond's troops who were close by with loaded muskets started from their sleep and commenced firing. An alarm of a general attack was raised, and the Nizam, escaping in haste, took refuge in the small fort of Khurdla (*Grant Duff*), where he was at once surrounded by the Mahrattas, and after three days was obliged to purchase his release by complying with all the Mahrattas' demands. This is known as the "Capitulation of Khurdla," and for a time was a crushing blow to the Nizam's power. The historians who describe this battle all speak in contemptuous terms of the Nizam's courage on this occasion, but it must be remembered that he was a very old man at the time, and also infirm, having only lately recovered from a dangerous illness. He was, besides, anxious for the safety of his ladies, and these possibly were the reasons which led to his flight; for, in earlier days, the Nizam, like all the rest of his ancestors, had been conspicuous for his courage. One thing is clear, and that is that a battle-field is not the place for ladies, and that the presence of a king of advanced age and in infirm health is calculated to be a hindrance rather than an advantage to his troops.*

Captured in this way in a trap, the Nizam had to submit to most humiliating terms. He had to yield a large slice of the western portion of his dominions, including Dowlatabad, Ahmednagar and Sholapur, with a revenue of thirty-five lakhs of rupees and an indemnity of three crores, and had also to send to the Poona court as hostage for the fulfilment of this treaty his principal minister, Azim-ul-Umrah.

One result of this unfortunate war was that the Nizam was bitterly disappointed at the want of support which he had received from the British force that were in his pay. He told the Resident that he no longer required their services, and asked him to withdraw them. This was done, and the consequence was that M. Raymond, with his French battalions, rapidly advanced in the Nizam's favour. The troops were greatly strengthened, and additional assignments of land were granted for their support. In the meantime, Azim-ul-Umra did not neglect his master's interest at Poona. Soon after the conclusion of the war (October, 1795), Mahdhoo Row, the Peishwa, died suddenly, not without a suspicion of foul play. In the intrigues which followed, Azim-ul-Umra was able

---

* One curious feature of the Nizam's army was that he had two regiments of women, who were called the "Zuffer Paltans" or victorious regiments. They were generally used as guards for the palace and zenana, and were regularly armed and drilled according to the French method. Briggs, writing in 1861, of the time he was at Hyderabad, as Assistant Resident, says that a few of the descendants of these female soldiers were even then in the service of Shumsul-Umra, and went through their exercise in his presence with many shouts of amusement and much laughter.

THE NIZAM AND THE MAHRATTAS

to obtain several important modifications of the terms, and soon afterwards returned to Hyderabad with increased power and influence. This, therefore, was the condition of affairs in 1795. British influence was considerably weakened, the Nizam had received a very serious reverse, and it seemed to him that, if he was to obtain any real support against the growing power of the Mahrattas he must depend upon the French troops entirely.

CHAPTER VIII

DISBANDMENT OF RAYMOND'S CONTINGENT

ONE of the results of the disastrous Kurdla campaign was that the Nizam was greatly disappointed in the support he could expect from the British alliance. His worst enemies were the Mahrattas and against them it was evident that, for the time at all events, the British, as the ally of both Powers, would give him little or no support. As regards Tippoo, the case was different.

Although the British were at peace with the Sultan, there was everything to be feared from his ambition and desire for revenge for his late losses. In order to guard against any aggression on Tippoo's part, it was absolutely necessary for the British to maintain a strong force, and any unprovoked attack on his part on any of their allies would have been the signal for a fresh war. On this side, therefore, the Nizam was comparatively safe; in fact, signs were not wanting that Tippoo would not be disinclined to make common cause with the Nizam. It was from the Mahrattas that he had most to fear. Although he had succeeded in obtaining a considerable reduction in the humiliating terms imposed after the capitulation of Khurdla, the Mahrattas had still enormous

DISBANDMENT OF RAYMOND'S CONTINGENT

money claims against him, which were unsettled, the interest on which grew from year to year, and which at any time might bring about a renewal of hostilities. But the Mahrattas had now a very large and constantly increasing force of well-drilled and disciplined troops, officered for the most part by Frenchmen, against which, as we have lately seen, the Nizam's irregular levies were absolutely of no service whatsoever. Unlike Falstaff's rabble they were not even fit as "food for powder," since they showed so little desire to face it. The only thing left for him to do was to strengthen his own disciplined contingent, taking advantage of the exact words of his treaty with the British that the force, though officered by French, was in reality a native force. Accordingly, as soon as this war with the Mahrattas was concluded, the Nizam dispensed with the services of the two British battalions, which, although they had served to replace troops employed at the front, had refused to take any active share in the hostilities. Coincidently with the dismissal, he ordered a large increase to Raymond's troops and assigned fresh districts for their maintenance. It was in vain that the British Resident expostulated and intimated that so much encouragement of the French portended serious changes in his relations with the English. (*Sir John Malcolm.*) These protests were not only disregarded, but a portion of Raymond's corps was sent to occupy the districts of Cuddapah and Cumbum, which the Nizam had obtained as his share of the Mysore spoils and which lay on the border of the Madras Presidency. At this step the Governor-General took alarm. "The measure itself," he remarked, "had a suspicious, not to say criminal appearance, and the strongest representations" were ordered "to be made to induce the Nizam to recall the detachment of Mr. Raymond." In case of refusal the Resident was even instructed to threaten the Nizam with the march of a body of English troops to his frontier, and the apprehensions of the English Government were increased by the discovery that certain French officers, prisoners in Madras, were suspected of a design to join Raymond and detected in this a project to escape. (*Briggs*, Volume I, Chapter IX.) But before it became necessary to take so pronounced a step, an event occurred in Hyderabad which showed the Nizam that it was not only foreign foes that he had to fear, but that there were even more dangerous enemies in his own household.

The Nizam had now attained a very advanced age and was in infirm health. The disaster of Khurdla was, there can be no doubt, to a certain degree attributable to this fact. His condition excited a certain amount of discontent among many of the younger and excitable nobles, who felt that in the crisis that was approaching a younger and more energetic ruler should be at the head of the State. Led away by these men and prompted by his own personal feelings of ambition, on the 28th June, 1795, the Nizam's eldest son, Ali Jah, fled from the capital and took refuge in the ancient royal city of Bieder. Here he raised the standard of rebellion, and was soon joined by a number of disaffected chiefs, bringing with them considerable levies. In a very short time this rebellion assumed a formidable and dangerous appearance. A few successes followed the first outbreak which served to attract more followers, and the Prince advanced towards Aurungabad. The first act of the Nizam was to recall the two British battalions which he had so lately dismissed, in order with them to replace Raymond's force which he had at once despatched against rebels. Raymond with his well-disciplined force had no difficulty in putting down this rebellion. At the first skirmish the Prince's hastily assembled levies broke and fled and the Prince himself escaped to Aurungabad. He was followed by Raymond and captured without any show of resistance. The Nizam at once despatched his minister to take charge of his rebellious son and bring him back to his presence. Whilst on the journey the minister ordered the Prince's elephant's *howdah* to be covered with a veil or *purdah*, as in the case when women travel. Whether the shame of this indignity was too much for him to bear, or whether he was afraid to meet his outraged father, it is impossible to say, but the fact remains that before he reached the capital the Prince Ali Jah committed suicide by taking poison.

Although this rebellion had been so easily suppressed, the Nizam was not slow to appreciate the additional security derived from the presence of the British battalions and they were accordingly retained in the capital. Their presence threw many difficulties in the way of Raymond, whose prompt action in the rebellion led to an even greater show of the Nizam's confidence. The force then consisted of about 12,000 men and was in a very high state of discipline. In spite of all obstacles, it is probable that its strength would have been still further increased and the French influence have become paramount in Hyderabad, as it already was in the leading Mahratta principalities.

The growth of the French influence amongst the Mahratta chiefs in the north of India forms one of the most interesting episodes of modern Indian history, but it is only possible here to mention the names of the leading French commanders of these subsidiary contingents. De Boigne, Perron, Dudrence, Filoz, Pedrons, Claude Martin, Bourquin, and the notorious Sumroo, are names to which are attached a great deal of interest and romance.*

The work of these men was the last desperate attempt of the French to recover the prestige and power wielded by Dupleix, Lally, and Suffrein, and to wrest from the rival English the Empire that was drifting into their hands, which, but for the supineness and lethargy of the French Government of the middle of the eighteenth century, would most certainly have been the heritage of France. Looking back now after the lapse of more than a century, it is easy to say that the idea of the French Empire in India was bound to fail, but about the year 1795 it was as near success as possible. Malleson thus describes the position (*Final French Struggles*, Book III) : " To enable the Princes of India to meet the English successfully in the field, it was necessary above all things to impart to their troops a thorough knowledge of European discipline and a complete acquaintance with the system of European strategy. To this somewhat venturesome task the sons of France bent themselves with untiring energy. They gave to it often their lives, almost always their every faculty. They had much to aid them. The native princes who employed them knew at least that their hatred of England was not feigned ; that they had nothing so much at heart as the humiliation of the rival of their own country. They, therefore, gave them almost always a confidence without stint. Their behests were but rarely refused. They worked under the avowed sanction and with the authority of the prince whom they served. And, if they did not succeed, their want of success is to be attributed rather to the jealousies which prevented combination amongst the native princes than

---

* Attention may here be drawn to Campton's *European Military Adventurers of Hindustan*, published by Fisher Unwin & Co., " Adventure Series."

to any shortcomings on the part of the ablest and most influential among them." At the period therefore at which we have arrived this French influence was at its zenith. In Mysore, Tippoo had, 6,000 miles away, caught the fever of the French Revolution. He suffered the Cap of Liberty to be received in his capital—Tippoo and Liberty!—and allowed himself to be called Citizen Tippoo. He was actively enlisting under his standard as many foreign adventurers as he could obtain, and, as subsequently transpired, had sent ambassadors to the French Governor of the Isle of France with overtures of alliance and a request for help. A similar letter had been sent to Bonaparte, who was then commencing his Egyptian campaign, which it was generally supposed would be followed up by an expedition to India.

We have seen what large forces were under the Mahratta princes, commanded by De Boigne, Perron and others, and now in Hyderabad Raymond was organizing a force which was in every way equal to theirs. If there had been anything like combination it seems difficult to understand how the British would have been able to withstand it. But it almost seems as if the hand of Providence was against the French, and that when success seemed to be almost within their grasp some unforeseen thing happened to shatter their hopes. In the midst of all his plans, and at the very height of his power and success, Raymond suddenly died on the 25th March, 1798, just six months previous to a crisis which proved one of the chief turning-points in the history of British influence in Hyderabad.

Raymond was succeeded by his next in command—a Fleming named Piron. This name is in some accounts of Hyderabad confused with that of Perron, the general in the Mahratta employ. Piron was however, a very different character, and had few of the qualities belonging to the man whose name resembled his. He had little of the tact of Raymond, and his influence over the troops under his command and over the Nizam was but very small. The Marquis of Wellesley had now arrived in India with the settled resolve to crush the power of Tipoo Sultan once for all.*

The Great Marquess, or as he was then called the Earl of Mornington, is one of the most prominent and brilliant characters in the history of the British Empire in India, over which he ruled for the next seven years. In the long voyage out he had ample time to reflect and resolve upon the policy he would pursue, and once resolved his was a masterful mind that would allow no obstacle to interfere with the attainment of the object he had in view. At the Cape of Good Hope, which was then largely used by officers on temporary sick-leave from India, he met Captain Kirkpatrick, who had come from the Hyderabad Residency to recruit his health, his place being in the meantime occupied by his brother, Captain Achilles Kirkpatrick. By him he was thoroughly posted up in the condition of affairs in the Deccan, and, in the Memorandum which the Governor-General elect drew up, his policy and the reasons for it are clearly laid down. In order the better to understand the events which were soon to follow in rapid succession, it will be as well to take a survey of the actual condition of India at the commencement of the year 1798.

* There is conclusive evidence that this was Lord Mornington's resolve before he landed ; at all events, that he expressed his intention so soon after his arrival that it is impossible to suppose that his words were not the result of a deliberately formed resolve. On the 17th May, 1799, after the fall of Seringapatam, Sir Alured Clarke wrote to Lord Mornington to congratulate him on the victory, and in a postscript to the letter, says, " I remember your observations of humbling Tippoo before the anniversary of your entering upon the duties of this Government, which took place precisely this day twelve months. (*Wellesley, Despatches*, Vol. I, p. 591).

The three great native powers at this period were Tippoo Sultan, the Nizam and the Mahrattas. They, occupied the whole of the territory from the Carnatic up to Delhi, with a long line of seaboard on the western coast extending from the north of Cochin up to Guzerat, excepting the Portuguese ports and the British dependency of Bombay. On the eastern coast the provinces of Cuttack and Orissa divided the Madras Presidency from Bengal and afforded an outlet to the sea. As regards the Carnatic it was almost entirely in the hands of the British. The Nawab, Mahomed Ali, was still the nominal ruler of the former portion of the Nizam's dominions, but he resided at Madras, and, though suspected of intriguing with Tippoo, he was practically under British influence. Of these three Powers Tippoo's was the one from which most danger was to be apprehended. For the last six years he had been carefully husbanding his resources and increasing the efficiency of his army. He was known to be waiting for an opportunity to recover the territory he had lost in 1792, and he looked upon the French as his natural allies, since they were the hereditary rivals of the English. Tippoo's possessions on the western coast gave him facilities for communicating with the French at the Isle of France, and as a matter of fact some 200 volunteers had recently landed on that coast from Mauritius and had been taken into his service.

The Nizam, although greatly reduced in power from what he had been fifty years before, was still in possession of an extensive kingdom, but with every year this power was being weakened, and the result of the battle of Khurdla had been to shake his kingdom to its very foundations. It seemed inevitable that, sooner or later, if left to himself, he must fall a victim either to the ambition of Tippoo or to the rapacity of the Mahrattas. Nizam Ali was now an old man, and, although he actually lived on for five years more, his decease was looked for daily. When that should take place a disputed succession was sure to follow and rival candidates were likely to be supported by Tippoo or by the Mahrattas. In the meantime, the growing power of the French contingent at Hyderabad was likely to prove an important factor in the coming struggle. If, as seemed likely, they should join hands with Tippoo, it was probable that they would prove irresistible and that the latter, openly joined by reinforcements of the French from Egypt, would become the predominating power in the south of the Peninsula.

The Mahrattas ruled over a more extensive territory than either of these two Princes, but their weakness lay in their mutual jealousies. The Peishwa at Poona was the nominal head, but the most powerful of the Mahratta princes was Scindia, who, as the protector of the blind old Emperor Shah Allum, and in possession of the enormous territories extending from Kandesh up to Delhi and Agra, was in a way representative of Imperial authority. Holkar ran Scindia close and both were anxious to make their influence at Poona paramount. The Bhonsla Rajah of Nagpur was the third great Mahratta power. He occupied the whole of the territory to the north of the Nizam's dominions, from Berar to the east coast at Cuttack. These Mahratta princes had all of them large armies with highly disciplined contingents officered for the most part by Frenchmen; so that here again came in the dangerous French influence, from which at that moment the school of English politicians, of which Pitt, Nelson and Wellesley were the representative spirits, feared so much. Every one of the Mahratta princes had large money claims upon the Nizam which they were ready to enforce by arms, and a general combination of their power would have been irresistible.

The policy which the new Governor-General had been instructed to uphold was the maintenance of the balance of power between the Native States as it stood in 1792 at the close of the first Mysore War. But this balance no longer existed, and had been materially altered by the Khurdla catastrophe. On the whole, it seemed likely that the Nizam, if left to himself, would have to apply to Tippoo for support, in which case that chief's power would become overwhelming. The Nizam's power had been greatly weakened; that of the Mahrattas had been increased *pro tanto*; Tippoo had recovered from the effects of the war of 1792, which he was burning to avenge; and a fresh element of danger had arisen from the French influence in Hyderabad, backed up by the mysterious, and therefore dreaded, ambition of the brilliant young French general, who had astonished Europe by his sudden descent upon Egypt.

The policy that Lord Mornington laid down to himself was first of all to dissolve the French contingent at Hyderabad and by substituting an English subsidiary force to prevent the Nizam from joining hands with Tippoo.*

Then the latter was to be called to account for his breach of friendly relations by his overtures to the

* There is nothing to show that Tippoo was ever afforded an opportunity of explaining his conduct, and there is a long minute of Lord Mornington in the Secret Department, dated 12th August, 1799 (reproduced by Wilks's " History of Mysore," Vol. II, Chap. LV), giving conclusive reasons why, since the overtures with the professed intention of exterminating the British, were an actual fact and constituted in themselves an act of hostility, there was no necessity to ask for an explanation of that which could not be explained; and that we were justified in making preparations for war without disclosing our knowledge. The whole minute is a most masterly production though we are not prepared to say that it is not open to objection.

French, and having crushed him by the Nizam's co-operation, together with that of the Mahrattas, to dispose of the remaining States separately. The method of dealing with them was to be the maintenance at each court of a British subsidiary force to the exclusion of the French, and by cutting the Native States off from the sea-coast to prevent them from having the power of affording a landing to a French army from over the sea.

The Nizam was, therefore, the first of the Native States that had to be dealt with, and as soon as the new Governor-General landed in Madras in May, 1798, on his way to Calcutta, he commenced to carry out his plans.

General Harris, then in charge of the Madras Government, was ordered to commence the collection of military stores, and to prepare a detachment of troops to be sent at a moment's notice to Hyderabad, and instructions were sent to the Resident to use every persuasion with the Nizam to disband the French troops. It had become a struggle for existence, and the presence of a large force entirely in French hands at the Nizam's court was likely to be a most dangerous element in the coming struggle. The minister, Azim-ul-Umrah, was a partisan of the English, and backed up the Resident's representation to the Nizam. The latter for some time was doubtful what to do; he was on the horns of a dilemma. On the one hand, he did not wish to throw the French trained troops over, for he would then be entirely dependent upon the English for support, but, on the other hand, he was afraid that, deprived of British support, he might be attacked by the Mahrattas, who were the enemies from whom he had most to fear, and could easily find ground for hostilities on account of their still unsettled claims, which amounted to about six crores of rupees. Finally, a compromise was arrived at. The Marquis, bolder than his predecessor, resolved to run the risk of offending the Mahrattas rather than allow a large force devoted to French interests to remain in Hyderabad, and accordingly he pledged himself to support the Nizam against any unjust demands of the Mahrattas, and to increase the British troops from two to six battalions. The Nizam thereupon engaged to disband the French corps, to deliver over the officers to the British Government as soon as the new British force should arrive, and to raise the subsidy which he paid for the maintenance of the British troops from Rs.57,713 to 201,425 a month. This treaty was signed on the 1st September, 1798.

"The way in which the disbandment was carried out was as follows : The French corps numbered 14,000 men, and it was necessary to take every precaution against the chance of resistance, so that nothing could be done until the arrival of the additional troops, which occurred on the 10th October. There was already a considerable feeling of discontent in the French corps. The rivalry to succeed to the deceased Raymond had produced a considerable amount of jealousy and animosity amongst the officers, whilst the men themselves were in a condition bordering on mutiny owing to large arrears of pay being due to them. Some of the men were absent on distant detachment duty, and altogether there were not more than 11,000 present at the headquarters in Hyderabad. After considerable difficulty, the reluctance of the Nizam to proceed to extreme measures was overcome, and the battalions of British, assisted by a strong body of the Nizam's horse, surrounded the lines of the French force, which was situated about two miles from Hyderabad, at the foot of the hill on which stands the house known as Asmangarh, near which is situated Raymond's tomb."

It is impossible to withhold a considerable amount of sympathy for the sufferers in this sudden dissolution and disbandment of a little army which had done such good service. It was dissolved not for any fault of its own, but in consequence of the exigencies of British policy, to which its existence was a menace and a danger. Kaye, in his life of Sir John Malcolm, who was employed as a principal actor in the final scene, says: "Viewed from the English side, the dissolution of the French corps was a masterpiece of policy. But the sympathies of our common humanity may yet be awakened in favour of the sufferers, when we contemplate the rending of all those ties which had bound the soldier and the officer together, and linked the united military body to the State. Doubtless, it was a necessity, but it was a cruel one. And, when the hour of parting arrived, it was not strange that there should have been a plentiful growth of subterfuge and evasion to delay the fulfilment of a stipulation so humiliating both to the French party and the Hyderabad court."

"The arrangements for the disbandment were carefully completed by the Resident, Kirkpatrick, and Major Malcolm. There were two brigades, one consisting of the two old battalions under Colonel Hyndman, and the other of the four regiments which had just arrived under Colonel Roberts. The former were moved up to attack the rear of the French camp; the latter were ready to advance upon its front. From such a disposition of the British forces there was no escape, and the French troops were completely at their mercy. In the meantime, the dissension in the French force had culminated in open mutiny. The officers, disunited and foreseeing the inevitable, had entered into negotiations with the Resident with the view of obtaining a safe conduct, which was promised them ; but the men, fearful of what might happen to them if they were abandoned by their officers, and clamorous for the pay due to them, rose in revolt and seized the persons of Piron and the other officers. When Malcolm reached the lines, the violence of the mutineers was at its height. In vain he endeavoured to make his way to the place where Piron was confined ; in vain he remonstrated ; in vain he endeavoured to persuade to men to suffer order to be restored to their ranks. They crowded tumultuously around him. They threatened to deal with him as they had dealt with their own officer. And doubtless, in the violence of their excitement, they would have fulfilled their threats ; but timely assistance was at hand. Among the crowd of the mutineers were some men who had formerly belonged to Malcolm's company in the 29th Battalion but had deserted to the French corps. They now recognized their old officer and went at once to his assistance. He had been kind to them in former days, and they had not forgotten his kindness. Lifting him up and bearing him away on their heads, they rescued him from the hands of the infuriated mob. Malcolm returned to the Residency and the mutiny continued to spread. It was an event to be welcomed, not to be deplored (though to the French officers concerned the position must have been an exceedingly unpleasant one). It was plain to the British diplomatists that it would render the dissolution of the corps comparatively easy. So measures were at once concerted for the accomplishment of disarming and dispersion of the disorganized mass. Early on the following day Colonel Roberts was instructed to draw up his detachment opposite the French lines and to summon the men to an unconditional surrender. If at the end of half an hour they had not complied with the demand, he was to attack them in front, and, as soon as Colonel Hyndman heard a shot fired, he was to open upon their rear. A party of 1,500 horse was placed under Malcolm, who was ordered to occupy their right flank and prevent escape in that direction, whilst Captain Green with another party of 500 horse occupied the left. Some time before Roberts's force came up Malcolm had reached his ground. The first French sepoys whom he met—a small party of deserters—fearing an immediate attack upon their camp, were in an extreme state of alarm. He exerted himself to allay their fears. He told them that if they fulfilled the required conditions no violence would be offered to them, and despatched them into the lines to give assurance of protection to their comrades. A deputation of subadars—native officers—came out to him and declared that they were ready to do anything that was ordered. On this he advanced into the lines. He found the whole body of sepoys panic-struck as were those whom he had first met. They had released their officers and were now disciplined and subdued by an overwhelming sense of their common danger. Malcolm assured them that if they laid down their arms in peace they would be protected by the British troops. They promised their prompt submission. The only condition which they urged upon the British officer was that the lines should be placed in the possession of the Company's troops, and not given up to the destructive plunder of the Mogul horse. Having reported to Colonel Roberts the favourable aspect of affairs, Malcolm drew up his detachment on the heights fronting the French lines. There he was speedily joined by the European officers of the French corps, elated with joy at their escape from the hands of their infuriated soldiery, and actually, in the conjecture that had arisen, regarding the English as friends and deliverers. The rest was soon accomplished. The sepoys left their guns, laid down their arms, and in the presence of the two lines of British troops moved off in a deep column to a flag planted on the right of their ground, followed by their wives and carrying their property with them. Not a shot was fired, not a drop of blood was shed. Eleven or twelve thousand men were thus dispersed in a few hours; and before sunset their whole cantonments with all their storehouses, arsenals, gun foundries and powder mills were completely in our possession. The celebrated French Corps of Hyderabad had passed into a tradition." (Kaye: "Life of Sir John Malcolm," Vol. I, p. 72.)

It was impossible to overestimate the importance of this event and its bearing upon the history of Hyderabad, and, indeed, of India. By the disbandment of the French corps the Nizam showed to the rest of India that he definitely decided to trust to the British alliance, and had, for good or for evil, resolved to throw in his lot with theirs, to trust to their protection and to be guided by their advice. The incident when it became known created a profound sensation throughout the Native States of India, and the immediate results were not long in revealing themselves.

CHAPTER IX

THE MYSORE WAR

THE disbandment of the French contingent at Hyderabad having been successfully carried out, everything was ready for the war with Tippoo. Bajee Row, the Peshwa, had promised his assistance, which indeed the Peshwa, as one of the signatories of the Tripartite Treaty of 1790, was bound to render, but, though a body of English troops was especially told off to co-operate with the Mahratta contingent, he rendered no actual assistance in the conduct of the war. The fact is that Bajee Row had no idea that Tippoo would be so easily conquered. He expected that the hostilities would be prolonged as had been the case in the former war, and that their result would be doubtful, and he therefore waited to see which side he should ultimately support. Indeed, at the very time that the siege of Seringapatam was proceeding, the Peishwa was entertaining Tippoo's ambassadors at Poona, with whom he was negotiating and had actually received from them no less than 13 lakhs of rupees purporting to be arrears on account of *chouth*. He was also negotiating with the Bhounsla Rajah of Nagpur with the intention, should the British arms suffer a reverse, of attacking the Nizam; but events were too rapid for him. No sooner had the French contingent been disbanded than the whole of the British force in Hyderabad, consisting of 6,500 men, with an equal number of the Nizam's army, marched towards Mysore, and joined the main army under General Harris at Vellore.

The force from Hyderabad consisted of the subsidiary troops under Colonel Roberts and Hyndman, and the Nizam's troops under Meer Allum. This portion of the allied army arrived at Chittoor, near the Mysore frontier, in advance of the main army, and here it was joined by Major Malcolm, who accompanied the Nizam's troops as Political Agent, and was of great service in preserving discipline and order on account of his personal influence. There was still a number of the French sepoys in the ranks of Meer Allum's regiments who were in a state of disorder, but Meer Allum delegated his authority to Malcolm, who, aided by the subsidiary troops, soon overawed and persuaded them into obedience, and subsequently the regiment contributed greatly to the success of the campaign. Meer Allum was so delighted with the success of his old friend Malcolm that he insisted upon his taking command of the entire infantry force. A European regiment, the 33rd, was attached to the subsidiary and Nizam's contingent, and the colonel of the regiment was—Colonel Roberts having expressed a wish to be relieved—appointed to command the whole of the Nizam's division. This colonel was Arthur Wellesley, brother of the Governor-General and eventually Duke of Wellington. Major Briggs says: "It was this circumstance (the relationship to the Governor-General) that rendered the appointment so acceptable to Meer Allum and so flattering to the Nizam that history may well afford to sink the question of military seniority which it involved."

Lord Mornington had himself come down from Calcutta to Madras to superintend the preliminaries in person; and Tiopoo, having refused to entertain the ambassadors whom the Governor-General proposed to send, war was declared. A second British army advanced from the western coast, and the two armies met and besieged Seringapatam, into which fortress, after a feeble resistance in the field, Tippoo had thrown himself. Nor did the siege itself last long. The preparations for a general assault were soon ready, it was delivered, and Tippoo himself fell, fighting bravely in the breach (1799). With him fell the Mahomedan rule in Mysore, and nothing now remained but a division of the spoil between the allies. Instead of wiping out the Mysore State entirely, in which case the Nizam would have been entitled to one half of the conquered dominions, it was deemed more politic to reconstitute the State. The central portion was made over to the descendant of the Hindu Rajah, whom Hyder Ali, Tippoo's father, had displaced, and the remainder was divided between the allies. The whole of Tippoo's revenue was estimated at ten crores of rupees, or 3,040,000 pagodas (the pagoda being reckoned at Rs. $3\frac{1}{2}$), and the following is the division as given by Grant Duff (*History of the Mahrattas*, Vol. II, Chap. 16):

To the new Rajah	1,360,000 pagodas
„ Nizam	530,000 „
„ British	537,000 „
For the maintenance of Hyder's and Tippoo's families	240,000 „
For Kummer-ud-Din	70,000 „
	2,737,000 (Rs. 9,446,000)

This left a balance of 263,000 pagodas, which was reserved for the Peishwa, for, although he had totally failed to carry out his engagement, it was deemed politic to allow him some share in the conquered territory. But this offer the Peishwa was unable to accept or refuse. It was by no means adequate to the share he would have received had he taken a part in the war. This no doubt was another reason for the resuscitation of the Mysore kingdom under a Hindu Rajah. As things turned out, to have divided the kingdom entirely between the Nizam and the British, as the two allies really concerned, would have had the effect of dangerously increasing the power of the former. By keeping a portion for the new Rajah, the shares of the new allies were naturally reduced, and rendered possible an arrangement to which we shall presently allude.* Had it been necessary to give to the Peishwa an equal third share of the conquered province, it is probable that the Mysore Kingdom would not have been reconstituted, or only on a very insignificant scale. But to the acceptance of this reduced share were attached conditions which were distasteful to the Peishwa. One of these was the establishment of a British Subsidiary Force to be stationed at Poona—ostensibly for the protection of the Peishwa against his powerful and dangerous vassals, Scindia and Holkar, but in reality in pursuance of the policy of Lord Mornington (afterwards Marquis Wellesley), to which allusion has already been made, namely, to build up the British Empire by means of British troops stationed in the Native States and maintained from the revenues of those States. The policy was in reality a development of that of Dupleix and Bussy, but Lord Wellesley was the first English statesman to recognize its great possibilities. To this condition the Peishwa was not personally

---

* That this was the real reason for the restoration of the Hindu Rajah, and not a sentiment of generosity, is clear from the Governor-General's despatch to the Secret Committee. (*Wellesley*, Despatches, Vol. I.).

averse; but he was afraid if he accepted it of incurring the resentment of his great chiefs. The second condition was that the British should arbitrate in all matters in dispute between the Nizam and the Peishwa. This condition, however, Bajee Row absolutely rejected, with the consequence that negotiations were broken off and two-thirds of the reserved revenue were given to the Nizam, whilst one-third was retained by the British. This therefore was the condition of affairs in the last year of the eighteenth century. This great enemy of the British power in South India had been annihilated. In the Deccan, the Nizam had become their devoted ally, dependent upon them for support against his chief enemies, the Mahrattas, who in their turn were disunited. Their rule still extended from Delhi to Poona, but the house was a divided one and therefore doomed to ruin. From Hyderabad to Cape Comorin British influence was now supreme.

But in order to make this influence permanent one thing more was needed. It was necessary to render impossible the recurrence of a hostile force such as Raymond's in the midst of the British sphere of influence, and accordingly in 1800 a new treaty was drawn up. It will be as well here to give a *résumé* of all the previous treaty arrangements so as to show at a glance the progressive nature of the relations between the Nizam and the British.

The first treaty was in 1759 (14th May), after the battle of Condore and the capture of Masulipatam from the French. The result of this war was that the power of the French on the east coast was broken. But it will be remembered that the Nizam Salabut Jung had given to Bussy the tribute hitherto paid by the east coast Rajahs, of whom Vizianagaram was the chief, in return for his undertaking to maintain the French contingent, the history of which appeared in a previous chapter. Under this treaty all the east coast districts were given to the English Company as an *inam* or free gift in the same manner as was done to the French. The Nizam (or Nawab as he is styled) undertook to compel the French troops to retire south of his dominions, and not to allow them to make a settlement in his country " on no account whatever, nor keep them in his service, nor assist them, nor call them to his assistance." The Vizianagaram Rajah was to continue to pay the same tribute to the Nizam as he had done before the time of the French, and all that the Company promised to do was not to assist the Nizam's enemies, nor to give them any protection.

The next treaty was in 1766 (12th November) and was executed between the Nizam and General Calliaud. In it the free gift of the five eastern Circars of Ellore, Chicacole, Rajahmundry, Mustaphanagar, and Murtezanagar was confirmed. In return the English engaged not only to keep a body of troops (number not specified) to settle the affairs of His Highness " in everything that is right and proper," but they also engaged to pay a tribute for the Circars of nine lakhs of rupees, namely, five for the three Circars of Rajahmundry, Ellore and Mustaphanagar, and two each for Chicacole and Murtezanagar when they should be put in their possession. Chicacole was to be given as soon as possible, but Murtezanagar (otherwise known as Guntoor) was to be allowed to continue in the possession of the Nizam's brother, Basalut Jung, during the Nizam's pleasure, or until the brother's death. As regards the payment of the troops to be maintained by the English, it was arranged that it should be made out of the five lakhs of tribute to be paid for the three Circars above mentioned, the Company to be answerable to the Nizam for any surplus, but in case of any excess to be themselves answerable. The same agreement in like manner was to hold good for the sums to be paid for the other two Circars, when settled. In case the troops of the Company should not be wanted, the tribute was to be paid each year in three instalments. The Nizam also bound himself to help the English with his troops under the same conditions, should occasion arise.

At the time of this treaty, the Nizam does not seem to have been aware that in the previous year the English had obtained a firman or *sunnad* from the Emperor Shah Allum, for the same five Circars as an *inam* or free gift. This, as has been shown in a previous chapter, was one of the reasons of the Nizam's temporary estrangement from the English, and of his alliance with the French, and in February, 1768, another treaty was entered into between Nizam Ali and the Company. This treaty is practically a confirmation of the previous treaty of 1766, but in it the gift from the Emperor is recited and an additional provision is made for the recognition by the contracting parties of the Nawab of the Carnatic, Wallah Jah. This appears to have been the first occasion on which the Nizam publicly recognized the Nawab of the Carnatic as an independent Power, and renounced all claim to any authority over the Carnatic for the future. In this treaty the number of troops that the English were bound to furnish was fixed at two battalions of sepoys, with artillery, officered by Europeans, and a further provision of mutual alliance and defence was made between the three parties—the Company, the Nizam, and the Nawab of the Carnatic. A further provision was

THE MYSORE WAR

also made that the English should take from Hyder Ali the district of the Carnatic Balaghat, and, in consideration of the Nizam relinquishing all his claim to the district, that the Company should pay him a tribute of seven lakhs of rupees. This latter provision, however, was never carried out, for soon afterwards the Company made peace.

In 1799 a treaty was made with the Nizam's brother, Basalut Jung. regarding the Circar of Murtezanagar, or Guntoor. This treaty gave very great offence to the Nizam, but need not be further alluded to, as it does not seem to have been acted upon; and eventually, in 1788, Basalut Jung having died, the district was handed over to the British in pursuance of the former treaties of 1766 and 1768.

The next agreement which we find is in the form of a letter from Lord Cornwallis to the Nizam, written on the 7th July, 1789, which was subsequently confirmed by the House of Commons and declared to be equal to a treaty. This letter was written immediately before the first war with Tippoo and recapitulates and confirms the previous arrangements. It begins by expressing the Governor-General's satisfaction that the Guntoor District had been handed over, goes on to specify that the number of British troops to be sent " whenever His Highness shall apply for them " shall consist of two battalions of sepoys of not less than 800 men each, and six pieces of cannon manned by Europeans, provided, however, that the troops are not to be employed against any of the Powers in alliance with the British, namely, the Peishwa and other Mahratta chiefs, the Nawab of Arcot (Carnatic) and the Rajahs of Tanjore and Travancore. The troops, however, when wanted, were to be paid for by the Nizam, and it does not appear that the cession of the Circars involved any obligation to maintain troops; in fact, the cession was one of sovereignty only, and the Company paid for the district a tribute of nine lakhs of rupees. In this respect, therefore, the Company's possession of the Circars was different from that of Bussy, who held them free of any tribute, in return for which he had to pay for his contingent out of the revenue.

The former stipulation about the Balaghat was confirmed in his letter, but was to take effect only if the existing peace with Hyder should be broken. This letter was written after the despatch of Meer Allum (Abool Cassim, as he is called) to Calcutta, where he personally conducted the negotiations with the Governor-General. These negotiations led to the treaty of 1790 between the three allies who were to take part in the war which was then impending—the British, the Nizam, and the Mahrattas. The allies agreed to furnish 25,000 infantry, and, if required, 10,000 horse to co-operate with the British army. If the horse were required they were to be paid for, but no stipulation was made regarding the payment of the infantry. It was, however, provided that any territory conquered should be equally divided between all the allies.

Then followed the war with Tippoo, in which the latter was compelled to sue for peace. This was granted by the treaty of Seringapatam (1792), under which certain districts were ceded, of which as his share the Nizam received Kurnool and Cuddapah, altogether about 30 lakhs annually.

Subsequent to this treaty occurred the enrolment of the French contingent under Raymond, the war with the Mahrattas ending with the battle of Kurdla, and the disbandment of the French contingent. Before, how-

THE MYSORE WAR

ever, this last event took place, another treaty, already alluded to, was arranged in 1798, in which it was agreed that the British should furnish a subsidiary force of not less than 6,000 men, including the existing two battalions, with artillery, at an annual cost of twenty-four and a half lakhs by instalments. In the event of there being any deficiency, the British were authorized to deduct the same from the tribute or *peshkash* paid on the Circars. This force was to be a permanent one but was not to be employed for the purposes of *sebundy* or collecting revenue. The British also agreed to contribute in the event of any dispute with the Mahrattas, and to uphold the Nizam in all that was right and proper.

We have seen how the disbandment of the French Contingent took place, and immediately afterwards occurred the second war with Tippoo, which ended in his defeat and death. Thereupon followed the treaty of 1800, in which the conquered territory was divided, the Nizam receiving as his share districts worth 19 or 20 lakhs of rupees, and subsequently, as the Peishwa declined to accept the position allotted to him, two-thirds of the Peishwa's share aggregating about five lakhs of rupees. This was therefore the condition of affairs when it was deemed necessary to place the subsidiary force at Hyderabad on a permanent footing, and to form a still closer alliance with the Nizam, both offensive and defensive, so that, in the words of the treaty, the affairs of the two nations should be considered as " one and the same in interest, policy, friendship and honour." Under this treaty the British agreed to add to the already existing subsidiary force in perpetuity two battalions of sepoys of 1,000 each, a regiment of cavalry 500 strong, and a due proportion of guns and artillerymen, so that the whole force should consist of 8,000 firelocks, two regiments of cavalry (or 1,000 horse), with the requisite artillery fully equipped, to be stationed in His Highness's territories. Roughly speaking, to judge from the former treaties, the cost of a regiment of foot 1,000 strong, or of cavalry 500 strong, together with the necessary artillery, appears to have been reckoned at one lakh of rupees annually, so that the total cost of this army of eight-thousand foot and one thousand horse may be calculated at nine lakhs of rupees monthly. In order to provide for the punctual payment of these troops, the Nizam ceded in perpetuity the whole of the districts which he had received as his share of the two wars with Tippoo. These districts were valued at about 73 lakhs of rupees, but the Company expressly undertook to bear any loss until they could be made to yield more.

As a matter of fact, it is doubtful whether there ever was a loss, and in a very short time they yielded considerably more than the cost of the subsidiary force. At the present time they yield from 180 to 200 lakhs annually, and consist of the four important districts in the Madras Presidency known as Bellary, Anantapore, Cuddapah and Kurnool. The Nizam on his part expressly refused to pay any possible increase, and so a complete payment in advance was made for the subsidiary force in perpetuity; in the words of the Treaty (Art. 8), " the cession of the districts shall be considered as a final close and termination of accounts between the contracting parties with respect to the charges of the said subsidiary force."

In the event of war, the Nizam agreed to support the above force with not less than an equal number of infantry and 9,000 cavalry, so as to form an army of a strength of 12,000 infantry (two battalions of the infantry being reserved for the defence of His Highness's person) and 10,000 horse, and to furnish as many more as he possibly could, a similar obligation resting upon the Company.* Certain other articles are also of importance. The Nizam undertook not to enter into negotiations with any other Power without consulting the Company, to commit no act of hostility against any Power whatever, and to submit all differences to the Company's Government for adjustment (Arts. 15 and 16); and in their turn the Company declared that they had no manner of concern " with any of His Highness's children, relations subjects or servants, with respect to whom His will is absolute."

As regards the payment of the subsidiary force, it was arranged that if the Zemindars of Shorapoor or Gudwal or any other subjects or dependents of His Highness's Government should withhold payment or excite rebellion, the whole force, or a portion of it, should be ready— in concert with the Nizam's own troops—to reduce such offenders to obedience. This clause appears to be in supersession of the clause in the former Treaty of 1798, where it was stipulated that the force should not be used as *sebundy*, or for collecting revenue. This is a point of some importance, and should be borne in mind.

It will be at once seen that this treaty is a very important advance in the policy which the great Marquis had resolved upon. Under the former treaties there was an alliance, and we undertook to furnish troops for which the Nizam had to pay. No permanent cession of territory was made to provide for the payment of these troops. The British still had to pay the stipulated tribute for the districts held by them, although they were authorized to treat that tribute as a security from

---

* Particular attention is drawn to this clause because it subsequently formed a ground for the establishment and maintenance of the Hyderabad Contingent.

which to provide for the payment of these troops. Under the earlier treaties the British were only required to furnish a stipulated number of troops when required by the Nizam, who could dispense with them when he liked, and it was only whilst they were actually employed in his dominions that he was liable to pay for them, and when withdrawn from his service the tribute had to be paid untouched. Under the treaty of 1790, a small force of two battalions was provided for, but even this was not permanent, for the Nizam, could as we have seen he did after the Kurdla campaign, actually dispense with them. In 1798 this Subsidiary Force was largely increased and made permanent, but still no arrangements were made for their pay by the assignment of territory. Although there can be no doubt that this was the ultimate end of the Governor-General's policy, he scarcely dared take so important a step. But, as soon as the Mysore War was ended and the division of the conquered territory had taken place, he commenced preparing the ground for this the basis of his policy. On the 6th November, 1799, a secret despatch was sent to the Resident (Captain J. A. Kirkpatrick), in which the outlines of a new treaty were sketched, under which the Subsidiary Force was to be increased by 2,000 men and a permanent provision to be made for their payment in perpetuity by an assignment of the whole of the districts, given to the Nizam as his share of the Mysore conquest. But the Resident was specially enjoined not to approach the Nizam on the subject at once, but to wait until his decease should appear to be imminent and then to make the execution of this treaty a condition of our placing his son, Secunder Jah, on the throne. This point is not alluded to in any of these histories, and it will therefore be as well to give chapter and verse for the statement.

Allusion having been made to the state of the Nizam's health, and the reason which would induce the Governor-General to support the succession of Secunder Jah in preference to the other princes, the despatch goes on to say:

"No obligation of treaty binds us to take part in any contested succession, arising either from the total silence of the Nizam respecting his intended successor, or from a disputable declaration of His Highness's intentions on the subject. Even in the case of an unequivocal nomination of a successor to His Highness, we should not be bound by the treaty of September, 1798, or by any other obligation to support that successor against any rival whose cause might be espoused by the Mahrattas."

. . . "Having stated the general principles which should govern our conduct in the conjunction under contemplation, I shall proceed to furnish you with an outline of the particular conditions on which I am willing to support the succession of Secunder Jah against all competition." Then follow the various provisions as subsequently embodied in the treaty, and the despatch continues: "Such is the outline of the terms upon which I propose to support and maintain the succession of Secunder Jah, *whether he would obtain the previous nomination of his father or not, or even if it should be pretended that His Highness had declared in favour of some other of his sons.* You will prepare without delay an instrument in the Persian language in conformity to the foregoing outline, in order that Secunder Jah (*at the moment of his father's death,* or when that event shall appear to approach) may be apprised of the terms on which we are ready to support his cause and may be enabled, by immediately executing a formal instrument, to accede to my propositions in a regular manner. . . . Secunder Jah must not be allowed to procrastinate his determination. *If at the end of a stated and short period he should not determine to accept the proferred Treaty, you will proceed in concert with Azim-ul-Omrah and Meer Allum to place one of the younger sons of the Nizam on the Musnud,* previously stipulating that the Prince succeeding to the Musnud shall fulfil all the conditions of the Treaty proposed to Secunder Jah."

Here is to be seen the mailed fist of the masterful Marquis, but the strange thing is that it is impossible to state from the materials available how the consent to the treaty was actually obtained. Nizam Ali did not die until 1803, but the treaty itself, as it appears in the official record, purports to have been concluded with Nizam Ali, and bears date the 12th October, 1800, and there is no letter from the Resident explaining what were the reasons that led him to depart from the secret instructions contained in this despatch. The foregoing extract is taken from *Wellesley's Despatches, Vol. II,* and the instructions were subsequently confirmed by the Governor-General's despatch to the Secret Committee of the Board of Directors, dated 25th January, 1800. This apparent alteration in Lord Wellesley's original intention is the more remarkable because the despatch of Captain Kirkpatrick goes on to say that, " although the objects proposed might be obtained from Secunder Jah with less difficulty previously to the death of the Nizam and that it would on that account be desirable that a negotiation should be opened immediately with Secunder Jah, there are many objections which occur to determine from such step. The attempt (if it should transpire either by accident or design) would probably lead to mischievous consequences; I am therefore of opinion that no such an attempt should be hazarded until the Nizam shall be at the point of death."

The position of the Nizam at the commencement of the nineteenth century was therefore very different to what it had been on the death of Asaf Jah in 1748, which may be summarized as follows. At the death of Asaf Jah the Nizam's authority nominally extended over the whole of Southern India as far as Trichinopoly and Tanjore. Now everything was changed. The result of the war between the French and the English had brought about the independence of Mohamed Ali as the Nawab of the Carnatic, and Hyder Ali was able to extend the Mysore Kingdom from the western coast to the banks of the Tungabudra. Towards the south and the west the Mahrattas made considerable encroachments in the direction of the Doab and Aurungabad. The Province of Malwa was lost to the Mahratta Chief, Scindia, and the greater part of Berar was in the possession of the Nagpur Rajah, whilst Khandesh had long since been ceded to the Mahrattas by Salabut Jung. On the east the coast zemindars no longer owed him allegiance, and, though he still continued to receive tribute or *peshkash* for these districts, it was paid by the British, who exercised all the rights of sovereignty which had previously been held by the Nizam without, as far as these districts were concerned, being bound to render any military assistance. Between 1750 and 1790 the Nizam's dominions had been enormously reduced in extent. The area over which he exercised sovereign rights was not so large as the present kingdom of Hyderabad, and over a great portion of this the Mahrattas levied *chouth*. After the first siege of Seringapatam in 1791 the result of the British alliance was a considerable accession of territory, but the Kurdla campaign showed that the Hyderabad State was unable to stand against the Mahrattas, and it was probably only owing to the dissensions amongst the Mahrattas themselves that the Nizam's power was not entirely crushed. The result of the second siege of Seringapatam was a further accession of territory, the whole of which, however, was ceded by the Treaty of 1800, except the portion between the rivers Krishna and Tungabudra. But in return for this cession the Nizam received the whole of the moral and material support of the British Subsidiary alliance. As long as British power remained paramount in India the Nizam was rendered safe from any outside attack and was greatly relieved from the burden of maintaining a large army. He was not entirely relieved, for he was bound under the treaty in case of war to co-operate with an army of not less than 6,000 foot and 9,000 horse, but compared with the enormous hordes maintained by Asaf Jah this was a comparative trifle. On the whole, though greatly reduced in size from what it had been fifty years before, the Nizam's dominions in 1800 were more consolidated and much safer from attack than they had been only a few years previously. The crisis in his affairs which seemed to have set in after the disaster at Kurdla had, thanks to the British Alliance, been successfully passed. There now only remained the Mahrattas to be dealt with in order to ensure to the Nizam complete safety for the future and in the next chapter we shall see how this danger was successfully averted.

CHAPTER X

THE MAHRATTA KINGDOM

THE sudden collapse of Mysore took the Peshwa and the Mahratta princes by surprise. At the moment a small force was sent out to co-operate, but it had scarcely crossed the Mysore frontier before Seringapatam had fallen and the war was over. The Peshwa had hoped that by waiting he might have secured to himself a better share of the spoil, but he waited a little bit too long and in the end overreached himself. Strictly speaking, as he had rendered no assistance worth speaking of, he was not entitled to any share of the conquered country, but a small portion was reserved for him of districts on both sides of the Tungabudra valued at about six lakhs of rupees annually, but coupled with them a stipulation was made that all matters of difference between the Peishwa and the Nizam should be submitted for the arbitration of the British and that he should receive a subsidiary force at his court on the same terms as the Nizam. To this stipulation he would not consent and the result was, as we have seen, that two-thirds of the Peshwa's share were given to the Nizam and one-third to the British. Under this arrangement, the Nizam received some increase apart from that portion which, after having been allotted to him, was subsequently

reassigned in payment of the Subsidiary Force, as related in the last chapter. This portion consists of the tract of country known as the Doab lying between the rivers Kishtna and the Tungabudra, the latter formed the natural boundary between the Nizam's and the Company's territories. In this way the last vestige of the ancient kingdom of Vijayanagar, which played so prominent a part in the early history of the Deccan, was cut in half. A descendant of the old royal family was still in possession of what had now dwindled down to a small zemindari, but the site of the old capital on the south bank of the river had for many years been deserted and the zemindar lived at Anaigoondy, a suburb of Vijayanagar, situated on the north bank.* The Rajah of Anaigoondy, as he is still called, thus became a subject of both states, holding lands on both sides of the river. The last Rajah died without any issue in 1886 and his widow subsequently adopted a boy, but the adoption was not recognized by the British Government, and the estate in British territory, together with the political pension paid to the family, was escheated. The Nizam's Government, however, more liberal to the last representative of their old enemy, recognized the adopted son and allowed him to remain in possession of his diminished estate. The present Rajah still lives in Anaigoondy, but in sadly reduced circumstances, his net income amounting to no more than about Rs. 20,000 per annum.

We must, however, return to the Mahrattas and to the position of affairs after the fall of Seringapatam. It will not be within the scope of this work to deal with Mahratta

---

* The Anaigoondy State is mentioned in the first Tripartite Treaty of 1788, between the British, the Nizam, and the Mahrattas, as one of those states which had been wrongfully annexed by Tippoo and which it was the object of the allies to recover. Practically, however, the Rajah cannot be said to have benefited by the result of the two campaigns.

affairs, except in so far as they are connected with those of Hyderabad, and they are therefore only alluded to in respect to that connection and not with the detailed accuracy which they would otherwise deserve. But, in order that the reader may properly understand the actual condition of India at the period at which we have now arrived, it is necessary to dwell somewhat more at length on the relative position of the different princes.

We have hitherto spoken of the English almost entirely with reference to their connection with the Nizam, which, indeed is the main object of this work; but it must be remembered that until very recently the English by no means occupied the prominent position in Central and South Indian affairs that one is apt to suppose. Until after the first Mysore War, their territory was confined to the Northern Circars and the extreme south of the peninsula. A very large portion of the Carnatic was still in the possession of the Nawab Mahomed Ali, and the remainder of South India, up to the Taptee and Godavery river, was divided between Mysore, the Nizam, and the Mahrattas. During the last decade of the 18th century, the Mahratta power extended enormously. The principal chiefs were Mahadoji Scindia, Tukaji Holkar, Bhonsla Rajah of Nagpur, and the Gaikwar of Baroda whilst the whole Mahratta sphere of influence extended from the source of the Krishtna in the South to Delhi and Agra in the North; and from Guzerat in the West, across India to Cuttack in the East. It is true that they all professed allegiance to the Peishwa at Poona and their conquests were nominally in his name. Scindia and Holkar shared between them the great province of Malwa, north of the Taptee, the former having his capital at Ujain, and the latter at Indore. It is impossible on a map to give anything like an accurate outline of their boundaries, for they were changing with each year. Scindia was by far the most powerful of the three princes, and his authority extended right up to Delhi and over the Doab or country between the Ganges and the Jumna. He was the custodian of the blind Emperor Shah Allam, and in his name he exercised imperial power, whilst the Emperor himself was kept in a state of miserable indigence. *

Scindia thus exercised a predominant influence over the enormous tract of country stretching from the Tapti up to the Sutlej, bounded on the west by the Sikh Kingdom of the Punjab and on the east by the Kingdom of Oudh, which still intervened as a buffer separating him from the English possessions in Bengal. The whole comprised, besides what is known as Hindustan, the whole of Central India and Rajpootana, including, it is

* The following letter written by a friend of Scindia, General de Boigne, conveys about the best description of the miserable state of the descendant of the great House of Timur. It is quoted by Herbert Compton (*Military Adventurers of Hindustan*, page 83): "Scindia sets Shah Nizam-ud-Din (known, as the 'Cowrie Father' from having been a Fakeer), over the Badshah, as the greatest scoundrel they could find. He does not give a farthing of money to the Badshah, or any of his people, affecting to console the poor old king that it is all the better for him, as no temptation can remain for another Goolam Kadir to seize upon him for the sake of plunder. Regularly every day he furnishes the old king with 2 seers (4lb.) of polao and eight seers of meat for himself to get cooked as he likes. This, with two loaves of bread, about the length each of a cubit, to suffice for breakfast, dinner, and supper, and he may get *masala* (spices and condiments) where he can. This, however, though it is to serve five persons, and the poor servants who can pick at it a bit afterwards, is living in clover in comparison with the rest of the royal household. They, poor creatures, without distinction, princes and princesses, nay queens, and old eunuchs and female slaves, have exactly delivered out to them to bake into cakes two seers a day of barley flour for every three of them, which they are to bake for themselves, and are thus afforded two-thirds of a seer of food a day. For liquors, from the king to the turnspit, they have nothing but water. The king's quincuncial party at dinner every day is made up of himself and his doctor, his son and heir, and a little favourite daughter, and the mighty boon of being one at this fine extra fare is fairly allotted to his 200 Begums one after another in turn; so that of the poor queens each has a prospect of what to them, after their miserable fare, must be a high treat indeed, a dinner and a half a year! I asked if the old gentleman would not wish to regale himself with beef now and then? Yes, he longs for it, but where is he to get it? The servants often apply in great misery to the unfeeling father (Nizam-ud-Din) for a little wages, when, after having been three or four months without a farthing, he will perhaps only bestow on them three or four annas, on another perhaps as much as eight annas. The old Nizam (of Hyderabad) sent the king, six years ago, 6,000 gold mohurs. Then every farthing got into Cowrie Father's hands, and remained there."

THE MAHRATTA KINGDOM

true, a large number of independent states, all of which were, however, more or less in subjection to him as lieutenant of the Emperor. It comprised also the State of Holkar, with whom he was constantly at war ; and if it had not been for the rivalry of these two chieftains, whose principal amusement seemed to lie in their sacking each other's capitals and raiding their respective territories, the map of India might have been different from what it is now. But the supremacy undoubtedly lay with Scindia, which was due to the large disciplined army maintained by De Boigne, the great French adventurer, who rose from the position of a common sailor to be almost the absolute ruler of a province nearly as large as his native country, France. De Boigne had a thoroughly efficient army of 40,000 men of all arms, officered by Europeans, and carefully drilled and disciplined ; and it was by means of this army that the great Mahadoji Scindia had acquired his predominance over other princes of India. Practically, Scindia was master of the whole country from Khandesh to Agra, extending over the principal portion of the province of Malwa and the Doab. The south eastern portion of this province was in possession of his rival Takoji Holkar, who had also a European-officered force which had been enlisted and trained subsequent to that of Scindia and was by no means so efficient. Holkar depended for the most part upon his cavalry, and he and the Nagpur Rajah, his neighbour to the south, were in the habit of extending their raids as far as Calcutta itself, of which, until just before the time of which we are treating, the existence of the " Maratha Ditch " was a standing proof. We have now arrived at 1800. Mahadoji Scindia and Takoji Holkar had both died very recently, De Boigne had retired and had been followed by Perron, Dowlut

Row Scindia had succeeded to Musnad of the Mahadoji, and Jeswunt Row (of illegitimate birth) to that of Holkar. Both of these princes were young men : the former was devoted to pleasure and dissipation, and the latter, a headstrong passionate man, was ambitious in the extreme and desirous of making himself supreme at Poona. The Peshwa himself was more or less in the hands of one or other of these great chiefs, but his minister Nana Furnavis, who is known as the Machiavelli of India, managed with extreme adroitness to steer a safe course between the two. Nana, however, also died in 1801, and with him disappeared all moderation from the Mahratta councils. It will be remembered that the Peshwa, Baji Row, acting under Nana's advice, had refused to receive the subsidiary force offered by Lord Wellesley as one of the conditions of participating in the division of the territory conquered from Mysore. After that war was over, one of the Mysore chiefs, Dhundia Vagh, refused to submit, and was followed by British detachments under Wellesley and Stevenson, until after a nine months' campaign he was at last defeated and killed at Kondgal (September, 1799), in the extreme south of the Nizam's territory, and for some time afterwards Colonel Wellesley remained in the vicinity of the Peshwa's country engaged in settling the districts recently conquered from Tippoo, whilst Colonel Stevenson was placed in command of the Nizam's subsidiary force. When Nana Furnavis died, Scindia was engaged in the northern dominions, and Jeswunt Row Holkar marched to Poona with an army determined to achieve an ascendancy in the Peishwa's councils. After some negotiations and an attempt to gain possession of the person of Baji Row, the Peshwa, the battle of Poona was fought, and, Holkar being victorious, the Peshwa fled to Bassein, where he sought protection from the

British. This was promised but only on the former condition that he would agree to entertain a British Subsidiary Force on conditions similar to those which had been accepted by the Nizam and should accept British arbitration in all disputes with that prince. This was the origin of the Treaty of Bassein (31st December, 1802), and the Peshwa was led back to his capital and installed on the *musnad* by Colonel Wellesley, who, at the head of the Mahratta Subsidiary Force, was able in a short time to reduce the refractory chiefs to obedience.

But the Treaty of Bassein was entirely opposed to the policy of the other Mahratta chiefs, and they regarded the interference of the British in Mahratta affairs with the greatest jealousy. Scindia and the Nagpur Rajah—who at this time was generally known as the Rajah of Berar, in which province he exercised a predominant influence, although nominally a great portion was still under the sovereignty of the Nizam—met together some fifty miles south of the Taptee in the Berar province. From a despatch of Lord Wellesley's it appears that the first intimation of their hostile intentions was given by the Nizam's agent who resided at Scindia's court, and measures were at once adopted by the Governor-General to meet any possible combination. As had been the case in the Mysore War, those measures were of a most complete character. Colonel Arthur Wellesley (afterwards the Duke of Wellington) was instructed to advance with the troops under his command, together with the Mahratta Subsidiary Force from Poona; Colonel Stevenson with the Hyderabad Subsidiary Force and the Nizam's troops acting in conjunction with Colonel Wellesley advanced to the Godavery on the road to Aurungabad; and General (afterwards Lord) Lake was ordered to hold an army in readiness to operate against Scindia's possessions in

Hindustan. Lord Wellesley was the more determined to crush the Mahratta opposition because he was still haunted by the bugbear of French interference. Perron, Scindia's general, was believed to be in communication with Napoleon, who in this year (1803) was crowned Emperor of the French, and to whose ambition and hostility there seemed to be no bounds. De Boigne was also supposed (erroneously as has since been proved) to be one of Napoleon's advisers in France itself, and the Mahrattas held access to the sea on both coasts, at several places on the west coast and at Cuttack on the east. Wellesley's policy was based on this conviction that the British could never be safe in India as long as they did not hold the whole of the seaboard. We have seen how effectually he had closed all the seaports in the south from attack. The same task was now to be performed in the north, and if possible the policy so successfully carried out at Hyderabad and Poona was to be followed at Oojjein (Scindia's capital), Indore (Holkar's), Baroda and Nagpur. French influence was to be destroyed and the princes were to be compelled to accept the British Subsidiary Force, which would undertake to defend them from all external enemies and would arbitrate between them in all their quarrels. The British were to play the part of the police of India and introduce order and rule in the place of anarchy and civil war. It was to be the commencement of the great *Pax Britannica* which was to open to India a new era of peace and prosperity. Negotiations were at once opened with the two Mahratta princes. At first they pretended that they had no hostile intentions. If that was the case, replied Colonel Wellesley, let them both retire to their respective capitals, Oojjein and Nagpur. To this they answered that they were willing to retire to Burhanpoor if the British armies would also retire within British limits. In other words, they would retire for fifty miles if the British would retire to separate destinations for 500, leaving the whole of the Nizam's country open to their combined attack. Colonel Wellesley took this as tantamount to a declaration of war, and at once commenced operations by storming Ahmednagar, which belonged to Scindia; and then, in co-operation with Colonel Stevenson, marched against the allies. Events followed as quickly as they had done in Mysore four years previously. The battles of Assaye and Argaum followed in rapid succession, and Gawilgurh, the last stronghold of the Rajah, and Berar and Nagpur, fell on the 15th December, 1803, and peace negotiations were concluded with him the 23rd of the same month, the campaign having opened in August of the same year. On the east coast, Colonel Campbell had overrun and conquered Cuttack, belonging to the same Rajah, and in the north General Lake, by a series of brilliant actions, had taken Aligarh, Agra, and Delhi, and, after gaining the battle of Laswarry (1st November), had made himself master of the whole of the country between the Ganges and the Jumna. In their last operations Lake was opposed by the celebrated battalions of De Boigne, now commanded by Perron, but they proved entirely unable to face the British Force. The result of the war was that Scindia and the Rajah of Nagpur had to make considerable concessions of territory, in which the Nizam as our ally received a share. The treaty does not contain the actual money value of this share, but it consisted of the whole of the districts west of the river Wurda and east of Khandesh, now known as Berar. Some of these districts were in the exclusive possession of Nagpur, and in the others the Mahrattas exercised a joint administration with the Nizam, known as *do amil*, under which the Mahrattas collected 60 per cent. and the Nizam the balance of the revenue. (*Berar Gazetteer*.) The Nizam also obtained certain outlying districts held by the Mahrattas in the midst of his territories, such as the fort of Dowlatabad, the fort and district of Jalna, some districts lying on the Godavery, and the country near the Ajanta Hills. The British got the fort and city of Broach, the fort and districts of Ahmednagar, and the whole of the territories held by Scindia in the Doab, including Agra, Delhi, and the country up to the Sutlej.

So far everything had succeeded with the Nizam and the British. The Peshwa's teeth were drawn by the presence of a subsidiary force, and the power of Nagpur and of Scindia had been greatly diminished by the deprivation of the territory they had forcibly possessed themselves of. By occupying Broach and Cuttack, the Marquis's policy had been further carried out and the Mahrattas were cut off from their remaining posts on both coasts, whilst Perron had been obliged to take refuge with the British; and Scindia's brigades officered by Frenchmen were disbanded. But the war was not yet over. It had opened with a series of brilliant successes, but it was doomed to end with some serious disasters.

Up to this point Holkar had taken no active share in the war. After the treaty of Bassein he was supposed to have expressed his willingness to sink his differences with Scindia and to make common cause against the British. Probably he did not think that operations would be so quickly concluded, and waited in order to secure better terms for himself. However this may be, at the end of the year 1803, he found himself isolated. The Nagpur Rajah had already submitted and Scindia had done the same (the actual treaty was signed on the 3rd

January, 1804.) The British power was now in the ascendancy at Delhi and in the Doab, and there seemed no chance of his succeeding to the position hitherto held by Scindia. Accordingly, he determined to try a last chance. One of his first acts was to put to death three Englishmen in his service, who, taking advantage of a proclamation issued by the Governor-General, had tendered their resignations. He then massed his army, consisting chiefly of Mahratta cavalry and Pindaris—a new race of soldiers, half camp-followers and half bandits, that had begun to form a new feature in conditions of warfare—near the British frontier. Lord Lake at once moved towards the Chambel, which was regarded as the frontier of British influence and hostilities commenced. Holkar's tactics were different from what those of Scindia had been. The latter, relying upon his European-drilled battalions, did not hesitate to meet the British in the open field ; but Holkar judging rightfully that his Mahratta troops were better suited to their traditional system of skirmishing and harassing, avoided anything like a pitched battle. For the first time circumstances were unfavourable to the Marquis's plans and combinations. The season was very advanced (June, 1804) ; the Deccan army under Colonel (now General) Wellesley, had withdrawn, and the column which had been ordered up from Bombay to march from Surat on Holkar's capital, Indore, was delayed. Lake sent on Colonel Monson with an advanced force to cross the Chambel. Hearing that he could not expect to form a junction with the Bombay column, and fearing that his supplies would run short, Monson commenced a retreat. He re-crossed the Chambel harassed by Holkar's cavalry at every step. On all sides the Mahratta light horse laid the country waste and prevented his getting supplies.

By degrees the troops became demoralized; detachments were cut off; guns stuck in the heavy mud and were captured; even the smallest rivers became impassable; and gradually the retreat degenerated into a rout, until at last, when approaching Agra, they finally broke and took refuge within the walls of the fort. This disaster was doubtless afterwards avenged and at Deeg Holkar's troops received a severe defeat from Colonel Frazer, who was killed in the action and was succeeded by the same Colonel Monson who had fared so badly; but the moral effect was a bad one, and at once raised the spirit of resistance in Scindia's bosom. After a series of desultory fights, Holkar had to vacate his own districts and take refuge with the Sikhs; his capital, Indore, was at last occupied by the Bombay columns, and there can be little doubt that Lord Lake would have effectually crushed all further resistance on the part of the Mahrattas, but a change had come over the spirit of British policy. The war had dragged on throughout the whole of 1804 and well into 1805, and the Directors at home had become alarmed at the results of the Marquis of Wellesley's policy. They had accepted the conquest of Mysore and the alliance with the Nizam with a certain amount of fear as to the responsibilities that would follow in their train. The minds of the merchants in Leadenhall Street had not yet grasped the idea of an Empire and had not yet got beyond that of an investment. No doubt, Lord Wellesley's forward policy had been eminently successful, but one war had led to another, and after each conquest there seemed to arise a fresh complication which could only be overcome by another war. Though the limits of the Empire were yearly extending, the "investment" was suffering. The money which should have been spent on commercial enterprise had to be wasted, as they deemed, on military expeditions, and in an interference with Native Princes, who, if left to themselves, would sooner or later cut their own throats. And to meet these expenses money in increasing quantities had to be sent out to India, loans had to be raised and liabilities incurred, whilst there were no corresponding profits to be made from merchandise. And now to crown all a check had occurred in the career of conquest. The capricious fortune of war seemed to have changed. This proved to be the last proverbial straw. The veteran Lord Cornwallis was implored to go out to India as if he were the only one who could save the country, and Lord Wellesley was recalled. This occurred in July, 1805, and the great Marquis had to leave India with his plans only half finished. His successor had only some ten weeks of life left, but it was sufficient to inaugurate a new policy. A hasty peace was patched up. Holkar's conquered districts were restored to him; he and Scindia were left uncontrolled by a subsidiary force and free to follow out their own devices with the Rajpootana States, with which Lord Wellesley had resolved to form a defensive alliance, and the elements were left of another war which was bound to break out sooner or later. One subsidiary alliance was formed, viz., with the Gaikwar of Baroda, who agreed to receive 3,000 men as a protection of his state, and so was cut off from the other Mahratta princes. The power of the latter, however, had been scotched, not killed, and even the Peishwa entertained hopes of being able some day to shake off a yoke which he found to be irksome and from which he had again derived no profit, for, owing to his apathy, his own forces had taken little or no share in the late war, and accordingly he received no share in the division of the spoil. The only one who benefited was the Nizam, who was again put in possession of ancestral dominions, which, but for his alliance with us, would have been lost to him for ever. The actual value of the estates thus recovered may be taken to have been about 30 or 35 lakhs of rupees annually although owing to the constant wars with which they had been ravaged they were greatly depopulated and deteriorated. But the Nizam had nothing to complain of. Since 1792 he had gained a considerable accession of territory, and, by parting with only a portion of it, he had acquired the right of permanent protection at no cost to himself. The 3rd Article* of the " Separate and Secret " clauses attached to the Treaty of 1800 had been faithfully carried out, and, although the battles of Assaye and Argaum had been won by Colonel Wellesley's force, the prestige of the Nizam had been greatly increased by the fact that the conquest of the Berar districts, which were now handed over to him, had been effected by his troops acting in conjunction with the Subsidiary Force under Colonel Stevenson.

* The last portion of this article (which still remains in force) runs as follows :— " It is, however, declared that, in the event of war and of a conquest partition of conquests between the contracting parties, His Highness the Nawab Asaph Jah shall be entitled to participate equally with the other contracting parties in the division of every territory which may be acquired by the successful exertion of their united arms."

CHAPTER XI

THE HYDERABAD CONTINGENT AND THE PINDARI WAR

WITH the accession of Secunder Jah and the end of the Mahratta war, there commenced an entirely new era for Hyderabad. The history of the last hundred and fifty years has shown it to have been a scene of constant and almost annual warfare. The country had been well-nigh devastated by the results of these perpetual struggles; in many parts it was almost depopulated, and in the absence of anything like a settled Government confusion reigned everywhere. The petty Rajahs and zemindars were frequently in a state of revolt; they were always turbulent and as dilatory as possible in the payment of their *peshkash*. The greater nobles enjoyed in their estates almost regal powers; they had the power of life and death and exercised a kind of *Imperium in imperio*—by one of the greatest of these families, a claim was put forward only a few years ago that the head of it had the right to put three persons to death every day.

Whilst the Government was constantly engaged with foreign enemies it was well-nigh impossible to regulate the internal affairs. Matters were left to adjust themselves as best they could. With the introduction, however, of the system of subsidiary alliance in the Deccan, matters assumed an entirely different aspect, as the Nizam had no longer any enemies of whom he need be afraid From being an open enemy, Mysore had become a friendly state. In Poona the British Subsidiary Force was sufficient to keep the Mahrattas quiet, and a similar but larger force was stationed at Hyderabad, which was a sufficient protection of his own dominions against any danger that might be expected from Scindia, Holkar, and Nagpur. To the extreme north-west of his dominions, at Baroda, there was another British Subsidiary Force; and to the east and west he had the allied British Presidencies of Madras and Bombay as his neighbours. The Province of Berar, recently reconquered from Nagpur, was still, it is true, in a considerable state of confusion, and, bordering as it did on the territories of Scindia and Holkar, whom the altered policy of Lord Cornwallis and Sir George Barlow had left independent, was still exposed to the ravages of the Pindaris. The Berar Province itself, from being a garden, had been converted almost into a desert. A large proportion of the inhabitants had either been killed or had emigrated, and it required a long series of years of careful nursing before it could recover its former condition of prosperity. But assured as it was now of protection from foreign enemies, if the Nizam's Government had devoted itself in earnest to the task of retrenchment and reform, it would not have been long before a period of prosperity would have been introduced. Unfortunately no attempts appear to have been made towards retrenchment, especially in the reduction of the large military levies, which under the modern system of warfare had become comparatively useless. The late Nizam had granted to the Shums-ul-Umra family no less than 52 lakhs of rupees' worth of *jaghirs* for the maintenance of the so-called *Paigah*, or feudal troops—a force which, though it may have been necessary twenty years before, was now no longer required for protection of His Highness's person. Besides this small army, there was an immense horde of irregular troops, infantry and cavalry, which were maintained by other noblemen, to whom assignments of land were made for that purpose. Almost all these noblemen resided in Hyderabad, where the Nizam held his court, and vast sums of money were spent in profusion and display. The whole revenue of the country (at least, such of it as the farmers or renters of the estates chose to send) was poured into Hyderabad, and scarcely anything was spent on the internal requirements of the country, such as roads, communications, and sources of irrigation. A certain amount of military the Nizam was bound to maintain, because under the treaty of 1800 he had undertaken to provide a force of 15,000 men to co-operate with the Subsidiary Force in the event of war. Amongst the troops thus entertained there were still a number of brigades officered by Englishmen and Eurasians.*

* Briggs gives the names of some of the officers employed, namely:—

Colonel Finglas	Irish (descendants still survive).
Captain Harding	English.
Captain Douglas	Scotch.
Major Johnstone	East Indian.
Captain don Torribio Paula Denis	Portuguese.
Captain J. Gordon	English.
Captain Freeman	East Indian.
Captain J. Fonseca	Portuguese.
Captain W. Palmer	East Indian.
Captain Guest	English.
Captain Bridges	English.
Captain Drew	English.
Captain Elliot	East Indian.
Captain Vincente	Spaniard.
Captain Blake	East Indian.
Dr. Silvester	Portuguese.
Signor Joachim	Portuguese.
Jose de Nunes	Portuguese.
Mr. Key	English.
Mr. Kullic	English.
Mr. Joachim Schmidt	East Indian (Dutch).
Mr. Plight	East Indian (Dutch).
Mr. Marten	Portuguese.

We have already heard of the Finglas Brigade, which had been raised as a counterpoise to Raymond's French troops. There were several other regiments of this description, officered by Europeans who had not enjoyed a regular military training, and it was in a great measure upon these regiments that the Nizam relied for furnishing the contingent he was bound to supply in case of war. They were accordingly employed for the most part in the western or Aurungabad division of the dominions, from which side danger was chiefly apprehended. Amongst officers of this stamp was a Mr. William Palmer, who had entered the Nizam's service in 1799, and had seen active service in the Mahratta War of 1803-4, under Colonel Stevenson, in Berar, by whom he had been appointed Brigade-Major. Of this gentleman we shall hear more later on.

It has already been narrated that Captain Achilles Kirkpatrick was the Resident at Hyderabad during the important events which occurred in the five years previous to Nizam Ali Khan's death. Captain Kirkpatrick exercised very great personal influence in Hyderabad during the nine years that he was Resident, and formed a romantic attachment to a young lady connected with the great family of Mir Alum. It is related that the young lady was about to be forced into a marriage which was distasteful to her, and that, rather than submit to it, she took refuge in the Resident's house, or rather zenana; for in those days it was not considered a reproach for a European official to conform in this respect with the customs of the country. This led to an intimate connection between the lady and Captain Kirkpatrick. He brought her openly to the Residency, "built for her specially, the *Rang Mahal*, and there made the usual public acknowledgment of marriage according to Mahomedan ritual,

by allowing garlands to be bound about his brow."
(Briggs's *Nizam*, Volume II, Chapter 1.)

From this union a son and a daughter were born,* but the connection was highly distasteful to Mir Allum, who made several representations on the subject to the Governor-General, Lord Wellesley. The Resident was called upon for an explanation, which was considered satisfactory, and in 1805 he went to Calcutta to confer with his lordship on political affairs, where he was suddenly taken ill and died on the 15th October, aged 41 years.

Captain Kirkpatrick was succeeded as Resident by Captain Thomas Sydenham, who continued in that post until 1809. For the first period of his administration he was a firm friend and adherent of Mir Allum, whom he caused to be appointed Minister in supersession of the Nizam's authority. The Nizam's assent to this arrangement is said by Briggs to have been "extorted from his timidity." Altogether throughout his reign Secunder Jah seems to have troubled himself very little about public affairs, and was content as long as he was left to his own amusements, and provided with sufficient funds to indulge in them. The great rival of Mir Alum at this time was one Rajah Mohiput Ram. This man the Resident caused to be sent to his jaghirs on the frontier, where he at once broke into revolt; he was, however, subdued without difficulty, and then went to Berar, where he created further disturbances, in the quelling of which the Mr. William Palmer who has been

---

* The two children were sent to England for their education, where the son died, but the girl grew up and married into a good English family. As Kitty Kirkpatrick she became known for her beauty and wit, and she was immortalised by Carlyle in *Sartor Resartus* as Blumhilde. A descendant of hers was serving in Secunderabad in a British Hussar Regiment in 1896, and was subsequently killed in the Benin expedition.

already mentioned was employed. Subsequently the Rajah took refuge in Holkar's court, by whom he was also employed. Here again he mutinied for arrears of pay, and being attacked by Holkar's troops was killed.

Mir Allum did not long survive his appointment as Minister, and in the question of his successor the Resident again opposed the wishes of the Nizam. The latter desired that the late Minister's son, Munir-ul-Mulk, should succeed his father, but Captain Sydenham insisted that Shums-ul-Umra should be selected, against whose appointment the Nizam had a strong objection on the ground that Shums-ul-Umra had been especially appointed to the great command of the Paigah troops in order to remove him from taking any share in politics and to secure him as adherent of the Nizam's person, to whose sister he was married. Eventually a compromise was arrived at: Munir-ul-Mulk was appointed nominal Minister but was compelled to sign a written engagement to take no part in the administration, "but to be content in the enjoyment of a stipend of about six lakhs of rupees per annum. The authority of the Government was vested in Rajah Chundoo Lal uuder the designation of the Minister's deputy." (Briggs' "Nizam," Vol. II, Chapter 1).

From this time forward for the next thirty-odd years Rajah Chundoo Lal was the principal power in the State. He was a man of great ability, and was intimately conversant with all the intricacies of Hyderabad intrigue. His policy was to make himself as amenable as possible to the British Resident, and at the same time to keep the Nizam quiet by supplying him with all the funds he required. By pursuing this policy he gained the active support of the Resident and of the Government of India, so much so that the Nizam became a mere puppet and kept himself in the seclusion of his own palace without taking any part in the public affairs of his kingdom.

Captain Sydenham resigned in 1809, in consequence of the Governor-General, Lord Minto, having expressed disapproval of the advice which he had given to the General Commanding the Subsidiary Force on the occasion of a disagreement with his officers. At the time he retired he expressed an opinion that the disorders of the Nizam Government were " too deeply rooted and too widely extended to admit of any remedy short of placing the administration of the country under the control of the Resident." He was succeeded by Captain Charles Russell, who in 1811 was succeeded by his brother, Mr. (afterwards Sir Henry) Russell. At this time the total army of the Nizam consisted of about 70,000 men, the greater part of which was of a most irregular and disorderly description. A very large proportion, especially of the cavalry, were quartered in the Berar Province where their presence was as much feared by the agriculturists as was that of the Pindari freebooters. A large number of infantry and cavalry were also stationed in the Aurungabad district. Some of these regiments were, as already mentioned, officered by Europeans and Eurasians, and were, comparatively speaking, in a greater state of efficiency. There were also several thousand men stationed in Hyderabad itself, remnants of the old French corps and of the Finglas Brigade. These, of course, did not include the irregular rabble of Africans, Arabs, and Afghans, who were maintained as military retainers of the noblemen, with whom the city swarmed, and whose presence rendered it unsafe for a European to visit the city unless strongly guarded. Although at this time the greater part of the

Deccan was at peace as far as any foreign invasion was concerned, still the whole of Central India (including Nagpur, Malwa, and Rajputana) was in a state of anarchy and confusion. The whole of this vast extent of country was ravaged in succession by the armies of Scindia and Holkar, and by the Pindaris, the principal leader of the latter being Amir Khan, the successful freebooter who after some eighteen years of predatory warfare, in which he was constantly changing from one side to another, was at last successful in getting himself recognized as the ruler of the small principality of Tonk. But large though the area of the country was over which these disorders spread, it soon became manifest that they must inevitably spread to the bordering British possessions. In order to maintain the turbulent and disorderly soldiery, fresh fields and 'pastures new would have to be sought out. The principal Mahratta chiefs— Nagpur, Scindia, and Holkar—were themselves becoming alarmed at the aggressiveness of the Pindaris, and were becoming uneasy at being rigidly restrained by the British boundary which encompassed them on all sides; the Peshwa at Poona also becoming dissatisfied with the comparatively peaceful rôle which the presence of the British Subsidiary Force compelled him to play, was secretly increasing his forces. It became evident that before long there would be another outbreak of war, and that the task which the great Marquis of Wellesley had been compelled to leave uncompleted would ere long have to be taken in hand again. But a war of this kind, in order to be effectual, would have to be conducted on a very large scale, and would tax the whole of the resources, not only of the British army, but also of the subsidiary allies of the British Government. But, large though the Nizam's army nominally was, it was manifestly out of the question to expect any efficient support from so badly armed and disciplined a force. Accordingly the new Resident, Mr. Henry Russell, resolved to reform and reorganize a small portion, at all events, of this heterogeneous force. He commenced with a body of about 2,000 men stationed in the old French gun foundry, not far from the Residency, and afterwards extended similar reforms to some of the infantry regiments stationed at Aurungabad, and some of the cavalry regiments in Berar, in which reforms the Resident was allowed a free hand by the Nizam's minister, Chundoo Lal. In order to maintain anything like a thorough state of discipline, it was absolutely necessary to ensure regular payment of the troops. This is exactly what the Hyderabad military authorities have never been in the habit of doing. If left to themselves the troops were allowed to remain in arrears of pay for months and months together, until at last they frequently broke into open revolt, tied their officers to guns and threatened to blow them away unless their arrears were discharged. This is what actually happened in 1812 amongst the troops, which, as above stated, were quartered in the old French lines at Hyderabad. After the murder of their commandant, Major George Gordon, by a mutineer, he was succeeded in the command by his brother, Major Edward Gordon. The soldiers again mutinied, tied their commanding officer to a gun, and threatened to blow him away unless their pay was given them together with a free pardon for their offence. (Briggs's " Nizam," Volume II, Chapter 4.)

The demands were acceded to, but, as there was no money in the Nizam's treasury, funds were furnished by the Resident, who afterwards so far departed from the promise held out to the mutineers as to insist upon the principal offenders being punished. It was this incident that caused him to take the necessary reforms in hand, and he at once commenced with the corps in question. The brigade thus remodelled consisted of two battalions numbering nearly 2,000 men, together with a train of one 24-pounder, four 6-pounders, and two $5\frac{1}{2}$-pounder howitzers. This force came to be styled the Russell Brigade, and was permitted to purchase ammunition and stores from the Company's arsenal at Secunderabad. Arrangements were also made by the Resident for regular payment of these troops from the *peshkash*, amounting to nine lakhs of rupees a year, which it will be remembered was paid by the British to the Nizam for the Northern Circars. This Russell Brigade formed the foundation of what has been subsequently known as the Hyderabad Contingent.

In the meantime, a large banking house had been formed in Hyderabad by Mr. William Palmer, who had retired from the Nizam's service in 1810. Mr. William Palmer was a gentleman of mixed blood, whose father, General Palmer, was for a long time Resident at the Court of Scindia and married a Mahommedan Begum. From this union there were three sons, one being Mr. George Palmer, who was a wealthy merchant and banker at Calcutta, and the others William and Hastings Palmer, who settled at Hyderabad. They took as partners a Mr. Samuel Russell (of the same name but no relation to the Resident), a native *sowcar* named Bankadi Das and Mr. William Currie, who though he held the appointment of Residency Surgeon, was, under the regulations then in force, allowed to embark in private trade. Subsequently, the firm took, as another partner, Sir William Rumbold, who had come out with the Governor-General, Lord Moira, better known as the Marquis of Hastings, and married a ward of that nobleman. Sir William Rumbold was not a mere adventurer: he was a grandson of Sir Thomas Rumbold, the notorious Governor of Madras, from whom he had inherited a considerable fortune. A portion of this fortune he embarked in the firm of William Palmer & Co.

The objects of this firm were not only banking, but also the development of the resources of the country. They embarked largely in the timber trade on the Godavery, and invested to a considerable extent in the cotton produce of Berar. In 1816 they obtained a licence from the Government of India to carry on their business as bankers, and to have pecuniary transactions with the Nizam's Government. This could not have been done without a licence, because under 37th George III, Chapter 142, Section 28, no European was allowed to have any financial transactions with Native States without the express sanction of the Governor-General in Council, the only reservation made being " that it should be at the discretion of the British Resident at Hyderabad, for the time being, to satisfy himself regarding the nature and objects of the transactions in which Europeans might engage under the permission accorded." The banking house, thus formed and authorized by the terms of the licence to be in communication with the British Resident, was of very considerable use to Mr. Russell in the military reforms which he was carrying out, which was especially the case in regard to the newly organized regiments at Aurungabad and Berar. Under arrangements with the Hyderabad Government, the firm guaranteed the regular payment of the troops, being reimbursed from time to time by the Minister, either by cash payments from the revenue or by assignments of land. Punctuality in payment was not, however, one of the chief points of the Hyderabad Government, and, as interest at the rate of

24 per cent. was charged on all outstanding balances, this item formed one of the firm's principal sources of profit. To modern ears this rate of interest sounds very high, but at the time we are writing of it was the ordinary rate of interest charged in all mercantile circles. So dear was money that the merchants themselves gave as much as 12 per cent. on deposits, and when making advances on a large scale to the Government they frequently had to borrow money themselves at 21 or even 24 per cent. Even at the present day, it is not uncommon to find that the charges for loans are from 6 to 18 per cent. and even more. It will be easily understood how, in the course of a comparatively short time this commercial firm became a most important factor in the Hyderabad State, and Mr. William Palmer and Sir William Rumbold took status amongst the most important residents of Hyderabad. They kept open house, and it is said that in the house of the former the table was always laid for at least thirty guests. They were lavish in their entertainments, and, being allowed access to the palace without the intervention of the Resident, were regarded by most of the principal personages of Hyderabad as being even of greater importance than the Resident himself. This prestige was greatly enhanced by the connection of Sir William Rumbold with the Governor-General's family, and the consequence was that the influence of this great banking firm overshadowed that of the Residency itself. As long as Mr. Russell was at Hyderabad this does not seem to have caused any friction. By means of this firm's support Mr. Russell was able to carry out all his reforms, and in about four years' time he succeeded in organizing a select and really efficient body of troops numbering about 7,000 men, formed of all arms. One portion of

this force, as already stated, was stationed at Hyderabad, but the remainder was garrisoned at Aurungabad and in Berar. These reforms, however, were not carried out for nothing; the *peshkash* of nine lakhs was soon found to be insufficient to provide for their payment, and by the year 1818 the cost of these re-formed troops, generally known as the Russell Brigade, amounted to 36 lakhs of rupees.

At the time of which we are writing the total revenue of the Hyderabad State could not have amounted to more than a crore and a half of rupees, or about one and a half million sterling, for the Mahrattas still continued to levy *chouth* over a considerable portion of the western districts. When it is further remembered that the Nizam still maintained a very large army and had also assigned more than half a crore of jaghirs for the upkeep of the Paigah force, it will be understood that the cost of this Russell Brigade constituted a very heavy drain, and that after meeting the demands of the Nizam there was but little left to cover the cost of administration. Chundoo Lal, however, knowing that these re-formed troops were a special hobby of the Resident, made no difficulties in supplying him with the necessary funds, whilst at the same time he furnished the Nizam with the money which he demanded. In this way there arose a period of financial embarrassment which lasted for at least 25 years more, and threatened in the end to plunge the State into a condition of insolvency.

In the meantime, the long-threatened war of extermination against the Pindari hordes had actually commenced in 1817. Lord Hastings' plan was to envelop them on all sides; from the south by the Nizam's Subsidiary Force; from the west by an army from Bombay; whilst he in person accompanied the grand army from the north and north-east. But no sooner had the Deccan Subsidiary Forces marched to take up their respective positions than fresh troubles with the Mahrattas commenced. The first to break into open revolt was the Peshwa, Baji Rao, of Poona. Taking advantage of the absence of the main body of the Subsidiary Force, he called in the whole of his available troops. The Resident, Colonel Barry Close, was just able to obtain some small reinforcements when the Peshwa's army advanced against him. The Residency was vacated and burned, and there followed the battle of Kirkee, in which, though little more than 1,600 British were attacked by thousands of Mahrattas, the result was a signal defeat of the Peshwa, who thereupon became a fugitive, until, after a year spent in hiding, he at last surrendered and was sent as an exile to Bithur, near Cawnpore, on the Ganges, where he afterwards resided, deprived, it is true, of his possessions, but in enjoyment of a princely allowance of £60,000 a year. It was here that he adopted as his son the afterwards notorious Nana Saheb. The example of Poona was followed at Nagpur. As soon as the British force had left for the Pindari war, the Rajah, or, as he afterwards pretended, his troops, without his consent, broke into open revolt. The battle of Setabaldi followed, with the same result as that of the battle of Kirkee, and although for the time the Rajah of Nagpur obtained better conditions than had fallen to the fate of the Peishwa he was effectually prevented from doing any mischief in future. But the infection of rebellion spread to the two other Mahratta princes, Scindia and Holkar, with the consequence that two years were occupied before the war was brought to a successful conclusion. The southern army was under the command of Sir Thomas Hislop. At the battle of Mahidpore, Hislop totally defeated

Holkar's army (December 21st, 1817). Holkar's submission followed, and in a treaty which was concluded on the 6th January, 1818, he entered into a bond of subsidiary alliance and agreed to reduce his troops to a contingent of 3,000 horse, and from this time forward he became a loyal ally of the British Government. After Holkar's defeat, Scindia also became more tractable, and the British troops were able to devote their attention to the Pindaris, who were divided into three bodies, headed by Wassal Mahomed, Curreem and Cheetoo. The two former were defeated in detail and their bands were broken up. Cheetoo's fate was even more tragic. After being followed and defeated in several engagements his followers gradually deserted him, until at length, when singly pursuing his flight, he was devoured by a tiger in the jungles near the fort of Aseergarh in Berar. " The Pindaris thus dispersed, without leaders, and without a home or rendezvous, were afterwards little heard of, though flying parties were seen in the Deccan until the termination of the war with the Peishwa ; they mingled with the rest of the population, but the real Pindaris still retain their name, though some have become active improving farmers." (*Grant Duff*, Volume II, Chapter 26.) A course of pacification followed rapidly. The Rajpoot States of Jodhpur and Jaipur were admitted to an alliance which freed them from all further danger from Mahrattas and Pindaris. What the ravages of these marauders in Rajpootana were has been described by Colonel Tod in the *Annals of Rajasthan*, a book which everyone interested in Indian history should carefully study. The Rajah of Bondi, who on a former occasion had been conspicuous for his loyalty in helping Colonel Monson during his disastrous retreat in the former Mahratta war, but had been ill requited by Lord Cornwallis and Sir George Barlow by being left to his fate, was now amply recompensed. All tribute was relinquished and the possessions usurped by Holkar and Scindia restored. Similar favours were shown to the Nawab of Bhopal, not only for the friendship of his ancestor towards General Goddard's army in the previous century, but for the zeal he had shown in the present war by selling his jewels to support troops.

The Peshwa himself finally surrendered on the 3rd June, 1818, and the war was finally brought to a conclusion by the reduction of the celebrated fortress of Aseergurh, after a siege of twenty days (9th April, 1819).

The foregoing is but a very brief summary of the last of the warlike proceedings in Central and Southern India. The whole story has been narrated by Grant Duff, who was himself an active sharer in the war itself, as well as in the pacification that followed. It only remains to be said that the Nizam's Subsidiary Force and the re-formed Russell Brigade took an active and most creditable share in the whole of the proceedings. After the close of the war, the Russel Brigade was highly commended by Sir Thomas Hislop for its zeal and efficiency. It took a part in the battle of Mahidpore, and the name of this decisive engagement is borne on the flag of the Hyderabad Contingent, by which name the force became known until its final absorption into the British Army under an agreement with the Nizam, dated the 5th November, 1902. Another portion of the force was engaged during this war in the reduction of the fort of Nowar. This fort was situated in a jaghir belonging to the Peshwa in the very heart of the Nizam's dominions, about twenty miles from the town of Nander, near the Godavery. The fort was strongly garrisoned by Arabs, and the siege lasted from the 8th to the 31st January, 1819, when it was carried with great gallantry by two battalions of the Russell Brigade, the 3rd battalion of the Berar Regular Infantry and a party of the Nizam's Reformed Horse, accompanied by a field battery and a small battering train. The name of this engagement is also borne upon the regimental standards. With this episode the period of warfare in the Deccan, which had lasted almost continuously for 170 years, may be said to have concluded. From this time forward *Pax Britannica* reigned throughout these disturbed regions, for on all sides they were surrounded either by British possessions or by tributary allies of the British power. It now only remains to be told what share fell to the Nizam for his co-operation. We cannot do better than quote from Grant Duff (Volume II, Chapter 27), who was himself one of the principal officers concerned in the settlements that followed :

" As to claims, the most important upon the British Government were those which regarded the settlement with its ally, the Nizam, but no arrangement of their mutual affairs could be made until it had been fully ascertained what surplus revenue the British Government should derive from the conquest. The advantages immediately gained by the Nizam were exemption from debts amounting to about 60 millions of rupees,* which on the most moderate estimate he could not have settled with the Peishwa without making cession of territory equal to ten lakhs of rupees a year. The shares of revenue within the boundary of the Subadar of the Deccan, which the Peishwa or his subjects had enjoyed up to the breaking out of the war and of which the Nizam now retained the collections, were more than equal to

* 6 crores—£6,000,000.

twelve lakhs of rupees a year, and the cessions which fell to him from the Governments of Holkar and the Rajah of Nagpur amounted to nearly six more; so that the Nizam obtained an addition of at least 28 lakhs of rupees of annual revenue."

CHAPTER XII

THE HYDERABAD CONTINGENT AND WILLIAM PALMER AND CO.

IT will be seen from the facts recorded in the previous chapter that the reforms carried out by the Resident in the Russell Brigade, the Berar Regular Infantry, and the re-formed Cavalry, which comprised together about 7,000 men (the different corps for the sake of brevity being hereafter styled the Hyderabad Contingent), were commenced and carried out in all good faith with the intention of rendering as efficient as possible the Contingent which the Nizam was bound under treaty to furnish. That these measures were eminently successful is shewn by the highly creditable manner in which the troops acquitted themselves during the Pindari war. It was, perhaps, unfortunate for the Nizam that the Contingent should have shown itself as efficient as it did; for the British Government became naturally reluctant to lose the services of so compact a little army which had proved itself to be so useful in a case of emergency. In addition, therefore, to the Contingent being a favourite hobby of the Resident as his own creation, and of which he was regarded as the controlling authority with all the powers of patronage at his disposal, it became a policy on the part of the Government of India that the

Nizam should be encouraged to continue the maintenance of so valuable a military unit. The minister Chundoo Lal was, as we have said, by no means disinclined to humour the Resident, and to defer to the wishes of the Government of India. For his own part he would probably have been quite willing to reduce the number of the Nizam's irregular forces, and so effect a saving in order to provide for the cost of the Contingent, but this was a matter which would naturally be very distasteful to His Highness; for according to his traditions it would lower his prestige to reduce his army, besides there were so many vested interests concerned that any step of this kind would have been highly resented and have raised against him a host of enemies, who would have rendered his position even more difficult than it was. Accordingly, Chundoo Lal temporized and gave a free hand to the great banking house of William Palmer & Co., to make the necessary advances for the upkeep of the Contingent. In this manner the Hyderabad Government became largely indebted to that firm, and in 1820 William Palmer & Co. proposed to adjust this indebtedness by consolidating it into a loan of 60 lakhs of rupees, which was to be paid off by regular instalments. The interest on this loan was to be reduced from 24 to 18 per cent., but the firm was also to receive a bonus of commission of 8 lakhs of rupees. The arrangement was recommended by the Resident, Sir Henry Russell, and sanctioned by the Government of India. In 1820, Sir Henry Russell retired, and was succeeded by his friend, Mr. (afterwards Sir Charles, and subsequently Lord) Metcalfe, who had been private secretary to the Governor-General, Lord Hastings, and was, of course, fully acquainted with Hyderabad affairs, which for many years had formed a subject for correspondence. He must have been fully aware of the embarrassed state of the country's finances, but immediately after his arrival he did not hesitate to put forward a request which he had brought with him from the Governor-General, that the Nizam would contribute a sum of 16 lakhs of rupees towards the improvement of the city of Calcutta. It was only natural that this request should have been taken as a command, and was at once complied with. How Chundoo Lal managed to raise the money we are not able to explain; but he was probably only able to do so by further borrowing of a ruinous description, the burden of which ultimately fell upon the unfortunate cultivators. When Metcalfe arrived in Hyderabad the house of William Palmer & Co. was in the very zenith of its prosperity. As already mentioned, the partners were profuse in their hospitality, while politically, owing to their financial relations with the Minister and the Nizam, they probably enjoyed more influence than the Resident himself, whose business communications were chiefly confined to the Minister. These financial relations were not merely confined to advances in money, as the firm also acted as general agents for the supply of European goods of every description, not only to the Nizam but also to the different noblemen who vied with each other in their profusion and ostentation. It would seem that when Metcalfe arrived he was not imbued with any hostile feelings against the firm; indeed, he was on intimate terms with John Palmer, at Calcutta, who was the brother of William Palmer, of Hyderabad; he was also a friend of Sir William Rumbold, who had married a ward of Lord Hastings, and he knew that his patron and friend, the Governor-General, was greatly interested in the latter's welfare. These considerations would naturally predispose him in favour of the firm, and, indeed, no one was more cordial in welcoming him than each of the principal partners; but, before he had been in Hyderabad many months, Metcalfe came to see that the influence of William Palmer & Co., was likely to form a most dangerous element in Hyderabad politics. The very connection of one of the partners with the Governor-General led the orientals of Hyderabad to suppose that his private influence with Lord Hastings was supreme, while the indebtedness of the Government to the firm, which could only be temporarily met by continual assignments of land, threatened before long to make them the paramount power in Hyderabad. Again, it soon became apparent that many of the officials connected with the Residency were pecuniarily interested in the firm's transactions, either by receiving an unduly high rate of interest on their deposits or else by receiving a share of the profits in return for investments. Metcalfe came to the conclusion that even at the sacrifice of his own prospects this overshadowing influence of the firm must be broken. Major Briggs, who was an Assistant at the Residency some years later, attributes the attitude which Metcalfe assumed to be due to personal pique at finding himself obliged, as it were, to play secondfiddle to the firm; but calmly reviewing the facts after a lapse of years it only seems fair to ascribe Metcalfe's action to conscientiousness. Had he been less conscientious, selfish motives alone would have induced him to remain quiet, and to support the firm, towards which he knew that the Governor-General, from whom he had everything to expect, was favourably disposed. This is the view which Kaye, in his *Life of Lord Metcalfe* takes, and it is one with which, knowing Lord Metcalfe's subsequent career and character, we feel bound to agree.

Before taking any active steps, Metcalfe made a lengthened tour throughout the Nizam's dominions, especially in those parts in and near the Berar districts, which had chiefly suffered in the former wars, and these he found to be nearly depopulated : the inhabitants had fled elsewhere, and the lands which were assessed at an exorbitantly high rate were left uncultivated and waste, owing both to want of money to pay for them and want of labour to cultivate them. Metcalfe accordingly introduced a system under which European officers were placed in charge of districts, the rates were to be reduced, and the cultivators were invited to return with the promise of protection. This arrangement was no doubt made with the very best intentions ; and, although at first great hopes were conceived regarding it, it does not appear to hove been successful in the end. Not only was the European supervision necessarily a costly one, but the dual management of Europeans and natives, especially when the latter found that their hereditary habits of peculation and corruption were interfered with, caused an amount of friction which made the whole arrangement very distasteful to the Hyderabad Government. Naturally, the European officials, when thwarted or opposed, appealed to the Resident, and this led to an interference which was scarcely consistent with Treaty arrangements. Subsequently, when the Nizam died in 1829, this arrangement was abolished by one stroke of the pen, and the old system of the native management was reverted to. It is difficult to give a correct description of what this system was, but suffice it to say that it was permeated throughout by corruption. Persons who had claims against the Government received assignments of lands, from the revenues of which they were supposed to reimburse themselves ; and, knowing that before long they would probably be replaced by others with similar claims, they naturally tried to feather their nests as much as possible. Others again offered to the Minister *nazars* by way of bribes, for the privilege of farming out one or more districts, and such persons always remained at head-quarters, and sent out their deputies to do their dirty work. Indeed, it not infrequently happened that the same district was farmed out to more than one person, from each of whom a *nazar* had been received, so that it became a proverb in Hyderabad that when a deputy went out to join a new district he rode with his face to the horse's tail in order to see whether his successor was following him. (See First Administration Report of the Nizam's Dominions for the Year 1884-5, Historical Review, Chapter XII). One of the results of Metcalfe's tour was to convince him of the dangerous nature of the influence of William Palmer & Co., and of the drain their demands upon the Government caused to the country. The consequence was that he made an official recommendation to the Government of India that steps should be taken to raise, at a more reasonable rate of interest, a loan sufficient to pay off the whole of the State's liabilities to the firm. In his proposals the Resident was even liberal in his wish to compensate the firm for the losses they would incur in having to bring their financial transactions to a close; and, in addition to the eight lakhs of rupees bonus which they had been promised under the loan just concluded, he recommended that a further sum of six lakhs should be given in the shape of compensation. But, liberal though his proposal was, it by no means corresponded with the wishes of the firm. Before sending off his despatch, Metcalfe showed a copy of it to the partners, and they at once forwarded a vigorous protest to head-quarters, Sir William Rumbold using the whole of the influence he possessed with the Governor-General to induce him to reject the proposal. He appears to have led Lord Hastings to suppose that Metcalfe was actuated by personal feelings against himself and the minister, Chundoo Lal, and Lord Hastings appear to have entirely sided with the firm; he was highly displeased that his former protégé should have sent up these proposals officially without having first consulted him on the subject, and the result was that for more than a year and a half the proposal was shelved, and Lord Hastings wrote to Metcalfe privately, with a considerable amount of irritation, pointing out to him what he conceived to be his disloyalty; adding that in return for his past services the Government of India was pledged to uphold Chundoo Lal. The result of this was that the firm became more influential than ever, and the Hyderabad authorities became convinced that the firm's influence was superior to that of the Resident. The minister, Chundoo Lal, even went so far as to ignore the Resident and send a communication to the Governor-General through the medium of Sir William Rumbold. All this no doubt caused Metcalfe a considerable amount of pain and embarrassment, but, in spite of the estrangement it had caused between him and his former patron, he conscientiously adhered to the course he had adopted, continuing to denounce the transactions of the firm, and to point out the political danger that was being caused by their influence, and by the association of so many officials in their affairs. He also pointed out the danger that arose from the constantly increasing expenditure on the Hyderabad Contingent, which he did not hesitate to describe as a mere " plaything " of the Resident, and used by him for the purposes of patronage (Kaye's *Life of Lord Metcalfe*, Vol. II, Chapter 2) In this he was undoubtedly right, for, as already pointed out, the whole of the Deccan was now in a state of profound peace. The Subsidiary Force was more than sufficient to afford ample protection to the Nizam within his own dominions, and outside of them he had absolutely nothing to fear for he was now entirely surrounded either by British territory or the territory of allied princes. Around him the *Pax Britannica* had been for the first time introduced, and whatever trouble he had to expect in future arose entirely from the disorganized state of his own dominions and finances. The disorganization of the dominions was in a great measure due to the disorganization of the finances, and this again was in a great measure due to the enormous drain caused by the maintenance of the Contingent and by the claims of William Palmer & Co. There seems to be no doubt that, had Lord Hastings acted with fairness and consideration towards the interests of his old and "faithful ally" the Nizam, he would not have encouraged him to maintain this expensive and unnecessary force. But this of course he never adopted; for, instead of helping him to reduce if not abolish the force entirely, for the next thirty years he actually deprecated any interference with it whatsoever. As the Contingent became an established fact, vested interests continued to grow up in connection with it, which became well-nigh impossible to sever. Like an avalanche, the evil continued to increase in volume and weight the longer it moved on, and although successive Governors-General spoke and wrote derisively of the expenditure, and although successive Residents pointed out the growing embarrassments of the Government, no one ever attempted to apply the knife to the sore which was sapping the vitals of the country. On the contrary, the Governors-General continued to insist upon the punctual discharge by the Nizam of the full cost of the force, and when under altered circumstances he began to fall into arrears we held him personally responsible.

But we are anticipating the course of events, and it is necessary to revert to Hyderabad in 1822. Finding the estrangement between himself and the Governor-General to be increasing, Metcalfe wrote a long statement of all the transactions of the firm and of the different persons involved in them, which he sent to Mr. John Adam, the senior member of Council, with a request that he would shew it privately to Lord Hastings. This paper completely vindicated Metcalfe's action, and justified all that he had done. Lord Hastings seems to have been convinced that it was impossible to support the firm any longer, and wrote to Metcalfe a very handsome letter of reconciliation in which he informed him that the proposed loan by which the Hyderabad Government's liabilities to the banking firm would be paid off, had been sanctioned. This generous overture was at once met by Metcalfe in the same spirit and the estrangement between the two friends came to an end. Lord Hastings' period of office had expired, and he left India on the 1st January, 1823, being succeeded by Mr. John Adam as Acting Governor-General. It was by this officer that the affair of William Palmer & Co. was settled. The debt due to them was paid by means of sixty lakhs of rupees advanced by the Government of India and remitted to the Resident at Hyderabad. The bonus of eight lakhs stipulated for by the firm on the loan of 1820 was disallowed, as were also six lakhs of rupees recommended by Metcalfe to be given as compensation for losses to the firm. William Palmer

& Co.'s claims were not only thus paid off, but the occupation of the firm was also gone and its influence entirely broken. Further transactions with the Nizam of a similar nature were prohibited, and with the departure of Lord Hastings, who was known to be the firm's chief supporter, the public withdrew their confidence and with it their business, and the consequence was that in a few months the firm of William Palmer & Co. had to declare itself insolvent. The loan thus advanced by the Government of India was subsequently liquidated by an arrangement under which the *peshkash* payable by the Government for the Northern Circars was permanently remitted. The *peshkash* amounted to nine lakhs of rupees, and Captain Hastings Fraser, in alluding to this transaction, says that the Nizam had to alienate this *peshkash* for little more than half its value, or, to be precise, Rs. 11,666,666, which amounts to 13 years' purchase.

Although there can be no doubt that it was a political necessity to break the influence which William Palmer & Co. were gaining in the Hyderabad State, it would seem that in the final arrangements the firm was treated with undue severity. They had undoubtedly rendered great service in advancing the funds to equip and maintain the Contingent before and during the Pindari War. Had the supply of the funds been left to the Nizam's Government, there can be no doubt that the troops would have been left unpaid and would therefore have become disorganized. In reference to the same Contingent, Metcalfe subsequently wrote in 1823 that the men had been left so long in arrears that they actually fell in the ranks from sheer exhaustion. Troops of this kind would, of course, have been utterly useless, and it was entirely due to the manner in which William Palmer & Co. came forward with the necessary funds that the Contingent was able to take the field at all. This they did without any guarantee from the supreme Government that their advances would be paid. Such services deserved more consideration than was ultimately shown to them. Nor can it be said that the rate of 24 per cent. for interest was exorbitantly high. It was the ordinary rate at the time which prevailed at Hyderabad, and was what the Hyderabad Government were in the habit of paying on their transactions to the native bankers.

In the discussion which subsequently took place in the India House, Sir Charles Forbes, the leading European banker at Bombay at the time, spoke regarding the rate of interest prevailing in India; he alluded to one transaction of the Government of India itself when they called for a loan in 1798, for which they actually had to pay with discount and interest no less than 34 per cent. per annum! He also added the following remarkable statement: "Now, sir, I have a letter in my pocket at this moment from Calcutta, which states that while some of the houses there are refusing money at four per cent. others are getting 12 per cent. for three months, this is 52 per cent. per annum." So much for the matter of interest; and it would therefore seem that, although it was necessary as a political expedient to destroy the firm's influence, the Government might well have afforded to treat them with greater liberality. Subsequently in February and March, 1824, the whole subject came on for discussion at the India House in the Court of Proprietors. This was brought about by a somewhat ill-advised proposal by some of Lord Hastings' friends for a testimonial in recognition of the services he had rendered whilst Governor-General. He had already been granted £60,000 after the close of the Pindari War and this fresh proposal was opposed. One of the grounds of the opposition was the interest which Lord Hastings had shown in the affairs of William Palmer & Co. It virtually became an attack upon Sir Henry Russell by the one side and upon Metcalfe by the other. Russell, in a very masterly speech, vindicated himself and also the firm. The whole discussion caused a good deal of excitement in London and party feeling ran very high. After six days' debate the original proposition to give Lord Hastings a further gratuity was lost. The mutual attacks upon Russell and Metcalfe fell through, and subsequently a half-hearted despatch was sent by the Board of Directors that the claims of William Palmer should if possible be satisfied This does not appear ever to have been done, but the Hyderabad Government continued to pay to William Palmer and his family certain handsome allowances amounting in the aggregate to Rs. 45,000 monthly, and, writing in 1861, Major Briggs says: " Mr. William Palmer still lives enjoying a green old age."

NOTE.—The authorities for this chapter are chiefly Kaye's *Life of Lord Metcalfe* and Briggs's *Our Faithful Ally*—two writers with diametrically opposite opinions.

CHAPTER XIII

MINISTRY OF MAHARAJAH CHANDOO LAL (*continued*)

PERIOD 1825 TO 1845

THE twenty-five years comprised in the period treated of in this chapter, although extending over a time of profound peace, are not marked by any of the triumphs of peace. The record unfortunately is not one of progress, but of deterioration, and at the close of the period it seemed as if nothing but a miracle could save the Hyderabad State from ruin. Not the ruin brought about by the armed forces of the enemy, as seemed so probable at the end of the previous century, after the battle of Kurdla; but financial ruin, which is sometimes even more fatal in its results. To use a homely phrase, it may be said of Hyderabad that during this period the State was not only burning its candle at both ends, but in the middle also; and, in pursuance of the policy of non-interference, it was allowed to continue in its career unchecked by what had been the allied, but had now become the paramount Power. The state of disorganization in the interior of the country has been described in a former chapter. This condition of affairs continued in even a more accentuated form, for a system of paying off one debt by contracting another can have but one inevitable result. Disorganized finances of a State must add to oppression and extortion in the interior. Whilst each official was endeavouring to make as much hay during the short period that his official sun was shining, all discipline and supervision were relaxed. The ryots or peasants were the sufferers, and as they are, in an agricultural country, the geese who lay the golden eggs, the revenues of the country continued to decrease, whilst the expenditure showed no signs of diminution. No attempt was made to reduce the huge number of irregular soldiery, for the maintenance of which enormous tracts of country were alienated; there was no falling off in the profuse expenditure of the court and its followers in the capital, and added to this was the annually growing expenditure on the Hyderabad Contingent, which, to use Metcalfe's phrase, had become the "plaything" of the Resident, its maintenance being the price that the minister, Chundoo Lal, had to pay for the unwavering support of successive Viceroys. Indeed, the maintenance of this force had become, to a certain extent, a necessity, for without its presence it is probable that the increasing exactions and corruptions in the interior would have produced ceaseless revolts and disorders; for under the treaty the services of the Subsidiary Force were only available against a foreign foe, and were not to be utilized for police purposes and the maintenance of internal order. The system introduced by Metcalfe, of employing English officials in the collection of the revenue and in the administration of the district, had not been found to work well. Although financially it was a success, it soon led to friction. There was a constant struggle between the British officials and the local authorities and the former naturally appealed to their own Resident. This dual authority was likely to, and actually did, cause unpleasantness. In Chundoo Lal's own words to Metcalfe, not long after the new system had been introduced, " there was not room for two swords in one scabbard," and, as the non-interference policy became more marked, the system was viewed with less favour by the Government of India. In 1829, Secunder Jah died and was succeeded by his son Nasir-ud-Dowlah, one of the first of whose acts was to abolish the whole system with a stroke of the pen, and neither the Resident nor the Governor-General attempted the slightest protest. In a short time the condition of the interior of the country became even worse than it had been before, although at head-quarters official correspondence between the Hyderabad Government and the Resident ran a smoother course. Chundoo Lal still continued to be minister, although he was now becoming an old man. His position and character have been well described by General Fraser, who was appointed Resident in 1838. In a confidential letter to the Governor-General, Lord Auckland, written soon after his appointment, he says, after describing the condition to which the country had been reduced : "It may appear remarkable that, under the circumstances I have described, the government of the country should have been maintained at all, and that the whole machinery of the State had not been destroyed or its movement stopped many years ago. This may in some measure be attributed to the Minister's personal character—the mild and clement disposition of which prevents him from ever committing a harsh or cruel act, his generosity and lavish disbursement of money, which secure him many friends and partisans, and the skill with which he has managed parties at Hyderabad, so far concentrating the whole power in his own hands as not to have had, for many years, a rival or antagonist to disturb the course of his administration, or to impair or call in question the autocracy (in the most absolute sense of the term) which he has created for himself. But the general tranquillity of the country and absence of any serious disturbance are, no doubt, principally to be ascribed to our support, to the presence of our troops, and to the close connection and friendship known to have always subsisted between the British Government and the Minister. Yet all these but account for the protracted existence of the Nizam's Government, which may still *consist with much wretchedness and degradation.*" After dwelling at some length upon the difficulty and danger of interfering by advice, the General goes on to say: " If your Lordship commands me to say whether any immediate suggestions have occurred to me in reference to the Nizam's dominions, the adoption of which might seem desirable, I am constrained to reply that, as long as Chundoo Lal lives, I apprehend little or nothing can be done. He is very old (between 77 and 78) and in all human probability the grave cannot be far removed from him. He has played the game of government long, and skilfully, a word which I use rather than ably, for I cannot ascribe to him genuine capacity, nor, still less, great talent. We have been the tools in his hand. Adroitly opposing the Nizam to us, or us at other times to his sovereign, as might suit the aim and object of the moment, he has contrived to keep the government—or rather the dictatorship—of the country in his hands for thirty years. Still, what his motives may have been, and how far soever actuated by self-interest and determination to uphold his own authority, he has been truly and essentially our friend.

But his death may cause embarrassment, which it will be desirable that we should, if possible, guard against by adopting some precaution. The debts of the State to *sowcars* will almost certainly be productive of financial difficulties; but, if any actual disturbance should occur on that score, it will probably arise from the claims of the Nizam's troops, Arabs, battalions of the line, horsemen and others, for payment of their arrears." The General then goes on to show the necessity of establishing an understanding with the Minister's successor, and passes in review the names of the different persons likely to succeed, concluding with the advice that, when a successor shall have been appointed in the ordinary course of events, a loan at 6 per cent. should be raised under the guarantee of the British Government in order to enable the Nizam to pay off the liabilities for which he was then paying 18 per cent. During the next few years this proposal was renewed but it was never actually carried into effect. In the meantime, the State's financial liabilities went on increasing, and in addition to the *sowcars* a new creditor appeared on the scene in the shape of the British Government for the pay due to the Contingent, which began to fall into arrears. A question was at the same time raised by the Government of India whether the whole of the pay of the British officers lent to the different native contingents should not be paid by those States. Hitherto the custom had been for the substantive pay of these officers to be met by their own Government, the especial allowance to which they were entitled being borne by the Native States. General Fraser deprecated the introduction of this rule as regards Hyderabad, on the ground that the Nizam was already inclined to ask for the abolition of the force and would certainly object to this new burden; and for the additional reason that if paid entirely by a foreign State the officers would be no longer amenable to the Mutiny Act.

In 1829, Sir Charles Metcalfe had already recorded a minute on this force in which he said: " The existence of a force paid by a Native State, but commanded by our officers and entirely under our control, is undoubtedly a great political advantage. It is an accession to our military strength at the expense of another Power, and without cost to us; an accession of military strength in an empire, where military strength is everything. The advantage is immense. But I cannot say that I think the arrangement a just one towards the Native State. The same circumstances which make it so advantageous to us make it unjust to the State at whose expense it is upheld." In the same minute, Sir Charles reviewed the whole position in Hyderabad in the following words: " We never conquered the Nizam's territories: our relation with that prince has always been one of alliance, and his alliance was once held to be of so much importance that the officer who negotiated the treaty establishing it was rewarded by a baronetcy. Since that period we have assumed much interference with the country, not warranted by any of our treaties. We effected the elevation of a Minister, who, emboldened by our support, ceased to be the Minister of his own Sovereign, and became in fact the reckless ruler of the country. . . . Our command of a considerable portion of the Nizam's troops still continues, but this is derived, not from any treaty, but from an arrangement with the Minister whom we supported, and who being in power finds this force essential for his own security and domination. . . . Not only is our command of the Nizam's auxiliary force liable to be withdrawn on the Nizam's requisition, but it is likely to cease from another cause. It gives an undue power to the Government over its own subjects and may lead to our being the instruments of oppression." After General Fraser's assumption of office he soon found that the Nizam was most reluctant to continue to bear the charge of maintaining the Contingent. The cost of this army he said in a letter to Lord Auckland on the 7th November, 1839, "already amounted to thirty-eight lakhs of rupees per annum (£380,000)—an amount which the Government finds it extremely difficult to pay, and which they pay, I believe, but very reluctantly, especially distributed as the army now is, tending not so much as it might to maintain the general peace of the country, and therefore not admitting of the disbandment of many of the irregular troops." But in spite of these representations the Government of India showed no signs either of reducing the cost or the numbers of the Contingent. An appointment to the force was looked upon as one of the prizes of the service, since each officer received an allowance in addition to his substantive pay, at the Nizam's expense. In 1829, these allowances (distributed among 123 officers) amounted to no less than Rs. 1,349,880 or $13\frac{1}{2}$ lakhs (£135,000)! As Colonel Hastings Fraser remarks (*Memoir of General Fraser*): "The Minister and the Contingent were in short the two points of incessant contact and communication between the Resident and His Highness on the one hand, and between the Resident and the Honourable Company on the other. The Minister was always to be maintained if he saved the Contingent from being dependent on the caprice of the ruler, and left it entirely to our discretion. The Resident was constantly told that above all things permanent security for the payment of these troops was to be 'sedulously sought for at every favourable opportunity,' and that, except with the great object in view, 'it were as well, perhaps, to avoid questions and propositions regarding the Nizam's army.'"

The policy of the Government of India at this time seems to have been to throw the whole of the military duties on the Contingent and to withdraw, if possible, the Subsidiary Force, the numbers of which had been fixed at "8,000 firelocks, 1,000 cavalry, and a due proportion of artillery," and the maintenance of which had been permanently paid for in advance by the cession of territory as provided for in the Treaty of 1800. In fact, immediately after General Fraser's appointment, Mr. Colvin, the Private Secretary to Lord Auckland, wrote to Major Moore, the Resident's Military Secretary, as follows: " Kindly let me know, after consulting Colonel Fraser, what portion of the Subsidiary Force could, in his and your opinion, be spared from the Hyderabad territories for other service in emergency. I should say at least half. For your fine army (the Contingent) is amply sufficient to maintain the general tranquillity of the country. But there should always be, doubtless, an imposing force near the city. Would it be ever safe to remove the Queen's Corps from Secunderabad?"* There can be no doubt in every impartial mind that the policy of the Indian Government was to make the Nizam pay a second time for military duties which at the opening of the century he had already handsomely paid for in advance. This was done against the Nizam's own wishes, and the minister who aided us in this policy was, therefore, imposed by us, even against his sovereign's wish. It was the cost of this second army which mainly

* *Memoir and Correspondence of General James Stuart Fraser*, by Colonel Hastings Fraser, p. 91 (London: Whiting & Co., 1885, Second Edition).

MINISTRY OF MAHARAJAH CHANDOO LAL

led to the subsequent financial embarrassments to the State, and, as Sir Charles Metcalfe had already said in 1829 : " It seems hardly fair, therefore, to hold either the Nizam or his minister responsible for the evil, situated as they are. In fact, we may perhaps more properly be regarded as responsible for them, having the power in our hands to remedy them and having shown that we were no ways scrupulous about making use of that power when we think fit to do so." (*ibid*, p. 86.)

Soon after General Fraser's arrival there occurred the revolt of the Nawab of Kurnool. This small state is situated on the southern bank of the river Krishna, near its junction with the Tungabudra. It had long been a vassal state of Hyderabad, and the then Nawab played a prominent part in the wars which followed the death of Asaf Jah. He had been the assassin who shot Nasir Jung before Gingee in the year 1750, and the leader in the attack on his successor in the Cuddapah district in March of the following year, in which affair Muzaffer Jung was killed. Subsequently the state became tributary to Hyder Ali, but reverted to Hyderabad in 1722, and was finally transferred to the Madras Presidency with the districts ceded by the Nizam in 1800. At the time of which we are writing there was a great wave of Wahabaism passing through India, one of the main objects of which was a subversion of the British power. Mubariz-ud-Dowlah, the brother of the Nizam, Nasir-ud-dowlah, became infected with this spirit and entered into correspondence with the equally disaffected Nawab of Kurnool. The ambition of the former was to supplant his brother in the Hyderabad State, and the object of both was to overthrow the British rule. Military attacks were conducted against the Kurnool Nawab by a detachment of the Madras Army, and some troops of the Contingent were marched to the north bank of the river in order to cut off the Nawab's retreat. Kurnool was subdued and taken without difficulty, the Nawab was sent into confinement, and the state annexed. A commission sat afterwards to enquire into the complicity of Mubariz-ud-Dowla, and having been found guilty he was confined to the state fortress of Golconda, where he remained for many years a prisoner. These incidents occurred in 1839 and 1840.

The somewhat favourable opinion which General Fraser formed of the minister, Chundoo Lal, seems to have undergone modification. As the years passed on and the disorders in the State continued to increase, he seems to have become convinced that no reforms were possible until a successor should be appointed. But the old man still clung to life and to office with an equal tenacity, and the Government of India was so pledged to his support that nothing could be done to remove him. But the debts and embarrassments of the State continued to increase. The regular army was always at least four months and often longer in arrears. Whilst these continued it was, of course, impossible to effect any reductions. And now the Contingent began to be left in arrears, and, as these were paid by the Resident, he was obliged to become an importunate creditor. At last the Minister in despair made a proposal to the Resident to mortgage districts valued at $4\frac{1}{2}$ lakhs of rupees, to be selected either in Berar, Raichur, or Bhir, in consideration of a loan of seventy-five lakhs of rupees. The cession was to be a permanent one (February 1843). This proposal did not meet with Lord Ellenborough's consent, which he declined to accord until it should come before him with the Nizam's authority (letter of 11th April, 1843), which does not seem to have been ever accorded.

Chundoo Lal's long tenure of power was now approaching its close. For many years he had been driven to all kinds of expedients to raise the money required for State expenses. To such shifts was he reduced that grants of land were issued in a most lax and reckless manner, so much so that subsequently the period of 1832 to 1839 was styled the prescribed period, and grants and *sunnads* issued during this time were not held as proof of title unless corroborated by further evidence. It would, however, be unfair to say that Chundoo Lal was alone responsible for this state of affairs. He himself was personally no gainer, and it is to his credit that with so many opportunities of profit and in such an atmosphere of corruption he eventually died a poor man. It is said that his son, Bala Persad, was by no means so conscientious, and accumulated a considerable amount of treasure, but there is no evidence of this. To this day the family remains a comparatively poor one, and the descendents of Chundoo Lal stand in the matter of revenue far below many of the other leading noblemen. By general consent, all writers on Hyderabad affairs attribute the financial embarrassments of the State to Chundoo Lal's misgovernment, but it would seem that they have not made sufficient allowance for the difficulties of his position. As long as the Contingent was duly maintained, the British Government refrained from interference, and, in order to meet this heavy expenditure—amounting to no less than 40 lakhs per annum, or about one-fifth of the total revenue of the State—and at the same time to supply His Highness with the usual funds, the Minister was compelled to plunge deeper and deeper into debt. Although in course of time General Fraser had got to regard the Maharajah Chundoo Lal as the main cause of difficulties, he seems to have been actuated by a genuine sympathy for the necessities of the State. He constantly advocated a more active interference, and this interference the Supreme Government as constantly refused to sanction. As the difficulties became more acute the proposal for a loan was increased to one crore of rupees (£1,000,000), with districts yielding 17 lakhs as security (1843). In reply, Lord Ellenborough was willing to advance the loan, but only on condition that the administration of the whole State should be handed over to the British Government; that an allowance should be made for the maintenance of the Nizam; and that all surplus of revenue over expenditure should be at the disposal of the British Government. It does not appear that this singular proposal was ever put before the Nizam, nor is it probable that he would have accepted it if it had been. In the meantime nothing was done; the difficulties continued to increase and the Minister by every means in his power endeavoured to retain his office. He did, however, tender his resignation rather in the hope of it not being accepted than otherwise. It was, however, accepted, but the Nizam showed great reluctance to appoint a successor with full powers. Ram Buksh, a nephew of Chundoo Lal, was appointed as Peshkar or Revenue and Finance Minister, and Nawab Suraj-ul-Mulk was nominated Vakeel of the Nizam to confer with the Resident. Having once been relieved from the presence of a Minister who had so long dominated over him, the Nizam appears to have been reluctant to relinquish the power that had fallen into his hands. He did, however, set seriously to work to discharge the State liabilities. A crore of rupees was taken from his own private treasure kept in the fort of Golconda and a sum of eighty lakhs of rupees in gold was taken from the palace in Hyderabad. Altogether

MINISTRY OF MAHARAJAH CHANDOO LAL

it is represented that he spent two crores from his own private purse, though it is to be feared that much of this did not reach the intended objects. For nearly three years this state of things continued. No regular Minister was appointed, and in spite of the Resident's frequent protests to the Governor-General nothing was done. There were other important matters which occupied Lord Ellenborough's attention in Scinde and the Punjab, and as long as the Contingent was maintained he appears to have troubled himself but little about Hyderabad. In fact, he seems to have been under the impression that no interference in Hyderabad would be effectual unless accompanied by a show of armed force, and for this he frankly wrote to the Resident that he had then neither the men nor the time to spare (letter of 27th February, 1844). But General Fraser did not want to make use of force or of a show of force, and with his knowledge of Hyderabad he constantly urged that a plain statement of the Governor-General's wishes would be quite sufficient. To these applications, however, he received no reply, and matters in Hyderabad were allowed to go on drifting. In June, 1844, Lord Ellenborough was recalled, and was soon afterwards succeeded by Sir Henry (Lord) Hardinge.

CHAPTER XIV

PERIOD 1845-50. LORD HARDINGE AND MARQUIS OF DALHOUSIE AS GOVERNOR-GENERAL. THE NIZAM'S RELUCTANCE TO APPOINT A NEW MINISTER WITH FULL POWERS. CONDITION OF THE COUNTRY. CONSTANT CHANGE OF MINISTERS. INCREASING DEBT. LORD DALHOUSIE'S RESOLVE AND ULTIMATUM. RESIGNATION OF GENERAL FRASER.

GENERAL FRASER'S idea had been that the removal of the Maharajah Chandoo Lal from power must result in an improvement of the administration, on the principle perhaps of any change being a change for the better. Matters indeed could not well be worse. The difficulty which the late Minister had found in raising money to meet the cost of the Contingent, added to the corrupt system of internal administration, led to constant abuses and oppression. As usual in India, the people bore this in silence. Not so, however, some of the larger landholders. Many of these, harassed on the one hand by continual demands for money, and seeing the relaxation of authority and the disregard of their own grievances, took the law into their own hands and revenged themselves for their own losses by depredations, not only upon their own ryots, but upon their neighbours, who, weaker than themselves, were subject to the same exactions. They were encouraged in this by the knowledge that, although the Contingent was stationed in scattered cantonments throughout the country, it would not be employed against them until an enquiry had taken place and the Nizam's Government had been able to satisfy the Resident of the "reality of the offence." This stipulation occurred in the Treaty of 1800 (Art. 17), and was intended as a safeguard against the troops being used for injustice and oppression. This, of course, meant delay, and the possibility of escape from punishment. In this way the Contingent intended for the protection of the Nizam's Government and country, whilst performing its duty in this respect, became the indirect means of preventing the people from obtaining redress from their oppression. In former times they would have found a natural redress in armed revolt led by their chiefs. The presence, however, of an armed and disciplined force prevented this, and, as it could not be used against their chiefs without enquiry and consequent delay, they were left to the mercy of those who should have been their immediate protectors, but who, oppressed themselves, became their oppressors.

As regards the Nizam, however, there can be no doubt that he felt a great relief by the removal of Chandoo Lal; for more than 40 years this old man had been the practical ruler of the country, and the Nizam and his father had been puppets in his hands. The Maharajah's policy had been to maintain himself in power by deferring in every respect to the wishes of the Government of India, as represented by the Resident. As Minister with plenary powers, every part of the administration was in his hands. Except as a last resource he knew that the British Government would not interfere in internal matters, and the Nizam could not, because none of the details of the executive were in his hands. The consequence was that, although the Subsidiary Army and the Contingent were an efficient protection of the Nizam's person and the country, they were of little or no protection to the people against oppression. The Nizam dared not remove his Minister, because he knew that the Resident and the British Government would support him, and, even when General Fraser became aware of the misgovernment that was being perpetrated, and showed himself in favour of a change, the Nizam scarcely dared consent. Living alone in his palace, ignorant of all State affairs and transacting no business with the Resident himself, he was easily persuaded that any change would be distasteful to the Government of India, who had so consistently shown themselves to be the supporters of his Minister. When, however, the change did take place and, owing mainly to the Resident's action, the Minister did send in his resignation, believing in his heart of hearts that the Government would not allow it to be accepted, the relief which the Nizam felt by the removal of a subject to whom he was in fact a subordinate was so great that he was averse to appoint another. He certainly nominated Ministers, but, as he refrained from bestowing upon them full powers, matters came to a deadlock. It had been the habitual custom for all subjects of public business to be settled between the Minister and the Resident, any settlement being subsequently ratified by the Nizam, as a matter of course. Now the Minister could settle nothing, and, since by etiquette the Resident could not discuss business with the Nizam, nothing was done.

Such was the condition of affairs at Hyderabad when Lord Hardinge arrived in Calcutta, in 1845, and one of the new Governor-General's first acts was to address to the

Nizam a letter of grave remonstrance (11th April, 1845), not only as regards the arrears due to the Contingent, but also regarding the effects of maladministration on the country itself. The Nizam was told " that, in the event of this state of things leading to serious and unhappy consequences, the British Government will not consent to put down by force of arms, troubles and opposition to your Highness's authority, manifestly caused by the oppression under which the people suffer in consequence of the maladministration of your Highness' Dominions." This warning had a certain amount of effect. Though still reluctant to invest his Minister with full powers, the Nizam made a strong effort to remedy the financial evil, so that in June of the same year the Resident was able to report that the Nizam had disbursed from his personal treasury about one crore and twenty lakhs of rupees (£1,200,000). It is doubtful however whether the disbursement of this large amount had been done in a judicious manner, for the Peshcar Rajah Ram Buksh was still unable to provide for the payment of the Contingent without allowing it to fall more than four months in arrears (*Life of General Fraser*, Chapter VI). In the meantime, the Governor-General and Lord Gough were engaged in the Sikh war and the conquest of the Punjab, and for the time their attention was devoted to the important negotiations which followed the battles of Moodkee, Ferozeshah and Sobraon. In the following year (1846), the disturbance anticipated by the Governor-General in his letter above quoted actually took place and five of the principal Zemindars enlisted bands of Rohillas and commenced plundering the surrounding country. The Nizam applied for the services of the Contingent to coerce them but the Resident declined to give the necessary orders until a month's pay should be given in advance to the troops in addition to the four months of arrears due, and until he himself had investigated into the complaints. The refractory chiefs, except one, protected by safe conducts, appeared before the Resident, and, in due course, made a peaceable submission, whilst the one who had failed to come in was " brought to obedience without actual bloodshed by the appearance of a detachment of troops in his neighbourhood" (*ibid*).

In September of this year (1846) the debt due to the British Government on account of the Contingent amounted to thirty-eight lakhs (£380,000), in addition to the four months' arrears, and called forth another serious remonstrance from the Government of India, with the result that in November of that year the Nizam at last conferred full powers upon the Minister, Suraj-ul-Mulk, the uncle of the afterwards celebrated Salar Jung. In his order of appointment the Nizam expressly says that he did so on the recommendation of the " undoubted well-wisher of the Nobles of the Court, Major-General James Stuart Fraser Bahadur," thus throwing, as it were, the responsibility for the appointment on the representative of the British Government, so that should it prove a failure he would be able to attribute some part of his embarrassment to their agency. This responsibility the Government of India was by no means willing to assume, and although, as General Fraser suggested, the best plan would have been to openly accept it, and by a cordial promise of support to crush all faction and intrigue, this course was not adopted, " partly by the settled practice of the Calcutta authorities, partly by an accident," and the result was, as reported by General Fraser in July, 1847, " most detrimental to the Minister."

The " accident " mentioned by General Fraser consisted in what the Government of India deemed a breach of official etiquette. In reporting to the Governor-General his appointment as Minister, Suraj-ul-Mulk addressed him as "the friend and well-wisher." This was a repetition of a phrase used forty years before by the Nawab Mir Allum on his appointment as Minister. There had been no occasion for a similar report to be made subsequently, because the Maharajah Chandoo Lal had never been really appointed as Minister, and, although he was the virtual Minister and was always treated as such by the Government and the Resident, officially he was only the Peshcar or Revenue Minister. At the time when Mir Allum reported his appointment, the relations between the Hyderabad State and the Government of India were very different from what they had become forty years later. At the commencement of the 19th century the Governor-General was actually a tributary of the Nizam, because he paid the Nizam tribute for the provinces he held known as the Northern Circars. He was therefore a subject of the Nizam, and in all communications styled himself "*niazmund*" or petitioner, whilst the Nizam in reply spoke of himself as "*Maba Dowlah*," or "Our Royalty." Since then, however, circumstances had altered. The British Government no longer paid tribute for the Circars, and had become in fact the paramount power in India. The Governor-General was no longer the petitioner of the Nizam, but in reality his superior, and therefore it was improper that the Nizam's Minister should address the Governor-General on terms of equality. But, although an alteration in the form of correspondence had been made when Secunder Jah succeeded in 1828, it had been forgotten to make any alteration in the form of correspondence between the Minister and the Governor-General. Hence when Suraj-ul-Mulk was appointed he merely followed the precedent of Mir Allum forty years before. It took the Government of India eight months to cut this Gordian red-tape knot, and then they pointed out the reason of the delay in acknowledging the Minister's letter reporting his appointment. No doubt the reasoning of the Governor-General was perfectly correct. The forty years that had elapsed had brought about an enormous change in the relations between the head of the Government of India and the native princes. He was no longer the "petitioner" or suppliant, whose representative had to take off his shoes before approaching a native prince, but he was now the "Paramount Power," whose expressed wish was accepted by every prince as an order, and it was therefore manifestly improper that a subordinate of the prince should address the Governor-General as an equal. Still, the matter was so simple that it could have been easily arranged by a few words of semi-official correspondence, without having had to incur the long delay which ensued before the Government of India recognized the appointment of the new Minister. In India a delay of this kind is always dangerous, and tends to weaken the position and the influence of the new nominee. The Nizam naturally thought that the delay meant a disapproval of his choice, and as this choice had been made at the recommendation of the Resident he reasoned to himself that neither the Resident nor the Minister enjoyed the full confidence of the Governor-General, consequently none of the internal reforms which the Resident was anxious to carry out were accepted by him, and for more than 18 months matters remained as unsettled as they had been before the Minister's appointment. The next step of the Government of India was calculated to continue this impression. One of the Resident's schemes was to appoint a Mr. Dighton as the Commissioner of one of the districts which it was intended should serve as a model for the revenue administration of the remainder of the kingdom. This appointment was approved of by the Minister and by the Nizam. Mr. Dighton was a gentleman well known, of good birth, of strict probity, and a favourite with all classes. He enjoyed the confidence of the Residency, the Nobles, the Government and of the Nizam. He would therefore seem to have been a most fitting person for such an appointment, but strange to say the Government of India would not sanction this nomination. The very fact of his being intimate at the Residency was deemed an objection, as being likely to raise a suspicion in the Nizam's mind that we wished to interfere in the internal administration of this country. The policy of the Government at this time, which we may safely say has been continued up to the present day, was to refrain from any interference whatsoever with the internal affairs of a native state, unless compelled to do so by a systematic maladministration calculated to produce an outbreak of the people. As long as matters did not reach this point, a policy of "laissez faire" was adopted in the dealings with native states, and when at last interference became necessary it was generally done by the means of an armed force, and spelt—annexation. This is a point upon which General Fraser, who seems to have been actuated with a sincere wish to remedy the evils which existed in the Hyderabad State, felt very keenly. His long experience of native princes, and of the change of conditions of affairs in India, induced him to form the opinion that all that was required was to make use of the moral influence which the British rule had acquired in order to suggest improvements. In such a case no armed interference was necessary. A wish would be regarded as an order, and a required reform would at once be carried out. Of course, this policy would throw a great responsibility upon the shoulders of the Resident, but it was a responsibility which our experience of administration in India shows he is always capable of bearing. Of the moral advantage to the native state of such a policy there could be no doubt. An improvement of the administration would of necessity take place without in any way jeopardizing its independence. On the other hand the "laissez faire" policy seemed calculated to pave the way to annexation and annihilation. It almost seems to the student of Indian history that at times the Government of India fostered this policy of non-interference in order to bring about the inevitable result. This seems to have been the impression caused in the mind of General Fraser. The General had the courage of his opinions and did not hesitate to express them with less reserve than was calculated to be acceptable to his superiors. Deeply interested as he was in the welfare of Hyderabad, he was profoundly disappointed at the refusal of the Government of India to support his system of reform. He wrote a private letter to Sir James Lushington, the Chairman of the Board of Directors, which is of such importance that it will be as well to quote it at length. The letter is dated 25th October, 1847, and is reproduced from the work from which we have already so frequently quoted. It runs as follows: "Improvement in Hyderabad has not progressed. I lament that such should be the case as there is no inherent necessity that it should be so. A little decision on the part of the supreme Government and its assent to what I recommended would have been sufficient. It is to this subject I wish to attract your attention and to obtain if possible the assent of the Court to some policy of their own devising, if not of mine, which may correct the evils of this Government, in the shame of which I may perhaps be made to participate, though I do not deserve it. I wish to induce the Court either to act with some vigour in this matter, or to acknowledge that they do not care to save the Nizam, and that he must be considered as bearing the exclusive responsibility of the ruin to which the Hyderabad State is hastening. The proceedings of the Resident here, to that extent only which has been sanctioned, cannot be of any use. A higher tone must be adopted to be of service. A continuance of its present course by the supreme Government will involve this country in the fate of Mysore.

"We are bound under the obligations of treaties to maintain the independence of this and several other native states, and until the treaties are infringed by the princes themselves, or the safety of our own provinces is in danger, we are bound to uphold them. All that I wish is that this should be done effectually, and in such a manner as to be at once consistent with the prosperity of a native state and with the general advancement of the Indian Empire in the path of good order and reform. It is not possible that so large a portion of India should be in a bad way without the adjacent districts being injuriously affected. We can adhere to our treaties in perfect good faith, and yet insist at the same time that the sustained independence of Hyderabad shall not impede the equally sacred obligations under which we are placed *not to allow our military protection of the Nizam to involve, as a necessary consequence, the misery and helplessness of his people.* We must not allow a barrier to be raised against the advancement of India in general in the ill-regulated condition of this particular State.

In the measures I have continuously proposed, the ulterior object has not only been a better administration for Hyderabad, but beneficial results for our own territory. Unhappily, in almost all instances, I have been prohibited not only from active interposition but from interposition at all. I need not enter into particulars. The evils of the Hyderabad Government and the state of disorder generally prevailing through the country must have been sufficiently well known at the Court of Directors when I was sent here by Lord Auckland. These evils continue as they were to this day. *Can it be the intention of the Court that they should remain so until some crisis arrives, which may afford a pretext for placing the Nizam's country under a Commission, with our train of English judges and collectors?* I cannot believe this to be the intention of the Court, and, if not, surely means ought to be adopted which may avert these consequences. Correction becomes more difficult by every day we remain inactive. The Government of India has in general expressed its concurrence in my views and wishes regarding the Nizam's affairs, but not in the measures which I have recommended as alone likely to accomplish those views. If my suggestions had been objectionable, let others be brought forward. Let me be favoured with commands, which I promise to execute, but let not the only commands be—to do nothing. This deliberate inaction appears to me to be as dishonourable to us as it is injurious to the Nizam."

The interference which General Fraser here advocates would seem to have been especially justified, because the British Government was, to a very great degree, responsible for the financial embarrassments into which the Hyderabad Government had fallen. For about 25 years we had so far interfered with Hyderabad as to compel the Nizam to maintain, at a cost of 40 lakhs annually, during a time of profound peace, a force which by treaty he was only bound to maintain in time of war. The chances of there being a war which would affect the safety of the Nizam's dominions had long since passed away. Whatever danger might accrue to the country would be from refractory landholders. Any such uprisings it was the duty of the Subsidiary Force to subdue, and for this provision had been made in the treaty of 1800. The Contingent therefore was really unnecessary, but finding a minister subservient enough to their views the British Government had so far interfered with the Nizam as to continue the maintenance of this force at the cost of nearly one-third of the total revenue of the state, entirely for their own purposes. There can be no doubt that the financial embarrassments of the Nizam had commenced with the necessity of constantly providing the funds necessary to pay for the Contingent. But, although no longer required for the purposes of war, no attempt was made to reduce either the numbers or the cost of the Contingent. The evidence on this point is overwhelming; from the Governor-General downwards, the Resident, and the members of the Courts of Directors who were best conversant in Hyderabad affairs, are all unanimous on this subject. General Fraser may perhaps be deemed a prejudiced person in this respect, but in the year 1848 he went away on six months' furlough and during his absence Colonel (afterwards General Sir John) Lowe, acted for him. We will quote from the letter which he wrote and left on record for the General's information on his return: " My opinion entirely coincides with your own respecting the cruelty, as I may well call it, that we have been guilty of towards the Nizam's Government, in keeping up for so many years the continued drain upon the revenues of his country of no less than forty lakhs of rupees per annum for the pay of the Contingent—in other words for purposes of our own, not of the Nizam's. Ever since 1819 there has been profound peace in the Deccan, and therefore, as it is only during "war between the contracting parties and any other power" that we can claim to be joined by 6,000 infantry and 9,000 horse of His Highness' troops, we have had no right by treaty to demand a single rupee for the Contingent during the whole of that period, upwards of 28 years. In the course of that time, however, we have actually drawn from the Nizam's treasury the enormous sum of 11 crores and 20 lakhs of rupees, of which a large portion has gone out of the Nizam's territory for ever through the remittances of the officers and sepoys, two-thirds of whom are from Oudh, Rohilkund and other parts of India, who annually take away their savings in hard cash to their distant homes, so that this huge drain not only exhausts the Nizam's treasury, but tends to impoverish his people by diminishing the amount of specie in his dominions. ". . . I remember to have pointed out to Mr. Colvin, in 1838, that since the year 1819, a Contingent of half the strength, costing 20 lakhs of rupees a year, could do precisely the same service for the Nizam's Government as the present force does, which costs forty lakhs."

This is what General Sir James Law-Lushington said on 24th April, 1848 : " The great difficulty is the state of the finances in Hyderabad, and something must be done to afford relief or the severe pressure must end in ultimate ruin. I have for some time been of the opinion that we have ourselves been the cause in a great measure of this difficulty, and have made exactions of the Nizam which we were not entitled to do by any treaty." He then alludes to the cost of the Contingent, which really the

Nizam was only bound to furnish *in time of war*, entailing a charge upon the Nizam's Government of forty-two lakhs of rupees every year; and goes on to say, "This demand swallows up nearly one-third of the country's revenues, and the consequence has been that the Nizam is now in debt to the British Government for sums advanced for the payment of the Contingent Force. Considering all these circumstances, I certainly am of opinion that the disbandment of the Contingent is a measure the propriety of which is worthy of the most serious consideration; for it cannot be denied that neither a continued maintenance nor the original organization is provided for by any existing treaty."

One more quotation from Lord Dalhousie himself. It is taken from a letter to General Fraser, dated 17th October, 1848. In it he says: "While I am not one of those who regard the Contingent Force as an oppression and an injustice, I yet think that we do not stand free of blame in respect to the footing on which we have maintained it. And, *whenever the Nizam shall manifest a sincere wish* to enter into an amendment of his administration, I shall be ready on the part of the Government of India to meet his endeavours to reduce the expenditure of his kingdom by entering on the consideration of the means of diminishing the *extravagant costliness* of this force and its appendages."

One example of the costliness of the force may be gathered from the fact that there were no less than five Brigadiers, each with a costly staff, and the force itself was scattered amongst six different cantonments, in each of which was the usual establishment of cantonment magistrate, police, etc.

It would therefore seem that General Fraser was actuated by a sincere sense of justice when he argued that, having once interfered, with the result of increasing the Nizam's embarrassments, we should now interfere with friendly help to improve the administration, so as to relieve him from those embarrassments. But neither Lord Ellenborough, Lord Hardinge, nor Lord Dalhousie seem to have understood the kind of interference which General Fraser advocated. What he wanted was, by a strong support of the Minister, aided by the Resident's advice, to introduce reforms in spite of the Nizam and of the various intriguers by whom he was surrounded. In the same way as the constant support which we had given to Chandoo Lal, in opposition to the wishes of two consecutive Nizams, had been the means of causing that Minister to play into our hands and offer no opposition to the maintenance of the costly Contingent, so a similar support given to Suraj-ul-Mulk, who was honestly anxious, in co-operation with the Resident, to carry out these reforms, would most certainly have enabled him to do so. But here the Resident was at once met with the answer that " the Nizam is an independent Sovereign and we cannot interfere with the internal arrangement of his dominions." It is significant that this argument never occurred to the Government of India when they brought pressure to bear upon Chandoo Lal to reform the troops which ultimately became the Contingent. A reform of a military body devoted entirely to our own interests was apparently not inconsistent with treaty rights, but a reform of the internal administration by which the Nizam alone would have benefited was so considered. Whenever General Fraser spoke of interference the answer was " we cannot now spare any troops." But troops were not what General Fraser wanted, he did not want an interference by armed force, but the permission to use a moral force, to which the Nizam would undoubtedly yield when once convinced that it was the wish of the Government of India.

Again, it will be noticed that Lord Dalhousie, whilst admitting the extravagant cost of the Contingent, does not make any attempt at reduction of that cost conditional on the Nizam manifesting a sincere wish to enter into an amendment of his own administration. Now one of the first steps towards such an amendment would have been the disbandment, and reduction in the expenditure, of the large army of mercenary troops which the Nizam still maintained, and which consumed nearly 75 lakhs of rupees annually out of the revenue of the country. It can well be imagined that if, with all the pressure the Resident was constantly bringing to bear upon him, the Nizam allowed the Contingent troops to fall into arrears, it was still more likely that he allowed his own troops to fall into still greater arrears. This was in fact the case, and, since it was impossible for him, without credit, to find the money to pay off these arrears, it was impossible for him to attempt a reduction in the expenditure without causing a mutiny. Of this fact a significant illustration occurred at the period of which we are writing.

Early in 1847, Suraj-ul-Mulk, in pursuance of his promises to the Resident to reduce expenditure, as a first step towards this object, made arrangements to disband about six thousand of the half-disciplined troops maintained in Hyderabad. On the first of May the Minister informed the Resident that these men refused to take their pay or to give up their arms, and that they had been joined by the whole of the rest of the line, who had placed their commandants under arrest, and insisted on being equally paid up their arrears of pay, when, they said, they would all take their discharge if required. On the third of May, the mutiny being still unabated, and the Minister's own life having been threatened, he applied for military assistance. The Resident at once ordered a force consisting of four companies of H.M. 84th Foot, two regiments of Madras Native Infantry and a detachment of Madras Artillery, with four nine-pounder guns, first to a spot called the foundry, about a mile and a half from the city walls, and then, when the "Line-wallahs" still refused to release their commandants, the General took possession of the very gate of the city. Two days were occupied in inconclusive negotiations and the troops were about to march upon the mutinous troops, when they tendered their submission and returned to obedience on the seventh of May; the reductions were then carried out and the British force withdrawn.

The Government of India were at first doubtful of the expediency of this very decisive action on the part of the Resident, but eventually gave a half-hearted approval. The whole incident, however, was so dangerous an experiment that the Minister scarcely dared to make another one in the same direction. No further reductions were therefore carried out, and the Minister's attempts to reduce the military expenditure appear to have begun and ended with this one incident. To the Nizam's mind, however, this occurrence together with the refusal of the Government of India to sanction the appointment of Mr. Dighton, before alluded to, seemed a proof that not only his Minister but also the Resident no longer enjoyed the support of the Government of India, and he was therefore obliged to remove the Minister, who had been appointed on the Resident's recommendation. This was done in the following year, and Rajah Ram Buksh was appointed in his place.

This appointment, however, was only temporary and was followed by that of a nobleman named Umjad-ul-Mulk, who, in his turn, remained for only one month, when the Nawab Shums-ul-Umra was appointed Minister. The appointment of this nobleman who was of the very highest rank, and who had been married to the sister of the late Nizam, was opposed to the tradition of the country. He was the head of the Paigah force, and as such was supposed to keep aloof from politics and to be exclusively in the Nizam's service. He was a nobleman of undoubted honour and universal esteem, but was thoroughly conservative in his opinions and disinclined towards reform. Matters, therefore, lapsed into their old groove, and financially the condition of the country went from bad to worse.

A curious incident occurred at this time which must be noticed: the Portugese Archbishop of Goa was the Patriarch of India, and claimed ecclesiastical jurisdiction over the entire continent. He was appointed by the King of Portugal, and the result was that his jurisdiction clashed with that of a great number of Roman Catholic missionaries appointed by the Pope and of the priests who were military chaplains to the British troops. These disputes sometimes took the form of a dispute regarding the possession of a church or chapel. In 1848 a dispute of this kind arose in Secunderabad, the British military cantonment of Hyderabad. A collision took place between the Goanese and the European priests, with whom the coloured Catholics and the Irish soldiers respectively took sides. A riot took place in which no very serious damage was done beyond the wrecking of the chapel in dispute. Some soldiers of the Queen's Regiment and of the Company's artillery had taken part in the riot, and one or two Irish priests were accused of having incited them to violence by words spoken at the altar; while the Vicar Apostolic, Bishop Murphy, was blamed for not having either previously forbidden or subsequently blamed the violent acts and words of his curates and his flock. A long enquiry was conducted by the Government of Madras under whose jurisdiction the Secunderabad troops were placed. The result was that the Madras Government called upon General Fraser to expel the bishop and the priests from the Nizam's dominions; this the Resident refused to do without referring the matter to the Government of India. There would appear to be no object to be gained in giving the details of the correspondence which followed; suffice it to say that a compromise was arrived at, the bishop was not expelled from the diocese, but was forbidden to enter Secunderabad where were situated his cathedral church, the principal schools, and the charitable institutions under his charge. For two years he could obtain no release from this anomalous state of affairs, but eventually sought redress in London, and then, by instructions from the Court of Directors, the prohibition was removed and he was allowed to return and resume the full exercise of his episcopal functions.

During the year 1849 no improvement took place in Hyderabad affairs. The debt still went on increasing, and now amounted to 64 lakhs of rupees. It is true that the interest which was formerly charged at the rate of 12 per cent. had been reduced to 6 per cent., but this item alone materially helped to increase the debt. Another warning was received from Lord Dalhousie in which it is stated that if early steps were not taken to clear off this debt " the Governor-General will feel himself under the necessity of taking such measures as shall be effectual both for ensuring those objects for which the faith of this Government is virtually pledged and for maintaining the security of its own interest." In a letter to General Fraser at the same time Lord Dalhousie emphatically repudiates the Resident's policy of friendly interference, to save the state from the ruin to which it was progressing. In a letter dated June 6th, 1849, he says : " I will rigidly act up to the requirements of the treaty with the Nizam. I will give him aid and advice. I will effectually take care that if he chooses to ruin himself in spite of aid and advice he shall not disturb the peace of British territory, or either injure or play with British interests, but I will not contravene the treaty on the pretence of protecting the Nizam, and I disavow the doctrine of our having any moral or political obligation to take the government of his country into our own hands merely because he mismanages his own affairs ; *and I recognize no mission entrusted to us to regenerate independent Indian States merely because they are misgoverned ; when we are invited, or our own interests affected I will act decidedly enough.*"

During this year a body of the Contingent was called upon to suppress a rising of some Rohillas in the Berar Province, a very smart and gallant affair took place on May 6th near the village of Gowrie in which Brigadier Hampton was severely wounded, besides three English and four native officers. There was a brilliant cavalry charge, in which the Rohillas were cut up and dispersed.

The remainder of the year was occupied in a repetition of the same old story. Delays in the matter of payment by the Nizam's Government and remonstrances and warnings from the Government of India. During this time we notice an increased acerbity in the tone of Lord Dalhousie's letters to the Resident, and an increased peremptoriness in his remarks about the Nizam and his State.

Although we have dwelt upon the Nizam's financial embarrassments, they were not really so great as may be imagined. The total amount of his indebtedness was not more than three years' revenue, and if he had only possessed credit he could easily have raised a loan sufficient to pay off all his debts. But loans in India, especially at this time, could only be made at high interest. He was debarred from attempting to raise a loan from European capitalists and the Government of India could not, or would not assist him. The Nizam therefore was reduced to a continual state of borrowing, and was compelled from time to time to raise money at high interest in one place to pay off the debts he incurred in another. Of course this meant that the interests of the country were neglected, the revenues decreased, and the liabilities swollen by interest and discount went on increasing. The minister, Shams-ul-Umra, found it impossible to carry on the government and in July, 1849, resigned his post. All that he had been able to do was to keep up the current payment of the Contingent, but the old debt had continued to increase.

Rajah Ram Buksh was then appointed, not as a Minister with full powers, but simply as Peshkar; this induced Lord Dalhousie to send another solemn warning in which the Resident was directed to require " that the whole amount should be discharged by the 31st of December, 1850. If on the arrival of that period the Governor-General's expectations were disappointed, his Lordship would feel it his duty to take such decided steps as the interests of the British Government demanded." Those decided steps it was well understood would be the exaction of territorial security for the payment of principal and interest; and, as the Governor-General must have been convinced that the Nizam would be unable to comply with this demand, a correspondence was at once commenced with the Resident regarding the most suitable districts to be handed over.

CHAPTER XV

The period which this chapter embraces, namely, 1851 and 1852, is occupied by a considerable amount of controversial matter. I have endeavoured as much as possible to refrain from entering into the details of this controversy, and have sought to confine myself almost entirely to the actual facts which occurred. The arguments advanced by General Fraser regarding the policy to be adopted towards the Nizam not having been accepted by the Governor-General, no object could be gained by entering into them here. They are all contained in Captain Hastings Fraser's book on the life of his father, General Fraser. To that book I am already largely indebted for the quotations I have made in the two preceeding chapters, and, should anyone wish to study this subject in further detail, I would recommend this book for the purpose.

THE first months of 1851 passed without any improvement in the financial condition of Hyderabad. Nothing was done towards the repayment of the old debt. The period fixed for its payment having passed, the Resident was busy in preparing instructions to the officers who were to be placed in charge of the districts to be held as security. These officers were Colonel Meadows Taylor, who for some years had, with the permission of the Nizam, been managing the small tributary state of

Shorapur under the Resident's orders, Mr. Bullock and Mr. Dighton. As the assignment was only to be a temporary one and the districts were still to remain under the Nizam's suzerainty, they were instructed to make no radical changes. The Resident sent to the Governor-General the draft of a letter which he suggested should be sent to the Nizam by the Governor-General. This letter was in consistence with his policy of friendly interference and management which by no means conformed to the plan Lord Dalhousie was inclined to adopt; accordingly, some time elapsed before an answer was received. In the meantime, events occurred which brought matters to a crisis. During the march of a detachment of British troops through H.H. the Nizam's Dominions a fracas occurred between them and some of the Nizam's irregular troops. This incident gave the Governor-General an opportunity which he did not allow to escape. As long as the differences between the Government of India and the Nizam referred to matters of finance Lord Dalhousie was inclined to show a certain amount of consideration to an old and faithful ally. But what he considered to be an affront to the head of the Empire, in the person of a detachment of British troops, could not be met with the same equanimity and forbearance. The letter dealt with two subjects, the disputes which had arisen between the Sepoys and some Arab soldiers, and the failure of the Nizam to fulfil his promises regarding the repayment of the debt. The Nizam was told that the former incident rendered him liable to the " indignation of the Government of India, whose power can crush you at its will." These are the words of the English letter, but in the Persian translation they were rendered " whose power can make you as the dust under foot, and leave you neither a name nor a trace." The letter then went on to call upon the Nizam to make over to the British Government a certain portion of his territory as repayment of the debt due to the British Government on the account of the debt due for the Contingent. He was told that no remonstrances or solicitations would be admitted, and that the Governor-General's determination was fixed irrevocably. (*Blue Book*, "Nizam's Debt," page 43.) It was also pointed out that a Minister should be appointed who would be a fit agent for transacting the important affairs between the Government of India and the Court of Hyderabad. The effect of this letter was like that of a bolt from the blue. No communication from the Governor-General to the Nizam had ever approached to this in severity of tone. Hitherto the Resident complained that the Government of India had not been decisive in the tenor of its despatches, and he was always recommending a policy of friendly interference, which if firmly insisted upon he was sure the Nizam would have agreed to. No doubt he would have done so, but Lord Dalhousie's policy was that an interference of any kind would be a violation of existing treaties, that nothing could be done unless the Government in pursuance of its own interest was compelled to interfere, and that then the steps to be taken should be of a drastic nature. In one way he was certainly right. The letter had the desired effect. The Nizam saw that in order to avoid a serious catastrophe he must awake from his lethargy and take a decided step. Suraj-ul-Mulk was at once appointed as Minister, and when, on the first of the month following (July 1st, 1851) the Resident waited on the Nizam to inform him of the districts which would be taken over, he was told that the Minister would pay the whole debt and also make arrangements for the regular pay of the Contingent.

This time the Nizam kept his promise, at all events in part. On the 15th of August the Nizam's Government completed the payment of the first instalment, more than half, of the debt due to the British Government, namely, Rs. 3,408,485.11.4, leaving the balance of Rs. 3,297,702.9.2 to be paid on or before the first of October, 1851. (*ibid.* page 67.) How the Nizam managed to pay this instalment is not exactly known. Some of it was taken from his private treasure and the balance by pledging some of his jewels to the native bankers. At all events the Nizam had shown himself in earnest, and for the present Lord Dalhousie was content to be satisfied, and matters were allowed to go on. Before long, however, affairs fell into their old groove. The current pay of the Contingent was only irregularly disbursed, and the balance of the debt, instead of being decreased, again began to rise. It was under these conditions that the year 1851 came to a close. The Minister doubtless was in earnest in his endeavours to carry out reforms. In internal matters, acting under the Resident's advice, much was done, but as regards finance he was powerless. There was no money in the country and in the words of the old proverb it was impossible to press blood out of a stone.

The early months of 1852 continued under the same conditions, but an attempt was made by the Hyderabad Government to put in a counterclaim against the British Government as the set-off to the debt due to them. This counterclaim arose as follows. During the forty years which had elapsed since the Contingent Forces had been stationed in separate cantonments, we had neglected to pay over to the Nizam's Government certain excise duties on liquor, which during that time had been wrongly credited to cantonment funds. These duties amounted to about a lakh of rupees a year, and would, therefore, reach the aggregate sum of about forty lakhs of rupees, which should have, but had not been credited to the Nizam. That this demand was justified is shown by the fact that it was subsequently admitted, and since 1853 these excise duties have been regularly paid to the Nizam's Government. But even General Fraser, inclined as he was to help the Nizam, was not able to admit the validity of this claim under the existing circumstances. The claim was one that was open to argument, whereas the debt was an acknowledged fact. He could not, therefore, admit a claim open to dispute as a set-off to an acknowledged debt. The latter must be paid according to the terms of the agreement, whereas the former might be left open to future consideration. As already mentioned, the claim was subsequently admitted, and has since been regularly paid, but the arrears which had accrued during forty years, and which apparently had never been claimed by the Hyderabad Government during that time have never been paid up to the present day.

The months in 1852 passed on, and not only was no further instalment of principal debt received, but also the current cost of the Contingent again began to fall in arrears, so that it became apparent to the Governor-General that the Nizam would be unable to fulfil his promise. Accordingly, a letter was despatched to the Resident in which the matter of assignment of territory was again dwelt upon. This letter was remarkable for an entire change in Lord Dalhousie's views regarding the status of the Contingent. Hitherto he had always maintained, not only that there was no injustice in the maintenance of the Contingent, but that its constitution was actually based on the treaty of 1800, because under that treaty the Nizam had agreed to furnish 15,000 men in time of war. In fact, in his letter of the previous year to the Nizam, the Governor-General had pointed out in so many words that the Nizam was bound under treaty to maintain the Contingent. In this letter, however, Lord Dalhousie expresses an entirely different opinion. He says: " If the Nizam should turn round upon us and deny the obligation existing by treaty, I am bound as a public man to say that I could not honestly argue that there was any other warrant than that of practice for upholding the Contingent; I could argue, and have argued, that His Highness's conduct has hitherto given that construction to the treaty and that till it is rejected and resisted there is an obligation upon him to support properly the force which, under that construction, he has allowed us to organize: but, if he were to take his stand upon the treaty, I could not argue that either the letter or the spirit of it bound the Nizam to maintain 9,000 troops of a peculiar and costly nature in peace because it bound him to give 15,000 of his troops on the occurrence of war." He then goes on to point out that either the Contingent is to be maintained in future, in which case it becomes absolutely necessary that an assignment of districts should be made so as to pay off the debt and also to provide for the regular payment of the force, or else it must be disbanded. But, even in this case, it would take some years before so large a force could be gradually disbanded, and therefore it would still be necessary for the Nizam to make an assignment of territory in order to provide, not only for the pay of the troops in the meanwhile, but also for the repayment of the debt; therefore whether the Contingent was retained or abolished, it became necessary for the Nizam to assign territory. The Resident was accordingly instructed to take the necessary steps. General Fraser's answer was very respectfully worded, but it was evident from the whole tone of his reply that although he obeyed he did not approve of his instructions. Lord Dalhousie had already stated in one of his letters that meekness was not one of his qualities and it is therefore probable that the attitude of the Resident was highly distasteful to him. An opportunity soon occurred for expressing his displeasure. For some time there had been a very disagreeable controversy between some of the senior officers of the Contingent which led to a court martial being held at Bolarum, its head-quarters. General Fraser, by virtue of his position as representing the Nizam, confirmed the proceedings of the court martial, and endorsed its remarks as regards one of the officers concerned. The Government of India in reviewing these proceedings, whilst agreeing with them, remarked that the Resident had appeared to have been actuated by the same party spirit which he blamed in others. It does not seem that this remark was justified, but at the same time it could not be received by an officer in the Resident's position except as a severe reprimand.

At the same time another incident occurred which tended to bring about the catastrophe which had for so long a time been hanging over the Nizam's head. In order to pay off the whole of the debt still remaining due to the British Government, the Nizam had resolved to pawn his jewels up to the value of about half a million sterling. It was contemplated to form a State Bank in Hyderabad, which was to be financed by the leading sowcars, and the managing director of which was to be Mr. Dighton, of whom we have so often spoken. To this bank the Nizam agreed to hand over his jewels, and received in return an advance of forty lakhs of rupees. Contrary to all expectation, not only was the bank successfully founded, but the whole of this transaction was faithfully carried out : the jewels were handed over and the money was sent to the Nizam. Before, however, he had time to pay it over to the Resident the Governor-General interfered. He refused to sanction the formation of the bank on the ground that, as one of the directors was a European, it would be contrary to the Act of George III, which prohibited all financial transactions between Europeans and native princes. This order, which was entirely unexpected, created a panic in Hyderabad. The Nizam, who had parted with his jewels, naturally held on to the money he had received, whilst the sowcars who had handed over the money to the Nizam in the expectation of being able to recoup themselves from the State Bank saw no way of getting their money back and wanted at all events to get the jewels as some sort of security. Mr. Dighton was thus placed in a very awkward position. He was responsible to the Nizam on the one hand for the safety of the jewels, and on the other hand he was equally responsible to the sowcars for the repayment of the money they had advanced. He managed to extricate himself from this dilemma in a very remarkable and thoroughly Oriental manner. The jewels were all kept in a safe in which were stowed different trays. The safe was locked with three different keys, each of which was kept by one of the persons interested. A meeting was called in order to form an inventory of the jewels to see that all was correct. The safe was opened and each tray was brought before the Committee, the jewels were counted and the tray was then carried back. But before they were replaced in the safe the contents of each tray were poured into a pair of jack-boots, the trays were placed empty in the safe, covered with their respective cloths and the safe was formally locked by the different members of the Committee, whilst the jewels were carried up to Mr. Dighton's room. That same evening Mr. Dighton started in a palanquin of one of his attendants with a box marked medical comforts. In this way carrying jewels with him to the value of half a million sterling he managed to get out of the Nizam's dominions; he reached Madras, got on board ship, and safely took the jewels to Europe, where they were deposited with a banking firm in Holland. This firm advanced the money necessary to pay off the sowcars, and eventually Salar Jung redeemed the jewels, had them brought back to Hyderabad and handed over to the Nizam. In this way no one eventually incurred any loss and the honourable conduct of Mr. Dighton and of Salar Jung not only redounded to their renown but was a foundation of the credit which the new Minister enjoyed for the next thirty years. In order to finish the narration of this episode we have been obliged to somewhat anticipate events, for the transaction was not terminated until about a year later. It is therefore now necessary to revert to Hyderabad.

These two incidents following so close after each other convinced General Fraser that he no longer enjoyed the Governor-General's confidence, and as at this time he received the news of his elder brother's death he resolved to leave India for good. Accordingly he sent in his resignation, which was at once accepted; he went home and never returned.

Colonel Lowe was appointed to succeed General Fraser, and came to Hyderabad with the draft of a treaty in his pocket, with which we must now deal.

CHAPTER XVI

THE BERAR TRUST

IT has been shown in the previous chapter how matters in Hyderabad gradually went from bad to worse, and how involved and entangled the finances of the State had become.

The result of Lord Dalhousie's warning in 1850 was that a couple of years later negotiations commenced, which resulted in the assignment to the British of certain districts in the Nizam's dominions.

The assignment of these districts led to much controversy which continued for many years, and which caused much ink to flow. In order to be able to judge impartially of the pros and cons of the question and fully to understand the situation it will be necessary to look back some years, to see what led up to the discussion and also somewhat to anticipate events by glancing forward, to see how this discussion was partly settled, some fifty years later. This will give a clearer view of the matter than could be obtained by merely confining the narration to the period in hand, and constantly harking back to this argument, which for the next 75 years played so large a rôle in the political foreground of Hyderabad.

It is now necessary to examine how the Berar Trust was created, and how it was administered, and for this purpose it will be necessary to sum up the situation.

It will be remembered that after the fall of Seringapatam in 1799, and the partition of Mysore, the British Government agreed to maintain a standing army of not less than 8,000 sepoys and 1,000 cavalry in Hyderabad, in order to protect the Nizam from his dangerous enemies. At that time he was surrounded by foes of the most ambitious and aggressive character. The Peishwa at Poona, Scindia, Holkar and the Bhonsla Raja at Nagpur were continually trying to filch from the Nizam some portion of his territory, and it seemed very probable that, between them all, the Nizam's dominions, unless protected by a strong army, would eventually be absorbed by one or more of these Mahratta princes. According to the treaty previously mentioned, drawn up in 1800, the Nizam made over the greater part of the territory which had fallen to his share in the partition of Mysore to the British, who, in their turn agreed to keep up, at their own cost, a force of not less than 9,000 men, thoroughly equipped and in every way efficient to defend the Nizam's dominions. This was the origin of the so-called Subsidiary Force. This force was available only to fight against a foreign foe, a special clause had been expressly inserted in the treaty that it should not be for *sillidari*, or police purposes, or for helping in the collection of revenue. But in the early part of this century the Nizam's dominions were full of turbulent and refractory zemindars. who, whenever they were strong enough, refused to send their tribute, and commenced disorders among themselves. Hence it was soon found necessary to organize a small but efficient body of troops for the purpose of quelling these internal disturbances. Such a body was formed in the year 1805, but, when two or three years afterwards it was sent into the field against some refractory noblemen in the Berar Province, it behaved in so mutinous a manner that it was evident that to be of any use it must be re-organized. In 1812 the Resident, Mr. Russell (afterwards Sir Henry Russell) undertook this re-organization, as has been shown in a previous chapter. Several regiments were formed and were officered by Europeans. From year to year the force grew in size and efficiency, and was known as the Russell Brigade. About the years 1817-1819 it numbered between seven and eight thousand, and took a very active and honourable share in the Pindari War. It was described by the General as one of the most gallant and efficient brigades of his army. By this time the cost of the little army had risen to over thirty lakhs of rupees per annum. The Nizam paid the troops, but, as we have seen, they were practically under the orders of the Resident, in whose hands lay all the patronage. The actual financing was carried out by the great banking firm of William Palmer & Company, to which were made large assignments of districts in the vicinity of Aurungabad, where the head-quarters of the force was situated. In this way the troops were regularly paid, though at a very heavy cost to the Nizam, since

Palmers' rate of interest was very high, being as much as 23 and 24 per cent. per annum. In 1820, Mr. Russell was succeeded by Sir Charles (afterwards Lord) Metcalfe, who, a short time after assuming office, took up a very hostile attitude towards the banking firm, as likely to become too dangerous a political power in the State. The result was that the pecuniary connection between the firm and the Hyderabad Government was taken over together with other liabilities by the British Government. Altogether the debt thus taken over by the British amounted to one crore and sixty lakhs (160 lakhs), in settlement of which the tribute of the Northern Circars, for which the British Government paid the Nizam seven lakhs, was abolished in perpetuity. Two years after this the firm of Palmer & Co. went bankrupt.

The payment of the Nizam's Contingent devolved, therefore, upon the Nizam's Minister, who, for twenty years from that date was Rajah Chandoo Lal. It was this Minister's policy to do everything in accordance with the wishes of the British authorities. The Resident was allowed a free hand with the Contingent, and he effected such changes and reforms as he pleased. Everything was conducted on a costly scale. There were no less than five Brigadiers, each with a full staff, and the officers received special and handsome allowances. Chandoo Lal, as has been shown, though a man of great ability, was reckless and extravagant. On the one hand he had to supply the Nizam with the necessary funds, and, on the other, he had to meet the constant drain of over three lakhs of rupees a month for the Contingent. In order to meet these liabilities he had recourse to loans. Large sums were raised from the sowcars at a high rate of interest, and assignments of districts were made to them in return. As a natural result the revenue fell off, and from year to year the Minister found it more difficult to raise the money to pay the Contingent. At length the cost of the Contingent crept up to forty lakhs of rupees, and gradually the pay began to fall in arrears. These arrears kept on growing until at last, in 1840, the British Government claimed fifty lakhs of rupees. For the next thirteen years there ensued a period of undignified squabbling.

In glancing back we find that in 1843 Chundoo Lal was removed as Minister, in which removal the Resident, General Fraser, was instrumental. A rapid succession of Ministers followed, and sometimes, for many months, there was no Minister at all. On the one hand, demands for money were made, and, on the other, excuses coupled with promises. Every now and then a sum would be paid on account, and then matters went on as before. During this time no attempt was made to reduce either the number of the Contingent or its expense. That the cost was far too heavy seems to have been admitted by all : but it was the Nizam's force, and he, knowing that it was efficient, never expressed a wish for its disbandment. We have seen how the debt due to the British Government gradually increased, and in 1849 amounted to 64 lakhs of rupees. Lord Dalhousie, the Governor-General, sent orders to General Fraser, the Resident at Hyderabad, to insist upon a settlement. A scheme was drawn up with the Nizam's Government, under which certain districts in the Berars were to be assigned to the British for a number of years until the debt was paid off The payment of the Contingent was still to continue as before. At the last moment, however, the Nizam made an effort. He almost exhausted his own treasury and succeeded in paying off more than half the debt due to the British in a lump sum. But, this one payment having been made, matters went from bad to worse. The arrears increased and at length Lord Dalhousie sent a warning to the Nizam that, if by the end of 1852 the matter was not properly settled, he would have to make arrangements for obtaining a material guarantee, not only for the debt, but also for the future regular payment of the force. Still there was no suggestion of reduction of expenses.

General Fraser was now no longer in Hyderabad, and Colonel Low was sent down from Calcutta with a new treaty to which he was to obtain the Nizam's signature. Colonel Low arrived early in 1853, and then followed the negotiations for the treaty, to which reference has been made in the previous chapters.

The first demand was that the Nizam should assign in perpetuity the Berar provinces and the Raichour Doab districts, in consideration of which the debt would be cancelled and the Contingent maintained by the British. This, however, the Nizam utterly refused to do. He was willing to cede the territory temporarily, but not in perpetuity, and it was only with great difficulty that he consented to agree to any cession at all. Negotiations went on, but success seemed as far off as ever.

The Nizam, as predicted by General Fraser, endeavoured to put off what he regarded as a calamity by passive resistance and protracted negotiations. When Colonel Low mentioned the matter of ceding the districts named in perpetuity, His Highness showed a great repugnance to making any such treaty, and replied, "God forbid that I should suffer such disgrace."

Lord Dalhousie had already intimated to His Highness that military force would be used if "His Highness the Nizam should reject the settlement that had been proposed for his benefit; and, if evil should consequently befall his State, the Government of India must stand acquitted of all blame towards him." On May 14th, 1853, Captain Cuthbert Davidson, then First Assistant Resident, wrote to the Minister Suraj-ul-Mulk, saying " that the Resident wished for the Minister's attendance in order to inform him that his negotiations with the Nizam were at an end, and he applied to the Government to move troops by to-day's post." Further on, in the same letter, Captain Davidson, added, that he had heard from his nephew in Poona " that the European regiment there had been ordered to hold itself in readiness to march on Hyderabad." This had the desired effect. On the same day the Minister notified to the Resident that the Nizam consented to sign the treaty, and this in reality was done two or three days later.

This treaty of 1853 contained a clause that any surplus over expenditure on administration should be handed to the Nizam and that the British Government was bound to furnish accounts. The objects of the expenditure were: (1) the maintenance of the Contingent at a numerical strength of 7,000 men; (2) the liquidation of the debt amounting to 48 lakhs of Halli Sikka rupees; (3) the payment of the cost of administration.

The treaty contained no stipulation regarding what the cost of administration should be, but, as will be shown from Captain Davidson's own words, there was a distinct understanding that the cost should not exceed 200,000 rupees. This statement from one of the principal officers concerned is conclusive as to the understanding between the high contracting parties, and, although the treaty itself contained no such provision, yet in equity this understanding must be taken to form one of the conditions of the trust. . Now it will be interesting to watch the way in which these conditions were fulfilled.

From the first year in which the treaty came into

operation the cost of the Contingent was reduced. Whereas in 1853 it is shown as having cost 40 lakhs, two years afterwards it cost only 24. This is a very remarkable reduction, As long as the Nizam was responsible for the payment no steps were taken to reduce the expenditure, but as soon as the Government of India took over the management, and were obliged to make the assigned districts pay, so as to meet the different liabilities, the cost was reduced to a reasonable figure. Nor could this have been done at the cost of efficiency, because, when two years afterwards, in 1857, the Contingent was called upon to take a part in the suppression of the great Mutiny, it did brilliant service, and received the well-deserved thanks of the General commanding the army, of which it formed a part, and the thanks of the Government of India. The question at once suggests itself : Why should not the Residency have been directed to carry out this reduction before, which proved so feasible and easy? Why should the unnecessary burden have been allowed to rest on the shoulders of the Nizam, until the accumulated load of debt threatened to bring the State to bankruptcy and ruin? The Governor-General is found bantering the Resident about his five Brigadiers, but there is no suggestion of economy that can be discovered until the Government of India's pockets are threatened with loss—then the reduction is prompt and drastic. A reduction of this kind effected five years previously would have wiped out the whole of the debt on account of which the Governor-General insisted on the assignment of the provinces.

During the period of 1853-60, the increase of the revenue in the Berars was gradual, but not very considerable, and did not exceed eight lakhs of rupees. The expenditure, however, on the Military Contingent was greatly reduced, and though it showed a tendency to rise it was in the last year of this period quoted at 26½ lakhs. As may be expected when the province was taken over by the British, it was found to be in a very backward state as regards public works. At first the outlay was very small, not more than 15,000 rupees, but in the latter year of this period it had increased to four and a half lakhs, by no means an extravagant charge. In the civil administration the increase of cost was more rapid, and it rose from eight lakhs in the first to nearly 22 lakhs in the last year. Still the receipts during the seven-year period showed a surplus over expenditure of 35½ lakhs.

In 1860 a new agreement was drawn up between the Nizam and the Government of India. The British Government in recognition of the Nizam's splendid loyalty to them in their hour of need, during the Mutiny of 1857, had resolved to bestow on him a substantial mark of gratitude for his loyalty during the Mutiny. Accordingly, the debt of fifty lakhs was remitted and the Raichur and Doab districts and Dharasoa were restored and only the Berars retained. The small Raj of Shorapur which had mutinied in 1857, and had been annexed, was given to the Nizam in full sovereignty, and some districts to the north of the Godavery were made over to the British in exchange. Under the treaty of 1857 the British bound themselves to render yearly accounts. This does not appear to have been done, at least officially, but under the new treaty of 1860, by authority of which the new assignments and exchanges were confirmed, a clause was inserted in which it was provided that in future no accounts need be rendered. It was in this manner that the new treaty was reconstructed. Presents amounting to £10,000 were given to the Nizam, and £3,000 to the Prime Minister, and, according to old-established custom, £15,000 were forwarded by the Nizam to the Governor-General, and, according to rule, paid by him to the Imperial Treasury.

As regards the administration of the Berars on the part of the British, much discussion has arisen.

The alleged debt of 1853, on account of which the Berars were assigned, having been cancelled, the Nizam clearly became entitled to the surplus revenue which had accrued during the period 1853-60, and which, as has been shown, amounted to 35½ lakhs, but subsequently the Accountant-General put in a claim for two items of Rs. 1,283,850, and Rs. 2,293,690 for civil and military expenditure respectively. The only explanation regarding these mysterious items, which were large enough not to have escaped attention when making up the accounts, is offered by a foot-note in the administration report, to the following effect :

"These amounts are stated to have been debited in the adjustment of certain area charges communicated by the Accountant-General to the Government of India, in letter No. 2123, 13/1/1865."

What must strike everyone as remarkable is, firstly, that these sums should have been lost sight of during the preliminary negotiations for the treaty of 1860, which occupied about a year, and should not have been discovered until five years afterwards ; secondly, that not having been discovered in 1860, when the treaty was concluded, the surplus as shown by the then existing accounts should not have been handed over to the Nizam in conformity with the treaty of 1853 ; and, lastly, it is a most singular coincidence that these two items, lost sight of for more than six years, should form the exact amount of the surplus which had accrued during the seven years' administration, and which ought to have been handed to the Nizam. When the arrear charges were discovered in 1865 the accounts had to be readjusted, and the opening year of 1861-62 shows a minus balance of Rs. 3,577,440. This, however, was adjusted by crediting against it the total surplus carried in the previous year. However, the administration of the province was carried out in a fairly economical manner. Only one lakh was spent on public works, nine lakhs on civil administration, and 24 lakhs on the Contingent, leaving an actual surplus of five lakhs.

The revenue went on rapidly increasing, and each year the surplus continued to grow, but still no actual money was paid over to the Nizam until the year 1867-8, when the surplus showed an accumulated balance of twenty lakhs unpaid, i.e., when in 1874-5 a regular annual surplus first began to be paid, there was an accumulated unpaid balance of about 50 lakhs of rupees. Hence, for over 20 years, the British Government had accumulated sums varying from 20 to 50 lakhs of rupees, for which no interest was paid and which the Nizam could not touch. This money nearly corresponds with the amount of the alleged debt due by the Nizam, when he assigned the districts in 1853. The actual amount in 1895 was Rs. 4,202,262. These figures are in round numbers.

As the years progressed the surplus of revenue over expenditure showed a remarkable tendency to shrink. In 1891-2 it was nearly 12 lakhs; then $7\tfrac{3}{4}$; then $7\tfrac{1}{3}$; then 5; then 2 lakhs; then, in 1896, 6 lakhs. Hence, the fact remains that, when the revenue was 73 lakhs twenty years before, there was a surplus of 13 lakhs, but subsequently, when the revenue amounted in round figures to one hundred lakhs, there was only a surplus of six lakhs.

The term " alleged debt " has been used and the reason for this expression must be stated.

For a period of 41 years from 1812-53 the British had levied and retained the excise revenues of the two cantonments of Secunderbad and Jalna. For those sums no accounts had been submitted, and though, in 1851, two years previous to the treaty of 1853, the Hyderabad Government put forward a claim that those receipts should be taken as a set-off against the amount of arrears, General Fraser, the Resident, refused to allow what he called a problematic claim to be credited in the settlement of an actual debt. But, subsequent to the treaty of 1853, it was admitted that those revenues properly belonged to the Nizam, and from that time they had actually been collected by His Highness. Colonel Davidson, writing in 1860, says in reference to this debt : " I have always been of opinion that, had the pecuniary demands of the two Governments been impartially dealt with, we had no just claim on the Nizam for the present debt of 43 lakhs of Company's rupees."

His Highness's Minister, in a note dated 19/8/1851, when pressed on account of arrears, of the Contingent, asked for the surplus of the abkari revenues of Secunderabad and Jalna, which was afterwards allowed to be a portion of the legitimate revenues of the Hyderabad State.

The Government of India carried these revenues, which in 1922 amounted to about one lakh annually, to their own credit from 1812-1853—say for 41 years. The above would have given the Nizam a credit of 41 lakhs of rupees without interest, against the debt claimed. Further His Highness was charged with interest from January, 1849, to May, 1853, at 6 per cent. on advances

THE BERAR TRUST

for the pay of the Contingent. This charge for interest amounted to $10\frac{1}{2}$ lakhs of rupees, although the Nizam earnestly protested against being made to pay any interest at all. In addition to this, when the Berars were taken over in 1853, part of the revenue consisted of custom duties. These duties were abolished since the province was considered as practically forming part of British India. These revenues, it had been agreed, should be accepted as payment for the Contingent; therefore, by abolishing these, the revenues were reduced *pro tanto*, and the sum of reduction in seven years, which would have amounted to 18 lakhs, should have been carried to the Nizam's credit.

By the foregoing, it can be seen that in 1853 there was really no debt to remit, but nevertheless from 1853 to 1860 the Nizam continued to pay interest, amounting to 18 lakhs, on this alleged debt. In the letter from Colonel Davidson, dated July 6th, 1859, he writes : " There is no doubt General Low allowed the former minister, Suraj-ul-Mulk, and the present one, Sarlar Jung, to suppose that our management would cost about 2 annas in the rupee, or about 12 per cent. of the revenue." As Colonel Davidson had been First Assistant Resident in 1853 and had conducted the negotiations, his statement is utterly unimpeachable.

In 1860, when the second treaty was drawn up, the cost of administration again formed a subject of preliminary discussion. At first the Government of India offered to bear all cost in excess of 2 per cent.—2 annas in the rupee—but the Nizam very generously said that he did not wish the Government of India to be too strictly tied down. The percentage is mentioned in the Governor-General's despatch to the Secretary of State, and is acknowledged by the latter official. Finally, Colonel

Davidson telegraphed and wrote to the Government of India that the cost of administration might be fixed at 25 per cent—4 annas in the rupee—" but this percentage we must engage not to exceed." (12/10/1860.)

At first when the Berars were taken over this tacit understanding was carried out. In the first year the cost of civil administration was eight lakhs out of a total revenue of 30—or a fraction over 3 annas in the rupee. As time went by, however, this proportion was exceeded, so that in 1859 the cost amounted to more than six annas in the rupee. When the obligation to render accounts was withdrawn by the treaty of 1860, we find the expenditure increasing by leaps and bounds. In fact it increased even more rapidly than the revenue. By 1894-5, the expenditure on civil administration alone rose to seven annas in the rupee. *The Pioneer* at the time pointed out that this was a cost out of all proportion to what was spent in the districts in British India, and was due to the extravagant manner in which the machinery of administration was conducted. Though the size of Berar (17,717 square miles) is only equal to two districts in the Presidency of Madras, it had the establishment sufficient to govern a whole Presidency.

The Berars were divided into six districts, officered by a full staff. It was this huge establishment that made the cost of administration so heavy, being more than $2\frac{1}{2}$ times the proportion expended in British India. It is difficult to understand why the cost of administration was allowed to increase until it amounted to four times to what it did when taken over.

It has been shown that the land revenue greatly increased during each decade. The following table will show the increase of expenditure under the heads of Public Works and the Military expenditure:

Year	P.W.D.	Military
1864-5	£49,098	£283,256
1874-5	£74,944	£270,907
1884	£114,198	£301,738
1894	£110,696	£397,472

Hence the reason why the Nizam's surplus showed signs of shrinkage was because the amount spent on Public Works, which should have been included in the amount allowed for civil administration, were charged separately. If the Public Works had been paid out of the Resident's 50 per cent. of the gross revenue, there would have been nearly five lakhs more available for the Nizam. As a matter of fact the Resident's expenditure was not 50 per cent. but 56 per cent.

It is the same story with the Military expenditure. There was, it is true, an increase in the force of the Contingent of 500 men, which about represents the strength of the artillery, which it was found necessary to add, in order to make the little army complete—but the small number in excess accounts in no way for the large annual increase. As *The Pioneer* pointed out at the time:

"The present system is evidently unfair to our ally, and a radical change is required. As long as we administer the trust we should do it in a businesslike manner—in the same way as we administer it in our own districts."

Enough has been said to show that the expenditure of the Berars was lavishly extravagant and it will be well once more to quote an article that appeared in *The Pioneer* summing up the situation:

"We first of all insisted upon the Nizam ceding territory on account of a debt, which afterwards was proved not to exist. We promised that the administration of the territory should not cost more than 25 per cent., and that we should annually give him the surplus. Relying on this His Highness left us a free hand in the treaty as regards administration and waived the right of asking for accounts.

"Taking advantage of this position we have increased the cost of civil administration alone to 43 per cent. and have spent about 13 per cent. in addition on Public Works and other items, which should have been included in the Civil Administration and have increased the cost of the Contingent to 41 per cent. In order to provide for what we call a working balance, we retain an accumulated surplus far beyond the amount required, for which we pay the Nizam no interest, and which very nearly represents the amount of the discredited debt for which he was compelled to assign the province."

In 1881-82 the total revenue amounted to 39 lakhs, but the civil expenditure had risen to very nearly four lakhs—or nearly 50 per cent. In 1891 the revenue was over one hundred lakhs, but the expenditure again amounted to more than 52 lakhs, or more than 50 per cent., and finally in 1901, the year when the accounts were made up, the revenue was 110 lakhs, and the expenditure 130 lakhs. This was the year after the first great famine that had ever visited Berar, and the expenditure, therefore, was abnormal, but, taking the year 1898-99 as a fair test, we find that the normal expenditure under the heads of civil administration, including the Public Works department, amounted to over 50 lakhs, or more than 50 per cent. of the gross revenue. All this led to much discussion and became a bone of contention. Undoubtedly under the British regime the province of Berar had greatly inproved. A larger area of the actually fertile land was under cultivation, hence the land was yielding larger crops, the ryot was more prosperous, and owing to better road communications criminals of all classes no longer found Berar the happy hunting ground it had been to them before the British took over the administration. In fact, Berar was looked on as the model province, and was spoken of as " the Garden of India."

It has never been suggested that the money used for Berar administration had been wastefully or improperly spent; on the contrary it was universally admitted that for every rupee spent a *quid pro quo* had been obtained. Everything was excellent of its kind. The buildings were fine, the roads admirable, the forest conservancy system good, and administration excellent. The only ground for complaint was that the money spent on administration in Berar was served out with a more lavish hand than was the case in other parts of British India. There were more officials per mile and per head of the population in that province than it was found necessary to maintain in other parts of India under British rule.

Before leaving the problem of Berar and passing on to consider other matters it will be as well to glance ahead and see how the matter was finally settled in 1902 between the Nizam, Mir Mabbub Ali Khan, and the Governor-General, Lord Curzon. As has been pointed out the steady rise annually in the cost of administration led to endless discussion. This was taken up by various papers headed by *The Pioneer*, and finally was the subject of a debate in Parliament. The result of this was that in 1902 an Agreement was executed by the Nizam's Government by which the Hyderabad Assigned Districts were leased to the British Government in perpetuity, in consideration of the payment to the Nizam, by the British Government, of a fixed perpetual rental of 25 lakhs annually, instead of the previous fluctuating surplus revenue, which on the average amounted to nine lakhs per annum. The Nizam's sovereignty was recognized by hoisting a flag and firing a salute annually on his birthday. This arrangement was confirmed by Lord Curzon, in Council, on December 16th, 1902. The British Government now retained the full and exclusive jurisdiction and authority in the Hyderabad Assigned Districts which they enjoyed under the treaties of 1853 and 1860 and were empowered to administer these districts in such a manner " as may seem advisable, and to distribute, organize and control the forces composing the Hyderabad Contingent. Due provision being made as stipulated by article three of the treaty, 1853, for the protection of the Nizam's Dominions. (See Aicheson's *Treaties and Engagements and Sunnads*, Volume IX, page 4.)

When it was known that the much vexed question of the Berars had been finally settled, satisfaction was not universal. For the last fifty years endless arguments had centred round this question, greatly due to the fact that the principals most vitally concerned stood aloof while the argument was carried on by outsiders who were not always actuated by impersonal motives. Great disappointment was expressed, in view of the greatly increased revenue, that the annual rental stipulated by Lord Curzon at 25 lakhs, good year or bad year, was not greater. At least double that figure had, according to the calculations, been estimated as due to the Nizam. Under the new arrangement the British Government was no longer compelled to keep up the Hyderabad Contingent, which was abolished, and for the maintenance of which the districts had originally been ceded. Some of the reasons for the disappointment that prevailed in Hyderabad were due to the fact that just before that period, when the agreement was executed, the finances of the Hyderabad State had been well organized and had revealed a degree of stability which would have ensured the regular payment of the cost of the Hyderabad Contingent. In fact, the Nizam offered to guarantee such payment, if Berar were restored to him, and there is no doubt that this undertaking would have been fulfilled. This proposal of His Highness, however, was not accepted. The question then arose: Was the British Government morally and equitably justified in those existing circumstances of retaining the province? Also was it justifiable permanently to sever from the Hyderabad State one of its most fertile provinces for the annual rental of 25 lakhs of rupees? Since 1902 the revenue of Berar has further largely increased and it shows signs of a steady rise owing to the extension of the railroads and the growing prosperity of India as a whole. The general impression is that the late Nizam reluctantly consented to the Agreement, under pressure brought to bear on him. It was estimated by people who had an intimate knowledge of Berar that, under normal conditions, the annual surplus, after defraying the cost of the Hyderabad Assigned Districts, would be fifty, and not 25 lakhs annually. Therefore it was felt that, if a permanent lease were the only solution, the British Government should have paid to His Highness the annual rental of fifty instead of 25 lakhs subject to periodical revision, in accordance with the growth of revenue, if the sovereignty of His Highness over these dominions was to be a reality and not a mere fiction.

On the other hand, the difficulties attending the return of Berar to the Hyderabad State, in view of the sentiments of its inhabitants, who had become more prosperous during British administration than they were before, necessarily influenced the problem. There is no doubt that, under the British, Berar, which had been a devastated area, where crime was rampant, was, by judicious handling, converted into one of the most fertile and prosperous provinces in India, where the inhabitants lead the normal life of peaceable citizens unmolested by bandits and dacoits.

This also was the history of Mysore—and has been the history of all native states or courts of wards that temporarily fell under the British administration. The general feeling in the Hyderabad State is that there should be a reconconsideration and revision of an agreement entered into between a powerful Government and its weaker but faithful ally, at a time when through famine the finances of Hyderabad were temporarily embarrassed.

Having traced the history of Berar we must now glance at the conditions prevailing when the Prime Minister, Sarlar Jung, took over charge of the administration, and note the changes inaugurated. We shall see from the extraordinary progress made by the State under his guidance how great a debt Hyderabad owes him.

CHAPTER XVII

DEATH OF SIRAJ-UL-MULK—MUTINY IN HYDERABAD—
THE RAJAH OF SHORAPUR
PERIOD 1853-58.

IN 1853 the Prime Minister, Siraj-ul-Mulk died, and his nephew, Salar Jung, with the approval of the British Government, was appointed to succeed him. This was, as we shall see, an admirable choice; nor was there anyone in Hyderabad who could so effectually have played the *Deus ex machina* as did the new Minister. It has been said that " nothing of him was ever hurried, no reform, however important, was carried out in hot haste. Though his policy was characterized by a wise and wary conservatism, that abhorred extreme measures, yet no man was less tenacious of old systems once their inefficiency had been proved." He was distinguished by a wonderfully retentive memory and a highly subtle, comprehensive understanding. But what most endeared him to the people was that his sympathies were wide and that he was eminently just. The level-headed policy of Salar Jung was shown in many ways, but specially so in 1857 when the spirit of unrest and sedition which pervaded Northern and Central India was manifested in Hyderabad itself. In the early part of that year when mutiny and bloodshed were rife, the Nizam Nasir-ud-Dowlah died and was succeeded by his eldest son, Afzal-ud-Dowlah. At the accession of this new ruler, the hopes of the dissatisfied were excited, and this led to an insurrection.

Before going further, it will be necessary for a moment to glance at the geographical position of Hyderabad. The actual extent of the Nizam's dominions is 95,337 square miles. In the north the State is bounded by the Central Provinces, in the south-west by Madras, in the west by Bombay, and in the north-west by Scindia, and the river Narbudda. Hyderabad, it will thus be seen formed a buffer between the Northern and Central Provinces where sedition was rife, and the Southern portions of this vast continent, which had not been affected by the insurrection. Therefore, His Highness's sympathy and policy were of the utmost importance. It was generally accepted that if the Nizam joined the mutineers the whole of India would take part in the rebellion. The popular saying was, " If the Nizam goes, all goes." Salar Jung, with his far-seeing policy, realized that the permanency of his sovereign depended on his loyal adherence to the British.

It was at this critical moment that the Nizam Nasir-ud-Dowlah died. The late Nizam had been very popular and his death was much deplored. He had been a ruler who was humane and was remarkable for his religious tolerance and his strict adherence to truth. He had also won the admiration of his subjects by his magnificent physique; he stood over six feet and was noted for his great bodily strength. As the young Nizam was still a minor a regency was proclaimed. The young prince left the Palace on the morning of his enthronement, seated on an elephant and attended by soldiers and all his court nobles. After the arrival of Colonel Davidson at the City Palace the ceremony of instalment began.

A bull had previously been sacrificed across the Nizam's path as His Highness entered the chief palace gate, and this was believed to be a propitious omen. His Highness was led to the *musnud* by the two Regents, Salar Jung and Shamsul-Umra, each holding one of his hands. The Resident then addressed the young Nizam and offered his congratulations. Colonel Davidson had only taken over office a month previously on the death of his predecessor, Colonel Bushby. Both the Regents and the Resident realized that a change of ruler in Hyderabad at this moment was most critical and every precaution was taken against a sudden rising. Nor were these fears groundless. The following month, in June, 1857, the walls of Hyderabad city were placarded with notices signed by some of the leading orthodox Moulvies calling on the " Faithful to murder the Feringhee." Colonel Davidson at once requested the General Commanding (General William Hill) to parade his troops in full marching order. Fortunately a perfect understanding existed between the Resident and the Prime Minister, both of whom were present at the review. The people, impressed by the number of troops and the *moral* of the men, were for a time quieted. This, however, did not last long. Two weeks later a large mob congregated near the Mekka Musjid and urged on by Moulvie Akbar raised the green flag, known as the holy standard, and proclaimed themselves ready to engage in a Jehad, or holy war, which had for its object the extermination of the Feringhee, or infidel. The cry " Din " was raised and urged on by their religious leaders, the mob were soon in a state of hysterical fenzy. On hearing this, Salar Jung immediately despatched a corps of Arab mercenaries and posted soldiers at each gate of the city. By this prompt measure the Prime Minister quelled the rising and life once more resumed its normal course. Superficially peace was restored, but below the surface sedition and discontent were surging. News from the outside world filtered in. Victories gained by the British were carefully concealed, and all the massacres of Cawnpore, Lucknow, Jhansi and Agra were discussed with grossly exaggerated reports among an inflammable people, among whom were interspersed adventurers from all parts of India, who were averse to any foreign custom or government. The following month, some thirteen Rohilla sepoys deserted from Buldana because some of their seditious companions had been shot. They sought an audience with Salar Jung, who insisted on handing them over to the Resident, much to their disgust. The Moulvies at once took up the cudgels in their defence and declared that Salar Jung had been guilty of an act of violation of sanctuary. This was made the excuse to again call on the people to engage in a Jehad. Some of the Moulvies actually pronounced Hyderabad *Darb Haram*, or an infidel country, where Mahomedans may wage a holy war. Once more a large mob collected outside the Mekka Musjid and marched on to the Residency. Here, everything was in readiness to meet their attack. The advancing mob was met with a charge of grape from the newly erected ramparts, followed by seven shots from the three big guns and a charge of the Nizam's troops. This caused the mutineers to flee in abject confusion and disorder. Thanks to the excellent understanding which existed between the Resident and Salar Jung, a serious catastrophe was averted. Had the Prime Minister not acted so promptly, and had the mutineers been given time to corrupt the city of Hyderabad, a general conflagration would have ensued. The results would have proved disastrous not only to the

Europeans but also to Hyderabad itself. For retribution would not have been long in coming, and, indeed, the history of Hyderabad as a separate state might never have been written from that date. As events turned out, however, it was proved that His Highness the Nizam and his Government had remained a staunch ally to the British throughout the Mutiny. This service rendered in the hour of need was not forgotten. The Nizam and the British Government realized from Salar Jung's masterstroke that in him they had a strong man and they were not slow in recognizing his worth and the following year, honours were awarded, first to the Nizam and then to Salar Jung.

Shortly after the mutiny in Hyderabad, it was decided to send a brigade formed of troops of the Hyderabad Contingent to act with the British troops in quelling the rising. This was an antidote to local irritation, and the success obtained by the Hyderabad soldiers greatly pleased their relatives, who promptly transferred their sympathies to the campaign in which their kinsmen were engaged.

No chieftain, except the Rajah of Shorapur, saw any reason to question the Nizam's judgment in this matter. The Rajah was a youth who had squandered his capital, financial, mental and physical, in orgies of wild dissipation and debauch. A rumour reached him that the British were about to disarm his state, and, intoxicated by promises held out to him by seditionists, the Rajah resolved to raise an army of rebels, levying Rohillas and Arab mercenaries for this purpose. On hearing this, Salar Jung issued an order that anyone taking service under the Rajah of Shorapur did so at the peril of losing any property he possessed in Hyderabad. The Resident at the same time sent an expeditionary force commanded by Major Hughes, to watch the western frontier, while another force was sent under Captain Wyndham to occupy Lingsagur. Captain Rose Campbell, one of the Resident's personal assistants, was also sent to endeavour to save the young Rajah from his own folly. Captain Campbell's efforts, however, proved useless, and he received messages from the Rajah's relatives that his life was in imminent danger, as a plot was on foot to assassinate him. Therefore, he joined Captain Wyndham and ordered him to march to Shorapur. According to the usual custom the Rajah sent out emissaries to meet the troops, and point out to them a favourable site for encampment. The spot indicated was a narrow valley surrounded by hills and rocks, but suspecting treachery Captain Campbell preferred an open plain. That night he, with 400 men and two guns, was attacked by a force of 7,000 men. Fortunately for him fresh reinforcements arrived in the morning and the mutineers were dispersed and overcome. The Rajah, realizing that the odds were against him, fled to Hyderabad and sought the protection of Salar Jung, who handed him over to the Resident, by whom he was tried.

In 1842 the Rajah's father had become so financially embarrassed that he could not fulfil his obligations to the Nizam. Consequently on his death the administration of the State temporarily passed into the hands of the British Government, during the minority of the young Rajah. The State was subsequently handed over to the heir when he attained his majority, in a flourishing and prosperous condition. Colonel Meadows Taylor had been intimately connected with Shorapur and knew the young Rajah from his childhood. Between the Colonel and his young ward there existed a sincere bond of affection. The Rajah always addressed the Colonel as "Appa" (my father). Things might have been different for the young chieftain had he remained under the wise and sympathetic guidance of Colonel Meadows Taylor, but unfortunately this officer's services were required elsewhere, and the young man, surrounded as he was by many who had their private axes to grind, soon drifted into zenana intrigues and wild debauch. Added to this, liquor and opium constantly consumed in increasing quantities soon affected the stability of his mental balance. On hearing that the young Rajah was a prisoner in Secunderabad, in the barracks of the Royals, Colonel Meadows Taylor obtained permission to visit his former ward. In the Colonel's reminiscences (*Story of My Life*) we are given an account of this interview, which is full of human interest and colour.

"The Rajah had deliberately rebelled against the British Government, and was to be tried for his life by a military commission, which would shortly assemble. As may be imagined he was deeply affected on first seeing me. Though handsome, his features showed unmistakable signs of dissipation and excess which I was sorry to see.

"'Oh, Appa, Appa,' was all that he could cry, or rather moan as he sat at my feet, his face buried in my lap and his arms clasped tightly around me. 'Oh, Appa, I dare not look into your face. I have done every crime. I have even committed murder.'"

At a subsequent interview the Colonel asked the Rajah if he wished see the Resident, but the young man shook his head.

"No, Appa," he replied, "he would expect me to ask my life of him, and this I will not do, for I deserve to die for what I did. And I will not ask my life like a coward, nor will I betray my people."

This speech, which the Colonel repeated to the Resident, pleased the latter greatly. At the final interview between Colonel Meadows Taylor and his former ward the Rajah asked what his fate would be.

"What do you think, Appa? Shall I have to die?"

"I think so," replied the Colonel gravely. "It would be wrong for me to give you false hope."

"It was not my own will, when I was in my senses, Appa," replied the youth.

The Colonel was deeply moved. "I do not reproach you," he said, "for I know all, but those who will try you do not. Speak the truth, as you have done to me."

"I will," he answered calmly, "but I would rather die than be imprisoned always."

"If you have to die," said the Colonel, touched at the nobility in his speech, "die like a brave man."

"I shall not tremble," he answered gravely, "when they tie me up to a gun. If you could be near me at the last I should be happier. Only, Appa, do not let me be hanged like a robber. Go now, Appa, I shall never see you again. Tell them all that I was no coward."

The guard on duty was touched at this scene so full of pathos, and spoke to the Colonel about the Rajah.

"He was like a child to me," answered the Colonel, "until evil people came between us, and temptations proved too strong for him."

When Colonel Davidson had the details of this interview he seemed deeply moved.

"Taylor," he said, "we will try to save the boy."

The trial took place and the Rajah was condemned to death, but, by special intervention on the part of the Resident on his behalf, the sentence was commuted to transportation for life. Shortly after this it was declared that the Rajah should be imprisoned in a fortress in

Chingelpet, in Madras, and he was told if he showed signs of reform his state, liberty and his power would be returned to him after four years' time.

Colonel Meadows Taylor was at Shorapur conveying to the senior Rani Rungama, and the other ladies of the zenana, the good news of the reprieve of the Rajah. Great joy prevailed in the palace, and the young wife asked the Colonel to come and visit her in her apartments. When he was announced, the young Rani, quite regardless of etiquette, first threw herself into his arms and then proceeded to dance round the room, overcome with joy at the idea of seeing her husband again. There was only one in the palace who shook his head in sorrow. It was the old *Shastri* (Hindu divine). The reason of his sorrow, he explained, was that some years previously the Rajah's horoscope had been taken, in which the statement was made that the Rajah would die before his 24th birthday and forfeit his State. This paper had been given into the hands of Captain Rose Campbell, who had carefully preserved it. The Shastri maintained, that, as his master's birthday was so close at hand he could not help feeling apprehensive until that date was over.

The ladies of the zenana laughed at this and continued their preparations for their long journey, as they had permission to join the Rajah at Chingelpet Fort. Many arrangements had to be made, for a journey to Madras in those days of slow transit was no light undertaking. Tradesmen bearing silks and embroideries for the Rani's adornment were waiting in the palace courtyard. An air of festivity was abroad. Suddenly the bells of an express runner were heard and excitement again rose to fever heat within the zenana, when it was made known that the runner had brought a despatch for Colonel Meadows Taylor from the Residency. The old Shastri was with the Colonel when the despatch arrived and watched every movement of his face as he read the message. Then suddenly leaning forward, with his quick intuition, he seized the Colonel's arm.

"Sahib, Oh Sahib," he wailed, "you need not tell me, my young master is dead."

This proved to be the case. The young Rajah at his first encampment had possessed himself of his escort's revolver and had shot himself. Though the general verdict was suicide, Colonel Meadows Taylor, from his intimate knowledge of the young man, maintained that it was not so, but that the Rajah impelled by curiosity had examined the weapon and had inadvertently pulled the trigger. However that may be, the strange prophecy had been fulfilled to the letter. By his presence and his extraordinary gift of insight and sympathy Colonel Meadows Taylor was able to prevent any further rising.

The young Rani, whose hopes had been raised only to be shattered in so tragic a manner, received a generous pension and provision was also made for the other ladies of the zenana.

The following year, in 1858, Queen Victoria's proclamation was read in all parts of British India, and also in Hyderabad. In this promises were given to all classes to respect the observation of their religious rites compatible with justice.

CHAPTER XVIII.

REFORMS INSTITUTED BY SIR SALAR JUNG PERIOD 1853-83

IN order to understand the value and nature of the service rendered to the Hyderabad State by the Nawab Salar Jung, it is necessary to glance at the administration of the State as it was when he became Prime Minister.

As we look back to the year when Salar Jung assumed the reins of Government, and compare the administration of the State in 1853 to thirty years later, it seems more like looking back several centuries than merely three decades, so great was the progress wrought by his genius for organization. In fact, as we become acquainted with some of the details of the administration of those days, especially in the Mofussil, it reads more like a tale from the Arabian Nights than a statement of facts that occurred within the last fifty years.

Owing to the chaotic state of government in Hyderabad, it was evident to all that things were in a very grave and critical condition when the Nawab Salar Jung, like the *Deus ex machina*, appeared on the scene of action. Drastic reforms of a very extensive nature were imperative, but the difficulty was to know at which end the tangled skein should be unravelled. Hyderabad, the capital, was by no means abreast of the times, and, in the

Mofussil mismanagement, oppression and crime were universal. Bands of marauders and highway robbers ruled by force of might, and were allowed to pursue their nefarious trade unhindered, for the simple reason that those in authority were in abject fear of them. In those days no police force existed, neither were there any courts of justice in the districts, so that the people had no means of redress.

The only Government officials in charge of the districts were the *talukdars* appointed by Government, who were mostly men of influence and position. According to custom, they were allowed two annas in the rupee for the expenses of collecting revenue. In most cases, owing to the unsettled state of affairs in the Mofussil, the *talukdars* preferred to live in the capital itself, and leased out their rights to irresponsible and inefficient subordinates, elected at their own instigation, men who were in no way answerable to Government and whose powers were not defined.

Other *talukdars*, again, by official misrepresentation, obtained sepoys in the army to collect their revenue. In both cases the money allowed by Government, for the sole purpose of collecting revenue, was not spent on the purpose intended. While the *talukdars* profited, their subordinates oppressed the people by fraudulent assessment. The *raiat* being without means of redress, became so impoverished that numbers of cultivators, rather than subject themselves to tyranny and oppression, left their hereditary lands, seeking a living in districts where conditions were more favourable. Thus hundreds of villages became depopulated and land formerly productive became barren. Consequently, it was evident that, under the conditions prevailing, both the interests of the State and also of the individual were endangered.

The first reform inaugurated by Salar Jung was by far the most important of all those introduced by him, namely, the abolition of the farming-out of revenue. Salar Jung, with his far-seeing policy, realized at once that the erratic revenue administration was indirectly responsible for the whole chaotic state of the Government. The talukdars were gradually dismissed and others appointed in their stead on smaller salaries, each man equipped with a staff of subordinates chosen by and directly responsible to Government. Owing to this new reform the rapacious policy of the talukdars collapsed. The people, no longer unduly taxed, were able again to make a living by cultivating the land, and deserted villages became inhabited once more. However, the dismissal of the old talukdars was by no means an easy matter. Some still had specified leases to run, while others, who were military chiefs, often set up a claim of *Fazilat*, or money advanced to Government, during pecuniary embarrassment. Government again set up counter claims for money levied by the contractors which had neither been remitted to the Treasury nor accounted for. These disputes caused lengthy and tiresome litigation. Hence, it is easy to understand that both tact and time were required to upset the old abuses and establish a system worked on lines that were sound and practical.

Up to the year 1853 the Government suffered from what might be described as a chronic state of financial embarrassment, consequently the man who was ready to lay down the largest sum as an advance to the state was in most cases the recipient of a taluka. As it often happened that, before the talukdar had held his post for more than a couple of years, he was ousted from it by a higher bidder, it naturally followed that his first object was to recoup himself for the money advanced. That this was done and a fair profit derived as well, is evident, or the competition for the charge of a taluka would not have been so keen.

For some time the land revenue had shown signs of a steady decrease owing firstly to the lack of a proper system of assessment, secondly to the gross mismanagement to which we have referred, and thirdly to the fact that Government had instituted a system of demanding revenue from the farmers in advance, to tide over the chronic financial difficulties which prevailed at that time. By demanding the revenue in advance the land could not be farmed out on such favourable terms. To show how great the loss to Government was from this topsy-turvy system we need only consider the instance of Pangal, which in twenty-five years showed a steady decrease in revenue during each successive change from Rs. 23,871 to Rs. 17,000. Under the old system each village was assessed collectively, any deficiency due to the relinquishing or desertion of fields by cultivators being made good by taxing other cultivators in excess, in order to recover the stipulated amount. This, however, was not the only vagary practised by those in authority, for the Government Agents, or rather their subordinates, had an elastic conscience. Assessment was constantly being enhanced and the terms agreed upon were not adhered to, but when these Agents were guilty of breach of trust no redress was available to the cultivator. Under this pernicious system, though the claims of the Government were limited, the claims of the talukdar on the unfortunate cultivator were unlimited, and there was no contact between the Central Government and the *Raiat*. Extensive and costly irrigation works which had formerly existed had been allowed to fall into ruin, for the talukdars, having only temporary power in the land, would not spend the necessary money, and the *Raiat*, already overtaxed, could not command the capital necessary for the purpose.

Having started the system of gradually dismissing the old talukdars, thus abolishing the farming-out of revenue, His Highness's Dominions were divided into five *subahs* (or counties), with 14 districts and 73 *tahsils*. A regular system of measuring each field separately and assessing it was also introduced. Under the new system, instead of making the assessments at harvest time, when the harvester was not allowed to touch his crops until assessment had been completed, assessment was made on a fixed scale at a certain date, and the harvester could dispose of his harvest when and how he chose.

A system known as *Takdama*, by which the cultivator was forced to advance a part of his revenue on pain of losing his crops was abolished. This also applied to another pernicious system known as *Batai*, which meant that Government fixed the price of grain at a price advantageous to the Treasury, making all *bunyas* buy at this rate and recoup themselves as best they could. It is easy to understand how this again fell heavily on the *Raiat*.

It was not long before the benefit of the revenue reform made itself felt all over the dominions. Not only did the revenue increase, but the cultivator once more became prosperous, barren lands became fruitful, and villages, some of which had been deserted for over a hundred years, again became inhabited.

The next step was to introduce a system of revenue survey through which the Government undertook to deal with the *Raiat* directly. Somewhat later a school for the training of revenue officers was temporarily established. This was done at the suggestion of the Director of Revenue, Mahdi Ali, and proved to be a great success. Pupils were selected from the nobility and well-to-do classes and after theoretical training were sent into the districts to learn the practical work. By this means the required number of revenue officers was obtained and the school having completed its object after about a year was closed. This new system of reform proved to be so excellent that, thirty years later the revenue of the State was nearly three times as great, while in Hyderabad city itself it had been more than trebled.

Having organized a sound system of land revenue Salar Jung next turned his attention to the administration of justice. During Chandoo Lal's ministry, in 1832-43, there were in the capital three Courts of Justice—the first in which civil and criminal cases were tried; the second, the Kotwali, or police court; and third, the court where religious disputes were heard. In all these courts, however, judgments were given orally, all proceedings were very brief and no record of litigation was filed. Hence, all depended on the personal integrity of the judge, and naturally under this regime many abuses crept in. Many of the nobles, for instance, declined to submit to these courts, and refused to appear when summoned, preferring to hold their own courts, where justice was administered by one of their own retainers, according to his individual ideas on the subject. Special cases, again were settled by direct appeal to the Minister. Under these conditions, naturally the rich man, with money and influence at his back, could do much as he pleased, without coming under the power of the law, while the poor man, who had neither of these powerful aids with which to press his cause, had little chance of obtaining justice. Bad as things were in the capital, however, they were much worse in the districts, for there

REFORMS INSTITUTED BY SIR SALAR JUNG

neither rules nor courts for the administration of civil and criminal law existed. In large towns like Aurungabad *Kazis* and sometimes *Amils* heard some of the cases, while in the villages disputes were settled by *Panchayats* (or village councils), consisting of *Patels* and *Patwaris* (head men of the village).

The merchants trading in His Highness's dominions were another source of terror to the people living in the Mofussil. Not only did they sell their wares at fabulous prices, demanding interest bonds after a few days, but these claims were enforced by lawless Arab retainers who were in their pay. This gave rise to much tyranny and oppression for the debtor was made responsible *nolens volens* for the maintenance of these wild, lawless retainers, who often on their own authority confiscated any household property that particularly took their fancy. The Afghan creditors, however, were infinitely worse, for they thought nothing of branding the bodies of their debtors and otherwise illtreating them. Here again the talukdars were fully aware of these proceedings, but having no police force at their back they dared not interfere, because of the possibility of a revengeful retaliation. For it was not an unknown thing for *Zemindars* and *Desmukhs* to be confined for some time in small houses, until they had executed fictitious bonds, for debts which they had not incurred.

Even worse was the fate of any unfortunate man who had been suspected of a crime, for he was forcibly seized and cast into prison, where he often lay for years awaiting his trial, and not infrequently died in prison, before he had been tried for an offence which he had not committed. Those, again, who were suspected of minor offences were often fined for years on end, whether they were guilty or innocent. It is not, therefore, surprising that dacoity and plunder were everyday occurrences, for the punitory force sent out to punish such offenders, not being trained, was as a rule quite inefficient to deal with these outlaws, or, if by chance the plundered booty was seized, the owner fared no better, for it only changed hands from the robbers to their pursuers, who usually looked on all such booty as their rightful perquisites. It was indeed a case of set a thief to catch a thief! Nor can we marvel at this when we read that the rank and file in such punitory forces received the munificent salary of Rs. 3 *per mensem!*

Thus it happened that those that wielded power were tyrants in every sense of the word. When those under them had cause to complain to the *Amil* they were often referred back again to the very person against whom they had complained, and it does not require much imagination to surmise that then the last state of the complainant was a great deal worse than the first! In most cases, therefore, people considered that discretion was the better part of valour and refrained from litigation, such as it was.

In the days of Siraj-ul-Mulk, the barbarous custom of mutilating prisoners was abolished, and, where it had been customary to amputate a hand, seven years' penal servitude was prescribed, and in the graver cases, where a hand and a foot would have been amputated, fourteen years were allotted. What the sufferings of these prisoners must have been, in those days, when neither antiseptics nor anæsthetics were known, seems to us almost impossible to contemplate, living in these days when anæsthesia is produced for the slightest operation. A decree forbidding *Suttee* had also been promulgated in Siraj-ul-Mulk's time, and both these reforms were studiously carried out by Salar Jung.

We have now seen the primitive state in which the great statesman found matters when he assumed the ministry. The extent of the reforms inaugurated, and the able manner in which they were carried out in thirty years' time by his administration represent a stupendous task. Hyderabad, at that time, was much like a noble ship tossed on a tempestuous sea, and nearing perilous breakers, when suddenly the master-hand of an expert mariner took her helm and slowly and surely steered her to a haven of safety.

Another important and far-reaching reform was the establishment of additional courts in the capital and the appointment in the districts of *Mir Adls and Munsifs* to administer justice there. A regular customs service was also introduced and the salt department organized.

The next noteworthy reform was the inauguration of a regular police service. This naturally could not be done in a moment, and as a temporary measure *Zillidars* were appointed to quell the turbulent state of the districts. These consisted of Arabs, Sikhs, Rohillas, Linemen, Peons, etc., some of whom were placed directly under the newly appointed talukdars, while others received their orders from a Central Committee.

As we saw in the last chapter, the districts of Raichur, Lingsugur, and Shorapur were restored to His Highness by the British Government in 1862. Now, in these districts an excellent police system had been instituted, and this was taken over and continued without any change until the year 1865 when the whole police force of the Nizam's dominions was reorganized. Then a separate force was provided for the city and for its suburbs and one for each district of the Mofussil. Though it was at first uphill work, the police gradually proved themselves equal to deal with the wild raid of the lawless

Rohillas, and a marked decrease of crime was very soon apparent. At first the police worked under the Board of Revenue, but later an Inspector of Police with the usual staff of superintendents was appointed.

Seing the state of pecuniary embarrassment into which His Highness's Government had lapsed in 1853, it is not surprising to find that the Government treasury that used to exist had fallen into disuse. There was, in fact, no Government Treasury at that date, Hindu bankers being permitted to fulfil that function. The natural result of this was that the State had no credit and Government servants received their salary most irregularly. All this was changed and not only was a treasury instituted, but Government servants were paid regularly.

A Secretariat under the Prime Minister and later a Board of Revenue were instituted in order to divide the *Divani** into civil divisions. So far the only divisions were *talukas*, which did not happen to coincide with the territorial division. The numbers of these *talukas* fluctuated annually, some years showing a record of forty, other years of sixty. This arose from the fact that no definite limit was assigned to each *taluka*. Finally, the restored districts were amalgamated and the whole country was divided into *subahs*, *talukas*, and *tahsils* on similar lines to the divisions which existed in British India. Each division was then classed into a grade according to its annual revenue and Government treasuries established in every division throughout the dominions. The result was that this scientific organization soon bore fruit. The country, hitherto depopulated and denuded of its rightful income, became fertile and prosperous once more.

* Divani—territory directly administered by Government, as opposed to Sarf Khas, i.e., His Highness's private estate, and to Sagu, a private estate of individuals, and Paigah, i.e., lands held on military tenure by certain noblemen. The word Divani is often used in Indian history. There is no English equivalent.

In 1853 there was practically no educational system for the public, though in the days of the kings of Golconda and Bidar, several *Madrassas* or Colleges were founded at which students were not only taught but also clothed and fed by the State. Owing, however, to constant campaigns and general mismanagement, the financial embarrassment, from which the Government was constantly suffering, caused these institution to lapse from want of necessary funds. Consequently, instead of instructing the students in Law, Theology, Logic and Philosophy, as had been done in former days, the boys were only taught the Koran and a few sayings of the Prophet, combined with a little penmanship. For the soldier in those days was of more service to the State than the scholar.

Sir Salar Jung saw how much the State was losing by this short-sighted policy, and the year after he assumed control he started an educational system on sound and practical lines similar to that established in other parts of India. Four years later an order was issued for the opening of two schools in every taluka, one to be conducted in Persian, the other in the vernacular. In all these schools History, Geography, Mathematics and Grammar were added to the usual curriculum. In addition to this, there were five branch schools situated at the five gates of the capital. At first all the schools were under the direction and control of the Board of Revenue, but later a separate Board of Education with the usual staff was instituted, and English was gradually introduced everywhere in the higher grade schools. There were a couple of independent schools as well as the State-aided ones. One of these was first started for the purpose of providing a sound education for the two sons of Sir Salar Jung and a few of the sons of the other leading nobles. An English University master was engaged and in a short time the results were so excellent that the numbers of the students increased rapidly and a larger staff of highly trained European masters had to be employed to meet the demand, in addition to a large staff of learned Moulvies and Indian scholars. This school eventually developed into a college now known as the "Nizam's College," and to the present day most of the sons of the nobles receive their education there. Another school for the people was founded by a philanthropist, Somasundrum Moodaliar, one of the enlightened Tamil Mudaliars that migrated to Hyderabad from Madras. In this school (which at the present day is known as the Mahbub College) Hindus, Mahomedans and Christians receive an excellent education and work in with each other quite harmoniously.

Female education was at this period totally unknown in Hyderabad, and if anything it was looked at rather askance. The Wesleyan Mission were one of the first to start a large training school for girls, but since then the *Patsala*, started and endowed by various Hindu philanthropists and entirely in the hands of Hindu management, has been one of the foremost to lead the way. The Church of England and Roman Catholic Mission also have done, and are doing, a splendid work in the educational line. Whether in State-aided, private, or mission schools, it was noticeable that the Hindu part of the community was always the first to profit by the new advantages offered, while the Mahomedans for some time were very apathetic.

As regards medical education, Hyderabad was not so far behind in this respect as might have been thought. A medical school had been started as early as 1845. Yet the women, both Hindu and Mahomedan, were

REFORMS INSTITUTED BY SIR SALAR JUNG

at a great disadvantage medically, for both were rigorous observers of the *purdah* system, and though there were in Hyderabad many fully trained medical men, both European and Indian, yet these were not admitted into the zenanas and consequently women and children were almost entirely in the hands of incompetent, unqualified women, who worked their cures by a combination of drugs and incantations. The result was obvious. Hundreds, nay thousands, of women and children endured endless agony, dying of comparatively simple ailments, for want of skilled medical attendance, for, though this was practically at their doors, custom prevented them from availing themselves of it. It has been said that a Nation's strength consists in its Workers, its Thinkers, and its Mothers. Sir Salar Jung realized this, and saw how great a drain preventible illness is on a nation's physique, and it was through his efforts that special medical aid was provided for the women of Hyderabad. Two of the first lady doctors were Miss Boardman (later Mrs. Belgrami), and Miss Dora White (later Mrs. Fellowes). The latter was at the Afzul Gunj Hospital for many years and did admirable work. *Purdah Nashins* flocked to her wards and in 1884 we read of no less than 3,000 new admittances and over 2 000 operations among the *gosha* women of Hyderabad being performed in that ward. Since that day the work has extended and there are now several European as well as Indian women doctors practising in the city, with a staff of English and Eurasian nurses under them.

Having considered at some length the principal reforms inaugurated by Salar Jung, we must now turn our attention to other matters of general historical interest. The year 1860 saw the awakening of Hyderabad to the necessity of a better means of transit. Until then the journey from Hyderabad to Bombay, or Madras, took many days to accomplish. The natives of small means still elected to travel in the old-fashioned bullock cart screened off by curtains, the value of which more or less betokened the status of their owner. Native nobles and Europeans, usually preferred to travel by tonga or on horseback, but the journey was a tedious affair, not unaccompanied by danger and dragged through many weary days. Indeed, we read in General Fraser's *Memoirs* that, on leaving Hyderabad in the year 1853 for Madras, General Fraser started in the first week in January, hoping as he expressed it " to arrive in Madras towards the end of the month as we are going down in slow marches."

From Bombay the Great Indian Peninsula Railway had extended as far as Wadi, some 121 miles from Hyderabad. In 1850 the Nizam decided to connect Hyderabad with Wadi by means of a railway. Consequently negotiations were commenced, and His Highness ceded certain territory to the British Government, who undertook the construction and working of the new line, which was to be known as the Nizam's State Railway, and was to be worked on the same lines as all the Government State Railways in India. Ten years later this arrangement was slightly altered, the British Government undertaking to manage the railway on behalf of the Nizam, who, with shareholders, provided all the capital and was to receive the profits. In connection with the railway the Nizam had granted to the British Government full jurisdiction within that portion of territory which was occupied by the Nizam's State Railway in the Southern Mahratta, the Dhond and Munmad or the Hyderabad Godavery Valley Railways, including lands taken up for stations and outbuildings and for any railway purposes. The introduction of the railway into

Hyderabad proved an invaluable asset to the State. Not only did it provide an easier means of communication in times of famine, but it gradually opened out the whole country, bringing the most benighted parts of the *Mofussil* into daily contact with a more advanced civilization. In consequence, agriculture and trade received a great impetus.

In 1861 a disagreement arose between the Nizam and the Prime Minister, the Nizam expressing a wish to remove Salar Jung from office and appoint another Minister. At this point, however, the British Government interfered, refusing to countenance this step. Some six years later fresh differences again occurred, but were amicably settled. On this occasion the British Government took the opportunity of impressing upon the Nizam the importance of giving his entire confidence to his Minister, pointing out what serious consequences the lapse into misrule would entail. The Nizam saw the truth of this argument. Shortly afterwards His Highness was created a G.C.S.I. It is curious to note that, when this honour was conferred on the Nizam, he was very loth to accept it, the reason being that the order was of a Christian origin, and the Nizam, being the leader of Islam in India, felt it unbecoming to his dignity to accept any Christian decoration. The Resident had much difficulty in persuading His Highness that this honour would add to rather than diminish his prestige. Eventually on hearing that the list of G.C.S.I. was headed by no less a person than the Prince Consort himself, His Highness decided to accept the new honour, but it did not give him as much gratification as had been anticipated. Three years later the same honour and a salute of 17 guns were conferred on the Prime Minister, Salar Jung.

In 1862 His Highness received a *sunnad* guaranteeing that the Nizam's succession should be maintained, provided it was in accordance with Mahomedan law. This greatly pleased His Highness.

In 1368 an attempt was made to assassinate the Minister while on his way to a Durbar. He was fired at in the streets of the city while seated in his Sedan chair. The culprit was immediately seized by the infuriated crowd who would have killed him had not the police intervened. The Minister serenely continued his way to the Durbar, where he was warmly congratulated by His Highness on his narrow escape. The prisoner, who had been taken to the palace, was condemned to death, but the Minister interceded for his life. To this, however, the Nizam would not accede, and the man was executed.

In the beginning of 1869 an important change took place in the affairs of Hyderabad. On February 26th, His Highness the Nizam died, and his son, Mir Mahbub Ali Khan, then not three years old, was placed on the *Musnud* by the British Resident. During the minority of the young prince the administration of Hyderabad was entrusted to Sir Salar Jung and Shams-ul-Umra. The British being anxious about the young prince's education, Captain John Clarke was appointed tutor to the Nizam, and he was succeeded by his brother, Captain Claude Clarke four years later.

In 1871 a further honour was bestowed on the Minister, who was created a K.G.S.I. by the Resident.

An exchange of villages was negotiated between the British and the Nizam in 1871, as Scindia had ceded to the British certain villages that he owned in the Nizam's dominions.

The following year Sir Salar Jung attended a Durbar held by Lord Northbrook, in honour of the Prince of

Wales' (later King Edward VII) arrival in India. On this occasion His Royal Highness presented the Minister with a sword and scabbard and a belt, set with precious stones, also with various personal mementoes of his visit in the shape of a gold ring and a gold medallion with the Prince's photo and motto on one side. Various valuable gifts were also sent to His Highness the Nizam, including some finely finished rifles and handsome pieces of jewellery.

A few years later in 1876 Sir Salar Jung received an invitation from His Royal Highness to visit England, and after having attended a Durbar held in honour of the arrival of Lord Lytton in Bombay, where he represented the young Nizam, the Minister sailed for Europe. He first visited Rome, where he had audiences both with the King of Italy and the Pope. Unfortunately during this time as the result of a slight accident Salar Jung broke his thigh-bone and in consequence he was delayed at Rome. As soon as he was able, he proceeded to England, where he was received with due honours by Queen Victoria, and attended an entertainment specially arranged for him by His Royal Highness. Everyone was impressed by the personality of Sir Salar Jung; not only was he attractive to all, as an Oriental nobleman and a foreign statesman, but also as a genial and cultured man of the world, whose conversational talent made him an honoured and welcome guest wherever he went The freedom of the City of London was conferred on him, and he was created a D.C.L. of Oxford. In fact, it was said that during this visit the Minister evoked an enthusiastic reception in England which was unprecedented.

In 1875 Shams-ul-Umra died and was succeeded by his half-brother, the Nawab Vicar ul Umra.

In 1877 the young Nizam attended by Sir Salar Jung

and Shams-ul-Umra attended the Durbar at Calcutta, on which occasion a salute of 17 guns was conferred on the latter.

During the Nizam's minority the two administrators endeavoured to regain the province of Berár, offering efficient security for the debt, and basing their appeal on the distinct understanding with Colonel Low that the districts were only made over "temporarily," as long as the Nizam might require the Contingent; but the appeals were not successful.

Of the various Residents with whom Sir Salar Jung worked, none were in more cordial relations with him than Sir George Yule. To show in what high repute Sir Salar Jung was held and how highly the British Government appreciated his work, it will be well to consider, verbatim, a despatch from Sir Richard Temple, dated August, 1867: "In the Deccan of late years," he writes, "the constitution, system and principles of the Nizam's Government are really excellent. This much is certain. That the results must be more or less beneficial to the country, is hardly to be doubted. Whether full effect is given to the intention of His Highness's Government throughout the Deccan, I cannot yet say, but independent testimony is constantly reaching me to the effect of great improvement being perceptible." (*Papers British and Native Administration of* 1869, page 69.)

It can be said with truth of Sir Salar Jung, that he introduced into every department a system which was practical and as near perfection as it could be, but naturally it was an impossible thing to expect that, to use Sir George Yule's words: "full effect should be given to the intention of His Highness's Government throughout the Deccan." Mistakes and delays in administration were bound to occur. but the mere fact of bringing so large a State as Hyderabad from a state of chaos into one of order and routine was in itself an Herculean task, and it required a great statesman to carry it out. We must remember that the Prime Minister was surrounded by intriguers, each ready to grind his own axe, and it required an extraordinary amount of discernment to differentiate between the sycophants and the well-wishers of the State.

Also in the annual return of *Moral and Material Progress*, 1867-8 (page 113), compiled at the India Office, we find the following:

"The efforts made towards reform have now placed the financial credit of the Nizam's Government on a satisfactory footing. It enjoys the confidence of the moneyed classes, and it can now raise money at very moderate rates instead of the usurious charges of former days."

Regarding assessment (*ibid.* page 114), we read that: "Pains have been taken more and more to render the annual settlements equitable and moderate," also "that all classes high and low connected with land or trade continue to flourish."

Referring to the new class of magistrate in the same annual (*ibid.* 1869, page 117), we read: "All these officers are well educated, though all have not done well, several had received their training in one of the British Provinces. Many discharged their duties with more or less efficiency, and many have by their firmness and uprightness brought credit to their department."

Again, Mr. C. B. Saunders, Resident, in 1869-70, thus speaks of the improvements of the previous years:

"It is hardly too much to say that the Hyderabad with which I became acquainted in 1860 was to the Hyderabad which was described, for example in the despatches of my predecessor, Sir Charles (afterwards Lord) Metcalfe, as the England of the present day is to the England of the Stuarts—a result essentially due, as the Government is aware, to the beneficent administration and sound policy of the present Minister, Sir Salar Jung, and to the support afforded him by my previous predecessor. Not only was the public treasury full, but the *annual income of the State exceeded the annual expenditure by about eight lakhs of rupees* (Rs. 800,000), while the credit of the Government stood proportionately high. Owing chiefly to the abolition of the baneful system of former times, by which the collection of revenue was farmed out to contractors, disturbances in the interior of the country became rare. The Hyderabad Contingent has not fired a shot, except on their own parade ground, since the suppression of the Mutinies. In no respect does the recent administration of His Highness's country contrast more favourably with the State of things prevailing twenty years ago, than in the regard to revenue matters."

Sir Richard Mead in 1880 after the inspection of the public offices wrote as follows to Salar Jung : " Now that I understand we have finished all that Your Excellency wished me to see in connection with the affairs here, I think I may assure you in this way of the very great gratification that has been afforded me by this opportunity of observing their condition and working. The work and records of the Survey Department appear to me to be admirable and leave nothing to be desired, and the care that has been bestowed on everything in this department was very striking. The Settlement operations are, of course, quite distinct from the Survey work, but I gathered that they are being conducted with equal care."

REFORMS INSTITUTED BY SIR SALAR JUNG

Statistics such as these (collected by the Imperial Famine Commission) show a remarkable improvement in the agricultural classes. People were not compelled to contribute to an income tax, a licenser or any such taxes, which in other countries have given rise to so much dissatisfaction among the agricultural and depressed classes. In General Fraser's *Memoirs* we read that: "The Berar districts certainly prospered under British Government and this proved an incentive to the Hyderabad State, if judged alone by land revenue, due to increased cultivation, by orderly conduct and the absence of crime among the inhabitants. The provinces ruled by the Hyderabad Ministry made quite as much progress as those under British rule."

In 1882 the Minister visited Simla and Lady Ripon in her diary records this visit and speaks of the personal pleasure that the Viceroy and herself had derived from meeting the Prime Minister of Hyderabad. Again reference is made to the charm of his personality.

It was proposed that Sir Salar Jung should accompany the young Nizam to England, but a sudden catastrophe prevented this plan from materializing. In February, 1883, the Grand Duke John of Mecklenburg arrived in Hyderabad and stayed at the Residency. With his usual hospitality Sir Salar Jung had arranged a series of fêtes for the distinguished visitor. On February 7th, a picnic had been arranged at Mir Allum lake. As usual His Excellency was in the best of health and a delightful and entertaining host. This was destined to be the last time that Sir Salar Jung appeared in public. After the picnic the Prime Minister returned to the palace and worked until midnight, and then retired to his private apartments. At about 2 a.m. he was seized with cholera. Medical attendance was at once secured and everything possible was done and the Minister seemed to be progressing favourably. The following day a panther hunt and a banquet had been arranged, and at Sir Salar Jung's express wish neither of these entertainments was postponed. He made a splendid fight for his life, but in spite of all efforts he suddenly grew worse and as the guests for the banquet arrived they were surprised to see the palace courtyard filled with mourning courtiers and retainers, who as is their custom beat on their chests and wept and wailed. The guests were shocked to learn that His Excellency had just died. There was great consternation all over the city as the news became public. Everyone was distressed at the death of one who always stood for justice and had in every sense been a friend of the people. His Excellency left two sons, the Nawab Mir Liak Ali and Saadut Ali, who on February 12th attended a Durbar to receive from His Highness the mourning *khillats* (white shawls). On this occasion His Highness completely broke down and was overcome with grief. Telegrams from all parts of India and from Europe poured in, deploring the death of one who had won the friendship of all with whom he had come into contact.

It is interesting to note that the family of Sir Salar Jung is descended from Sheikh Omar Karman of Medina, who settled in India in 1656. Sir Sarlar Jung was the 33rd descendant in the 9th generation. The Sheikh's son married into a noble family, espousing the daughter of Mulla Ahmet Nait, by whom he had two sons.

During his boyhood Salar Jung's family suffered from pecuniary embarrassment. He was a very delicate child, but became stronger as he grew up. As a boy one of his great amusements was to ride a captive giraffe. It is said that, when Salar Jung was seized with typhoid fever, his grandfather, Munir ul Mulk, became very much alarmed and performed the *Tasad* ceremony, praying that any evil that should befall the child be transferred unto the grandfather instead. Shortly after this the gradfather died, but the child recovered.

Sir Salar Jung was accorded a great State funeral with military honours, but the regal pomp of the obsequies was not so impressive as the genuine grief of the people. Arabs and Rohillas followed in the procession weeping. On the third day the usual custom of placing flowers on the grave was carried out, but on this occasion the crowd appropriated every flower as they were anxious to keep some memento of the great man whose bounty they had known and whose personality they had loved.

The Resident in his letter to the Government of India says:

"Every British officer who has had the honour of his acquaintance feels his death as he would that of a friend. No royal master ever had a better servant.

"His name has been inscribed on the roll of India's great men. Of this illustrious man the whole country is a tomb. He was for thirty years the trusted adviser and friend of His Majesty's representative. His example has done much to make society here quite different to what it is anywhere in India. He was in the best sense the foremost gentleman of the place. In no place in India are benevolent institutions of all kinds endowed so largely.

"I shall always consider it an honour and privilege to have been associated with him. Nothing in him was ever hurried. No reform, however important, carried out in hot haste. Wise and wary conservatism and abhorrence of extreme measures characterized the Minister."

Sir Salar Jung was known to be fond of poetry and

art, and particularly of reading history and pursuing any study which led to practical results in statecraft.

Centralization was a great distinguishing feature of his administration. In his personal life he was religious though without having a narrow sectarian spirit. He observed daily the prayers and fasts prescribed to be followed by those of Shiah persuasion. His Excellency was in his 57th year when he died.

In many ways this great statesman reminds one of the Controller-General of Finance in France at the time of Louis XVI—the famous Turgot. Both were men of the highest moral integrity gifted with an extraordinary power of organization. Both found themselves surrounded by a veritable network of corrupt and degrading conditions, which they proceeded to tear away, if not with ease, at least with determination. Again, in both cases the people whom they had to manage had for some time been suffering cruel and grievous wrongs at the hands of the nobles and men of position. Owing to their extravagance, the people were ground down, unduly oppressed and unjustly taxed. Both men in a short time worked wonders and inaugurated very far-reaching reforms. The difference was that, in the case of Sir Salar Jung, he was fortunately allowed to work out the reforms he had advocated; whereas Turgot after a while found himself hampered on all sides. Had Louis XVI been a minor and Turgot been Regent, or had he been able to carry out his programme with all it involved, those terrible pages of the French Revolution, so red with bloodshed, might never have been written. But alas! for France, though Turgot was recognized by a large party as a champion reformer, and loved by the people, a weak, extravagant King, surrounded by a corrupt Court, became tired of the words "*reduce expenditure*," and Turgot was dismissed. Gradually the reforms which he had advocated so strongly were forgotten and the country lapsed again into mismanagement, extravagance and misrule, resulting in one of the most stupendous and dramatic of revolutions.

If Sir Salar Jung had not been allowed to carry out his reforms, as he did, it is difficult to say what the fate of Hyderabad might have been. For oppression and misrule are inevitably the forerunners of a revolution. Therefore, in estimating the services which Sir Salar rendered to Hyderabad, we must not only consider the benefits which the State has derived from his administration, but also the evils which his sound policy averted.

In the *Gazette* His Highness speaking of Salar Jung says :

" His generosity, courage, justice charity, kindness and modesty were known to all ; his faithfulness and attachment to his Sovereign were unequalled. He was ever willing to sacrifice self to the well-being of his country and fellow-subjects. He was one who was beloved by all."

This was His Highness's tribute to the Minister who had so faithfully served his royal master and had steered the barque of State through many storms into calmer waters.

Sir Salar Jung was not only one of the most eminent men that Hyderabad has ever produced, but one of the greatest of India's sons.

APPENDIX

No. 1.

AFSUR-UL-MULK.

Name: MIRZA MAHOMED ALI BEG. *Religion:* Mohammedan.

Titles: Received the titles of Afsur Jung and Khan Bahadur, 1840; Afsur-ud-Dowlah, 1895. Raised to Afsur-ul-Mulk after Delhi Durbar, 1903; C.I.E., Jubilee Honours, 1897; K.C.I.E., 1911; M.V.O.; A.D.C. to H.E.H. The Nizam.

Services: Afghan War, 1879-1880 (medal); Black Mountain Expedition, 1888 (medal, mentioned in despatches); China Expedition, 1900 (medal).

Appointments Held: Raised and commanded 1st and 2nd Lancers Hyderabad Imperial Service Troops; Hon. Colonel 20th Deccan Horse; Hon. A.D.C. to Lord Hardinge, Viceroy of India, 1911; on Staff of Count von Waldersee during Boxer Rebellion, 1901; on Staff of Imperial Service Cavalry Brigade, Indian Expeditionary Force, Egypt, 1915; on Staff Indian Cavalry Corps, and A.D.C. to Sir John French, 1915-16; Commander-in-Chief, His Exalted Highness the Nizam's Regular Force and Imperial Service Troops, 1917. As A.D.C. to H.H. the Nizam, Sir Afsur represented Hyderabad at the Coronation of King Edward VII, 1902.

N.B.—Sir Afsur introduced Tent-pegging and Polo in Hyderabad, and was Captain of the famous Palace Polo Team. He has raised the system of beating for tigers into a veritable science.

No. 2.

Title: NAWAB FAKHR-UL-MULK BAHADUR.

Name: MIR SAFARZ HUSSAIN. *Born:* 1858. *Religion:* Mohammedan (Sect Shiah).

Additional Titles: SAFDAR JUNG, MASHIR-UD-DOWLAH.

Appointments Held: Moin-ul-Maham (Assistant Minister) in the Judicial Police (Postal and Educational Department); Member of the Cabinet Council from 1893-1917.

No. 3.

Title: NAWAB SIR FARIDOON MULK BAHADUR.

Name: FARIDOONJI JAMSEDJI. *Born:* September, 1849. *Religion:* Parsi.

Additional Titles: K.C.I.E., C.S.I., C.B.E., Jung and Dowlah.

Appointments Held: Officer in the Revenue Department; First Taluqdar of Aurangabad; Commissioner of Survey and Settlement; Private Secretary under Sir Sarlar Jung II; Private Secretary to Sir Asman Jah, Prime Minister, Sir Vikar-ul-Umra, Sir Kishan Persad, and Sir Sarlar Jung III; Private Secretary to H.E.H. the Nizam; Member and Vice-President of the Executive Council.

APPENDIX

The son of Sir Faridoon, Mr. Rustomji Faridoonji, is Commissioner in the Central Provinces. Two brothers, Nawab Burzoo Jung and Mr. Sorabji Jamsedji, held the rank of Subadar in the Hyderabad Service.

No. 4.

Title : SIR SARLAR JUNG III.

Name : MIR YUSUF ALI KHAN BAHADUR. *Religion :* Mohammedan.

Son of Sir Sarlar Jung II. *Born :* 13th June, 1889.

Titles : Sarlar Jung.

Appointments Held : Prime Minister to H.E.H. the Nizam, 1912-14.

No. 5.

Name : COLONEL R. NEVILL, C.I.E.

Appointments Held : Entered the Nizam's service, 1874; became Commander of H.H. the Nizam's Troops; Appointed C.I.E. for services rendered to the Colonial and Indian Exhibition in 1886, as the Nizam's representative. Died in 1897.

No. 6.

Name : A. J. DUNLOP, ESQ., C.I.E., C.S.I.

Appointments Held : Minister of Revenue, entered the Nizam's service from the Berar Commission, 1883; 1885, Inspector-General of Revenue, Imam Commissioner, Chairman Board of Irrigation, Survey Settlement Commissioner, Senior Member Board of Revenue; 1889, Famine Commissioner, Administrator Court of Wards, Customs Department, Administrator Abkari Department (Liquor, Opium, Ganja). Retired 1912.

Increase in State Revenue during his 31 years' of service, Rs. 14,270,853.

Born : 7th April, 1848. *Died :* 1919.

Son of Henry Dunlop, Craigton House, Lanark.

N.B.—Mr. Dunlop was appointed by Sir Sarlar Jung I. and his work has been the foundation of the prosperity of Hyderabad. The ryots who had formerly no security of their holdings now cannot be disturbed. Land formerly unsaleable now realizes 10 to 20 times the assessment.

No. 7.

Title : NAWAB IMAD-UL-MULK.

Name : SYED HUSSAIN BILGRAMI. *Born :* 1844. *Religion :* Mohammedan.

Educated Bhagalpur, Patna, and Calcutta. Matriculated from Hare Academy in 1861, and graduated in 1866 with distinction.

Appointments Held : Professor of Arabic at the College, Lucknow; Personal Assistant to Sir Sarlar Jung I, 1873-76; appointed Private Secretary to Sir Sarlar Jung I, 1876. Subsequently Director of Education to H.H. the Nizam; Member of India Council, London. In 1911 was appointed Private Secretary to H.E.H. the Nizam.

Titles Held : Imad-ud-Dowlah, Imad-ul-Mulk, Ali Yar Khan Bhd: Motoman Jung.

INDIAN NAMES AND THEIR MEANING

ABKARI.—Duty levied on alcohol, Excise Customs.
AMIL.—Governor, Collector of Revenue, Finance Administrator.
BATAI.—Rent of land paid in kind, division of crop between Ailkwator and Zemindar or Government.
CHOUTH.—A fourth, a tax levied by the Mahrattas on the lands raided or conquered, quarter of the regular Government assessment.
DEISHMUKH.—A Mahratta official in charge of a group of villages.
FAUJDAR.—A military term, an officer in charge of a considerable body of troops.
INAM.—A gift, land granted in fee simple free of all conditions.
JAGHIR.—Land granted by the Mahomedan rulers to one at the head of a body of troops of varying numbers. The Jaghir was granted for the upkeep of the troops.
KAGIS.—Judges.
KHILLAT.—A dress of honour conferred by Mahomedan Princes on deserving officials and others. It might include in addition to the dress, jewels horses, elephants and arms.
MADRASSAS.—Mohammedan College.
MUSNAD.—Throne.
NAZAR.—An offering made by an inferior to a superior, in token of fealty, submission, congratulation, etc. Under the name of an offering it is sometimes a heavy exaction, imposed on appointment to office or succession to property, at other times merely a formality.
PANCHAYAT.—A Village Council, generally of five, to assist the Patel in deciding the cases.
PAIGAH.—Lands held on military tenure by certain noblemen.
PATEL.—A head man in the village—in all matters except accounts.
PAKIVARI.—One of the head men in the village whose business is to keep the accounts.
PESHKASH—Tribute.
PURDAH.—A veil or curtain. PURDAH NASHIN.—Veiled Woman.
SHASTRI.—A Hindu divine.
SANAD.—Originally a Royal ordinance.
SAGU.—Private estates of private individuals.
SURDESHMOOKI.—A tax similar to Chouth, consisting of one-sixth over and above the chouth.
SARFI-KHAS.—H.H. The Nizam's private estates.
SEBUNDY.—Three monthly or quarterly payments in connection with irregular native troops, used in the collection of revenue or police work.
SILLIDARI—Police.
SOWCAR.—Moneylender.
SUTTEE.—Widow burning.
TAKDAMA.—Cultivator advances revenue to Government on his crop.
TALUKDAR—Collector of Revenue.
TASAD.—A religious ceremony whereby the petitioner prays that illness may be averted from some person specified and that it may instead be borne by the petitioner.
ZEMINDAR.—A large landowner, the Mahomedan equivalent to the Mahratta deishmukh.
ZILLIDRA.—An officer in charge of a Zillah or district.